Sharing Faith

SHARING FAITH

A Comprehensive Approach to
Religious Education and
Pastoral Ministry

The Way of Shared Praxis

Thomas H. Groome

HarperSanFrancisco
A Division of HarperCollinsPublishers

SHARING FAITH: *A Comprehensive Approach to Religious Education and Pastoral Ministry.* Copyright © 1991 by Thomas H. Groome. All rights reserved. Printed in the United States of America. No part of this book may be used or reproduced in any manner whatsoever without written permission except in the case of brief quotations embodied in critical articles and reviews. For information address HarperCollins Publishers, 10 East 53rd Street, New York, NY 10022.

FIRST EDITION

Library of Congress Cataloging-in-Publication Data

Groome, Thomas H.
    Sharing Faith: a comprehensive approach to religious education and pastoral ministry: the way of shared praxis / Thomas H. Groome. —
        1st ed.
            p.   cm.
    Includes bibliographic references and index.
    ISBN 0–06–063496–0 (hard: alk. paper).
    ISBN 0–06–063497–9 (pbk.: alk. paper)
        1. Christian education. 2. Pastoral theology. I. Title.
    BV1471.2.G688 1991
    268—dc20   90–55797
                                                                            CIP

91   92   93   94   95   FAIR   10   9   8   7   6   5   4   3   2   1

This edition is printed on acid-free paper that meets the American National Standards Institute Z39.48 Standard.

To Colleen

Grá mo chroi

Contents

Preface

This book is about any and every event, occasion, and community concerned with "sharing faith." I write particularly from a Christian perspective and propose a comprehensive approach for doing Christian religious education and pastoral ministry. The central focus is the way of "shared Christian praxis." I first introduced "shared praxis" to a wider audience in 1980 with *Christian Religious Education: Sharing Our Story and Vision.*[1] It addressed six foundational questions to Christian religious education, identified most readily as: what, why, where, how, when, and who. In response to the how question, I proposed a shared praxis approach. Thereafter the way of shared praxis has attracted significant interest and has been used with apparent good effect in a great variety of educational and ministerial situations.

Since *Christian Religious Education* was published, I have continued to learn about the approach of shared praxis. I benefited greatly from many reviews and critiques the book received. My clarity of thinking has been enhanced especially by the students I have worked with in graduate courses at Boston College and elsewhere, and by many participants in seminars, workshops, and conferences across the United States and beyond. I have also learned from using shared praxis in a variety of other settings: for adult education and theological reflection, in community renewal and planning programs, in social justice work, in preaching, counseling, retreats, in teaching theology to undergraduate students at Boston College and in teaching fifth-grade CCD. I have learned from reading and research in relevant literature and in literature that at first did not seem relevant at all. I have learned especially from writing the *God with Us* (1984) and *Coming to Faith* (1990) religion curricula. Ranging from kindergarten to eighth grade, these programs are now widely used in Catholic schools and parishes throughout North America. Creating them has occupied much of my writing and research time over the past ten years. I was fortunate to work in partnership with a host of gifted colleagues—publishers, editors, designers, and artists—and have received many comments from teachers and students who use them; this curriculum project has been a primary source of both theoretical and methodological clarification of the shared Christian praxis approach.[2]

Ten years later, this book is in dialectic with *C.R.E.*; it assumes and affirms some things the earlier work said, critically appropriates other aspects, and goes beyond *C.R.E.* in significant ways. Part I (chaps. 1–3) deepens the philosophical foundations of the shared praxis approach and particularly its epistemological underpinnings. I have been convinced for some time that the "learning outcome" of Christian religious education[3] should be more than what the Western world typically means by "knowledge"; that it is to engage the whole "being" of people, their heads, hearts, and life-styles, and is to inform, form, and transform their identity and agency in the world. But from a religious education perspective, the primary literature of Western epistemology is a mixed heritage. It has assets for us but also a negative, even destructive, underside. Part I, then, makes an attempt to reconstruct from the Western epistemological tradition foundations that can better serve our purposes. Readers without a strong background in philosophy may be tempted to begin with Part II; however, I have tried to write Part I in accessible terms, and I hope the effort it may ask is rewarding.

Part II (chaps. 4–10) explains in detail the rationale for and workings of the movements of shared Christian praxis. This is a significant elaboration on what I summarized in *C.R.E.* (chap. 10) and reflects what I have learned of the approach over the past ten years.

Part III expands the possible uses of shared praxis to functions of ministry other than what we might readily identify as Christian religious education. This reflects my convictions (a) that all ministry has an educational dimension and (b) that an educational style like shared praxis can suggest an apt approach to other functions of ministry. I review ministry in general (chap. 11), liturgy and preaching (chap. 12), social ministry for peace and justice (chap. 13), and pastoral counseling (chap. 14). Chapter 15 summarizes my understanding of the theological convictions and spiritual commitments that an approach like shared Christian praxis asks of religious educators; I weave it together as my pedagogical creed.

I portray shared Christian praxis as a metaapproach to education in Christian faith and pastoral ministry. By "metaapproach" I mean an overarching perspective and mode for proceeding that can be readily adapted to a great variety of teaching/learning occasions and ministerial tasks. Shared praxis is not simply a teaching *method* in the typical sense of the term. In fact, as I explain in Part II, one can use many different methods and teaching models to effect its commitments and movements.

I am a Christian religious educator whose ecclesial context is the Catholic tradition and community of the Christian church. This praxis is my first source of reflection. I intend readers to bring their own praxis into dialogue with what is here and to appropriate it to their own situations and communities of faith. But I hope my book can be a resource for religious educators far beyond my mainline Christian community and perspective. From personal experience and conversations with Jewish and Unitarian Universalist religious educators, I am particularly convinced of the potential of a shared praxis approach in those traditions. The sponsoring community can supply the middle term: "shared Christian (or Jewish, or etc.) praxis." Clearly too the commitments and dynamics of shared praxis can be honored in education that is not overtly religious.

I write first for people who intend to educate others in Christian faith, that is, to be religious in a Christian way. This includes bringing participants to understand the Christian tradition, to learn from it,[4] and to be shaped by it in their religious identity and historical agency. These "Christian religious educators" may be publicly designated for such work, be "professionals" or volunteers, be parents, guardians, clergy, teachers, or administrators, may educate in families, communities, or congregations, in parochial schools, Sunday schools, or parish programs, resource the religious education ministry of a whole school or congregation, or attend to a particular aspect of it, and so on. Education in Christian faith, however, is not my exclusive but rather my primary focus. For instance, I reflect also on my teaching of undergraduate theology courses at Boston College, where the intent is more obviously, to use Gabriel Moran's distinctions, teaching people to understand Christianity than that they become Christian.[5] I hope some of these reflections are helpful to people who, as Moran describes it, "teach religion" (see note 5).

I am aware of the particularity and limits of my primary focus, and how it is shaped not only by personal faith but by my social/political context. The separation of church and state proviso of the United States Constitution (First Amendment)[6] is so strictly interpreted that not only is education in particular faith traditions excluded from the public school curriculum but so too is "teaching religion" (arguments for an alternative interpretation notwithstanding).[7] With little exception, activity that can be readily recognized as religious education in the United States is, in fact, Christian, or Jewish, or Muslim, or Buddhist religious education, and is sponsored by particular faith communities. The great majority of religion-related schools were founded and are supported by private funding to "teach people to be religious in a particular way" (Moran; see note 5). This is markedly different from, for example, Britain, where religion is taught as an academic discipline in state schools. Yet, again, my hope is that what I write here may be helpful to people in different social, cultural, and political situations.

The note format used throughout is as follows. All works quoted or cited are listed in the Bibliography. In the notes for each chapter only the author's surname and the title, often shortened, are given. The Scripture quotations are from the New American Bible unless otherwise noted. Many works quoted were written before consciousness about exclusive language; when I have changed them, I enclose the interposed word or words in brackets. The National Council of Teachers of English now permits use of *they, their,* or *them* to refer to an indefinite singular pronoun—a return to the practice of medieval English. Contrary to how we were taught, instead of "Everyone knows he is to decide for himself," it is now grammatically acceptable to say, "Everyone knows they are to decide for themselves" or, as Shakespeare said, "God send everyone their heart's desire." I often use this construction to avoid the cumbersome "him or her" and like expressions.

Acknowledgments

This work would never have come to publication without the help and support of a great host of people. I can express my gratitude to only some of them here. Many friends read different parts of the manuscript and offered helpful comments. For this invaluable service I thank especially Dr. Ann Louise Gilligan and Dr. Katherine Zappone, two friends and former doctoral students with me, whose work at The Shanty in Dublin is an eminent example of the education I write about here; Dr. Raymond Devettere, who again critiqued my philosophy sections (he did likewise for *C.R.E.*); my good friends and colleagues at the Institute of Religious Education and Pastoral Ministry, Boston College, and especially Dr. Claire Lowery and Fr. Robert Imbelli, who read chapters 14 and 15, respectively, with their expertise in pastoral counseling and systematic theology; Fr. Richard Ling and Paul Covino, who did likewise for chapter 12 on liturgy; Rev. Louis Roy, O.P., another fine colleague at Boston College, who read chapter 3 with special attention to the section on Lonergan; my wonderful niece Annette Honan, who read much of an earlier draft and has taught me more than I have taught her, although she has been one of my finest students;and Liam Wegimont for his perceptive critiques of the philosophical sections.

I thank my friend Harold Daly Horell, who made many helpful comments on much of the manuscript and worked diligently to check many quotations, notes, and bibliographical entries. I thank Dr. Kate Siejk, who contributed research time to an earlier draft of the notes, and Karen Wood, who carefully read and gave editorial advice on the whole manuscript. I thank Robert Lynn and the Lilly Foundation for making available a small research grant. I am deeply grateful to John Loudon of Harper San Francisco, who served again (as he did for *C.R.E.*) as my editor. He is surely one of the "best in the business," and this is a better book because of him. I also thank Georgia Hughes and Mimi Kusch of Harper San Francisco, who helped bring it to publication. Of course, none of these people are responsible for the book's shortcomings.

Apart from my family, the two people to whom I am most indebted at the end of this work are Helen Blier and Kevin McGuire. Kevin began the project with me almost five years ago and typed the early drafts. Helen took over when Kevin found more gainful employment; she brought the added gift of insights from her own fine work as religious educator. Beyond being most diligent about every aspect of the manuscript, they have been my friends. Kevin was a most generous "pinch hitter" until the end, and Helen's great care for the project seemed tireless, even in the "extra innings."

I thank the Groome family, both here and in Ireland, for their love and support over the years; they are the roots to which I constantly return and find new life. I thank the Griffiths, who have welcomed me into their family. My dear friend and "mother-in-love," as I came to call her, Mary Ann Griffith, constantly encouraged me as the project unfolded and began to seem endless. The faith, integrity, and courage with which she faced a far greater struggle gave me a living witness of holiness of life. I hope a little of her spirit and love are reflected here to her memory; Mary Ann went home to God a few days after I told her I was "finished."

Finally, I thank my wonderful spouse, Colleen Griffith. I benefitted greatly from her fine expertise in theology and religious education as we talked through much of what is here. She read every page of the manuscript in draft form and was my severest, albeit most supportive, critic. In dispirited moments her infectious spirit has sustained mine. More than this, she has been the principal sacrament of God's love for me over the past five years of our marriage. Our life and love together is the deepest expression I "know" of shared Christian praxis. To her, *Cailín grá mo chroi*—the woman love of my heart—I dedicate this book.

Thomas H. Groome
Boston College
Easter 1990

PART I

FOUNDATIONS

Prologue

God guard me from those thoughts men think
In the mind alone;
He that sings a lasting song
Thinks in a marrow bone.

W. B. Yeats[1]

CHRISTIAN RELIGIOUS EDUCATORS have a growing conviction that the "lasting song" of Christian faith must be nurtured in and arise from "the marrow bone" of people, that we cannot settle for engaging "the mind alone" of our co-learners. In Part I, I attempt to further clarify and augment the emergence of this paradigmatic shift toward educating the whole "being" of people in Christian faith. This Prologue serves to focus the central themes of Part I and to indicate how I use its more technical terms.

Though seldom referred to explicitly, my angle of vision throughout Part I is a shared praxis approach to faith education. My concern is not this approach per se, however, or for clarifying its philosophical underpinnings, although that may well be achieved. Here my hope is to contribute to broadening the philosophical foundations of Christian religious education beyond epistemology and people's ways of "knowing" to embrace ontology and people's whole way of "being" as human beings in the world. I do not propose that we abandon concern for "knowledge"; far from it. Obviously, as is rightly assumed of all education worthy of the name, Christian religious *education* is to promote "knowledge" of some kind and to actively engage people's minds in achieving it. I argue throughout that critical rationality should be a constitutive dimension of the processes used to bring people "to *know* their faith." Though there may be little agreement on what is meant by "knowledge,"[2] epistemology—deliberate attention to the dynamics, sources, and reliability of human knowing—is of foundational concern to Christian religious educators.[3] In chapter 2, especially, I engage some of the chief architects of the Western epistemological tradition to critique their inadequacies and retrieve insights that contribute foundations more likely to promote the holistic "learning outcome" intended by Christian religious education.

The nature and purposes of Christian religious education require that we promote personal cognition as a critically reflective, dialectical, and dialogical process that encourages a "right relationship" between knower and known in a community of discourse *and* that we broaden our concern beyond simply cognition. The incarnational principle that stands at the heart of Christianity demands a pedagogy that is grounded in and shapes people's ontic selves—their identity and agency in the world. For instance, our aim is not simply that people know about justice, but that they be just, not only understand compassion but be compassionate, and so on. We are, then, to attend to all dimensions of human "being" and articulate our most basic philosophical foundation and task as ontological rather than simply epistemological. We need to make an "ontological turn"[4] in the very foundations of Christian religious education.

The key terms of Part I will be explained in detail as the work unfolds; however, initial clarification of some of them seems in order here. I use *ontology* not primarily in its traditional meaning as "the science of all being" but more in the Heideggerian sense of the "being" of ourselves as we exist in an agential relationship with historical reality.[5] (It might also be called philosophical anthropology.) Thus, an "ontological turn" in our pedagogy encourages educators to engage and inform, form, and transform the very "being" of people in the world. I use the term *being* in both its noun sense, as in *human being* (the traditional category of essence), and in its verb sense, as in the act of be-*ing* (the traditional category of existence). To indicate when I so use "being" in this combined noun/verb sense of human identity and agency, I italicize it.

I sometimes use the term *epistemic* ontology to reflect our educational interest and to signal my central conviction that epistemology and ontology, "knowing" and "being," should be united in the philosophical foundations of Christian religious education. Though ontology remains the noun and thus the primary focus, the modifier *epistemic* reflects the educator's interest in enabling people to attend to the consciousness that arises from their whole "being" as agent-subjects-in-relationship. And I will often use this latter phrase to indicate how participants are to be both engaged and formed by religious education; it is to honor and empower people as agent-subjects-in-relationship.

In this cumulative phrase, I use the term *subject* to signify the intrinsic value of persons qua persons, a meaning heightened when we think of subject in contrast to object, the latter always being something of a qualified value. I preface it with *agent* to emphasize the originating and historically responsible dimensions of human "subjectivity"; "*agent* subjects" are to be consciously aware, reflective, discerning, and responsible people. *Agent* as a modifier of *subject* also helps to avoid the possible connotation of the latter as a position of subordination as in "subject to." I use agent-subjects-*in-relationship* to indicate that the authentic "being" of people is always realized "in relationship" with others in time and place. We are not to be egocentric monads in self-sufficient isolation; we achieve authentic subjectivity by caring for and receiving care from other people.

The last term to be indicated briefly here is *conation*. I am prompted to revive this ancient term because it carries a holistic meaning. All education intends some learning outcome. When Christian religious education is grounded in an "epistemic ontology," and treats people as "agent-subjects-in-relationship," the learning outcome effected includes but is more than what is typically meant by knowledge or cognition. *Conation,* I argue, is a more comprehensive term than *cognition* and more adequately names the learning outcome intended by Christian religious education. For now, by conation I mean what is realized when the whole ontic being of "agent-subjects-in-relationship" is actively engaged to consciously know, desire, and do what is most humanizing and life-giving (i.e., "true") for all. And for people who find the term too strange, I also use *wisdom* as a synonym for conation.

Chapter 1 reflects on the nature and purposes of Christian religious education to articulate the rationale for an ontological turn and indicates the foundational shifts it demands. Chapters 2 and 3 parallel each other as exercises in deconstruction and reconstruction respectively. Chapter 2 reviews some of the chief architects of epistemology in Western philosophy in order to discern its liabilities and assets in formulating an epistemic ontology to ground Christian religious education. Building on these historical insights, and combining them with more contemporary literature and convictions from my own praxis, chapter 3 attempts to construct a schematic statement of the dimensions and dynamics of "being" to be engaged to promote conation in Christian faith.

Chapter 1

Educating for Conation in Christian Faith

1. The Nature of Christian Religious Education

When we intervene in people's lives to educate them religiously in Christian faith, *what are we doing?*[1] I propose that Christian religious education shares with all religious education three constitutive characteristics: it is a transcendent, an ontological, and a political activity.

A. Education that is intentionally "religious" is clearly a transcendent activity. In attempting to "bring things together again" (a meaning suggested by the Latin root of *religious*) in the context of ultimacy, it attempts to nurture to awareness and lived expression the human capacity for the transcendent. In other words, it encourages people to interpret their lives, relate to others, and engage in the world in ways that faithfully reflect what they perceive as ultimate in life, that is, from a faith perspective. A Christian perspective lends particularity to how people experience and live their relationships with *the* Transcendent, for example, as a personal God who loves all humankind. But by nature, Christian faith education shares with all religious education this transcendent dimension.

B. By nurturing people's capacity for the transcendent, religious education attends to, engages, and shapes their whole way of "being"—a profoundly ontological activity. It engages what is most deeply human and is, we hope, a humanizing affair. In a sense, all education has this "human" characteristic in that its primary intent is to *educate people*, a tautological truth but one hidden by educational language that refers to the "things" taught as "subjects." The "subjects" teachers teach are *people*, not the "things" about which we teach. Even educators who see their task as exclusively epistemological typically hope that the knowledge they foster will make a substantive difference in people's lives—in their "being." It would seem patently true, however, that religious education is to make a fundamental difference in how people realize their "being" in relation with God, self, others, and the world. The transcendent and ontological aspects of the enterprise are symptomatic of each other, and both are clearly suggested by the word *religious*. (The particularity of *Christian* will be more evident under my statement of purpose.) But what of *education*? It suggests a third characteristic that marks all educational activity, regardless of its qualifiers.

C. In the philosophy of education literature there is little consensus about the nature of educational activity of any kind. For most people, it means "schooling" whose primary activity is didactic "instruction." But viewing the essential nature of educational activity as schooling/instruction is a misguided reductionism that I hope to help dispel throughout these chapters. Education includes but is more than schooling, and teaching/learning can include but is more than didactic instruction. I contend that the essential characteristic of all education is that it is *a political activity*.

I regard as "political" (from the Greek *politike*, meaning the art of enabling the shared life of citizens) any deliberate intervention in people's lives that influences how they live their lives as social beings in history, that is, as agent-subjects-in-relationship. In this broad but traditional sense of "politics," one can readily recognize, as both Plato and Aristotle first recognized,[2] that all education is political. The knowledge to which it gives people access, how it does so, and the influence it has on people's "characters," all shape how people live their lives together in both the private and public realms. Its power is hopefully of persuasion rather than coercion, but is as real nonetheless. In a teaching/learning event power and knowledge combine to form how people respond to the deepest questions about what it means to be human, how to participate with others in the world, and the kind of future to create together out of their past and present. If we recognize people as "beings in place and time" (elaborated on in chapter 3), that is, as historically located and interdependent agents in whose present context there resides the corporate consequences of their past and the shared possibilities of their future, then education is, as Huebner says, "the futuring of the person and the futuring of a society."[3] It is a value-laden activity that greatly affects how people live their time and shape their place together as historical subjects in the body politic. Educational activity is eminently political; to deny this separates "knowing" from "being."

Rather than lessening its political nature, making education "religious" augments its political dimension. Nothing is more politically significant than shaping the ultimate myths of meaning and ethic by which people live their lives. And I can think of nothing more value-laden and intentional about shaping how people interpret, relate to, and engage in the world than education in Christian faith. This is not to gainsay the transcendent dimension of Christian religious education. My point is to affirm precisely what Christians believe—that God calls them to incarnate their relationship with God in a communal way of life patterned on the life of Jesus, whose historical commitments were profoundly social.

Anticipating the next section on the reign of God, the center of Jesus' preaching and thus the focus of Christian faith is that people are to effect in history the values of God's reign, love and justice, peace and freedom, wholeness and fullness of life for all. Such values cannot be lived apart from other people or from the public realm. The very symbol "*reign* of God" is itself an eminently sociopolitical one; it makes the notion of a "private" (i.e., nonpolitical) Christianity a contradiction in terms. It demands that what God wills—fullness of life for all—be done on every level of human existence: personal, interpersonal, and social/political.

Nothing could be more political in its intent and consequences than the "great law" of God's reign as preached by Jesus, that people love God *by* loving their neighbor as themselves, with neighbor having no limits and love demanding justice. Education in Christian faith clearly should shape the lives of people as agent-subjects in *right* relationship with God, self, other people, and all creation. Thus it intervenes in people's lives as a profoundly political activity, albeit often unrecognized as such. Though the Christian church, as Vatican II noted, "is bound to no particular form of human culture nor to any political or social system,"[4] it is impossible to educate for love, justice, peace, and so on toward all humankind and remain "apolitical."

Christian religious educators should recognize that "politics" permeates their whole curriculum—what they teach through content, process, and environment. In giving people access to a faith community's Story and Vision, religious educators make choices about which collective memories to make present and toward what end, what paradigms of meaning and criteria of action to propose to people. These are political issues. For example, we can present a version of Christian tradition that legitimates present ecclesial and social/political arrangements, and/or a privatized account of Christianity that anesthetizes people's sense of social responsibility. On the other hand, we can choose to uncover and make accessible the subversive and emancipatory memories from the tradition that call our lives and situations into question and heighten our commitment to the sociopolitical responsibilities of Christian faith.

Likewise, *how* we teach and the kinds of teaching/learning environments we create reflect political choices. On the one hand, we can employ teaching processes that treat people as dependent objects rather than as agent-subjects, that rob them of their word and capacities for reflection, imposing our own thoughts, worldview, and version of Story/Vision upon them as hardened ideology. On the other hand, we can choose processes and create environments in which people are actively engaged as participating subjects in events and communities marked by relationships of inclusion and mutuality, where they are enabled to speak their own word in dialogue with others, to deal critically and creatively with their own reality, to appropriate and see for themselves the truth in the faith handed on, and come to decision together as

responsible subjects of lived Christian faith. In sum, the whole curriculum, explicit and implicit, and indeed the "null curriculum,"[5] that is,
what we choose not to teach, have significant political import.

2. The Purposes of Christian Religious Education

I propose that the biblical symbol that best expresses the overarching
telos of being Christian and thus evokes the *metapurpose* of Christian
religious education is the "reign of God." True, of course, the reign of
God symbolizes the metapurpose of all Christian ministry. For Christian
religious education, however, it provides the ultimate hermeneutical
principle for what to teach from the tradition, the primary guideline
for how to teach it, and the direction of its politics. Promoting this
ultimate purpose of God's rule in people's lives calls up the more immediate and interrelated pedagogical tasks of educating, by God's
grace, for lived Christian faith and for the wholeness of human freedom that is fullness of life for all.

A. For the Reign of God

I recognize that this symbol is an ambiguous one for our time and
has understandably come in for critique. From a feminist perspective,
"*King*dom" of God appears patriarchal. This is one of two reasons I
favor the word *reign;* the other is that "reign" is a more accurate translation of the Hebrew *malkuth Yahweh* and the Greek *basileia tou theou,*
which refer to an act of reigning rather than to a particular realm or
domain. It has been criticized too as reifying God's "will" into arbitrary
law to test and control humankind, regardless of the promptings of our
own wills. Some claim it reflects an "imperialistic" mentality, implying
that God's rule triumphs without human effort or responsibility. In
addition, it seems an outmoded symbol from a bygone era.[6]

There are many proposals of alternatives to replace it: democracy,
commonwealth, commonweal, rule, realm, or *kin*dom of God; new creation, new age, and so on. Though I appreciate their intent and am
open to a replacement more appropriate to contemporary consciousness, I find none of those suggestions adequate to express the multiple
meanings that the traditional symbol carries. In continuing to use
"reign of God" as the most comprehensive symbol of the telos of Christian faith, I recognize with Sallie McFague that like "all language about
God," it "is a human construction and as such perforce 'misses the
mark.'"[7] Further, as a linguistic symbol it functions as a metaphor—a
word or phrase that denotes an action or object that belongs properly
in one context but is used in another to suggest a likeness or analogy
that amplifies or makes more vivid something that deserves to be highlighted (e.g., the ship *plows* through the water). A metaphor never describes something exactly as it is; as such, "reign of God" is a "likely

account rather than a definition."[8] It is always, as Perrin claimed, a "tensive symbol";[9] that is, it has inexhaustible meaning that can never be fully stated. Its criticisms and limits notwithstanding, I continue using it to symbolize the metapurpose of Christian religious education for the following reasons.

Christian religious educators are to teach the faith tradition of the Christian community; we cannot easily abandon its central symbols and metaphors unless they are irretrievable as life-giving and emancipatory in our present situation. First, by using *reign* of God it seems possible to retrieve the symbol as inclusive and active rather than as an exclusive and static place. Second, rather than interpreting it to represent an arbitrary "will" of God that is imperialistically imposed on all, regardless of human cooperation, reign of God must be interpreted within its scriptural meaning of God's covenantal relationship with humankind. In the covenant, what God *wills* is love and freedom, peace and justice, wholeness and fullness of life for all, favoring the "lowly" and showing "no partiality" to the mighty. (See Wis. 6.) God takes humankind into partnership to realize these values, which reflect, in fact, the best interests of ourselves, others, and all creation.[10] Far from being imperialistic or arbitrary, God wills for us what, at our best, we will for ourselves and others. What then does this symbol pose metaphorically as the metapurpose of Christian religious education?

In the Hebrew Scriptures, the actual term *reign of God* is rarely used, but convictions about the reality that the symbol came to represent in Jesus' time were vital to Hebrew faith: God's saving activity in the midst of human history; God's intentions, on behalf of which God is ever active, that all people come to live in peace and justice, love and freedom, wholeness and fullness of life (*shalom*) and that creation be brought to final completion; the responsibilities that the covenant places upon the people to do God's will now—to live in right relationship with God, self, others, and creation after the model of how God relates to humankind. Jesus preached the reign of God in continuity with these core convictions of his Jewish roots, making it a comprehensive symbol of the central theme and purpose of his life. He presented himself as God's definitive agent in history for the advent of God's reign; he radicalized its law by making universal love of others as ourselves the measure of our love for God; he made its only criterion of membership that people do God's will on earth as it is done in heaven. Reclaimed at first by political, hope, and liberation theologians but now well established in "mainline" Christian theology, the reign of God, or some alternative that approximates its meaning, is seen by much contemporary scholarship as the central symbol for understanding the meaning and purpose of Christian faith. It epitomizes the centrality of eschatology to Christian existence as a historically meaningful and purposeful life lived.

Contemporary Scripture scholars and theologians disagree a great deal about the meaning of God's reign; the different positions reflect the tensions in its biblical roots[11] and the variety of ways it has been understood throughout history.[12] Though it will always be a "tensive" symbol, a consensus view reflective of contemporary scholarship can be outlined; I propose the following ten statements as elements of such a consensus. The first three reflect more the Hebrew Scriptures and the other seven the New Testament, but all are in cumulative continuity with one another. Together they constitute what I intend to invoke when I use "reign of God" throughout as the metapurpose to guide the praxis of Christian religious education.

1. Reign of God is a symbol of God's sovereignty over all creation and history, heaven and earth, now and always. It reflects the faith that God is the only God who is to reign in people's lives.

2. Reign of God evokes both God's intentions for and God's activity in history; it symbolizes God's intentions of peace and justice, love and freedom, wholeness and fullness of life for all, and for the well-being of creation (*shalom*), and it symbolizes that God is active in partnership with human agency to effect these universal intentions.

3. Because God is active with humankind on behalf of God's intentions, on the one hand, the reign of God is first and always a gift that comes by the grace and power of God. On the other hand, God has called humankind into covenant that requires us to live toward the realization of God's reign. What God wills *to* us—fullness of life for all—is God's will *for* us, that is, the rule by which we are responsible to live. The reign of God is both gift and responsibility, promise and command.

4. In Christian faith, the reign of God can be spoken of as "already begun," as "coming now," and as "not yet" fulfilled. It has already been initiated definitively in Jesus, the Christ, in that he is God's irrevocable promise of commitment to its final victory; it is "coming now" as people do God's will; and it is "not yet" in that its completion will be radically new at the end time.

5. In Christian faith, the gift of God's reign and its catalyst in history were incarnated in Jesus, the Christ. Through the saving event of Jesus, God empowers people to choose, but without violating their freedom, to live free *from* the power of sin in all its forms and *for* the values of God's reign on all levels of their existence.

6. In continuity with his Hebrew roots, Jesus' whole life purpose was that God's will be done now and all people brought to wholeness and creation to completion. He lived with an apocalyptic urgency for the reign of God. In his life, Jesus made it clear that all people are welcome to live as participants in God's reign. He had, however, a special outreach and compassion toward the poor, the oppressed, the marginalized. He radicalized its law of love—that we love God *by* loving our neighbor as we love ourselves, with neighbor unlimited—as the only measure of membership in God's reign.

7. Knowing that it is always God's gift, Jesus never said, "Go build the reign of God," but he made clear that his disciples are in a covenantal partnership with God and one another, with responsibility to bring forth its fruits. His disciples are to do God's will on earth as it is done in heaven by following Jesus' way of life and living in right relationship with God, others, selves, and all creation. As in the Hebrew Scriptures, the reign of God in Jesus is a symbol of both hope and command, promise and responsibility.

8. The reign of God has profound meaning for us, personally and interpersonally. Personally it is realized in authentic love and care for the self; it is marked by inner peace, realization of one's dignity and worth, recognition and development of one's gifts, by a sense of hope and joy in life, a satisfying of what one needs, physically, socially, and aesthetically for wholeness of life. Interpersonally, the reign of God calls people to a lifelong conversion of deepening relationship with God and of turning toward their neighbor with all that love requires (justice, peace, respect, etc.).

9. In the social/political realm, the reign of God means that Christians and their faith communities should publicly reflect its realization in their lives and ecclesial structures and participate as a "public church" in society that helps effect its eminently social values of life for all.

10. We are to trust in God's promise to bring God's reign to completion at the "end time." But we must participate, however, in realizing this promise within and through human history. Its covenant is a true partnership. If we refuse our part, if we choose alienation instead of "right relationship," death instead of life (Deut. 30:19), God does not rescind our freedom to so choose. We cannot act irresponsibly to the covenant and presume that God will intervene to save us from the consequences, even should that be our own annihilation.[13]

God's reign as the metapurpose of Christian religious education highlights the enterprise as an ontological one, demanding pedagogy that engages and forms people's very selves to be historical agents of God's reign. The heartfelt response to the "myth" evoked by this symbol arises from the depths of our "being" and reflects the deepest eschatological impetus of humankind. Though it is a central biblical symbol, its myth is a universal one[14] that arises from the "deep heart's core" (Yeats). The mythical longings it represents—for peace, justice, love, freedom, equality, gentleness, wholeness, well-being for us and all creation—are our best sentiments for "the land of heart's desire" (Yeats). Only by engaging people's whole "being" as agent-subjects-in-relationship are we likely to educate them for the reign of God.

B. For Lived Christian Faith

Though "reign of God" can symbolize the metapurpose that guides what is taught by content, process, and environment, the more immediate existential purpose of Christian religious education is to promote lived Christian faith in the lives of participants. It is to be an instrument of God's grace to inform, form, and transform people in realized Christian faith toward the reign of God. (Old Aristotelian distinctions can be helpful here: reign of God is the "final" purpose of Christian religious education; lived Christian faith is its "formal" purpose, i.e., what it is to "form" in people's lives.)

Regarding faith, religious educators must first recognize that our work is no more than a secondary, "instrumental" cause; God is always the "first cause" (Aristotle again!). Faith is never "produced" by human "doing, it is God's gift." (Eph. 2:8). The gift reaches first to the inner core of a person and disposes toward a relationship with God. Yet, if this a priori gift is to come to explicit and a posteriori expression as Christian faith, then the Christian community must make accessible and nurture people in the specificity of its faith tradition.[15] Its religious educators are commissioned (see Rom. 10:15) with a primary responsibility in this ministry.

Lived Christian faith should shape the whole venture of Christian religious education; our educational interest is Christian faith as realized in people's lives. As such, lived Christian faith is a holistic affair that engages the whole of people's "beings": their bodily, mental, and volitional capacities; their heads, hearts, and life-styles; cognition, desire, and action; understanding, relationship, and service; conviction, prayer, and agape. As Jesus expressed concerning the great commandment, Christian existence is to engage all of people's hearts, souls, minds, and strengths (see Mark 12:28–31, etc.). In its most complete expression, *lived* Christian faith is the action of agent-subjects who through an interdependent community of Christian faith engage in a threefold dynamic of historical activities: *believing, trusting,* and *doing* God's will.

1. There is a cognitive/mental dimension to Christian faith; it is a believing activity that reflects conviction and decision. Religious faith of any kind affords a perspective for interpreting life, a way of making meaning out of existence, pattern out of chaos. In its interpretive and meaning-making activity we recognize the mental dynamic of being in faith. As people interpret their lives from a religious perspective and bring a religious pattern of meaning and ethic to their own experiences, their reason, memory, and imagination are engaged in a profoundly cognitive activity. Its dynamic engages them in efforts to recognize, understand, evaluate, and come to decision about deep convictions that enable people to have an ultimate perspective to make sense out of life and engage in the world. When faith as a human universal is given expression by a community of people through a particular tradition of religious faith, members of the community are expected to "know," come to personal conviction about, and choose to embrace the essential beliefs and values proposed by that tradition.

Christianity in particular is founded on the conviction of the primordial expression of God's self-disclosure in Jesus, the Christ, and, before him, in the people Israel. As an identifiable community of faith since then, Jesus' disciples have responded to God's revelation in history and have attempted to live their lives in its light. From that "original" revelation and Christian praxis over time, particular convictions about how to live life meaningfully and ethically have emerged in what we recognize as "the Christian faith." This tradition is mediated symbolically in many ways, including written scriptures, creeds, doctrines, and dogmas—in symbols that represent *beliefs* of the community. When we stand as a community at worship "to proclaim our faith" we begin by declaring, "*I believe . . .*" Though not all Christian beliefs are of equal importance to Christian identity (there is, as Vatican II stated, a "'hierarchy' of truths since they vary in their relationship to the foundation of the Christian faith"),[16] yet membership in Christian community both nurtures and expects conviction about its constitutive beliefs as part of the activity of *lived* Christian faith.

If people are honored as agent-subjects of their faith, then education for "believing" must engage them in *mental* activities in the best sense of that term and do so within the guiding/testing context of a Christian faith community. All of people's mental capacities for critical reflection (reason, memory, and imagination) are to be engaged in the process of recognizing, understanding, appropriating, and deciding about the tradition's beliefs and coming to conviction about them. Beliefs should never be simply conveyed and received as what Whitehead called "inert ideas"—"that is to say ideas that are merely received into the mind without being utilized, or tested, or thrown into fresh combinations."[17] Critical cognition (which varies according to developmental readiness)[18] is necessary if people are to truly make inherited beliefs their own and have personal conviction about the truth that is in them, if they are to have what Newman called "real" as distinct from notional assent. To pose Christain faith as demanding "blind submission" to the stated beliefs of the community reflects a lack of faith in both the believers and the beliefs themselves; it implies that it is impossible for a person to have an "intrinsic" but only an "extrinsic" faith as a Christian (Allport's terms). People can know a "belief" to be true, and make it their own as agent-subjects, only as they personally recognize its internal coherence and persuasiveness, its external consistency with what they know from their own lives, and when it is found to be effective in enabling them to make meaning out of and to engage responsibly in life. Christian faith is always realized and sustained in a community of like-minded disciples, but specific beliefs require personal conviction and "investing of one's heart"[19] if they are to shape lives.[20] There is, then, a cognitive and convictional component to Christian faith, yet belief alone cannot be made synonymous with the fullness of realized Christian faith.

2. There is an affective/relational dimension to Christian faith; it is a trusting in one's relationship with God in Jesus that is nurtured and realized in relationship with a Christian faith community and that shapes one's relationship with all humankind.   At the heart of lived Christian faith is a relationship of loving trust in a personal God who saves/liberates humankind in Jesus Christ. Beyond conviction of beliefs, this fiducial dimension calls people into a loving relationship of absolute trust in God as one's firm foothold on the mountainside of life, the "stone that has been tested . . . as a sure foundation" (Isa. 28:16). Like all relationships, faith is primarily an affair of the heart. Toward God our heartfelt relationship is most readily realized in worship and prayer that express sentiments of praise and adoration, thanksgiving and repentance, petition and commitment. As always with the covenant, one's relationship with God both shapes and is shaped by the quality of our relationships with other people. More than any other dimension, this affective/relational activity of Christian faith reflects its communal nature. When historically realized, Christian faith is always ecclesial; it is both nurtured by and the source of Christian community through which a people may live in right relationship with God, themselves, others, and creation.

Christian religious educators have the task of nurturing people's growth in Christian faith as agent-subjects-*in-relationship*. First, they are to foster the spiritual growth of participants to become ever more deeply in love with and trusting of the One who is Love and who is most to be trusted. This requires particular attention to spiritual formation as people of prayer, personal and communal, verbal and contemplative. Second, the relational dimension of lived Christian faith requires education to form people in identity as members of a Christian community, ever renewing its life as well. And third, we are to educate people for a deep and abiding bond of loving-kindness and justice toward the whole human family.

3. There is a behavioral/obediential dimension to Christian faith; it is an activity of "doing God's will" in the world.   Matthew's Gospel has Jesus declare that to enter God's reign it is not enough to recognize and proclaim God as our God; we must also do what God wills (see Matt. 7:21). Christian faith is realized through living with the justice and peace, wholeness and fullness of life that God wills, and such praxis is itself a source of deepened faith. The Christian dispensation particularly emphasizes that faith is realized in love. Though "love" has traditionally been distinguished from "faith," in the existential life of Christians they exist together, as Aquinas claimed, as necessarily as do "matter" and "form."[21] Or, as Paul says, "Faith expresses itself through love" (Gal.5:6). Without Christian love and the justice it demands, faith is not realized; it is not *lived* Christian faith. Though we can indeed have belief and trust without doing God's will, such refusal of faith praxis is precisely what we mean by sin—not by Christian faith. "Faith without works is as dead as a body without breath" (James 2:26).

Christians do not typically think of this dimension of obedience as an ingredient of faith itself but see it, instead, as a consequence of faith. I am proposing that obedience to God's will is of the substance of Christian faith.[22] Christian praxis is not only an expression but also a source of deepened trust and more convinced belief. We have been socialized to think that faith begins either with belief that leads to trust and then action (a typically Catholic emphasis), or with trust that leads to belief that leads to praxis (a typically Protestant emphasis).[23] However, both the Hebrew Scriptures and the New Testament often favor the sequence of the praxis of faith first. John has Jesus explain that "if you live according to my teaching, you are truly my disciples; then you will know the truth, and the truth will set you free" (John 8:31–32). Note the sequence from Christian praxis, to trusting relationship, to "knowing" the truth. In our curriculum construction it is important not to think of any of the dimensions as invariably prior to the others or of faith as realized in any fixed sequence. Only God's grace is prior to all three; they are then symbiotic with and constitutive of one another.

The behavioral aspect of faith demands that Christian religious education be grounded in and a shaper of people's historical praxis. Its curriculum should engage the present praxis of participants, bring them to reflect on it, teach the tradition with practical intent, and invite a faith response that realizes the values of God's reign in their lives and world. Opportunities for living in Christian faith should be integrated into the curriculum rather than regarded as ancillary, or worse yet of no educational significance.

This holistic understanding of lived Christian faith clearly pertains to people's whole way of "being" in the world. Realized Christian faith is an ontic affair from which no dimension or dynamic of our "being" can be excluded. As Tillich well said, "faith . . . is an act of the total personality."[24] Much of the history of Western religious education is marked by the assumption that there is a direct correlation between religious knowledge and lived faith, that to impart "knowledge about" is adequate to promote Christian identity and agency; we must transcend this partial assumption. Religious education for lived Christian faith is an ontological enterprise that is to inform, form, and transform people in heads, hearts, and life-styles; it is to engage nothing less than the "marrow bone" of people—together.

C. For the Wholeness of Human Freedom That Is Fullness of Life for All

Regardless of what church we grew up in, most people likely remember being taught that if we live our Christian faith we will save our souls (get to heaven, find justification, salvation, etc.). However it was stated in one's particular tradition, the Christian church throughout its history has taught that there is an ultimate (even eternal) consequence to living or not living one's Christian faith. I affirm this traditional truth that there is an existential consequence to Christian faith that should be reflected in the praxis of Christian religious education. However, I recast it in language theologically more reflective of contemporary scholarship and, I trust, more engaging for our time. My contention is that *both the impetus for and the consequence of people living in Christian faith is the wholeness of human freedom that is fullness of life for all, here and hereafter.*

Such freedom is to begin now within history and to be ever coming to realization on the personal, interpersonal, and structural levels of human existence. Our confidence, in Christian faith, is that we will be completely free in God's eternal presence and will finally have "life to the full"(John 10:10). However, precisely because the freedom that God makes possible in Jesus is not simply for souls later but is to begin within history, freedom as an intentional purpose should suffuse the whole enterprise of Christian faith education. I argued above for recognizing the political as well as the transcendent dimensions of religious education. Here I say that we must educate as if we know that the intent of its politics is freedom. Only thus will Christian religious educators empower Christians to participate, as their covenant requires, in God's salvific and emancipatory praxis in history.

The language of freedom is comprehensive enough to include all the values of God's reign (justice, peace, love, reconciliation, hope, joy, mutuality, equality, and so on) and at the same time is sufficiently focused to both empower and critique the praxis of Christian religious education. Christian faith, however, claims that our own efforts to live for God's reign are empowered by the grace of God, which, in the Christian covenant, is mediated through the historical event of Jesus, the Christ. In effect, then, I am proposing *freedom* and its related terms, *liberation* and *emancipation,* as the most adequate words in our time for talking about the historical consequences and responsibilities for Jesus' disciples of his life, death, and resurrection.

Since the beginning of the church, orthodox Christian faith has affirmed that the Jesus event has significantly changed our human condition, augmenting its potential for fullness of life and orienting us effectively toward God and God's intentions for us. But from the beginning too the church has struggled to express this transformation in language meaningful for different times and places (usually called soteriology). It has constantly asked the question, posed best perhaps by Anselm, *Cur Deus homo?*—Why did God become a human person? For the first Christians, Paul offered a number of images to describe the historical consequences of Jesus for humankind: salvation (Rom. 1:16), justification (Gal. 2:16–21), reconciliation (2 Cor. 5:18–20), redemption (Rom. 3:24), freedom (Gal. 5:1), transformation (2 Cor. 3:16–18), new creation (Gal. 6:15), expiation (Rom. 3:25), new life (1 Cor. 15:45), adoption (Gal. 4:4–6), sanctification (1 Cor. 1:30), forgiveness (Rom. 3:25). Subsequently, there emerged three major "models" for understanding the work of Jesus *for us*. The "classic" model images Jesus as the *Savior* who has saved humankind from the powers of evil and conquered the principalities that threaten to destroy us. The "Latin" or "satisfaction" model images Jesus as the *Redeemer* who buys humankind back from bondage and pays the price for its sins by making satisfaction to God's justice. The third, more favored by Eastern Christianity, is that Jesus as *Divinizer* has restored the divine image to humanity that was wounded or lost by original sin and is the catalyst for us living into our full potential for God.[25] The classic phrase of Athanasius summarizes well: "God became [human] so that [humans] might become God."

All such imagery and "models of atonement" emerged in different cultural and historical contexts from our own and are not necessarily effective for teaching the import of the Jesus event in a way that meaningfully engages contemporary consciousness and empowers the kind of historical praxis needed in our time. In fact, unless they are interpreted with caution and with awareness of their originating cultural context, the classic and satisfaction models, especially, can have unfortunate consequences.[26] On the other hand, while we search for new imagery to engage the imagination of our time, we can affirm the symbolic truth that the traditional models mediated in their context. As I see it, their truth is as follows: that in Jesus, God acted in a new and definitive way to save all humankind from every form of personal and social oppression, from all the powers of sin and forces of evil that hold us bound, even death being robbed of its final victory (*Savior*); that because of Jesus' life of at-one-ment with himself, God, and others, realized in total faithfulness to his own truth of God's reign, a qualitative new possibility has emerged for all humankind to live with the freedom, justice, and peace that comes from "putting things right" (*Redeemer*); that through Jesus all humankind has been empowered, as yeast leavens dough, with a new potential to say yes to life and to God and thus to reflect the glory of God through fullness of life (*Divinizer*).

When the life-giving truths reflected in the traditional soteriological symbols are subsumed into a contemporary understanding of the praxis of the historical Jesus and interpreted within present consciousness of sin as both personal and social, and when Christian soteriology is understood to point to a historical task for here as well as a promise for hereafter, then Christians can truly confess the import of Jesus Christ for human existence with the symbol Liberator. To this confession one must add the caveat that Jesus as Liberator represents humankind before God in its struggle for true freedom but is not a substitute for human effort and responsibility.[27] Far from depriving us of the task of opposing sin and working for true freedom on all levels of "being," Jesus' living, dying, and rising empower disciples to participate in liberating historical praxis through a faith that does justice with love.

Christians should not glibly claim that humankind is "free" in the face of so much evidence to the contrary. Like all Christological statements, "Jesus is Liberator" is also an eschatological one, and his disciples are to be engaged in its historical realization. To forget our responsibilities for freedoms yet to be realized is to deny the historical significance of Jesus.[28]

It is crucial that Christians be clear about "the freedom made possible in Jesus," or such language will also be problematic for our time. For example, American culture tends to understand freedom in an individualistic way—that the individual is to be free *from* internal compulsion and external constraint and *for* making his or her own choices. Though there is some truth in such a bourgeois understanding, the freedom that Jesus makes possible transcends its undue individualism. In Christian faith, Jesus sets people free *from* sin, personal and social, calls them to struggle *against* the consequences of sinful choices and structures, to be free *for* living in right relationship with God, self, others, and creation and free *to* create structural arrangements that enable others to so live.

The freedom Jesus makes possible is to begin now on all levels of existence; this is how we are to live in faith and hope of its final completion in God's eternal presence. It is a *personal* freedom that heals our inner brokenness, assures us of God's never-ending mercy, and sets us free to truly love ourselves, and God. For our *interpersonal* relationships it is freedom to say yes to the neighbor with love that does justice and to create liberated zones of "right relationship." It is a *sociopolitical* freedom that empowers us to refuse the deadening power of sinful social structures and to create political arrangements that promote fullness of life for all people and, as Paul said, for "creation that groans and is in agony" to be set free (see Rom. 8:22). The freedom made possible by Jesus will be completed as eternal and total freedom with God; meanwhile, within history it empowers disciples to live and continue in the struggle to realize "the wholeness of human freedom that is fullness of life for all."

To interpret the life, death, and resurrection of Jesus from a liberationist perspective makes evident the appropriateness of posing freedom as an existential purpose that is to shape the praxis of Christian religious education. First, *his life* for God's reign is a model of freedom and a catalyst for fullness of life for all (John 10:10). When he came into the synagogue at Nazareth to launch his public ministry, Jesus drew upon "the most important revolutionary social innovation in Jewish history, the Year of Jubilee"[29] to state his purpose. He saw himself as bringing good news to the poor, liberty to captives, sight to the blind, release to the oppressed, health to the sick, life to the dead, forgiveness to sinners (see Luke 4:18–19). His ministry of healing and forgiving, his care for the poor and suffering, his outreach to the excluded, his refusal of cultural mores that reflected sexism, racism, and class bias, his opposition to oppressive politicoreligious structures, his criteria for judging disciples, his understanding of the unity of the love commandment—all point to his lifework as emancipatory and humanizing for the human condition.

His suffering and death reflect the solidarity of God with oppressed, powerless, and suffering people. Because he refused to use coercive power to achieve his goals, and because his death resulted from the integrity of his life, Jesus' cross gives new meaning to human suffering by turning its destructive impulse into life-giving power. Through his faithfulness to God's reign, even unto death, he modeled freedom from the power of sin and freedom for his disciples to side with the outcast, the maltreated, the powerless, the oppressed, the excluded, the reviled. Jesus' *resurrection* and "that God raised him from the dead" (Rom. 10:9) is a symbol of freedom and new life for all, here and hereafter. United with Jesus in his dying and rising, we too can live with new life (see Rom. 6:3–11). Even the ultimate oppression of death has lost its sting (1 Cor. 15:55). In Christian faith we recognize that "freedom is what we have, Christ has set us free," that we are to struggle to realize freedom for all and not become slaves again (Gal. 5:1).

Freedom as an existential purpose of Christian religious education also has pedagogical advantages: it lends to it a language that is engaging, consciousness-raising, and praxis oriented. It is an *engaging* language for our time, when issues of justice and liberation have taken on an urgency that, for example, the threat of slavery and the need for ransom likely had when the image of Jesus as Redeemer first emerged. It is *consciousness-raising* in that it prompts people to think socially as well as personally, historically as well as "eternally," about the effects of sin *and* the import of Jesus. It is *praxis oriented* in that it prompts people to take on the historical responsibilities of Christian faith. By contrast, "salvation" and "redemption" can be heard today as fully accomplished in Jesus and requiring only "playing it safe" so as not to lose what has already been won.

To educate for human freedom that is whole and life-giving highlights the ontological task of Christian religious education: it is not simply to inform people about the freedom made possible in the paschal event of Jesus but to form people as well to participate in the transforming struggle to realize the passover to freedom for all. This unity of "knowing" and "being" means shaping the ontic selves of participants as agent-subjects of such freedom in place and time toward eternity. Pedagogy for lived Christian faith that is emancipatory requires the foundation of an "epistemic ontology"; that is, it must engage and form people's consciousness of their own "being" in time and place with the intent of true freedom for all.

3. Shifts in Foundation and Outcome: "Remembrance of Being" for "Conation" or "Wisdom" in Christian Faith

Seeing Christian religious education as an ontological enterprise high-lights the nurturing function of a Christian faith community. (I only note this here; it is a primary theme in Part III.) Because people's ontic selves are shaped, in large part, by their social/cultural context, forming people's "being" in Christian faith identity and agency needs a vibrant Christian faith community. The ideal will never be realized perfectly in any situation, but we can at least be clear about what is most desirable and attempt to approximate it as best we can: the more Christian religious education can form a Christian community within the environment of its teaching/learning events, and the more faith filled is the community that surrounds its participants and sponsors the enterprise, the more likely will be their education in Christian identity and agency. School-based religious educators who see their educational task as an ontological one will do well to deliberately foster a Christian community among participants, and, insofar as possible, to help nurture such an environment within the whole school. Likewise, church-sponsored schools cannot relegate the faith formation of students to the religion class but should attend, insofar as permitted by the political context, to fostering a Christian environment in the ethos of the whole school.[30]

The nature and purposes proposed above and the "ontological turn" they require signal a shift in how to perceive the intended learning outcome of Christian religious education and thus in how we structure its pedagogy. I have already introduced the term *conation* as a more adequate term than *cognition* in this regard. It is important for the remainder of this work that I describe more completely what I mean by the term *conation* and then by the "remembrance of being" it demands in the dynamics of teaching/learning events.

A. "Conation" (or Wisdom)

As a Christian religious educator my intention has been to contribute to pedagogy that promotes a learning outcome that includes and yet is more than what is typically meant by *cognition*, even in the richest sense of the term. Not only are "value concepts" like justice, love, mercy, and so on to be realized in people's very "being," but even the most "cognitive concepts"[31] are to be appropriated by people in a way that shapes their identity and agency in the world—their cognition, their affections, and their behavior. I am also convinced from my experience of it that the approach of shared Christian praxis is far more than "cognitivist."[32] To capture what it is beyond this, however, is not easy with the language of *knowledge* and its cognate terms.

In my search for a language pattern that would reflect the holistic intent of a knowing/desiring/doing that engages and shapes the whole "being" of people as agent-subjects in the world, I encountered this word *conation* and its related terms.[33] *Webster's Third New International Dictionary* defines *conation* as "the conscious drive to perform volitional acts." This implies consciousness, desire, will, and action; it encouraged me to investigate the historical roots of the word to see if it might be reclaimed and reconstructed to help describe the learning outcome of Christian religious education. I am well aware that the word has been largely lost to common usage, and though it has a significant philosophical history, it is rarely used in contemporary literature. For people not convinced of its potential, I also suggest the word *wisdom* as an approximate synonym and a term more resonant with Christian tradition. At the end of chapter 3 I further suggest that a pedagogy for conation in Christian faith intends to foster ongoing *conversion*— intellectual, moral, religious, and social as the learning outcome of Christian religious education. Again, the word *conversion* is more resonant than *conation* with common Christian discourse. However, I am convinced that the demise of *conation* in Western tradition was concomitant with the triumph of "the mind alone" and of a very disembodied, dehistoricized, and patriarchal "mind" to boot. The emergence of a more holistic mode of knowing/desiring/doing the truth warrants the revival of *conation* and its related terms.

    Conation has its immediate root in the Latin *conatus*, meaning "a conscious effort or endeavor." The verb form, *conari*, means to deliberately make an attempt. Cicero used *conatus* in a technical sense to refer to the intentional movement of "spirit" by which we maintain ourselves in existence.[34] It is sometimes still employed in psychological literature to identify the third aspect in the traditional tripartite division of the mind, as in cognitive, affective, and conative, the latter being taken to refer to willing or volition.[35] Plato is usually footnoted as the original author of this division.[36] It is true that *The Republic* designates a tripartition of the "soul" (*psyche*) as rational (*logistikon*), appetitive (*epithymetikon*), and "spirited" (*thymoeides*).[37] The latter aspect has a distinctly ethical quality in Plato's opinion and is the ability to enforce the decisions of reason against the inclinations of the appetites. But there is no etymological (or philosophical) continuity between the Greek *thymoeides* and the word *conation*. In fact, the weight of opinion seems to be that the Greek root of *conation* is *kinesis*, meaning motion or movement, and *kinoun*, meaning active agent or efficient cause. Plato attributed self-motion to the whole soul, not simply to the third aspect of it, and posed *kinesis* as the source of all activity and existence. In *Theaetetus* he wrote, "Motion [*kinesis*] is the cause of that which passes for existence, that is, of becoming."[38] In animate organisms *kinesis* is the self-realizing power of their being. Thus, from a Platonic perspective conation is not one activity of the *psyche* but the more holistic capacity and disposition people have to realize their own "being"; it is the agency that undergirds one's cognition, affection, and volition.

This sense of the term is amplified in Aristotle. Among other meanings, Aristotle used *kinesis* to describe the process by which anything moves itself from potency to act—the activity of realization as "being."[39] Human kinesis is a reflection of the actualizing activity of the First Mover (*proton kinoun*), who always moves to choose and realize "that which is most pleasant and best" because "the essential actuality of God is life most good and eternal."[40] Thus, one suggestion by Aristotle is that human kinesis is the ethical realization of one's "being," of moving to do the good.[41] Unlike the gods, however, humans move only intermittently to actualize our potential for the good because kinesis is "wearisome" for us.[42]

Aristotle claimed that human kinesis begins with sensation (*aisthesis*) and the perception of the good by reason/intuition (*noesis*); this gives rise to desire (*orexis*) that is guided by deliberate choice (*proairesis*) and moves the person from potency to act in choosing the good. In this holistic usage by Aristotle (see note 41 for variations) there is a sensate, a rational, an affective, and an agential dimension to human conation, and it has the ethical intent of doing the good; it is the correlate of praxis rather than theoria (see chapter 2, note 49). It seems, then, at least in continuity with its earliest philosophical roots to use *conation* to describe activity by persons as agent-subjects who, moved by sensation, reason, and desire, choose to realize their ontic selves with historical responsibility.

The most complete elaboration of conation in the history of Western philosophy is by Baruch Spinoza (1632–1677), for whom it was a foundational concept in his philosophy of self-preservation. Drawing from the ancient Stoics,[43] from Cicero,[44] Augustine,[45] and Aquinas,[46] Spinoza posited that all "nature" has an active impulse toward self-preservation; all animate things have an impetus to realize and persist in their own "being." He called this active disposition *conatus* (translations of Spinoza typically retain the Latin term): "The conatus to preserve itself is the very essence of a thing,"[47] and again, "The conatus with which each thing endeavors to persist in its own being is nothing but the actual essence of the thing itself."[48] In other words, the conatus of human beings is their capacity and active disposition to realize their own identity and agency in the world. In fact Spinoza identified conatus as the central trait of human existence. This general impetus for realizing our own "being" expresses itself through a variety of conati (capacities and dispositions) that reflect the body, the emotions, and the mind. The body's central conatus is its capacity and disposition for physical action;[49] the conatus of the emotions is the ability and propensity for desire;[50] and the conatus of the mind is its power and disposition to think and come to understanding.[51] Further, he also saw our conatus for "being" as guided by an ethical intent. Drawing from Aquinas, who was echoing Aristotle, Spinoza posed the various conati by which humans actualize themselves as always intending to choose and do the good.[52]

For Spinoza, then, human conatus refers to the active dispositions of people by which their corporeal, cognitive, and volitional capacities are engaged as they realize their own "being" (noun and verb) toward what is true and good. After Spinoza, however, his notion of conatus, and the term conation, faded from attention and use in Western metaphysics. Hobbes (1588–1679) and Leibnitz (1646–1716) both used conation as the human disposition toward self-preservation. But it never became a central concept in the epistemological literature, where one might expect to find it, largely, I believe, because Western epistemology suffered, as Heidegger charged, "a forgetfulness of being"; that is, "knowing" was severed from "being."

Most of the standard dictionaries and glossaries of philosophical terms do not include a definition of conation at all. As one brief insert notes, in philosophy "the concept has largely fallen into disuse."[53] It was not, however, entirely eclipsed. For example, the 1925 edition of Baldwin's *Dictionary of Philosophy and Psychology* has a helpful definition of conation as understood at the time: "The theoretical active element of consciousness, showing itself in tendencies, impulses, desires, and acts of volition."[54] In other words, conation is theoretical consciousness that is motivated by desire to move the will to act.[55] As Baldwin's definition indicates, the term never lost its recognized potential to signify a unified activity of cognition, affection, and volition, the active force of people's whole "being."

In continuity with its historical roots, my own understanding of conation emerges first from the recognition that we humans have a fundamental eros that moves us to realize our own "being" in relationship with others and the world. This "will to being" prompts us to exercise our sensate, cognitive, affective, and volitional capacities (what Spinoza called "conati") to place and maintain ourselves as agent-subjects in relationship. Though this generative source of us as historical agents is an original disposition, the eros to realize our identity and agency is profoundly relational rather than isolationist or self-sufficient. Our ontic "being" as humans is always "being toward" the world and "being with" others. Further, when exercised according to the proper form inherent in it, our conatus for "being" can transcend both subjectivism and determinism; it prompts us into "right relationship" with others and the world, to be shaped by and a shaper of our own situation in place and time.

This ontological vocation and capacity to become agent-subjects-in-right-relationship can, of course, be frustrated by personal choices and by situations or social structures that militate against one so becoming. But the spark of a person's conatus for such authentic "being" can never be entirely quenched, as long as life remains. It is a constant cohesive structure at the heart of human existence that prompts us not to remain in a state of passivity, isolation, or ignorance but rather disposes us for meaningful and responsible action, affection, and cognition. Our conatus for "being" has an innate ethical disposition that tends to move and subsume our reflection, desire, and will to appropriate the good and the truth by doing them.

In gist, then, the exercise of this foundational eros for actualized, meaningful, responsible, and relational human "being" can be called "conative activity," and the ongoing realization of such activity can be called "conation." Thus, conative activity engages people's corporeal, mental, and volitional capacities, their heads, hearts, and overt behaviors, their cognition, desire, and will as they realize their own "being" in right relationship with others and the world and contribute in ways that are life-giving for all. Conative activity is that which is most eminently "human." Conation, then, emerges and is realized as the whole ontic "being" of agent-subjects actively engaged in partnership with others to consciously know, desire, choose, and responsibly do what is most humanizing and life-giving for all. Our conation of life both reflects and arises from our whole way of "being" as agent-subjects-in-relationship—from our sensations, actions, cognitions, affections, choices, decisions—it is both consequence and source of who we are and what we do in time and place. In gist, it is our style of "being."

What now does it mean to propose "conation in Christian faith" as the desired learning outcome of Christian religious education? Clearly it engages a person's whole "being"; it subsumes cognition, affection, and volition in synthesis as a self-in-community who reflects and realizes Christian identity and agency. Christian conation means "being" and becoming Christian. Pedagogically this poses the task of informing, forming, and transforming people in the pattern of lived Christian faith—to know, desire, and do with others what is ingredient to being Christian in right relationship with God, self, others, and creation after the way of Jesus. It means educating people's "character" to realize the believing, trusting, and doing that is constitutive of lived Christian faith in the world. In fact, the old catechism answer to the question, Why did God make you? reflects what I mean by conation in faith—"to *know, love* and *serve* God in this life."[56] The unity of knowing, loving, and serving God by knowing, loving, and serving one's neighbor as oneself after the way of Jesus makes for specifically Christian faith conation. To educate people's "being" in such discipleship should permeate the whole curriculum—its dynamics, content, and environment.

Wisdom: To name the holistic learning outcome proper to Christian religious education, I believe the term *wisdom* can be used, and in continuity with its history, as a synonym for *conation.* I will typically rely on the latter term because it seems more suggestive than *wisdom* of including a critical/theoretical aspect, and *wisdom* tends to be associated unduly with what is ancient or with being old. However, it is a plenitudinous term with a rich biblical tradition, and Christian religious educators can appropriately state their intended learning outcome as "Christian wisdom."

Roland Murphy, writing of wisdom in the Hebrew Scriptures, describes it as "elusive" and "exceedingly complex"; "the many faces of wisdom cannot be captured in any logical schema."[57] There are a variety of words in Hebrew that carry the meaning "wisdom": *hokmah,* or a variation, is the most frequent, but its synonyms *binah, sakal,* and *tebunah* are also used. Over the span of biblical tradition, wisdom evolved from connoting a technical skill, to a practical mode of living, to an ethic of life, to personification as a divine partner and something truly of God. Nevertheless, some features of its biblical meaning are suggestive for using *wisdom* to describe the desired learning outcome of Christian religious education.

In the earliest tradition, wisdom is often portrayed in a morally neutral way as a craft or technical skill (Exod. 31:6) or as a kind of cleverness (2 Sam. 14:2). Later it emerges as a practical wisdom of life that brings success, respect, personal well-being, and so on. Such prudence comes from reflection on experience (Job 12:12) but is also learned from the tradition of the people (Prov. 19:20) and from people of recognized wisdom (Isa. 19:11). Regarding the latter, it appears that after the beginning of the monarchy, a special class of wise women and men emerged (2 Sam. 14:2) dedicated to a more academic study of wisdom. By the time of Jeremiah they had taken their place alongside prophets and priests as a major religious and social influence (Jer. 18:18). Thus emerged an intellectual dimension to wisdom—it was seen as both an intellectual and practical virtue—but its locus was the *leb* (Eccles. 10:3). This word is typically translated "heart," but in Hebrew Scripture *leb* reflects the total person: it is the center of *affections* (Ps. 4:7), the *intellectual* source of thought and reflection (Isa. 6:10), and the seat of *volition* and conscience (1 Sam. 24:5). Thus, wisdom is an activity of the whole person and pertains to their whole "being."

In the post-exilic period wisdom becomes more obviously a gift of God and an ethical response to God's revelation and law. The wise person does God's revealed will, and especially justice, compassion, and peace (Prov. 2); the fool is the sinner (Ps. 14:1). Wisdom is truly of God (Job 28); God's wisdom is reflected in God's saving deeds (Isa. 1:2) and in nature (Prov. 3:19) and is personified as the craftsperson God employs in the work of creation (Prov. 8:30). Humankind can come to share, though imperfectly, in God's wisdom, but always by God's gift (Prov. 2:6) rather than by human effort alone. In fact, the beginning of wisdom is the "fear" of God (Job 28:28), in the sense of respect for God manifested by loving obedience to God's will. The promised messiah is to have God's "spirit of wisdom" (Isa. 11:2).[58]

In the New Testament, Luke has Jesus present himself as wiser than Solomon (Luke 11:31); Paul portrays Christ as "the wisdom of God" (1 Cor. 1:24); James, ever conscious of praxis, teaches that true Christian wisdom is in works of peace, mercy, kindness, and justice (James 3:17–18). We hear Paul encourage the Philippians, "In your minds you must be the same as Christ" (Phil. 2:5, JB). However, Paul was using "mind" as suggested by the biblical *leb* (see Isa. 65:17; Jer. 19:5, etc.) to propose that people adopt the attitudes and commitments that were characteristic of Jesus. To take on "the mind of Christ" is to be educated to one's "marrow bone" in Christian wisdom. Consistent with the later Hebrew perspective, in the New Testament and throughout Christian tradition, wisdom was understood as a gift of God's Spirit that leads people to know, desire, and live in right relationship with God, self, others, and creation.

In the philosophical tradition of the West, attention to wisdom was overshadowed by an obsession with rational certainty; nevertheless, wisdom has a substantive subtradition. Blanchard, summarizing, writes that wisdom "may be accompanied by a broad range of knowledge, by intellectual acuteness and by speculative depth," but it cannot be equated with these or "with the elaboration of theories." Rather, wisdom's major features are "reflectiveness" and "sound judgment" regarding "the means and ends of practical life." He explains, "By reflectiveness is meant the habit of considering events and beliefs in the light of their grounds and consequences." Blanchard describes judgment as discernment from reflection on experience or from the cumulative experience of the race and as able to choose appropriately both the ends and means of living toward the good and the truth.[59]

It seems appropriate to its history and adequate to how it is likely to be heard to propose "wisdom in Christian faith" as the learning outcome of Christian religious education. Like conation, wisdom can be used to refer to a holistic human activity that includes cognition, affection, and volition and engages and shapes people's whole "being" in ways that are historically responsible and life-giving for self and others. Wisdom pertains to one's identity and agency, it is realized in one's very "being." Such wisdom arises from reflection on one's own life, from dialogue and the example of other "wise" people, and from reflection on God's wisdom as revealed through Scripture and tradition; it requires the context of dialogue and testing of a "wisdom community."[60] Pedagogically Christian wisdom presents the task of informing, forming, and transforming people in the "character" of Christian faith. And the truly wise are those who so live.

B. "Remembrance of Being"

In chapter 3, I outline the aspects of human identity and the dynamic structure of human agency to be engaged in educating for conation or wisdom in Christian faith. For now, the understanding of conation proposed above is sufficient to bring to some of the dominant architects of the epistemological tradition of the West in order to uncover what is constructive or debilitating to a conative pedagogy. Although this tradition is overwhelmingly cognitivist, I turn to it for two reasons. First, there is indeed a knowing/cognitive dimension to the task of Christian religious education and we can learn something from classic epistemological positions about how to promote authentic cognition. Second, we must unlearn much of what this tradition has bequeathed to educators. For our interest it has taken some significantly wrong "turns," for example, its cognitivist quest for rational certainty and its exclusiveness. But educators need to know both its assets and liabilities if they are to reconstruct from it and beyond it pedagogies for conation in Christian faith.

I review the literature with the hermeneutics of a Christian religious educator. The task of educating for the reign of God, for lived Christian faith and human freedom, are operative interests I bring to the epistemological tradition, and these purposes provide criteria to evaluate its assets and liabilities. As philosophical literature, however, it should also be evaluated on its own terms. We need a philosophical criterion that reflects the conative interest of Christian religious educators yet is appropriate to appraise the positions of Plato, Aristotle, and others.

In keeping with my contention that the foundation of a conative/wisdom pedagogy is an "epistemic ontology," I employ the operative criterion of "remembrance of being" to evaluate the adequacy of traditional epistemological positions to our interest. My understanding of the term *being* has been influenced by Heidegger's work and his notion "forgetfulness of being" has been suggestive for what I mean by "remembrance of being." In dialogue with the relevant aspects of Heidegger's thought, I make three points about "being" and two about "remembrance," then offer a summary of what I intend by "remembrance of being" as an evaluative criterion of epistemological positions (chapter 2). Later I use it as a ready guideline for pedagogy that honors an "epistemic ontology" for conation or wisdom in Christian faith (chapter 3).

1. I use *being* to refer to the being of ourselves, to how human beings *are*. To attend to "being" is to turn intentionally to us as historical agent-subjects-in-relationship and to our consciousness of the phenomena that arise from our lives in the world. This point is prompted by Heidegger's insistence in *Being and Time* that to know "being as such" requires turning to the "being" of those who inquire about it, that is, to ourselves.[61] For Heidegger this means turning to *Dasein,* sometimes rendered in English "human being" but more faithfully to his intent "the Being that belongs to persons as we inquire about the meaning of our own being."[62] In sum, then, "remembrance of being" calls for turning to the consciousness of our own "being" as historical agent-subjects-in-relationship.

2. *Being* includes its meaning as a verb—as in "be-ing." To suspend the rules of English grammar, "being" involves all the ways that humans "do be" in the world, all our *acts* of "being." In its verb form, our "being" is profoundly relational—it is "being toward" or "being with." Pointing to human "being" as a verb echoes Heidegger's emphasis on the essence of *Dasein* as "existence." In fact, Heidegger has been read to claim that human "being" is nothing other than a verb—that we have no essence other than our existence, that we become who we "do be"

by our own agency. He wrote, "The essence of *Dasein* lies in its existence."[63] I also diverge from him in this, which prompts my third point about "being."

3. *Being* includes its meaning as a noun—as in "I am a human being." *Being* refers to the identity we have and our inherent existential structures as humans. In contradistinction to Heidegger (see note 63), I am convinced that human beings have an ontic "essence" that is not solely our own creation. The ultimate ground of our "being" is God, the most actual of Beings, in whose image and likeness we are created and in whose Being our "being" shares. Though our own choices and actions and our social/cultural context shape our becoming, who we become does not depend entirely on our own agency or historical influences. To borrow Yeats's phrase again, there is a "marrow bone" to us that is prior to and prompts our identity and agency.

4. By "remembrance" here regarding "being" I mean the activity of consciously bringing to "mind" (engages reason, memory, and imagination) for understanding, judgment, and decision, all that arises from our whole "being" in the world. Such "remembrance" is the counteractivity to what Heidegger accused Western philosophy of—a "forgetfulness of being."[64] He claimed that Western philosophy, by erecting metaphysical systems about "being," had severed knowing from people's experience of "being," epistemology from ontology, and thus the "knower" both from themselves and from what is known. "Remembrance" means attention to the consciousness of the knower as she or he is related to the world as a historical agent-subject; for people to "remember being" is to be aware of who they are and what they do in time and place.

5. The second meaning I intend for "remembering" is more readily indicated if I hyphenate the word—"re-membering." Re-membering calls us to recognize that our "being" is shaped by "memberships" in time and place. We return with detail to this point in chapter 3. For now, I highlight that to re-member is to bring to consciousness how our situation in place and time shapes our "being" and the responsibility that we, as *members,* have to reshape our context not only for our own authentic existence (as Heidegger would have it)[65] but also for the well-being of others and of our world.

In summary then, *to be marked by "remembrance of being," a way of "knowing" and/or a pedagogy must engage the whole "being" of participants as agent-subjects-in-relationship, enable them to bring to mind the consciousness that arises from their "being" with others in the world and to discern how they are both shaped by and are to be responsible shapers of their place and time together.* Lest this technical explanation of "remembrance of being" sound too cumbersome or confusing in the work of deconstruction (chapter 2) and reconstruction (chapter 3) ahead, I note that "remembrance of being" can function as a commonsense criterion. Whenever we find epistemological positions that exclude some aspect of human "being" from the process of knowing, we will recognize "a forgetfulness of being" and something unlikely to contribute to a pedagogy for conation. Insofar as positions reflect the aspects and dynamics of who and how we are in the world, we can draw upon them to fashion a pedagogy for wisdom in Christian faith.

Chapter 2

Epistemology Re-visioned: In Search of Conation

Epistemology is the branch of philosophy that inquires about the nature, sources, and reliability of knowledge.[1] What does it mean to know? How do we come to knowledge? How do we know what we know is true? These are the questions that occupy epistemology. Responses offered to them at the beginning of Western philosophy established some patterns that have continued ever since; noting them here may help interpret what follows.

In the ancient world, people thought the gods alone were the owners and sources of knowledge, and humans could know only what the deities shared with them.[2] Recognition of human agency in knowing came in circa 600 B.C.E. with the pre-Socratic philosophers. They insisted that people are agents of their knowledge and paved the way for metaphysics—the rational inquiry into the nature and meaning of all that exists. But these first philosophers soon had to face the prior questions of the nature, sources, and reliability of knowledge itself.

It was probably the Sophists (fifth–fourth centuries B.C.E.) who raised epistemology as a pressing issue. These were wandering teachers who came to Athens from foreign cities to literally sell their knowledge. Because their livelihood depended on their success, the Sophists often attached themselves to ambitious young politicians who needed training in rhetoric to be used as persuasion for whatever idea seemed politically expedient. Their facility with words enabled the Sophists to convincingly defend paradoxical positions. This skill, however, raised the threat of relativism and the question, Is any human knowledge true or reliable? The Skeptics[3] offered one response. As their name ever after denotes, they denied the very possibility of reliable knowledge and placed the whole philosophical enterprise in crisis. Skepticism was itself rejected with a vengeance, most eminently by Plato and Aristotle, but those who argued for reliability of knowledge were soon divided by what they regarded as its source—one emphasizing the role and reliability of *reason*, the other the role of *sense experience*. Thus two general schools of epistemology emerged; though there are many variations within each one, they can still be called rationalism and empiricism.

Rationalism situates the origin and form of reliable knowledge in the intellect. By reasoned intuition, some first principles can be recognized. By rational deduction and logical analysis from those foundational propositions, other ideas follow in a descending hierarchy of truths. *Empiricism* claims that experience is the first source of true ideas. Thought begins from sense experience, and in the battle cry of empiricists, "Nothing is ever in the mind that was not first in the senses."[4] For the rationalists, then, true ideas, insofar as we can know them (and there are both dogmatists and skeptics among them), come from our use of reason alone. For empiricists, true ideas, insofar as we can know them (and there are relativists and positivists among them), begin always with sense experience.

Given this early pattern of the debate, and because of the social ideologies of the time, three other persistent features can be recognized in the tradition, albeit shared differently by rationalists and empiricists. First, the gauntlet thrown down by skeptics caused the founders of Western epistemology (and their descendants) to overreact with a quest for rational certainty and thus tended to limit reliable knowledge to ideas that are *certain*. Thereafter both rationalists and empiricists sought rational certainty, presuming that such is the mark of true knowledge; the difference between them was only methodological. The limiting of knowledge to ideas and of truth to rational certainty (rather than, e.g., truth as what one does in faithfulness to the perceived good) was a "forgetfulness of being" from the start; it echoes humankind's "original sin" of seeking to have knowledge "like gods" (Gen. 3:5).

Second, preoccupation with rationally certain ideas encouraged a dichotomy between knowing and "being," theory and praxis, mind and will, with a one-way relationship from the former as source to the latter as point of application. Even the pragmatists, the empiricists too, and certainly the rationalists failed to maintain a dialectical unity between life and thought; everyday historical activity was not taken seriously as both source and realization of ideas. This hierarchical dualism between theory and praxis, along with the assignment of the quest for rational certainty exclusively to trained academics, led to denigration of the praxis of ordinary people as a reliable way of knowing.

Third, the placement of rationally certain ideas at the top of a hierarchy of knowledge within a patriarchal culture encouraged what Sandra Harding calls an "androcentric ideology." This ideology insisted on a dichotomy between the "rational mind" and "prerational body and irrational emotions and values," and "linked" "men and masculinity . . . to the former and women and femininity to the latter."[5] It excluded women from the processes, structures, and social power of "real" knowing. Evelyn Fox-Keller summarizes Western epistemology as marked by a triumph of mind, ideas, and men over body, nature, and women.[6] This "triumph" also encouraged the myth of "objective" and "value-free" ideas that are "undistorted" by the physical, emotional, or aesthetic of life or by relational considerations.

In the review that follows, I do not pretend to decide perennial debates that have marked epistemology; that is beyond my scope and far beyond my competence. I am only proposing some re-visioning of some of the primary architects of the epistemological foundations on which Christian religious education and, indeed, all Western education functions. I mean only to suggest how this tradition must be relativized and dialectically appropriated if the purposes of Christian religious education and the learning outcome of conation or wisdom in Christian faith are to be fostered. I begin with the first great architect of the rationalist tradition—Plato.

1. Plato: Ideas Over All

Plato (c. 428–c. 348 B.C.E.) is among the greatest philosophers of Western tradition. Born in Athens at the end of its golden age (it surrendered to Sparta in 404), Plato studied with the great Socrates for at least eight years and was profoundly influenced by him. From Socrates, Plato become convinced that the human soul or mind (neither word quite translates his word *psyche*) has a constant aspiration (an eros) to reach for the morally good, which can be known by rigorous thinking; that the happy and responsible life of virtue is based on certain knowledge through which mind directs will to choose the good; that the foundation of good government is not democracy, because it relies on the opinions of common people who are leading an "unexamined life," but rather rule by philosopher kings, who, because of their reliable knowledge, will do justice by the people. Reacting to the Sophists and Skeptics of his day, Plato pointed to the unquestionable truths of mathematics as instances of rational certainty and set out to establish that we can have certain knowledge, to describe what it is and how we come to it, and to distinguish it from mere opinion.

There are, said Plato, two kinds of reality: the changing, "becoming," and thus unreliable world of sense objects in space and time and the unchanging world of ideas or eternal "forms."[7] Through our bodies and by our sense experience we can come to opinions about the world of "becoming" but not to reliable knowledge of the world of real and substantial "being." For Plato, it is by reason, unaided by sense experience, that we come to certain knowledge of the most real world of "being"—the world of forms (*eidos*). These are eternally true and unchanging ideas that lie outside the domain of temporal, material nature (e.g., objects of thought like a triangle or a concept like "the good"). Plato's word *eidos* is translated as both "form" and "idea." Our word *ideal* is probably more suggestive of what he intended, in that the world of forms is not so much the ideas in our mind as the universal and unchanging objects of our thought. The forms represent the ideals of perfection that exist in a transcendent world, the eternal standards against which we humans measure our imperfect experiences of them in everyday life. For example, when we say that something is beautiful, we recognize that it is not perfectly so but approximates some ideal standard of beauty. Because reality is only a faint shadow of the real world of forms, we cannot know them from experience but by reason alone. As Fox-Keller notes well, in defining "the proper object of knowledge as lying entirely outside the domain of temporal, material nature," for Plato, "mind undergoes a parallel purification: as nature is dematerialized, so is mind disembodied."[8]

Plato's "disembodied mind" is epitomized in his famous allegory of the cave.[9] The denizens of the cave are the great mass of humanity who rely only on sense experience. They sit with their backs to the light, facing a wall on which they can see the shadows but not the substance of reality—the world of forms. Only by turning away from the shadows of sense experience and coming up into the sunlight of reason can one gain true and certain knowledge of the essences of reality. A life in the light of reason is one of certain knowledge and thus of virtue—the life of the true philosopher. People who attain it have a responsibility to try to release from the cave those deluded by the shadows of experience.

Plato depicted his process of reliable knowing most graphically in the image of a line that the reader is to "cut into two unequal parts to represent in proportion the worlds of things seen and things thought, and then cut each part in the same proportion."[10] It is best to imagine this as a perpendicular line, divided into four parts from the bottom up to represent four human efforts to know. The bottom two parts (designated AB and BC) pertain to perception of the sense world, and the second two (CD and DE) to our knowledge of the world of ideas. There is a clear and qualitative dividing line between them (at point C). The two lower parts, because they are body dependent, provide mere opinion. The two upper parts, drawing upon the mind alone, provide knowledge, and the fourth part certain knowledge, of the forms.

The most sensory experience of the visible world (AB) is recognized by imagination, whose object is images.[11] It gives us the most untrustworthy opinion—conjecture. For Plato, poetry, painting, sculpture, drama, and religious ritual are totally unreliable as ways of knowing. The second level of perception of the sense world (BC) is of concrete things, recognition of sense objects. This activity can perceive only the world of flux and change, the world of "becoming"; it gives rise to belief, but that is still a form of opinion (albeit slightly more reliable than conjecture). It cannot be a source of true knowledge and virtuous living.

To come to knowledge, people must leave the bodily world of senses and passions and cross over into the qualitatively different world of mind and its ability to reason by itself and within itself. For "knowledge of true being," wrote Plato, we must be "rid of eyes and ears and, so to speak, of the whole body" and employ "the mind alone."[12] On level three (CD) of the ascending hierarchy, the first level of reliable knowledge, Plato says that discursive reason (without examining its assumptions)[13] draws images from the sensory world to understand certain ideas in mathematics or the natural sciences: images, for example, of triangles or circles, or of air, water, or fire. Knowing the forms of such things is true knowledge and beyond mere opinion, but precisely because knowledge of them is tied to particular instances in the visible world, and thus depends at least partially on human bodiliness, such understanding does not bring people to the highest forms—to knowledge of the true, the good, the beautiful. This is reserved to the level of "pure reason."

		OBJECTS	THOUGHT	
Intelligible Unchanging World of Reason	E	Highest Forms (Ideals)	Reason (Intellectual Intuition)	Reliable Knowledge
	D	Forms of Science and Mathematics	Understanding (Discursive Reasoning)	
	C	*Line of demarcation between opinion and knowledge*		
Visible Changing World of Senses	B	Sense objects	Belief	Mere Opinion
	A	Images	Conjecture	

The fourth level (DE) gives rise to the most certain knowledge of the highest forms. Here, the intuition of pure reason, unaided by images or sense objects or discourse, can recognize the universal and unchanging truths of the intelligible world of forms. The mind can then reason dialectically from these ideas (i.e., analyze their essences and assumptions) to see their relationship to one another and to logically deduce other truths in a descending hierarchy.[14] Plato believed that the human soul has an eros for this most real, universal, and unchanging world of forms, to withdraw from bodily influences and think for itself about clear and certain ideas.

If they are independent of bodily experience and sensory images, we can well ask Plato where such ideas come from. His answer was that the forms are already in the mind or soul by transmigration from previous lives. Ideas are already in the mind as sight is already in the eye, and we simply recollect them by *anamnesis,* by reminiscence.[15] Though the proddings of sense experience may help to bring them to consciousness, the forms are known by the immortal soul, where they are latently present in memory and recognized by rational intuition.

Plato's understanding of knowledge and knowing became the foundation for all the great rationalists and idealists after him. His legacy for Christian religious education is ambiguous; each of his possible assets for a conative pedagogy has a corresponding and weightier liability. The assets reflect a "remembrance of being" and the liabilities a "forgetfulness." I can think of at least three couplets of assets and liabilities.

A first asset is Plato's conviction that there is, beyond sense perception, a reliable source and measure of truth that is not of our construction alone. People who believe in God can claim no less.[16] On the other hand, the hierarchical dualism he posited between mind and body in the pursuit of such truth caused him to dismiss historical knowledge and what is most human as unreliable for truth and virtuous living. By situating truth outside time and history, he encouraged an unqualified ideationalism. This often distracted Christians from their historical responsibility to "do the truth with love" and encouraged them to seek instead an individualistic and otherworldly salvation. Further, disparaging of the historical as a way of knowing threatened the historicity of divine revelation, a central conviction of Christian faith. Christians believe that God reveals Godself in creation, life, and the events of history and that "the truth" did not remain otherworldly but became flesh in a person. This truth is not to be simply known about in our heads or sought in another world but historicized now by living like Jesus. In gist, excluding the body from human knowing encourages Christians to ignore the incarnational aspect of their faith—the truth incarnate in Jesus and to be incarnated in their own time and place.

A second asset is Plato's wise affirmation of the role of clear thinking and right ideas/ideals in human effort to make meaning and live virtuously; at least he intuited that "knowing" is to shape "being"— a conative sentiment. He proposed an ideal of perfection that draws us forward by desire, which is clearly resonant with how the reign of God should function in Christian living. On the other hand, his claim that knowing the ideals of the good, the just, and so on will lead people to so live becomes patently false as we "remember" our own "being." We often fail to do the good we know (see Rom. 7:19). Here too, by dismissing historical "being" as a way of knowing, he failed to see the role of praxis in forming people's wills in the habit of virtue. And though Plato presumed that clarity of thought would lead to virtuous living, he excluded from reliable thinking the function of imagination, so crucial to moral decision making.

A third asset is Plato's conviction about the innate desire and capacity people have for knowing and recognizing the truth. Contra Plato, this capacity is shaped by experience, but a "remembrance of being" indicates that our ability to know the truth is present in us even before experience. This is not explained by transmigration of the soul that carries in memory the truth learned in previous lives but by an innate structure of cognition that shapes our experience and our understanding and judgment of it (a position significantly developed later by Kant). Plato's sense of a universal capacity for knowledge should have heralded inclusivity and active participation by all in the process of knowing. However, he was eminently exclusive and elitist in who he perceived as agents of knowledge. For Plato, knowledge is best joined with power and placed in the hands of an elite and exclusive group of men who are to rule the rest. His ideal Greek was an educated man, and though his sexism was amplified in Aristotle, he saw women as less capable than men of being the philosophers who rule the people.[17]

2. Aristotle: Living "Three Lives"

Aristotle (384–322 B.C.E.) became a pupil of Plato's at the Academy in Athens at eighteen and remained under his master's tutelage for about twenty years. After Plato's death, perhaps disappointed at not being named his successor, Aristotle left the Academy and eventually opened his own school, the Lyceum. He never left behind Plato's influence, however; in epistemology especially Plato remained both his mentor and his foil. Aristotle rejected Plato's theory of a separate world of ideal forms; he said that forms do not exist apart from the matter of the visible things to which they give form. Conversely, sensible things are not the poor, shadowy reflections of an ideal and transcendent world; their substantial reality resides in things themselves. Consequently, knowing begins with the study of nature, real things, everyday life, as presented by the senses and experience. On the other hand, he was determined not to limit "knowledge" to the experiential and practical. The Sophists of his time claimed that philosophical knowledge is of value only if it can be used to direct practical behavior. Though we will note Aristotle's concern for the practical and political, he saw the Sophist position as reductionistic and posing a threat to the great intellectual enterprise of Greek philosophy. He defended theoretical knowledge as a value and satisfaction of itself and not simply a means to practical or productive ends. In his never quite successful attempt to honor both empirical and rationalist positions and theoretical, practical and productive interests, we discern Aristotle's understanding of knowledge and of the ways of knowing.

Contra Plato, Aristotle rejected the notion that for reliable knowledge one must transcend sense experience. Lived experience is a source of reliable knowledge for directing practical (*praxis*) and productive (*poiesis*) activities. Beyond that, theoretical or "scientific" knowledge (*theoretikos episteme*) is stimulated by sense experience, which gives first intimations through historical instances of universal ideas. The dynamic of moving from particular sense perceptions to universal ideas seems to be by twin processes of induction and abstraction. Inductively, the senses present "sensible forms" of particular things to the mind/soul. At first the psyche's sense perception is by a "passive intellect" that simply inducts into itself the form of the thing perceived, much as wax receives the imprint of something but not the thing itself. Then an "active intellect" takes over to abstract universal ideas from particular instances provided by the senses. It is not simply the repetition of sense experiences, however, that creates universal ideas; they are recognized by the intuition of active intellect. Thus, if the dynamic of sense experience and passive intellect functions "from the bottom up," the active intellect has its own independent activity that functions "from the top down." By intellectual intuition (*nous*), a person can discern self-evident principles "of things that are of necessity."[18] From such certain first principles, the mind can proceed downward by dialectical reasoning to scientific knowledge (physics, math, or theology/first philosophy) or upward to wisdom (*sophia*), which is "the most perfect of the modes of knowledge . . . as regards the things of the most exalted nature."[19]

It seems that, for Aristotle, though the mind is stimulated by sense experience, rational intuition has its own source of knowing beyond the instances of experience. (One wonders if for Aristotle the mind's innate capacity for universal ideas played much the same role as the world of forms did for Plato.) But though he may not have abandoned it, Aristotle modified Plato's cognitive ladder by claiming that experience provides reliable knowledge for practical and productive activities and is stimulating, somehow, for theoretical knowledge as well. This modification also led him to revise (but not abandon) Plato's social stratification of knowing, no longer confining it to an elite group of philosophers."

Aristotle shared Plato's conviction that the ultimate purpose of all knowledge is to live a good and happy life according to virtue, and that the best life is lived according to the highest virtue.[20] Having broadened the source of reliable knowledge beyond "pure reason," Aristotle recognized that people other than philosophers can be happy and virtuous, leading him to analyze the ways of life that are available to a "free" and "refined" man (exclusivity intended: for Aristotle, free people were adult male citizens). This analysis led to his famous tripartite division of "ways of life" (or "ways of being"?). Each one is a mode of engaging intelligently and virtuously in the world: *theoria, praxis,* and *poiesis.* They give rise respectively to theoretical/scientific knowledge that is an end in itself, to practical/political knowledge of how to live ethically in society, and to productive/creative knowledge of how to make things or art. Because I argue that pedagogy for conation in Christian faith must engage and promote critical reflection, ethical action, and imaginative creativity and attempt to reconstruct Aristotle's notion of praxis to subsume theoria and poiesis as foundation of a conative pedagogy, I will dwell on Aristotle's understanding of each of the three lives in some detail here.

Theoria. For Aristotle, this is the life of theoretical and disinterested reflection on nonsensible realities. Its purpose is to discover first principles and to reason downward from them to scientific truths or upward toward transcendent and divine wisdom (*sophia*), the most perfect knowledge. Theoretical knowledge is an end in itself, because it brings joy by satisfying a natural desire we have for it.

There are three "faculties of the soul" (capacities of the psyche?) that give rise to and are developed by the life of theoria: rational intuition (*nous*), by which necessary and universal principles are recognized; the power to reason syllogistically (*episteme*) from first principles to scientific knowledge; and theoretical "wisdom" (*sophia*), which includes both *nous* and *episteme* but goes beyond them and above them, in that "wisdom [*sophia*] is both scientific knowledge [*episteme*] and intuitive intelligence [*nous*] as regards the things of the most exalted nature."[21] This divine wisdom requires transcending the physical world to enter into interior contemplation of things eternal. The greatest happiness for humankind is the life of historically detached contemplation;[22] it is most virtuous and best because it is most akin to the divine. Aristotle believed that God is removed from purposeful activity in human history and absorbed in rational contemplation—in the thinking of thoughts. People can approximate God's life of theoria "in virtue of something within [us] that is divine."[23] Thus, he concluded, "Among human activities that which is most akin to the divine activity of contemplation will be the greatest source of happiness."[24]

Praxis. Aristotle understood human praxis,[25] the second way of life open to "free citizens," as constituted by "twin moments"—one of engagement and one of rational reflection, with each dependent on the other. Praxis[26] is conduct done reflectively and with historical purpose, or, conversely, it is reflection and intentionality that is realized in human conduct. Aristotle's most frequent use of the term *praxis* was to describe reflective and purposeful human activity of any kind. Yet he used it most precisely to describe ethical conduct according to "right reason" in political life. The purpose of praxis is further praxis, not rationally certain ideas. Its "knowing" both is expressed in and arises from reflective and responsible living in society. Reflecting the social stratification of his time, for Aristotle, social praxis excluded women, children, and slaves and is superior to the life of poiesis of the craftsperson.

Aristotle wrote that "there are three elements in the soul which control action [*praxis*] and the attainment of truth, namely, Sensation, Intellect, and Desire." He added, "Of these, Sensation never originates action, as is shown by the fact that animals have sensation but are not capable of action [*praxis*]."[27] It seems sensation is more a precondition than a source of praxis in the sense that experience of the world is a requirement for intelligent engagement with it. The "intellect" involved is practical or "calculative"[28] that enables people to live by "right reason" rather than being swayed by sensual appetite. This practical reasoning differs from the speculation of theoria in that here reasoning is not an end in itself but has the practical intent of making right judgments concerning ethical action. It discerns the general principles that apply in particular situations to guide right decisions.[29] Then desire (*orexis*), informed by practical reasoning, moves the will to choice (*proairesis*), which is "desire and reasoning directed to some end";[30] thus, "right choice" is the "efficient cause" of praxis.

When a person engages sensation, practical reason, and right desire and acts on right choice, praxis is an expression and formative source of what Aristotle called *phronesis*—prudence or practical *wisdom*. He defined prudence as "a truth-attaining rational quality concerned with action in relation to things that are good and bad for human beings."[31] A "prudent" person both knows and acts toward the "right ends" and with the "right means" to achieve the greatest good. Practical wisdom is an "intellectual virtue"[32] in that it involves rational reflection. Yet its intent is practical rather than theoretical; the prudent person has both the ability and the disposition to apply rationally discerned and generally true principles to particular circumstances, to make the right practical judgment and to act accordingly.[33]

Praxis for Aristotle is clearly a cyclical and holistic process. It begins with historical engagement and employs practical reason and right desire to choose further right praxis. Its exercise both arises from and forms people in virtuous character.[34] Of the "three lives," it is most clearly concerned with wisdom or conation.

Poiesis. In its most general sense, poiesis for Aristotle was the intelligent way of life and knowing that is productive and creative, usually of concrete artifacts. The producing involves and the product expresses a kind of knowledge, but though praxis is reflective doing, poiesis refers to some kind of artistic or skilled "making."[35] The creative science par excellence for Aristotle was poetics, to which he devoted an entire treatise, but poiesis also included the professions (medicine, law, etc.) and the crafts of the artisans, his most frequent use for the term.

The "faculty of the soul" that prompts the life of poiesis is what Aristotle called *techne*—sometimes translated "art" but also "skill" or "craft." For Aristotle, *techne* refers to both fine art and to utilitarian production, to sculpture and to stone cutting (see note 35). There is a rational quality to the practice of an art, at least a technically oriented rationality. This is precisely what makes poiesis a valid way of knowing and an expression of knowledge. He writes, "Art [*techne*] . . . is a rational quality, concerned with making, that reasons truly."[36] But there is clearly another dimension to art besides rational knowledge with productive purpose. Taking medicine as an example, Aristotle explained that "if a man has theory without experience and learns the universals, but does not know the particular contained in it, he will fail in his treatment: for it is the particular that must be treated."[37] In addition to rational knowledge, then, art requires practice, in the sense of doing a particular thing repeatedly to develop the ability to do it well. Conversely, from practicing a skill, not only does one develop the ability to do it well, but one also comes to discern the principles involved in the art of it.

What of imagination in poiesis? In contrast to Plato, Aristotle saw imagination as essential to all rational activity; he noted often that "the soul never thinks without a mental image."[38] Further, he said it has a role in prompting desire and thus praxis; he wrote, "The living creature . . . is not capable of [desire] without imagination."[39] Beyond this, however, we cannot detect any developed sense of imagination's creative and ethical function as understood today. At times Aristotle posed memory and imagination as symbiotic activities that belong to the same "part of the soul,"[40] with imagination drawing its images from what is already in memory by a process of imitation (*mimesis*). On the other hand, he also made clear that imagination is not simply an exercise in duplication. It involves constructing and creating, and this is especially evident in the art of poetry. Though everyone has a "natural instinct for representation," poets have the gift of imagining and proposing what might be rather than simply reporting what already is.[41]

For Aristotle poiesis was the lowest and least reliable way of knowing. At times he wrote appreciatively of the poets and the service professions, but reflecting his social bias he considered poiesis the lowest form of social life for a citizen and the least reliable way of knowing. With the gender bias of his context, Aristotle considered women's domestic work to be the very lowest form of poiesis.[42] He failed to recognize the social significance and way of knowing of women's socially assigned nurturing labor. In one sense he was correct in not categorizing childbearing and child rearing as simply productive; as Nancy Hartsock, commenting on this, writes, "One does not (cannot) produce another human being in anything like the way one produces an object such as a chair."[43] However, Aristotle's exclusion of work socially assigned to women from what was appropriate for a free citizen meant that no way of life open to women was deemed to have social freedom or significance, that their domestic work was not considered "real work," and that what Hilary Rose calls "women's caring labor and the knowledge that stems from participation in it"[44] was excluded as a valid way of knowing and form of knowledge. To subsume the creativity of poiesis into a pedagogy for wisdom/conation we must reject Aristotle's debasement of it as class biased and sexist.

The "Three Lives" and Hints for Conation

In spite of recognizing that sense experience is at least a stimulant to theoretical reasoning, Aristotle hierarchized and trichotomized the "three lives" from one another.[45] Both must be rejected in pedagogy for conation in Christian faith, the hierarchy on theological grounds and the trichotomy because it reflects a "forgetfulness of being." First, Aristotle found legitimation for theoria as the highest wisdom in his understanding of God as a God of "thought," removed from all concern or engagement in human history. The Hebrew and Christian Scriptures, however, portray a God of love and justice who is actively engaged in covenant with all humankind and with a special favor for the poor, oppressed, and marginalized. The way of "being," and thus of "knowing," most like this God's is the life of historical praxis and poiesis that is life-giving for all. Second, even a momentary "remembrance of being" indicates that all intentional participation in life is marked by theoretical, practical, and poetic/productive activities, with all three in constant concert to realize our "being" in place and time.

On the other hand, Aristotle's delineation of the "three lives" and his affirmation of each as a valid way of knowing "the truth,"[46] if they are woven together and honored pedagogically as co-constitutive activities of our "being" in the world, begins to suggest the holistic engagement needed to promote conation or wisdom. Likewise, his attempt to include both the empirical and the rational in the dynamic of "knowing" (though never satisfactorily explaining their relationship) signals a "remembrance of being" to be reflected in pedagogy for conation/ wisdom. I turn now to consider the "three lives" to indicate what to reject and what to retrieve from his understanding of them. Then, I hint at how I hope to subsume all three into a conative pedagogy.

Aristotle's theoria reflects a "forgetfulness of being" in presuming a mode of knowing and form of knowledge that is ahistorical, dispassionate, and disinterested. As with Plato, we can affirm his commitment to reason and logical thinking, but his perception of its dynamics must be roundly rejected when we "remember" the sociology of knowledge and of the human psyche. On the other hand, his emphasis on the contemplative aspect of rational activity is an asset for a conative pedagogy. Aristotle's contemplative life is not the same as authentic Christian contemplation. (See note 22.) Yet his recognition that there is "something within [us] that is divine"[47] reminds us to honor the capacity for spiritual wisdom within all people and to recognize mystical, and numinous dynamics in the process of coming "to know as we are known" (see 1 Cor. 13:12).[48]

In Aristotle's notion of praxis, we must reject both his separation of it from theoria and its relegation to an inferior social and cognitive status. This is especially imperative for an "epistemic ontology" to ground education in Christian faith. At its core, Christianity is realized as an historical praxis; in the Hebrew and Christian Scriptures, one's real "knowledge" of ultimate truths and one's doing of God's will are symbiotic. So too we must reject his separating of praxis from productive and creative labor (a dichotomy not challenged until Marx) and recognize both the "forgetfulness of being" involved (the very language that articulates and shapes human praxis is an act of "poiesis") and the class and gender bias reflected in their separation. On the other hand, we can affirm his predominant notion of praxis as including all reflective activity that engages the whole person in sensation, intellect, and desire to come to practical understanding, judgment, and ethical choice. In fact, as Aristotle posed praxis as the social expression of *kinesis*, and of *phronesis*[49] I find warrant to propose a holistic understanding of praxis as the source and expression of conation and wisdom.

Regarding poiesis, we need to reject Aristotle's limiting of it to "productive" labor that produces "things," thus excluding reproductive and "caring labor" that forms people. Further, he was wrong to relegate "work" to the periphery of worthwhile life and to disparage it as a way of knowing. As Aristotle found theological legitimation for his social biases toward poiesis in his notion of God, on the same basis Christians must reject his position. We believe that God is the originating and continuing creator and loving parent of humankind and that we, as likeness of our creator, participate in God's ongoing creative and procreative activity in history.[50] A pedagogy for conation in Christian faith must engage people's capacities and activities of poiesis, but reconstructed beyond Aristotle to include all the creative, imaginative, and life-giving "work" of all humankind. Further, his separation of human production/creativity from the mental labor of reflection and from the praxis of social ethics helped pave the way for the "technical rationality" of a later era, with its potential to destroy both self and society. Yet, in his recognition of poiesis as a virtuous life and a valid way of knowing, Aristotle took a significant step beyond Plato. His understanding of memory and imagination was limited, but he had some sense of the role of both in creative human agency.

These criticisms notwithstanding, I believe we find in Aristotle's "three lives" the rudimentary activities that, woven together, constitute a "remembrance of being" and that when engaged pedagogically are likely to promote conation or wisdom. Anticipating here what I later outline in detail, I believe educators are to engage, weave together, and hold all three activities in a symbiotic unity—the theoretical/contemplative (theoria), the practical/political (praxis), and the creative/imaginative (poiesis). When the three are reformulated and combined in a conative pedagogy of Christian faith, the "theoretical" dimension is reflected in at least three ways: by contemplative activity to discern God's self-disclosure in present reality; by critical reasoning on people's own "being" in time and place and on the meaning of the Christian faith for the present; and by a narrative activity that goes beyond Aristotle's dehistoricized notion of theoria and makes accessible the practical wisdom from God's revelation to this community over time—Christian "Story." The pedagogy is "practical" in that it arises from, engages, and intends to shape people's "being" in time and place, and thus has a dynamic suited to conation in Christian faith. The "creative" dimension is honored by attending to people's historical visions and to the Vision of God's reign by enlivening their imaginations and empowering their wills to be co-creators of it now.

Conceptually, I subsume what Aristotle intimated by the "three lives" into a holistic understanding of "being," and I designate the historical realization and consciousness of our "being" in time and place as the activity of praxis. I pose *praxis*, redefined beyond but also resonant with Aristotle's most general use of the term, as synonymous with "being" in the world because: (a) of the three "lives," it can be most readily reconstructed to subsume the activities of the other two; (b) from its history it seems most capable of the three to designate human "being" in time and place; and (c) it has a clear correlation with wisdom and conation, as Aristotle intuited (see note 49). In the pedagogy of shared Christian praxis, I propose placing people's shared reflection on their "being" in time and place and their reflection on Christian Story/Vision in a dialectical relationship that is mediated by an imaginative/creative activity akin to poiesis.

3. Christian Faith and Greek Philosophy: Unlikely Partners

With severe selectivity required in such a condensed story of Western epistemology, between Aristotle and Descartes I only note the initial encounter between Greek philosophy and Christian faith, then highlight the epistemologies of Augustine and Aquinas. I select them because they are the great "Christianizers" of Plato and Aristotle, respectively, and surely two of the most influential architects of the church's educational praxis—where its operative epistemology is most evident.

We could expect that Christian disciples and Greek philosophers would first perceive each other as unlikely partners. Christianity was in continuity with its Jewish roots, and the Hebrew and Greek worldviews are markedly different. For the Hebrews and for Jewish faith, God is not a cosmic intelligence who gives rational design to creation according to a world of ideal forms (Plato) or a removed and disinterested "first mover" whose only activity is "thought" (Aristotle). Instead, God is imaged as like a loving person who created and sustains creation with abiding care, who made people in God's own likeness to be partners with God and one another; though transcendent "other," God is also immanent in human history with loving-kindness and saving compassion and actively present on behalf of fullness of life for all. In Hebrew faith, the world and history are not unreliable shadows (Plato) or distractions from God (Aristotle) but the loci of God's self-disclosure and saving activity. The happiest life of greatest wisdom and highest virtue is not rational contemplation of ultimate ideas but obedience to what God wills for all—shalom, the intent of God's covenant with people. "Knowing God" is not an activity of pure reason or of disengaged contemplation of ideas by an elite few but a profoundly historicized, relational, loving, obediential, and egalitarian process in which the truly wise person is the one who lives peace, justice, compassion, as God wills. Greek philosophers had come to rely on reason, logic, and dialectic to know rationally certain ideas. The Hebrews too had a strong commitment to study, but for wisdom they turned to the faith testimony of their ancestors to whom, they believed, God had revealed Godself and how they were to live as God's people. How could "revelation" be reconciled with Greek commitment to metaphysics?

Christianity at first looked like an augmentation of a Hebrew worldview and "way of knowing." In Christian faith, the "incarnation" of God in Jesus, the Christ, is the ultimate act of divine praxis in history. Jesus is confessed as the divine word made flesh as model for how to do God's will, and disciples are to follow his "way" of loving God by loving their neighbor as themselves. Divine truth is appropriated, not by achieving certainty of ideas, but by coming into right relationship with God and Jesus, whom God sent (see John 17:3). "The (one) without love has known nothing of God" (1 John 4:8), and it is by *living* as Jesus' disciples that people come to know truth that sets them free (see John 8:31–32). Far from belonging to an epistemically privileged few, the first Christians heard Jesus invite all, with a special outreach to the marginalized, into an "inclusive discipleship of equals."[51] As Nicholas Lobkowicz asks rhetorically, How could this movement "embrace the extreme intellectualism of the pagans"?[52]

At first, the Christian attitude toward Greek philosophy was one of extreme caution. The *Didache* (c. 100 C.E.), perhaps the first great catechetical document outside the canon of the New Testament, makes clear, with an anti-Gnostic tone, that Christian faith is "a way of life" that welcomes all and requires strict moral praxis supported by prayer and worship in a community of service.[53] When Gnosticism emerged as a movement among Hellenistic Christians, it was recognized and condemned as heresy. In their overassimilation of philosophical ideas into Christianity, Christian Gnostics claimed that faith is only a stepping stone to *gnosis,* a mystical and secret knowledge reserved to a few rather than a way of life for all. Against them, Irenaeus (c.130–c.200 C.E.) made the argument on behalf of orthodox Christianity that the Scriptures and the church carry the life-giving truth and practical wisdom needed for salvation, and it is available to everyone.[54]

On the other hand, even the New Testament authors were aware that the Christian gospel needs to be "redacted" according to the cultures of its listeners. "Inculturation" increased as the Christian movement spread out of its Jewish environment and into the Hellenistic and Gentile worlds. On finding himself with an audience of philosophers in the Areopagus at Athens, Paul was clearly concerned to couch his message in a way more likely to be heard (see Acts 17:22–34). As the great Christological and Trinitarian controversies emerged, patristic writers recognized that orthodox Christianity needed the thinking and terms of Greek philosophy to combat the heretics and give a systematic articulation of Christian doctrine. There were Christian authors who shared the skepticism of Tertullian that "Jerusalem has no need of Athens."[55] More realistic writers, however, recognized the potential assets in Greek philosophy for bringing the church to creedal clarity. The school of thought readiest at hand was Neoplatonism.

Neoplatonism, as its name implies, was a revision of Plato's thought, mixed with some elements from Aristotle and mystical religions.[56] Plotinus (205–270 C.E.)[57] expounded its central positions and saw himself as clarifying the thought of Plato. He said all that is truly real and really true lies beyond the sensory and historical in a hierarchical world of "thought" or "mind." At the top of the hierarchy is "the One" (also called "the Good"), the ultimate reality and divine source of all that is. Below "the One" is the "intellectual principle" (*nous*) that embraces Plato's world of ideal forms, and below this is the "universal soul." Individual souls have "reason" because they share in this "world soul" and are emanations of "the One." The rational soul, unaided by the body, is the source of all sensation, perception, and knowledge; its highest activity is rational contemplation of "the One." Contemplation is supported by "theoretical reasoning," which Plotinus understood as the soul's capacity to find reflections of the ideal forms in physical creation. But the process and purpose of all rational knowing is not to know the world, oneself, or how to live but to come into mystical communion with "the One."

Even Plato's practical notion that people who come into enlightenment are to return to the cave to release its denizens from mere opinion, was absent from Plotinus. Benedict Viviano says that as Christians embraced a Neoplatonist quest for "an enlightenment of soul which led to union with the One in a blissful spiritual eternity beyond this vale of tears," the symbol of God's reign as an intrahistorical task correspondingly diminished.[58] Certainly in the Neoplatonism that dominated philosophy for almost a thousand years, theoria as rational contemplation and scientific reasoning came to triumph as the most preferred life and the only reliable way of knowing. Praxis was disparaged as unreliable for cognition, and it was overshadowed by the contemplative life as a way to "perfection."[59] The "productive," and even more so the reproductive and care-giving life was dismissed as a degraded way of "being" and never a way of attaining "real knowledge."

Some remained (and remain) skeptical about "the rationalism of the pagans," yet Christian scholars recognized the need to forge a "Christian paideia,"[60] a system of thought that could clarify and express Christianity in terms resonant for Greek philosophy and culture. Most likely the first systematic attempt was carried on at Alexandria, the center of Neoplatonism and site of a school of Christian catechesis.[61] Clement (c.150–c.215 C.E.) and his student Origen (c.185–c.254), both much influenced by Neoplatonism, were the most significant voices there and led the efforts to forge a Christian paideia. As catechists, however, they recognized the challenge of presenting Christianity in metaphysical language without reducing it to a system of ideas. Were they successful? The reviews are mixed. Some still claim that their "ideationalism" was heretical to Christian faith.[62] I prefer the majority opinion; I appreciate their initial efforts to bring faith to understanding and culture to "the faith."[63] Standing on their shoulders, Augustine of Hippo was more successful in developing a Christian paideia.

Augustine: Truth Already Within

With Constantine and the Edict of Milan (313), Christianity began to emerge as the established religion of the Roman Empire; its perspective shaped the social, cultural, and intellectual life of the West thereafter. No one person was more influential in forming the thought patterns of "Christendom" than Augustine of Hippo (354–430). Augustine saw his task as weaving together revelation and reason in a coherent theology to promote the "spiritual wisdom" of Christian faith (see note 87).

In describing how people come to "know their faith," Augustine first affirmed that faith is by God's grace, which moves the will to believe. Faith is a gift prior to understanding. In fact, "a certain faith" is the "beginning of knowledge,"[64] and Augustine often quoted the phrase (suggested to him by Isa. 7:9), "Unless you believe, you shall not understand."[65] He also insisted on the normative role of scripture and church teachings for instructing people in Christian beliefs and morals. Yet Augustine was convinced that faith must move beyond blind assent; it needs to be made intelligible and complete by reason, and for this philosophers can be helpful. He "confessed" that Neoplatonism had saved him from Manichaeism[66] and skepticism; it remained his philosophical viewpoint thereafter and shaped especially his epistemology.

Reflecting Plato, Augustine said that there is a clear division between the intelligible and sensible worlds[67] and that the soul/mind is the only source of what qualifies as "knowledge." Soul, he believed, is always related to body "as ruler to ruled."[68] As a farmer might use a plow, so soul/mind uses the bodily senses, but the latter are never the efficient cause or originator of knowledge. He wrote, "Man [sic] as he appears to us is a rational soul, making use of a mortal body."[69] But by presenting the "capacities of the soul" as reason (or intelligence), memory, and will, Augustine went beyond Plato, most significantly with will. Further, in this threefold schema of the soul's "capacities," Augustine did not claim that they are separate faculties; they are symbiotic activities that arise from the same soul. Reason, memory, and will, though recognizably distinct, are as much one as God is One.[70] The soul is reason as the source of understanding; the soul is memory of what the soul already knows and of its images for the future; the soul is will that initiates human action by desire and choice. How did Augustine understand each capacity in the process of knowing?

Reason. Augustine saw the soul/mind as capable of two kinds of reasoning. The first is the "gaze of the mind" when turned upward by the eros of will toward God, eternal truths, the ideal forms, the virtues as moral principles, and so on; this is a superior form of reasoning or contemplation. The second is when reason is turned downward by the will toward temporal and sensible things. The gaze upward leads to wisdom (*sapientia*), and the gaze downward to knowledge (*scientia*), and the former is of greater value than the latter.[71]

This distinction between the "gazes" of the mind meant that "there are two kinds of things which are known: one, the knowledge of those which the mind perceives through the senses of the body, the other of those which it perceives through itself."[72] For knowing what is known independently of the senses, the mind possesses a kind of spiritual sight or inner illumination because it is a reflection of the mind of God.[73] Note, however, that the mind is sole agent and efficient cause of knowledge through the bodily senses. Sensation and perception are actions of the mind through the body, used as a tool; for Augustine, mind can act on body but never body on mind.

Memory. Augustine saw memory as the great "treasure" chamber where we retain all we already know, whether by thought itself, by thought about sense objects, or "through the testimonies of others."[74] Further, memory is the storehouse of our capacity to recognize and judge the truth or falsity of our thoughts. In a very Platonist sentiment, all learning is a kind of "remembrance" or recognizing of knowledge already in the soul.[75] Knowledge and wisdom are not in memory by transmigration (as in Plato), however, but by the presence of God in Christ to the inner person. Christ is "that teacher within" whom we consult as "a truth that presides within."[76] Nor is memory only to recall and recognize what is already known; it also has "treasures of countless images" that it brings to imagine "future actions, events and hopes."[77]

Will. For Augustine, willing is ingredient to knowing because a person must first will to seek knowledge to even begin the process; he also recognized, of course, that one can will to turn away from the truth. Reason and memory, being turned by will to perceive truths and standards of how things should be, then offer the will new choices. But having perceived what is in keeping with "the rule of a true and right reason,"[78] the will, prompted by God's grace and the desire for happiness, must function as the agency of free choice to choose and to do what is good and true.[79] The will, then, is the function of soul that exercises choice, and wisdom and knowledge known by reason and memory is to lead to "certain willing."[80] The will, however, has the ability to choose according to *caritas* (love), which leads to truth and the good, or to *cupiditas* (concupiscence), which leads away from them. For Augustine, as for Plato, true knowledge is the source of virtuous living, and the happy life comes from "joy in the truth."[81]

Augustine's epistemology had a profound influence on theology and education throughout the remainder of the medieval period and indeed into our own day. I think it has at least three significant assets for conation in Christian faith, and also three serious liabilities. Again, the assets reflect a "remembrance of being," and the liabilities a corresponding "forgetfulness."

First by way of asset is Augustine's insistence on the unity of reason, memory, and will in both their source and their functioning. He said all knowing is by "the mind alone," in that it is the efficient cause of knowledge, but he had a broad and integrated understanding of mind amazingly similar to what modern psychology means by the psyche. For Augustine, the soul/mind's activities of reasoning, remembering, and willing interweave as people both know the truth and do God's will. His balance was lost in Western epistemology, especially with Descartes, when reason alone triumphed, dismissing memory as unreliable, and directing the will to obedience. Augustine, even more than Plato, also recognized the need for unity between thought and action and for reciprocity between the contemplative life of union with God and the practical life of Christian virtue—a conative sentiment.[82]

There is an asset too in the role Augustine attributed to memory. Pedagogically, he suggests the importance of people's own memory of life lived, that is, their own story, as a source of wisdom and knowledge. His appreciation of the revelatory capacity of personal remembrance is reflected especially in his treatise *The Teacher*.[83] His catechetical praxis turned people to what was already present in their own memories, as well as to the memory of the community and its faith narrative in scripture and tradition. The latter is an emphasis in Augustine's "First Catechetical Instruction," where he outlined how to present salvation history in a narrative style. When these two writings are placed in dialogue within the ambit of his emphasis on the role of memory in wisdom and knowledge, we can hear Augustine calling for a catechetical process that attends both to people's own stories and to Christian Story.

A third and related asset is Augustine's affirmation of "the truth that presides within" and the capacity of all people to recognize the truth of God's word when made accessible to them. Pedagogically, this suggests that people must be engaged as agent subjects in knowing their faith, as active participants who come to know for themselves rather than passive receptacles who simply imbibe the knowledge of the teacher. I'm convinced that Augustine was as opposed to "banking education" as is Paulo Freire today. As he once asked wryly, "For who would be so absurdly curious as to send (their) child to school to learn what the teacher thinks."[84]

A liability is Augustine's hierarchical dualism between mind and body. Among other consequences (some already noted in Plato) one must conclude that because the soul acts on the body, faith made reasonable may lead to praxis but historical praxis never deepens people's faith or understanding of it. Similarly, for Augustine, reliable knowledge leads to willing virtuous actions, but he ignored that the praxis of virtue shapes people's *habitus* of life and the tenor of their thinking.

Second, though he saw memory as having an imaginative function, it was a very limited one. For Augustine, the images in memory come only from sense objects and thus always turn the person downward toward knowledge, never toward God and true wisdom. The latter movement arises only from "imageless thought."[85] The imaginative and creative activities of poetry and art (poiesis) have no place, for Augustine, in coming into right relationship with or contemplation of God.

Third, and most debilitating for church education into our own day, the great conceptual endeavor he posed for uniting faith and reason was an exclusive one. To begin with, not only did he exclude the body as an efficient cause of knowledge and set the mind to rule over it, but he identified men with mind and women with bodiliness. Thus Augustine argued for the social and epistemic privilege of men and legitimated for Christians the sexism of Plato and Aristotle. Further, for all his egalitarian sentiments in *The Teacher,* Augustine saw theology as exclusive to "the educated," which in his church context meant male clergy. He said there are two ways of coming to understanding in faith, "by authority and by reason," and added, "Although the authority of upright men [*sic*] seems to be the safer guide for the uninstructed multitude, reason is better adapted for the educated."[86] This encouraged the church to assume that the common people are to be instructed as passive recipients by a pedagogy based on a "theory [from authority] to practice" epistemology.

Thomas Aquinas: First in the Senses

Scholastic theology emerged at the beginning of the second millennium when the rediscovery of Greek philosophy, with a preference now for Aristotle, offered a new day for forging a Christian paideia. The Scholastics had fresh determination to marry philosophy with the truths of Christian revelation and to construct a rationally defensible and systematic presentation of Christian beliefs. Their attention to the relationship between faith and reason left a rich legacy to the church's educational ministry, but one can only regret that the Scholastics were not equally concerned for the relationship between faith and praxis. Methodologically, they moved away from the style of a prayerful reading of Scripture that had marked the theological method of the first millennium. Favoring Aristotle's mode of theoria but neglecting its contemplative dynamic, they developed an approach of scientific reasoning. In consequence, the overall purpose of Scholastic theology was more a quest for rational knowledge about God than for spiritual wisdom toward holiness of life.[87] A separation ensued between theology and spirituality that enfeebled both.

No one joined the renewed effort for a Christian paideia with more determination and greater influence than Thomas of Aquino (c.1225–1274). Aquinas was eclectic in his philosophical sources,[88] but his primary mentor was undoubtedly Aristotle, to whom he referred simply as "the Philosopher." Aristotle's influence was especially evident in Aquinas's understanding of knowledge and of the dynamics of knowing.

Like Augustine, Aquinas saw faith as prior to religious understanding and knowledge; one believes in order to understand. Likewise, he was careful to distinguish truths reached by reason from those received on divine authority from Scripture and the teaching of the church, with the latter truths functioning as guide and norm for reason. Yet, like Augustine, Aquinas was also convinced that faith must seek understanding, that reason can confirm and complement the truths of revelation. In epistemology, however, the similarity between the two ceases. Aquinas's theory of knowledge was at least as different from Augustine's as Aristotle's was from Plato's. Unlike Augustine, Aquinas insisted on the unity of soul/mind and body as constitutive of the person; they depend for their action on each other.[89] The body is always an active participant in knowing, and universal ideas are known by abstraction from their instances in sense experience[90] (Aristotle) rather than by inner illumination of the mind alone to know a world of ideal forms (Plato and Augustine).

The theme song of Aquinas's epistemology is often and rightly cited as, "Nothing is ever in the mind that was not first in the senses" (note 4); all knowing begins with sense perception. The soul has two intellectual capacities. One is "passive" or "sensitive" and receives the data of sense perception (Aquinas called it passive because the senses, not intellect, are the active agent in collecting sense data). The other is "active" and turns the "phantasmata" (images) presented to it from the senses into thought "by abstraction from the conditions of individual matter."[91] As the senses are stimulated by experience, the passive intellect begins to be aware not of disembodied forms but of real things in themselves. Passive intellect has the inner powers of "common sense," memory, imagination, and "particular" reason.[92] It uses these powers to gather data from experience, to organize the data into images for the active intellect, and to discern the meaning of particular things. Its judgments of meaning and value are always of the concrete and the "contingent."

The active intellect takes its images from the passive and enables people to have universal ideas in matters for "intellectual knowledge" and ethical principles in matters for action.[93] By the active intellect we can abstract from sense data our understanding of the general nature, meaning, and value of things, come to universal ideas, and understand the revealed truths of God. Its ability for discursive reasoning moves us beyond understanding of particulars to judge according to universal categories and to discern whether ideas are true or false, decisions good or bad. Knowledge of the most abstract metaphysical and theological truths and of the universal principles of ethical action always begins from sense experience, which provides at least "the material cause" of all knowledge. (See note 93.)

Aquinas sided with Aristotle in refusing to draw a line of demarcation between sense knowledge and universal ideas, between experience and reliable cognition. However, he at least tried to avoid Aristotle's trichotomizing of the "three lives." He was certainly more successful in maintaining unity between the theoretical and practical activities of intellect, and thus between theological knowledge and Christian praxis. He could sound very Aristotelian at times, as if the theoretical activities (*sapientia/sophia, scientia/episteme,* and *intellectus/nous*) are separate from practical reason (*prudentia/phronesis*),[94] but his intent was only to distinguish them for analysis, not to separate them as distinct faculties. He insisted that "the speculative and practical intellects are not distinct powers," and though one can claim that the practical intellect intends the good and the speculative the truth, it must be recognized that "truth and good include one another." He explained: "The practical intellect knows truth, just as the speculative, but it directs the known truth to operation."[95] The whole intellect (active and passive, theoretical and practical) functions to provide the will with the knowledge and moral principles it needs to make free choices concerning truth and goodness.

Aquinas was also more appreciative of poiesis than Aristotle was. He maintained that "the life of art" is both an intellectual habit and a moral virtue.[96] It was Aquinas's understanding of God that prompted him to maintain a unity in all "ways of life" and "being" despite Aristotle's separation of them into a hierarchy. God is not a removed divinity of passive contemplation but a God who is fully "Act." God fully realizes within God's "Being" the true, the good, and the beautiful and is actively present in human history as ground of their realization. God prompts people from potency to act in their own "being" and to be co-agents with God and others for the well-"being" of all creation. Because our "being" participates in the "Being" of God, we have the capacity, by God's grace transforming and working through our "nature," to become responsible historical agents who know the truth, do the good, and create the beautiful.[97] For Aquinas, then, theoretical, practical, and creative activities are united in human "being" and "becoming."

Aquinas had also a profound influence on church education and especially on Catholic religious education. We have much to both learn and unlearn from his legacy for a pedagogy for conation or wisdom in Christian faith. The following points, suggestive rather than exhaustive, seem most salient. On the positive side, Aquinas's position is marked by a "remembrance of being" in the unity he proposed between soul/mind and body in the process of knowing (albeit with "hierarchical ordering")[98] and likewise by the unity he maintains between theoretical and practical reasoning. Both reflect his attempt to blend empirical, theoretical, and practical perspectives. Because he claimed all knowing begins with the senses, Aquinas has been called the first great empiricist. But avoiding naive empiricism, he insisted on the role of intellect in knowledge and in enabling will to choose according to "right reason." When this epistemology is coupled with his faith in Scripture and the teachings of the church, we can recognize a theological method that is reflection on life experience in light of Scripture and tradition. None has argued more coherently than Aquinas for the compatibility and affinity between the mysteries of Christian faith and the truths that are knowable from human experience. Aquinas's mode of "faith knowing" is echoed in how I describe a shared Christian praxis approach.[99]

Second, Aquinas has a sense of the dynamic structure of "knowing" that resonates with our experience of what we "do" when we "know." For Aquinas, "knowing" begins with *attention* to and *comprehension* of the data of experience. Then we employ the agent intellect that is both theoretical and practical to come to *understanding* and *judgment* of the truth and the good, and this enables the will to make right choices. What is truly "known" by people as their own is not "poured in" from outside but their own dynamic and personal appropriation of knowledge as agent-subjects. Such, I believe, is akin to the dynamics of a conative process.[100]

His assets, however, remained more potential than actual in what the church drew from Aquinas for its educational ministry. Honoring people's experience in the world, their capacities for theoretical and practical reasoning, and the dynamics of the knowing process he intimated never became operative in the church's catechetical ministry. Instead of a pedagogy in which people actively and self-consciously participate from their own life praxis, after Aquinas Catholicism especially embraced wholeheartedly a style of presenting "truths" already assembled in metaphysical language (often from Aquinas) and requiring unquestioning assent from the people.[101] Some of this passivity and exclusion, however, must be laid at the feet of Aquinas himself.

To begin with, Aquinas situated faith in the intellect rather than the will (contra Augustine) and thus encouraged a very rationalized presentation of "the faith." Aquinas also was entirely patriarchal in how he understood the active intellect and the capacity for discursive reasoning. He saw rationality as a male prerogative that legitimates male domination: "Woman is naturally subject to man—because in man the discretion of reason predominates."[102] An even more general exclusion of all "common people" is evident in his actual practice of teaching them. His teaching style, from what we can tell, was more a didactic monologue than a Socratic dialogue or an engagement of learners as active participants in the teaching event. It is as if he recommended an experiential/reflective mode of knowing for such "experts" as himself but "the people" were to be taught in a didactic manner what experts had assembled for them as the teaching of the church and the Scriptures. This is evident in his most concise statement on education, *De Magistro (The Teacher)*,[103] and in his *Catechetical Instructions*, the only example we have of Aquinas in a process of public catechesis.[104] It would seem that in catechesis at least, Aquinas, like Augustine, was not faithful to his own epistemology.

Aquinas, of course, had his Catholic critics in John Duns Scotus and William of Occam, but Thomism, not the Franciscan school,[105] shaped the later educational ministry of the Catholic church. The Reformers rejected Scholastic rationalism and understood faith as the gift of God's grace that moves the will to an act of trust in God who saves, rather than the mind to assent to doctrinal formulations. In religious education, however, Luther was the great popularizer of the catechism question-and-answer approach, and Calvin followed his example.[106] Thus the church, both Catholic and Protestant, turned toward "the modern era" using a pedagogy far removed from a conative one. We now pass in our epistemological overview[107] to the great architect of modern rationalism—René Descartes. He brought the triumph not only of the "mind" but of "*reason* alone" to new and dizzying heights.

4. René Descartes: A Doubter, No Doubt?

No one has been more intent on certainty or turned more completely to reason alone to find it than René Descartes (1596–1650). By his time the Renaissance had created a deepened confidence in human ability to know. A new "scientific" view emerged—more akin to what we mean by science—that claimed that human reason, unaided by divine revelation and independent of any church authority, is capable of knowing reality and directing the course of human affairs. In the midst of this intellectual élan, one can imagine the reaction when Michel de Montaigne (1533–1592), a maverick philosopher of the time, threw down the gauntlet of skepticism again.[108] No one took it up more determinedly than Descartes.

Descartes resolved to find one sure foundation upon which to build a system of certain knowledge that would silence the skeptics forever. He claimed that the knowing process of mathematics, his model too of certain knowledge, consists of two procedures—intuition and deduction. Rational intuition gives rise to self-evident principles (e.g., a straight line is the shortest distance between two points). Deduction follows by inference and logical reasoning to absolute certainty. Descartes set out to find such certainty for all the sciences. I review his epistemology as follows: first, what constituted the certainty he sought; second, where he turned to find it; and third, the method he used in the quest.

Descartes was searching for one certain idea that could serve as "an unshakable foundation" (*fundamentum inconcussum*) for all knowledge. He wrote, "Archimedes used to demand just one firm and immovable point in order to shift the entire earth; so I too, can hope for great things if I manage to find just one thing, however slight, that is certain and unshakable."[109] This Archimedean point must have three characteristics to satisfy Descartes's criterion of certainty: it must be an idea so self-evidently clear in itself that it is impossible to doubt it; be distinct, stand alone independent of any other idea; and be of something that exists, because it is to be the source of knowledge for all else that exists.[110] In sum, Descartes was in quest of a *clear* and *distinct idea* of an *existing thing* to serve as the foundational axiom for a deductive system of certain knowledge.

Where did he turn to find it? Like all the rationalists before him (and many more after him), Descartes turned to the mind and even more particularly to *reason* alone, dismissing senses and feelings, memory and imagination, as untrustworthy and incapable of playing any part in the quest for rational certainty. Significantly, he turned not to "mind" in general but specifically to his *own* mind, to the activities of his own rational and solitary consciousness.[111]

Descartes posited a total and substantial separation between mind (*res cogitans*) and body (*res extensa*). He claimed that mind can exist and function apart from body and apart from what he considered the bodily influenced functions of memory and imagination; reason can function in and of itself to provide clear and distinct ideas, even of existing things. He recognized that the senses, imagination, and memory can assist the intellect in knowing physical or corporeal matters but offered no adequate explanation of how body and reason interact[112] other than to insist that even sense perception is by the agency of mind alone.[113] Beyond that, "When the intellect is concerned with matters in which there is nothing corporeal or similar to the corporeal [i.e., clear and distinct ideas], it cannot receive any help from those faculties [i.e., of the body]."[114]

In his quest for certainty, Descartes ironically announced that he was committing himself to a method of doubt. He resolved to set aside every previous belief and opinion for which he could find even the slightest doubt. He explained, "Anything that admits of the slightest doubt I will set aside just as if I had found it to be wholly false; and I will proceed in this way until I recognize something certain, or, if nothing else, until I at least recognize for certain that there is no certainty."[115] He proceeded to reject all knowledge that comes from everyday experience and from the natural sciences; because it depends on our bodies for sense data, it must be doubted. He could find no reason to doubt the clear and distinct ideas of mathematics—so he invented one. Suppose, he said, there is an evil spirit that deceives us in all we think we know with certainty. Descartes admitted this doubt was "hyperbolic," but asserted there is at least the possibility that a malevolent demon has deceived us into a false sense of certainty. Even mathematics, then, does not yet provide an Archimedean point that is beyond doubt.

Finally, in triumph, Descartes came to an undoubtable truth: "I think, therefore I am"—his famous *Cogito, ergo sum.* Eureka! Because I'm thinking, I therefore must exist, and I cannot doubt that I do. Even if I suspect that an evil spirit is deceiving me, thus causing me to doubt, I cannot doubt that I'm doubting. Doubting, however, is a form of thinking, and, though I may doubt *what* I think, I cannot doubt *that* I think. Because thinking requires a thinker, I have a clear and certain idea of something that exists.[116] With this certain idea as foundation,

Descartes took the next step and concluded that our very essence is to be "a thinking thing," independent of the body. He wrote, "I am, then, in the strict sense only a thing that thinks; that is, I am a mind, or intelligence, or intellect, or reason . . . a thinking thing."[117]

He said "the cogito" (as it came to be called) is an innate idea; it is always already within us and known by reason alone.[118] But he knew he must push beyond if it was to serve as a foundation for all knowledge. How could it serve as a verifier of other innate ideas that arise from intuitive reason—cause, substance, mathematics, and so on? What if we *are* deceived in such ideas, if a malevolent God is the cause of them? Descartes's response was to use "the cogito" argument to prove the existence of a good and veracious God, who, far from being a deceiver, is both author and guarantor of all our intuitive ideas.

Descartes's central argument[119] for the existence of God can be set out as follows: we have the idea of an infinite and all-perfect God; this idea could not be produced by our finite selves but only by something that has the same infinite reality as the idea of it; therefore God exists.[120] Because God is perfect, we can be certain of the reliability of all our intuitive and innate ideas and can proceed to rationally deduce from them other certain knowledge.[121]

Descartes still had to explain error; how does error arise if our intellects are always capable of certainty? His solution was to attribute it to the will. For Descartes, will is the faculty of judgment concerning the truth or error of an idea presented to it by the mind. (But if one perceives an idea as certainly true, how can one refuse assent to it?— thus the circularity of his argument and the token and rationally directed role he assigned to will.) The way to avoid error is to restrain the will from judgments about things for which the mind does not have clear and distinct ideas, with the dangerous implication that error on someone's part is the result of ill will.[122]

Descartes's rationalism and unqualified dualism between mind and body have had enormous influence on Western epistemology. In spite of his unbridled "forgetfulness of being," I can think of two assets he left for a conative pedagogy. Through his influence, Western philosophy shifted to the individual subject as the agent and source of knowledge. Diverging from Plato's rationalism, Descartes posed ideas as emerging from the content and activities of one's own intellect rather than from an unchanging world of ideal forms. This shift was deepened but not doubted by philosophers after him. I critique his individualistic and ahistorical understanding of "thinking" below, yet his turn to the subject as the agent of cognition affirms the role and responsibility of each person in their own knowing and knowledge.

Second, his critics cast doubt on the authenticity of Descartes's method of doubt (Was it genuine or only a method for finding the certainty he never really doubted in the first place?). Nevertheless he helped initiate the practice of critical reasoning in the process of knowing. His method of doubt entailed a healthy skepticism toward "authority" of any kind and stimulated what we now call a hermeneutic of suspicion. The church reacted negatively at first to such critical thinking but eventually embraced it through critical biblical scholarship and dialectical theology.

Descartes's liabilities, however, far outweigh his assets. I list three pertinent ones to be avoided in a pedagogy for conation or wisdom in Christian faith. First, Descartes's epistemology has a greater "forgetfulness of being" than that of any philosopher before him. In fact, our "being" is constituted by thinking alone ("I am a thing that thinks"). In addition to maintaining hierarchical dualism between mind and body, he associated memory and imagination as well as sensation with the body and assigned a token and rationally controlled function to the will, thus reducing the "mind" to reason alone (Plato posed memory as crucial to the functioning of even "pure reason"). Descartes may have found the suggestion for his cogito argument in Augustine (see note 116), but he overlooked the unity Augustine proposed among reason, memory, and will. Further, the disembodied knowing that he championed, and his portrayal of nature as a "clockwork universe" that functions according to mechanical and rational principles implanted in it by God (see note 112), prompted the use of reason as a tool applied to the world without ethic or awareness of interest. This encouraged irrationalism in the practical sciences (in the sense of lacking self-reflection and ethical concern); one outcome of this is the technical rationality of our day, with its potential for ultimate destruction. On this Cartesian point, Colleen Griffith writes, "Truth that purports to transcend bodiliness is inevitably tyrannical. Bodiless truth contributes nothing to the advancement of the human enterprise."[123]

Second, Descartes equated knowledge with rational certainty that is reached by scientific reasoning with such intensity that the "common sense" knowledge of people from their historical praxis was now excluded with a vengeance from Western education. This encouraged the church to teach in a dogmatic and doctrinaire mode, excluding any sense that the praxis of people is an integral part of their curriculum. The church now more obviously presumed (a) that it has such rational certainty in its Scriptures and official teachings and (b) that "the faith" must be presented in a deductive mode and as rationally certain if the "common people" are to give it their commitment. Descartes's conviction that modern science requires a rationally certain foundation disposed the church to presume that Christian faith needs a similar one (how ironic that "rational certainty" and "faith" would be so conjoined). The consequence in Christian religious education was a kind of fundamentalism by the church concerning "the truth" (as rational certainty) it already presumed to possess, a discouraging of the critical thinking that Descartes might have intended, and a preoccupation with orthodoxy to the neglect of orthopraxis.

Last, though he championed personal rational thinking as the source of truth, for Descartes this was a ruggedly individualistic and nondialogical activity, and he had no awareness of the influence of social context and psychological states on people's thinking. The intellect works in a dehistoricized vacuum, and thinkers can come to certain ideas in solitude, without bias or interest, independent of any community of discourse or need for dialogue. Such historical naïveté and isolationism is a clear "forgetfulness of being" and unsuited to a conative pedagogy. In Descartes, these sentiments reflected his disembodied notion of the human subject. However, his epistemology also reflected, as we have noted in so many authors, his concept of God. For Descartes, God is self-sufficient and perfect Rationality, the guarantor of ideas and the removed "first mover" who sets the mechanics of creation in motion (see note 112) but is no longer engaged in human history. If he had remembered the active God of the Hebrew and Christian Scriptures, the God of covenant who calls us into partnership with Godself and one another, he might have had a more relational, dialogical, and historical understanding of knowing.

5. Empiricism: What You See Is . . .

By tradition empiricism is identified as a British school of thought. Its modern architects were two great British philosophers, the English John Locke (1632–1704), and the Scottish David Hume (1711–1776); the Irish philosopher Bishop George Berkeley (1685–1753) is usually listed (and erroneously as "British") along with them, although his credentials as an empiricist have been questioned.[124] Locke and colleagues were influenced by their English "empiricist" predecessor Francis Bacon (1561–1626). (See note 107.) Its exponents today are variously called logical empiricists, scientific empiricists, and logical positivists, but there is still a strong British influence among them, with Bertrand Russell (1872–1970) a significant recent voice.[125] In the sciences, empiricism usually means that scientific (i.e., reliable) knowledge is assembled by a process of "objective" and measurable research on observable data, the results of which are verified by further empirical data gathering and experimentation. In everyday speech it usually means "to look at the facts," with the presumption that "the facts speak for themselves." Empiricism's historical roots, however, which I first noted among the ancient Greeks, suggest a broader meaning for it.

The years following Descartes witnessed a great expansion in industry and trade and, concomitantly, in the scientific investigation of the physical universe. Newton and others took up Descartes's depiction of the universe as a machine (see note 112) and proceeded to investigate its mechanical laws with amazing results. Everything, they believed, from an apple falling off a tree to the movement of the planets can be explained by cause and effect laws of physics. Ironically, however, this scientific investigation of nature also encouraged a rejection of Descartes's deductive reasoning from rationally self-evident axioms. An epistemology emerged convinced that reality is not something upon which we impose our innate ideas; on the contrary, nature and even human nature reveal themselves to us if we but investigate their observable data, the empirical evidence that they offer. This was a more thoroughgoing empiricism than any before it.[126]

There is much divergence among Locke, Hume, and Berkeley, with Hume a total empiricist, Berkeley a metaphysician and idealist at heart, and Locke a more balanced voice somewhere between them. But they are united in their rejection of Descartes's rationalism in general and of his notion of innate ideas in particular and thus are classified together as empiricists. I concentrate on Locke here as the most representative of the three; his influence on the politics of Western culture has significantly shaped its operative epistemology.[127]

John Locke

Locke set out to construct an adequate theory of knowledge and was convinced that metaphysics, rationalism in particular, had led us astray. He appealed to "common sense" to prove that the data of experience is always the primary and efficient source of reliable knowledge. Everyone recognizes, said Locke, that we move by induction from experience to concepts, and then to general ideas. Note that the outcome is, as it is for the rationalists, "ideas." Locke, however, didn't equate reliable knowledge with rational certainty and allowed for probable knowledge and "degrees of certainty."[128] Neither was he a skeptic or total empiricist. He accepted the certainty of mathematical reasoning and distinguished between ideas of the senses and ideas of reflection. The latter, however, arise from the operation of our mind, shaped by experience, on the ideas of the senses.[129]

Locke believed that the bête noire to be destroyed was the Cartesian notion of innate ideas. For Locke, there are no ideas "born into us." Everything we know arises from reflection on sensible data, and the "mind" with which we reflect is itself formed by previously lived experience. At birth the mind is not a "closet" filled with innate ideas but a "tabula rasa," or blank tablet (a phrase Locke borrowed from Aristotle).[130] In a classic summary statement, he wrote, "Let us then suppose the mind to be, as we say, white paper, void of all characters, without any ideas; how comes it to be furnished? Whence comes it by that vast store, which the busy and boundless fancy of [humankind] has painted on it with almost endless variety? Whence has it all the materials of reason and knowledge? To this I answer, in one word, from *Experience;* in that all our knowledge is founded, and from that it ultimately derives itself."[131]

To explain how physical objects cause their ideas in our mind, Locke posed his "causal theory of perception." He portrayed this as a "realist" position that recognizes that the qualities of things exist in the things themselves and cause us to perceive the ideas we have of them by sensory stimulation.[132] By "idea" he meant any perception, thought, or understanding the mind receives from sense data.[133] He distinguished between "simple ideas" of sensation and complex ideas of reflection.[134] The first is an immediate perception we have of the primary qualities of things (solidity, extension, shape, etc.). Complex ideas are produced in us by combining simple ideas and by our apprehension of what he called the secondary qualities of things (color, sound, taste, etc.). These qualities do not really exist in the bodies outside of us, said Locke, but are subjective effects produced in our mind by the primary qualities we perceive through sense data.[135] In sum, all general ideas are abstracted from and "caused" by their instances in sense data (as in Aristotle), but in the process of knowing them, the mind is both shaped by and dependent on experience (a notion very unlike Aristotle's, and what a total contrast to Descartes!).

Bishop Berkeley took Locke's "realist" empiricism in an idealist direction. Berkeley claimed that all knowing begins with sense perception, but the material world does not actually exist except as an idea in the mind of God; God communicates ideas of the material world to us by a "law of nature" that stimulates our sense perception.[136] David Hume pushed empiricism to the other extreme. He claimed that sense data totally control our mind and that mind is no more than a collection of previous sense impressions. With no recognition of a substantial mind or self to evaluate the truth or falsehood of what the senses present (the self is only "a bundle of perceptions"), Hume was driven to a position of total skepticism.[137]

Empiricism contains a central insight to be reflected in a pedagogy for conation in Christian faith; this is its insistence that the personal sense experiences we have of our world are constitutive of human knowledge and knowing and shape our ontic selves. We can never settle for a naive or positivistic "taking a look" kind of empiricism (I outline Lonergan's critique of this in chap. 3); nevertheless, to be marked by a "remembrance of being," a process of conation must include "the empirical" as a constitutive component. It is imperative to affirm this for education in a faith that is incarnational to its core and claims that we come to "know God" through God's recognizable activity in creation and in history—our own, and the history of the faith community over time.

On the other hand, empiricism of whatever variety is marked in many ways by "forgetfulness of being," and an empirical pedagogy is insufficient for wisdom in Christian faith. To begin with, there is no concerted recognition of the "knower" as an agent-subject or of the mind's innate capacities for knowing. Epistemologically, Hume was quite logical in pushing empiricism to skepticism; ontologically, too, if we are formed entirely by the data of experience, we must logically conclude that we have no freedom or agency in our "being" and "becoming." Second, empiricism tends to presume the "objectivity" of observation and to be unaware of the social influences and interests of gathering and interpreting data. This critique pertains to all the authors reviewed thus far but seems pressing here as an antidote to any "empiricist" sentiment that knowing is "taking a look." Third, with all knowledge grounded in sense experience, it is never clear in empiricism how we appropriate the truths recognized and systematized by other people around us and before us. For example, it is not clear how the tradition of biblical revelation can be appropriated in an exclusively empirical process. In fact, to make place for revealed truths within his epistemology, Locke said they must be accepted on faith alone "in contradistinction to reason," with their acceptance not influenced or aided by experience.[138] In addition to encouraging an "irrational" Christianity, this position ignores what I later portray as a conative correlation between people's own stories and Christian Story. Fourth, the empiricist understanding of "experience" seems to be totally passive—something that we simply "undergo" as our senses *note* the data. That our personally initiated engagement in the world as agent-subjects (our praxis) is also a source of knowing is overlooked. For empiricists, to know the truth is to have an accurate correspondence between our ideas and the data of reality. Absent from an empirical mind-set is the notion that truth is also a practical task to be done, and that our appropriation of it can be deepened by our efforts to live it and to change reality.

6. Immanuel Kant: Knowledge by Construction

A brilliant thinker who broke new ground in Western philosophy, Immanuel Kant (1724–1804) was above all an epistemologist; the dynamics of knowing and the reliability of knowledge were his first concern.[139] Kant had two abiding purposes: to defend religion from what he perceived as the threat of rationalism; his strategy was to place religion beyond the realm of theoretical reason. Second, and in reaction to Hume, he intended to save science from skepticism and establish a reliable way of knowing for all the sciences.

Kant claimed we have three basic faculties of the mind that enable us to engage intelligently in the world. We have *intuition,* which operates in concert with imagination to enable us to make unified representations of sensibilia, that is, to have *perceptions* of things. Second, we have *understanding,* by which we grasp perceptions and turn them into *concepts* for understanding. Third, we have *reason,* which unifies concepts of understanding, judges them, and moves to universal ideas; reason also has functions and ideas that arise from within itself.

Kant was ever adamant that "ultimately [there is] only one and the same reason which has to be distinguished simply in its application."[140] Within "its application," however, he distinguished between theoretical and practical reason. Theoretical reason (close to what we now mean by scientific) is reason directed to knowing the everyday world around us. Kant called the judgments of truth that theoretical reason makes *syn-*

thetic a priori.[141] They are synthetic because their basis is experience; they are a priori because they also arise from categories of thought that are in the mind prior to all experience. Kant analyzed theoretical reasoning in his *Critique of Pure Reason* (1781).[142] Practical reason, ironically, is reason aimed at knowing the supersensible world, what Kant presumed to be above experience and beyond the stimulus of the senses. Practical reason knows ideas that have no objects in sense reality (God, immortality, and freedom). It proposes the moral imperatives that ought to be obeyed and is totally rational in that its ideas are generated entirely by the mind itself. Kant analyzed this function of reason in his *Critique of Practical Reason* (1788).[143]

Theoretical Reason. Kant was convinced that one dimension of scientific knowledge comes from experience *and* another dimension is contributed by the mind alone, independent of and prior to experience. In this, he claimed, he had united and affirmed the basic truth of both empiricists and rationalists and had transcended their opposition with a new synthesis that explained the dynamic relationship between sense data and theoretical reason (i.e., finally erasing Plato's line of demarcation). He considered his achievement comparable to "a Copernican revolution."[144]

The core of Kant's Copernican revolution is as follows. Theoretical reasoning begins with sense experience. Our senses intuitively provide *perceptions* of reality as the "raw material" for the understanding mind to form into *concepts* and eventually into *ideas* and *scientific truths*.[145] The mind, however, is an active and structuring agent in this knowing process. It has a priori "categories" of thought,[146] independent of experience, that make perception of experience possible in the first place and turn our perceptions into concepts for understanding and judgment. In other words, what we know is as much structured by the knower's mind as it is shaped by the world known. The interaction between the subject knowing and the object known is what Kant called "the biology of thought"—to which we now turn.

Kant began the *Critique of Pure Reason* by saying, "There can be no doubt that all our knowledge begins with experience," and then hastened to add, "but . . . it does not follow that it all arises out of experience."[147] This is a subtle but very important distinction; we begin from experience, but knowledge does not come from experience alone. The world of sensibilia stimulates our senses, and by intuition we gather our first perceptions of things.[148] Then the faculty of understanding takes over to form these perceptions into concepts that are "thought."[149] We will see presently the role of imagination in the transition from sensibility to intelligibility. First it will help to note the "categories of understanding" by which, Kant said, we make things intelligible.

Kant distinguished categories of sensation and categories of thought. Categories of sensation are the transcendental intuitions or "forms" we have of *space* and *time;* they make perception of sensations possible in the first place. Categories of thought make understanding and then *synthetic a priori* judgments (see note 141) possible after sensations have been received from intuition. Both the "intuitive forms" of space and time and the categories of understanding are a priori in the mind. This is why Kant called them "transcendental" categories; they are formal structures of the mind itself and universal functions in all theoretical knowing.[150] The "intuitive forms" of space and time and the categories of understanding are not, then, innate ideas in the Cartesian sense. Rather, they are a priori structures that make experience first possible and then understandable. They are not "already knowledge" before experience but give rise to "knowledge" on the "occasion" of experience. There are two stages, then, in the process of working from the raw material of sensations into the end product of understood ideas. First is the coordination of sensations by the a priori "intuitive forms" of space and time. Space is our sense of an outer world in which all things are located; time is our inner sense of continuity and ongoing identity.[151] Everything we experience is perceived through the categories of space and time; they are, as Kant said, "conditions of experience."[152] At the second stage the a priori categories of thought take over to think perceptions from experience into concepts of understanding, that is, rationally understood ideas. In the transition from perceptions to conceptions, imagination plays a key mediating role. Imagination, for Kant, possesses schemata or organizing capacities that take multiple stimuli from sense experience and form them into a unified image. His word for imagination, *einbildungskraft*, literally means "the power of shaping into one";[153] it is the capacity to bring unity among varied perceptions. It is imagination that enables understanding to activate appropriate thought categories so that perceptions may emerge as concepts.

The thought categories of understanding operate at the postperception stage on the unified images that have been prepared by sensation and imagination. Kant listed twelve of these innate structures of thought, three each under the broader categories of quantity, quality, relation, and modality.[154] By way of example, I take Kant's category of causality (listed under relation). We are not born with the *idea* of causality. Yet, on the occasion of a cause and effect experience, reason activates this a priori category from the mind's own formal structures, and we recognize that every effect has its cause, or that this particular effect must have a cause. We know that it must have a cause not from experience but from the very structuring pattern of our minds activated on the occasion of experience.[155] In other words, we must already have the category of causality in our mind's structure in order to recognize an experience of it. So too is it with all the categories of understanding. We know concepts from experience because of the pure thought categories into which understanding subsumes experience.

Beyond understanding, Kant had a role for the activity of theoretical reason in its own right, and with its own distinctive intent. He explained that what the categories of understanding do to the data of the senses, reason does to concepts presented to it by the understanding.[156] Thus, as understanding forms concepts, reason, by inference, "endeavors to reduce the varied and manifold knowledge obtained through the understanding to the smallest number of principles (universal conditions) and thereby to achieve in it the highest possible unity."[157] Theoretical reason aims ultimately to provide us with what we judge to be unified, systematic, and universal ideas that form the sciences of knowledge.

Practical Reason. Notice that the outcome of theoretical reasoning is ideas and scientific knowledge. Kant limited such knowledge to whatever could begin from sense experience. But this posed a dilemma! Could such theoretical knowledge be "practical" in the sense of shaping the ethics of human conduct and the practice of religion? And if not, then what is the source of morality and belief in God? Kant admitted that theoretical knowledge could have a technical practicality by providing principles or rules for producing things. But that is a limited and improper use of the term *practical.* For Kant "practical" knowledge is knowledge of moral norms of conduct, knowledge of God, immortality, and freedom—things, he claimed, that do not have objects in the observable world of experience but belong in the supersensible or metaphysical realm, beyond the reach of theoretical reason. For example, that people ought not to lie is a valid norm, but its validity cannot be established from experience, because people often lie. Kant claimed we need a more reliable source of such a norm, some built-in capacity that enables people to know the moral law by vivid and immediate moral reasoning. Such reasoning is indeed practical, in that it moves our wills to do the good.[158] However, its judgments must be *analytic a priori* (i.e., immediately evident because of an inner structure of practical reason that functions independently of experience; see note 141) because *synthetic a priori* judgments that take our own historical experience into account cannot be relied on for ethical norms and metaphysical truths.

The precepts and ideas of pure practical reason are known *a priori.* In other words, Kant believed morality and religious faith are divorced from all experience, from all personal interests, from all consideration of the circumstances in which we are to act morally and believe in God, immortality of the soul, or freedom. Morality and "faith" are based on the inner a priori structure of pure practical reason. In a sense, we "just know" such matters and existentially cannot say much more about their basis.[159] As Kant wrote, we know them by "an objective necessity arising from *a priori* grounds."[160] His intention was to change the basis of religion from speculative theology to morals, from theoretical creeds to practical conduct that is simply "willed."

"Assuming that pure reason can contain a practical ground sufficient to determine the will,"[161] Kant set out to find an absolute, universal, and necessary moral law that can be known by all regardless of experience. As Descartes sought an unshakable foundation for rational knowledge, Kant proposed a categorical imperative, an unqualified and unconditional moral command upon which all morality can be based. It ran: "So act that the maxim of your will could always hold at the same time as a principle establishing universal law."[162] In other words, our fundamental imperative is to act the way we want everyone else to act in like matters (echoes of the Golden Rule: "Treat others the way you would have them treat you," Matt. 7:12). Actions are good when we do them in obedience to our inner sense of duty to this categorical imperative. Kant believed this law is so universal, it is accessible to "even the commonest and most unpracticed understanding without any worldly prudence."[163]

Concerning the three primary supersensible realities of interest to practical reason—freedom, God, and immortality—Kant said freedom is a necessary condition of morality. Only if we are free do the dictates of the moral law make sense. Conversely, we experience freedom only as we act according to the dictates of practical reason. Having posited freedom as an a priori of pure practical reason, Kant concluded that God and immortality are also necessary conditions if the categorical imperative and its free exercise are to make sense to the will. In effect, Kant was asking, Why be moral, if there is no God and we are not immortal? God and immortality are necessary postulates of practical reason; without them, it is faced with unanswerable contradictions (antinomies, Kant called them). Since we know that the moral law binds us as a "fact of pure reason," we are therefore morally bound to ascribe reality to God and immortality to ourselves. We do so, said Kant, not out of any speculative reasoning that proves or explains such truths but out of the convictions that arise from the "natural order" (see note 163) of pure practical reason.

Kant and Conation. Kant's influence on the operative epistemology of the West (seen especially in the severing of science from ethics) has been enormous, and his epistemology has serious impediments to a conative pedagogy. However, I can think of three aspects of Kant's thought that are assets to promote wisdom in Christian faith.

His insight that all knowledge is in fact constructed by the active agency of the knower in interaction with the world must be remembered and honored in a conative pedagogy. We are not spectators before reality (contra "banking" education); nor may we simply impose our ideas upon the world in a willy-nilly solipsism. Kant insightfully proposed a balanced and interactive relationship between subject knowing and object known, not collapsing the tension to terms of either-or, and this perspective is essential to pedagogy for conation. In his analysis of the dynamics of theoretical reasoning, Kant initiated a process of "thinking about thinking" that was later picked up on as a way to critical consciousness. Such potential, however, is nowhere recognized by Kant. In fact, his insistence that the a priori categories of reason are unaffected by experience is a "forgetfulness of being" and a hindrance to critical consciousness. Jean Piaget and other developmentalists took up and affirmed Kant's suggestion that there is an inner structure to the human capacity for knowing but demonstrated empirically that it develops chronologically in interaction with the environment.

Second, Kant's "biology" of theoretical reasoning offers the first explicit analysis (we noted an implicit one in Aquinas) of the activities we perform as we come to know the world; some such dynamic must be engaged by a conative pedagogy. We begin with sense data (albeit identified as phenomena);[164] intuition and imagination combine to weave data into perceptions; understanding and its categories move perceptions to conceptions; reason judges and creates unity in ideas and systematic knowledge in the sciences. As far as it goes, this describes the basic structure of cognition and resonates with common everyday experience of how we come to know. For conation, however, we must transcend Kant's separation of theoretical from practical reason and push the dynamic to decision and choice for responsible historical praxis.

Third, the categories of space and time as constitutive of knowledge must be attended to in a pedagogy for conation. Rather than taking a sense of time and place for granted, however, as Kant implies (i.e., as a priori), a conative process should enable people to intentionally engage and come to consciousness of their location in time and place. Rather than a priori categories, then, our time and place shape us and are to be shaped by us.

I can think of at least two major liabilities in Kant that we must avoid. First, nothing could be more detrimental to conation than Kant's separation of theoretical from practical reasoning. In this he hardened the old dichotomies between theory and praxis, understanding and will, science and ethics with the potential for terrifying consequences. After Kant, scientific knowing could more readily become technical rationality that only asks "how to do it," with no sense of ethic or self-critique beyond technical efficiency. By dividing theoretical from practical reasoning, Kant left science without an ethic and attempted to place ethics and religion beyond the monitor of critical reason. As Jane Flax summarizes it, the division between epistemology and ethics was "blessed by Kant and transformed by him into a fundamental principle derived from the structure of mind itself." A consequence was to establish "a rigid distinction between fact and value" and thus to "consign the philosopher to silence on issues of utmost importance to human life."[165] A wisdom pedagogy must transcend Kant's dichotomy between theoretical and practical reasoning.

Second, Kant said that it is impossible to come to faith knowing or ethical conviction from life experience or from one's own active engagement as an agent-subject in history. This is a forgetfulness of both the Being of God and our own "being." God of Hebrew and Christian Scriptures reveals Godself and will in the context and events of history. And a moment's reflection on our identity and agency reminds us that our "being" in faith is shaped, in large part, by our historical experiences. Contra Kant, Christian religious education must bring critical reason to faith and ethics and likewise enable people to draw upon their own life experience and praxis as sources of their identity and responsible agency in faith.

7. Some Contemporary Sources for Conation

From Plato, Aristotle, Augustine, Aquinas, Descartes, Locke, and Kant I have indicated some broad contours of the dominant epistemological tradition in Western philosophy, up to and including the modern period. That their positions have shaped the church's praxis of faith education is beyond doubt, and likewise that none of their positions provides an adequate foundation for a conative pedagogy. Informed by their assets and intending to transcend their liabilities, I attempt to weave an epistemic ontology as the philosophical foundation of Christian religious education (chap. 3) and, more important, propose a pedagogy that can be effective for conation/wisdom in Christian faith (chaps. 4, 10). In addition, four significant movements in philosophy between Kant and the mid-twentieth century can contribute theoretically and practically to a conative process. (More recent authors are drawn upon in chap. 3.) These are Marxism, phenomenology, existentialism, and pragmatism. An already lengthy chapter does not allow much elaboration of their epistemologies, but I briefly review their insights that seem most salient to our interests.

A. Marxism

Karl Marx (1818–1883), the primary architect of Marxism,[166] is identified as many things (political philosopher, social revolutionary, economist) but rarely as an epistemologist. Yet, in the overall corpus of his works,[167] we can recognize an epistemology, and one relevant for conation. Marx favored what can be called a "praxis way of knowing" and, with Hegel, was responsible for reviving the term in Western philosophy. For Marx, praxis is the productive activity of people done reflectively in a social context. "Knowledge" arises from engaging reflectively with productive labor in the world to transform it; true knowledge is what is "done" to transform the social and economic structures of society in emancipatory ways. Marx's notion that productive labor is the most basic form of social praxis subsumed Aristotle's category of poiesis as integral to, rather than separated from, politics but, alas, he tended to limit historical praxis to productive labor. However, I have written elsewhere on the assets and limitations of Marx's understanding of praxis.[168] Here I highlight his key insight (for which even conservative sociologists give him credit)[169] about the sociology of knowledge. To appreciate this aspect of Marx's thought it must be set within his understanding of economics as the determining force in human history.

Marx wove together his understanding of Hegel's dialectics of history and Feuerbach's materialism as "dialectical materialism." Its basic claims are that all reality is reducible to matter, that history evolves dialectically by a process of class conflict, that the classes are distinguished according to their economic relationship to matter—either as owners or workers. Marx claimed that in a capitalist economy the dialectical process of production and reappropriation by producers of what they produce is preempted by "owners," who control the means of production and take the "surplus value" of workers' labor as their own. Because "workers" do not control the means of production or the products of their labor, Marx claimed, their condition in a capitalist system is one of alienation and exploitation. Marx was convinced that an economic restructuring toward a classless society of common ownership is the only way to destroy alienation and bring people to true freedom and subjectivity as historical agents.

As a thoroughgoing materialist, Marx insisted that all thought and culture reflects the material conditions, and especially the economic conditions, of life. All human ideas, values, laws, politics, social and economic structures, and so on constitute a superstructure that both reflects and arises from the economic infrastructure of society. People's consciousness and knowledge, said Marx, is shaped by their social location and by the structures of ownership, exchange, distribution, and so on in which they are located. In a pithy summary, he wrote, "The mode of production in material life determines the general character of the social, political and spiritual processes of life. It is not the consciousness of [people] that determines their existence, but on the contrary, their social existence determines their consciousness."[170] In other words, everything we know about the world and about ourselves is shaped by the context in which we know it and by the form of our labor in society. Marx's notion of social existence as coextensive with one's economic condition was broadened by later authors and is now perceived as one's whole social/cultural context and condition in place and time. However, these writers still appreciate Marx's insight about the "sociology of knowledge." Sheila Greeve Davaney gives a helpful summary of how it is at present perceived: "There is . . . no such thing as objective, universally valid experience or knowledge. Human beings and our knowledge are irrevocably historical and hence conditioned by time and place."[171]

Marx's economic interpretation of history is certainly limited and so too his solution to its woes. Obviously his atheism and materialism are in conflict with basic tenets of Jewish and Christian faith (although, ironically, he was a powerful stimulus for Christians to rediscover the this-worldly dimension of their eschatology).[172] Yet clearly his insight that our "knowing" and thus our very "being" is powerfully shaped by our social/cultural context must be honored in a pedagogy for conation. It should invite participants to develop a critical consciousness of the influence of all social and cultural conditions on their "being" in the world, to see the reconstruction needed, and to commit themselves to the social responsibilities of Christian faith.

B. Phenomenology

Phenomena here refers to the objects of experience as they present themselves to consciousness. Phenomenology as an epistemology recognizes that all knowledge, meaning, and truth is grounded in our "life-world" of experience, where our consciousness first encounters phenomena through prereflective (i.e., pretheoretical) acts of perception, imagination, and language. People's "knowing," then, has its origin in our historical experience of "things themselves" as they are present to our own consciousness, rather than in any objectified theory about things as others tell us that they are. For phenomenology, knowledge and truth are not found primarily in objects known or in subjects knowing but in the relationship between them—between the world and the activities of our own consciousness.

Phenomenology first developed in German universities in the period prior to World War I. Its primary architect was the German-Czech philosopher Edmund Husserl (1859–1938). Husserl, like so many before him, was searching for certainty in the face of skepticism, a certainty for philosophy akin to that of mathematics. He concluded that the *cogito* argument of Descartes does not prove the existence of a subject who can think independent of sense experience but rather the existence of our own consciousness that is always directed toward phenomena. The more we can see the world through a pristine experience of its phenomena, the more likely we are to know the truth about it. Far from being independent of sense experience as Descartes contended, consciousness operates in relationship with the phenomena presented to it. Consciousness is always "consciousness of" something to which it attends, and its attending bestows meaning or value according to its own inner structures as it relates to phenomena of existence. Husserl intended to give a "biology" of consciousness akin to what Kant had offered for the dynamics of theoretical reason.

For Husserl, we understand phenomena and know the essences of them not by an empirical or "objective" analysis of "things in themselves" but by analyzing the activity of our own consciousness as it intentionally attends to and structures its perceptions of phenomena. Thus, the meaning of the objective world is how it engages human consciousness (how it appears to us), and the meaning of our subjective consciousness is the mode with which it opens us to the world (how we look at it).[173] Husserl gave a special role to intuition in the interactive relationship between consciousness and phenomena. First we have "individual intuitions" of ordinary experiences. Then, we go beyond immediate or "natural" awareness to "essential intuitions" by which we intuit the essences not just of particular things but of universal truths.[174] Here imagination has a key function as we move from particular instances of a phenomenon to its universal essence. For universal essences Husserl used the term *eidos,* the same Plato used for the ideal "forms." For Husserl, however, essences do not exist in a transcendent world of ideas but in our own human consciousness—a kind of "subjective idealism."

To reach for "eidetic" knowledge, that is, the very essences of life, requires essential intuition to "bracket out" or place in suspension all presuppositions that distract us from the activities of our own pure consciousness and from our own innermost self ("transcendental ego," he called this). "Bracketing" brings to consciousness a method of doubt similar to what Descartes applied to the mind. Husserl wished to "put out of action" or "nullify" everything that distracts pure consciousness from encountering the essential phenomena of things. Operationally, such "bracketing" means becoming aware of our own baggage—all the theories, attitudes, interests, ideologies, and so on that we usually bring to reality—and suspending all of it—its assumptions, interests, biases—so that reality can speak for itself to our consciousness. Only thus, said Husserl, can our consciousness see for itself what it really sees and why it sees it, rather than simply seeing what we want to see or what others want us to see.[175] When our own consciousness is operating without outside influence and we encounter phenomena without perspective, then we can know the essential and certain meaning and value of those phenomena.

There is a deep "forgetfulness of being" in Husserl's assumption that we can ever have such a pristine and presuppositionless view of reality. Moreover, he was wrong in posing an individualistic and internal analysis of consciousness as the source and measure of essential truth. Nevertheless, he had significant insights for a conative process; three are particularly worth noting.

First, phenomenology turns to our agential consciousness as primary in the activity of knowing and prompts us to become aware of the phenomena presented to us by our own conscious activities. Such self-consciousness is crucial to knowing both ourselves and the world as agent-subjects. This calls for a pedagogy that invites people to reflect on their consciousness of their own "being" in the world. Second, Husserl's emphasis on analysis of our own consciousness (what might be called a second level of reflection), holds the potential of critical consciousness. A pedagogy that helps people to uncover what they are bringing to interpret their lives in the world can encourage a critical consciousness that in turn can empower emancipatory praxis for self and others.[176] Third, and related, Husserl's naïveté about "bracketing" notwithstanding, there is a valid sentiment undergirding it for religious educators as they interpret and explain the texts of the tradition. It is essential to be aware of what one is bringing to the text if the text is to "speak for itself." Only with awareness of our own subjectivity can we hope to allow the texts to bring *their* meaning to the present.

C. Existentialism and Heidegger

Existentialism looks to Søren Kierkegaard (1813–1855), "the melancholy Dane," as its founder. It embraces such a variety of positions and authors,[177] most of whom reject the appellation existentialist, that it is very difficult to describe, and a definition of existentialism contradicts its anti-systematic stance. Existentialism eschews the quest for universals and certainties and gives priority instead to individual existence. I take the work of Martin Heidegger (1889–1976) as a significant instance and point up some aspects that support a conative pedagogy.

Heidegger saw human existence as an alienated state of meaninglessness and abandonment, a situation of "thrownness" in which the only hope of authenticity is to face with rugged resolve the dread of one's own death. This is a far cry from the faith, hope, and love proposed for Christian identity and agency. Nevertheless, I have found insights in Heidegger's early work especially that contribute at least to the backdrop of an epistemic ontology. This is probably because he attempted to challenge a civilization that he believed had committed a "forgetfulness of being" by selling out to technical rationality; his intention was to make it once again "at home in Being."[178]

Through the influence of his teacher Husserl, Heidegger's basic approach was phenomenological. However, he gave Husserl's phenomenology an existentialist twist; that is, he pushed beyond an examination of consciousness to an examination of "being." He opened Husserl's "brackets" to "let in existence" and contended that the original source of meaning is not consciousness of the world but our "being-in-the-world" with its existential structures, moods, projects, and so on. Heidegger was convinced that previous philosophers had hidden our own "being" from us; their metaphysical systems and objectified abstractions do not describe or help us understand our own "being-in-the-world." He set out to investigate the most foundational aspects of our "being" as they present themselves to consciousness. By uncovering the existential structures and moods of "being" that shape our consciousness, we will also know how and what we know. The following are key characteristics of his ontology.

The Centrality of Existence. In chapter 1, I noted Heidegger's work as a turn to the "Being of beings," to *esse* rather than *ens*, to *human being* as a verb rather than a noun. His intent was to "think Being as such" by an analysis of the beings who can think about being, namely, ourselves. To investigate "Dasein"—the being of human beings as we inquire about our own being—Heidegger focused on the activities of human "existence," on the multitude of things we do as "beings in the world."[179] He rejected the notion that we have a stable "essence" to be investigated. Existence is our only "essence"; we make our "being" what we choose to make it.

Alienation and Thingification. Human beings are in a state of alienation, a "homelessness" in the world that separates us from one another and from our own consciousness as subjects. We are depersonalized and made "an anonymous one" by superstructures such as bureaucratized government, giant business corporations, big religious institutions—by all the vast, impersonal powers, which have a life of their own and cause us to succumb to the controlling habits and conventions of everyday existence. This alienation from our own true selves tends to "thingify" us, to turn us into objects. The temptation, said Heidegger, is to accept such "everydayness" and become an anonymous entity among "das Man"—the faceless "they" in which our individuality is obliterated and responsibility avoided.

Authentic and Inauthentic Existence. The first step away from alienation is to become conscious of our "thrownness" as "beings-in-the-world." By "thrownness" Heidegger meant that we find ourselves in the world without knowing the whence or whither of our being "there." The "facticity" of Dasein's "thrownness" must be taken with radical seriousness; we are beings in a world of "givens"—cultural, social, psychological, economic conditions—and our possibilities are already limited by them. Yet there is an existential structure at the depth of our existence, said Heidegger, whereby we refuse to be determined by what is and can strive for what might be. This is authenticity. It means taking responsibility for the open horizon of our existence and realizing our potential to become originating subjects of historical agency. Inauthentic existence means turning away from one's own possibilities for true being, accepting oneself as a fixed entity rather than an open possibility, and settling for the endless distractions of everydayness as one of the faceless crowd—das Man. Only by our free and responsible actions in the world can we come to authentic being.

Dread, Death, and Care. Heidegger posed "dread" or "anxiety" (*angst*) as a pervasive mood of the human condition. Unlike fear, which has a particular object, dread is the anxiety of "nothingness"—that our whole being is undergirded by nonbeing. The most ultimate of all existential anxiety is the dread of death, that we are "being-toward-death." But dread, if we face it with courage, can be a prelude to "care" or "concern"; this is when the conscience of Dasein is awakened to transcend thrownness, alienation, and anxiety and to truly "care" for our own being. Thus "dread" awakens "conscience," which leads to "care" for "being" and enables us to live authentically, to take responsibility for who we become in history. Only when we embrace our own temporality and understand ourselves as "beings-toward-death" can we live authentically and be agents of our "ownmost" being and becoming in the world.[180]

Heidegger's most significant contribution to a conative pedagogy is not so much in what he achieved (he abandoned the project begun in *Being and Time,* see note 178) as in what he perceived as needing to be done and hoped to accomplish. In gist, he attempted to reunite epistemology with ontology, knowing with "being," making the latter primary, and posed "knowing," insofar as it was his concern, as the consciousness that arises from attention to "being." I believe he intended to construct an "epistemic ontology." He posed our "being" rather than our "knowing" as the original foundation of our relationship with the world and articulated the consciousness he had (epistemic) of the pervasive structures and moods of human "being-in-the-world" (ontology). "Existence" as the originating source of truth and meaning suggests a teaching-learning dynamic that engages the whole "being" of participants and enables them to turn to and express the consciousness that arises from their own "being-in-the-world." Though I prefer (for reasons I outline in chap. 4) the word *praxis* to name reflection on one's participation in the world, I believe Heidegger's notion of "consciousness of being-in-the-world" is certainly resonant with and a significant aspect of what I intend by praxis.

Heidegger's second asset may seem strange when noted, yet it has an echo in Christian theology. Perhaps more than any philosopher in the Western tradition he looked honestly into the "abyss" and faced the possibility that there is no world of meaning and truth "ready-at-hand" for us to discover. He concluded we are faced with thrownness, facticity, alienation, thingification, anxiety, and death, yet we are responsible for the meaning we make, who we become, and what becomes of us all. Put in more theological terms, Heidegger is an extreme statement of the brokenness of the human condition, that we are capable of choosing the "nonbeing" of sin, of destroying ourselves and others. Christian faith calls people to trust that the ground of their "being" is a loving, caring, sustaining, saving, and merciful God rather than "no ground" or "the abyss" (*abgrund*), yet Heidegger's portrayal of our condition can ring true to our "existential" reality. His emphasis on our historical responsibilities can serve as antidotes to both Pollyannish liberalism and "cheap grace." Education for conation in Christian faith should challenge people, with apocalyptic urgency, to live now for God's-reign-in-the-world, filled with active hope for its realization but also with some wise dread of ultimate destruction.

In chapter 1 I noted my disagreement with Heidegger's limiting of our being to "existence" and his forgetting that there is also an "essence" to us not entirely of our own making. This, too, reflects Heidegger's forgetfulness of the "ground of Being" and his posing "no ground" instead. He also has a profound liability for pedagogy in Christian faith in the rugged individualism and self-sufficient resolve he proposed as the way to authentic existence. Heidegger often wrote that Dasein is co-Dasein, but most of his critics agree that his appreciation of relationship was more linguistic than real. For Buber, authenticity can be found only in an I-Thou relationship; for Heidegger, it is worked out in solitude. For a conative pedagogy in Christian faith, our existentialist mentor is Buber rather than Heidegger. From a Christian perspective, Heidegger's position is an unmitigated form of Pelagianism in which we are to make ourselves who we ought to become by our rugged will and individual efforts. Wisdom in Christian faith will always entail our will and effort, but we are also to trust that our will is prompted and our effort sustained by the gift of God's grace. And though we must face death, we do so through a community of faith and with hope that even death has been conquered by love.

D. Pragmatism

From the Greek *pragma,* meaning "things done," its etymology indicates the interest pragmatism has in results. I note pragmatism here, however briefly, because as an American contribution to Western philosophy we may suspect that it reflects something rooted deeply in North American consciousness. It has greatly influenced American education; in addition to Charles S. Peirce (1839–1914) and William James (1842–1910), it numbers John Dewey (1859–1952) among its leading exponents.[181] Here I point only to its emphasis on the "practical" in the sense of recognizable results as the motivating interest of knowing and the measure of truth.

For Peirce, its originator, the muddles of metaphysics can be cleared up most readily if one attends to the "practical" consequences of ideas; its consequences are the best indication of an idea's "meaning." In his key essay "How to Make Our Ideas Clear" (1878) Peirce offered a classic statement, oft quoted as the heart of a pragmatic view: "In order to ascertain the meaning of an intellectual conception one should consider what practical consequences might conceivably result by necessity from the truth of that conception; and the sum of these consequences will constitute the entire meaning of the conception."[182]

William James went beyond Peirce's concern for meaning and proposed practical results as the ultimate measure of truth. For James, the truth test of any idea is its fruitfulness in practice. "True ideas" are ones that work, that bring about satisfactory and "good" results; and "the pragmatic method" is "to interpret each notion by tracing its respective practical consequences."[183] Dewey echoed these sentiments. For Dewey, knowledge arises from "reconstruction" of experience that, among other things, imaginatively perceives alternative ways of acting; truth is what is warranted by its verifiable results. "Confirmation, corroboration, verification lie in works, consequences. . . . 'By their fruits shall ye know them. . . .' The hypothesis that works is the true one; and truth is an abstract noun applied to the collection of cases, actual, foreseen and desired, that receive confirmation in their works and consequences."[184]

There is an asset for a wisdom pedagogy in pragmatism's emphasis on historical consequences. Christian faith is to be "done." Jesus preached his gospel as a way of life to be lived. Christians are to be known by their fruits (Matt. 7:20) more than by clarity of ideas.[185] On the other hand, a purely pragmatic interest would be reductionistic for religious education. Pragmatism can lead to relativism, making no distinction between necessary and contingent truths and establishing "what works" as the only criterion of right and wrong. The praxis of

Christian faith must be based on principles of meaning and ethical norms beyond instrumental utility. Christianity is eminently "practical," but its practicality should not be reduced to the simply pragmatic. Oftentimes education in Christian faith brings people to awe, to wonder, to reverence, and into communion with ultimate mystery. Such outcomes are indeed practical—they change us—but not pragmatic in the instrumentalist sense.

8. The Shift Toward an Epistemic Ontology

In these recent movements, we notice the beginnings of an "epistemic shift" that can help religious educators to make an "ontological turn" in the philosophical foundations of our pedagogy. We would be misled, however, if we were to presume that the debilitating aspects of the dominant epistemological tradition have been transcended. As Jane Flax notes, our operative epistemologies are marked by "dualisms of subject-object, mind-body, inner-outer, reason-sense," and even the critiques of them are still "not adequately grounded in human experience."[186] In addition to such dualisms, a hierarchical ordering still marks Western epistemology, exemplified in what has been aptly called "a triumph of the mind," with "mind" equated with reason since Descartes. This augments the severing of "knowing" and "being" that pervades the whole Western tradition. Flax writes, "In philosophy, being (ontology) has been divorced from knowing (epistemology) and both have been separated from either ethics or politics."[187] "Forgetfulness of being" and "triumph of mind" combine to encourage education that perpetuates unjust social arrangements, precisely because it excludes significant aspects of human "being" and the majority of human beings from the "knowledge" that wields social power; it maintains an epistemic privilege of a few over the rest. To redress this pyrrhic victory of the dominant rationality, "knowing" and "being"—all of "being" and all human beings—must be reunited and especially in our pedagogy.

Lest I be misinterpreted, I affirm the contributions the mind and especially critical rationality of the post-Enlightenment era has made and must continue to make to Christian theology and religious education. My claim that the "triumph of reason" has been debilitating to the conative interests of religious education does not mean that the assets of critical rationality should be excluded from its pedagogy; I am convinced that the positive legacy of the Enlightenment era must be reflected in the dynamics of Christian religious education. Though the Enlightenment was naive in its undue confidence in reason to solve all human problems, and though it emphasized individual autonomy to the neglect of interdependence, its positive values and achievements must not be left behind—its insistence on the role of critical reasoning to promote human well-being, its emphasis on the rights of the individual (liberty, equality, pursuit of happiness, etc.), its championing of people's right to think for themselves. That I very much favor critical reasoning in faith education is amply evident in my description of an "epistemic ontology" (chap. 3) and of shared Christian praxis.

Post-Enlightenment "reason" has made at least four contributions to Christian theology and education: (1) it has raised awareness of how all symbolic mediations of "Christian faith" are historically conditioned, thus helping to prevent the reification of its symbols and their abuse as legitimations of destructive ideologies; (2) it has stimulated biblical scholarship to a critical reading of what is behind, in, and before the texts, helping to uncover their "surplus of meaning"; (3) it has given impetus and tools for a critical theology that can reformulate and reconstruct the Christian tradition in dialectic with different times and cultures, thus contributing to its vitality as a living tradition; (4) it has helped Christians to recognize their socially conditioned assumptions, ideologies, and interests, this "critical consciousness" contributing to ongoing conversion in the social responsibilities of Christian faith.

Education in Christian faith must build upon the contributions from critical reason; its pedagogy should help participants to rise to Kant's challenge of the Enlightenment—"dare to think." But critical reasoning must be explicitly reunited with analytical remembering and creative imagining and the "whole mind" subsumed into a pedagogy that honors and engages people's whole "being." However, even as we attempt to do more than engage people's minds, we must recognize that it is far from inevitable in our context that we even do as much.

Technical Rationality. There seems to be an operative epistemology in "developed" society and popular consciousness that bespeaks more a "demise of the mind" than its "triumph," a distorting of what the Western tradition, beginning with Plato, has meant by rationality into a kind of technique for control and production. Max Horkheimer, probably the first to sound an alarm about it, called it instrumental reasoning, but it is often identified now as technical rationality.

Technical rationality is moved by an instrumental interest in "what works" to produce "results." It does not engage "knowers" as "thinking-persons-in-relationship" with reality but functions as an adversarial stance toward nature, society, and other people; it obliterates the dialectical relationship that should exist between knower and known if knowledge is to be life-giving and historically responsible. Horkheimer explains that this "instrumental reasoning" in society employs the mind in a one-dimensional, utilitarian logic that excludes memory and imagination and concentrates only on what it claims are objective and empirical "facts" in order to promote commodity production and bureaucratic management.[188] As such, it brings about "rationality with reference to means and irrationality with reference to human existence."[189]

The kind of "objectification" necessary to concentrate only on the "facts" and to treat everything as an instrumental tool requires, says Horkheimer, a "loss of memory,"[190] and the refusal to think of outcomes beyond "what works for control" demands the suspension of imagination. Technical rationality "requires the kind of mentality that concentrates on the present and can dispense with memory and straying imagination."[191] As a result, "speculative thought is altogether liquidated,"[192] and people "are acting more and more like machines."[193] Severed from memory and imagination, from past and future, and so from people's own "being" in time and place, technical rationality is without self-engagement, critique, or ethic and thus has the capacity to destroy us.[194] In contrast, what I call a "humanizing rationality" brings knowers and known into a dialectical and right relationship of care that is life-giving for self, others, and creation.

Let us note that even a text like the Scriptures can be studied with a technical instead of a humanizing rationality. The former approaches the text as an "object" to be "mastered." Claiming to be without historical interest, it proceeds to analyze the Bible's "technical" details, to dissect its parts, to note its "facts" and "data," to uncover its context, to recognize its literary forms and sources, but intentionally excludes any sense of personal relationship with the text or of its import for one's life. The "product" is "knowledge about" the Bible and a sense that one is in control of the text—certainly enough to pass an exam about its "data," to do well in a biblical quiz. Much scripture scholarship, in the professed interest of "scholarship," often appears to encourage such an exclusively technical rational approach to the Bible, reflecting a dichotomy between "knowing" and "being," and reducing "knowing" to "knowing about."

In contrast, a humanizing rationality in biblical study can also be academically rigorous and employ the tools and "criticisms" of modern Scripture scholarship. However, it enters into a personal relationship with the text; one becomes engaged with it as with a friend. The student enters into a self-investing dialogue with the text as a source of meaning and ethic for life. Beyond concern for its "data," she or he asks such questions as, What has this meant for people's lives? What does it mean for me and for us now? How is my and our life reflected in and illumined by this text? What am I bringing to it, and what am I to take away from it? How am I and how are we to respond to it, to draw life from it? A pedagogy for conation in Christian faith can honor the best of critical scholarship and employ a humanizing rationality if it is grounded in an epistemic ontology.

Feminist Epistemology. Technical rationality is pervasive, not only in the production of technical commodities, where it may have a place, but throughout society. However, there are hopeful signs of awareness of its dangers, concerted resistance to it, and efforts to forge a more humanizing "epistemic." These alternatives reflect a "remembrance of being"; they work to reunite epistemology with ontology and to include all beings in what counts for "knowledge." Not surprisingly, the movements toward such an "epistemic ontology" are emerging from groups of people previously excluded from the knowledge enterprise and thus from social power.

Sharon Welch points to liberation movements in society and, of particular relevance to religious educators, to the *theologies* of liberation, as posing "an epistemic shift that is shattering the foundations of Western knowledge and action." She also notes the work of Michel Foucault as offering "an incisive, unsettling description of this shift."[195] Foucault says that an "epistemic shift" is being caused by "an insurrection of subjugated knowledges," that is, by the emergence into voice of what had been disdained by people with "knowledge control" as "naive knowledges, located low down on the hierarchy, beneath the required level of cognition or scientificity."[196] This "shift" and "insurrection" is forging fundamental changes in who participates, what counts as knowledge, and how it emerges.

The critiques of establishment epistemology and the posing of alternatives that I have found most compelling are in the literature of "feminist theory."[197] Its influence has been evident in the deconstructive work of this chapter and is a constant perspective throughout the constructive work of chapter 3. Here it will help to summarize a few central themes from feminist theory that contribute to an epistemic ontology.[198]

Feminist theory recognizes that women, women's "experience," and as Evelyn Fox-Keller states, "those domains of human experience that have been relegated to women: namely the personal, the emotional, and the sexual"[199] have been excluded from or treated as marginal to the epistemology of the West. Because "knowledge" has been correlated with "power" (an insight first articulated by Bacon), the upper-class male hegemony over what counts for knowledge has both reflected and maintained the social oppression of women. Male epistemic privilege has expressed itself, as Jane Flax notes, in ways of knowing separated from "being" and marked by false dualisms; the consequence has been "distorted forms of knowledge" that are destructive.[200]

Alternatives demand that "the multiplicity of experience," and thus all beings, be included in the enterprise of knowledge.[201] Feminist theorists insist that women and women's "experience" be at least fully honored epistemically, and some argue for the "epistemic privilege" of a feminist perspective as a source of more life-giving, ethically responsible, and less distorted "knowledge."[202] Here Josephine Donovan offers a very helpful summary statement of "the determinant structures of experience under which women, unlike men, have nearly universally existed." She then delineates "how these historical structures may have contributed to the formulation of a particularly female epistemology and ethic."[203]

> First and foremost, women have experienced political oppression. They have not had substantial political power in society, and have not been in control of the realities that have shaped their lives. Second, nearly every-

where and in nearly every period, women have been assigned to the domestic sphere. . . . Third, women's historical economic function has been
production for use, not production for exchange. . . . Fourth, women experience significant physical events that are different from men's.

Donovan then surmises that these "conditions" of women have led to "a
particular epistemology" that reflects,

> a fundamental respect for the contingent order, for the environmental
> context, for the concrete, everyday world. Women more than men appear
> to be willing to adopt a passive mode of accepting the diversity of envi-
> ronmental voices and the validity of their realities. Women appear less
> willing to wrench that context apart or to impose upon it alien abstractions
> or to use implements that subdue it intellectually or physically. Such an
> epistemology provides the basis for an ethic that is non-imperialistic, that
> is life-affirming, and that reverences the concrete details of life.[204]

Extrapolating from Donovan's summary and from other relevant
literature, I see a feminist "epistemic shift" making at least the following
contributions to an "epistemic ontology":

1. It offers both theoretical clarity and political power to a social
   struggle whose epistemological import is to include the whole
   person and all people as agents and participants in what
   counts for knowledge.
2. Its mode of "knowing" is one of partnership and dialogue and
   of recognizing the contextuality and "interest" of all knowledge rather than seeing knowledge as "objective" and value
   free.
3. It has an intentional ethic of care that emphasizes relationship
   and responsibility rather than individual rights and rational
   certainty.[205]
4. Because of social gendering and patriarchal structures, "wom-
   en's ways of knowing" may often have to originate from "silence" to then move through other "modes" of knowing. From
   the work of Mary Belenky and her colleagues, however, it
   seems a feminist epistemic has a cumulative impetus toward
   "constructed" and constructive knowledge that transcends the
   dualisms that have plagued Western epistemology.[206]

Chapter 3

The Dimensions and Dynamics of "Being" Engaged for Conation in Christian Faith

I am convinced that a conative pedagogy, adequate to educate in the wisdom of lived Christian faith and human freedom toward the reign of God (see chapter 1), needs the philosophical foundation of an "epistemic ontology." This means that our teaching should reflect an "ontological turn" to engage all the dimensions and dynamics of human "being" and be epistemic in that it turns participants to the consciousness that arises from their whole "being" as agent-subjects located and related in place and time. Here I attempt to clarify an "epistemic ontology" and more precisely to describe the dimensions and dynamics of human "being" to be consciously engaged in a pedagogy for conation in Christian faith.

The organizing question of this chapter is, *What pedagogical activities are required by an epistemic ontology to educate for conation/wisdom in Christian faith?* Clearly the religious educator needs some functional schema of appropriate pedagogical activities. It should suggest how the curriculum (i.e., content, process, and environment) of specific teaching/learning events are to be effected. To this end I propose a fivefold taxonomy of pedagogical activities. Each activity honors some aspect of "being" as one comes to identity and agency in Christian faith and so reflects an epistemic ontology. Though I distinguish them, existentially these activities overlap and function as an orchestrated unity within a teaching/learning event. In sum, I propose that pedagogy for conation in Christian faith do the following:

1. Engage the "being" of people in their *self-identity* as "agent-subjects-in-relationship"
2. Engage the "place" in which people's "being" is realized

3. Engage people's "being in time" and the faith tradition of the Christian community over time
4. Engage people's dynamic structure for conation
5. Engage people in decision for their "truth" in Christian faith

1. Engaging People's "Being" in Their Self-identity as Agent-Subjects-in-Relationship.

The emphasis of this first category of pedagogical activities is human "being" qua self-identified subjects, from *our* side of personal agency in the world. (The world side of the relationship is the focus in section 2.) Existentially, of course, this perspective is a fiction if it views persons in an ahistorical way. As agent-subjects we are always in relationship with the world; our self-identity emerges and is maintained by our location in social place and historical time. The angle of vision, then, is our*selves* as related and situated beings, and I focus here on the dynamic capacities of people by which they express their identity and realize their agency in the world. I often refer to these capacities as *personal conati* (borrowing from Spinoza) in that they are the originating sources of our "being" and thus of conation. I call them "dynamic capacities" because they are both abilities and dispositions for some expression of our agency as subjects in the world. The task, then, is to delineate the conati that can be recognized in people qua agent-subjects—in our personal "aliveness"—and so are to be intentionally engaged in a conative pedagogy.

It is helpful for educators to have ready at hand a reminder of what to engage in a teaching/learning event. The schema that follows is suggested by the notion of "self-identity," which I take to mean the sense we have of being "selves" with continuity over time.[1] In schematizing our personal conati around self-identity, it seems wise to take a phenomenological rather than a metaphysical approach, that is, to attend to the aspects of our "selves" that appear in our consciousness of "being" rather than to a "theory" of the person.

The most immediate phenomena we notice about ourselves is that we have bodily, mental, and volitional *aspects* (literally, "ways of looking at"). In the commonsense meaning of the terms we perceive the phenomena of our bodiliness, our minds, and our wills, and we recognize them as sources of identity and agency in our one "being." We recognize further that though body, mind, and will function in concert as our "selves," each aspect has capacities and dispositions for "being" that can be identified with it.

Our corporeal, mental, and volitional conati are many, and one could readily assemble a long list of them with only a few moments of reflection on the question, What are the things I typically do as an alive human being? However, a more memorable schema emerges if we combine our sense of corporeal, mental, and volitional capacities with the recognition that self-identity entails our sense of the past, present, and future. As "selves" we are constantly engaged with appropriating our past, dealing with our present, and forging our future. This, combined with our three most obvious aspects, suggests a schema of human conati for "being" and thus the activities to be engaged and brought to consciousness in a conative pedagogy. People have dynamic capacities for corporeal/maintaining, mental/remembering, and volitional/inheriting of the past; corporeal/engaging, mental/reasoning, and volitional/relating in the present; and corporeal/regenerating, mental/imagining, and volitional/committing toward the future.

Schema of Personal Conati as "Agent-Subjects-in-Relationship"

CORPOREAL	MENTAL	VOLITIONAL	
Maintaining	Remembering	Inheriting	of the past
Engaging	Reasoning	Relating	in the present
Regenerating	Imagining	Committing	toward the future

I emphasize again that all our "timely" conati—bodily, mental, and volitional—operate in concert with one another; they are functional "aspects," not separate faculties, of the one "self." Corporeal conati make possible and shape reflecting and willing; mental conati influence what we choose and how we experience bodiliness; volitional conati animate mental and corporeal activities. This symphonic interrelationship is especially operative as teachers engage them and bring their activities to consciousness in teaching/learning events. My situating of some activities within a particular aspect of us will often reflect no more than a degree of emphasis in our perception of their dynamic. For example, I place the activity of language within our mental aspect, but communication of any kind also depends on activities of body and will. Clearly every pedagogical event will not equally engage every human conatus and all their possible combinations and will not equally bring their activities to consciousness. The theme, context, participants, and so on usually call for more attention to some than others. But all of them should be engaged over time, and educators can neglect none consistently if they intend the learning outcome of conation/wisdom.

Body, Mind, and Will: Aspects of Human "Being"

The Corporeal. I use "corporeal" here for the whole physical aspect of human "being." Surely the most obvious phenomenon we notice about our "selves" is that we are what Merleau-Ponty called "body-subjects," and all of our consciousness is "embodied consciousness."[2] Even the generic pronouns we use of people—some*body*, every*body*, and no*body*—remind that as persons we are bodies. The space we occupy, the location we have in "place," the active presence we are in "time" is first and foremost as embodied selves. As and through our bodies we first sense our own "being," initiate action, experience the world, and communicate with others.[3] Richard Kearney, with a pithy summary that reflects Merleau-Ponty's central philosophy, writes, "The body is not an object amongst others, to be measured in purely scientific or geometric terms, but a mysterious and expressive mode of belonging to the world through our perceptions, gestures, sexuality and speech. It is through our bodies as living centres of intentionality . . . that we choose our world and that our world chooses us."[4]

Our bodies are not simply containers for our mental and volitional aspects. Rather, the first (sequentially) source of agency and consciousness is our embodied "being," and it gives an incarnate quality to how we exercise our mental and volitional conati. As Colleen Griffith writes, the body is "the contextualizing organism" that provides "all the anatomical systems and functions that make consciousness and agency possible."[5] This must not be heard as another version of the body as servant to the mind—an old theme. The body has its own conati for placing the "self" as subject and agent of one's own "being" in the world. These are the active dispositions of our bodies to maintain our incarnate selves in continuity with the past, to engage bodily in present time and place, and to physically make and do things that regenerate our own and other "bodies" for the future.

The body is its own source of "sensuous wisdom" that is constitutive of conation. This point has been convincingly demonstrated by the pedagogy of Maria Montessori, which engages participants in physical interaction with sensorial materials as the first source of learning.[6] The greatest resource and highest expression of body wisdom is "aesthetic activity." Aesthetic activity originates from the body's dynamic capacity to act upon and give its own form to material reality and to estimate according to its own sensuous gratification the appropriateness of any material form. The proper intent and outcome of aesthetic activity is the creation and/or appreciation of "art." I understand art as any sensible expression or representation of what is or might be that prompts people to see the ultimate in the immediate. Clearly art engages the mental and spiritual aspects of both creators and recipients, but the first impetus to create it and our ability to appreciate it originate in the form-giving or aesthetic disposition of our bodies toward the world.

A pedagogy for conation includes and engages the activities of people's corporeal conati and brings participants to express the consciousness that arises from their "bodied wisdom." Recognizing, however, that people's corporeal conati can be used for destructive as well as creative and life-giving purposes, a conative pedagogy also attempts to educate and form the physical dispositions of participants to create and do what is most humanizing for all in wisdom.

Mental. This is our ability and disposition to engage life with thoughtful comprehension, to construct an intelligible world for ourselves and to appropriate some measure of meaning and value from it. In concert with our bodies, and moved by our wills, our minds function to perceive and recognize, to understand and comprehend, to discern and judge, and, prompting our physical agency and will, to decide and choose about ourselves and the world around us. Not only are people capable of these activities of mind, we can also be conscious of performing them—we can reflect on our own reflecting.

Our minds have conati for reasoning, remembering, and imagining. That "by which" we reflect are our reasons, memories, and imaginations. Further (continuing to draw on Aristotle's schema of "causes"), that "on which" we exercise these dynamic capacities is our life in the world; that "for which" we exercise them is to appropriate the truth about ourselves and the world; and that "with which" we reflect is symbols and especially language. Our mental conati enable us to create language and symbols to externalize our "selves" and to represent our "world" to self and others; our language, in turn, shapes us and how we perceive our "world."

Note well that remembering, reasoning, and imagining are not separate faculties but functions of the one mind; they always function together, yet should not be reduced to one another. To paraphrase Augustine, they are functions of the one mind that cooperate to remember with reason and imagination, to reason with memory and imagination, to imagine with memory and reason.

Remembering, reasoning, and imagining are constitutive of our "being" as agent-subjects in the world and thus are ingredient to conation. Educators must engage these conati of participants both in their own right and to bring the activities of their corporeal and volitional conati to consciousness. Engaging their mental activities and enabling participants to bring consciousness of them to expression is integral to both the content and process of a conative curriculum. And people's own reflective capacities are engaged not simply as curriculum for a particular occasion but also to form them in the habit of thinking—to become *thinkers* for themselves.

The Volitional. This is our capacity to make choices about and to effect the substance and form of every expression of our identity and agency in the world. The will animates our corporeal and mental activities but has conati particular to the functioning of the will itself. The latter are our active dispositions to inherit and draw life out of our past, to relate with affectivity in the present, and to commit ourselves with responsible and creative agency toward the future.

It is also suggestive of its dynamic to designate this volitional aspect of us as "spiritual." In terms of the Adamic myth, our spiritual (from *spirare,* to breathe) aspect is the breath of God's life that enlivens us to engage humanly in the world with a will to life. This "aliveness" of our "being" has traditionally been called the "soul," but the term has fallen out of use in philosophical literature. "Soul," however, is still a rich term for the spiritual aspect of us that we readily recognize in our consciousness as the "heart" that gives us passion, desire, commitment, relationality, and "will" for life.

This volitional/spiritual aspect of us is also the predominant location of our affectivity and "feelings." I say "predominant" because feelings are a will-o'-the-wisp that can prompt and arise from any aspect of our "being." Some feelings originate and are felt in the body (hunger, thirst, etc.); others are mentally induced and felt, especially by memory and imagination (satisfaction, regret, hope, anxiety, etc.). Yet the most appropriate location for human affectivity seems the volitional/spiritual aspect of us; feelings prompt and are prompted by our "will" and "heart" for life.

Like mental conati, our volitional capacities are not distinct faculties of the "soul" but interdependent functions of the one person; inheriting, relating, and committing are always symbiotic with one another and interrelated with all our other conati. A conative pedagogy intentionally turns people toward and engages them in activities of "willing" and brings them to express the consciousness that arises from their volitional activities. The proper intent of the choices we make is to do "right actions" and thus to become virtuous actors who live in "right relationship" with self, God, others, and creation. Though acts of volition regarding past, present, and future are ineluctable, nevertheless we do not inevitably use these conati in virtuous and life-giving ways for self and others. A conative pedagogy, then, is also structured to form participants in the habit of choosing what is most life-giving for all—a life of wisdom.

A. Maintaining/Remembering/Inheriting—of the Past

1. Corporeal/Maintaining. We have a corporeal conatus to maintain ourselves in well-"being." This dynamic capacity impels us to feed, satiate, rest, shelter, clothe, and care for our bodies. When physically threatened, our embodied instinct is to preserve ourselves. Beyond this, the body also has from its beginning an incarnate disposition and need for physically expressed love and relationship. Small babies can die from malnutrition or exposure but can also waste away (*marasmus*) if they are not cuddled and physically loved.

From its "being" over time, the body has an incarnate wisdom that it carries and maintains within itself from the past into the present and future. Its store of wisdom is truly "biographical" in the sense suggested by the word, from *bios graphia*, literally, "what is written on our bodies." The body knows skills developed along the way, has intuitive wisdom sharpened by experience to recognize what is good for it as well as danger and threat; it has a reliable sense, tested over time, of what is gratifying or disagreeable. Because of their conatus for maintenance, our bodies carry and remember all we have been through—joy and pain, health and sickness, love and hate, satisfaction and hunger, and so on. Even what our mental memories "forget," our bodies likely "remember"; our whole biography is "lodged deep in the memories of the body, which forgets nothing."[7]

Appropriately, then, a conative pedagogy actively engages and turns people to the time-tested wisdom that they already carry in their bodies. It also encourages people in the disposition to cherish, respect, and care for the well-being of their own and others' bodies. Remembering that people's bodily estates impinge upon and shape the learning process, educators create teaching/learning environments that are appropriate to people's physical comfort and general well-being and sensitive to participants' age, sex, race, economic class, and so on. A conative pedagogy especially encourages participants to attend critically to how their bodies may have been disvalued over time by age bias, sexism, racism, and consumerism in their culture.

2. Mental/Remembering. This is our active disposition of mind to bring to consciousness our personally owned information, thoughts, convictions, feelings, and images that we have learned from experiences and from other people. It is the conatus to reclaim for oneself as "living knowledge" (Derrida) what one already "knows" qua agent-subject-in-relationship (social remembering is described in section 2). Though memory can be used for simple recall, or to retrieve something that was "stored" by rote memorization, remembering that brings previous knowledge to life again entails analysis and reclaiming of it with a renewed sense of its wisdom or value. Here Derrida, borrowing from Plato in the *Phaedrus,* offers an interesting distinction between "knowledge as memory and nonknowledge as rememoration."[8] The former is what Plato means by anamnesis, which entails, says Derrida, "the active reanimation of knowledge, for its reproduction in the present." In a sense, such remembering, which I characterize as "analytical," is a kind of re-dis-covering of what one already knows as a living wisdom again. The "nonknowledge of rememoration," on the other hand, simply recalls something by some mnemonic device; it is, as Derrida notes, a "passive, mechanical simulation or 'mimicking' of knowledge."[9] This recalling can have a limited place in a conative pedagogy, but the fullest meaning I intend for mental/remembering here is "calling to mind again" (from its root *re-memorari*) and seeing from analysis the meaning and import of what one already "knows."

Analytical remembering may be of the world around us or of ourselves as the "self" emerges from our own life story. Remembering something from one's life story is particularly affective; it is difficult to remember one's own story dispassionately and without emotion. Analytical remembering is also a primary source of our self-identity; in fact, without it we lose our self-identity and thus our sense of historical agency.[10] Likewise, analytical remembering can uncover repressed memories of the self that if left "forgotten" can hold us bound; remembering them can bring healing and emancipation. Remembering, then, can have various levels, from simple recall to the depth work of psychoanalysis.

The typical teaching/learning event is not appropriate for psycho-analysis, but a wisdom pedagogy engages the conatus of people for remembering as bringing to mind again through active analysis what participants already "know" of their world and, as appropriate, of themselves. Recall can also be appropriate in such pedagogy, but ana-lytical remembering of "living knowledge" is constitutive to one's "be-ing" as agent-subject, and thus is integral to a pedagogy for conation. When it seems appropriate to encourage participants to commit some-thing to memory by rote, memorization should come *after* understand-ing and appropriation, so that when recalled it may be a source of living knowledge rather than simply a "mimicking" of knowledge. (I comment further on memorization in chapter 10.)

3. *Volitional/Inheriting.* I use "inheriting" to designate the conatus of our wills to make our own—to become heirs to—the wisdom of our bodies, the memories and stories of our lives, and the cumulative will to life that we have lived thus far. It is our dynamic disposition to say "fiat" to our "self"-constituting activities over time, to say yes to who we are from who we have been. The proper intent of such "inheriting" is to reclaim our identity by choice rather than simply accepting for ourselves what Cooley called "a looking-glass self" from the past, or fatalistically allowing it to determine who we become as if we are held bound by it. Our conatus for volitional/inheriting enables us to decide for ourselves who we are, to act according to our own deepest truth, to maintain our dignity and autonomy as agent-subjects, even in situations of the most abject control.[11] What we inherit from our own lives is always influenced by our context and draws upon the wisdom of our bodies and the memories of our minds. But volitional/inheriting has its own conatus that both reflects and nurtures our agency as historical subjects.

A pedagogy for conation engages participants in activities of volitional/inheriting and invites them to claim their "ownmost" and deepest truth, to act faithfully to the best "selves" they already are. It also invites participants to share the consciousness that emerges from acting true to themselves and to their personal tradition regarding the themes of the curriculum. A conative pedagogy intends to form par-ticipants in the disposition to discern and claim what is life-giving from their "inherited" identities and to refuse and move beyond what is destructive from the influences of their past.

B. Engaging/Reasoning/Relating—in the Present

1. *Corporeal/Engaging.* This is the dynamic capacity we have to physically experience and act with "manual" agency upon the world and others. It is difficult to think, even analytically, of physical engaging apart from volitional/relating, and, of course, they shape each other; yet we recognize that our bodies have their own impetus to relate physically with the world. As corporeal "beings" we cannot keep to

ourselves but constantly reach out to physically receive from and act upon the world. In our "being" we have a nonrefusable conatus to physically engage in life; thus such activity is a source of conation or wisdom.

The term *engaging* as I intend it here includes but goes beyond what empiricists have meant by "sense experience." Engaging is indeed receiving through our senses the stimuli of sensibilia *from* the world, but it also includes our physical action *on* and *in* the world as creative agents. Thus corporeal/engaging includes what we are manually doing and creating, as well as what we are physically feeling and receiving in our encounter with reality and others. In fact we can notice three phenomena from our being physically engaged. I call them our "feelings," our "sensings," and our "labors." The first is what we experience of our bodiliness in itself; the second arises from our active reception of the data of reality; and the third comes from our physical work on the world around us and with others.

Our bodies experience *feelings* of which they are also the originating locus—of being tired or rested, hungry or well fed, cold or warm, and so on. Our minds and wills can have a hand in them (we can choose to get a good night's rest), yet our bodies are their first source and site (volitional feelings of love, joy, hate, and so on are reviewed below as "emotions"). We can, however, bring them to consciousness and expression as a source of "sensuous wisdom." By our *sensings* I mean the sensible data we appropriate through our senses of seeing, touching, tasting, hearing, and smelling. Our *sensings* are the beginning of and give perspective to rational cognition, and they also add to and are appropriated by the "sensuous wisdom" that the body carries in its own biography. By *labors* here I mean our productive and reproductive activities by which we either work on and create out of material reality or physically engage in and manually care for our own and others well-"being." Both "labors" are expressions of the body's aesthetic capacity and disposition. The productive can be as sublime as creating a work of art or as ordinary as bringing dishes from dirty to clean. Undoubtedly, a great work of art (and perhaps even washing dishes well) engages conati beyond corporeal/engaging, yet productive and creative labor originates from the body's impetus to give sensible form to things of nature they would not have otherwise. Reproductive and sustaining labor also has an aesthetic aspect in that it reflects a felt appreciation for self and others and is an expression of the body's "sensuous wisdom."

The body's wisdom from its maintaining activity over time and from its present physical engagement with world and others typically flows on into reflection and volition, but of itself it is sensuous rather than ratiocinative or volitional in origin. The body "knows" and has its own felt truth and meaning—an "organic inner wisdom" that is "body logical" before reason-logical.[12] This wisdom has been excluded or marginalized in Western education, but a pedagogy for conation must turn people to and bring them to express their consciousness and body wisdom from their corporeal feelings, sensings, and labors. This attention is also a source of formation for participants' aesthetic capacity to engage in the world in ways that are humanizing and life-giving for all.

2. *Mental/Reasoning.* This is our dynamic capacity to engage reasonably in life. Reason prompts us to question and interpret reality, to understand the meaning of it and of ourselves within it, and to judge the adequacy of the understandings we reach. Mental/reasoning has an *intuitive* ability to recognize self-evident truths, an *inductive* ability to analyze evidence and reach comprehension, and a *deductive* ability to reason logically from principles to conclusions. Mental/reasoning also has a capacity for transcendence that can go beyond, as it were, the immediacy of reasoning in two significant ways. First, as we reason, we can self-consciously attend to, understand, and evaluate our reasoning activity—reason about our reasoning. Second, we are capable not only of looking reasonably "at life" but also of looking "through life" to the Ground of its meaning. The first transcendent reach is the capacity for critical consciousness and the latter for a contemplative consciousness.

Pedagogy for conation sponsors people to reason and, according to their developmental readiness, to think critically and contemplatively for themselves. All of people's reasoning capacities are employed and brought to expression in a wisdom pedagogy—to understand and judge, to reason intuitively, inductively, and deductively to truth about themselves and their world. This is eminently appropriate in a pedagogy for conation in Christian faith. The whole theological tradition of Christianity reflects the conviction that although faith is a gift of God, we need to bring our faith to understanding. Christian religious education should bring people to reason for themselves about their own lives in faith and about their faith tradition as it is made accessible to them. Without mental/reasoning, critical questioning, and what Kenneth Leech calls "creative doubt," participants are less likely to become agent-subjects of their faith in the world. Leech says insightfully that when people are educated to "believe everything without question," with advent of the first serious doubt they can readily "cease to believe anything."[13]

3. *Volitional/Relating.* This is our dynamic disposition as an "I" to relate intentionally and with emotion to our perceived "selves" (i.e., to a "me"),[14] to others, creation, and God. Volitional/relating is intentional in that we consciously choose it and affective in that our will is moved by desires and feelings that arise from our bodies, our memories, our imaginations, and from within the will itself as the source of our passion for "being." Emotions that are volitional (as distinct from body feelings of hunger, thirst, etc.) include our longings and fears, hopes and despair, joys and sorrows, laughter and tears, enthusiasm and indignation, esteem and contempt, trust and mistrust, love and hatred, tenderness and wrath, admiration, veneration, reverence, dread, horror, terror, and so on.[15] These emotions prompt and influence how

we choose to relate to our world of meaning and value and they shape our relationships on every level of existence—personal, interpersonal, and social/political. The proper intent of volitional/relating is "right relationship" with self, others, creation, and God. As so evident, however, we can and often do misdirect our wills to isolation and injustice rather than to right relationship.

Pedagogy for wisdom engages people's volitional/relating capacities and activities. Contrary to the stereotypical kind of dispassionate discourse (sometimes called "academic") presumed necessary to promote "cognition," the more a teaching/learning event can emotionally engage, inspire, delight, move, and rouse the hearts of participants, the more appropriate it is for conation. This pedagogy also turns participants toward and brings them to express the consciousness that arises from any realization of their relational activities, in a way that seems appropriate to the focus of the curriculum on a particular occasion. The pedagogue must strive to create an educational environment likely to form people in "right relationship," that is, to provide a context whose emotional climate and learning dynamic is itself marked by right relationship.

C. Regenerating/Imagining/Committing—Toward the Future

1. *Corporeal/Regenerating.* Our bodies have a capacity and active disposition for regenerating ourselves, others, and society. This conatus reflects the will to future well-"being" embedded, as it were, in our very genes and gives us an instinctive disposition to avoid what threatens and do what sustains our own and others' lives into the future. Existentially it is often indistinguishable from corporeal maintaining and engaging, yet we can note three aspects of our conatus for corporeal/regenerating. First, we have a corporeal conatus for our own ongoing salubrity; when our bodies are sick or wounded they have an amazing ability to heal themselves. Second, our disposition for corporeal/regenerating prompts us to be life-giving for others. Humans have a genetic impetus to give life through procreation and a natural disposition to nurture and protect the new life we bring into the world, not just for the sake of their future but for our own as well. Whether our disposition for procreation is exercised or not, we constantly direct our regenerating capacity to the corporeal life of others, through activities of protecting, sheltering, feeding, hugging, teaching, and so on. Third, we take physical care for the future of our social and cultural worlds. Colleen Griffith is correct in describing our bodies as "sociocultural sites"; they are the primary loci where society and culture position themselves.[16] Our bodies, then, are sources of physical agency for the continuation and regeneration of our sociocultural world.

A wisdom pedagogy engages people's conatus for corporeal regenerating and brings them to express the consciousness that arises from such activities, both to learn from them and to educate this conatus to be life-giving for all. The latter requires keen attention to the likely and preferred outcomes of people's corporeal/regenerating activities and encouraging participants to listen to their own body wisdom as they act toward the future. We can refuse or suppress the promptings of this conatus for life and choose death for ourselves, for others, and even for our human community. By helping people to listen to the promptings of their bodies for life, a conative pedagogy can enable participants to refuse the destruction with which technical rationality and unethical wills at present threaten us.

2. Mental/Imagining. Everyone has a conatus to imagine, but the creative dynamic of this capacity makes every description only partial. Imagination ranks with affectivity (to which it is closely allied) as a gadfly among the conati. The nature of imagining is to break the limits of every schema and, as here, to highlight its limitations. I place it within the mental aspect of us and as a conatus toward the future, but it also functions in the borderlands between body and mind, mind and will, will and body,[17] and helps us to bring the past into the present for the future. Within our mental activities, reason and memory require its images to function.

I describe this will-o'-the-wisp as our dynamic capacity to see *what is* and its likely consequences and to see *what is not yet* but either can be or should be. My summary suggests that imagination has a fourfold function. (a) It enables us to see what "is." In this, imagination functions to "shape into one" (Kant) our corporeal and intuitive activities by providing schema of the stimuli that arise from experience, and it presents understanding with perceptions that it can fashion into concepts, enabling us to recognize and understand what "is." (b) Beyond Kant's notion of it as organizer of sense data, imagination also has an anticipatory function that enables us to see both the conceptual and practical consequences of what "is." Conceptually its impetus can lead us on, if appropriate, to see the universal in particulars; practically it enables us to anticipate the likely or intended consequences of human action. Regarding what is "not yet," (c) imagination leads us beyond the paralysis of settling for what is, and enables us, as Kearney says, "to begin to imagine that the world as it is could be otherwise."[18] This is what he calls the poetic power of imagination, its disposition for *poiesis*. And (d), imagination entails "the ethical demand to imagine otherwise."[19] In its ethical impetus, imagination "can open us to the otherness of the other" and enliven our sense of responsibility for what is most humanizing and life-giving for all.[20] Especially in its latter three functions, imagination both awakens and is prompted by emotion and particularly by desire. It is impossible to see the consequences of what is or the possibilities of what might be or should be and remain dispassionate.

Pedagogy for conation must intentionally engage participants in imaginative activities to express the consciousness that arises from their acts of imagination, and to see for themselves what is and its consequences, what is not yet but can be or should be. Imagination is difficult to kill, but it can be stymied or controlled (and, alas, sometimes by forms of education). A conative pedagogy deliberately avoids anti-imaginative practices, and positively encourages participants to "use their imaginations."

3. Volitional/Committing.   We have the conatus to consciously choose and make commitments that shape how we live toward the future for ourselves, others, and creation. Volitional/committing permeates and draws upon all of the other conati. It operates explicitly in concert with corporeal/regenerating and mental/imagining and with the other volitional activities of inheriting and relating to bring to historical expression the stance of people as agent-subjects toward the future. It is the key human conatus that enables us to be social creators and re-creators in our time and place.

The proper intent of this dynamic capacity for chosen commitment is right living or orthopraxis on every level of our "being"—personal, interpersonal, and social/political. When it functions according to "right desire," which is itself informed by "right reason" (Aristotle), such praxis forms people in the habit of virtuous living, it nurtures them in wisdom. Volitional committing, then, is both expression and source of human conscience—of what enables us to discern rightly and to do what is fitting, true, and good. Existentially, of course, we do not inevitably exercise this conatus according to its intent of right living. We can choose to create destruction, settle for falsehood, and do evil; we are capable of sin. A pedagogy for conation, then, must actively engage people in making chosen commitments and provide a community where there is resource, sponsorship, testing, and opportunity to make and practice right commitments. It should turn participants toward the consciousness that arises from the praxis of their decisions and bring them to express it. It is to encourage people to question and discern in dialogue the likely consequences of their commitments and to give them a sense of empowerment in their own agency for orthopraxis in every arena of their lives.

To conclude this first piece of a five-part mosaic of the dimensions and dynamics of "being" to be engaged in a pedagogy for conation or wisdom in Christian faith, I reiterate that all the personal conati outlined in this schema overlap and function in concert with one another. Whether or not the reader agrees with my delineation of our personal conati, my more general point (which I hope elicits agreement) is that a pedagogy for conation is to engage, not necessarily on all occasions but certainly over time, every dynamic capacity of its participants. Nothing of our human condition should be excluded or neglected in a conative pedagogy. In sum, engaging people's whole way of "being" as agent-subjects in the world, turning them toward and bringing them to express the consciousness that arises from their activities, and forming them to exercise their corporeal, mental, and spiritual capacities according to their proper life-giving intent is all integral to the content, method, and environment—to the curriculum—of a pedagogy for conation.

Our personal conati, however, bring us into a two-way relationship with a public sociocultural world of meaning and value that is already established in its ideologies and structures. Our own "life world" (Husserl) always exists in dialectic with a systemic reality that shapes our identity and agency and to which our life contributes; we are agent-subjects in "place" and "time." Section 2 elaborates on how education for conation calls for a pedagogy that promotes a dialectical engagement by participants with the whole "place" in which their "being" is realized.

2. Engaging the "Place" in Which People's "Being" Is Realized

By "place" here I mean the social and cultural world in which people realize their "being" and continue to "become" in interaction with it. The social sciences indicate that who we are, what we do, and who we become is greatly shaped by *where* and among *whom* we have been socialized. As Huebner writes, "We are our relationships."[21] A pedagogy for conation must bring participants to critically and creatively attend to their sociocultural situation, both to draw life from it and to become agent-subjects-in-relationship who contribute to it as a "place" that is humanizing for all. To allow people to "forget" the contextuality of their "being" helps ensure they are determined by their "place" in history. The "socialization theorists"[22] of religious education have convinced us of the formative influence of the social/ecclesial environment on people's faith identity and have helped the church to attend deliberately to its communal life as a primary source of Christian nurture. My point here, however, is that the whole "place" of participants is to be critically engaged in the dynamics of a conative pedagogy; to appreciate this, it will help to have a working understanding of the process of socialization (or as anthropologists prefer, enculturation).

A. The Facticity of Culture and Society

Our "place," or what sociologists usually mean by "reality," is socially constructed in that it results from the expressive (culture) and relational (social) activities of people over time. Further, culture and society have a "givenness" of their own with powerful forms of self-maintenance and legitimation. *Culture* (from the Latin *cultura*, "cultivated"), in its most general sense, refers to everything that human beings create (as distinct from what is produced by nature) in order to express themselves and to make the world a more habitable and hospitable "place." In the social sciences, culture refers to all the symbols through which a particular people create and express a common form of life together with shared patterns of meaning, attitudes, and values. Clifford Geertz gives an oft-cited definition of culture as "an historically transmitted pattern of meanings embodied in symbols, a system of inherited conceptions expressed in symbolic forms by means of which [people] communicate, perpetuate and develop their knowledge about and attitudes toward life."[23]

Society (from the Latin *socius,* "companion") refers to the more institutional structures we create to mediate human relationality; it includes all the public agencies—political, economic, religious, educational, legal, military, and so on—that arrange our common life together. Society is the more systemically structured aspects of culture, although a particular society can have a variety of cultures within it. As distinct from a natural or organic group,[24] a society usually has some explicit or implicit rationale, is bonded together by an agreed-upon social contract, and has some degree of voluntary and enduring cooperation for the well-being of its members. Culture and society are so intermingled in the existential life of people that I usually refer to them together as our "sociocultural context," or use their synonym—"place." Note too that the church is like a sociocultural context; it has institutional structures and symbols of shared meaning, attitudes, and values, even as it is historically located within and influenced by particular sociocultural sites. The church is an agency of socialization and a recipient of it from its historical context in the world.

Our sociocultural world is created by the human urge to externalize ourselves and enter into relationship and common life with others, yet our social structures and cultural patterns take on a "facticity" of their own. As Durkheim explained, they exist *sui generis,*[25] that is, in their own right. We cannot wish away the structures and symbols of our sociocultural situation and expect them to disappear. In fact, even minor changes can come slowly. Our "place" has such facticity for a number of reasons. First, it erects elaborate systems of restraint that serve to keep members within its boundaries and systems of constraint to promote what is perceived as the common good. Max Weber analyzed how restraint and oversight for the common good are exercised by "authority" of some kind that, if necessary, has the power to exercise "legitimate violence" to protect its interests when threatened from either within or without.[26] Beyond authority, as sources of social maintenance, Berger lists economic pressure and the less formal "mechanisms of persuasion, ridicule, gossip and opprobrium."[27]

No social reality, however, can survive for long on submission to authority or by the force of social pressure. A society's expectations and regulations need to appear reasonable to members and warranted by their common good. Every sociocultural entity needs "systems of legitimation" and "plausibility structures" that make present arrangements seem both legitimate and reasonable;[28] these, in turn, reflect some generally accepted "ideology" of the group. The word *ideology* can be used with both negative and positive connotations (e.g., Marx and Mannheim respectively). Here it means a comprehensive worldview that enables people to make sense out of things as they are and thus makes their sociocultural environment seem legitimate and plausible.[29] Often a people's social ideology itself has a transcendent form of legitimation—a "sacred canopy."[30] Its symbols preside over the whole "place" and bless its "facticity" with an aura of ultimate justification. (This is not to say that religion is no more than an ultimate justification of social maintenance; clearly it can and must often be a source of social subversion and reform.)[31] We now turn to how this "social construction of reality" socializes its members and the import for a conative pedagogy.

B. The Agent-Subject/"Place" Dialectic

"Place" Shapes "Being"/Knowing. The sciences of sociology, psychology, and anthropology agree that our self-identity is shaped, in large part, by the sociocultural context in which we are first raised (primary socialization) and later live our lives (secondary socialization).[32] Each social science has its own language and concepts for explaining the process of socialization,[33] but none doubt that our "being" who and how we are emerges through interaction with our sociocultural environment. John Westerhoff offers a comprehensive description of socialization as: "the lifelong formal and informal ways one generation seeks to sustain and transmit its understanding and way of life; seeks to induct its young into and reinforce for its adults a particular set of values and responsible adult roles; and seeks to help persons develop self-identity through participation in the life of a people with their more or less distinctive ways of thinking, feeling, and acting."[34] This means that we are never mere observers in our "place"; rather, we take on as our own its patterns of meaning and role models, its attitudes and values as constitutive of our identity, and this interiorization disposes us to be agents of social maintenance.

It would be wrong and misleading to portray the formative influences of people's sociocultural situation as simply limiting and determining their identity. On the contrary, our "place" is always our first source of life and well-"being." We could not even survive and certainly not live humanly without the nurture of our sociocultural environment. From our very birth, we depend on others, on their love and care, and on social structures and cultural patterns for "being" and "becoming" human. Likewise, for Christian identity and agency we need the initiating and nurturing context of a Christian faith community. Such community, of course, is always intermingled with our secular "place," even as human and faith identity/agency are always intertwined.

The symbiosis between "being" and "knowing" makes the influence of one's "place" on "conation" readily evident. In chapter 2 I credited Marx with the basic insight of "the sociology of knowledge." Max

Scheler (1874–1928) first pushed beyond Marx's claim about economic structures and argued that the whole social construction of reality shapes human knowledge, that all consciousness reflects its location in time and place.[35] There is disagreement among sociologists about how determining the context is for human knowing,[36] but many would agree with Sheila Greene Davaney's summary statement: "Human beings and our knowledge are irrevocably historical and hence conditioned by time and place."[37]

"Place" conditions one's "being" and "knowing," therefore a pedagogy for conation in Christian faith must bring participants to attend to and engage their whole sociocultural context, secular and ecclesial. However, the power of socialization raises the question of how "place" should be engaged pedagogically and with what intent.

A Dialectical Relationship? The power of socialization poses a profound question for our very "being" as agent-subjects. Can we become our own autonomous person, or are we never more than the product of our socialization? Are we determined by our context, or is there a dialectical relationship between people and their "place"? This question, in turn, goes to the very heart of all education and raises the question of its *raison d'être*. Educationally, the question is, What is the relationship between socialization and education—should education promote a dialectic between people and their "place," or should it simply be an intentional agency of socialization?

Clearly, responses to these questions depend a good deal on one's understanding of a "dialectical" relationship. My understanding of "dialectical" is in the Hegelian tradition but I use it (unlike Hegel) of our own "being-in-relationship" and, avoiding Marx's exaggeration of Hegel's position, do not see its "second moment" as inevitably negation.[38] There are three aspects to a dialectical moment: one of affirming, giving assent, or accepting; an aspect of questioning and *possibly* of refusing or negating; and a "moving beyond" that subsumes the first two moments in a new realization of "being." (As becomes more evident below, similarity in the dynamics of dialectic and dialogue makes them "next of kin"—an old insight, see notes 38 and 58—and close allies in a conative pedagogy.) To inquire, then, if there is a dialectical relationship between people and their sociocultural context is to ask, Are we the creatures of our sociocultural world, determined and shaped by its formative forces (i.e., no dialectic) or do we come into historical agency for our own "being" by accepting some of our contexts' influence, refusing or adapting some, and forging a synthesis that reflects new life for ourselves as agent-subjects and for our sociocultural situation?

From the briefest "remembrance of being" we know that there is a dialectical relationship of some extent between people and their "place." We recognize that we have grown and changed in ways other than as prompted by our environment. We have not turned out exactly as our primary socialization recommended; we are quite different from siblings or others who were formed by the same primary context as ourselves. Growing to adulthood we have at times refused the influences of our "place" and transcended it to become agents and decision makers with a measure of personal independence and initiative toward our sociocultural situation. We are naive to underrate and ungrateful to disparage its formative influence on us, yet we recognize a dialectical relationship between ourselves and our "place." In fact, social scientists no longer dispute that there is a dialectical relationship of some kind between people and their social world; what they disagree on is the extent and quality of the dialectic.[39]

Echoing the weight of contemporary social science literature on this issue, my own position is that the dialectic that takes place inevitably between "objectively assigned reality" and our "subjectively appropriated identity" in the process of socialization is quite minimal. Though socialization nurtures our identity, both human and faith, its inner dynamic is maintenance of people in expected "roles" and of the social reality in its "status quo." For identity *and* agency in Christian faith, socialization alone is insufficient, in and of itself, to promote ongoing conversion in people's faith journey, the renewal of the faith community itself, and the ministry of the church to be a sacrament of social transformation. As the church educates, so the church needs to be educated. The very dynamic of its pedagogy should be likely to encourage a dialectical relationship between people and their "place," both secular and ecclesial. Only thus is it likely to contribute to both nurture and ongoing conversion of people in Christian faith conation.

My conviction that religious education can and must be a dialectical activity comes first from my own praxis over the years; I have experienced what is also the overwhelming conclusion of developmental researchers (Kohlberg, Gilligan, Fowler, et al.) that the typical socialization by church and society forms the great majority of people in a conventional level of faith and moral development (i.e., they accept what is recommended by their social context). This is empirical "evidence" that socialization is not likely for most people to foster a personally owned and intrinsic faith. My theoretical clarity, however, has been informed by the "critical social theorists"[40] and especially by the work of Jurgen Habermas. Building on earlier critiques by Horkheimer and others, Habermas identifies the "suspension of reflection" and "deadening of consciousness" caused by technical rationality and challenges its controlling influence on people's identity and agency. He argues that we can intentionally promote reflection that is personally and socially "self-reflective" in a community of authentic discourse and thus heighten the dialectic with our social context. What follows is the gist of his relevant thought.

In a schema that he takes to be self-evident, Habermas classifies people's engagement with their social reality as taking place in three modes of interaction—our work upon the world, our communication through symbols with one another, and our participation in social structures—labor, language, and politics. Each mode of engagement is, in fact, a "way of knowing" reality (echoes, surely, of Aristotle). However, each mode has its own "knowledge constitutive interest,"[41] in other words, a particular concern and perspective that undergirds it and shapes the kind of consciousness that emerges from its mode of engagement.[42]

Habermas says that our *work* upon the world has the instrumental interest of "technical control."[43] When we engage in producing something our only interest is to empirically analyze reality to know how to control it for production. This does not promote a dialectic between ourselves and our social reality; it brings us to technical know-how but not to critical consciousness. Our *communication* with others has a "practical interest"[44] of maintaining and promoting understanding within our traditions and communities of discourse. It enables people to interpret their world as it appears to be according to shared "preunderstandings." However, this practical interest makes such hermeneutics unlikely to encourage people in a dialectical relationship with their sociocultural world.[45] The third mode of social engagement, however—participation in "politics"—can be undergirded by an "emancipatory interest" that reflects the human quest for freedom.[46] When an "emancipatory interest" is at the forefront of our social praxis it can promote a dialectic between people and their "place." This interest, however, requires a *critical reflection* upon ourselves as historical agents and on all our social praxis. For Habermas, critical reflection means to uncover the personal and social geneses of one's "being" in the world, to unmask the interests, assumptions, and ideologies of one's own praxis and of one's sociocultural context.[47] Reflection that does so is capable of releasing repressed dialogue and of unmasking ideologies that legitimate forms of domination and repression, and it encourages us in historical/political action to recreate our lives and sociocultural world in emancipatory ways[48].

Whether one agrees with Habermas's schema and *his* depiction of the "ways of knowing" (see note 45), he at least helps to highlight that people's everyday work and relationships are not likely to promote an emancipatory dialectic with their sociocultural situation. We are most interested in "getting by" and "getting along" rather than in changing ourselves and the world. Such a dialectic, however, can be and needs to be intentionally promoted. The dynamic of it enables people to critically reflect with emancipatory interest on their own historical praxis and on the praxis of their sociocultural context. This is a key insight for religious educators, and is foundational to the shared praxis approach (chapters 4–10) to conation in Christian faith.

The dynamics of Christian religious education should encourage participants to critically reflect on the context in which they exercise their conative activities. Critical reflection on present social reality is necessary for a dialectic of sufficient quality to promote the ongoing conversion of participants, the reformation of the church, and the transformation of society.[49] Without it, the domination and destruction of which all sociocultural situations, secular and ecclesial, are capable remain unchallenged, and Christian religious education, reduced to acting merely as an agency of socialization, fails to honor its ultimate purpose of God's reign. What is this critical reflection? I give a philosophical description below; in chapter 7 I describe how to effect it in teaching/learning events.

C. Critical Reflection on the "Place" of Human "Being"

Our personal conatus for reflection engages activities of reason, memory, and imagination. However, human "being" is always socially located and mediated. For conation, then, we must bring reason, memory, and imagination to self-consciously attend to our "place" and to critically reflect on how it shapes and is to be reshaped by our "being". A pedagogy for conation enables participants to bring to consciousness and name their own conative activities qua subjects, and it must also structure its teaching/learning dynamic to enable people to remember, reason about, and imagine regarding what is "going on" in their "place," the influence it has on their own "being," and the agency they are to exercise toward it. Reflection that is socially critical requires religious educators to prompt participants to do *analytical and social remembering, critical and social reasoning, creative and social imagining* regarding their own conative activities and on the "public life" of their sociocultural situation, that is, to reflect on what they are doing in their own "life world" and on what is "going on" around them, to them, and to others in their public "place."[50] (In chapter 7 I describe socially critical reflection as participants reflecting *on the context of their praxis* and *on the praxis of their context.*)

Analytical and Social Remembering. As noted earlier, we often use our personal memory for simple recall, but its fullest expression brings to life again, with renewed appreciation, the personal wisdom of our past. With analytical and social remembering, however, we move beyond the subjective function of recalling or reappropriating past wisdom to do social historical analysis of our own activities and of the "public life" of our "place." We remember the psychological conditions and the social influences that are at the genesis of our actions *and* the historical conditions that have shaped the public life of society. Analytical and social remembering, then, has two overlapping intents: to uncover (a) the historical influences that shape what we do and (b) the social/historical genesis of what society does.

A. Social remembering that attends to the historical conditions that influence our own conative activities is a "re-membering" in the sense of recognizing how our various "memberships" have influenced us and what we do as historical agents in the world. Social remembering enables us to see our identity and actions in their historical context, to notice for ourselves the influence on who we are, what we do, and what we "see" of where we have been and who we have been "with."

B. Likewise, analytical and social memory enables people to uncover the communal narrative that is sedimented in their sociocultural reality, secular and ecclesial. It can dis-cover the political interests and social ideologies that historically have shaped the "public life" of our "place." More positively, social remembering also searches for the often forgotten but life-giving memories from a people's tradition that can dispose them to refashion present social structures and cultural patterns. In fact, our "interest" in critical social remembering is always emancipatory—to reclaim what is life-giving in our memories and in the traditions of our people, to question rather than fatalistically accepting old bondages, to not simply repeat the past but to build upon the truth of one's own and society's "story," to faithfully go beyond past influences in ways that are emancipatory for oneself and society as well.[51]

Critical and Social Reasoning. When our personal conatus for reasoning as agent-subjects becomes critical and social, it takes on a more explicitly contextual function. By critical social reasoning we reflect on the social situation of our activities and on the social "reasons" or causes of society's "public life." The personal function of critical reasoning is to reflect on the influences of our present "place" on all our conative activities, including our mental ones. Likewise, socially we can question and interpret the structures and patterns, interests and ideologies that cause the "public life" of our social cultural context to be as it is. Such critical reasoning that asks "why" with a social consciousness of our own actions and of society's life can bring us to recognize and transcend our socially mediated biases and the biases of society that shape our lives in the world. An emancipatory interest undergirds critical social reasoning; by it we intend our lives to be more than the product of our social context, and likewise we intend to question and move our sociocultural world beyond its present limits.

Creative and Social Imagining. Our personal conatus for imagination becomes socially focused when we engage it to see the social consequences and responsibilities of our own activity, to see the consequences of society's "public life" and what society can and should do to help make and keep life human for all. Creative social imagination takes present "reality" with radical seriousness and yet refuses to settle for it, for either oneself or one's social group. By it we refuse to allow the self to be centered in the self, or society to be "held bound" in its dominant interests and ideologies. By creative and social imagining we move to interdependence as selves and as societies with a sense of responsibility to "the other" whose life is impinged on by our own social praxis and by the praxis of society.[52] It prompts us to act together for the life of the world and gives hope that our solidarity can be humanizing for all. As such, creative social imagining has an emancipatory interest.

To summarize, a pedagogy for conation in Christian faith brings participants to the constantly overlapping and interrelated activities of analytical and social remembering, critical and social reasoning, creative and social imagining about their own conative activities and the "public life" of their society. This critical reflection promotes a dialectical relationship between people and their "place." As such, it is likely to promote the "learning outcome" of conation in Christian faith and is appropriate to the ultimate purpose of God's reign in the world. In chapter 7 I describe the pedagogical activities educators employ in teaching/learning events to engage both the personal and social emphases of critical reflection. Here it is enough to note that educators have a facilitating role of bringing participants to critical reflection and enabling them to do it intentionally and self-consciously.[53] The more immediate question for here is, if critical reflection is constitutive of a conative curriculum, what kind of discourse and community does this suggest for an event of pedagogy?

D. The "Language World" of a Conative Pedagogy

Language expresses our "being" and shapes it as well. One explanation of its ontological power is that its shared meanings, values, attitudes, and expected roles of a "place" are mediated symbolically to participants, and language is our first and primary symbol system. As we appropriate and use the language of our context, we interiorize as our own the world of meaning and values carried in its language. Both the life-giving resources and the pathologies of our sociocultural situation are mediated to us primarily through language. In Heidegger's oft-quoted summary statement of its ontological power: "Language is the house of Being";[54] we realize our own "being" as we "dwell" in language.

Its ontological power and their ontological task highlight the care that religious educators must take for the "language-world" they facilitate in teaching/learning events. The language we model and encourage has great significance for how our pedagogy engages and forms people's "being," for whether it is simply an intentional instance of socialization or an occasion of critical and dialectical education as well. Our purposes as Christian religious educators and our intended learning outcome can be defeated or promoted by the language we use for ourselves and God, for life and creation. This theme echoes throughout this book, but here I propose a general principle: *The language world created by Christian religious education should reflect and propose to people a deep conviction of the profound dignity and worth of all people, a mode of relating that is based on the justice of "right relationship," mutuality, and partnership, a worldview that is humanizing for all and care-full of creation.* Conversely, language that disvalues or degrades people, that is chauvinist, oppressive, or exclusive on any basis, that is mechanistic, controlling, or destructive should be absent from the language patterns of religious educators.[55]

Within a teaching/learning event, we can distinguish between the "content" of its language and the "dynamic of *discourse*" that it creates.[56] Regarding content, in light of the guideline above, a conative pedagogy is intentional about using and encouraging language that is likely to engage and form participants' "being" in dignity, right relationship, and responsibility. And the "dynamic of discourse" we sponsor in a conative pedagogy should be one of dialogue among all participants.[57] Dialogue is required for people to bring their consciousness of their conative activities to expression; they must have opportunity to speak their own word and to hear the word of one another. Likewise critical reflection on their lives and "place" requires dialogue among all participants. Without an environment of dialogue, mutual exchange, and communal testing in a teaching/learning event, critical reflection can deteriorate into personal arbitrariness and/or total relativism.[58] Christian religious educators must be convinced about the kind of discourse needed and be committed to intentionally promoting it. To clarify the kind of dialogue and conversation[59] most likely to educate for conation in Christian faith I find the work of Buber and Habermas most helpful.

Buber's understanding of relationship and dialogue was shaped by his Hasidic tradition and by his existentialist philosophy.[60] Both brought him to recognize and criticize two prevalent errors of our age—individualism and collectivism; the former honors only a part of us and the latter treats us only as a part.[61] Over against these errors Buber posed "community" as *the* alternative. He characterized community as "the being . . . with one another of a multitude of persons" in which one "experiences a dynamic force . . . a flowing from I to Thou." He noted that community requires a "vital dialogic, demanding the staking of the self."[62]

To have community and dialogue, people must choose a personal rather than a functional mode of relating, an I/Thou rather than an I/It way of "being" together. The latter may be appropriate at times in our day-to-day relating to things,[63] but if we relate to others only as "It," we diminish our own humanity. I/Thou relationships are essential to realizing our ontic vocation as human beings.[64] Buber poses five characteristics of an I/Thou relationship of community and dialogue: it (1) engages the whole of one's "being" and of the other's "being"; (2) requires that one be truly present to the other; (3) is marked by genuine openness; (4) is characterized by agapaic love; and (5) has a profound sense of responsibility for and loyalty to the other.[65] Such too is the desired dialogue of pedagogy for conation in Christian faith.

When Buber's characteristics of true community and conversation are fulfilled, I believe participants experience what Habermas calls a situation of "communicative competence . . . the mastery of an ideal speech situation."[66] Habermas's work brings further clarity to the dialogical "place" that is the ideal and goal of a conative pedagogy.[67] He claims that for critical reflection on social reality to be emancipatory and to promote the dialectic between the "life world" of the self and the "systemic world" of our sociocultural context, we do best in a situation of "communicative competence."[68] Habermas describes this "communicative action" as a situation of nondistorted reciprocal communication that is oriented to mutual understanding according to commonly held validity claims.[69] Contrary to interests of personal "success" or "strategic advantage," "communicative action" takes place in a situation of mutuality between participants; it happens when the "symbolic interaction" of language is free of domination or manipulation and there is no compulsion to agreement other than the persuasiveness and validity claims of a particular position.[70] In less technical language, it is an honest and fair conversation among partners in quest of the truth.

What Habermas means by "communicative competence," I call "authentic dialogue."[71] He readily admits that "a speech situation determined by pure intersubjectivity is an idealization" and indeed a "utopian ideal."[72] Yet this ideal is presupposed in every act of communication that purports to be an authentic act of discourse. Although Habermas overclaims for both the feasibility and transforming power of such conversation,[73] we can strive to create the ideal in a wisdom pedagogy.[74] The more we approximate it, the more our pedagogy will encourage a dialectic between participants and their "place," and thus conation in Christian faith. We also need true dialogue for the third activity of a conative pedagogy—honoring the "whole time" of participants; to this we now turn.

3. Engaging People's "Being-in-Time" and the Tradition of the Christian Community over Time

A. The "Time" of Our Lives

Kant distinguished space and time as the intuitive forms we have for perceiving and organizing experience of the world; he portrayed them as the most basic categories of thought. His distinction suggests our attention to both "place" and "time" in this chapter. We are not interested in them, however, as transcendental categories of thought that are unaffected by our "situation-in-life" but as aspects of historical existence in the world that shape our very "being." As I used "place" above for our sociocultural context, here "time" refers to the whole history in which we live, both our own and the history of our people— the "time of our lives."

It is difficult to distinguish "place" from "time" in our consciousness. Existentially, we experience spatiality and temporality together, and each one impinges on what we perceive of the other. Inevitably, then, we have already attended to temporality in our previous reflections on the activities of agent-subjects qua subjects and on the social "place" of our "being." Self-identity is one's sense of continuity over time, and our corporeal, mental, and volitional activities, each in their own way and together, attend to the past, present, and future of our "being." Likewise, because our "place" is always realized in "time," critical social reflection entails remembering (past) and imagining (future) as well as reasoning about its present. Nevertheless, we must attend to and engage the temporality of existence in its own right precisely because it is a dimension of our "being" and thus is constitutive of a pedagogy for conation.

To honor our temporality, conative pedagogy brings participants first to share their own stories and visions, that is, what they perceive is behind, around, and in front of their lives in time and place. When people bring their own historical activities to expression, critically reflect on them and on the reality of their sociocultural situation, they are, in fact, sharing their own "stories" as "beings in time" and their perceived and/or preferred consequences of present praxis, that is, their own "visions." Pedagogy that honors and engages people's sense of their "time" helps them to appreciate themselves as agent-subjects in history, to recognize and share the resources and wisdom they have from "the time of their lives." It encourages people to think historically and thus responsibly about themselves and their lives in the world. Further, it lends to the pedagogical dynamic a narrative and practical language pattern of discourse. This praxislike pattern is most appropriate to a conative pedagogy precisely because human "being" has a profoundly narrative structure. As Gerkin notes, "praxis . . . always involves an essentially narrative structure," and it is "by means of stories of the self and of the world around us [that] we hold together events, persons, and experiences that would otherwise be fragmented. To be a person is therefore to live in a story."[75] Here, I make explicit that all our stories give rise to visions; and to honor people's "time," a curriculum must enable them to perceive, express, and critique the visions in their stories as well.

A pedagogy for wisdom in Christian faith must also give access to and promote appropriation by participants of Christian Story and Vision.[76] By this I mean the whole ongoing faith narrative and practical wisdom of the Christian people over time. People can come to their own identity and agency in faith through dialogue and dialectical hermeneutics between their stories/visions and the Christian community's Story/Vision.[77] The stories and visions of participants from their own time and the Story/Vision of a faith community over time are constitutive of a conative curriculum in Christian faith.

When I offer the theological rationale for the movements of shared praxis, I present the reasons why Christian religious educators must attend to and engage the stories and visions of participants and make accessible the Story/Vision of the community of faith, as the theology of revelation undergirding the approach. Here, however, as I delineate the dimensions and dynamics of an epistemic ontology, my argument for engaging people's "whole time" in a conative pedagogy is more philosophical; in fact, it reflects my understanding of time.

B. Of Time and Temporality

The understanding of time that undergirds a conative pedagogy is suggested to me by Augustine and Heidegger. Augustine, in *The Confessions*, wrote, "What, then, is time? If no one asks me, I know; if I want to explain it to someone who does ask me, I do not know."[78] Traditionally, Western philosophy has favored Aristotle's explanation of time as a measure of motion along an imaginary line of history.[79] This "linear" perspective thinks of past, present, and future as three distinct and separate "times." The past is past; the present is all that is present; and the future is not yet. But Augustine challenged this linear understanding and argued that if pushed to its logical conclusion, the "present" ceases to exist, in that time present becomes time past as soon as it comes into existence. Any given point on the line of time can be subdivided so minutely into past and future that the present disappears into "nontime" between them. But this robs us of "our time" and makes us think of time as something objectified outside us that flows past us and in which we are not engaged.[80]

Over against Aristotle's linear notion, Augustine proposed a holistic understanding in which all time—past, present, and future—has its existence in "time present." He wrote, "If future and past times exist . . . they are there neither as future nor as past, but as present. For if they are in that place as future things, they are not yet there, and if they are in that place as past things, they are no longer there. Therefore, wherever they are, and in whatever they are, they do not exist except as present things."[81] Augustine explained that if we use the traditional terms of past, present, and future, we must intend them to mean the "present of things past, the present of things present, and the present of things future."[82] In contemporary language, for Augustine, people experience time as their own "being-in-time," and the consequences of our past and the possibilities of our future exist in our "present time."

Augustine's holistic and existentialist understanding of time did not prevail in the West. Aquinas favored Aristotle's more linear and objectified understanding[83] and so, it seems, did most Western philosophers.[84] Eventually Heidegger revived a more holistic and subjective understanding of time that echoes the sentiments of Augustine and is more appropriate, with some revision, to a conative curriculum.

Heidegger explicitly located time in the existential human being—in Dasein. Time *is* for us, because we are. As we *are* in time, so time *is* in us, not as an object outside of us but as the very ground and unity of our "being."[85] To experience our unity as "beings in time," however, we cannot think of time as a trichotomized thing outside us. We need instead a holistic and subjective sense of time and of the temporality of existence.

Heidegger says that we existentially experience time as what is to come, the present, and what has been. But these experiences are descriptions of our own ontological being—they are how we exist. We are "beings in time" who constantly lean into the future from the past in our present. In other words, we are not observers of a cycle of past, present, and future—an assembly line of "nows" that come to us out of the future only to be lost immediately into the past. Instead, we *are* within time, we "have time" rather than being "had by time," and the time that we have is most truly who we are. The past, present, and future exist for us, in us—in our own temporality. Remembrance of my/our own "being" may help to clarify Heidegger's notion of human temporality.

My past as a person and indeed the past of my people is not "past and gone" at all. It is with me now, shaping what I think and what I write on this page. Without this past I would not have words or grammatical rules, concepts or images with which to construct these sentences. Likewise you the reader can comprehend what I am writing only because of the past you have had; it is operative in your present act of reading with recognition, comprehension, judgment, and decision. In other words, our past is very much present to us in this encounter. Likewise, our future is always suspended in and shaped by whatever present time we have now. As you read, the future influences how you interpret, decide, and so on in the present moment, and this present encounter may make some difference to what you do in the future. In other words, the future is not simply "not yet"—it is already taking form in and giving form to our present time, which also holds the consequences of our past.

For our "being," time is its existential unity. To engage people's "being" pedagogically requires that we engage their "whole time." This is their "time present" that holds the consequences of their past and the possibilities of their future. Honoring the "whole time" of participants in a teaching/learning event enables them to attend to their "present time," to their past and to the past of their people that influences the present, to their own future and to the future of their people that is being shaped in their present.[86] Diverging from Heidegger's notion of it, I add four other points about time that are relevant to a conative curriculum.

First, our human experience of temporality is of "time together," in that we live our time authentically in right relationship and community with others. Our very temporality calls us into "being with," in the sense of being *present* to others. A Christian perspective highlights that we are to live the time of our lives in community, in solidarity with and care for others. Second, we are capable of shaping our "times" together, of giving our history new directions. Alone we can be overwhelmed by our "thrownness" and become merely creatures determined by "the crowd" (*das Man*). But with others, we can be agent-subjects who "make history"; we can give time a direction it would not have without our intervening agency. Our temporality, then, gives us a sense of historical responsibility, of "duty" for our time.

Third, attending to our "time" lends a sense of reverence as well as duty, and so is a source of "being religious." I draw this point from Whitehead, who stated it well, and in the context of education. "The present contains all that there is. It is holy ground; for it is the past, and it is the future." Education must attend to "present time," and as such, it is religious; in fact, "the essence of education is that it be religious." Whitehead explained: "A religious education is an education which inculcates duty and reverence. Duty arises from our potential control over the course of events. Where attainable knowledge could have changed the issue, ignorance has the guilt of vice. And the foundation of reverence is this perception, that the present holds within itself the complete sum of existence, backwards and forwards, that whole amplitude of time, which is eternity."[87] Pedagogically, when we truly honor people's present time, it turns us toward eternity.

My fourth point is to emphasize, from the perspective of Christian faith, that in our "time" together we find cause to hope, even as we recognize our own temporality. Heidegger contended that to live authentically "in time" we must face the facticity of death. True indeed! But in Christian faith, temporality and death are not faced "like those who have no hope" (1 Thess. 4:13) or who have hope only in their own rugged resourcefulness. Rather, we cherish the eternal value of the time of our lives when we live it in right relationship and can have confidence in One whose living and dying has conquered death to live now in hope for eternal time.

C. Curriculum as Concern for Human Temporality[88]

Whether one assumes a linear and trichotomized understanding of time or an existential and holistic one has significant implications for how one educates; this is reflected most particularly in curriculum decision making. I illustrate this claim by reviewing briefly the traditional points of emphasis that have been operative in the "curriculum field."[89] There are various schemas for delineating the "curriculum ideologies" of education,[90] but here it is helpful to note three traditional emphases in curriculum construction: (1) the *disciplines of learning*, (2) the present *experiences and interests of learners*, and (3) what is needed for the *well-being of society*.[91] The advocacy of the three corresponding schools of curriculum theory is that curriculum should be constructed primarily— few would say exclusively—(1) from the disciplines and traditions of learning in which students are instructed; (2) from the learners' present experiences in community, encouraging them to discover knowledge according to their own activities, interests, needs, and aptitudes; (3) from material that prepares learners to function effectively in society and/or, as Schiro highlights, to reconstruct society according to "some conception of the nature of the good society" (see note 90).

All three curriculum emphases—on disciplines, learners, and society—are undoubtedly valid, but neglect of or undue emphasis on

any one of them, so often the case in both general and religious curricula, reflects a trichotomized understanding of people's own "time"
and of the time of the educating community. The disciplines of learning school reflects the perennial responsibility of all education to hand
on the wisdom and learning that has emerged from the praxis of people before the present generation; without "traditioning" the wholeness
of people's time is not honored. Yet undue emphasis on it leads to
relying only on what Dewey called "the funded capital of civilization"[92]
and to teaching it in a didactic and "from past to present" manner. This
excludes the stories and visions of participants as a source of wisdom
and may not attend sufficiently to people's need to function effectively
in society or to their responsibility to engage in its reconstruction.

An exclusive emphasis on the present experiences and interests of
participants as the source of curriculum tends to forget the wisdom of
the ages before us and fails to encourage responsibility for the future.
This emphasis does not give people reliable resources with which to
interpret present experience, and without such "memories" and "images," they have less sense of responsibility for their common future
and for renewal of the community.

An exclusive emphasis on educating people to (a) function effectively within and maintain society or (b) help reconstruct it, places undue emphasis on the future. A. The "social efficiency" model (see note
90) tends to neglect the subversive memories from the tradition that
help to restructure society and can overlook the need for a dialectic
between society and its individual members, between the faith community and its sociocultural context. B. To unduly emphasize "social reconstruction" can neglect attention to "the wisdom of the ages," forget
learners' own appropriate needs and interests, and distract them from
living and celebrating their "present time." In sum, if we opt for any
one emphasis exclusively or unduly we choose, in terms of "time," for
either the past, or the present, or the future and neglect the "whole
time" of participants—personal and communal.

A conative curriculum must reflect a holistic understanding of time.
It should honor and be responsible to the past and future of the community in its present, the past and future of participants in their present. Further, it should enable them to appropriate both "times" to each
other as their "whole time," from which they have life-giving resources
and to which they have significant responsibilities. In more educational
terms, Christian religious educators must engage and make accessible in
teaching/learning events (1) the whole Story of the faith community, (2)
the stories and visions of participants, (3) the whole Vision of the faith
community.

1. The Whole Story. By "Story" here I mean the faith tradition
handed on to Christians and the contemporary understanding, celebrating, and living of it in their faith community. I use Story as a metaphor for the whole faith life and practical wisdom of the Christian
community that is congealed in its Scriptures, symbols, myths, rituals,

liturgies, creeds, dogmas, doctrines, theologies, practices, spiritualities, expected life-styles, values, art, artifacts, structures, and so on. It is a comprehensive metaphor for all that realizes or reflects the faith of Christian people over time and in our time. Theologically the Christian Story is the distillation and symbolic mediation of God's self-disclosure to this people and their ancestors in faith over time, and how they have attempted to understand it and respond. Sociologically, as with any people, their Story gives Christians their particular identity in faith, binds them together as a community, enables them to make meaning out of chaos, and invites commitment to an ultimate center of value.

In chapter 8, I review hermeneutical principles to guide the educator in choosing how and what to make accessible out of Christian Story. For now, I refer to the "whole" Story here to make the point that educators should plan the curriculum with a scope and sequence that consistently makes the Story accessible in all of its manifestations (i.e., not Scripture alone, or doctrines alone, or liturgy alone) and that allows it to speak for itself, "warts and all." The curriculum should also teach the Story's subversive memories, its often forgotten sources of new life that can turn present personal or social arrangements and perspectives upside-down. Likewise, rather than making it sound complete and perfect, and thus beyond questioning, the curriculum should be honest (as appropriate to age level, context, etc.) that even the church has used Christian Story to prevent "life to the full"—lest we repeat our sins. To reflect the faith of the Christian community over time, educators should tell the Story of the community's virtues *and* vices, its faithful living of its truth *and* its distortions of it, its saints *and* sinners, its heroes *and* scoundrels; they should make accessible their Story's consoling *and* confronting dimensions, its nurturing *and* subversive memories, its affirmations *and* its judgments of us, how it has been used to promote the quality of human life *and* how it has been abused to legitimate oppression and injustice.[93] Through the "whole story" of their community over time, Christians are more likely to live their faith with meaning and responsibility appropriate to the "present time."

2. *The "stories" and "visions" of participants.* Participant's stories express their own lives in history, their sense of identity and agency over time. Their stories draw together and express the consciousness of their conative activities regarding past and present, and what emerges from their critical remembering and reasoning about their activities in social "place" and "time." For participants educated or influenced by a Christian community, their own stories are already shaped by Story of the community; likewise, their interpretation of their own stories will reflect pre-understandings suggested by their community Story. And yet people's own stories reflect the wisdom of their historical lives; sharing them is constitutive of a conative curriculum.

The visions of participants arise from their imaginative reflection on their "being" in time and place and express their sense of responsibility and opportunity, their perceived and preferred consequences, the hopes and concerns that they recognize and imagine for their present and future lives in the world. People's sense of their own visions emerges especially from their conative activities of regenerating, imagining, and committing as agent-subjects and from creative and social imagining regarding what can be and should be done about their own and society's future. When people speak their vision about any aspect of their lives, they "know" what it means "for me and for all." A conative pedagogy places participants' visions in dialogue and dialectic with the Vision of the community, but they must express them first as constitutive of the curriculum.

3. *The Whole Vision.* Vision is a metaphor for the possibilities and responsibilities, the promises and demands, that are prompted by the Christian community's Story. Christian Story is never told as entertainment or out of nostalgia for the past. Educators make it accessible so that people may draw life from it—meaning and ethic for their present and future. The comprehensive Vision for Christian faith is the reign of God. This ultimate symbol represents a reality we are to begin to realize in the present, even as its completion comes to meet us and draws our present and future into it. For the present, Christian Vision gives hope and promise, but it also places demand and responsibility upon us to participate by God's grace and with urgency in the coming of God's reign of fullness of life for all and for creation. Christian Vision is the practical intent of its Story; this is how we are called to live now and into our future.[94] Educators must see to it that the Vision is proposed to people to educate for wisdom in Christian faith.

4. Engaging People's Dynamic Structure for Conation

A. *The Dynamic Structure of "Being"*

Thus far I have proposed that for religious education to reflect an "epistemic ontology" in the interest of conation, its pedagogy is to intentionally engage and encourage to expression the consciousness that arises from the historical activities of participants as agent-subjects; promote a dialectical engagement with their "whole place" through critical and dialogical reflection on their own "being" and on the "public life" of their society; enable them to share the stories and visions of their "time" and to encounter the Story/Vision of their faith community over time. At this point, the dynamics of a teaching/learning event for conation in Christian faith needs to subsume and move beyond these three genres of activities. It must enable participants to place the consciousness that emerges from "present praxis" in place and time (i.e., reflection on their own activities and the "public life" of their society) in dialogue and dialectic with Story/Vision of Christian community, in order to appropriate these "sources" of wisdom to each other and come to decision for lived Christian faith toward God's reign. As one imagines these activities unfolding existentially, they begin to reflect a cumulative dynamic within the pedagogy that lends impetus for participants to move to conation. In this section 4 I claim that people already have as existential to their "being" an inner structuring capacity that when honored and intentionally engaged provides a cumulative dynamic toward conation. First I delineate this inner dynamic structure and indicate how a pedagogy for conation is to engage it.

To focus the kind of cumulative dynamic I am describing it helps to hearken back to some points outlined in chapter 2 about the dynamics of cognition, that is, what we do when we are "knowing." In reviewing Aquinas, I noted his attempt to delineate the sequence of dynamic activities that people perform in coming to knowledge; we begin by attending to experience of reality, then move by reasoning to understanding, and thence to judging the true and the good. Kant went a step beyond Aquinas by explicitly claiming that we have such an a priori structuring capacity for knowledge and by attempting to delineate "the biology" of theoretical reasoning, that is, the dynamic capacities we have to appropriate data from experience, to "construct" knowledge and then science out of these data. Since Kant, philosophers, and then developmental psychologists (e.g., Piaget) have accepted and researched his claim that people have an inner dynamic structure of cognition, which prompts us to the appropriate activities for "knowing."

My proposal here, however, is that our conative process proceeds with a dynamic similar to *cognition,* albeit more holistic because conation engages the whole "being" of people—their corporeal, mental, and volitional aspects. Because of the "forgetfulness of being" that has marked the epistemological literature of the West, there has been no attempt to delineate the dynamic structure of conation. However, a schema very suggestive of our conative dynamic can be found in Bernard Lonergan's delineation of the dynamic structure of cognition. In fact, Lonergan insists that the activities of an existential subject in coming to cognition are similar for the dynamic structure of one's "moral being." I appropriate and adjust Lonergan's description of our "cognitive structure" from the perspective of what I proposed in sections 1–3, and with an eye to the holistic understanding of truth I propose in section 5 to follow.

B. Lonergan on the Cognitional Structure

Lonergan is convinced that people can discover within themselves, in the data of their own consciousness, "the dynamic structure of their cognitional and moral being."[95] People have "by the eros of the human spirit" an impetus to exercise this inner dynamic, which, in fact, reflects our capacity for self-transcendence.[96] By self-transcendence Lonergan means the ability to see beyond the immediate and the "given," to move beyond "taking a look" at sense data and settling for what "appears" to be, and reaching instead with intentional consciousness (i.e., doing it and reviewing how well we are doing it) from the sense realm into the realms of the intelligible, the true, the good, and ultimately the "holy."[97] In gist, we have the dynamic capacity and the impetus to intentionally appropriate "a world mediated by meaning"[98] and can consciously review ourselves performing this activity.

Lonergan claims this "eros of the human spirit" for "meaning" provides the ground and shapes the pattern of all authentic human cognition. Further, he detects in the operations of consciousness a pattern of dynamic activities that all people perform in the act of true cognition. He calls these universal activities "transcendentals"[99] because everyone who "knows" performs them in coming "to know"; everyone who asks, "What am I doing when I am knowing?"[100] detects these activities going on within. Lonergan writes, "In the procedures of the human mind we shall discern a transcendental method, that is a pattern of operations employed in every cognitional enterprise." These basic operations "have a prior existence and reality in the spontaneous, structured dynamism of human consciousness."[101]

What are these transcendentals of "knowing"? Lonergan writes, "Now in a sense everyone knows and observes transcendental method. Everyone does so precisely in the measure he [sic] is *attentive, intelligent, reasonable, responsible.*"[102] Their converse, "inattention, oversight, unreasonableness, and irresponsibility" lead to alienation from one's own self, and in the social realm to "cumulative decline."[103] I will outline how he understands these four activities, the transcendental notions and values for which they reach, the precepts they demand of "knowers," and the levels of consciousness to which they give rise for existential subjects.

The transcendental activities are four sequential operations that constitute our efforts at authentic cognition, namely: attending, understanding, judging, and deciding. Cognition begins by intentionally attending to the data of experience. From attending, one moves by intelligent inquiry to understanding, to making the data of experience intelligible. However, "experience and understanding taken together yield not knowledge but only thought."[104] To "know" we must push on to the third activity, "reason,"[105] by which we determine the conditions for something to be so and judge the truth or falsehood of what we understand. The existential subject does not, however, stop there; judgment leads us on to decide responsibly about what we perceive to be "truly good."[106]

Lonergan says each transcendental activity has its own "active potency,"[107] that is, something for which it aims. The "potencies" can be for either transcendental notions (ideas) or values,[108] and they are, sequentially, the "given" (i.e., the "world of immediate experience"[109]), the intelligible, the true, and the good. Correspondingly, we reach for these notions or values by following the four transcendental precepts, which are Be attentive, Be intelligent, Be reasonable, Be responsible.[110] These activities are imperative for authentic cognition or valuing; as we honor them we can move from attending to our experience of the "given" data, to understanding the intelligible, to judging the truth, and to responsible action for the good.[111]

Lonergan says that when intentionally followed, the four transcendental activities bring people to ever higher levels of consciousness, ever deeper as subjects into the world mediated by meaning. He lists the four corresponding levels of consciousness as the empirical, the intellectual, the rational, and the responsible. He writes,

> There is the *empirical* level on which we sense, perceive, imagine, feel, speak, move. There is an *intellectual* level on which we inquire, come to understand, express what we have understood, work out the presuppositions and implications of our expression. There is the *rational* level on which we reflect, marshal the evidence, pass judgment on the truth or falsity, certainty or probability of a statement. There is the *responsible* level on which we are concerned with ourselves, our own operations, our goals, and so deliberate about possible courses of action, evaluate them, decide, and carry out our decisions.[112]

Summary Diagram

Transcendental Activities	Transcendental Notions and Values	Transcendental Imperatives	Levels of Consciousness
Attending	The given	Be attentive	The empirical
Understanding	The intelligible	Be intelligent	The intellectual
Judging	The true	Be reasonable	The rational
Deciding	The good	Be responsible	The responsible

Lonergan claims further that for people to come to authenticity as subjects by this dynamic, it is not enough to perform its activities by an unreflective impetus; we must come to "self-appropriation" of our doing them, that is, recognize and review ourselves doing them. One is to perform intentionally the dynamic activities of cognition but also to be aware of oneself performing the activities of attending, understanding, judging, and deciding. By "introspection," or reflection on ourselves performing the four transcendentals, says Lonergan, we can "objectify" the contents of consciousness and become aware of ourselves intentionally performing the four activities.[113] Only by such consciousness of our own knowing processes and of ourselves as knowers can we be true subjects of our cognitive activity, he claims.[114] Therein lies the difference, at least for our interest here, between what Lonergan calls "undifferentiated" and "differentiated" consciousness.[115] The former is when a person is not intentional and self-conscious of being attentive, intelligent, reasonable, and responsible. Differentiated consciousness, by contrast, emerges when we "objectify" the contents of our cognitive activities and review how we are attentive, intelligent, reasonable, and responsible. In other words, differentiated consciousness—and

Lonergan would say authenticity as a self-transcending subject—comes from bringing the four transcendental activities to our performing each of the transcendentals themselves. For example, in the act of consciously attending, we are also to attend to, try to understand, judge, and decide about the quality of our attending, and so on.[116] In everyday terms, to be true selves and to truly "know," we must think, and must think about our thinking.

Lonergan refers to the dynamic structure of cognition as "a rock on which we can build."[117] If we perform its activities with intentional consciousness, it can bring us to authentic cognition, to differentiated consciousness, to self-transcendence, and ultimately, I believe Lonergan would say, to God. I disagree with Lonergan's apparent inattention to the influence of our "place" on the inner structuring transcendentals, and I see an unmitigated individualism in how he portrays one performing the transcendental activities with intentional consciousness.[118] I also resist his overconfidence in the power of "cognition" for social transformation (see note 114). Yet I agree with his claim that doing the transcendental activities with intentional consciousness helps to overcome what he also calls, citing Heidegger, "a forgetfulness of being."[119] Conversely, a "remembrance of being" in pedagogy calls for engaging participants in consciously, intentionally, and dialogically performing all four transcendental activities. The dynamic Lonergan outlines reflects a cumulative process that is pedagogically appropriate to promote conation in Christian faith *if:* people attend to their historical activities in the world through conversation with others; understanding emerges from an intentional dialectic with their sociocultural context through critical reflection on their "being" in place and time; the practical wisdom of one's own story/vision is shared and tested in a community of dialogue (see note 118); participants have access together to the practical understanding and wisdom of Christian Story/Vision; they are brought to judgment as dialectical appropriation of the community Story/Vision to their own; we invite participants to decision for their "owned truth" in Christian faith. It may aid clarity here to make explicit how the dynamics of our cognitive structure are engaged in the three activities of a conative process as outlined thus far, and then to indicate the dynamics yet to come.

First, recall that any one of the transcendentals may be our focused activity in a particular moment—for example, understanding. If, however, we are self-conscious and intentional about it, then in fact we are applying all four of the transcendentals to the activity of understanding—we are attending to, understanding, judging, and deciding about our act of understanding. Thus, when the religious educator sponsors participants to intentionally engage and bring to expression in conversation their consciousness of their corporeal, mental, and volitional activities as agent-subjects, to critically reflect on their socially located praxis and the praxis of their sociocultural world, to share their story/vision of their historical time and to encounter the tradition that emerges from the whole time of their faith community—participants constantly employ the four activities of attending, understanding, judging, and deciding to do all of the above. In addition, instead of having to constantly check oneself to be sure that one is performing the transcendentals self-consciously, the dialogical dynamics of a conative pedagogy encourages the "objectification" of the contents of consciousness and the application of "the operations as intentional to the operations as conscious" (see note 116).

However, the three aspects of "being" I've outlined can be identified specifically with either of the first two transcendentals as their primary conscious activity. First, bringing people to engage and express the consciousness of their historical activities responds to the transcendental precept "be attentive" (albeit requiring all four transcendentals to do that self-consciously). I believe we have pushed beyond Lonergan, and cognition, however, in that this first dynamic activity of conation consciously attends, not simply to the "givens" of one's immediate sense world, but to the data in consciousness from the agent-subject's own active engagement in the world, from all of one's corporeal, mental, and volitional activities, from one's making, thinking, relating, feeling, engaging, and so on. The basis of conation is not simply what we observe but our whole "being" and how we intentionally "do be" in the world, that is, our own historical praxis.

When pedagogy prompts people to employ analytical social remembering, critical social reasoning, and creative social imagining to critically reflect on their historical activities and on the "public life" of their society, the primary intent is understanding, and it honors the second precept "be intelligent" (again employing all four to do it self-consciously). We have expanded beyond Lonergan's transcendental notion of understanding by recognizing the sociocultural context that shapes understanding and by encouraging a dialectical interpretation of present praxis, personal and social. To promote the dialectic, I proposed not simply inner self-reflection but critical and social reflection as well, capable of uncovering the socially shaped constitutive interests that undergird our own historical activities and the "public life" of our "place." Further, my proposal that understanding be reached through dialogue in a community of "communicative competence" reflects a historically located and incarnate subject; in contrast, Lonergan's inattention to dialogue in coming to understanding reflects a more transcendental notion of the "subject," one less appropriate to educating for conation.

When educators sponsor participants to appropriate and bring their "whole" time to expression as their stories and visions and to engage the Story/Vision that emerges from the time of their faith community, our intent is still primarily for *understanding* the intelligible. This activity enables participants to recognize, comprehend, and test in dialogue the practical wisdom from the narrative of their own lives and of their faith community over time. It goes beyond Lonergan's portrayal of being intelligent, however, in that (a) teachers create situations in which participants share in dialogue, not simply their conceptual clarity but also their practical wisdom from life, and (b) they intentionally give participants explicit access to the narrative practical "understanding" of the faith community over time. The latter activity, of course, is required for conation in explicitly Christian faith; Lonergan was describing the dynamic structure of cognition in general.

It seems that in the activities of a conative pedagogy outlined thus far, the transcendental activities of *attending* and *understanding*, have been well honored. In this section 4, however, I contend that people's whole dynamic structure should be engaged in order to promote wisdom in Christian faith. It remains then to explain how educators for conation honor the transcendental activities of judging and deciding. Below I focus on the place of judging in Christian faith conation and in section 5 on the fourth transcendental—deciding.

C. Judging in Coming to Conation

Judging has a commonsense meaning of applying some criterion to discern and measure something on a continuum between truth and falsehood, right and wrong, the aesthetic and the ugly, and so on. Lonergan lends precision to this common sense meaning and suggests the crucial role judgment plays in the dynamics of conation. In general, he describes judgment (the third transcendental activity) as marshaling evidence to evaluate the hypotheses put forward by understanding to account for the data that come from attending. Judgment establishes the conditions for something to be so and evaluates whether this particular thing *is* so or not. "Observing lets intelligence be puzzled, and we inquire. Inquiry leads to the delight of insight, but insights are a dime a dozen, so critical reasonableness [i.e., judgment] doubts, checks, makes sure."[120]

Lonergan also describes judgment as central to how people appropriate *for themselves* "the world mediated by meaning"; "the full act of meaning [for us as subjects] is an act of judgment."[121] He outlines four "functions of meaning" for people as subjects: (1) cognitive, which shapes what we know and believe; (2) efficient, which shapes what we make and do; (3) constitutive, which shapes who we become, and (4) communicative, which shapes what we share with others.[122] These functions of meaning are operative in every "realm" of our lives.[123] In other words, judging is our way of appropriating "meaning" for ourselves, and it constitutes what we know, how we act, who we become, and how we relate to others on every level of existence. Religious educators for conation must structure pedagogies to encourage participants to judgment; it is essential to their "being" human. I propose that they are to promote judgment as an act of *dialectical appropriation*, and

I turn to Piaget to help explain what I mean by "appropriation" in the dynamic of judgment.

Appropriation. Piaget describes the process of "knowing" something for oneself as two interactive activities of assimilation and accommodation; through them we transform what we know and are transformed by what we know. Assimilation is the process by which we incorporate into our present epistemological structures what we experience and do in the world. In the process, our "genetic cognitive structure" acts upon and modifies what appears from life as we make it our own.[124] By accommodation, our cognitive structure is itself modified and changed in response to the incoming data. As Piaget explains, "The filtering or the modification of the input is called assimilation; the modification of internal schemas to fit reality is called accommodation."[125] The two combine as appropriation; it is making something our own (assimilation) and being reshaped as agent-subject in the process (accommodation). In a pedagogy for conation, the dynamics of judgment are equivalent to the dynamics of appropriation; it is "seeing for ourselves" what something means *for us* and reshaping our own "being" in the process.

I have two further points here. First, appropriation/judgment must engage the whole person as agent-subject in "place" and "time." Conative appropriation requires pedagogy to encourage judgment that engages the corporeal in that it is grounded in the incarnate subject; the mental in that it rationally discerns and weighs evidence, remembers past experiences, and imagines consequences; and the volitional in that it engages desire and will to form people's values and motivate their choices.[126] This highlights the practical interest of conative judging; it reflects what Aristotle called *phronesis*—prudence. Second, as Lonergan insists, the activity of judging is located in the existential subject, in the ontic "being" of the person.[127] We are influenced by our location in "place" and "time," but ultimately are responsible agents of what we know, do, and become and how we relate to the world.

The Dialectics of Appropriation. As intimated in Piaget's notions of assimilation and accommodation, we are to maintain a dialectic within appropriation between our "selves" and what we "know." The dialectics I already proposed in the relationship between people and their "place" for critical understanding should now be present in the dynamic of judgment. A dialectic is essential if appropriation is to avoid subjectivism and objectivism. This point is particularly germane to religious education, which, as Lonergan says, has often been marked by either an "insistence on objective truth"[128] in more traditional approaches or by subjectivism in the more liberal ones.

Christian religious educators are to prompt the dialectics of judgment especially as participants' own stories and visions are placed in a "meaningful" (in Lonergan's understanding) encounter with Story/Vision of their faith community. As participants express their stories and visions and have explicit access to community Story/Vision the educator is to structure the encounter between these two "sources" of conation as a two-way dynamic of affirming, questioning, and moving beyond. Thus, participants are to see for themselves how the Story/Vision affirms, questions, and calls them beyond their own and their society's present praxis. Conversely, the process is to enable participants to discern the ways that their own stories/visions affirm, question, and forge beyond the version made accessible and the present living of their Story/Vision in the community. This kind of dialectical appropriation by agent-subjects-in-relationship prepares participants for completion of the conative dynamic and circle with *decision*.

5. Engaging People in Decision for Their "Truth" in Christian Faith

In chapter 1, I summarized conation as "what emerges when the whole ontic being of 'agent-subjects-in-relationship' is actively engaged to consciously know, desire, and do with others what is most humanizing and life-giving (i.e., the 'truth') for all." People are to realize conation through their whole "being." A conative pedagogy, then, invites decision, with a sense of the personal responsibility and historical significance for self and others of decisions made. That the dynamic structure of conation is to result in decision making is also suggested by Lonergan's description of the dynamics of cognition. If authentic cognition by an existential subject is to eventuate in decision making, how much more it is required for *conation* that arises from and renews a person's historical praxis, one's whole way of "being" in the world. Clearly a pedagogy for wisdom engages the conative structure of participants with the practical intent of decision making; chapter 10 elaborates on how educators can encourage participants, themselves included, to self-consciously and intentionally make decisions. The issue to be clarified here is the intent of decision making in a conative pedagogy.

In a sense conation/wisdom in Christian faith, the oft-stated learning outcome of Christian religious education, is an expression of intent, but within the dynamic of conation itself, what is the formal purpose of its choosing? We need a sense of what we are deciding about in this teaching/learning event; that is, what we are giving form to. This sense of telos should be likely to focus and motivate the agency of participants and give them a compelling sense that this decision engages my/our life, that it's about us and how we live. Because I attempt to describe an "epistemic ontology," it will be well to state the formal intent of its decision making in more philosophical terms. About what, then, are participants in a conative pedagogy, reflective of an "epistemic ontology," to come to decision?

I give a summary indication in my description of conation—that people choose to know, desire, and do with others what is most humanizing and life-giving (i.e., *the truth*) for all. This needs further elaboration, and especially of what I mean by "truth" here, but it at least alerts us that the decision making in a conative pedagogy includes but cannot be exclusively cognitional—the predominant emphasis in Western philosophy regarding the "truth"; it engages the whole "being" of participants in the *outcome*, as well as in *origin* and *process*.

Including in it both "the true" and "the good" (see Lonergan's "active potencies" of judging and deciding),[129] I name the formal intent of decision making in a conative pedagogy under the rubric of "the truth," and that specifically Christian religious education engages people in decision for "their truth in Christian faith." The "Christian faith" aspect makes explicit that in Christian religious education, a conative pedagogy will pose decision making in dialogue and dialectic with a Christian Vision of meaning and value; it also alerts here to the cognitive, affective, and behavioral dimensions that are integral to decision making in such faith. That we invite people to decision for "their truth" in Christian faith is not to encourage subjectivism but to signal that the decisions elicited are to emerge from and shape participants' own "being" as agent-subjects-in-relationship. "Their truth" of any kind is not something "objective" or "apart" from them that is imposed from the outside in, but a relationship into which people enter, with and for their whole "being." I am encouraged to designate the formal intent of decision making in a conative pedagogy as "the truth" because (a) it can engage participants with an existential sense of focus, agency, and the historical significance of what they are deciding; (b) the Bible portrays "truth" as an *historical activity* that engages the deepest integrity of people's whole "being" as agent-subjects-in-right-relationship with God, self, everyone, and creation; and this clearly epitomizes the decision-making intent of a conative process.

A. Dimensions of "The Truth"

From the discourse in the Fourth Gospel between Jesus and Pilate, we get an inkling of how Jesus, in continuity with his Hebrew tradition, understood "the truth" and also a sense of the common skepticism about defining it. Jesus says, "The reason I was born is to testify to the truth. Anyone committed to the truth hears my voice" (John 18:37). Jesus saw "the truth" as residing at the core of his identity, as central to his purpose and the witness of his life, as a commitment to be made in order to "know" it. For his part, Pilate asks, probably in cynical jest, "Truth, what is that?" (John 18:38), apparently expecting no answer because he presumed none to be possible. However, we must at least try to describe it here, and specifically as the intent of inviting participants to decision in a conative pedagogy.

The Cognitive. In describing "the truth" intended by a conative pedagogy as more than a cognitive achievement—as engaging and forming people's whole "being"—we must be careful not to leave behind its cognitive aspect and portray it exclusively as fiducial and agential. There is certainly a cognitive dimension to conative truth. What this may be most readily clarified by returning briefly to the epistemological traditions of the West, even with their markedly rational emphasis. There we find three principal understandings of "truth," the correspondence, the coherence, and the pragmatic;[130] each has a suggestion for the cognitive dimensions of conative truth.

The *correspondence theory* says "truth" measures the verity of stated propositions; a statement is considered the truth and true if it "corresponds" with the "facts." Aquinas had a classic statement of this position: "Truth is the correspondence of the mind to reality" (*adequatio intellectus ad rem*).[131] Finding truth means "matching up" our experiences with our beliefs.[132] As might be expected, this theory is favored by empiricists—the measure of truth is correspondence of statements with sense data. Although contemporary philosophy generally agrees that the correspondence theory is inadequate to account even for the cognitive dimension of truth,[133] nevertheless, it reflects something that conative truth must include. Conation reflects people's whole "being" in the world. There is, then, an "empiricism" to conative truth; it ought to "ring true" to our historical experience. In Christian religious education, what people know from their engagement with reality encounters the historical tradition of Christian faith, which is, in a sense, a further source of "empirical" data to which they must attend. We need at least resonance, if not correspondence, between what we know from our own "being" in the world and what we know from the data of the tradition if the latter is to "ring true" for us.

The *coherence theory* says that stated propositions are true if they are harmonious, consistent, and make sense within a comprehensive, rational system.[134] As might be expected, this theory is favored by rationalists; truth is in propositions arrived at by deductive reasoning from rational foundations. It does not question the overall schema within which a particular "truth" may fit quite well, and thus overlooks the historicity of thought. Again, however, it has an affirmation that conative truth must include; for people to recognize the truth as agent-subjects, it must make overall rational sense and have coherence within their perspective. Though coming to own and be owned by "the truth" does not depend on rational coherence alone, a proposition is less likely to shape our commitments if it appears irrational to us. Of course the truth should confront us and call our present "ecology of meaning" into question, but we need it to be coherent with our worldview, and, in Christian faith, to our overarching sense of its Story/Vision, if it is to elicit our commitment as agent-subjects.

The *pragmatic theory* says "the truth" is what fulfills the test of being useful, expedient, practical. Something is true according to the measure that it "works," that it has "cash value" (James).[135] Pragmatism has little time for the wisdom to be learned from "the lilies of the field" or for "foolishness of the cross," yet wisdom in Christian faith must have a profoundly "practical" aspect. When Jesus was asked by John's disciples "Are you 'He who is to come,' or do we look for another?" he pointed to his praxis as the warrant of his identity—he helped blind to see, cripples to walk, deaf to hear, lepers to health, the dead to life, and "the poor have the Good News preached to them"(Matt. 11:3–5). Likewise for Jesus' disciples, their faith and "the truth" of it should "work"!

Weaving together the affirmations from each of these schools of thought, conative truth has three characteristics: (1) it "rings true" to what people "know," even intuitively and pre-reflectively, from their engagement in the world; (2) it makes sense within their overarching life-perspective, and faith-wise, within the overall meaning structure of their faith tradition; (3) it is warranted by "practical" results. But all three theories, even the pragmatic, presuppose that "the truth" is what we *know* and can state in propositions; conative truth is broader than this. Beyond corresponding to what "is," conative truth often creates what might be or ought to be; instead of being simply coherent within present systems of meaning, it often calls "the systems" into question; its wisdom is not always expedient but often courageous and perhaps foolishness in the eyes of the world. As basis for a more transforming and holistic portrayal of "truth," we turn to the biblical tradition.

A Biblical Perspective on Truth. In the Bible, the common Hebrew and Greek terms for truth, *emeth* and *aletheia* respectively, carry meanings like steadfastness, faithfulness, constancy, reliability, integrity; as Kittel writes, biblical truth is "a reality that is firm, solid, binding."[136] In the Hebrew Scriptures, God above all *is* truth (Isa. 65:16, Jer. 10:10, e.g.), is rich in truth (Exod. 34:6, e.g.), does the truth (Neh. 9:33, e.g.). People are to pray for and seek God's truth in the sense of "God's ways" of fidelity in covenant love and action (Ps. 25:5, e.g.). In the prophetic tradition especially, truth, justice (*sedaqa*), and steadfast love (*hesed*), says Couturier, are "almost synonymous words" that "define true religion in Israel" and epitomize what must be trusted and done in fidelity to the covenant.[137] Of truth in Hebrew Scripture, Joanna Dewey writes, "in all . . . instances, the emphasis is upon reliability; something or someone true will stand up under testing. For the Hebrews, truth was moral and relational, not intellectual." She adds, by way of contrast, that the Greek philosophical sense of truth "is primarily intellectual; truth is known, not trusted or relied on."[138]

In the New Testament, *aletheia* is used mainly in Johannine and Pauline writings, and in continuity with the Hebrew sense of *emeth*. For John, God especially is true (John 3:33, e.g.); Jesus shares in God's truth (John 1:14, e.g.) and reveals God's truth to the world (John 18:37, etc.). In fact, in his incarnate "being" Jesus *is* "the truth" (John 14:6) and sends "the Spirit of truth" (John 15:26). Christians are to live into the truth (John 16:13, e.g.), to worship God "in Spirit and in truth" (John 4:33–34); to "know the truth" they must live as Jesus' disciples (John 8:31–32). To know "the one *true* God" and Jesus Christ "whom God has sent" is clearly relational and obediential and thus the means of "eternal life" (John 17:3). In fact, anyone "who claims 'I have known Jesus Christ' without keeping his commandments, is a liar; in such a one there is no truth" (1 John 2:4). Paul too uses "truth" primarily in a Hebrew sense: the truth proves to be reliable (2 Cor. 7:14, e.g.), is realized by obedience (Rom. 2:8, e.g.), is expressed in a life of love—"the path of truth" (Gal. 5:6–7). Truth is synonymous with sincerity, and they are the opposites of malice and wickedness (1 Cor. 5:8, e.g.).

Clearly the biblical depiction of "truth" calls people beyond a purely cognitive notion of it; it is "the good" that is done and trusted as well as known in a rational sense. In fact a synonym for truth in the Bible is "fidelity," a helpful term here because it carries a historicized meaning for us. In truth as "fidelity," the Bible places dual emphasis on the relational and the moral; the truth can be trusted and is the good that is done faithfully.

The Relational. A relationship of trust and an ethic of care mark the biblical sense of the truth (much as I noted in chapter 2 of a feminist epistemic). Biblically one clings to the truth with visceral trust as anchor of one's "being" on the mountainside of life, and people's own "truth" is realized in their care for others. The old English word for truth, *troth* (as in "I pledge my troth"), suggests a similar meaning of committing oneself to trust and to be trustworthy with the integrity of one's whole "being." Truth as a fiducial relationship means to trust in the ultimate trustworthiness of life, of ourselves, of other people, and to act trustworthily toward all, that is, out of integrity to the core of our "being" with care for ourselves, others, and creation.

The ultimate basis of truth as trust and integrity is the conviction that the very Ground of our "being" is trustworthy and acts trustworthily with care toward us. This cannot be appropriated by "cognition" alone nor verified with rational certainty. In fact, to "own" and to be "owned" by such truth—to decide for God's trustworthiness—is to enter more into mystery than certainty. Such truth calls us into self-transcendence in the sense of "letting go" of the control and power we can feel from rational certainty; instead we trust that we have our "being" and well-"being" because we are "held" lovingly by gracious Mystery. Truth as a relationship of trust with God and life brings us to awe, to reverence, to worship, to a "felt" sense of the goodness and sacredness of life, of the gift of creation, of the dignity, value, and unity of all humankind. This truth is realized in love and "right relationship."

We are agent-subjects in trusting and acting trustworthily, but we never come to "the truth" by our own doings or deserts alone. Rather truth comes to meet us, and we as much allow ourselves to be found as we find it, to be owned by it as to own it. Parker Palmer writes: "I not only pursue truth but truth pursues me. I not only grasp truth but truth grasps me. I not only know truth but truth knows me. Ultimately, I do not master truth but truth masters me. Here, the one-way movement of objectivism, in which the active knower tracks down the inert object of knowledge, becomes the two-way movement of persons in search of each others."[139] In Christian faith, the high point of "the Truth" coming to meet us was in Jesus, the Christ. And still the "one true God" continues to reach out to all humankind as subjects with grace-filled invitation, and thus we are both responsible for and capable of responding in covenant relationship of "the truth."

The Moral. This second emphasis of "fidelity," and here the third aspect of the truth that engages decision making in a conative pedagogy, is the moral imperative of doing what should be done, and in Christian faith, living faithfully to our covenant relationship with God in Jesus Christ and all humankind. This ethical aspect emphasizes the historical and praxislike nature of conative truth or true wisdom. Ultimately, our "truth" in Christian faith is an ethic of life to which we are responsible and accountable in every arena and level of existence. Christianity appears most "untrue" when its community of disciples fail to embody in history the truth they claim to profess as their own.[140]

Conative truth in Christian faith is not only an ethic *of* life, but an ethic *"for* life" as well. In chapter 1, I claimed that human beings have an ontological will to life, a conatus for "being." Here, under the rubric of "truth," I note that humans have a will, not just for living, but for living well, for living responsibly, for living faithfully, for living fully— for living in ways that are humanizing and life-giving for all. We can discern this ethic *for* life in a remembrance of our own "being." At our "deep heart's core" (Yeats) we recognize that our best intentions are for life to the full, for ourselves and for others. Complementing this "remembrance of being," the "one true God" reflected in Scripture is imaged as totally and irrevocably "for life," as committed to the well-being of all humankind, with a "preferential option" for those to whom life is denied. Made in God's image and likeness, we share in this biophilia of God; our truth as human beings and in Christian faith is to do what is humanizing for all. Patently we have the ability to choose falsely, to choose death rather than life (Deut. 30:15), yet our faith is that by God's grace we can choose life over death and do *the truth* with love. (See 1 John 3:18.)

To summarize, pedagogy in Christian faith is to engage people's capacities for decision making and create a teaching/learning dynamic that invites them and gives opportunity to make decisions with the intent of choosing their conative truth in Christian faith. This truth is *cognitive* in that it "rings true" to and is meaningful (i.e., makes sense) for people's own lives, *relational* in that it prompts people to relate to life as trustworthy and trustworthily, and *moral* in that people realize it as an ethic of and *for* life. Religious educators are to sponsor and invite participants to decision for knowing, desiring, and doing with others what is most humanizing and life-giving (i.e., "the truth") for all.

In chapter 1, I proposed *wisdom* as a synonym for *conation* to describe the intended learning outcome of Christian religious education and have often so used it throughout. In light of what has been said here about people's "truth," in Christian faith, it is also clarifying for decision making in its pedagogy to recognize Christian religious education as a process that intends conversion. The act of deciding for conative truth and wisdom is always an occasion of ongoing conversion and a moment when people grow in their own fidelity and authenticity as human beings.[141]

B. Decision Making and Ongoing Conversion

In a very real sense, all the activities and dynamics of a conative pedagogy is an education for ongoing conversion. As participants attend to their own historical activities, reflect critically on present social praxis and share in dialogue their own stories/visions, have access to Story/Vision of the Christian community, and engage their whole conative dynamic structure to come to dialectical appropriation of Story/Vision and to decision for their "truth" in Christian faith, such pedagogy is a catalyst of ongoing conversion. It functions in the lives of participants as a resource for lifelong nurture and renewal in Christian living.[142] It has potential as a conversion process because, by God's grace, it can shape the Christian identity and agency of participants, and thus form them in the *habitus* of Christian faith.

I use "habitus" here in its old Scholastic meaning as the disposition of a person, formed over time, that shapes their identity and agency in a particular kind of "being."[143] To come into the *habitus* of Christian faith, which in fact is to take on Christian "character," requires education in the understanding, desire, and disposition to so live. But as Aristotle pointed out wisely, we are nurtured in the habit of any virtue by the praxis of it. Likewise, people's ongoing nurture *and* renewal (i.e., conversion; see note 142) in Christian identity and agency is realized by the praxis of their "truth" in Christian faith, and, pedagogically, by decision making to so live. The dynamic of decision making in a conative pedagogy, then, lends itself to the lifelong process of conversion. Lonergan's threefold description of conversion as intellectual, moral, and religious readily correlates with the notion of conative truth I have outlined.

Lonergan explains that decisions that are "responsible and free" are not the work of "a metaphysical will" but rather of conscience; making good decisions forms good conscience, and that, in fact, is a process of conversion.[144] To delineate more precisely what I mean by conversion, I draw upon Lonergan's threefold categorizing of it.[145] He explains that "conversion may be *intellectual,* or *moral* or *religious*," and the coalescing of all three aspects constitutes a "transformation of the subject and [the subject's] world."[146]

Intellectual conversion is a shift in how people "know" reality so that present "horizons" are broadéned and we expand "the sweep of our interests and of our knowledge."[147] It requires turning away from the "exceedingly stubborn and misleading myth" that knowing is simply taking a look at the data of experience; it moves beyond naive realism that presumes reality is as it appears to be and that the "looker" is objective in what he or she sees.[148] By intellectual conversion we turn instead to "know" by intentionally employing all four of the transcendental imperatives—be attentive, be intelligent, be reasonable, be responsible—and to self-consciously performing them. It is a process of turning "to truth attained by cognitional self-transcendence."[149] As I understand it, then, intellectual conversion is refusing to be held bound by one's socialized perspectives and moving instead to a critical consciousness that expands one's horizons for "the truth," wherever it can be found.

Moral conversion, Lonergan points out, entails changing "the criterion of one's decisions and choices from satisfaction to values."[150] By it, we move to congruence and consistency between the values we claim and the ones we live by. Moral conversion is "realizing" one's values in "moral self-transcendence";[151] by it a person consciously and intentionally goes beyond "self-satisfaction" to choose and do what is truly moral.

Religious conversion is ultimately the act of falling in love with God. It is "being grasped by ultimate concern. It is otherworldly falling in love. It is total and permanent self-surrender without conditions, qualifications, reservation."[152] This radical relationship of loving trust is both the "efficacious ground" and "ultimate fulfillment" of human conversion.[153] Operatively such religious conversion is the gift of God's grace, but existentially it requires our free cooperation with its gift.[154] In Christian faith, religious conversion is loving God by loving one's neighbor as oneself, as God is revealed and we are empowered to such love by Jesus Christ.[155]

Lonergan says all three aspects of conversion operate in concert.[156] In keeping with the dynamics of conation described here, I make more explicit than Lonergan a social aspect of conversion. This is not so much a separate category as an emphasis that should be present in each of the three aspects.

Social conversion works in concert with the intellectual, moral, and religious but gives each one a distinctly social perspective and telos. *Intellectually,* social conversion means coming into critical consciousness that enables people to discern the reality, the sources, and the consequences of oppressive sociocultural arrangements and to imagine social structures that are life-giving for all. *Morally,* social conversion moves beyond "personal self-transcendence" and turns people to socially transcend the "givens" of their context, in that they do not settle for them but participate in the historical struggle for structures congruent with the values of peace and justice. *Religiously,* social conversion means realizing the conviction that there is no apolitical way to be in love with

God; that falling in love with God is historicized as we do the truth in love by our neighbor, through political concern for the sociocultural contexts in which our neighbor dwells. The social dimension of specifically Christian religious conversion also calls Christians into solidarity and agency in a community of faith—the church—that is itself always in the process of reformation/conversion as sacrament of God's reign. The dynamics of pedagogy that educate people in Christian faith conation are also likely to prompt ongoing conversion—intellectual, moral, religious, and social.

What I have described in this chapter poses the operational task of intentionally structuring teaching/learning events and pastoral praxis to promote conation/wisdom/conversion in Christian faith. The remainder of this book presents "shared Christian praxis" as one approach to honoring and organizing all these activities and dynamics of conation within intentional moments of religious education (Part II) and in pastoral praxis (Part III).

PART II

AN APPROACH: SHARED CHRISTIAN PRAXIS

Prologue

RELIGIOUS EDUCATORS and pastoral ministers need an intentional "way of being with" people in ministry, an approach to their work that realizes both sound principles and effective practice. To this end, and building on the foundations laid in Part I, I propose a "shared Christian praxis approach." I call it an *approach* because it is neither a theory alone nor a method alone but a reflective mode of going about the historical tasks of religious education (Part II) and pastoral ministry (Part III). The word *shared* reflects its participative and dialogical style; it engages people in a partnership of common discernment and decision making based on "present praxis" and Christian Story/Vision. I call it *Christian* to signify that in Christian religious education the approach makes accessible to participants the Story/Vision of the Christian community over time and enables them to appropriate it to their lives. (A shared praxis approach used for faith education in other traditions would, of course, reflect their particularity.) I propose it as a *praxis* approach because I'm convinced that engaging people's "present praxis," that is, their reflection on their lives in the world, is an effective way to originate a pedagogy that honors the philosophical foundation of an "epistemic ontology" and intends conation or wisdom. In chapter 4 I offer a detailed description of how I intend the term *praxis*. For the transition and correlation between Part I and the rest of this work, however, I indicate here how the foundation of an "epistemic ontology" is honored by a pedagogy grounded in present praxis. The key, of course, is the correlation of "praxis" with the central term of Part I: "being."

For Christian religious education to reflect an "ontological turn" and an "epistemic ontology" in its foundations calls for a pedagogy that engages the whole "being" of participants as agent-subjects in place and time and the consciousness that emerges from their historical "being."

A pedagogy that so engages people originates with reflection on and in any mode by which people realize themselves as historical agents in the world *and* from reflection on what is mediated to their "being" from their social/historical context. This, however, is what I mean by "present praxis" when I pose it as the origin of a conative pedagogy. To engage people's "present praxis" in a teaching/learning event is to turn them (a) to the consciousness that emerges from and the agency expressed in their whole "being" as "agent-subjects-in-relationship" (i.e., their conative activities in place and time) *and* (b) to consciously reflect on the social praxis—the "public life"—of their sociocultural situation. This means bringing people to reflect on whatever is "being done" by them, from them, through them, and "going on" around them, to them and to others. Thus to reflect on one's "being" in place and time is to reflect on present praxis. One's praxis is consciousness of one's whole "being" in the world as an agent-subject-in-relationship. Thus, a pedagogy that reflects an "epistemic ontology" can be described as originating with people's historical praxis.

Chapter 4 presents a brief overview of the components of a shared Christian praxis approach and a summary of its "movements," and offers some general comments on the process that might not be evident in the detailed description that follows. I intend this overview to be a friendly guide for the reader throughout the ensuing chapters, to help make explicit the overall dynamic of the shared Christian praxis approach and how its various components and movements work together. Chapters 5–10 review the focusing activity and the five recognizable movements that blend together as shared Christian praxis in its fullness.

I am convinced that few people are totally new to a shared praxis approach. Some may be already familiar with my own previously published descriptions of it; some may have experienced it in the *God with Us* or *Coming to Faith* religion curricula or in other curricula that are intentional about honoring its principles and dynamics. I wager, however, that many who are unfamiliar with shared praxis as I describe it are using some form of it already. I say this because I believe it is grounded in and prompted by a "remembrance of being." Educators and pastoral ministers will do well to consciously bring their own approaches to reflect on this one. The dialogue between my description here and one's own work will clarify and bring greater intentionality to the approach that is most appropriate to one's own gifts and situation.

Chapter 4

An Overview of Shared Christian Praxis

1. The Constitutive Components

Putting together what I intend by each of the three words in the term, "shared Christian praxis" is *a participative and dialogical pedagogy in which people reflect critically on their own historical agency in time and place and on their sociocultural reality, have access together to Christian Story/Vision, and personally appropriate it in community with the creative intent of renewed praxis in Christian faith toward God's reign for all creation.*

To unpack this dense description I explain separately the three words that constitute its title, beginning with the last one, *praxis*.[1]

A. Praxis

Praxis is difficult to define precisely and, as evident already, I use the term with different levels and shades of meaning. Here I must describe its constitutive aspects when posed as the origin and ongoing dynamic of a pedagogy for conation in Christian faith. It will help first to clarify a point that has been raised about my previously published descriptions of praxis.

I indicated that to engage people's "present praxis" in a pedagogical event is to turn them to the consciousness that emerges from and the agency expressed in their whole way of "being" as "agent-subjects-in-relationship" in place and time, that is, to reflect on whatever is "being done" by them, from them, through them, and is "going on" around them, to them, and to others in their sociocultural context. However, this is clearly a significant expansion of the term beyond, for example, where we last paid concerted attention to it in Aristotle. Indeed Aristotle also used the term widely to describe any kind of practical activity and saw it as both source and expression of "conation" (see chapter 2, note 49). However, he used *praxis* most precisely to refer to public political activity.

In the understanding I pose here, although I recognize and emphasize a political dimension to every aspect of human "being" in the world (the personal" is also "political," as feminist theorists insist), nevertheless I do not confine *praxis* to the public work in society that the term *political* typically identifies. *Praxis* as the defining term of this pedagogical approach refers to the consciousness and agency that arise from and are expressed in any and every aspect of people's "being" as agent-subjects-in-relationship, whether realized in actions that are personal, interpersonal, sociopolitical, or cosmic. The relevance of this point will be more evident as I describe the dynamics of a shared praxis approach. For now, it is enough to say that though there are many themes in Christian faith for which a conative pedagogy most appropriately originates from people's public political praxis (for example, issues of social justice), it is neither necessary nor always pedagogically appropriate for all possible life themes of Christian faith to originate from explicitly political praxis (e.g., a doctrine like the Trinity).[2]

I move now to describe my own understanding of praxis as constitutive of a conative/wisdom pedagogy and its "aspects" (i.e., ways of looking at it) in the life of an existential subject that educators engage in a praxis-based educational event. Recall that Aristotle distinguished between theoria, praxis, and poiesis as "ways of life" and "knowing" and separated them from one another. They corresponded, respectively, to the contemplative/speculative life that brings knowledge of the divine or of first principles, the practical life marked by purposeful and reflective action, and the productive life of creativity. After Aristotle, praxis and poiesis disappeared from Western epistemology, dismissed as unreliable ways of knowing. Theoria, understood under Neoplatonist influence as speculative reason, triumphed as the only mode of cognition presumed capable of providing "certain" knowledge. With Hegel, praxis as reflective historical activity began to be understood again as a valid way of knowing if held in dialectical tension with theoria. Its source in human agency was clarified by Marx, and more recent philosophers have extended both its reflective and its active aspects far beyond Marx's understanding of them. In contemporary literature, praxis usually refers to purposeful human activity that holds in dialectical unity both theory and practice,[3] critical reflection and historical engagement.

This contemporary notion of praxis has expanded and united the activities that Aristotle assigned to the first two "lives." In my depiction of its aspects, I also explicitly include what Aristotle intended by poiesis—the creative/productive life[4]—and identify present praxis as our whole way of "being" as agent-subjects in place and time. In gist, I am proposing the term *praxis,* albeit redefined, as the most capable of subsuming the activities and carrying the combined meanings that Aristotle assigned to the three separate "lives." Thus, praxis can be viewed and pedagogically engaged from three perspectives: it has active, reflective, and creative aspects. They overlap and unite as one in the existential life of agent-subjects in the world.

The *active* aspect of praxis includes all the corporeal, mental, and volitional activities by which we intentionally realize ourselves as agent-subjects in place and time. In the personal realm, "present action" includes what we are intentionally doing and making in the world and what we are receiving from, "doing" with and "making out of" what is "going on" in the sociocultural reality around us. Socially, "present action" includes the whole "public life" of our social context and what is "going on" or being realized there. Reflecting a holistic understanding of "time," attending to and engaging this active aspect includes looking to the consequences of the past and the possibilities for the future that are congealed in "present" praxis. Thus, a praxis-based pedagogy turns people to and engages their immediate present action but also the past and future in their personal present and the past and future in the present of their social situation.

The *reflective* aspect of praxis is critical reflection on one's own and society's historical "actions." From chapter 3, and when realized most completely, critical reflection engages people in analytical and social remembering, critical and social reasoning, creative and social imagining regarding "present action." Its intent is a critical consciousness about present "action," of the sources and consequences of our social reality and of our own activities within it. This reflective aspect of praxis can be identified as "theoretical" in that it enables people to express and comprehend in dialogue with others the consciousness that emerges from their "being" in the world. It also helps people to clarify the perspective through which they personally interpret and appropriate the "theoretical" formulations that have arisen from the praxis of their communities—secular and religious—during their history. However, participants have access to and encounter the "theoretical" of Christian faith not as metaphysical ideas, as in Aristotle's "theoria," but as the practical understanding and wisdom that has emerged from the faith life of the Christian community over time.[5]

The *creative* permeates the two aspects already described; the *active* includes producing as well as doing, and critical *reflection* includes creative and social imagination. However, there is a distinctly creative *aspect* to all human "being" (not a separate life, contra Aristotle) and thus to present praxis. It is pedagogically important that we highlight it here in its own right, although we cannot pin it down precisely, because it is prompted by this will-o'-the-wisp, imagination. First, we can identify as creative the impetus within praxis for ongoing praxis, the fact that our reflection/action forms and disposes us to so continue. Aristotle rightly identified this as its ethical interest and even recognized the role of imagination in awakening desire and moving the will to renewed praxis.[6] Going beyond Aristotle (and Kant, etc.), I propose that the creative/ethical aspect of praxis should permeate its theoretical, practical, and productive expressions precisely because each should engage imagination and desire, and all should be ethically responsible. Human creativity is present within both *action* and *reflection* and also mediates between them as people imagine what is yet to be done and made.

Aristotle misled us in separating the practical from the productive and both from the theoretical probably because he underrated the role of imagination and did not recognize the social responsibility or equality of all three. It is, in fact, poiesis/imagination that holds what Aristotle identified as theoria and praxis in a dialectical unity as people realize their "being" in the world as agent-subjects-in-*right*-relationship. This point is pedagogically important because the creative aspect of human "being" has a constitutive function in the originating praxis of a conative pedagogy *and* throughout its unfolding dynamics. In the shared praxis approach this is reflected especially in the role of imagination throughout all its movements.[7]

All three aspects—active, reflective, and creative—are a unity in people's "present praxis." However, because of its cumulative dynamic as a pedagogy, different moments of the shared praxis approach can focus on and engage any one aspect of participants' praxis more concertedly than the other two. Because of the unity of the three aspects, and indeed the unity of the three modes of conative activity (chapter 3, section 1), we can still call what people attend to in a particular moment "present praxis," albeit with an emphasis on one aspect. I make this note here because I sometimes refer to the focusing activity and movement 1 of this approach as turning participants toward and engaging their present praxis, personal and/or social, around a particular generative theme, even though the dynamics of the process will deepen the reflective aspect (e.g., in movement 2) and the creative aspect (e.g., in movement 5) to promote renewed praxis in Christian faith. Given the cyclical nature of human praxis, such less precise use of the term seems at least appropriate if not, at times, unavoidable.[8]

B. Christian

When used as an approach to specifically Christian faith education, shared praxis makes accessible to participants a Christian Story and Vision that emerges from the faith of the Christian community in our time and over its history. Clearly Christian Story and Vision should not be idealized as monolithic. There are many stories within "the Story" and many versions it can be given; there are various consequences or slants of emphasis that different Christian denominations propose as or exclude from its "Vision." As Tracy argues, Christianity, like all traditions, is marked by "plurality," and by profound cognitive, moral, and religious ambiguity . . .";[9] given its historicity and perennial "surplus of meaning" it could not be otherwise. Chapter 8 deals in detail with hermeneutical principles to guide how and what to make accessible from Christian Story/Vision. Here, for now, I use Story and Vision as metaphors to symbolize the whole historical reality of "the Christian faith" and the demands and promises that it makes upon the lives of its adherents. In sum, the Christian Story/Vision includes God's self-disclosure to the people of Israel as mediated through the Hebrew scriptures; it has its highpoint in Jesus the Christ, who Christians believe is the "heart" of God's Story/Vision for humankind; and it symbolizes the Christian tradition since then and the living faith to which disciples are called in the community of Jesus.

I use Story as a metaphor because here it means more than its everyday sense, as in "story telling." It suggests a narrative practical language for our discourse in teaching it, but its form is more than a narrative of the faith tradition. Story symbolizes the living tradition of the Christian community before us and around us (the church) as it takes historical expression in a myriad of different forms, all of which constitute "the Christian Story." These forms include scriptures, traditions, and liturgies; creeds, dogmas, doctrines, and theologies; sacraments and rituals, symbols, myths, gestures, and religious language patterns; spiritualities, values, laws, and expected life-styles; songs and music, dance and drama; art, artifacts, and architecture; memories of holy people, the sanctification of time and celebration of holy times, the appreciation of holy places; community structures and forms of governance; and so on.

The Vision prompted by Christian Story is ultimately the reign of God—the ongoing coming to fulfillment of God's intentions for humankind, history, and all creation. More immediately in a pedagogy, Vision is a metaphor of all that the Story means for and expects of people's lives—the demands and responsibilities, hopes and promises that Christian faith signifies for adherents. It calls people to realize the pattern of meanings, ethics, values, worship, practices, and so on reflected in Christian Story toward furthering God's reign in the world. In the existential lives of Christians and Christian communities their Story and Vision are two sides of the same coin—the unfolding of God's reign in the world. This is why I often write them here as Story/Vision and refer to them in the singular. Neither one, however, can be neglected in a pedagogical event when the intent is wisdom in Christian faith.

We return many times, and especially in chapter 8 (movement 3), to the pedagogy of Christian Story/Vision. Here, however, a prior issue is the pedagogical rationale for using these metaphors. Are Christian religious educators well advised to use Story and Vision to symbolize their whole tradition of Christian faith and its import for people's lives, and is the narrative mode of discourse that they imply likely to be effective in a conative pedagogy?

Story implies events and characters, beliefs, values, and emotions, a past, present, and future, a beginning, a middle, and an end. *Vision,* in this context and used alongside *Story,* connotes a renewing and creative process that invites discernment, choice, and decision. Together they imply a narrative practical language pattern of presentation and discourse. By narrative here I mean a historically reflective language as compared to a metaphysical one—an existential language that describes what is, has been, will be, or should be. Narrative language is discourse that reflects how interaction among people, events, values, and ideas is historically realized; it expresses practical meaning and wisdom that arises from and has consequences for history.[10]

Often, of course, it will be wisest to name the various expressions of Christian Story/Vision as they are—creeds, commandments, sacraments, and so on. However, there is a pedagogical effectiveness in imaging the whole tradition of Christian faith and its import for people's lives through the metaphors of Story and Vision. Both metaphors and their narrative mode seem particularly appropriate to the general tenor of Christian faith. In its Hebrew roots and at the heart of the Christian dispensation we find a call to practical wisdom and historical commitment with constant notes of remembering and anticipating. In its pedagogy especially, this encourages a narrative practical discourse for the community to express its faith identity and to envision how they are to live as a people of God in history.

The biblical faith of Israel is expressed in a great variety of literary forms and language patterns—stories, dramas, poems, instructions, laws, proverbs, prophecies, and so on. It has "instruction from the priests . . . counsel from the wise . . . messages from the prophets" (Jer. 18:18). Yet the overall structure that binds these expressions of faith together and reflects communal identity is a practical narrative—the story of God for their lives and of their lives for God. The response of Israel to cardinal questions of identity and meaning—often asked by the children in recognizably "teachable moments"—was to tell their Story (see, e.g., Exod. 12:26–27; 13:8, 14; Deut. 6:20–25; Josh. 4:6–7, 21–25). Over time it became a narrative of creation, fall, promise, call, slavery, exodus, covenant, land, judges, kings, prophets, exile, return, and so on. This Story, by enabling the Israelites to remember their identity, shaped their faith life in the present and prompted them to lean forward into the future and the fulfillment of God's promises. It was within and through this overarching narrative that the Israelites knew (and Jews know today) the faithfulness of their God, their own identity, and how to live as a people of God. Likewise, in the New Testament we find a great variety of literary forms. But they are unified in the life of the storyteller Jesus as a practical narrative from birth to resurrection—a life story that forms disciples in a way of life. The metaphors Story and Vision and a narrative/practical language pattern for making Christian tradition accessible to people seem indigenous to the very character of Christian faith. So too they are fitting and effective for a conative pedagogy in Christian faith in the following aspects.

Historical and Practical. The metaphors Story and Vision and a narrative language pattern are effective in teaching the historical and practical nature of Christian faith because they reflect that this faith tradition is rooted in history, that it arises from God's activity among humankind—among the people of Israel, in the historical life of Jesus, in the Christian community over time—and is to shape its adherents now in their whole way of "being" in the world. A narrative pattern of discourse conveys this sense of historicity and practicality; it reflects and teaches that Christianity is always about and for praxis. This narrative mode serves as an antidote to the tendency to reduce Christianity to a system of ideas or to ignore the historical responsibilities of Christian faith. Johann Baptist Metz writes about the typical metaphysical language and categories of theology: "My criticism . . . is principally directed against the attempt to explain the historical identity of Christianity by means of speculative thought (idealism), without regard to the constitutive function of Christian praxis, the cognitive equivalent of which is narrative and memory."[11]

Belonging and Ownership. Story/Vision and a narrative practical style of making them accessible promote among people who share this Story a feeling of belonging to the community that carries it, a sense of ownership of the community assets and of responsibility for its Vision. As people appropriate Christian Story/Vision as their own, the very metaphors themselves encourage a sense of inclusion; an owned Story becomes "my/our Story," a chosen Vision is perceived as "my/our Vision." As symbols of their faith, they encourage Christians to recognize to whom they belong and the community in which they are included—the great host of Christians before them and around them who are gathered by this shared Story and Vision into one community of faith over time. Because the metaphors Story and Vision encourage collective ownership of the tradition, they discourage the notion that any one group controls the community wisdom and parcels it out to the rest. They are egalitarian metaphors symbolizing that everyone in the community should have equal ownership of and access to their shared Story and is equally responsible for its Vision.

Engaging and Dialogical. We are engaged by a story well told. A "good" story is a mirror of life in which we find ourselves reflected. It is a "remembrance of being" that illustrates and illuminates our own "being" to us. Through its praxis we come to reflect on our own. Without coercion, a narrative pattern of discourse invites people into its story and has the capacity to engage our very "being"—and thus can shape our identity and agency. Religious educators can draw upon this engaging power of narrative with particular effect to teach aspects of Christian tradition that are formulated in more metaphysical language. For example, the metaphysical language of the creeds and dogmas of Christian faith can deter people from personal engagement with them as existentially meaningful to their lives. But they can be made accessible and more engaging with narrative practical language. Creeds and dogmas are symbolic expressions of the convictions Christians have come to and the commitments they have made over their history. They are the "punch lines" of long-winded stories. As such, they can be appreciated by people and appropriated to their own lives most readily if catechesis is presented in narrative language that articulates their practical wisdom for life.

Likewise, the metaphors Story and Vision can encourage people to dialogue and conversation with the reality they represent. Presented as a system of ideas, the Christian faith tends to promote debate or at best discussion. When symbolized by the metaphors Story and Vision and made accessible by a narrative language pattern, the tradition appears more ongoing and life-giving, less reified or finalized, more "something to talk about." Good stories have a "surplus of meaning"; we can return many times and find aspects not noticed in previous encounters. Vision implies ever shifting horizons. Its open-endedness invites people into dialogue.[12]

C. Shared

The word *shared* points to this approach as one of mutual partnership, active participation, and dialogue with oneself, with others, with God, and with Story/Vision of Christian faith. Before describing how its actual dynamics are shared ones, I offer a brief rationale for why this or any other approach to education in Christian faith should be a "shared" process. This aspect cannot be taken for granted. Neither our society, so marked by individualism and competition, nor the church, which can be so magisterial and/or clericalized, dispose us to think of pedagogy in Christian faith as a "shared" affair. Further, both society and church have an image of teacher as answer person and maker of meaning; correspondingly, students are "receptacles" (Freire) of the knowledge and consumers of the meaning they are taught. Over the history of Christian religious education, both "teachers" and "tradition" have often taken on an authoritarianism that negated the word of participants.

The rationale for a process of partnership, participation, and dialogue can be briefly stated: Christian religious educators are educating for faith identity/agency that is radically communal, and our pedagogy should be likely to promote our purpose. Christian identity/agency always means membership in the Christian church, which is to be an "inclusive discipleship of equals"[13] who constitute the Body of Christ. According to Paul, "We, though many, are one body in Christ and individually members one of another" (Rom. 12:5), because "it was in one Spirit that all of us, whether Jew or Greek, slave or free, were baptized into one body" (1 Cor. 12:13). A "private" Christian is a contradiction in terms. Every Christian is a member of the Body of Christ, and no one is less a member of it than any other Christian. "You, then, are the body of Christ. Everyone of you is a member" (1 Cor. 12:27). So "there does not exist among you Jew or Greek, slave or free [person], male or female. All are one in Christ Jesus" (Gal. 3:28). Christians cannot view such statements as empty rhetoric or eschatological promises. They should be at the foundation of Christian communities now, and how they educate must be radically communal. Only a "shared" process in which the voices of all are welcomed and heard can fully satisfy the purpose of Christian religious education.

The "shared" component of this approach points to two constitutive aspects of the process: (1) the communal dynamics that are to take place within a teaching/learning event; (2) the kind of dialogue and dialectic it encourages between participants' present praxis (stories/visions) and Christian Story/Vision. The former is a dynamic of partnership, participation, and dialogue. The latter is a two-way "dialectical hermeneutics" in which participants' praxis and community Story/Vision are placed in dialogue and dialectic to encourage appropriation and decision for lived Christian faith.

1. Partnership, Participation, Dialogue.
Partnership. By partnership I mean a relationship that transcends the stereotype of teacher delivering and students receiving knowledge; instead, every participant contributes according to their teaching/learning style. Partnership both reflects and promotes the I/Thou relationship already noted (in chapter 3) as most appropriate in a conative pedagogy. In a teaching-learning partnership, one experiences oneself as an "I," as an agent-subject-in-relationship who is responsible for one's own and others' learning and sees other members as a Thou to whom and with whom one is responsible for the teaching/learning event.

Letty Russell's work has encouraged partnership in all forms of ministry.[14] She describes it as marked by ongoing shared commitment, common struggle, and communal interaction.[15] We realize partnership in attempting to be partners; Russell writes, "We learn to be partners by being partners." Christian religious educators are to "provide the context of community where people can experience partnership."[16] I agree!

True partnership demands a kind of ongoing conversion of all participants. It calls the teacher to a new self-image, away from answer person or controller of knowledge and into "being with" participants in a subject-to-subject relationship. Partnership does not mean a false egalitarianism in which teachers forgo their responsibilities as enablers and resource persons; it means being willing to learn as well as to teach, to listen as well as to talk, to be questioned as well as to question, to use one's training and resources to empower rather than to control the teaching/learning partnership. For other participants partnership encourages conversion away from dependency as "objects" into their own agency as "subjects" of their faith, to value their own word rather than waiting upon the word of "authority," to accept responsibility for their own and one another's learning.[17] A community cannot wait until there is perfect partnership before proceeding, but Russell is right when she reports that it can emerge if a teaching/learning community is intentional about it and employs a process that encourages partnership.[18]

Participation. Closely related to partnership but worthy of emphasis in its own right is the participative dimension of this *shared* approach to faith education. By it, I mean that we intentionally structure the process to encourage people to express, reflect, encounter, appropriate, and make decisions, while respecting each person's participative style. If partnership moves away from dependency, participation moves away from passivity; it engages all the conative activities of participants and their whole structure of conation. Participation enables people to be agent-subjects of wisdom rather than "spectators of knowledge" (Dewey).

Dialogue. In chapter 3 I proposed dialogue and the testing discernment of a community as constitutive of a conative pedagogy and "communicative competence" as its ideal. We are to structure the communal dynamics of a *shared* praxis approach to foster dialogue and conversation with oneself, with others, and with God.

Paradoxical as it may seem, true dialogue begins with oneself. At bedrock it is a reflective conversation with our own story/vision. Shared praxis is structured to promote a personal dialogue precisely because it invites people to both consciously and intentionally engage their dynamic structure of conation. Second, the dialogue with others is an honest sharing of one's own story/vision and an empathetic listening to their word and expressions in true conversation (see chapter 3, note 59). If authentic, it includes both affirmation of self and others and confrontation of self and others. It is an event of mutual discovery and discernment—sharing our lives and wisdom with others and discovering both theirs and our own in the process. Third, *shared* praxis encourages participants in dialogue with God. In "the space between," as Buber called it, participants can experience the presence of the "Spirit of truth" (John 16:13). Whenever people come together to reflect in dialogue on their lives and on Christian Story/Vision, in order to discern and choose how to respond in faith, they are in dialogue with God as well as with themselves and with one another; shared Christian praxis is a "prayerful" process.

In summary then, partnership, participation, and dialogue are integral to the group dynamics of *shared* praxis. These "values" grow and are realized in its praxis. Undergirding all three communal aspects the approach encourages participants to acts of faith, hope, and love within the very teaching/learning community itself. *Love* is asked of all and realized most eminently in willingness to truly listen to others. Listening should not be merely a polite waiting for another to finish speaking. Listening with the heart is an act of profound love requiring deep empathy, a "passing over" into the place of the other to hear "from the inside" what she or he is saying, both explicitly and implicitly. *Hope* is asked of and nurtured in participants to move beyond fear, defensiveness, and hardened positions and to be open to what is being discovered and un-covered together. And *faith* is needed as an act of trust—trust in the communal process, trust in oneself, trust in others, and, ultimately, trust in God's Spirit to move within the event and its community. Shared praxis asks trust of participants, that all are intent on seeking "their truth" and that the Truth is seeking them.

2. Dialectical Hermeneutics Between "Praxis" and "Christian."

Hermeneutics is the science of interpretation. It includes activities of figuring out and explaining the meaning of something—typically a text, but also a symbol, an event, and so on. Shared Christian praxis entails hermeneutics throughout, in that it brings participants to interpret both present praxis and Christian Story/Vision. I noted above, however, that its "shared" dimension also signals the interpretive relationship between present praxis and Christian Story/Vision. Here I only suggest the kind of critical and dialectical hermeneutics it sponsors as people bring present praxis to interpret Story/Vision and bring Story/Vision to interpret present praxis (chapter 9 gives details).

First, shared praxis invites people to hermeneutics that are critical in a dialectical sense of their own and of their society's praxis. As participants attend to present praxis and reflect on it with critical reason, analytical memory, and creative imagination, they may affirm aspects of it, question or reject aspects, and discover ways in which their interpretations invite them beyond present praxis. Likewise, as educators make Christian Story/Vision accessible in a pedagogy, they bring hermeneutics of retrieval, suspicion, and creativity to their interpretation and explanation of it.

Beyond such critical hermeneutics of both present praxis and Story/Vision, when participants place these two sources in dialogue (movement 4 especially), the two-way dynamic is well described as "dialectical hermeneutics." This is the moment of judgment and dialectical appropriation described in chapter 3, section 4, as essential to pedagogy for conation. As participants bring Christian Story/Vision to interpret present praxis, there are aspects that the Story/Vision may affirm and aspects it questions and perhaps judges as inadequate or even sinful; it also symbolizes promise and demand that calls people to more faithful Christian living. Likewise, as the approach prompts participants to bring present praxis to interpret Christian Story/Vision, again, there are aspects of it they affirm and cherish and aspects of present understanding and living of Christian faith that are called into question and refused if necessary (the Story *has* had its distortions), and because of its "surplus of meaning," participants can construct a more appropriate understanding of the Story and ways of living more faithfully into the Vision of God's reign.

With its three major components outlined, I summarize the pedagogical movements that typically constitute shared Christian praxis when it is fully effected in an intentional teaching/learning occasion of any kind. The next six chapters explain these movements in detail.

2. The Movements of Shared Christian Praxis

In its complete expression, shared praxis as an approach to education in Christian faith can be enacted by a focusing activity and five subsequent pedagogical movements. I use the term *movement* intentionally. It implies that shared praxis is a free-flowing process to be orchestrated, much like the movements of a symphony or a dance. The movements have a logical sequence as I name them (akin to the structuring dynamics of conation), but in an actual event they often overlap, recur, and recombine in other sequences. Typically this approach is most effective when an intentional teaching/learning event—class, seminar, workshop, pastoral encounter, sermon, retreat—has some particular historical issue or life-centered theme as its focus of attention. (Chapter 5 will elaborate on how themes can be chosen or emerge, and how to proceed in events that do not have one focused theme.) When a group has a "generative theme" (Freire) for common attention, shared praxis begins with a focusing activity.

Focusing Activity

The focusing activity turns people to their own "being" in place and time, to their present praxis, and establishes a focus for the curriculum. Typically it does this most effectively by engaging participants with shared focus in a generative theme for the teaching/learning event. It may do this by sponsoring a present action of it or by turning them toward some aspect of their historical reality in the world to recognize the theme as it is operative in present praxis. The focusing activity may also turn participants to present praxis through an engaging symbol so that as people look through it they begin to recognize a particular aspect of their own and/or their society's praxis. This likely leads on to or the symbol can continue to serve the function of a generative theme.

Movement 1: Naming/Expressing "Present Praxis"

Movement 1 invites participants to "name" or express in some form their own and/or society's "present action," typically of a generative theme or around an engaging symbol, as they participate in and experience that praxis in their historical context. Depending on the focused generative theme, this expression of consciousness of present action varies in both content and form.

With regard to content, participants can depict how the theme is being lived or produced, dealt with or realized, "going on" or "being done" in their own or in society's praxis; they can express their sentiments, attitudes, intuitions, or feelings toward it, the operative values, meanings, and beliefs they see in present praxis of the theme, their perceptions and assessments of it, their commitment regarding it, and so on. In form, present action can be named or expressed through a recognizable activity, in making and describing, in symbolizing, speaking, writing, gesturing, miming, dancing, that is, through any form of human expression. As people bring their conscious and historical engagement with a generative theme to expression—an aspect of their present praxis—they fulfill the intent of movement one.

Movement 2: Critical Reflection on Present Action

Movement 2 encourages "critical reflection" by participants on what was expressed as "present action" in movement 1. Critical reflection can engage people in any or all the activities of critical and social reasoning, analytical and social remembering, creative and social imagining. The intent is to deepen the reflective moment and bring participants to a critical consciousness of present praxis: its reasons, interests, assumptions, prejudices, and ideologies (reason); its sociohistorical and biographical sources (memory); its intended, likely, and preferred consequences (imagination).

Movement 2 enables participants to come to a critical appropriation of present praxis in their "place" and "time" and, metaphorically, to share in dialogue their own "stories" and "visions."

Movement 3: Making Accessible Christian Story and Vision

The third movement makes accessible expressions of Christian Story and Vision as appropriate to the generative theme or symbol of the learning event. Its Story symbolizes the faith life of the Christian community over history and in the present, as expressed through scriptures, traditions, liturgies, and so on. Its Vision reflects the promises and demands that arise from the Story to empower and mandate Christians to live now for the coming of God's reign for all creation.

Movement 4: Dialectical Hermeneutic to Appropriate Christian Story/Vision to Participants' Stories and Visions

In movement 4 participants place their critical understanding of present praxis around a generative theme or symbol (movements 1 and 2) in dialectical hermeneutics with Christian Story/Vision (movement 3). In the fullest expression of its dynamic, participants ask, How does this Christian Story/Vision affirm, question, and call us beyond present praxis? And, conversely, How does present praxis affirm and critically appropriate the version of Story/Vision made accessible in movement 3, and how are we to live more faithfully toward the Vision of God's reign?

Such dialectical hermeneutics between the two sources of Christian faith conation/wisdom (present praxis and Christian Story/Vision) enable participants to appropriate the Story/Vision to their own lives and contexts, to know it for themselves through judgment, and thus to make it their own as agent-subjects in the larger Christian community and in the world.

Movement 5: Decision/Response for Lived Christian Faith

Movement 5 offers participants an explicit opportunity for making decisions about how to live Christian faith in the world. In keeping with a holistic understanding of Christian faith (chapter 1) and of conation or wisdom therein that engages people's whole "being" in "place" and "time" toward "truth" that is cognitive, relational, and moral (chapter 3), responses chosen by participants, depending on the generative theme or symbol, context, and so on, can be primarily or variously cognitive, affective, and behavioral and may pertain to the personal, interpersonal, or sociopolitical levels of their lives. Decisions too may be personal ones by each participant or be made by the consensus of the learning community. Whatever the form or level of response invited, the practical intent of the dialogue in movement 5 is to enable participants—by God's grace working through their own discernment and volition—to make historical choices about the praxis of Christian faith in the world. As long as they maintain continuity with the central truth claims and values of Christian Story, reflect the faith of the broader teaching/learning community—the church—and are creative of the Vision of God's reign, they are likely to be appropriate decisions for lived Christian faith.

3. Reflections on the Shared Praxis Approach

Before a detailed description of the workings of shared praxis, I offer four general comments: (1) it is a "natural" approach for which people have a ready disposition; (2) it is likely to educate for a "public church"; (3) it is an instance of a broad-based pastoral movement to honor people as agent-subjects of their faith; (4) it is an "inculturation" approach that can place "the gospel" and "the culture" in dialogue for their mutual enrichment.

A. A "Natural" Approach

The many details of the next six chapters about how to enact shared praxis in a variety of contexts could make the approach sound so complex and daunting as to deter people from employing it. I might give the impression that only teachers highly trained in the process, with well-prepared participants, can use it. Nothing could be further from the truth. My experience of using shared praxis in many different situations and with people of all age levels has convinced me that it is an approach for which we have a natural affinity. In fact, I wager that we come to appropriate much of what is most significant for our lives by some form of a "shared praxis" process—a reflection on life and on "the wisdom of the ages" in dialogue with others. How indigenous the dynamics of shared praxis are to people was clarified for me by a particular experience.

I was visiting a friend who has a son, Joey, then about seven years old. As she and I were chatting in the kitchen, Joey suddenly came charging through the back door of their home, crying loudly, hair tousled, shirt torn, and nose bleeding. He had obviously been in a fight. (No doubt here about the life-theme for attention.)

His mother did what any parent would do: took him in her arms and asked urgently, "Joey, Joey, what happened?" (movement 1—inviting him to express his "present action"). He proceeded to describe, in colorful detail, the terrible things his playmate Johnny had just done to him, how Johnny had knocked him to the ground and beat him up; it sounded as if Joey were lucky to escape with his life. His mother was listening and attending to him, bathing his cuts and bruises, and satisfying herself that he had no serious injuries.

Joey finished his story and was consoled by his mother, and the excitement abated. Now she asked gently, "Well, why do you think you had such a bad fight with Johnny?" and a dialogue began. Beyond this "reasoning" question, she reminded Joey that this was the third fight he had been in recently, whereas he previously had not fought at all. She asked him to imagine what could happen if he continued fighting this way (movement 2—reason, memory, and imagination brought to "present action"). From his "critical reflection" Joey began to recognize he was not nearly as innocent as he first made it sound and in fact had helped start the fight.

Their conversation shifted as my friend, without scolding, began to explain to Joey some of her own "wisdom of the ages" (movement 3). It was not an explicitly "Christian" faith statement but more a sharing of the wisdom she has gained over the years. She assured Joey she was sorry Johnny had punched him in the face and felt Johnny was wrong to do so. She explained, however, how fights get started, what we can do to avoid them, and the dire consequences they bring if we don't. She mentioned how wars happen between nations when they just want their own way and won't "talk things over" (Story/Vision).

Then she asked Joey what I overheard as an appropriation kind of question: "Am I making any sense to you?" (movement 4). A kind of "dialectical hermeneutics" ensued between them; Joey could see some of the wisdom in what she said but also protested, "Mom, you weren't out there, you didn't see what he did to me." (True!) As the dialogue came to an end, she asked, "Well, what are you going to do about it?" (movement 5). He protested, "What can I do?" She made a few suggestions: he could offer to make peace with Johnny (No way! "Mom, he'd hit me again!"); he could ask their friend Pedro to help them make up, and so on. They talked awhile about possible courses of action. Finally she said, "Well, *you* have to figure out what to do about it," gave him a hug, and left Joey to his own decision.

The dynamic I observed unfolding between parent and child seemed quite "natural" to them, yet it reflected the movements of shared praxis (and, I should add, this friend had never read any of my writings!). By portraying shared praxis as a "natural" mode for people to interact around significant life themes or occasions, I do not mean that it is simplistic. It requires intentionality and planning by educators and an art to facilitate it refined only in the praxis. Given the educational approaches into which people have typically been socialized, it may be experienced by many as a paradigmatic shift, in facilitation and participation. However, with a little time, people can discover they have an affinity for it, that it comes somewhat "naturally" to them.[19]

B. A "Public" Faith Approach

Mainline North American churches are growing in awareness that they are to live a "public" faith, a faith that is socially and politically responsible rather than focused exclusively on sacral concerns. Christian faith demands that its claimants join the public discourse and the political struggle for a better world. This aspect of Christian faith was until recently identified exclusively with liberation communities and theologies, but it now permeates the "establishment" church. An emerging literature calls for a "public" theology and church[20] and for a "public" religious education.[21]

In *The Church in the Education of the Public*, Seymour, O'Gorman, and Foster argue well that Christian religious education is not simply to serve as an intra-ecclesial agency of church maintenance but must retrieve its task to educate and shape "national values, ideology, and lifestyle."[22] I say "retrieve" because they point out that in America "the educational task of the Church . . . in the colonial period had been to embody social life and meanings." However, "in the national period [the task] became the gathering of members and the nurturing of the children of those members."[23] For the American context at least (the European state churches tradition would differ), this development was a serious loss to the "public" sphere and a reduction of religious education to a churchy affair that often allowed people to forget the social responsibilities of Christian faith. We must refuse what they call "the continual domestication of the churches' education" and move it beyond ecclesial nurture to also play "its role in the wider educational ecology."[24]

My claim in chapter 1 that Christian religious education is to inform, form, and transform people in identity and agency for the reign of God has already pointed to the sociopolitical aspect of "being" in Christian faith; I elaborate on this perspective in chapter 13 on peace and justice ministry. I believe shared praxis is one fitting approach to educate for a "public" church and Christian faith. Although it both engages and nurtures the socializing role of the faith community, it also promotes a dialectic between participants and their contexts, social and ecclesial, and between the Christian faith community and its sociocultural situation. By beginning with the historical praxis of participants, promoting critical social and historical analysis thereof, moving through

Christian Story/Vision with emancipatory interest to return to renewed praxis of faith that is lived for God's reign of justice and peace, shared praxis educates for a "public" church and faith. Its very dynamics make it capable of shaping people's politics as much as their prayers.

C. An Emerging Approach

There is a growing pastoral movement, especially at a grass-roots level, to create faith communities and styles of ministry that engage people as full participants in the life of the church, as agent-subjects rather than dependent objects of their faith in the world. One aspect of this movement is to take seriously people's own historical praxis as a starting point for religious education and pastoral ministry, and for "doing theology." A shared praxis approach is a clear instance of this broader movement.

Perhaps its most amazing instance is the Basic Christian Community movement, so significant now in Third World churches and growing in the First World.[25] When participants meet together for group discernment and support, these "base communities" typically seem to intuitively begin with their present historical reality. They reflect together in dialogue on the praxis of their lives in light of their Christian faith, in order to move to pastoral planning for renewed faith praxis. As yet there appears to be no agreed-on explanation of how the base community movement first emerged;[26] it seems to be a response to existential needs that arises from "the base" rather than a program initiated by the hierarchy or the application of some theory to practice.[27] In Christian faith, one can recognize it as a movement of the Holy Spirit.

In North America, the Rite of Christian Initiation of Adults (RCIA), so widespread in Catholic parishes and receiving initial interest now in mainline Protestant denominations, gives credible signs of being an instance of a community- and praxis-based movement of church renewal. In fact, many parishes implement its catechetical component with a very creative adaptation of a shared praxis approach.[28] The Renew Movement is also a praxis-based approach to promoting congregational renewal.[29] Alongside these grass-roots movements and often in dialogue with them, an emerging literature proposes and helps to clarify a praxis-based approach to religious education and pastoral ministry. A little of it has been influenced by my own work,[30] but much is emerging from different sources and primarily from people's growing insistence that they be engaged as participating subjects in the teaching/learning and pastoral praxis of their faith communities. I briefly describe two of many approaches[31] as instances of an emerging movement in religious education[32] and pastoral ministry.

James Whitehead and Evelyn Eaton Whitehead propose a model for pastoral ministry built on "three sources . . . the Christian Tradition, personal experience, and cultural information."[33] By "Christian Tradition" they mean something very similar to what I intend by the metaphors Story and Vision. "Experience" refers to "the personal experience of the minister and the collective experience of the community in which the reflection is taking place." By "cultural information," they intend "that sort of understanding, conviction, or bias in the culture which contributes explicitly or implicitly to any theological reflection in ministry."[34] These three sources are then "correlated" by a "three-stage method" of attending, assertion, and decision.[35] The sources and dynamic are clearly resonant with what we have reviewed above as shared Christian praxis.[36] They propose a way to enable people to "do theology" together in a pastoral context. Shared Christian praxis has also been and continues to be so used.

A second model of the same genre is the method of social analysis developed by Joe Holland and Peter Henriot. I draw extensively upon their work in chapter 7 to highlight the social analysis aspect of critical reflection. Here I mention only the skeletal outline of their "pastoral circle"—a model for doing social analysis in a pastoral context to promote action for justice. In summary, they write, "A social analysis that is genuinely pastoral can be illustrated in what we can call the 'pastoral circle.' This circle represents the close relationships between four mediations of experience: (1) *insertion*, (2) *social analysis*, (3) *theological reflection*, and (4) *pastoral planning*."[37] Beginning with insertion, the process engages "what people are feeling, what they are undergoing, how they are responding . . . the experiences that constitute primary data." From this first moment, the dynamic moves to social analysis, which "examines causes, probes consequences, delineates linkages, and identifies actors." The third moment, theological reflection, is "an effort to understand more broadly and deeply the analyzed experiences in the light of living faith, scripture, church social teachings, and the resources of tradition." The cumulative dynamic of these three moments leads into pastoral planning, which asks, "what response is called for by individuals and by communities? How should the response be designed in order to be most effective not only in the short term but also in the long term?"[38]

These two contemporary samples, their complementarity with each other and with shared praxis make the point that an educational and pastoral approach grounded in historical praxis to promote Christian conation/wisdom is an emerging process "whose time has come."

D. An Inculturation Approach

Inculturation is a newly coined term that the church and pastoral theologians now use widely to name the appropriate relationship between "faith and culture." Tillich wrote, "Religion is the substance of a culture; culture is the form of religion."[39] His point was that every faith tradition becomes intertwined with its cultural contexts; it shapes, and its expression is shaped by, the culture of its adherents. The appropriate relationship between faith and culture (actually cultures) is as urgent an issue for our time as faith and reason was for an earlier era.

Of course, faith and culture was an issue for Christianity from the beginning. In the very Incarnation, Jesus Christ took on the culture of one particular people, time, and place but intended "the gospel" to be preached to the ends of the earth. Even the fact that there are *four* Gospels indicates that its different base communities shaped the earliest Christian kerygma. Disciples have had to "indiginize" the gospel ever since, not simply transfer it. Pope John Paul II states: "The synthesis between culture and faith is not just a demand of culture, but also of faith. A faith which does not become culture is a faith which has not been . . . thoroughly received, not fully lived out."[40] However, global awareness, modern communications, and the universalizing of Christianity give the faith and culture issue particular exigency in our time.

The Second Vatican Council stated repeatedly that Christian faith is "bound to no particular form of human culture."[41] Better that "each nation develops the ability to express Christ's message in its own way," so that "a living exchange is fostered between the Church and the diverse cultures of people."[42] Karl Rahner, in an oft-cited essay, proposed that Vatican II marked the beginning of a new "epoch" in church history—the shift to a truly universal church.[43] The pluralism of a "world church," however, creates tension with the dominant but culturally determined (Western) version of Christianity. Much of what European evangelists presented as "the gospel" was in fact a cultural form of Christianity; the church must now welcome and encourage other cultural expressions.

The Council's call for "living exchange" between faith and culture reflects awareness that there is something of God in all human reality, that God is actively present and revealing Godself in the existential life situations of all peoples. From the "faith" perspective, however, inculturation must retain what is constitutive of Christian tradition without loss of its permanent legacy, what speaks to every time and place. Honoring both "partners" in the relationship is a most difficult challenge, and Christians have not always proceeded wisely.

Schineller highlights the following inadequate ways of relating faith and culture: *imposition,* forcing an already culturally embedded Christianity on new cultures, with no appreciation or respect for what is already there; *translation,* transferring symbols of Christian faith to a culture without creative modification in accord with local customs or thought patterns; and *adaptation,* adjusting the cultural trappings of Christianity to "fit" the context but engaging in no real dialogue with the local culture.[44] Pastoral leaders now propose better alternatives, many of which are complementary to one another, for example, indiginization, contextualization, incarnation, localization, and so on;[45] however, the term and process now most favored is *inculturation.*[46]

We've seen, of late, a "veritable explosion of literature on inculturation,"[47] and there are many definitions of the term itself.[48] I understand it as *the process of historically realizing the intimate relationship between "culture" and "the Christian faith" so that (a) Christian faith is expressed in people's lives through symbols and modes native to their culture; (b) it is a source of transformation for its cultural context; (c) each cultural expression of it renews and enriches the universal Christian community.*[49] Thus, inculturation must honor the culture and the gospel and enrich both.

There is still much disagreement about the theoretical underpinnings of inculturation. A crucial issue is how to establish the core of Christian faith to be realized in every time and place; even if this is always already culturally embedded, how do evangelists find its "dynamic equivalence" in cultures new to Christianity?[50] Inculturation also requires models for doing it that honor both Christianity and culture in their encounter.[51] Shared Christian praxis as a style of ministry (Part III) is one possible model.

Movement 1 begins with people "naming" their present reality as they perceive it, not as a "missionary" tells them that it is. Rather than canonizing their present "culture," movement 2 encourages people to reflect critically on it, to discern the assets and liabilities of their place and time; they can draw upon the social sciences for such analysis (chapter 7). Movement 3 makes accessible Christian Story/Vision in its many forms. The style of making accessible (chapter 8) avoids imposition and is beyond translation or adaptation, yet it is faithful to the tradition, open to its new possibilities, and seeks the "dynamic equivalence" of its essentials for the lives of these participants. Movement 4 encourages people's own appropriation of the Story/Vision in a dialectical hermeneutic with their historical reality. Movement 5 invites them to live Christian Story/Vision in their sociocultural situation in ways transforming of the context and that enrich the universal Christian community. Shared praxis can be used in education or evangelization as an inculturation approach.

Chapter 5

The Focusing Activity in Shared Praxis

The focusing activity turns people to their own "being" in place and time, to their present praxis, and establishes a focus for the curriculum. Typically it does this most effectively be engaging participants with shared focus in a generative theme for the teaching/learning event. It may do this by sponsoring a present action of it or by turning them toward some aspect of their historical reality in the world to recognize the theme as it is operative in present praxis. The focusing activity may also turn participants to present praxis through an engaging symbol so that as people look through it they begin to recognize a particular aspect of their own and/or their society's praxis. This likely leads on to a generative theme or the symbol can continue to serve the function throughout the event.

To review in detail the focusing activity and each of five subsequent pedagogical movements, I use a common format in the next six chapters: a description of the *nature and purpose* of the pedagogical activity, the *rationale* for it, *procedures* for effecting it, and some practical considerations for the educator in *developing the art of facilitating* this aspect of a shared praxis approach. At the end of each chapter an appendix gives some examples of the activity to clarify what is involved and to stimulate the reader's own creative thinking about it. At the end of Part II, I append an overview of each movement.

1. Nature and Purpose of Focusing Activity

By way of purpose, note first that the focusing activity is to turn people to their present praxis, to some aspect of their lives in the world with shared focus. There can be events when a community does not have a precise and common life theme at the outset; nevertheless, the opening dynamic engages an aspect of present praxis. They may first establish shared focus around an engaging symbol that turns them to aspects of present praxis from which the generative theme(s) likely emerges as the movements unfold. For example, an adult Bible study may come to focus on praxis by "looking through" a passage of Scripture to then name in movement[1] the aspects of present praxis it brings into view. Typically, however, the dynamics of the process are enhanced and likewise participants' sense of being a community with common purpose, if the focusing activity establishes a common "generative theme" (Freire's phrase) that shapes the core curriculum of the whole event. It should at least raise up a generative symbol for participants' lives that prompts them to turn to an aspect of their own praxis. A long-term program could have an overall generative theme or symbol (e.g., to deepen commitment to a faith that does justice, to study Mark's Gospel), but a specific educational event within an extended program likely needs its own more immediate focus to establish its curriculum, and one that is manageable for a particular occasion.

A *generative theme* is some historical issue—question, value, belief, concept, event, situation, and so on—that is likely to draw participants into active engagement because it has import and meaning for their lives. Likewise, a generative symbol is one that is readily identifiable for these participants and is likely to engage them personally. Whether it is an ordinary symbol or, as is often the case in religious education, a religious symbol from the faith tradition (e.g., the Bible) it should be presented in the focusing activity in a way that turns participants to some aspect of their present praxis; participants are not so much to look "at" the symbol as to look "through" it to their own situation in life. Since a generative theme is often established within the dynamics of a teaching/learning event through a symbol, and a generative symbol of peoples' praxis usually leads on to a common life theme or can continue to function as the praxislike focus throughout the event, to avoid repetition I often write of both them and symbol here simply as the "generative focus." Whether the focus is around a theme or a symbol (or a symbol of a theme), it should be "generative" in that it turns to an aspect of present praxis that is to establish and engage participants with something of interest to their very "being" in the world.

Most often, the generative theme signals to participants, and from the beginning, the vital core of the curriculum to be attended to throughout this whole event. Then it functions akin to what Sophia Cavalletti, in her Montessori approach to religious education, calls a "linking point." By this she means "an especially striking element that emphasizes the vital nucleus of the theme. The linking point should introduce us into the heart of the subject in such a way that it gives us, in a flash, the global intuition of the essence of the subject we are considering."[2] The generative theme then should be of life import to participants, pertain to their very "being" in place and time, and, when possible, intimate the core of what the whole event is about.

Second, the focusing activity is to *engage* the interest and participation of people, as agent-subjects, in the learning event. Engagement clearly correlates with whether or not the event has a theme that is a life-centered and generative one for participants. But even if a theme is generative for this group of people, they need to perceive and experience it as such. Educators are to establish the theme in an invitational and evocative manner, with a style that is likely to engage people's personal interest and participation. Engaging people in a generative theme should evoke a sense that "this is about us—of real import to our lives." Active engagement as agent-subjects is essential if the process is to be a conative one for participants. Third, the focusing activity establishes a *shared focus* of attention among participants. It brings into view a common sense of the core curriculum they are attending to together. Participants are likely to have very different perspectives on the theme and different levels of consciousness concerning it, but their shared enterprise proceeds most readily if they have a common sense of a generative theme.

The nature and purpose of the focusing activity unfolds as a unity. Insofar as the two can be distinguished, I note that the typical nature of the focusing act is either to sponsor a present action of the generative theme or to turn participants to some aspect of their lives where it is operative in present praxis, personal and/or social. Echoing this second option, if the generative focus is established through a specific symbol, it should be engaged in a way that turns participants not so much to the symbol itself (that is the curriculum in movement 3) as to what it means for and how it functions in their lives, that is, to some aspect of their present praxis brought into "view" by the symbol. Whether it sponsors an action of the theme outside or within the immediate teaching/learning event, or turns people, symbolically or otherwise, to a theme as already operative in present praxis, the focusing activity engages the "being" of participants in their corporeal, mental, volitional activities and/or focuses them on what is "going on," being realized, dealt with, or happening concerning the theme in their context. Which aspect of "being" people primarily engage, and whether they turn to personal or social expressions of present praxis (or both), depends on the variables of the event (participants, time, them, etc.). The intent, however, is to focus on an aspect of present praxis. Participants express their consciousness of that "action" in movement 1, reflect critically on it in movement 2, and so on.

That the focusing activity can be a "present action" of a theme, or raise into focus an expression of it as already operative in present praxis, or be a symbol that turns people to aspects of present praxis, thus serving as the focused theme of the occasion, calls for five further points of clarification. First, the pedagogy can begin with a communal action around the theme *within* the immediate teaching/learning event itself. In a sense, this is a symbolic action in that it reflects the generative theme as operative in participants' lives and not simply within this event. For example, if a group of younger children engage with the theme "new life" (perhaps to correlate the Story/Vision of Resurrection in movement 3) and it is early spring, an appropriate focusing activity would be to take a "field trip" to experience together and notice the signs of new life in nature. Similarly, a unit on "faith as trust" might begin with the shared activity of a "trust walk" within the event itself. Many of the opening activities in published curricula are suggestive of such thematic action within pedagogical events.

Second, there typically are limits to the extent of "present action" of a generative theme that a group can effect within an educational event. However, every intentional event in a praxis-based pedagogy is a moment of heightened education within the overall historical praxis of participants. Yet, it cannot always be presumed that participants already have a significant praxis of a particular theme in their present lives; sometimes the overall program needs to encourage a historical praxis of the theme by participants outside its specific teaching/learning events to serve as their focusing activity. For instance, in praxis-based pedagogy on social ethics, engagement in specific works of peace and justice should be encouraged as integral to the curriculum. Such praxis can arise from decisions in the fifth movement of an earlier event, or be a constant expectation of participants, as, for instance, in the "service-based" programs sponsored by many high schools and colleges. The Pulse program at Boston College, for example, an undergraduate course of studies on the social responsibilities of Christian faith, expects participants to engage in some social justice activity for ten to twelve hours per week throughout the academic year. Such action "outside" serves as a remote focusing activity for the intentional teaching/learning moments. It is also, in a sense, a symbolic expression of work for justice in participants' lives; they cannot presume that the mandate of justice is fulfilled by ten to twelve hours a week for one year. Also, when participants come together in class to name and reflect on their praxis, they typically need something that functions like a symbol to give a shared focus to their dialogue and to the aspect of Christian Story/ Vision they attend to in movement 3.

Third, very often there are generative themes that are operative already in the lives of participants, before the formal educational event begins. For example, parents of young children in an event focused on "how to share our faith with our children" already have both a personal and social praxis of this theme to which they can attend. For themes already clearly operative in present praxis, the focusing activity is to enable participants to recall or recognize what they are "doing" or what is "going on" regarding this life theme. In these instances, we can also characterize the focusing activity as presenting a symbolic expression of the theme as operative in present praxis. Here the focusing activity functions symbolically in that it brings diffuse actions, experiences, memories, social realities, and so on into a common generative theme that participants recognize and engage together. It is clarifying to image this type of focusing act as functioning like an icon, in that participants look at it and then through it to recognize their own and/or society's present praxis of this theme in their lives.

Fourth, the action sponsored or turned to in the focusing activity can be one that is overtly religious, or one that has no immediately evident faith dimension, or one in which the faith dimension is yet to be uncovered. Note particularly that when a specific symbol is engaged as the focusing activity it can be an everyday one or an explicitly religious one. Many themes present a choice whether to begin with an ordinary or a religious symbol; the choice is best made according to what is likely to actively engage participants and turn them to present praxis.

Fifth, it should be remembered that the fundamental intent of the focusing activity is to turn people to their present praxis. Given inevitable diversity in this, there can be occasions when no uniform theme emerges from the focusing activity, but participants continue to reflect throughout the event on a variety of themes that are particularly "generative" to them. I have sometimes experienced this in scripture study groups when a particular passage is read as a symbol for the focusing activity. As participants bring their "being" in place and time into relationship with the text, and look through it to name some aspect of their present praxis (movement 1), a variety of life themes may emerge, and participants may carry them throughout subsequent movements. This poses a particular challenge, however, to the educator in movement 3 (to choose one theme or try to honor a number of them), and the dialogue throughout may be quite diffuse. Typically the "shared" dynamics of the process are most effective when a particular theme is established from the beginning or emerges out of the focusing act.

2. Rationale for Focusing Activity

The theological rationale for beginning this approach by turning participants to present praxis is an aspect of the understanding of revelation that undergirds it. A philosophical rationale for the focusing act was outlined in chapter 3, section 1; here I offer a more theological one around the theme of revelation. The overall theology of revelation reflected in shared Christian praxis unfolds gradually as we review each of its movements. At the outset, however, we can describe a constitutive aspect of it that undergirds this focusing activity and, indeed, the first two movements.

Beginning a pedagogy for conation in Christian faith by turning participants to present praxis in place and time reflects at least two theological convictions: (a) that God is actively revealing Godself and will in the everyday history that is people's lives in the world, and (b) that people are agent-subjects within events of God's self-disclosure and can actively encounter and recognize God's revelation in their own historicity through reflection on their present action in the world. Existentially we realize the two together, but it may clarify matters to say something about each.

A. The Hebrew Scriptures reflect Israel's faith that God revealed Godself to them through God's deeds in history on their behalf, and that God was/is actively and ever present in the midst of the people. "I will set my dwelling among you, and will not disdain you. Ever present in your midst, I will be your God and you will be my people" (Lev. 26:11–12). Likewise, in continuity with their Hebrew roots and reflecting the historicity of the Jesus event, the Christian Scriptures have a keen sense of the historical source and import of God's revelation: that God is engaged in human history and discloses here how people are to live as a people of God. My point in this rationale for the focusing activity of shared praxis is that God has not withdrawn God's revealing presence with the finalizing of the Scriptures. In Christian faith, they render access to the "primordial" revelation of the tradition (refer Macquarrie) and are normative symbols of God's revelation, but God continues existentially to reveal Godself and will to people in every time and place.

This turn to present praxis as revelatory is at least suggested by the shift in mainline Christian theology away from a purely doctrinal or propositional model of revelation, as if it were special information conveyed to us from outside of history, to what Dulles calls the "revelation as history" model.[3] Dulles explains, "Finding the propositional model of revelation too authoritarian and abstract, some theologians of the nineteenth century, followed by a great throng of twentieth-century theologians, have maintained that revelation occurs primarily through deeds, rather than words, and that its primary content is the series of events by which God has manifested himself [*sic*] in the past."[4] Dulles goes on to summarize this model's understanding of the content and form of revelation: "The content is the great deeds of God in history—events which, seen in their mutual connection, manifest God as the Lord and goal of history. The form of revelation is primarily that of deeds or events, especially the climactic events of the death and Resurrection of Jesus, in the light of which the previous history of revelation in God's dealings with Israel is at once confirmed and reinterpreted."[5] My claim here is resonant with this historical model of revelation (and I return to it in chapter 8), but it also goes beyond how this model has been typically understood.

As Dulles notes, the "revelation as history" model points to "the great deeds of God in history" and, for Christians, to "the climactic events of the death and Resurrection of Jesus." Shared Christian praxis honors this aspect of the historical model of revelation, but its focusing activity reflects the related conviction that the present praxis of people's lives—their own history—can be a source of God's existential revelation and experienced presence to them *now*. This is so precisely because God's tent is yet pitched among humankind, in Christian faith the Risen One is still with the community of disciples, and the Spirit of Truth has come as promised to guide them to recognize their God and God's will for their lives in the world (see John 16:13). As Rahner wrote, "The very commonness of everyday things harbors the eternal marvel and silent mystery of God and [God's] grace."[6]

Further, by using "present praxis" to describe this existential source of God's self-disclosure, I emphasize that revelation can emerge through our active engagement in history as agent-subjects.[7] I say *can* emerge because we must not canonize historical praxis as if it inevitably reflects God's intentions for humankind. On the contrary, and as I elaborate in chapter 7, people must bring an epistemic realism to critically question and discern what is of God's reign in present praxis and what is sinful and contrary to God's intentions, as these intentions are symbolized and normatively in Christian Story/Vision.

The Bible makes clear that it is in doing God's will that people most readily encounter God's self-disclosure. For the Hebrews, to know God is to do God's will, especially justice to the weak and poor (see, e.g., Jer. 22:15–16). In fact, throughout the Hebrew Scriptures, "The fundamental point to grasp is the closeness, amounting to virtual identification, between pursuit of justice and the knowledge of God."[8] Jesus also claimed that by doing the truth we come into the light.

As is most amply evident in movement 3 (chapter 8), shared *Christian* praxis is clearly committed to making accessible the Story/Vision— the "classic" revelation symbolically mediated through the scriptures and traditions of the Christian community. Clearly the approach does not limit God's revelation to present praxis. However, the approach reflects the conviction that people are not likely to be educated in Christian faith apart from their own historical praxis. Knowledge "about" God or "of" God may be transported from the outside in but conation/ wisdom, the kind that shapes conviction and commitment, begins most readily from present praxis.

James Barr explains that the Bible can speak to us "with authority" precisely because it "is built upon cumulative experience."[9] The most effective way to begin to appropriate Christian Story/Vision as our own is to replicate the process by which it came about, that is, reflection on life. Bernard Cooke writes that "the basic experience of life that each of us has is the first and fundamental word that God speaks to us."[10] Apart from present praxis, Christian Story/Vision seems foreign to people rather than "familiar"; they are more likely to simply accept or reject the version they hear as a cognitive exercise than to critically appropriate it to their own "being" in the world.

B. The focusing activity also reflects a conviction that people are agent-subjects within events of God's self-disclosure; that we are not tabulae rasae or "passive receptacles" into which revelation from "outside" life is transported and deposited but partners in events of divine-human encounter. For revelation, as with every aspect of human relationship with God, the initiative comes from God's side of the covenant; God comes to meet us in self-disclosing ways. But people are agent-subjects of revelation in that through reflection on their own present praxis in the world they can encounter, recognize, and appropriate God's ongoing self-disclosure in their existential lives, *and* through such "everyday" revelation people are likely to appropriate God's "primordial" revelation in conative rather than simply informative ways. Enabling people to turn to and share their reflections on "present action" in the world is constitutive of a conative curriculum in Christian religious education.

This aspect of the theology of revelation operative in shared praxis also reflects a dimension of the theological anthropology that undergirds the approach. I attempt a more comprehensive statement in chapter 15; here I note only the theological conviction about our "being" that undergirds the focusing activity and draw upon the work of Karl Rahner to do so.

Rahner is convinced that all faith "knowing" begins from our own human "being"[11] because of what he calls the "supernatural existential" embedded in human existence. There are certain basic structures of "being" that characterize every person and make human existence specifically human. He calls them "existentials" and lists three as self-presence (i.e., the ability to reflect consciously on ourselves), freedom (i.e., the ability to choose with self-actualizing consequences), and self-transcendence (i.e., the disposition to reach beyond ourselves for meaning, ethic, etc.). Permeating all the "structures" of human "being," however, is the "supernatural existential"; it provides both ground and horizon of human existence. The "supernatural existential" is like the Godly constituent that always "already graces" the human condition; it is "the innermost center of the Christian understanding of existence."[12] We possess this "structure" in our "beings" because of God's a priori self-communication to us, even before our response to God's initiative. It is an a priori and universal offer of God's grace that qualifies the ontic being of humankind with a distinctive affinity for and orientation toward God; likewise, it enables our capacity to recognize and respond to God's loving outreach to us. We first experience this capacity and aptitude for God in the depth of human existence itself.[13]

For existential subjects, God's self-revelation always originates, albeit in an unthematic way, in the depths of human existence,[14] precisely because of our God-gifted "supernatural existential"—it gives us capacity to encounter and recognize God's self-communication. Thus, every human "experience" can have a transcendental dimension in that it reflects "an unthematic and anonymous, as it were, knowledge of God."[15] At first this might look like a natural knowledge of God, but it is always already more than natural—it is prompted by God's grace, working within.[16]

We can be agent-subjects in the divine-human encounter of revelation, and this agency is always realized within history. Through historical reality and in dialectic with it, we realize our capacity to recognize and respond to God's self-communication.[17] Through what is realized and reflected on as human "being" in the world as well as through the symbols of what Rahner calls "categorical revelation" (i.e., the biblical and formal expressions of the faith tradition), God discloses Godself and will in the lives of existential subjects. In fact, it is because of the former that people can appropriate the revelatory capacity of the latter in conative ways. Thus, people's own history in the world as well as Christian Story/Vision mediate God's revelation, and, by God's grace, people can be agent-subjects who encounter, recognize, and share with others God's self-disclosure in their lives. Such theological anthropology as warrant for turning to present praxis as an existential source of revelation did not begin with Rahner. The Bible reflects both the historicity of revelation and people's ability to be agent-subjects in the encounter because of what is already within them. In the book of Deuteronomy, Moses says:

> For this law that I enjoin on you today is not beyond your strength or beyond your reach. It is not in heaven, so that you need to wonder, "Who will go up to heaven for us and bring it down to us, so that we may hear it and keep it?" Nor is it beyond the seas, so that you need to wonder, "Who will cross the seas for us and bring it back to us, so that we may hear it and keep it?" No, the Word is very near to you, it is already in your mouth and in your heart for your observance. (Deut. 30:11–14, JB)

John speaks of "the truth that lives in us and will be with us forever" (2 John 1:3). A central conviction of Christian faith is that the Spirit of Truth has come as promised and now reminds Christians of all that Jesus taught (John 14:20) and guides them to the truth (see John 16:13). In chapter 2 I noted Augustine's conviction that we have a "Teacher that presides within"—the presence of God to us. And the long tradition of the *sensus fidelium* (sense of the faithful) in the church reflects the conviction of Christians that, by baptism, they have the guidance of the Holy Spirit who helps them, as Newman put it, to know "from life" by a "sort of instinct" God's truth for their lives.[18]

To this theological rationale for the focusing activity, I add two points of emphasis. First, although God continues to existentially disclose Godself and will in and through human history, it cannot be presumed that "present praxis" reflects what God wills to be done, and it is far from inevitable that people recognize and respond to God's self-disclosure in their own lives. Our present praxis can be sinful, and by hardness of heart we can refuse or "miss" God's revelation in our lives. Even well-meaning attempts to do God's will need critical reflection and discernment in dialogue with a faith community and in dialectic with its Story/Vision. Second, turning to present praxis in the focusing activity is not simply an effective entrée into the Story/Vision of the community (movement 3); it is a constitutive part of the curriculum. For conation in Christian faith, a pedagogy must turn its participants to their own historical reality and praxis in the world.

3. Procedures for the Focusing Activity

A. Selecting a Theme

I am proposing shared praxis as an approach to any event of intentional religious education in Christian faith; thus the variety of possible themes, contexts, and time frames, age levels and backgrounds of participants, makes it difficult to delineate guidelines for selecting a generative theme that are equally relevant for all occasions. However, guidelines are clearly needed in the distinctly "political" activity (see chapter 1) of establishing a generative theme that shapes the core curriculum of a teaching/learning event. Three general guidelines, which typically function in concert and cumulatively, are suggested (1) by the intent of establishing a generative theme, (2) by the "shared" dynamics of the approach, and (3) by the primary sources of wisdom in Christian faith—present praxis and Christian Story/Vision.

1. The generative theme should be or symbolize some aspect of present praxis that is likely to engage people's active participation in the teaching/learning event because it has import and meaning for their lives in the world.

This guideline is attended to in every instance of selecting a generative theme; it needs no elaboration. In practice it means that what people are "doing" and what is "going on" in their context, that is, present praxis in their place and time, is a primary consideration in selecting a generative theme for any educational event.

2. Selecting a generative theme or symbol should be consistent with the commitments of a shared-praxis approach and especially, as far as existentially possible, with its "shared" dynamics of partnership, participation, and dialogue.

This guideline proposes the *ideal* that all participants actively and explicitly engage in selecting a generative theme. That, however, is not often feasible and sometimes not even advisable (e.g., with young children). In all instances, however, participants must be at least tacit partners, in that their praxis, interests, needs, and so on are seriously considered by whoever is entrusted with selecting the theme. Distinguishing between vocal and tacit participation and giving some examples of both may help clarify this guideline.

Vocal Participation. The ideal scenario—all participants involved in selecting a generative theme—is usually with adults and in a volunteer/ pastoral context. Some examples! With adults who meet regularly in

an ongoing program of faith education, the theme for a particularoc-
casion can emerge from the community, often at the end of the previous session. I have also worked with groups who spend their opening
time together reflecting on life events since they last met; usually a
common focus for attention emerges. This is likely most effective with
ongoing communities whose membership is constant, that are familiar
with the process, and that have people who can provide ready resource
for the third movement. If the fifth movement of a previous event has
led to corporate action by a group, that praxis can suggest the generative theme of the next meeting.

There are also contexts in which participants, besides considering
present praxis in choosing a generative theme, take into account the
general topic of study designated for the whole program. For example,
in a group studying Luke's Gospel together, the different life-themes
are also suggested by the sequence of the Gospel, from chapter to chapter, or perhaps from pericope to pericope. Even here, however, choosing a generative theme within a chapter that perhaps has a variety of
possible life foci can be worked out in dialogue by all participants, including whoever has primary responsibility for facilitating and being a
resource (whom I designate the educator). For such events, the focusing activity may be the groups' reading of a piece of text and selecting
from it the life theme(s) they wish to attend to together, or simply
allowing it to emerge as they name the aspects of present praxis that the
text as symbol brings into view. On these occasions a group may not
always establish a uniform theme, but the dynamic can still unfold as
people share what emerges from the encounter between the text and
their present praxis; in a sense the text, intentionally read as an icon of
their own praxis, is their generative theme.

Tacit Participation. When it is not feasible or does not seem advisable
to involve all participants in choosing the core themes of a curriculum,
their praxis, interests, and needs must still be explicitly considered by
the educators if what is chosen is to be generative for them. Here the
educator(s) and/or the sponsoring community have primary responsibility for selecting the theme. The broader their consultation, however,
the more likely is the theme to be an engaging and appropriate one.
Using insights from cognitive, moral, and faith development research,
and drawing on contemporary social awareness and commentary, the
selector(s) of the theme must consider the developmental readiness of
participants and their social/historical context—the place and time of
their lives. Educators should be keenly conscious of the "politics" of all
such curriculum decision making, that the themes selected and not selected influence how people will live their lives in society.

3. *Selecting a generative focus should attend to both present praxis and to
Christian Story/Vision, albeit with varied emphases depending on the age level,
purpose, occasion, and so on of the event.*

This guideline reflects the commitment to honor the whole "time" of participants, including the Story/Vision that emerges from their faith community over time. The task, then, is to find generative themes that are "adequate" to people's praxis in order to engage them in the teaching/learning event, and appropriate to Christian Story/Vision so that it can be comprehensively made accessible over time to these participants. For this latter concern, the option to engage a specifically religious symbol that turns to present praxis is particularly relevant.

Harking back to the schools of curriculum theory outlined in chapter 3, section 3, may help to clarify this guideline. In brief, three points of emphasis in selecting curriculum are according to (a) the disciplines/ traditions of learning, (b) participants' present praxis, interests, and learning needs, and (c) what is needed to prepare people to function effectively in society and/or to reconstruct it to promote the good of all. I also noted that all three emphases should be represented in the curriculum of a conative pedagogy in Christian faith. Since guideline 1 above calls attention to present praxis in thematic selection, this third guideline can highlight that the Story (the "discipline of learning" in this instance) and the Vision of God's reign (responsibility for personal and social future) must be considered in formulating themes for occasions of shared Christian praxis.

Attending to Christian Story/Vision as well as to present praxis in selecting a generative theme helps educators to avoid a subjectivist pattern of simply asking, What do you want to talk about today? and allowing the conscious interests and felt needs of participants to determine the core curriculum. Ralph Tyler makes a helpful clarification when he contends that whereas people's needs and interests should be consulted in curriculum construction, learning *needs* must also be judged according to a desirable norm, and education should broaden and deepen students' interests. Otherwise their "interests" will not be themselves educated, and their presently "felt" needs will limit their education.[19] Christian Story/Vision can broaden people's interests and be guideline and source of the life-themes for their education in Christian faith.

Even while honoring this guideline, there are many occasions when present praxis is still *the* primary emphasis in selecting the theme (guideline 1). For example, people may draw the generative theme for a particular occasion primarily from participants' present praxis, and then movement 3 makes accessible the narrative practical wisdom of Christian faith regarding the theme. But there are occasions when the Story and Vision are *the* primary considerations in choosing a generative theme. Then the educator's task is to discern a life-theme or an aspect of present praxis reflected in the Story/Vision being attended to that is likely to also engage participants because they can recognize it as of import to their lives and as operative in their present praxis. The designated purpose of a particular program or event might suggest such a theme. For example, in a program to help parents or guardians to prepare young people for confirmation, Christian Story/Vision of confirmation is a primary consideration in selecting generative themes. Those selected must be themes operative and generative in the present praxis of participants, but to honor the designated purpose of the program they must also be adequate to serve as a praxislike entrée into substantive presentations on confirmation.

Attending to Story/Vision to establish generative themes is most significant in formal programs with younger people, as in Sunday schools, parish programs, and parochial schools. Whether they employ a "homegrown curriculum" (Wyckoff's phrase) or a professionally published one, such formal programs intend to inform, form, and transform participants in explicitly Christian identity and agency, and thus are responsible to teach Story/Vision of Christian faith. Their "core" curriculum should have a scope that corresponds to participants' age level and a sequence appropriate within the overall Story/Vision. Distinct events in a program should originate with a praxislike theme that is generative for *these* participants *and* an effective correlation with the aspect of Story/Vision for attention (movement 3). In most contexts, honoring this guideline will be primarily the educator's responsibility. If a published curriculum uses a shared praxis approach, one would hope that its generative themes are adequate to engage the present praxis of participants and appropriate to serve as an entrée over time into comprehensive encounter with the constitutive themes of Christian faith. However, it is often advisable or necessary to adapt such published curricula to a particular occasion, time frame, group, or other factor.

A different instance in which Story/Vision may be the primary consideration in thematic selection is in formal theology or religion courses in high school, college, or graduate school. Frequently, the Story/Vision for attention in such courses is not limited to Christian tradition, yet the responsibility to attend with academic rigor to Story/Vision of whatever tradition is being considered is primary in selecting generative themes. Here again, giving this guideline primacy must not exclude the other two. Themes are selected by consulting, either explicitly or tacitly, the lives of participants and should be likely to engage people and turn them to present praxis. However, the themes are also selected from life issues reflected in Story/Vision itself so that they can readily lead participants to actively and personally engage the tradition(s) in movement 3. For example, in a school-based course on Christology, the teacher has the responsibility to see to it that participants investigate the topic with competent scholarship, albeit around generative themes of life import for them.

These three guidelines typically function in concert, although at times with one of them emphasized because of the circumstances of a particular event. They can help to select appropriate generative themes for most teaching/learning events.

B. Creating an Appropriate Teaching/Learning Environment

The "shared" dynamics of participation, partnership, and dialogue constitute the appropriate environment of a shared praxis approach. We cannot expect such a "community" context to be fully present at the beginning of any program, nor indeed, given the human condition, is it ever perfectly realized. But it can emerge through the actual praxis of such a pedagogy and as people make a conscious effort for participation, partnership, and dialogue. A conscious effort to create a "shared" environment is necessary throughout all the movements, but it seems especially important to establish it at the beginning. The educator, as the one accepting primary responsibility for effecting the educational event, can be a catalyst for participants to create an environment where truly *shared* praxis can begin to take place. The educator and the group are to attend deliberately to both the psychosocial and physical aspects of their environment.

Psychosocial Environment. The interpersonal ethos in which shared praxis takes place ought to be conducive to participation, partnership, and dialogue. What is called for is an ethos marked by hospitality that both arises from and helps create an environment of trust among participants. As suggested by Padraic O'Hare's analysis, a hospitable learning environment offers people both psychological and intellectual hospitality.[20] He describes psychological hospitality as "a deep struck spirit of acceptance and compassion for the groping pilgrim."[21] Participants should be able to feel "at home" and experience a sense of welcome for themselves and empathy for their issues. There should be no semblance of discrimination of any kind but a deep respect for all participants that creates the sense that their being together is "holy ground."[22] An environment of *intellectual* hospitality is free of ossified positions or knowledge control. It invites participants into dialogue to grapple with and question their lives, their world, their faith tradition; to agree and disagree; to be affirmed and confronted; to come to critical understanding, tested judgments, and responsible decisions—to truly "think" for themselves and with one another as agent-subjects-in-relationship.

Such inclusive hospitality reflects and nurtures a growing level of trust. When participants are new to one another, events may best begin with community-building of some kind. This can be done in a great variety of imaginative ways; when appropriate, serendipitous and fun group activities can be effective "ice-breakers" and "trust-builders."[23] With adults, introductions and statements about why people are present and what they hope to learn together can begin building trust. With any group—regardless of occasion, theme, or age level, whether a once-only gathering or a continuous community, meeting for the first time or the fiftieth—participants are engaged in a teaching/learning covenant together; it helps to bring this shared purpose to consciousness as the foundation for their communal process.

One church in a racially mixed neighborhood that had been torn by racist incidents invited its congregation to an evening of discernment to discuss what they should do in response to rising racial tensions. They chose to use a shared praxis approach to facilitate the meeting. Participants, over one hundred, were racially diverse, and a good deal of tension and anxiety were present as the group assembled. The educator began with an opening statement along the following lines: "Can we assume that we are all here to reflect together on the racial tensions in our neighborhood and to discern the best ways to respond to this crisis in light of our common Christian faith?" He then asked them to raise their hands to agree or disagree; everyone seemed to agree. He then invited participants into racially mixed groups of four and gave some suggestions for nonthreatening ways to establish themselves as dialogue groups and to share their hopes for what might come out of the evening. After this initial covenanting and sharing of common hopes (with the noise and laughter level rising in the room), the focusing activity was completed by three people, well rehearsed, role-playing a racist incident, very similar to a recent one in the neighborhood as widely reported in the media. Movement 1 began by inviting participants to express their sentiments and reactions in response to the role-playing and then their perceptions of the situation in the neighborhood. The process flowed on. The evening reflected the possibility of trust emerging, even in very tense situations, when an educator brings people to consciousness of a shared covenant and appeals to their best hopes and desires.

Physical Environment. An emerging literature on "educational ecology" highlights the importance of physical environment to the quality of the teaching/learning dynamic.[24] A shared praxis approach is enhanced if the physical environment is conducive to dialogue, participation, and partnership. It seems to work best in "soft" rather than "hard" physical environments, that is, where the lighting, colors, and textures are soft and warm rather than hard and cold. It is also enhanced by "circular" rather than "linear" designs and by seating arrangements that are movable for small-group dialogue. However, most of us rarely get to teach in such a physical environment. What of the drab church basement with terrazzo floor, bright lighting, and hard school-desks; or the lecture hall where the architectural lines and fixed seating all point toward the lectern and blackboard?[25] Under such conditions you can only do the best you can, but it is always possible to do something to make such spaces more hospitable, more conducive to a "shared" process. If possible, seating can be arranged to create a sense of "physical presence" with everyone making eye-to-eye contact with someone else. In large gatherings it is most effective to divide into groups of two, three, or four with opportunity to share with the whole group on occasion, maintaining this group dynamic of small and large throughout the process. The space and group can be organized so that everyone can speak directly to at least one other person and has the opportunity to be heard by the whole group should she or he so desire and if time allows.

C. Ways to Effect the Focusing Activity

The focusing activity can be a common praxis either outside of or within the teaching/learning event, or it can be a representation of a generative theme that is already operative in the participants' lives and context, or similarly a distinct symbol presented in a way that turns participants to an aspect of their present praxis. Clearly, the focusing activity can be effected in an endless variety of ways. Participation in a "shared praxis" outside the teaching/learning event is most appropriate with themes of a social/ethical nature. However, when participants come together for intentional educational events, it is most effective that they bring their shared activity into common focus around a generative theme. For this, a symbolic representation of their praxis outside the event can engage them in shared discourse within it. This can be a concrete symbol of their present praxis (what Freire calls a "codification"),[26] or it can be as simple as an opening statement that focuses the attention of participants on their common praxis.

A common social praxis outside the event is not always possible, however, nor does every life-theme in Christian Story/Vision correlate explicitly with political/social action in people's lives. For some themes the focusing activity may be a common praxis within the ambit of the actual educational event: a group project, a nature walk, a field trip, a liturgical celebration, a movie, a demonstration, a case study, a role-playing or drama, for example. Or participants may need only to recall or recognize the present praxis of a theme in their lives and context. Here the icon used, whether a distinct symbol or something symbolic in a more general sense, to turn them with common focus to relevant present praxis may be as varied as a story, a poem, a puzzle, a picture, an artifact, a drawing, a scripture reading, a ritual, a descriptive or evocative statement, an instance or example, and so on.

Concentrating specifically on a focusing activity within an educational event, I can think of four guidelines for an effective one.

First, and most obviously, *a focusing activity sponsors some common praxis or turns people to attend to an aspect of present praxis that reflects the generative theme.* (This guideline does not gainsay my earlier note that a theme or themes may not have been predecided before the focusing act but can emerge later in the process.) Some of my most unsatisfactory experiences with this approach have been when the initial act did not focus people on present praxis and instead gave the impression that this event was a "theoretical" discussion of "ideas." By contrast, if the focusing activity engages people with present praxis at the outset, the dynamic of a shared praxis approach is well under way.

Second, *a focusing activity engages participants; it should elicit their active participation as agent-subjects in the teaching/learning dynamic.* For this, the sponsor(s) of the focusing activity must be attentive to participants' ages and backgrounds, to their political, economic, and cultural contexts—what makes them tick and so what is likely to get them involved. Consonant with Dewey's claim that the greater the aesthetic quality of an "experience" the more likely it is to be educational,[27] I have found that when the focusing act has an aesthetic dimension it is more likely to engage participants. True to my claim (chapter 3, section 1) that the aesthetic originates in people's corporeal activity, I have also found that the focusing activity is typically very effective when it engages people physically and in sensory ways.[28]

Third, *typically the focusing activity is to establish, and should at least move participants toward, a shared sense of their common curriculum, and as it pertains to present praxis.* Its intent is to help all participants to recognize clearly the core curriculum for attention—everyone should have a sense of "what this is about."

Fourth, as *the focusing activity proposes a theme, or sense of the shared curriculum, it should be a "manageable" one for these participants on this occasion.* This guideline means that a particular event not "take on" too much (major themes can, of course, be apportioned and sequenced over a number of events). The focusing activity is most effective when it engages an aspect of present praxis to which participants can attend without diffusion and without feeling overwhelmed by the breadth of the issue. I was once facilitator of a shared praxis group that met around the theme of "being Christian parents today." This proved to be so broad a topic, however, that the conversation had no common focus, and the process broke down. For their next meeting, participants chose to focus on peacemaking in a Christian family, and the process seemed to unfold with far more cohesion and focused conversation. The difference, I believe, was that the latter theme was more "manageable" than the first.

4. Developing the Art of Facilitating the Focusing Activity

We develop the art of facilitating a shared praxis approach most readily by using it reflectively, that is, in the praxis. However, I conclude each of these chapters on its movements with some reminders that may be helpful to religious educators who take this approach; I have gleaned them from my own or other people's praxes over the years.

First, from many events of shared praxis, both as teacher and as participant, I recognize that the dynamics of the process are enhanced if a clear generative theme is established with the focusing activity, and if the educators especially have a clear sense of it and keep the focused theme to the fore of both their own and the group's consciousness in subsequent movements. Staying with the theme throughout is undoubt-edly easier when all participants have a sense of what the theme is and a sense of responsibility to attend to it. Openness to development and reformulation of the theme is appropriate as the process unfolds; ed-ucators must always respect the diversity of needs and perspectives in a group, which means that even common themes are engaged dif-ferently by all. These nuances notwithstanding, educators should be aware that all groups are capable of digressing in nonhelpful ways (e.g., avoidance). For reasons that can be readily surmised here, digression happens especially at movement 2—the moment of critical reflection. It is most obviously the educator's service to the educational dynamic to bring the dialogue back to the theme when people appear to lose sight of it. Doing this gently is an art learned only in the praxis, but having a clear perception of the generative theme is an important first step.

Second, the educator, or whoever is responsible for facilitating the focusing activity (and that can alternate in a group of older participants familiar with the process), is to turn participants to present praxis, and as typical around a focused theme, with a dialogical style. This means doing it in a way that respects participants, that clearly welcomes their participation and evokes conversation rather than closing it off. A di-alogical focusing activity presents the theme as an issue for engagement rather than as a problem solved or a case closed. The following example illustrates what the educator should *not* do!

A group of devout Catholics was meeting to reflect on the moral issue of birth control. For a focusing activity, the educator began with the symbolic gesture of holding up a copy of *Humanae Vitae* (the papal encyclical of 1968 on the issue) and then delivered a summary of what he considered to be "the clear teaching of the church's magisterium on birth control" as opposing any form of artificial contraception. When he posed movement 1 questions, inviting people to name their own attitudes toward and ways of dealing with this issue, there was almost no response other than apparent agreement with the church's official po-sition. But, of course, the focusing activity had not disposed them to enter into dialogue. (A brief summary statement of a theme could be an appropriate focusing act, but not one like this that "closes" the issue.)[29]

Third, after the educator, or whoever is responsible for it, has con-structed a focusing activity for a specific teaching/learning event, it helps to ask the following questions:

Does this activity turn people to an aspect of their own present praxis?

Is it likely to engage participants with what is a generative theme in their lives?

Will it establish a common focus that is clear and manageable, and around which participants can readily express their present praxis in movement 1?

Does it establish the generative focus in a way that evokes and clearly welcomes dialogue?

Appendix

All of the following instances of the focusing activity took place in on-going groups whose members knew one another well and had already established a significant level of trust.

1. A lesson with eighth-graders on their image and understanding of God was focused by the story of Michelangelo being chosen by Pope Julius II to paint God in the act of creation on the ceiling of the Sistine Chapel. The story is a dramatic one of how at first Michelangelo refused, for two reasons: he did not know what his own image of God was; and he felt that no matter what he painted, given the topic, he would surely fail and be a laughingstock among other artists. When Julius forced him to accept the assignment out of "obedience," he is reported to have asked, "What image of God should I paint?" Pope Julius, never famous for his piety, is alleged to have said, "You must find your own image, Michelangelo." The outcome is still there on the roof of the Sistine Chapel.

The story was effective in that it engaged students with the theme and enabled them to look *at* and *through* Michelangelo's dilemma to their own operative image of God. When the first movement began—with such questions as, If you were given the same commission as Michelangelo, what would you do to find your own image of God? What image do you think would emerge? How does your image of God influence your daily life?—the students had many praxislike expressions to offer around the theme.[30]

2. A group of Catholic sisters met for a renewal day around a theme—The Dance of Our Hearts: Claiming Our Ministry as Sisters of Saint Joseph. The focusing activity entailed a very powerful and beautiful dance drama. Based on a medieval French story, "Le Jongleur de Dieu," the drama was adapted to tell of a wonderful ballerina whose greatest gift was her ability to dance and to inspire other people to dance. As the drama unfolds, she joins an abbey where she is forbidden to dance but must do other things more appropriate to the cloister. Broken in body and spirit, she finally decides to dance—"against the rule." Her abbess, whom she does not know is watching, is moved by the prayerfulness of her performance and gives her permission to dance to her heart's content. But it is too late; the drama ends with the ballerina dancing her way into the heavenly court.[31]

The power of the dance drama seemed to conjure up in participants a great variety of identifications and memories, both joyful and sad. When the first movement asked them to describe "the dance of my heart as minister" there was ample evidence of its effectiveness. It was fruitful as well at movement 2, prompting participants to uncover and reflect critically on occasions when the dance of their hearts had been or is denied and to imagine how it might be renewed.

3. In a less elaborate instance, a group of people was studying the Gospel of Saint Luke together. The assigned passage for attention in this event was Luke 4:16–22, the story of Jesus coming into the synagogue at Nazareth to begin his public ministry.

The group had engaged in many different and creative focusing activities in previous meetings. This time the designated educator (it varied from meeting to meeting) did an interpretive and somewhat dramatized reading of the Gospel passage. She prefaced the reading by inviting participants to place themselves imaginatively in the synagogue congregation at Nazareth and to notice, as Jesus speaks, what aspects of their own lives and contexts come into view; what seems impoverished and in need of "good news," what blindnesses need sight, what captives need to be liberated and prisoners released, what a "year of favor from God" would mean for them personally and for our society now. When movement 1 invited them to express the present praxis that came into "view," this focusing activity had proved effective. Note, too, that in this instance the text being read in an engaging way and turning participants to aspects of present praxis was the focusing act. In a sense, the theme at the outset was the text but as an icon of peoples' present praxis; it can continue to be the focusing theme throughout subsequent movements, and especially for the more formal exegesis of movement 3. Also on this occasion, although the naming of present praxis in movement 1, as prompted into "view" by the text, could be loosely grouped in the area of social justice, there were in fact a variety of specific themes expressed within this general topic. This, however, did not obviate the process; participants could still have shared dialogue in the social analysis of movement 2, and the exegesis of movement 3 could have a social hermeneutic of interest to most participants' concern.

Chapter 6

Movement 1: Naming/Expressing "Present Action"

Movement 1 invites participants to "name" or express in some form their own and/or society's "present action," typically of a generative theme or around an engaging symbol, as they participate in and experience that praxis in their historical context. Depending on the focused theme, this expression of consciousness of present action varies in both content and form.

In content, participants can depict how the theme is being lived or produced, dealt with or realized, "going on" or "being done" in their own or in society's praxis; they can express their sentiments, attitudes, intuitions, or feelings toward it, the operative values, meaning, and beliefs they see in present praxis of the theme, their perceptions and assessments of it, their commitments regarding it, and so on. In form, present action can be named or expressed through a recognizable activity, in making and describing, in symbolizing, speaking, writing, gesturing, miming, dancing; that is, by any form of human expression. As people bring their conscious and historical engagement with a generative theme to expression—an aspect of their present praxis—they fulfill the intent of movement 1.

1. Nature and Purpose of Movement 1

The intent of movement 1 is to enable participants to name or express an aspect of their own and/or their society's present praxis, and this is typically done around a generative theme brought into focus with the opening activity. I add the term *express* to emphasize that movement 1 activity can be realized by means other than words. Words, spoken or written, are the most obvious way to name present praxis in a peda-gogical event, but participants can also express themselves through action, mime, gesture, drawing, painting, music, dance, symbolizing, and other means, or can use a combination of forms. What matters is that participants "objectify" or symbolize their own consciousness of present praxis. They "put it out there" so that they can stand back and look at it with critical reflection in movement 2. As representation of present praxis, the expressions made in movement 1 are to reflect an aspect of what participants "do" or experience "being done" in their historical context, that is, the consciousness that emerges from their whole "being" as agent-subjects-in-relationship in place and time.

Although movement 1 names/expresses present praxis, it is not a falling away from a praxis mode of education. For people to learn from present praxis by attending to it in an educational event, they must begin by naming or expressing their consciousness of it. But this is not a theoretical activity in an ahistorical sense of theory (theoria). When people name their own present praxis, that very act is itself a moment of praxis. In response to comparable criticisms of his praxis approach to literacy education, Freire defends his initial activity of making a symbolic expression of present praxis (what he calls "codification") as essential to the opening dynamic of education that originates with historical praxis: "We do not mean to suggest that critical knowledge of [person]-world relationships arises as a verbal knowledge outside of praxis. Praxis is involved in the concrete situations that are codified for critical analysis. To analyze the codification in its deep structure is, for this very reason, to reconstruct the former praxis and to become capable of a new and different praxis."[1]

Participants can express their consciousness of (1) their own, or of (2) their society's praxis, or their perception of (3) both. Which to invite depends on the theme of the occasion and what seems most likely to engage participants in the dynamic of movement 1. A creative educator will want to do it differently on various occasions, especially with an ongoing community. Some learning events and themes suggest an invitation to expression of participants' own praxis, others to expression of an aspect of social praxis, and still others an expression of both, beginning with the personal and moving to the social, or vice versa. An example of the latter was an event with graduate students focused on the purpose of Christian religious education. The questions posed in movement 1 were, When you look at your own praxis as a Christian religious educator, what are you educating for? When you look at what goes on in your church community, what does its primary educational purpose seem to be?

Young children are more readily engaged in movement 1 when the educator invites them to express their own action regarding a theme; this reflects their psychosocial development. Personal questions could be as simple as, for example, asking after a focusing story, Who reminds you of yourself in the story? Does something like this ever happen to you? Can you tell about it? With topics that participants might experience as threatening, and especially in new groups where the trust

level is not yet well established, it may be less discomforting to begin
with what appear to be expressions of society's rather than one's own
praxis. For example, with a group of male clergy reflecting on sexism
in the church, movement 1 began with a group brainstorming on "some
of the ways in which our church discriminates against women." The
group, made up of more traditional men, had no trouble coming up
with a rather large list, to much surprise. To have begun with "Name
the ways in which you discriminate against women in your church"
would not have been pedagogically advisable in this group. Invariably,
however, as people name their society's praxis they also begin to recognize their own participation in that praxis.

When people seem to express only the consciousness that comes
from their own personal praxis in movement 1, movement 2 can turn
them to their society's praxis to encourage critical reflection as social
analysis of their personal praxis. For example, work with a group of
young adolescents on the theme "our hopes for new life" (in which
movement 3 catechesis was on the resurrection of Jesus), movement 1
included asking them, after a good deal of general discussion, to write
out their personal understanding of success and what influence their
notion of it has on their everyday lives, and then their own operative
understanding of failure and how they deal with it. In movement 2,
they questioned social praxis when they reflected on how the typical
understandings of success and failure operative in society were influencing their own.[2]

Whether naming their own or their society's praxis in movement 1,
participants' consciousness of that action can be an expression of what
they see "going on," being lived or produced, dealt with or realized in
the present praxis of which they are agents or that they experience in
their society. They bring to expression their consciousness of whatever
is "being done" by them, through them, around them, or to them, by
others and to others. They can express such consciousness as their sentiments, attitudes, feelings, or intuitions as they look to an aspect of
present praxis, and typically around a focused theme; the operative
values, meaning, and beliefs they see in its present action; their descriptions, perceptions, and assessments of it; their commitments and
values regarding this praxis—that is, the consciousness that comes from
any aspect of their conative activities as agent-subjects in place and time.
And though the educator invites *present* praxis to expression in movement 1, "present" here reflects an existential understanding of "time"
(chapter 3, section 2), that is, the "present" that carries the consequences of the past and the possibilities of the future.

I have four further points of clarification about the nature and
intent of movement 1. First, the distinction I make between participants' own praxis and their society's praxis should not be exaggerated,
as if there were a dichotomy between them. Personal and social praxis
are woven together as warp and woof in the fabric of our "being" and
historically are never separate. The personal is always somehow social,

and vice versa; it is not possible to speak truly about one without at least intimating the other.

Second, every expression we make about present praxis is already an interpretation and one shaped by the person's sociocultural context in place and time. In fact, we have no *human* experience if we do not interpret it. Our "knowing" any "action" is realized by our interpretation of it, and our interpretation is shaped by the socially constructed languages, perspectives, beliefs, and so on that we bring to "reality."[3] In the dynamics of shared praxis people reflect critically on the social/historical grounds of their interpretations in movement 2, but social influences are already present in movement 1 expressions. Thus, everyone's expression in movement 1 should be welcomed as an authentic interpretation, but they should not be treated as if they are "objective" or "value-free" reports of what is going on in present praxis. That is historically naive and works against dialogue and critical reflection in movement 2.

Third (and my first two points notwithstanding), a crucial requirement for movement 1 is that people make expressions that are truly their *own*. They are to speak their own word about present praxis and express what engagement with an aspect of it prompts in their own consciousness. Here the educator has a significant role to be catalyst of a hospitable environment in which participants can take the risk to share their own perception of present praxis rather than settling for what they intuit as expected by the group or by their social/ecclesial context. They are to have their own say rather than saying what they are supposed to say.

Fourth, movement 1 can invite an expression of praxis that is consciously motivated by religious faith or of human praxis in which the faith dimension is as yet prereflective. Again, even as I make this distinction (and resonant with my second point above), I recognize that in North America, at least, people's sociocultural reality and thus their praxis is significantly shaped by the symbols of the Jewish and Christian traditions. Hans-Georg Gadamer argues convincingly that we are always born "belonging to a tradition" that shapes our ontic identity, and this tradition is at least in part "religious."[4] We may presume to be naming only human praxis, but it is often shaped by religious symbols, and our interpretation of it likewise.

2. Rationale for Movement 1

Our reflections in chapter 5 on the theology of revelation that undergirds a turn to historical praxis in faith education also serves as theological rationale for movement 1. Likewise, the philosophical rationale for movement 1 is the position I argued in chapter 3 that the conative activities of participants as agent-subjects in place and time should be consciously engaged and shared in dialogue to originate a pedagogy for

wisdom in Christian faith. Indeed, originating such pedagogy by turning participants to their lives in the world is not a new insight; all the
great educational theorists of the modern era have argued for it.[5] In
our pedagogy, however, we educators have been slow to change old
didactic ways that reflect a "theory to practice" epistemology. This is at
least as true of religious educators as of any other kind. We have had
only limited success in designing pedagogies that honor and engage
people's own praxis and also honor and make accessible "the faith
handed on." Shared praxis is designed precisely to do both and to be
readily enacted in an educational event.

The rationale for movement 1 that I can make more explicit here
is why the process brings people *to express their own consciousness of present
praxis*. One can wonder if it would not be enough for the educator to
simply summarize for the group what she or he presumes their present
praxis to be. Or, more expedient still, could we not take it for granted
that participants are already well aware of present praxis of a theme
and proceed immediately to the third movement? Either style would be
more efficient in "covering the subject" (an unfortunate but telling
phrase in educational parlance).[6] Why then express present praxis in a
community of dialogue, a process that can seem "inefficient" to people
accustomed to nonparticipative pedagogies? On this question too, some
philosophical rationale was intimated in my claims that dialogue is essential to promote conation (chapter 2, section 2). We can add to this
now in the context of movement 1 of shared praxis.

To begin with, to symbolically express ourselves and our historical
reality is constitutive of us as agent-subjects-in-relationship. Our use of
language and symbols both arises from and shapes our consciousness,
identity, and agency. In a conative pedagogy, then, participants' self-
expression is essential to their "being" and becoming agent-subjects-in-
relationship. Freire argues that "the learners must assume from the
beginning the role of agent subjects"; this requires that the pedagogy
honor "the radical, human need for expression."[7] Without such
representation of their consciousness to others, people have no sense
of their own "word" and remain caught in a world of "silence."[8] By
contrast, when this need is honored in an educational community of
dialogue, that testing context can save self-expression from subjectivism and individualism. As this is true in the general context of life,
so too it is true in matters and communities of faith. People's identity
and agency in faith are greatly enhanced when they express to others
their existential encounters with God's self-disclosure in their lives.
Without this they are more likely to be "dependent objects" than
"agent-subjects" of their faith. Likewise, we need to share and test our
representation of our historical consciousness and to have it further
enlightened in a faith community if it is to be a reliable source of God's
self-disclosure and if our faith is to be a communal one.

Second, expressing an interpretation of present praxis and placing
it in dialogue with other people's expressions is essential for responsible

freedom and social transformation. Naming reality for ourselves rather than accepting it as already named for us can be a firststep to reshaping it. Here again, I echo Freire's insight that "speaking one's word" in dialogue is intrinsically related to "transforming reality."[9] Participants in every struggle for emancipation and social transformation are empowered by naming reality as they see it and testing their expressions in a community of dialogue; from this, the critical consciousness needed for emancipatory action is likely to emerge. In the context of Christian faith education, it seems that bringing people to their own expressions of present praxis in dialogue with one another is integral to realizing the purpose of God's reign.

My deepest conviction about participants' expressing present praxis in movement 1 arises from my own teaching experience and from others' use of this approach over the years. I have often been amazed by what Reuel Howe called the "miracle-working power of dialogue"[10] in this first movement as people expressed their own consciousness of present praxis. In such naming together, participants can experience a sense of surprise and discovery, as what may have been taken as self-evident or obvious is brought to expression and "the obvious" is recognized as significant. Such "epiphanies" also lend impetus to the critical reflection of movement 2.

3. Procedures for Movement 1

Enabling people to express their consciousness of present praxis and typically around a generative theme, like any of the movements, can be done in myriad different ways. The "action" brought to expression here can be any intentional human activity or any aspect of what constitutes the participants' "life-world" in their social historical context. Likewise, and as noted, people's consciousness of present action may come to expression as their sentiments, attitudes, feelings, or intuitions toward a life theme; the operative values, meaning, and beliefs they see in its present action; their descriptions, perceptions, and assessments of it; their commitments and values regarding it—that is, whatever comes into consciousness from what one is "doing" or from what is "being done" historically regarding some generative theme. Similarly, the modes of expression here can be any form we have—vocal, literal, physical, aesthetic—of expressing our own "being" and consciousness of historical reality. As long as the activity elicits from participants their own "naming" of an aspect of present praxis and typically around a common generative theme for the learning occasion, it is appropriate to the purpose of movement 1.

The most obvious mode, of course, is the written or spoken word. People can share a descriptive or interpretive report, respond to a question or questionnaire, give an analogy,[11] make an association of ideas,[12] and so on. Given my proclivity for words, I most often employ the verbal in my own teaching. However, educators more creative and artistic than I regularly employ mime, movement, drawing, dance, play drama (especially with young children), painting, making of a symbol, and other modes of expression in movement 1. A large group of church leaders reflecting on the theme of church leadership used symbol making, for example. After an initial focusing statement, participants moved into small working groups with an array of construction materials. Their assignment was to construct a symbol that represented their own experience of and participation in church leadership in their present ecclesial context. As each small group presented its symbol, the whole group first named what it saw, and then its architects described what they intended by it. This expressive exercise engaged a good deal of identification and recognition from all participants and created some level of common consciousness of how they perceived present praxis of leadership in their church.[13]

Typically the educator renders the service of posing the questioning activities of movement 1. However, I have participated in events where having engaged in a focusing activity, people originated their own praxislike questions about the theme. As participants become accustomed to this approach, they should be encouraged to put questions to one another as appropriate to each movement, in the style of a good conversation.

I have learned, often from mistakes, two guidelines for the group "sharing" moments of this approach. I present them here to guide the procedures of movement 1, but they are relevant to movements 2, 4, and 5 as well. (1) Insofar as at all feasible, everyone should have an opportunity to speak their own word or share their expression of present praxis with at least one other person, if they so choose. (2) Activities should never be structured in a way that forces anyone to share anything they are not ready to share.

1. How and to what extent the first guideline is honored clearly depends on the size of the group and the allotted meeting time. In small gatherings everyone may have opportunity to share with the whole group, but movement 1 may require subdividing larger communities into smaller working groups of three or four or even pairs for everyone to have an opportunity to share with someone. This guideline does not mean, however, that everyone must share on every occasion and at all movements—even when group size and time permit. In continuing groups that grow together as teaching/learning communities, a few thorough expressions may reflect the present praxis of participants well enough to allow them to proceed to movement 2.

2. Educators must avoid all coercive tactics, any that force people to speak or make them uncomfortable if they do not. For example, it is important, even in small gatherings, not to "go around the circle." When larger gatherings are invited into small groups for dialogue, the educator can emphasize to participants that they should feel free not to join a group (and continue reflecting on their own movement 1 ex-

pression instead) or that they may join a group and simply listen to other participants. On some personally sensitive themes, and especially with older children and adolescents, there may be relatively little sharing in the general group at movement 1 or 2. In these instances, some form of journal writing can be effective in encouraging people to their own expression and to critical reflection. Although little of this writing may be shared in the group, the dialogue has begun, at least with oneself, and it may eventually be shared with a trusted friend, teacher, or parent.[14] Also, we should not presume that the more reticent members are not participating; they may well be actively engaged in the dialogue as they listen to other people's expressions. The educator's challenge is to be a catalyst for a hospitable environment that respects the participative and learning style of each person.

4. Developing the Art of Facilitating Movement 1

Whatever aspects of present praxis are invited to expression, whatever modes of expression are encouraged, and however the group sharing is enabled, participants typically encounter a generative theme or symbol in movement 1 as a "question," in the sense of an issue of life import; they engage it as agent-subjects in dialogue with one another. Not only do they attend to this "question" in movement 1 but it permeates the entire process as the dynamic of conation unfolds through critical reflection and community understanding to appropriation and decision. To facilitate movement 1, then (and indeed movements 2, 4, and 5), the educator needs to be ever developing the requisite art of (a) formulating appropriate questioning activities and (b) facilitating the process of group sharing and listening.

Appropriate Questioning Activities. As participants grow accustomed to a shared praxis approach and become a teaching/learning community together, the various movement questions and questioning activities may be increasingly generated by the group itself, especially with older participants. As such a community emerges, the initiating role of the educator appropriately recedes. It seems "false liberalism," however, to expect this of every occasion and with all participants (e.g., young children). Typically, educators render the service of seeing to it that appropriate questioning activities are generated for each movement; even in groups well acquainted with the process they usually retain primary responsibility for enabling the dynamic of shared praxis to unfold. The first movement asks a shift of consciousness of educators, especially those new to such an approach, away from a self-image as "answer person" to "question poser." In preparing to teach, educators have typically been socialized to first think in terms of "what will I say?" Teachers are never robbed of their own word in shared Christian praxis, and they see to it that a Christian Story/Vision is made accessible in movement 3. However, in preparing to facilitate the dynamics of a shared praxis event, the educator's first concern is, What will I ask? and, How will I ask it? One can learn the art of constructing and presenting appropriate questioning activities throughout the process only by trial—sometimes error—and always by reflecting on one's efforts, knowing that perfection is seldom possible and rarely necessary. What follows may aid self-reflection on one's art of posing questions.

Crucial to constructing questioning activities appropriate to the dynamics of shared praxis is to *keep consciously in mind the specific intent of each movement.* Applying this principle to movement 1 here, the educator must remember that movement 1 is to elicit from participants an expression of their own consciousness of an aspect of present praxis. As educators construct movement 1 questioning activities, they should ask, Will this activity enable people to discern and express their own consciousness of present praxis, personal and/or social, and typically around a shared and generative theme for the learning occasion? In Lonerganian terms, the questioning activity in movement 1 should bring people to intentionally and consciously *attend* to an aspect of present praxis, to recognize and test their perceptions of it, to choose what to express of their perceptions, and how to express it. In less technical terms, movement 1 should help participants to see and share what they really think is going on—inside and out—about a life issue. The following steps may help the educator (or the team, if working in partnership) in formulating appropriate questioning activities for movement 1, and especially, as is typically the case, when a common generative theme has emerged from the focusing activity.

1. Be clear yourself on the generative focus and the aspect of present praxis that participants have already engaged through the focusing activity.
2. Imagine what might be appropriately elicited from this community in response to this generative theme or symbol, remembering that the hope is to elicit people's *own* expression. "Think praxis" is helpful in formulating movement 1 questions (likewise in movement 5).[15]
3. Use open-ended questions rather than questions likely to bring a yes or no response (e.g., "Describe what you do about *x*," rather than "Does *x* make you feel uncomfortable?").
4. Imagine a questioning activity and mode of expression that would be effective in eliciting *your own* consciousness of present praxis.
5. Try out the procedure first on yourself; notice what it elicits and how effectively it brings you to express some aspect of present praxis. When it is effective for you, it is likely to be likewise for the group.
6. Now, with a sense of what needs to be elicited and a mode that has been effective for yourself, construct the questioning

activity, adapting it as necessary to the age level, context, time constraints, and so on of this event.

7. Carefully avoid invasion of participants' privacy. There is a qualitative difference between "personal" and "private" questioning activities; it is possible to bring people to their own personal expressions of present praxis without violating their privacy.

8. Later, reflect on how effective the activity seemed to be and why. Critical reflection on one's efforts develops the art of posing appropriate and effective questioning activities.

Promoting Sharing and Listening. Ideally, the whole community is responsible for the dynamics of movement 1 as a dialogical activity; this can be increasingly realized as members become comfortable with the process and one another. Again, however, the educator renders the service of being a catalyst of community conversation. Beyond encouraging trust and hospitality, and maintaining the group's attention on its generative theme (chapter 5), I have found the following counsels helpful to enable dialogue in movement 1.

1. In every context, the educator is to proceed with the kind of gentle inviting to expression that clearly manifests to participants that their own word about present praxis is not only welcome but essential to the curriculum of this teaching/learning event. Among well-established groups this may well be taken for granted, and the educator's facilitating role at movement 1 can be minimal. I have also worked, however, with groups of adults who had previously been socialized into what Freire calls "a culture of silence," that is, to believe that their own word is of no value, and that they wait upon the teaching of an authority. In these situations too, the educator can proceed on course, with patience if the initial level of participation is less than desired, but without losing confidence in people's ability and eventual readiness to speak their own word. This too is Freire's counsel. He discovered in his work with uneducated peasants in northeastern Brazil that people socialized into a "culture of silence," when given opportunity to express themselves and believe the invitation is authentic, do so with relish. And Freire's point notwithstanding, the educator should also remember that there are always aspects of our lives that we truly know but may not be able to name or express. Mystery always remains in life, and often brings us to the limits of what we can name, even while we know it well as what Polanyi calls "personal knowledge."

2. It is often appropriate for the educator to pose probing questions during movement 1 dialogue to prompt people to more complete expressions of present praxis. As the trust level increases, participants often begin to ask probing questions of one another. Such probing, however, must be done with great sensitivity and only to enable clarity and completeness of expression; it should never sound like interrogation.

3. As full participants in any event, educators may well model the intent of movement 1 by bringing their own consciousness of present praxis to expression—when they discern that this facilitates the dialogue of the group. I nuance this counsel precisely because often there are situations, with young children especially, in which if the educator lays out a strong expression of present praxis in movement 1, participants tend to repeat what she or he said. This danger recedes, however, as people grow accustomed to the process and to trusting the educator.

4. Whether teachers "talk" at the first movement depends upon the context, the group, and other factors, but there is never a situation in which they are not to listen. The educator's authentic presence in the community and investing of the self in the process should be reflected by an active and empathetic listening, a "leaning toward others"[16] that hears not only what they express explicitly but also what they say "between the lines." Educators must be sensitive to the feelings involved, to the risks being taken, and to the broader sociocultural context of participants. Such loving and empathetic listening helps to establish the kind of communicative competence intended by the dynamics of a shared praxis approach.

5. In facilitating this and all subsequent movements, the educator can encourage the dialogical dimension by seeing to it that there are times of silence. This is often difficult for educators and participants alike; we have been socialized to presume that nothing is being learned unless someone is talking. In fact, silent periods may be the most effective times for dialogue with oneself and with what others have already shared.

6. Beginning here and throughout all the movements, a shared praxis approach to Christian religious education asks educators to invest themselves as agent-subjects in the teaching/learning dynamic. A detached, nonengaged stance as a technician of the process is neither authentic to the approach nor likely to be effective. Given its wisdom intent, it asks an investment of the "self," that educators allow the generative theme to engage the core of their own "being." Writing of authentic education, Buber explains, "Only in his [sic] whole being, in all his spontaneity can the educator truly affect the whole being of his pupil. For educating characters you do not need a moral genius, but you do need a man [sic] who is fully alive and able to communicate himself to his fellow beings." Buber adds that such educating "demands presence, responsibility; it demands you."[17] Sound advice!

Appendix

1. In movement 1 activity with fifth-graders focused on the theme "Reminders of God's Presence," the children were invited to do as follows: "Try writing a four-line poem in which every line tells about something that reminds you of God's presence. Do not worry about rhyming your

poem." After some writing time, those who wished were invited to share their poems with the group and to explain how they respond to their everyday signs of God's presence. The exercise seemed to be fun, creative, and also effective in bringing the children to express their own sense of God's presence in their lives and how they respond.[18]

2. An instance that exemplifies the variety of dimensions of one's praxis that can be elicited in movement 1 was a unit with high school students entitled "The Church's Mission of Service." The focusing activity turned participants to look at "the social conditions in our country." Then, movement 1 invited written responses, later to be shared if participants so desired in groups of two or three, to a series of praxislike questions or statements. A sample follows:

a. When I hear about people who are out of work I think . . .
b. When I hear about people who are on welfare I think . . .
c. When I see stories about the homeless on television I feel . . .
d. When people talk to me about racism, I want to say . . .
e. When someone says that sexism is rampant in both church and society, I know . . .
f. I think that old people are . . .
g. If someone were to ask me to help out in a soup kitchen I would respond . . . [19]

3. I take the third instance from a program that uses a shared praxis approach to teach improved farming methods in a Third World situation. I have never experienced this program firsthand but have heard reliable reports of it. I cite it also as a reminder that shared praxis can be used for other than faith education.

When the farmers of an area have assembled in a group, for focusing activity the educator often simply presents for view a set of immediately recognizable symbols for these participants of their farming. After some identifying of what the symbols mean for them, it is clear that the theme is their farming praxis and that everyone is welcome to participate in a conversation about it. Then, movement 1 invites the group to begin describing, as accurately as it can, how it farms in this village—a kind of general brainstorming. By all accounts, there is reluctance at first and an attitude of "but we all know what we do here." As the naming process continues, there is growing discovery and some amazement as they recognize how they *do* farm. Having "objectified" their farming praxis, they then move on (movement 2) to reflect critically on why they farm this way, what influences their farming methods, how effective they are, who benefits and who suffers as a consequence, and so on.

Chapter 7

Movement 2: Critical Reflection on Present Action

Movement 2 encourages "critical reflection" by participants on what was expressed as "present action" in movement 1. Critical reflection can engage people in any or all the activities of critical and social reasoning, analytical and social remembering, creative and social imagining. The intent is to deepen the reflective moment and bring participants to a critical consciousness of present praxis: its reasons, interests, assumptions, prejudices, and ideologies (reason); its socio-historical and biographical sources (memory); its intended, likely, and preferred consequences (imagination).

Movement 2 enables participants to come to a critical appropriation of present praxis in their "place" and "time" and, metaphorically, to share in dialogue their own "stories" and "visions."

1. Nature and Purpose of Movement 2

To portray the nature and purpose of movement 2, it may first help to correlate its dynamics with the corresponding activities in a conative process (chapter 3, esp. section 2). As evident from the two previous chapters, the focusing activity and movement 1 of shared praxis reflect and honor, approximately, the first activity and dynamic of a conative pedagogy (chapter 3, section 1). In other words, they encourage participants to intentionally attend to and express the consciousness that arises from their own conative activities as agent-subjects regarding the generative theme of the learning occasion. I say approximately because movement 1, in addition to eliciting one's personally originated praxis as an agent-subject, often invites participants to name the present action of their social context regarding the focused theme. However, it is always participants' *personal* consciousness of present praxis (their own, or society's, or both) that is brought to expression in movement 1. Now, reflecting the succeeding dynamics of conation, movement 2 engages and enables participants to reflect critically on their whole "place" and begins to honor their whole "time." (This is completed in movement 3, which makes accessible Story/Vision from the faith community *over time*.) In Lonergan's terms, the "dynamic intent" of movement 2 is "self-conscious understanding," but I prefer "critical consciousness," that is, the consciousness that emerges from peoples' critical reflection on present praxis to understand and imagine how this praxis is shaped by and can reshape their location in place and time. I have found three perspectives on movement 2 activity that help to clarify its nature and purpose with a view to effecting it in a pedagogical event.

First, movement 2 is *critical reflection* by participants on the present action expressed in movement 1. Lest it be lost sight of in the detailed analysis below, this is the most essential activity of movement 2: *critical reflection on present action that is shared in dialogue*. It represents a deepening of the reflective moment in this praxis-based pedagogy. Second, it is helpful to recognize that movement 2 activity is a critical and creative hermeneutic of present praxis, an activity of discerning what to affirm, what to refuse, and what needs transforming in one's historical "reality." Third, the dialogue of movement 2, flowing out of movement 1, can be portrayed metaphorically as participants' sharing their own "stories" and "visions"; that is, they express the truth of their own lives as perceived from their location in place and time.

1. Critical Reflection. The intent of critical reflection is to encourage participants in critical consciousness and appropriation of present praxis, to promote a dialectic among them and their location in place and time. Critical and historical consciousness emerges as participants un-cover and dis-cover together the personal/social sources of and reasons for present praxis and discern its consequences. People's ability for critical reflection emerges gradually and likely corresponds to the stages of the various aspects of human development as delineated by Piaget and others. It can begin, and thus should be nurtured, at least with the first signs of concrete operational thinking, that is, at about five or six years of age.[1]

The most complete expression of critical reflection in movement 2 has participants engage in critical and social reasoning, analytical and social remembering, creative and social imagining of both their own and society's praxis regarding a generative theme.

Critical and social reasoning enables participants to uncover the reasons for present praxis and how it is influenced by their context in place and time, to scrutinize the interests, assumptions, prejudices,[2] and ideologies[3] that it embodies and the pre-understandings they bring to interpret it. *Analytical and social remembering* prompts participants to a critical analysis of the sociohistorical and biographical sources of present praxis and the historical influences that shape how they name it. *Creative and social imagining* enables participants to see the intended and likely consequences of present praxis for both self and society and empowers them to imagine and make ethical choices for praxis that is personally and socially transforming. Together these activities of movement 2 amount to people reflecting critically on the context of their praxis and the praxis of their context. I note three further features of the critical reflection of movement 2.

First, the consciousness it encourages is a new level of theoretical understanding, but it is not "theoretical" in the ideational and disinterested (theoria) sense. Instead, because it arises from reflection on what is "being done," such historical consciousness is marked by *practical* intent; critical reflection on present action has the impetus, enlivened by imagination (poiesis), of further praxis. Second, the critical reflection of movement 2 prevents the activity of movement 1 from falling prey to a naive empiricism or positivism in that it intends to uncover the historical and structural conditions of present praxis and the sociology of one's own interpretation of it. On the other hand, its critical reflection also rejects the ahistorical and disembodied cognitivism of Descartes, and indeed of Enlightenment metaphysics, precisely because it reflects on one's own historical being and what is "being done," and even on how this reflection is shaped by one's social situation. As such, movement 2 deepens (i.e., beyond movement 1) people's mental activities of reasoning, remembering, and imagining in both their critical and socially attentive dimensions. But because present praxis is the focus of attention, participants' corporeal and volitional capacities continue to be engaged as substantial to the reflection. Thus, rather than an activity of "the mind alone," the critical reflection of movement 2 engages the whole "being" of participants as agent-subjects in time and place.

Third, critical reflection on present praxis is constituted by an emancipatory interest in that it intends to "decode" the historical reality that our location in place and time mediates to us "coded" (Freire). Rather than accepting uncritically what first appears to be as what "is" and "ought" to be, critical reflection can uncover the personal and social biases, ideologies, and so on in present praxis and in our own naming of it. As a process of what Freire calls "unveiling reality,"[4] critical reflection enables participants to remember the historical/social sources of present praxis that might otherwise be forgotten, to dis-cover its "reasons," interests, assumptions, and so on that might otherwise go unnoticed, and to imagine new possibilities beyond the "inevitable" outcomes of present praxis. As a constitutive activity of shared Christian praxis, critical reflection encourages "disbelief" as well as belief, "disbelief" especially toward the controlling myths, both inside and outside us, that maintain structures of domination—sexism, racism,

economism, consumerism, age bias, militarism, and so on.[5] Critical reflection on present action *can be* a source of both personal and social
emancipation.[6]

2. Critical/Creative Hermeneutics. We can also characterize the
critical reflection of movement 2 as a critical and creative hermeneutics
of present praxis. It i *hermeneutical* in that people interpret and explain
to themselves and one another the meaning and value of some aspect
of what they are "doing" or what is "being done" in their context; it
is *critical* in that they attempt to see what to affirm, question, or refuse
in present praxis; it is *creative* in that they envision the historical possibilities and ethic of a new praxis. I noted (chapter 6) that
movement 1 is already an interpretation of present action; it expresses
the consciousness that arises from participants' own and their society's
action regarding a generative theme. It is as if present action is the
"text" for interpretation in movement 1; then movement 2 deepens the
critical dimension of the hermeneutics by encouraging participants to
reflect on the "context" of the "text," that is, on the social location of
present praxis in place and time. The dynamic of movement 2
encourages participants to see how their historical situation shapes
present praxis (personal and social), shapes their own interpretation of
it; and it helps them to imagine how they should refashion it.

Movement 2 hermeneutics may be thought of as having two foci: (a)
present praxis of a generative theme or symbol and (b) each participant's understanding of the dialogue going on within the event itself.
(a) As participants engage critical reflection to interpret an aspect of
present praxis, they find actions of personal and/or social praxis they
can affirm as life-giving; they often find aspects to question or reject as
problematic or destructive; and they will imagine ways to create a new
praxis that is more humanizing for themselves, others, and their social
situation. (b) A hermeneutics goes on in movement 2 (and indeed
throughout the whole process) by each individual participant toward
the group dialogue. This happens as each participant listens to and
interprets the emerging conversation and consciousness of the group
regarding present praxis. In any group dialogue, people experience
their own interpretations shifting and clarifying as they listen to others.
The dialogue of movement 2 encourages each participant and the community to discern in dialogue what is true in their interpretations of
present praxis, what is false or inaccurate, and what needs to be added
to both one's own and to the group's interpretation.

Movement 2, like all hermeneutics, needs criteria to guide its accuracy and adequacy of interpretation. People's interpretations of present praxis cannot be left "up for grabs." In the dynamics of a shared
praxis event, the educator typically renders the service of seeing to it
that community dialogue is tested by appropriate criteria. Before proposing such criteria, there are two points to keep in mind about an
event of shared *Christian* praxis. First, there may be already operative in

second movement activity, at least implicitly, criteria suggested by a Christian faith perspective; they are often raised by participants in the dynamic of movement 2 dialogue (e.g., someone saying, "That doesn't seem very Christian to me"). In chapter 8 I pose the "reign of God" as the metacriterion for interpreting Christian Story/Vision in movement 3, to guide the dialectical hermeneutics of movement 4 (chapter 9), and the decision making of movement 5 (chapter 10). In movement 2, however, the educator at least can be conscious of God's reign as an ultimate criterion of interpretation and allow it, if only implicitly, to shape the questioning activities she or he proposes. Second, an existential guideline of discernment is always operative in the dialogue of the learning community itself. As participants approximate a situation of "communicative competence," their dialogue provides a corporate means of testing, affirming, and correcting their hermeneutics of present praxis. This testing dynamic of the group, however, itself needs criteria by which each participant and the group as a whole can evaluate its interpretation of present praxis. Here I draw upon the criteria David Tracy has developed for "interpreting common human experience."[7]

Tracy's first criterion is "meaningfulness," and by it he intends that an interpretation be "genuinely disclosive of our authentic lived experience."[8] Thus "true" interpretation of present praxis should enable participants to make meaning out of their lives, to see "the sense" of them, and (I would add) to see the consequences of present praxis as well. Second, an interpretation should have "meaning as internal coherence."[9] This means that it should fit into an overall and coherent perspective on life, that it be "appropriate" within the system of rationality people bring to present praxis. And third, an interpretation should be "true" in that it is credible to what one already "knows" from life. For Tracy, this means testing an interpretation for its "adequacy to experience"—people should recognize it as "true to life" and a likely source of further truth.[10] Here, I refer to my holistic understanding of truth (chapter 3, section 5); to be true to one's "own truth," an interpretation of praxis should be conceptually, relationally, and morally "adequate" for one's life in the world.

In less technical terms, a critical interpretation of present praxis should (a) help people see the meaning and consequences of their lives and of their present social reality, (b) make sense in that it "hangs together" with coherence, and (c) "ring true" to people and enable them to live their truth in the world. Although the testing dynamic of group dialogue stimulates these criteria, the educator renders the service of encouraging participants, in one way or another, to ask in movement 2, Are we coming to see the meaning and consequences of present praxis? Do our interpretations "sound logical" to us? Do they "ring true" to our lives and empower us and others in life-giving ways?

   3. *Sharing by Participants of Their "Stories" and "Visions."*   This is a third perspective for viewing the nature and purpose of movement 2

activity. As participants reflect critically on present praxis, interpret it, and test their interpretations, what they speak arises from their own "being" in place and time. As an aid to facilitating the process, we can characterize this dialogue as people's own "stories" and "visions."

This third perspective brings into focus the dialogical aspect of movement 2 activity, and it is not necessary to dwell further here on a rationale for it. As people need to express their present praxis (movement 1), likewise they need to share in dialogue their critical reflection on it. If the teacher alone does the critical reflection and hermeneutics of praxis in movement 2, even very insightfully, it is not as likely to shape people's commitments as it is when they do it themselves in conversation. What can be amplified here about the dialogue of movement 2 is (a) its quality, (b) its purpose, and (c) its substance.

A. The dialogue of movement 2 should have the quality of Buber's I/Thou relationship. As in movement 1, but more urgently in this moment of critical reflection, participants' listening and sharing is to reflect and promote a presence and openness to one another as "subjects" in partnership. The aim is to approximate Habermas's ideal of communicative competence: that interaction be marked by mutual respect for one another; be free from domination or manipulation; have no compulsion to agreement or consensus other than the persuasiveness of a particular perspective as it is tested by the discernment of the teaching/learning community.

B. The purpose of movement 2 dialogue is to prompt participants to critical consciousness of their lives and world. Movement 2 certainly entails a testing of interpretations; it is not a false liberalism or "niceness" in which everyone passively accepts everyone else's reflection as if it were a final word. However, it is more a dialogue than a debate as participants express and hear reflections on present praxis not for polemical or strategic success (Habermas) but with the common purpose of gaining critical consciousness of it.

C. The "substance" of the dialogue in movement 2, that is, what participants bring into public discourse, is their own honest perceptions and interpretations of present praxis. When movement 2 unfolds as intended, its discourse is not to repeat dehistoricized ideas or metaphysical concepts that participants have heard elsewhere and may use to make points here. Instead, the dialogue expresses the existential truth they are coming to appropriate from critical reflection on historical praxis and their discernment of the responsibilities they have for future praxis. It seems appropriate then to identify the substance of this dialogue as participants' own *stories* and *visions*. Here, too, I use these terms metaphorically; they do not mean a purely anecdotal or "story-telling" pattern of discourse (more appropriate, on occasion, in movement 1). Movement 2 discourse is more critical and analytical than anecdotal; it expresses participants' critical reflection and tested interpretations of present praxis. On the other hand, to achieve the intent of movement 2, the educator may do well to structure its questioning activities to elicit a narrative practical response (instead of simply asking why in a conceptual mode, e.g., asking, What do you think has brought you to that value, or action, or perspective, or hope?).

To summarize its nature and purpose, critical reflection on and critical and creative hermeneutics of present praxis of a generative theme or symbol, shared in dialogue as participants' "stories" and "visions," are central features of the same movement 2 activity. It intends to bring participants to critical consciousness of present praxis in that they recognize the personal and social origins of it and reasons for it, envision how it might or ought to be refashioned, and test their discernment in a community of dialogue.

2. Rationale for Movement 2

I offered a philosophical rationale for this movement 2 activity in chapter 3 (esp. section 2): that pedagogy for conation in Christian faith must enable people to reflect critically and in dialogue on their lives in place and time, and thus promote a dialectic between participants and their social/historical context. Here, however, and focusing on the critical reflection of movement 2 of shared Christian praxis, I add first a religious education reason and then a more theological one. To appreciate why a specific rationale is even needed for critical reflection as constitutive of a process of faith education, I situate my comments against the backdrop of some current attitudes evident among some ecclesial leaders and some theorists of religious education, albeit held for different reasons.

Some ecclesial authorities are at best indifferent and at worst antagonistic toward any kind of critical reflection in Christian faith education. The indifferent attitude asks, in one way or another, Why bother?—Why bother people with critical reflection and consciousness-raising in their faith life? Surely no more is needed than to catechize, primarily children, in the beliefs and morals of a particular tradition, in "facts" that are already well established as "the faith handed down." Critical reflection *may* be appropriate for theologians and Scripture scholars, but "ordinary" people certainly do not need it. Let the specialists or church authorities establish the beliefs, meanings, and morals of the tradition that teachers are to deliver "faithfully" (i.e., unquestioningly) to people. The overtly antagonistic version of this attitude (usually a biblical or doctrinal fundamentalism) sees critical reflection at worst as a lack of faith and at best as a threat to people's faith identity.

Both indifference and antagonism to critical reflection in faith education can be expressions of elitism or knowledge control. They may also be mixed with the vested interest of maintaining power over people's lives and of seeing "ordinary" Christians more as "dependent objects" than "agent-subjects" of their faith. Developmentally, to exclude critical reflection tends to arrest people at stage three of their faith journey (the stage at which they rely on whatever "authorities" say). Ironically, the antagonistic view reflects a lack of faith in both people and the tradition, as if people's reflection were prone to error and "the faith" could not "hold" under analysis.

Some scholars of religious education not only distinguish but separate "a schooling/instructional" paradigm from a "community of faith/enculturation" paradigm.[11] They posit further that the schooling paradigm (often called "religious education") is to be "good" education; as such, it should entail critical reflection. Rossiter calls this "an intellectual study" that leads to "knowledge and understanding of religion";[12] Moran refers to it as "academic instruction in religion" that helps people "to understand religion."[13] In the "faith formation in community" paradigm, however (often called catechesis or Christian education by Catholics and Protestants respectively), critical reflection does not have (Moran) and should not have (Rossiter) a central place. Moran describes this second paradigm as "teaching people to be religious in a particular way" and recognizes that schools can have a role in this; Rossiter, however, calls for "a creative divorce" between the two paradigms.[14]

Undoubtedly, these paradigms as distinguished have phenomenological warrant; they reflect a typical "division of labor." The socialization paradigm gives little place to the role of critical thinking in faith formation. Its theorists often recognize the need for it but offer little suggestion for critically reflective education to encourage a dialectic between the person and his or her faith community or between the faith community and its social context. But rather than settling for this division of labor or arguing in its favor, I believe there is urgent need to challenge it.

In *Christian religious education*[15] a separation of "education" from "formation" is false and debilitating to its purposes (see chapter 1) and intent of conation or wisdom; wherever Christian religious education takes place—school, congregation, or family—it is to engage the very "being" of participants as agent-subjects and include an activity of critical reflection as I describe for movement 2 of shared praxis. To do otherwise is to settle for a narrowly cognitivist epistemology that separates "knowing" from "being" instead of honoring an epistemic ontology as the foundation for education in Christian faith.

Of the faith enculturation paradigm, I refer to the positions argued in chapter 3, section 2: that the inevitable dialectic between individual and context, and between a faith community and its social situation, is not sufficient of itself to encourage the maturation in faith of participants, the reformation of the faith community, and the transformation of society. We cannot presume that our faith communities or our society are places of critical consciousness; as history gives witness, the former have often been accomplices with the latter in "thoughtless injustices."[16] The nurture essential to "being" and becoming in Christian faith, needs—and by intention—a critical "thoughtfulness," because rigorous intellectual probing is also constitutive of formation in faith identity and agency. Every nurturing context needs a dynamic of critical reflection that helps raise people's consciousness to "see" their reality as it is and especially to see the poor, oppressed, and excluded, to recognize why things are the way they are, who is benefiting and who is suffering, and to imagine what people of Christian faith can and should do as agents of God's reign in the world. A "thoughtful" dynamic can be intentionally promoted in all aspects of the church's ministry—in its preaching, counseling, worshiping, and so on (see Part III). Likewise, Christian-identified families, partnerships, and small communities can be intentional about critically questioning their lives and world from the perspective of Christian Story/Vision.

Regarding the schooling/instructional paradigm, although its faith-nurturing dynamic differs in style from what happens in congregation or family, nevertheless significant nurture goes on in schools. By their very environment and ethos, schools inevitably "nurture" people, so, to expand and echo Bushnell's point about families, in Christian schools (parochial schools, Sunday schools, etc.), let the nurture be Christian and intentionally so.[17] Nor can we presume that school-based Christian religious education inevitably entails a critically reflective and consciousness-raising dynamic. Giroux makes a compelling argument that schools are typically "sites of socio-cultural reproduction" that states use to maintain ideological control rather than to promote critical consciousness and social transformation.[18] As much could probably be said of church-sponsored schools.

The shared praxis approach, whether used in school, parish, or family for Christian faith education, is capable, I believe, of both nurture and critical education.[19] It nurtures through its communal dynamics of participation, partnership, and dialogue and through its conative dynamic that begins and ends with people's praxis. Its critically reflective aspect is evident in the critical and dialectical hermeneutics of Story/Vision (movements 3 and 4) and the decision making of movement 5, but it begins and is the central activity here in movement 2. I can now draw together the rationale for movement 2: its critical reflection is warranted (a) for good education and (b) to heighten through critique and dialogue the revelatory potential of present praxis.

Good education. Christian religious education should be good education.[20] Good education has a humanizing import in people's lives that informs and forms them in how to think critically, act responsibly, and create imaginatively.[21] John Dewey is often cited glibly as claiming that experience is educational. But Dewey, to my knowledge, never said precisely that. He did say that experience *can* be educational *if*—if we "reconstruct" it—which, for Dewey, means question it, ask why of it, imagine and test its consequences, and so on, that is, reflect critically on it.[22] Education should promote the reconstruction of experience by engaging critical intelligence and so nurture "the formation of careful, alert, and thorough habits of thinking."[23] Religious education, whether in school or community, must intentionally promote activities of critical reflection if it is to be good education.

Beyond forming "thorough habits of thinking" (Dewey) critical reflection on present praxis is integral to forming people's moral character. The life of virtue is embodied in chosen and responsible historical praxis. Echoing Aristotle's time-honored insight (chapter 2, note 34), moral formation requires reflection on and in practice (praxis), or, again, the kind of practical reflection that Hannah Arendt aptly called "thoughtfulness."[24] Movement 2 of shared praxis is an instance of the thoughtfulness that can form people, over time, in the character and habit of orthopraxis. Its reflection on action and coming to decision (movement 5) in dialogue with others and with Christian Story/Vision helps participants avoid both subjectivism and relativism in moral decision making.

Ethical formation clearly requires critical reasoning and analytical remembering but highlights the importance of creative imagination in movement 2, and indeed throughout the whole process of shared praxis. Educators, both general and religious, have neglected people's capacity for imagination in their pedagogies.[25] One place (I note others later) to redress this neglect is in the area of moral formation.[26]

Imagination is rooted in history and begins with present reality—it is not mere fantasy. Nevertheless, it has a creative capacity that brings people to perceive what can be and should be, to fashion new possibilities beyond the "givens" of life; in this way it fuels our moral impetus to do what should be done and to create things as they ought to be. Kathleen Fischer writes, "The imagination not only shows us a possible future; it evokes the energies needed to participate in the coming of that future." And again, "We are beginning to recognize that the deepest sources of our moral behavior are found in the life of the imagination."[27] Our imaginations can be a source of prophecy, of new life that has not been before. Ricoeur says that "the imagination is, par excellence, the instituting and constituting of what is humanly possible; in imagining possibilities, human beings act as prophets of their own existence."[28] Its prophetic impetus and capacity to evoke ethical response makes imagination, here the creative and social imagination of movement 2, significant in moral formation. Critical reflection, then, with a special emphasis on its imaginative activity, is a crucial ally in educating people to think critically and to act responsibly, and so it is essential to educating people in Christian faith.

Heightened revelatory potential. The second and more theological reason for the critical reflection of movement 2 is to enhance the revelatory possibilities of present praxis. As noted, turning to an aspect of present praxis in the focusing activity and expressing it in movement 1 reflects the conviction that God is disclosing Godself and will in people's existential lives and that we are agent-subjects in such "everyday" revelation. Here, apropos movement 2, I add that the revelatory potential of present praxis is enhanced by people's critical reflection upon it to discern what is and what is not of God's will, and it is heightened further when they share their reflections in a community of dialogue.[29] My claim here is that the more deeply we move into a truly critical consciousness of our lives in the world, the more likely we are to uncover God's revelation therein of how we are to live as a people of God. Both critical reflection and a community of dialogue heighten the revelatory potential of present praxis; I say a word about both.

As Dewey insisted that experience needs reconstruction to be truly educational (see note 22), so too the revelatory potential of people's historical praxis is heightened if they reflect critically on it. The deeper our levels of reasoning, remembering, and imagining, the more likely we are to uncover the transcendent that is imminent in our lives, the "beyond" present in the everyday. Critical and social reasoning can enable people to uncover their historical reality as it is, to see its sin and grace, to recognize God's presence and how God's will is or is not being done. Through analytical and social remembering, people can recognize the pattern of God's self-disclosure in their own biographies and in the history of their people and can perceive the "salvation history" of which their lives are a part. But of the three activities of critical reflection, again, creative and social imagination is most crucial to uncovering the revelatory potential of present praxis.

There is growing consensus among theologians that revelation is mediated to human consciousness through symbols, through what Dulles calls "symbolic communication." He explains: "According to this approach, revelation never occurs in a purely interior experience or an unmediated encounter with God. It is always mediated through symbol—that is to say, through an externally perceived sign that works mysteriously on the human consciousness so as to suggest more than it can clearly describe or define. Revelatory symbols are those which express and mediate God's self-communication."[30]

But if revelation is symbolically mediated, whether in a normative way through the primordial symbols of the faith tradition or in an existential way through the events and realities of everyday life, we recognize that revelation comes to meet us first in our imaginations; we reach through the ordinary to the "extraordinary" present in it by the impetus and power of imagination. Mary Warnock writes, "It is the function of imagination to see more in an object than meets the regular eye of sense . . . that there is something more, that there is never an end, is the sense generated . . . by imagination."[31] In a similar vein, Kathleen Fischer describes imagination as "the bridge which joins God and the earth . . . the human power that opens us to possibility and promise."[32] Through imagination we are most likely to first encounter, recognize, and respond to God's revelation in our lives. "It is on the level of the imagination that we first encounter the divine in this world, for revelation is always given through the material; it is always symbolic, pointing to the ultimate through the finite. It is also on the level of the imagination that we formulate our initial response to the encounter with the divine; faith finds expressions first as myth and ritual, sacrament, symbol, image and story."[33] George Bernard Shaw has the following dialogue in his play *Saint Joan:*

> JOAN: I hear voices telling me what to do. They come from God.
> ROBERT: They come from your imagination.
> JOAN: Of course. That is how the messages of God come to us.[34]

The dialogical dimension of movement 2, and indeed of the whole shared praxis approach, heightens the revelatory potential of present praxis. This reflects the Jewish and Christian convictions that God's word is always for a people, and its interpretation is best discerned and tested in the midst of a community of faith. Christians believe that Jesus' promise to send "the Paraclete, to be with you always, the Spirit of truth" (see John 14:16) has been fulfilled. They're convinced that God's Spirit now enlivens the Body of Christ, making the community of Jesus' disciples "the temple of God" in which "the Spirit of God dwells" (see 1 Cor. 3:16). The Spirit works in the midst of and through the community, especially to guide its discernment of God's revelation for people's lives. From a Trinitarian perspective, the Spirit functions in "the between"—between God the Creator and Jesus the Liberator, between God and humankind, and between ourselves and others. Buber was convinced that the "truth" is discovered in "the between" of an I/Thou relationship. Likewise, God's Spirit of truth is especially operative through the dialogue and communal discernment "between" participants intended in a process like shared praxis.

3. Procedures for Movement 2

To facilitate movement 2 the educator needs to (1) be keenly aware of its nature and purpose, and (2) know how to construct questions and questioning activities that engage critical reason, memory, and imagination toward present praxis. I already described the nature and purpose of movement 2 activity, and chapter 3, section 2, offered a more philosophical description of the three activities of critical reflection. My concern in this section is specifically pedagogical. It elaborates how *critical and social reasoning, analytical and social remembering,* and *creative and social imagining* can be engaged in an existential event to reflect critically on present praxis and to bring participants' critical interpretations into dialogue. These three activities coalesce as the critical reflection of movement 2, yet the educator needs to be clear about the functions of each and know how to construct questions and questioning activities of reasoning, remembering, and imagining as appropriate to different events.

A. Critical and Social Reasoning

I described *reasoning* in chapter 3 as arising from our personal conatus to question and interpret our world, to make sense out of it and meaning within it. I described *critical social reasoning*, first, as the effort to reason critically (according to developmental readiness) about our own initiated praxis with attention to the social context that shapes both our personal praxis and our thinking about it and, second, as social analysis of the praxis going on in society. In other words, we can recognize two emphases in critical social reasoning: (1) an introspective activity that engages our own subjective consciousness to attend to the content and context of our reasoning about present praxis and (2) an outward-looking activity by which critical reason questions the social structures and cultural ethos that cause present praxis to be as it is. Both aspects, of course, overlap and existentially are seldom separated. For identification, I call the first *critical personal reasoning*, and the second *critical reasoning as social analysis*.

1. Critical Personal Reasoning. For clarity and completeness of description, this activity can also be distinguished into two interdependent aspects: (a) questioning present praxis with the discerning dynamic of one's own rationality and (b) uncovering the sociology of one's own act of thinking about present praxis. Less technically, critical personal reasoning means looking at whatever is going on and asking oneself, Why are things this way, and why do *I* see them as I do? The first dimension moves beyond the thinking of movement 1 (which essentially asked, What is our present praxis?) and invites participants to logically analyze through their own rational capacity as agent-subjects *how* and *why* things are the way they are. This aspect of personal reasoning in movement 2 employs the conceptual functions of the mind to come to understanding (echoes of Kant) about present praxis. It can be intuitive to comprehend self-evident truths; it can be inductive to analyze evidence to come to comprehension; or it can be deductive to reason logically from principles to conclusions.

We engage the second aspect of critical *personal* reasoning—thinking about one's own thinking—when we ask why we see and understand things the way we do, and we question the adequacy of our understanding of present praxis. In Lonergan's terms, this emphasis of critical thinking attends to, reasons about, judges, and decides concerning one's attempts at understanding present praxis. It already entails some social analysis—albeit of our own understanding—in that it intends to uncover the socially influenced assumptions, ideologies, interests, and so on that shape how we understand and comprehend present praxis. This second emphasis of critical personal reasoning attempts to uncover what we are bringing to our reasoning activity from our own situation in the world and how that influences our understanding of present praxis.

By way of procedure, I note first that the communal dialogue of movement 2 helps to prompt participants in both aspects of critical personal reasoning. But educators can encourage both emphases through a great variety of reflective activities. Essentially they ask, in one way or another, What do you think are the reasons for present praxis, and why do you think you think that? For example, in an eighth-grade event focused on justice as right relationship, movement 1 invited participants to describe three present relationships in their lives, one with a family member, one with a friend, and one with someone they considered "different" from themselves. Movement 2 activity was built around two sets of questions: Why do you think your relationships are the way they are? What is influencing you to describe them as you do?

2. Critical Reasoning as Social Analysis. With this emphasis, participants bring critical reasoning to the social realm of present praxis; they discern its social agency and the contextual influences, ideologies, interests, and assumptions (i.e., "reasons") that shape it. Here critical reason functions as an aspect of social analysis. In social analysis, people think systemically about present praxis and how it is shaped by the interrelated "systems" of a whole sociocultural reality. Holland and Henriot write, "Social analysis is simply an extension of the principle of discernment, moving from the personal realm to the social realm."[35] Through social analysis, participants can become critically aware of the context of present praxis and comprehend the social whole of which present praxis, one's own or one's society's, is a part. Essentially one asks, What are the social structures and the cultural ethos that shape present praxis of this theme or symbol to be as it is?

Holland and Henriot describe social analysis as people "seeing the wider picture"[36] by analyzing four aspects of their sociocultural context: "(1) the *historical* dimensions of a situation; (2) its *structural* elements; (3) the various *divisions* of society; and (4) the multiple *levels* of the issues involved."[37] I situate the historical emphasis of social analysis (1) under social remembering below. In analyzing the structures of their society (2), participants can look, for example, at its economic design (labor, ownership, production, exchange) or at its political order (structures of government, military, police, judiciary, church, education, family, etc.). Cultural divisions (3) call for analysis of social stratification and arrangements based on money, sex, race, age, ethnicity, religion, and so on and the ideologies that legitimate these divisions. People can analyze their sociocultural reality at any or all levels (4) on which the praxis of a particular generative theme is operative—local, regional, international, or cosmic.[38] As an emphasis I add to this schema that by social analysis in movement 2 of shared praxis, people are to uncover the social interests, ideologies, and assumptions that undergird present praxis, that is, the operative social "reasons" for it being as it is.

Procedurally, the educator should remember that this social aspect of critical reasoning is not a disinterested or value-free activity; it has the emancipatory interest of promoting "right relationship" and historical responsibility by participants in their own social agency and in the agency of society.[39] Honoring that interest, however, need not diminish the rigor and thoroughness of the systematic analysis. The educator and participants can draw insights, as appropriate, from the various critical social sciences—anthropology, sociology, psychology, political science, and so on.[40] Even something as simple as quoting relevant social statistics can help to deepen people's level of social analysis in movement 2 (e.g., with seventh grade: "Homelessness has increased 100 percent in the United States between 1983 and 1988. What do you think are some of the causes of this increase?") Critical reasoning about society is also deepened by the dynamic of communal dialogue as participants bring to awareness their analysis of social structures and cultural arrangements. And the social criticalness of people's reflections is heightened if they participate in resisting forms of social oppression or cultural domination.

Social analysis may at first appear complex and daunting for both educators and participants. If it is constantly neglected, however, critical reflection can readily become a narrow psychological analysis of ourselves or others that tends to "blame the victims" in society. When Christians neglect social analysis, they fail to take seriously the social structures of both sin and grace. People can submit any aspect of present praxis to social reasoning through questions or questioning activities along the following lines:

· How is this aspect of present praxis shaped by the social structures and systems within which it takes place?
· What cultural divisions, values, and attitudes, what ideologies, interests, and assumptions impinge upon and shape this present praxis?
· Who exercises the power that most influences present praxis to be as it is?
· To whose benefit and to whose loss is the power employed?[41]

Not all these questions are posed on any one occasion. Whether to emphasize critical personal reasoning or social analysis or to engage people in both, what questions to pose and how to pose them, depends on the theme, time available, readiness of the group, and so on. A form of social analysis can begin with young children as long as its questioning activities are directed to concrete issues—to honor their concrete operational thinking. For example, in a lesson with third-graders in which movement 3 was a catechesis on the Great Commandment, movement 2 was introduced by suggesting, Let us try to think of all the things in our families, school, neighborhood, and even in our country that make it difficult for us to really love others and to truly love ourselves. They entered into what for third-graders was a significant level of social analysis.

B. Analytical and Social Remembering

When people direct analytical and social remembering to present praxis, they can uncover the influences over time that engender one's own praxis and the historical influences that have shaped the praxis of society. Analytical and social remembering also has two emphases: one directed by participants toward their own biography and how it shapes their personally initiated praxis, the other to the history of their sociocultural context and how it shapes their society's present praxis of the theme. For identification, I call the first aspect *analytical remembering of one's biography,* and the second *analytical remembering as social archaeology.*

1. Analytical Remembering of One's Biography. For participants' own praxis, analytical memory is their personal anamnesis by which they recall and analyze its sources in their biographies over time. Through analytical remembering, we attempt to recognize the constitutive sources of our "being" that are "written in our life" (*bios graphia*). By analytical remembering about a particular aspect of present praxis, as here in movement 2, we attempt to uncover and recognize how our personal story is shaping both our own praxis and our interpretation of our society's praxis. Analytical memory, then, is "remembering where we're coming from" as we reflect on present praxis, personal and/or social.

This aspect of analytical and social memory is directed to people's own biographies, but we can recognize both an inward and an outward movement to it. It looks inward, insofar as possible and appropriate in a pedagogical event, to uncover the patterns of agency embedded in participants' own psyches. As analytical memory looks to one's own psyche, however, it must also begin to look through it and outward to the sociocultural influences that have shaped one's psyche and agency over time. We can identify this outward-looking aspect of analytical memory as "re-membering," in the sense that it brings to mind one's various "memberships" (class, race, nationality, gender, sexual orientation, age, etc.) and how they and their ideologies have shaped one's present agency. Such "re-membering" clearly overlaps with critical and social reasoning, but its focus is to recognize how one's memberships over time shape one's own present praxis. In keeping with the fundamental thesis of psychoanalysis, the conviction is that such remembering by the self of the self, in its personal and social origins, can be a source of new life for oneself as agent-subject. It also reflects, here for the individual person, the biblical conviction that "remembering" brings healing and salvation, whereas "forgetting" causes alienation and bondage.

Procedurally, for personal analytical remembering, the educator fashions questioning activities that prompt participants to uncover the personally owned and socially formed aspects of their "being" that shape their praxis and their interpretations of society's praxis of the theme. In one way or another, and as appropriate to the occasion, the educator poses the question, How have our own biographies shaped our present praxis of this generative theme or symbol and our perspective on what is "going on" around us?

The depth to which an educator encourages such analysis needs to be carefully discerned and monitored. Educators must take account of the group, the context, the occasion, the theme, the time available, their capacity to facilitate and the capacity of the group to support such analytical remembering. I've participated in an adult group where the trust level grew to allow an amazing level of depth in our personal analytical remembering. A favorite and effective movement 2 question in that group was, What aspects of our own biographies are shaping our present praxis and perspectives on this theme? Participants seemed to have an instinctive sense of what was "personal" and yet appropriate in the group, and what was "private" and more appropriate for a one-on-one counseling context. With young children I have often facilitated this personal memory aspect of movement 2 by asking them to tell a story about something that might be behind their present praxis of the theme. Undergraduate male students who had expressed stout resistance to anything like a feminist consciousness in movement 1, were assigned to write a paper on the theme, What influence does my own maleness and what my background has taught me about male and female social roles have on my present attitude toward feminist consciousness? A similar questioning activity could have been posed if the issue were racism, age bias, or some similar topic.

2. *Analytical Memory as Social Archaeology.* This is the role of memory in social analysis. In social analysis of present praxis, critical reasoning and analytical remembering constantly function in concert; for clarity and effective pedagogy, however, we can distinguish critical reasoning as attending to the contemporary structural context and ideological ethos that shapes present praxis, whereas analytical memory focuses on the history of that context and ethos over time. Using the distinctions of chapter 3, reason attends more to "place" and memory more to "time." Holland and Henriot make a similar distinction: "The social system needs to be analyzed in terms of time—historical analysis—and space—structural analysis."[42] When people analytically remember the "time" of their "place," they perform a social archaeology in that they can uncover the layers of sedimented social history that are impinging on present praxis. In social analysis participants engage such remembering to uncover the history behind "the wider picture."

Critical social remembering can help dispel reification of present praxis in that it uncovers its historical genesis, not out of curiosity or nostalgia, but with a practical and emancipatory interest.[43] Conversely, without such remembering, present praxis can take on an aura of inevitability, appear unchangeable, thus robbing participants of their sense of historical agency.

As people uncover the social history of present praxis, an emancipatory interest also prompts them to search out the "dangerous memories" embedded in the communal narrative behind this present praxis. These life-giving memories are "dangerous" (popularized by Metz) in that they subvert rather than legitimate oppressive and unjust aspects of present praxis. A powerful source is the remembrance of suffering. Walter Benjamin contends that emancipatory praxis in the present is "nourished by the image of enslaved ancestors rather than that of liberated grandchildren."[44] A second source of dangerous memory is recalling the "pockets of resistance," the prophetic voices and struggles for freedom in the communal history of present praxis.[45] Kearney argues that "the project of freedom can easily degenerate into empty utopianism unless guided in some manner by the retrieval of past struggles for liberation."[46] Butkus summarizes: "Dangerous memory refers to the remembrance of suffering and injustice and to the remembrance of freedom as it takes shape in commitment to and action for justice."[47]

Procedurally, educators facilitate analytical remembering as social archaeology, by posing, as appropriate, questioning activities that ask, What are the historical influences, traditions, customs, behind society's praxis of this theme? They might also ask, What in our shared past could encourage us to change present praxis? Again, however, the format of these questioning activities, and the depth and thoroughness of their social archaeology, varies a great deal according to the particular occasion—participants, time, theme, and so forth. It is often enhanced by historical research. For example, in a learning unit with graduate students on misogyny in the church, and particularly in religious education and pastoral ministry, we spent significant time on the social/ecclesial history of patriarchy and the suffering it has caused. Examples were raised of women in history who were models of resistance to sexism and struggled to make the church a discipleship of equals as envisaged in the praxis of the historical Jesus (this is also an instance of movements 2 and 3 overlapping; I take up variations and combinations of the movements in chapter 10). Younger participants can also be prompted to do social archaeology of present praxis by the story of a person who is a "dangerous memory." In an event with seventh-graders on the social values of Jesus, with a special emphasis on his respect for people, the focusing activity raised up the theme of racism. In movement 1 participants described the instances of racism that they experience and see in their own lives and society. Movement 2 began with a social remembering of some of the historical roots of racism in America and then retold the story of Harriet Tubman and her work with the underground railroad. Her story helped participants uncover some of the suffering caused by racism in America and gave them a significant model of resistance to it.[48]

C. Creative and Social Imagining

In concert with critical reason and memory, the educator engages participants in creative and social imagining about present praxis in movement 2.[49] By creative and social imagination participants can see the consequences, possibilities, and responsibilities of present praxis, personal and social, and how it can or should be reformed for the well-"being" of all. Again, then, as with reason and memory, we can distinguish for analysis a personal and a social aspect to the imaginative activity of movement 2. For identification, I call them *creative imagination for the person* and *creative imagination toward society*.

1. Creative Imagination for the Person. Imagination contributes to our self-understanding and, beyond this, suggests responsibilities and possibilities that engage our wills and creativity for the well-being of ourselves and others. In self-understanding, imagination functions most obviously in concert with memory; together they enable us to weave our lives into a narrative pattern, to "know" the "stories" that give us identity over time and into the future. On the "far side" of self-understanding, and when it is focused on present praxis, creative imagination helps people to envision what is not yet but can be or should be; it brings into focus the hopes and ethical responsibilities people have for their future. It enables us to see the "visions" that arise from our "stories." In this, imagination is the creative catalyst that recombines old images and constructs new ones to pose expanded horizons and responsibilities for reshaping present praxis toward an open and life-giving future. As this will-o'-the-wisp functions on the borderlands between body, mind, and will, between past, present, and future, imagination gathers people's stories and engages their affectivity and wills to encourage historical commitment.

Procedurally, the educator's task is to invite participants to imagine the consequences of their praxis and to envision how an aspect of present praxis can be or should be reshaped to promote the well-"being" of all. To this end, I often ask questions that begin, What do you imagine . . . ? What if . . . ? How can we . . . ? What will be . . . ? What are the likely . . . ? What should you . . . ? Whatever stimulates participants to think about the consequences—likely, preferred, or demanded—of their own agency in the world is appropriate to the personal function of imagination in movement 2. The group dialogue here helps people to test their "visions" as they share them and hear the visions of others. The educator, however, can see to it that the community does not lapse into passive acceptance of anyone's "visions" and gently bring participants to scrutinize how humanizing they are for self and others.

2. Creative Imagination Toward Society. Creative imagination toward the praxis of society as focused around a generative theme or symbol (and one's own participation in that praxis) enables participants to recognize its likely consequences, to imagine what can be or ought to be refashioned in social praxis, and to envision how to act in solidarity with others as agents of social transformation. Such imagining is focused on present reality, yet is most eminently the ethical and utopian impetus of movement 2 critical reflection. This impetus is heightened after movement 3 proposes the Vision of God's reign regarding the generative theme. Even in movement 2, however, social imagination should encourage what Freire calls "an announcing of new possibilities that pose a utopian challenge for all."[50]

Procedurally, the educator can encourage social imagination toward present praxis by questioning activities that invite participants to reflect along the following lines: "Looking at our description of what is happening in society regarding (whatever is expressed in movement 1), what are its consequences? What can or ought to be changed? How can we act together to change it?" As these questions suggest, creative and social imagining is integral to social analysis of present praxis. However, when participants do not directly experience the sometimes unjust and destructive consequences of present social praxis, it is important to promote not only analysis but empathy for those who do; in this, imagination can play a crucial role. Personal imagining with a social aspect to it can encourage such empathy. For example, in an event with eighth-graders on the fourth commandment, the second movement posed a social analysis of how American society typically treats retired persons. The movement opened with some reasoning and remembering activities; then it engaged imagination as follows: "Imagine that you are sixty-five and retired. You are told that your Social Security should be enough to take care of you. How will you feel? Will you have enough to live on? How do you imagine others will feel about you? What will be your greatest fears? What can you contribute to the happiness of others?"[51]

Theorists who describe the dynamics of imagination emphasize that it cannot be hurried, that we need "pause" and some "distance" from an issue or question to allow our own images to emerge.[52] The educator should be mindful of this in movement 2 and remember that imagination continues to be engaged throughout movements 3, 4, and 5 of a shared praxis event. To conclude on procedures for critical reflection in movement 2, I reiterate three points. They have important procedural implications, and given the dissecting above, they could be missed.

First, the activities of reasoning, remembering, and imagining constantly overlap and coalesce as a unified process of critical reflection. Reasoning requires images that are resourced by memory; remembering requires ideas and images to interpret and appropriate memory's resources; imagination is tested by reason and dips into the "well" of memory for its "materials." Likewise, there is constant overlapping within each one between personal and social. All the various dimensions coalesce as critical reflection on and creative hermeneutics of an aspect of present praxis that uncovers what to affirm and cherish, what to question or refuse, and what can be or should be refashioned for the good of all and all creation.

Although recognizing the symbiosis of reason, memory, and imagination, my second point is that in any one event of shared praxis it is neither advisable nor even possible for an educator to devise questioning strategies to engage all three activities and their various personal and social emphases. My outline above is only to indicate the depth and variety of questioning activities that promote critical reflection. Typically the educator is responsible for discerning what aspects of critical reflection seem most appropriate to engage regarding present praxis of a theme. This discernment considers the time available, the size and readiness of the group, their ages and backgrounds, the need for variety in ongoing learning communities, and every other aspect of the occasion. The educator may place emphasis on critical reason, or on analytical memory, or on creative imagination—personal or social—or some combination. Without making rigid distinctions, events focused on ethical themes (e.g., justice) more obviously call for social analysis in movement 2 than events in which movement 3 is concerned with a doctrinal symbol, for example, the Blessed Trinity. The key for educators is not so much to remember all the possible options and combinations, but to have a "felt sense" of the kind of critical reflection to encourage at movement 2. Then in an existential event they will be able to choose and pose questions and questioning activities from the array of possibilities that are appropriate and effective for the particular occasion.

My third point concerns the recurring question of "readiness" (see chapter 1, note 27, and note 1 of this chapter), clearly an issue for whether and how to structure the reflective and hermeneutical activities of movement 2. Here, I believe religious educators need be attentive to both *kairos* and *chronos* time. *Kairos* time means discerning if this is "the right time" to pose a particular questioning activity, depending on such factors as the trust level in a group, people's emotional openness to the issue, the groundwork already done, even people's physical alertness and the time of day (Augustine advised teachers to introduce nothing new in the afternoon!). For *chronological* timing, religious educators can draw upon the research of developmental psychologists, as long as it is taken more as descriptive than prescriptive. Teachers can encourage children moving into concrete operational thinking (five to seven years old) in incipient forms of critical reflection as long as they pose questioning activities in concrete terms about children's own life praxis. For example, with kindergarten children on forgiveness, movement 2 activities were built around the following questions:

· Tell about a time when you felt hurt by someone. How did you feel? (memory)
· Why do we sometimes need to say, "I'm sorry," to other people? (reason)

· Imagine how people feel when we hurt them. Imagine how they feel when we say, "I'm sorry." (imagination)[53]

4. Developing the Art of Facilitating Movement 2

To facilitate movement 2 activity, it is imperative to keep in mind its nature and purpose: to bring participants to critical reflection and interpretation of present praxis relating to a generative theme or symbol and to share their discernment in dialogue. As the trust level deepens and familiarity with a shared praxis approach grows in a teaching/ learning community, participants share more readily in facilitating movement 2. Typically, however, and especially with younger participants, the educator renders the service of creating the questioning activities. Many of the counsels I offered for the focusing activity and movement 1 are relevant for movement 2 as well:

· Promote an environment that respects and welcomes the contributions of all participants.
· Maintain the reflection of the group on present praxis, typically around a common focus.
· Invite people's *own* reflections.
· Encourage group dialogue and discernment to test the remembering, reasoning, and imagining of all.
· Provide opportunity for all to speak, according to style of participation, but never force anyone in particular to expression.
· Try out any envisioned questioning activities on oneself first and note how effective and appropriate they are.
· Ask probing questions, without sounding like an interrogator or violating people's privacy.
· Model the intent of movement 2 if it is likely to promote critical reflection and dialogue.
· Adapt the questioning activities to the age level, situation, time available, and other factors.
· Maintain a presence of active and empathetic listening.
· Allow time for silent reflection.
· Be willing to invest one's "self" in the teaching/learning dynamic.

Movement 2, however, poses its own particular task of facilitation; I have found the following counsels helpful.

1. Be realistic about the challenge of critical reflection for all of us, and realize that many people are unaccustomed to a reflection/action pedagogy in faith education. Critical reflection, as Dewey warned of "reconstruction," can be "painful." Ira Shor, a notable proponent of "critical teaching," points out that our society is "crowded with interferences to critical thought" and "submerged in a host of cultural mystifications."[54] Critical reflection does not occur inevitably; nor can we

presume that the institutional sponsors of Christian religious education, whether in parish or school setting, want such reflection to take place. On the other hand, I have found that through the dynamics of shared praxis and as participants become an educational community, even people unaccustomed to it can achieve a significant depth of critical reflection. Groups new to such a process often begin with what seems like superficial or anecdotal participation in movement 2. A moment typically emerges, however, when some person's contribution moves the group dialogue more deeply into critical reflection. Educators are to proceed, then, conscious of the challenge but equally confident that in a supportive environment and with appropriate questioning strategies, the "shared" dynamics of the group will become a catalyst of critical reflection.

2. The best questioning activities for movement 2 are open-ended ones that signal to participants that there are no "right answers" the teacher is waiting to hear. People guessing at what an educator has already decided is the antithesis of movement 2 of shared praxis. This doesn't mean that the educator pretends to be without opinion on the questions posed. It requires that he or she pose questions that are genuine questions to be struggled with and be truly open to surprises and new insights from the dialogue that ensues.

3. The questioning activities of movement 2 should not give participants the impression that they must defend their expressions shared in movement 1. To this end, I have found it helpful, when possible, to fashion questioning activities that elicit from participants a practical narrative response, to express their reflections in the pattern of their own "stories" and "visions." For example, movement 2 activities can be prefaced with introductions that say, in one way or another, "Let us try to explain to ourselves how we have come to hold such positions (or do such things . . .); let us be aware of who or what has influenced us, then try to imagine the likely consequences and whether or not we are happy with them." Inviting people to explain their consciousness of present praxis *to themselves* lets them know that they are not defending their own or their society's praxis but explaining its causes and consequences. There is a subtle but significant shift between asking why of someone's expression of present praxis (disposing them to defend it) and asking, "Why do *you* think you do (feel, think, etc.) as you do?" A form of this questioning can be posed with any age level.

4. Movement 2 is never an exercise in dispassionate analysis. As people share "stories" and "visions," they entail both joys and sorrows, fears and hopes. Remember that people's whole "being" is invested in what they express as their critical reflection on present praxis; it is impossible to recognize and share one's own story and vision dispassionately. When painful reflections are expressed, I have found that groups with a sense of identity and solidarity can usually provide a supportive community. The educator, however, has a special responsibility in this regard and may need to be available for support outside

the immediate event. When something painful or personal emerges that does not seem appropriate for group attention, it may be wisest to say something like, "Can you and I talk about this afterward?" and then move the dialogue back to its curriculum focus. Afterward, the educator will discern whether the issue simply needs the support of a friend or is a serious psychological problem that requires professional help. (See chapter 14.)

5. Educators need to remember that their style of facilitating movement 2 is never "value free." The questions we pose are not neutral, nor are the analytical tools and insights we may employ from the social sciences. Writing of social analysis, Holland and Henriot note, "We always choose an analysis that is implicitly linked to some ideological tradition. The claim to have no ideology is itself an ideological position!"[55] Be aware, then, of the values and principles of selectivity in the questions we pose. It is also advisable, especially with older participants, to make one's "ideology" self-evident to the group.

6. There is a prophetic dimension to movement 2 activity. Whenever we invite ourselves and others to uncover the origins, "reasons," and consequences of present praxis, and to become aware of the "tinted lenses" through which we interpret it, we are being prophetic. Prophecy, of course, often requires courage and risk taking and confronts the educator as much as other participants. Here again, the educator has responsibility to be a prophetic presence in the community, to encourage and be open to the prophetic gifts of all participants.

7. Problems with the level of dialogue—for example, lack of participation by some or dominance by a few—may, with good effect, be put to the group as a "problem to be solved." This heightens the sense of communal responsibility for facilitating the event and can be a catalyst for bringing more reticent participants into the conversation.

8. Often there is overlap and overflow between movements 1 and 2. As "movement" implies, shared praxis is not a lockstep but free-flowing process. There are events when movement 2 kinds of questions are best raised in immediate response to movement 1 expressions and, conversely, when movement 2 reflections prompt a recasting of what was expressed in movement 1. With larger groups it can be advisable for the whole community to work together at movement 1 in some form of "brainstorming," move into small groups for the in-depth analysis of movement 2, and conclude with comments from the small groups to build the whole community consciousness. Conversely, the first movement can be done in small working groups, and then movement 2 questions posed as the naming of movement 1 is shared in the whole community, and so on. I cite these variations (and add to them at the end of chapter 10) to make the point that the task is to honor the "intent" of any one of the movements rather than its "mechanics."

I conclude this chapter with reflection on the transition from movement 2 to movement 3. That the opening movements bring to expression, either explicitly or implicitly (identifiably religious language may not have been used yet), an aspect of God's existential self-disclosure in participants' lives is a primary conviction of the shared Christian praxis approach. Its overarching dynamic also reflects the assumption that critical reflection on praxis gives participants recognized and tested stories and visions with which to approach Christian Story/Vision as made accessible in movement 3. In chapter 9 I elaborate on the point that because both arise from God's self-disclosure through the existential realities of human history, there is a "family resemblance" between participants' stories/visions and the Story/Vision of the faith community; this readies participants to encounter Story/Vision in a way that they can "see it for themselves" and appropriate it with resonance to their own reality in movement 4. For example, people's own praxis with slavery and liberation, with suffering and new life, enable them to appropriate as their own the Story/Vision of Egypt and Exodus, of Cross and Resurrection.[56]

These convictions notwithstanding, educators need to facilitate the transition from the first two movements to movement 3; a kind of "linkage" needs to be made, especially with younger participants. A fourth-grader once told me about her Sunday school class: "First we do a lot of fun things. But then we have to sit down and talk about God and stuff like that." In shared praxis terms, the linkage between the opening movements and movement 3 was not being made in the little girl's class.

We can effect linkage in many ways, both at the end of movement 2 and at the beginning of movement 3. However, I have found activities involving imagination to be *the* most effective source of transition. (This lends some empirical weight to my earlier claim that in Aristotelian terms poiesis is the mediator between theoria and praxis.) This is especially effective when I use an imagination activity at the end of movement 2 to introduce explicitly religious language resonant with the catechesis of movement 3, if such is not already present. For example, in a fourth-grade event, when movement 3 was a catechesis on God's reign in Jesus, the opening movements focused on the children's perceptions of the present state of their world, how they feel about that and why they think things are the way they are. These activities employed no specifically religious language. However, movement 2 was completed with this activity: "Imagine that Jesus is sitting and talking to you. What do you think are some things that Jesus wants us to do to make our world a better place for everyone?"[57] Imagination made the linkage between the opening movements and movement 3—the praxis of Jesus for the reign of God.

Appendix

1. In an eighth-grade event with a catechesis in movement 3 on the fifth commandment, the opening activity focused on the sacredness of hu-

man life. Movement 1 invited the young people to express their attitudes about their own lives and the lives of others. Movement 2 was built around a combination of social reasoning and imagining. Because this lesson was published in the Coming to Faith religion series, I reproduce movement 2 here as it appears in the student text. The teacher's guide gives suggestions for enacting these questions as communal dialogue:

> Life can be threatened in many ways today. Some ways are obvious, such as physical violence and murder. Others are less obvious but equally destructive. Consider the following statistics:
>
> · A large percentage of high school seniors have experimented with marijuana and cocaine.
> · There are several million problem teenage drinkers in the United States
> · Every five seconds, a teen has a drug/alcohol-related accident.
> · Death rates have dropped in all categories in recent years except 15- to 24-year-olds, where it rose. The U.S. Surgeon General believes this rise is the result of accidents and suicides involving drugs and alcohol abuse.
>
> What do you think those statistics say about the typical attitude of American teenagers toward life? Discuss together why these statistics are so high.
>
> Statistics about television viewing can also be alarming. One analyst claims that by the time a person is eighteen, he or she will have seen 40,000 murders and over 100,000 acts of violence on television.
>
> What do you think that kind of violence in the media does to people's attitudes toward life? Do you recognize any influence it may have had on your own attitudes? Can you share them?
>
> Why do you think people find violence entertaining?
>
> Imagine that you are the chairperson of the respect life group in your school. List several topics for your next meeting. What will you propose as a line of action for each topic?[58]

Notice especially how social statistics are drawn upon to enhance the level of social analysis and imagining.

2. With graduate students in an event that focused on the context or influence of social "place" on religious education, we built movement 2 around the following questionnaire.

A Reflection on My Social Context

At 6 or 7 Years   Self-Identity Today

1) *Family Context*

Relationship with parents: Describe your worldview:

With siblings:

Dominant outlook on life: Value system:

Attitude toward you:

2) *Neighborhood Context*

Kind of house: Self-image:

Who were your friends?

Kind of neighborhood: What continuities do you
                                                       recognize over time?

3) *School Context*

Attitude of school toward you: What discontinuities?

You toward school:

4) *Church Context*   Sources of change?

Quality of parish life:

Dominant image of God:

5) *Cultural Context*

Ethnic background:

Proposed sex roles: What can you learn from your
                                                       own social formation for your
                                                       ministry today?

Racial attitudes:

6) *Class Context*

Economic bracket:

Attitude toward possessions:

7) *Political Context*

Liberal/conservative/radical:

The questionnaire was presented question by question with pauses after each in a guided reflection; people shared their responses according to readiness, first in small groups and then with the whole class. It was an interesting attempt to combine personal biography with social analysis and to bring participants to awareness of the origins of their self-identity and faith identity. It is also an example of the flexibility of the movements, in that participants responded to the questions on the left side of the page before the ones on the right; in a sense, they did movement 2 before movement 1.

3. The third instance is from an undergraduate theology course, specifically from its opening unit on theological anthropology. This unit, entitled "A Christian Understanding of Human Existence," was spaced over one month of a semester, with two and a half hours of meeting time each week. The focusing activity (part of which was reading and discussing a novel that focuses the anthropological question) and movement 1 prompted participants to an expression of "My everyday (i.e., operative) understanding of myself as a person." Movement 2 reviewed a variety of responses to the anthropological question from psychology, sociology, philosophy, anthropology, and literature. However, the constant questions throughout our review of this material were, Who or what has influenced our understanding of ourselves? Is it adequate to our own experience? What are its likely consequences? What do we want to change in how we understand ourselves and others?

Chapter 8

Movement 3: Making Accessible Christian Story and Vision

The third movement makes accessible[1] expressions of Christian Story and Vision as appropriate to the generative theme or symbol of the learning event. Its Story symbolizes the faith life of the Christian community over history and in the present, as expressed through scriptures, traditions, liturgies, and so forth. Its Vision reflects the promises and demands that arise from the Story to empower and mandate Christians to live now for the coming of God's reign for all creation.

1. Nature and Purpose of Movement 3

In the opening movements of shared Christian praxis participants express in dialogue their critical reflection on their own and/or society's present praxis relating to a generative theme or symbol. Metaphorically, they appropriate and share together their own stories and visions from an aspect of present praxis. Next, movement 3 makes accessible to participants a Story/Vision of their faith community as it pertains to (and often originally suggested) the focused theme. This Story/Vision symbolizes the Christian tradition of religious faith. As participants have critically interpreted the "text" and context of their lives, so the educator now brings critical hermeneutics to the texts and contexts of Christian Story/Vision, to make it accessible (movement 3) and to prompt participants to critically appropriate its meaning and truth to their lives (movement 4). Chapter 4 reviewed the suitability of Story and Vision as comprehensive metaphors of Christian faith and the narrative style of access they imply. Here they are general referents of the content and style of movement 3 of shared Christian praxis.

Christian Story is made accessible in movement 3 of shared *Christian* praxis as the primary symbolic mediation of God's revelation. Story is a metaphor of the historical roots and realization of Christian faith over time and in its present community—the church. The Christian Story reflects God's historical revelation through God's covenant encounter with humankind in the people of Israel, in Jesus the Christ, and in the community of Jesus' disciples since then. It is mediated and expressed in myriad forms: in scriptures, traditions, and liturgies; in creeds, dogmas, doctrines, and theologies; in sacraments and rituals, symbols, myths, gestures, and religious language patterns;[2] in spiritualities, values, laws, and expected life-styles; in songs and music, dance and drama;[3] in art, artifacts,[4] and architecture; in memories of holy people, sanctification of time and celebrations of holy times, and appreciation of holy places; in community structures and forms of governance, and so on.

Both *Christian* and *Story* can be ambiguous here; a word on each to clarify. First, *Story* often means something that someone "made up"—a nonhistorical fiction. Anderson cautions that using Story for Christian tradition should not diminish the conviction that "the God of the Bible is the God who acts historically, in real events and concrete circumstances"; we must avoid the impression "that the Bible is *only* story."[5] Clearly every Christian Story reflects human interpretation and creativity, but it is not just a made-up story. I use the metaphor precisely to signify that Christian faith originates from the events of God's self-disclosure in history. This is a "real" story in its origins, and its import has real meaning for people's lives in every time and place.

Second, by *Christian* here I only mean to signal whose "internal history" of religion is made accessible in explicitly Christian faith education. I do not intend to encourage what Macquarrie calls "the parochial prejudice that God has granted one and only one revelation of [God's] self."[6] Ironically, for Christians to so claim is to deny the universality of God's love, a central tenet of their faith; as Vatican II stated well, God's "providence . . . , manifestations of goodness and . . . saving designs extend to all people."[7] Even the specific Story of Christian faith includes a tradition that is, in a sense, "external" to it, in that Christians "inherit" from the Hebrew tradition but do not own it. They believe it is confirmed and reinterpreted by the Jesus event, but it is revelatory in its own right and reflects the divine-human covenant of the Jewish people that God has not revoked. Further, when people use shared praxis in another religious tradition (or traditions, as in Unitarian Universalism), they draw movement 3 from their particular resources. Even specifically Christian religious education often has contexts and themes in which movement 3 is enhanced by access to other religious traditions. Here Christians should recognize and appreciate, to quote Vatican II again, "the truth and grace" of other religions and approach them in a spirit of "dialogue and collaboration."[8] Nevertheless, in using shared praxis to educate people in Christian identity and agency, movement 3 makes accessible a *Christian* Story as the particular source of wisdom in faith and through which "the truth and grace" of other traditions can be appreciated.

Christian Vision is a metaphor of the promises and responsibilities that arise from the Story for the lives of people who claim it as their own. Every aspect and expression of Christian Story has various invitations and implications for how Christians live their lives. For instance, to say with faith that God is love is to commit oneself to be a loving person;[9] to say with faith that God forgives us is to recognize that we are to forgive others (see the Lord's Prayer). Similar examples could be given for every expression of Christian Story. Access to it shapes people's lives now and into the future. Vision, then, is a metaphor of the whole eschatological aspect of Christian faith—that it is to be done, to be realized, to be brought about. It is synonymous, both immediately and ultimately, with the symbol "reign of God."

Christian Vision, of course, does not provide a blueprint for life or easy answers to the problems and complexities people must face.[10] But it tenders truths by which to make meaning, ethical principles to guide decision making, and virtues to live by; it offers images of promise and hope to sustain people and of responsibility and possibility to empower historical agency towards God's reign. In the nature and purpose of movement 3 activity, Vision refers the educator's task to propose the historical import of Christian Story for the lives of participants. The educator is to raise up as Vision the promises and judgments of Christian faith, its gifts and responsibilities. The Vision should reflect God's promises of shalom and wholeness, yet empower people in their historical responsibility to work in partnership for the realization of what God wills—peace and justice, love and freedom, wholeness and fullness of life for all. Educators are to teach the Vision of Christian faith as something *immediate* and *historical,* in that it calls people to do God's will on earth now as if God's reign is at hand, and as something *new* and *ultimate,* in that it always calls people beyond their present horizons of praxis in faith until they finally rest in God.

2. Rationale for Movement 3

Every approach to *Christian* religious education must intentionally teach Christian Story/Vision; in fact, to offer a theological rationale for this seems redundant. To take on identity and agency appropriate to any faith community, individual members need to have access to and make their own the Story/Vision in relation to which the community as a whole finds identity and agency.[11] Chapter 3 offered a philosophical warrant for the activity of movement 3. In gist, a conative pedagogy reflects an epistemic ontology; as such, it engages the consciousness that arises from people's whole "being" in place and time (movements 1 and 2) *and* the wisdom and traditions of learning from their community over time (movement 3) and enables participants to hold these two sources of wisdom in a dialectical hermeneutics for appropriation (movement 4) and decision (movement 5). To forget the "wisdom of the ages" is a "forgetfulness of being." Or again, the old Aristotelian trichotimizing of "being" is transcended by a conative pedagogy because it engages praxis (movements 1 and 2) and theoria (movement 3) and places them in a creative relationship (poiesis) to promote renewed praxis. The theoria, however, is not ahistorical metaphysical ideas but practical wisdom from the Christian community over time. What we can develop here with benefit is the theology of revelation that undergirds the third movement.

Christian Story/Vision as Revelatory. The shared praxis approach has already been employed in Christian faith education by a variety of communities that span a broad spectrum of theological opinion. This "empirical" evidence indicates that various theologies of the revelatory content and form of Christian Story/Vision can undergird movement 3 activity while yet using the approach appropriately to its dynamics. Nevertheless, this breadth of possibility does not mean that the theology of revelation one brings to movement 3 is inconsequential, or that every perspective is equally appropriate for this kind of pedagogy. How religious educators perceive the revelatory potential of Christian Story/ Vision *should* influence *how* they make it accessible and *what* of it they make accessible. To honor the dynamics of shared Christian praxis requires at least a conviction that Christian Story/Vision is *a* symbolic mediation of God's revelation of Godself and will over time in the people of Israel, in Jesus, and through the Christian community since then, and that it has the potential to be revelatory in this time and place.

Further, its dynamics suggest that either an extremely fundamentalist or an extremely liberal attitude toward the community Story/ Vision is inappropriate for this kind of pedagogy. The former makes the opening movements superfluous and the closing ones impossible. If the ultraliberal perspective rejects the potential of Christian Story/ Vision to be a serious partner with historical praxis in discerning God's will for the present, then the educator would bypass movement 3; the process, however, would not then be shared *Christian* praxis. Thus, while I recognize the position I propose below reflects my own faith and its "mainline" Christian perspective, my intent is to pose one model of revelation that is appropriate to the dynamics of shared Christian praxis. To this end, I turn again to Dulles's scheme of the "models of revelation" and particularly to "revelation as doctrine" and "revelation as history." Dialogue with them, and with his preferred model of "symbolic mediation," helps me articulate what the theology of revelation undergirding movement 3 is and is not, as I propose it.

"Revelation as doctrine" or "the propositional theory" understands revelation as "divinely authoritative doctrine inerrantly proposed as God's word by the Bible or by official Church teaching";[12] it is a set of "clear propositional statements attributed to God as authoritative teacher."[13] For conservative evangelical Protestantism these statements are found in the Bible, which is literally true as God's own written word; for neo-scholastic Catholicism these propositions are also found in the doctrinal teachings of the Catholic church. For both, however, revelation is "an impersonal body of objective truths" that "transmits conceptual knowledge by means of words (or speech)."[14]

Clearly, this model of revelation is not appropriate to movement 3 of shared Christian praxis. As Dulles notes, it overlooks the historicity of God's self-disclosure, forgets "God's presence in one's own life and experience," excludes a "faith that probes and questions," and prevents dialogue with people of other faiths.[15] Revelation as doctrinal propositions views the Bible and Christian tradition as what Elisabeth Schüssler Fiorenza calls an "archetype" (as distinct from a prototype; see below); it "takes historically limited experiences and texts and posits them as universals, which then become authoritative and normative for all times and cultures."[16] To approach Christian Story/Vision as an archetypal "impersonal body of objective truths" would frustrate the dynamics of all the movements of shared praxis. Yet this model reflects two closely related truths that should not be lost, because of their typical overstatement, to the theology of revelation in movement 3, namely: (a) for Christians, their Story/Vision has a "normativity" in discerning God's revelation, and (b) among its many normative symbols, there are propositional truth claims (e.g., God is one; God is triune; the creed, etc.).

People can well resist the notion of its "normativity" if taken to mean that the Story/Vision is a reified and already determined "absolute" that cannot be interpreted according to its text and context, and ours. This is not what I intend. The hermeneutics of movement 3 must be informed by both the best of critical biblical and theological scholarship and by contemporary consciousness, and especially by what emerges from life-giving communities. By normativity I *do* mean that when approached with the kind of hermeneutical guidelines I propose below, the symbolic expressions of Christian Story/Vision are sources of *trustworthy guidance* for people in the present to discern together who their God is and how they are to live as a people of God. This trustworthy guidance is reflected in both the overarching hermeneutical perspective suggested by the Story/Vision and in its particular beliefs, meanings, values, and ethics.

Theologically the normativity of Christian Story/Vision reflects the trust that God has never allowed this faith community to go totally astray in what they express as God's self-disclosure in their history; that in fact they have been and are guided by God's inspiring Spirit in bringing it to symbolic expression. The basis of such "normativity," however, can also be stated philosophically because it reflects an aspect of existential human experience. Every identifiable "people" recognizes a community won and owned wisdom that has arisen out of their shared

life from generation to generation. They usually express this cumula
tive "wisdom of the ages" in symbolic forms (myths, law codes, etc.) to
render it accessible and "lively" for subsequent generations. Such symbols have a normativity for their particular people in that they propose
and help them hold together a common form of life with shared patterns of meaning, attitudes, and values. David Tracy explains that classics are symbols that "disclose permanent possibilities of meaning and
truth"; because they reflect time-tested wisdom, they can disclose "compelling truths" in different contexts and thus have "some kind of normative status."[17] Existentially, Christian Story/Vision functions as a
"classic" for the faith life of Christian communities.

Of its propositional truth claims, I recognize that the Story/Vision
of Christian faith is expressed through many symbolic forms besides
propositions. Further, the ones it proposes are shaped, and sometimes
distorted, for the present by the contexts and language in which they
first emerged; their "truth" for this time and place must be ever re-
dis-covered. Yet its propositional truth claims are substantive expressions of Christian tradition and serve as "benchmarks" of a Christian
community's identity and expression of God's revelation in history. One
cannot reject the substance of the Nicene Creed (its language *is* in need
of reform) or propose as revelatory that "God is hatred" and also claim
Christian identity. Christian religious education, here in movement 3 of
shared praxis, must teach the propositional truth claims that are constitutive of its Story/Vision, not as hardened facts from outside to be
blindly accepted, but as instances of "trustworthy guidance" of God's
revelation for the present.

In chapter 5 we reviewed Dulles's second and "historical model" of
revelation. As its name implies, "God reveals himself [*sic*] primarily in
his great deeds . . . especially those which form the major themes of
biblical history."[18] For this model, "the Bible is . . . not primarily the
word of God but the record of the acts of God . . . an interpreted
account in which the interpretations are so basic that they become 'integral parts of the acts themselves.' '[19] The understanding of revelation
that I propose for movement 3 activity has close resonance with this
model of revelation. Story/Vision of Christian faith can be revelatory
for now because it symbolically expresses the faith convictions from the
"cumulative experience" of our people's encounter with God's saving
deeds over history.[20] However, I go beyond Dulles's portrayal of the
"revelation in history" model.

Existentially, God reveals Godself, not only through the accounts of
"the great deeds of God in history" but in the ongoing life of faith
communities in the world. I made the latter point as theological rationale for the opening movements, but here it pertains to the form and
style of making Christian Story/Vision accessible in movement 3. The
very historicity of God's revelation, and the historicity of the human
expression of its meaning, call for the "original revelation" in the narrative of God's primordial saving deeds to be made accessible as a dy-

namic "prototype" of revelation for the present. Elisabeth Schüssler Fiorenza explains that a prototype, unlike an archetype, requires critical interpretation for other contexts and reformulation in light of contemporary consciousness.[21] An archetype is taken as closed and final, requiring normative applications; a prototype is more a suggestive resource for interpretation. This means that Christian Story/Vision provides authoritative resource for interpreting the meaning and value of present praxis, and likewise present expressions of Story/Vision are themselves reinterpreted for contemporary appropriation by the consciousness that arises from present praxis. Pedagogically, then, this means that movement 3 makes community Story/Vision accessible to participants not as a closed message in final form from the past but with a style that prompts participants to place it in dialogue and dialectic with their own stories and visions.

Drawing insights from the strengths and weaknesses of each of five models (see chapter 5, note 3), Dulles makes his own constructive proposal of revelation as "symbolic mediation." He writes, "According to this approach, revelation never occurs in a purely interior experience or an unmediated encounter with God. It is always mediated through symbol—that is to say, through an externally perceived sign that works mysteriously on the human consciousness so as to suggest more than it can clearly describe or define."[22] He describes symbol as "a sign pregnant with a plenitude of meaning which is evoked rather than explicitly stated."[23] Dulles argues that seeing revelation as "symbolic mediation" has distinct advantages: symbols promote "not speculative but participatory knowledge"; they have "a transforming effect"; they actively engage people in a way that has "a powerful influence on commitments and behavior"; and they introduce us "into realms of awareness not normally accessible to discursive thought."[24] In other words, symbols engage our whole "being" as agent-subjects; they can change us, shape our commitments, and "give insight into mysteries that reason can in no way fathom."[25]

These advantages that Dulles lists are in fact pedagogical ones. To understand and make accessible Christian Story/Vision as "symbolic mediations" of God's self-disclosure over time and in the present encourages educators to attend very deliberately to the life-giving quality of the language and symbolic world they create with participants. Educators need to weave together symbolically rich expressions of Christian tradition and make them accessible in ways likely to engage people in personal encounters with Story/Vision rather than simply proposing, as "critical scholarship" tends to do, a technical and "objective" analysis of its "texts." Likewise, movement 3 activity should harness the potential of life-giving symbols to change people in life-giving ways, to invite commitment, and to draw people into experiences of mystery and worship rather than only into "discursive thought." To realize movement 3 as symbolic mediation of God's revelation to this faith community over time also encourages participants to appropriate

Christian Story/Vision to their own lives in the world and can influence their decision making.

And a final point before summarizing. As with the theology of revelation undergirding the opening movements, an aspect of the theology of revelation I propose for movement 3 is that the most reliable context for encountering, testing, and appropriating God's self-disclosure through symbols of Christian faith is within the ambit of a Christian community—the church. I elaborate on this aspect below under hermeneutical guidelines (see note 9 especially). From the foregoing reflections, I can draw together a theology of revelation that I propose as appropriate, from a "mainline" Christian perspective, to undergird movement 3 of shared Christian praxis.

The Christian Story/Vision symbolically mediates through a great variety of forms, and with normative import for Christians, the prototype of God's revelation of Godself and will through the events of their history to the Israelite and Christian peoples, and primordially in Jesus, the Christ; as people actively engage and personally appropriate, within a community of faith, the inspired scriptures and symbols that reflect and make accessible Christian Story/Vision, they can discern God's self-disclosure and will in their present time and place.

3. Procedures for Movement 3

How then is "the educator" to proceed with "making accessible" Christian Story/Vision in movement 3? Note that I highlight the term *educator* to signal that I use it here with great breadth of meaning. The primary "educator" is the particular faith community that sponsors the event or program—typically some expression or agency of "the church." Theologically this can be said of all the movements, but it has particular relevance in movement 3. For example, it is the responsibility of "the educator" to see to it that Christian Story is faithfully made accessible and its Vision proposed; this means that "the church" must provide educators it commissions in its name with curriculum resources and training to fulfill the hermeneutical tasks and the "making accessible" of movement 3. As I outline hermeneutical guidelines for movement 3, it is clearly impossible for every religious educator, and especially volunteer teachers, to have the scholarly expertise necessary to fulfill all of them by their own initiative. However, with reliable training and well-informed resources—both responsibilities of the sponsoring community[26]—the procedures I outline can be honored by any religious educator, professional or volunteer.

Second, within a particular event, the "designated educator" can be the facilitator of the opening movements, or someone else within the teaching/learning community, or a visiting resource person invited for a particular theme, and so on. Within the event, the "educator" could also be the whole group taking responsibility for making the community Story/Vision accessible to one another, perhaps with subgroups working in hermeneutical circles and sharing with the whole group, or everyone having access to research by each participant. In other words, however it is accomplished, participants have access in movement 3 to a Christian Story/Vision; for convenience, I designate the agency of this making accessible "the educator."

The educator's activity in movement 3 is essentially a hermeneutical one; she or he interprets and explains the aspects of Christian community Story/Vision as appropriate to the generative theme(s) or symbol(s) of the occasion and in dialogue with the stories/visions of participants. Procedurally, the educator's task is to discern both *what* to make accessible from the Story/Vision and *how* to make it accessible to participants. Each existential situation requires particular responses to these questions—what and how—in ways that we cannot anticipate here for all occasions and contexts. We can, however, suggest some principles to guide the hermeneutics of movement 3 regarding *what* to make accessible. I dwell on these in this section 3 and propose nine procedural guidelines for movement 3. Section 4 offers suggestions for *how* to make accessible a Story/Vision.

The Hermeneutical Task and Guidelines of Movement 3

The Greek verb *hermneuein* means both to interpret and to translate, thus implying dual activities of establishing the meaning of a text and expressing its meaning in a context for which it is not immediately evident. The contemporary science of hermeneutics retains these emphases and attends to both interpretation and explanation of the meaning of a "text." Palmer describes hermeneutics as the process of "bringing to understanding" *and* "making familiar, present and comprehensible" to others the meaning of something that is "other or foreign."[27] Ricoeur advises that, although interpreting and explaining can be distinguished, they are never separate activities. There is a dialectical relationship between them and their joint intention is "comprehension," or what he also calls "appropriation"; Ricoeur summarizes, "to make 'ones own' what was previously 'foreign' remains the ultimate aim of all hermeneutics."[28]

Because of its close correlation with biblical exegesis, for a long time the focus of hermeneutics was written texts. Dilthey and Heidegger broadened hermeneutics to include the interpretation and explanation of any expression of human self-awareness. To appreciate their point it helps to remember that no "meaning" is entirely immediate to human consciousness but is always indirect or mediated to us symbolically, if only through language. We cannot interpret our own consciousness by some "pure" phenomenology of it (despite Husserl); we always take a "hermeneutical detour" into our psyches through symbols of the external world that themselves carry and reflect a world of meaning from their historical context. Thus we are always interpreting ourselves and the world around us; hermeneutics is ontological, that is, an aspect of our "being" in the world. We are hermeneutes of every symbol of meaning that we encounter, and existentially we encounter nothing but symbols of meaning (i.e., not "meaning as such," unmediated). Thus, I use "text" to refer to the hermeneutical focus of movement 3 but include in it any symbolic mediation of Christian faith.

Every "text" of meaning originated in a historical context; it reflects, then, a meaning that it meant for its creator and first "audience." Yet as a symbol of human meaning it can have meaning for this "audience" today that is likely not the same as for its original situation. In other words, a text of meaning has an archaeology and a teleology, an "original meaning" that can only be approximated now, and a meaning for this context that was likely not perceived by its original audience. The hermeneute steps into the back and forth between interpretation and explanation, between "meant" and "meaning"; Gadamer likens this to the dynamics of a conversation.

Ricoeur distinguishes between the meaning "of" a text (i.e., as it speaks for itself with its own meaning), the meaning "behind" a text (i.e., what it reflects of its context and might have meant for its original audience), and the meaning "in front of" the text (i.e., what it might mean for the present context). By discerning the meaning "of" and "behind" a text, the hermeneute honors what Ricoeur calls the "objectivity" of the text, that is, allows it to speak in its own right. However, "the sense of a text is not behind the text but in front of it"; the hermeneute's task is to uncover the world of meaning and possibility that the text opens up for the present. "The text's career escapes the finite horizon lived by its author. What the text means now matters more than what the author meant when he [or she] wrote it."[29] Ricoeur recognizes that laying out the meaning "in front of" or "before" a text is more "subjective," in that it engages the inner life of the interpreter. But both the "objectiv*ism*" of technical exegesis and "subjectiv*ism*" of reading into the text at will can be avoided if hermeneutics is a personal encounter with the text in which one recognizes oneself as interpreter and interpreted, as well as a critical analysis of the text and an explanation of it in a community of discourse.[30]

For the hermeneutic of movement 3 and especially its Vision aspect, Gadamer adds an important emphasis on "application."[31] For Gadamer, this is a third aspect of hermeneutics that suffuses interpretation and explanation. His point is that all hermeneutics has a practical intent in that it attempts a "fusion" of the horizon of the text and the horizon of the interpreters.[32] The "fusion" takes place as the interpreter recognizes her or his own horizon as reflected in and expanded by the horizon prompted by but also beyond the situation of the text itself.[33] Because every act of hermeneutics intends this fusion of horizons, "application is neither a subsequent nor a merely occasional part of the phenomenon of understanding, but codetermines it as a whole from the beginning."[34] For Gadamer, all hermeneutics is to change the interpreter and has an ethical interest of practical wisdom akin to what Aristotle meant by phronesis. This point has general significance for all hermeneutics in that it belies the possibility of "disinterested" interpretation, so often the pretense of a "technical rationality" approach to texts; all interpretations of texts of meaning have historical interests and consequences. For movement 3 of shared Christian praxis, Gadamer highlights the educator's task of bringing the practical interest of God's reign to the hermeneutics of every aspect of the tradition, of making the Vision a prior interest in interpreting and explaining the Story, rather than only its applications "afterward." This practical interest encourages a relational hermeneutic with the text rather than simply a technical exegesis.

That religious educators are to be, among other things, hermeneutes of Christian Story/Vision has not been recognized, even by ourselves. The more magisterial and doctrinally conscious traditions of the Christian church especially have socialized their educators to presume that someone somewhere else has already established the complete meaning of the texts of the tradition and our task is simply to teach "it" clearly—free of our own interpretive acts. Undoubtedly, religious educators are responsible for teaching the tradition of the faith community that commissions them to educate in its name, but this cannot mean approaching the tradition as if, in Dewey's terms, it is "predigested knowledge" and the educator is simply to "ladle it out in doses."[35] And, as the science of hermeneutics has become apparently more complex, we have evidence of a new "magisterial" attitude—that those not professionally trained in the languages and skills necessary for exegesis must now wait upon the word of the scholar for what a text meant or means.

Christian religious educators are indeed guided by the canon of scripture and traditions of the church and should make available a version of the community Story/Vision that reflects the best of contemporary scholarship. Yet we must lay to rest the false notion that religious educators are not engaged in hermeneutics when they teach a Story/Vision of faith in an existential event. Apropos movement 3 of shared praxis, there are at least three reasons for religious educators to engage in hermeneutics and to have reliable resources and training to practice it well. They are suggested by the reality of human existence, the style of a shared praxis approach, and the nature of Christian Story/Vision.

Hermeneutics is a highly developed science but also a constitutive activity of human existence. It is not the preserve of experts but rather, as Bernstein says, an "ontological and universal" activity that is "integral to our very being."[36] We cannot but be hermeneutes in our world. This is surely heightened when a religious educator mediates the texts of a faith tradition with practical intent to a contemporary situation and community. If educators pretend to simply pass on an already formulated tradition without interpretation, they are historically naive; as human beings, we cannot avoid choosing some things to emphasize, others to minimize, and some slant of application. Even in the catechism approach, the "answers" were explained; no educator can explain anything without engaging in a hermeneutical activity. It is more appropriate, then, for educators to be conscious of and intentional about their hermeneutics and have reliable guidelines for getting on with it.

Second, the flow of the movements of shared praxis calls for a hermeneutics of Christian Story/Vision in movement 3 to be adequate to the stories/visions of participants as expressed in the opening movements. The dynamic of shared praxis clearly recommends the educator to make Story/Vision accessible in ways that give it a "familiar" ring for participants. This is how they can discern the "family resemblance" between their own stories/visions and Story/Vision of their faith community. Without "linkage" between movements 1 and 2 and movement 3, their Story/Vision will sound "foreign" to people and of no real import for their lives. Only the educator *in situ* can do the interpretation, explanation, and application of community Story/Vision in a way that correlates with the praxis of a particular group of participants.

Third, responsible hermeneutics by religious educators is essential to the procedures of movement 3 of shared praxis because of the very nature of Christian Story/Vision. The questions the educator brings to it from the first two movements, coupled with its "permanence and excess of meaning, always demand interpretation, never mere repetition."[37] Because it functions as a "classic," the Story/Vision of a faith community cannot be repeated as some clear-cut package of "predigested knowledge" (Dewey) handed out on every occasion and in the same way. The very canon of scripture, as Sanders argues, "is located in the tension between two poles, stability and adaptability, with hermeneutics as the mid-term between them."[38] Likewise, the creeds, dogmas, doctrines, and every other expression of Christian Story/Vision have both stability and adaptability that must be honored by the "mid-term" of hermeneutics.[39] Without it, educators carry on some form of biblical or doctrinal "traditionalism" that promotes what Pelikan calls "the dead faith of the living" rather than appreciating the tradition as "the living faith of the dead."[40]

Beyond honoring its "stability and adaptability" (Sanders), its "permanence and excess of meaning" (Tracy), the religious educator should also be keenly aware of the distortions and aberrations in Christian Story/Vision over time and avoid repeating the destructive interpretations it has been given. There is evidence strewn across the pages of history of lamentable "Christian" teachings and practices that approved of racism, blessed unbridled capitalism, encouraged anti-Semitism, legitimated sexism and patriarchy, allowed Christians to be irresponsible toward their ecology, and so on. This historical evidence, coupled with the practical and life-giving intent that should guide the educator in making accessible Christian Story/Vision, heightens the imperative of responsible hermeneutics by the educator in this movement 3. Its political implications alone highlight the imperative that religious educators avoid arbitrariness and personal preferences in effecting it; they need reliable hermeneutical guidelines and resources. There is no one Christian Story/Vision that the educator can make accessible in final form and for every learning occasion. Brueggemann is eminently correct when he writes that "the hermeneutical enterprise is something church educators can no longer regard as outside their responsibility."[41]

In the procedures of movement 3 of shared Christian praxis, the educator's hermeneutics has two responsibilities: (a) to honor the texts of Christian faith in their own right with interpretations appropriate to the tradition and (b) to propose explanations and applications that respond adequately to the praxis of participants, and with a view to appropriation and decision making in movements 4 and 5. To help the educator fulfill these responsibilities, I propose nine hermeneutical guidelines. None of them can stand alone or is sufficient unto itself; cumulatively they can guide the educator in fulfilling the hermeneutical task of movement 3. The first three guidelines pertain to the pre-understandings religious educators are to remember as they approach the "texts" of Christian Story/Vision (section A); the second three pertain to the hermeneutical acts and interests of educators in interpreting the texts themselves (section B); and moving "in front of" the texts, the last three guide educators' explanation/application (section C).

A. The Pre-understandings the Educator Brings to Christian Story/Vision

The great modern exponents of hermeneutics have established that there is no such event as a "nonperspectival" or "objective" or "presuppositionless" reading of any "text" of meaning. We always come to texts with what Bultmann first called "pre-understanding," or what Gadamer calls the "bone-structure of understanding" in place, in other words, with already formed perspectives that shape our interpretation of it. In fact, the best hope of honoring the text's "objectivity" is to be aware of the "subjectivity" we bring to interpreting it.[42] For religious educators in movement 3, there are at least three sources of pre-understanding they should be aware of and consciously bring to a text: (1) the overarching sense one already has of the import of the whole Story/Vision for people's lives from previous encounters with it over the years and in a Christian community, (2) the personal interests and perspectives educators have from their own sociocultural context in place and time, and (3) the questions and issues suggested by the dialogue of participants in the opening movements.

Guideline 1: The "first criterion" for the hermeneutics of movement 3 of shared Christian praxis is the reign of God.   Every interpreter of Christian tradition already has some general sense of its overarching meaning and import for life within which to interpret a particular expression; she or he has a sense of the picture of which this is a piece. In interpreting a particular text, one's prior understanding can be enlarged and transformed, yet we need some grasp of the whole to begin the dialogue with a part. This is what all the great exponents of hermeneutics (Schleiermacher, Dilthey, Heidegger, Gadamer, Ricoeur, et al.) recognize as "the hermeneutical circle," from a general pre-understanding in our subjectivity, to the text, and then back to reformulate one's pre-understanding. Lonergan uses the analogy of a sentence: "One grasps the meaning of the sentence by understanding the words. But one understands the words properly only in light of the sentence as a whole."[43] Taking "the sentence" as an analogy of the whole Story/Vision, we see that our prior sense of its overall meaning shapes how we interpret a "word" within it, which enlarges our understanding of "the sentence," and the circle goes on.

Every hermeneute brings an overarching pre-understanding to any text. I propose, however, that Christian Story/Vision itself suggests a "first criterion" or "metacriterion" for an approach like shared Christian praxis. This overarching criterion functions like a "canon within the canon" of Story/Vision; it is our most dominant sense of what the prototype of Christian faith *always* means *for us*. It guides the educator's hermeneutics of particular expressions and is the primary guide when deciding what to teach. Clearly, we need a symbol for this "first criterion," and especially for our pedagogy, in which we often must use it "on our feet." In chapter 1 I suggested that the "reign of God" is the comprehensive symbol, suggested by the tradition itself, for the heart of what Christian Story/Vision means for people's lives. Here I propose it as the metacriterion to guide the hermeneutics of movement 3. We need only summarize this symbol as a hermeneutical guideline.

The reign of God can symbolize God's intentions for humanity and creation. It summarizes the Story of how God has intervened and continues to intervene in history with the "goodwill" of freedom, justice, peace, love, wholeness, and fullness of life for all, and the integrity of creation. It is a symbol of the covenant into which God calls humankind as co-partners to live according to God's "goodwill" toward us. The God of Abraham and Sarah, Moses and Miriam, is God who wills us shalom and calls us to so live as if God reigns in our lives. The center of the life of Jesus is his commitment to God's reign; his praxis fulfills its law of love, is a catalyst of "fullness of life" for all, and he invites disciples to live likewise. In the "dangerous memories" of Jesus' life of resistance to everything that denied fullness of life to anyone, of outreach to marginalized people and outcasts, of suffering with us and rising to new life for humankind, Christians find model and empowerment to live for the reign of God by doing what God wills on earth as it is done in heaven. In our own time the hermeneutical import and urgency of this central symbol is deepened by the critical consciousness that emerges from communities of faith who actively struggle against its antitheses and to create social structures that promote its values; that is, people who truly live for God's reign show best what it is about. Some find this symbol dated, or problematic for other reasons (see chapter 1), and I appreciate their reservations. However, the tradition suggests it; I believe it can be a symbol of all that Christian faith means for people's lives and human history, of all that the Christian community can be and should be, of all that we can be, should be, and will become in God's eternal presence. Alternatives to it need to mean as much.

As the "first criterion" of hermeneutics in movement 3, "reign of God" means that educators approach every particular expression of Christian Story/Vision with the bedrock conviction that God is a God of life and love, who intends freedom, peace, and justice for all, who is active in history to realize God's "goodwill" and calls people into covenant to so live. This conviction permeates and colors every interpretation and explanation and application of every aspect of Christian Story/Vision. It suffuses hermeneutics with practical and emancipatory interests. As educators interpret any text of Christian Story/Vision, "reign of God" encourages them to interpret in a way that empowers and liberates participants as responsible agent-subjects, to bring participants into right relationship with God, self, others, and creation, to encourage critical consciousness about the personal biases and social structures that deny fullness of life to all, to prompt solidarity with the oppressed and encourage praxis on personal, interpersonal, and social/political levels that promote the values of God's reign. Conversely, interpretations of the tradition that do not promote the realization of God's reign on all levels of people's existence—that do not encourage them to live as disciples of Jesus—are false by this criterion and should be avoided as unfaithful to God's intent for humankind.[44]

Guideline 2: Religious educators are to remember the interests and perspectives they bring to every text of Christian Story/Vision from their own "life" in place and time.   Even with the reign of God as one's metacriterion, educators must remember the interests, perspectives, and "tinted lenses" they bring to the text from their social and cultural "situation in life." In other words, the bedrock interpretive framework we bring to the texts of the tradition is shaped not simply by our general sense of the "canon within its canon" but also by our own social biography. In hermeneutics we are never without what Tracy, echoing Gadamer, calls "the history of the effects of . . . culture," because they are in "the very language we speak and write."[45] But we can be aware of and critically appropriate the influences of our psychic state and social biography, to the point that our personal perspective does not blind but, in fact, enlightens our interpretations of the texts—helps us see what might not be seen by others from a different "situation in life." It is when we forget what we bring to the text from our context that we read into it what we want to find there, according to our interests.

It is important that religious educators be self-critically conscious of both the psychological dispositions and social perspectives they bring to the hermeneutics of movement 3. Looking to our own psyches, we should be conscious of any biases, fears, vested interests, and closed-mindedness that we bring to interpret the texts of the tradition. On the positive side, religious educators must try to maintain a genuine open-ness to the potential of the text to enlarge their horizons, an expectancy that God can disclose Godself through these texts as they symbolize God's revelation in times past. Of hermeneutes' *social* perspective, they need to remember the political interests and ideologies prompted by their historical context, the assets and liabilities these have for herme-neutics of texts of Christian faith.[46] And it is important to regularly recall how our denominational allegiance shapes our interpretation of the text.[47]

Guideline 3: Religious educators are to remember what they bring to the texts of the tradition from the stories and visions of participants.

In movement 3 of shared Christian praxis, the stories and visions of participants should shape the questions and issues the educator brings to interpret texts of Christian Story/Vision. Religious educators in movement 3 go to the texts of the tradition with the practical interest of making accessible in life-giving ways what pertains to the genera-tive theme(s) or symbol(s) of the learning occasion, in light of which participants are to reinterpret and re-envision their own and/or their society's praxis. The educator must be conscious of the age levels, backgrounds, contexts, and so on of participants and consciously re-member their interpretation of present praxis in the opening move-ments. Otherwise, participants are not likely to perceive the "linkage" between their own and the Story/Vision of their faith community, thus making appropriation and decision making less likely in movements 4 and 5.

B. *Hermeneutics of Retrieval, Suspicion, and Creative Commitment to the "Text"*

The second threefold set of procedural guidelines refers to the hermeneutical acts and interests that religious educators bring to in-terpret texts of Christian faith. Aware of their "pre-understandings," educators turn to the "texts" of Story/Vision with a critical hermeneutics that has dialectical aspects. The meaning and import of the texts are to be discerned by a threefold schema of activities: (a) to recognize and affirm the truths of the text, (b) to question or refuse the limitations and/or errors in its dominant interpretation, and, (c) as appropriate, to reformulate or construct new horizons of meaning and ethic beyond how it is currently understood and lived. As so often with such distinc-tions, existentially these aspects constantly overlap. Using the terms popularized by Paul Ricoeur, the first two moments of affirming or reclaiming and of questioning or refusing call for hermeneutics of *retrieval* and *suspicion*.[48] To complete the dialectical tripod, I call the third leg of it a hermeneutics of *creative commitment*.

To honor these hermeneutical activities in movement 3 does not require, of course, that each individual educator is to originate the scholarship needed to do these activities well, or that he or she alone carries responsibility for them. These three especially highlight the fact that "the educator" in movement 3 includes the "church"—the whole sponsoring faith community, locally and universally. The designated educator *in situ* must have reliable resources informed by the teaching/learning of her or his Christian community, who commissions or sponsors the educator to teach in its name. However, I place "church" in italics to indicate that I intend a particular meaning for it in this teaching/learning context. Anticipating what I explain below, as an authoritative resource and interlocutor in the hermeneutics of movement 3, "church" has three recognizable sources of its teaching and learning: the official church *magisterium* (whatever its form in particular denominations), the research of its *scholars*, and the *sense of its faithful*.

The hermeneutics of movement 3 is informed by the sponsoring community's consensus understanding of its faith tradition, however this "magisterial" consensus emerges or is expressed. Likewise, it should be informed by the research of those trained in the original languages of the tradition and in the scholarly skills of critical biblical and theological research. And as reflected throughout the history of Christianity, hermeneutics of its Story/Vision should be informed by the "sense of the faithful" that emerges from the historical efforts of Christians to live faithfully as disciples of Jesus. Regarding this *sensus fidelium*, I'm convinced that religious educators should listen especially to the consciousness that emerges from communities actively engaged in the works of peace and justice for the realization of God's reign in history. The "hermeneutical privilege of the oppressed,"[49] makes such critical consciousness a compelling resource as educators interpret Christian Story/Vision.

Guideline 4: The educator employs a "hermeneutic of retrieval" to reclaim and make accessible the truths and values symbolically mediated in the texts of Christian Story/Vision.   In movement 3, the educator engages in a hermeneutic of retrieval to discern, affirm, cherish, and make accessible to participants the life-giving truths and values in Christian Story/Vision. This activity is clearly required by the very responsibility of shared *Christian* praxis to educate participants in Christian identity and agency. Commitment to a hermeneutic of retrieval reflects the faith conviction that, far from leading the Christian people astray over their pilgrim past, God has been leading them into life-giving truths about God, themselves, and how we are to live as a people of God.[50] Expressions of its Story/Vision reflect the judgments of meaning and ethic, truth and value to which this community has come and to which it calls its members now; they should be retrieved and made accessible by pedagogy for wisdom in Christian faith.

The life-giving truths and values of the "faith handed on" cannot be presumed upon or made accessible by repetition; as Tracy writes, "Its permanent achievements can and must be won, over and over again" through "a hermeneutics of retrieval by means of which humanity may enrich its present impoverished lot."[51] The educator's interest in hermeneutics of retrieval is to discern and make accessible the truths and values of this Story/Vision in ways that illumine the present reality of people's lives *and* encourage them to live Christian faith in the world. In other words, the hermeneute is concerned for both the conceptual *and* the moral appropriateness of her or his interpretations of texts and of their adequacy to people's lives.[52] This means that a hermeneutic of retrieval in movement 3 must consciously attend to the Vision of Christian faith as well as to the texts of its Story.

For hermeneutics of retrieval, educators clearly need to draw upon scholarship in Bible, theology, and history. Religious educators need not be personally so trained, but they need resources that give them access to the insights of scholars about the meaning of and behind texts of the tradition. Retrieval is also guided by any consensus understanding articulated by the community's magisterium about this expression of Story/Vision, even as encounters with the texts in teaching/learning communities are a source to the magisterium in its task of deepening and renewing its interpretations. Likewise, retrieval is informed by the "sense of the faithful" about what is true, life-giving, and to be cherished from the tradition. Critical consciousness from praxis for God's reign gives a special alert to the truths of the tradition to be retrieved.

Guideline 5: The educator employs a "hermeneutic of suspicion" to uncover mystifications and distortions in the dominant interpretations of Christian Story/Vision and to reclaim its "dangerous memories."   The educator's task in hermeneutics of suspicion is first to look out for false consciousness and distortions in original texts and/or in their accepted interpretations, to un-cover negative consequences they may have had over history or still legitimate now. This "suspicion" also means being alert for subjective errors in one's own interpretations. The educator's final intent, however, is not negative criticism but, beyond "demystification" (Ricoeur), to un-cover from the texts of tradition the subjugated or forgotten memories that can give new life.

A hermeneutic of suspicion reflects awareness that God's revelation is always mediated in particular historical circumstances and through culturally conditioned symbols. People who interpret those symbols are "to refuse all absolutizations, all claims that human, historical, interpretive matters elude relativity and corruption."[53] To make absolute any expression or interpretation of a faith tradition is to ossify and deaden it; to forget that there have been distortions and corruptions reflected in Christian Story/Vision is historically naive.[54] Religious educators should approach the faith tradition with a healthy suspicion and, as educators, help people to recognize that "much that has been proudly told must be confessed as sin; and much that has been obscured and silenced must be given voice."[55]

I emphasize that a hermeneutic of suspicion is not a negative exercise but an eminently positive one. It attempts to recognize and refuse what is destructive in texts of the tradition[56] and it searches for their "dangerous" or "subversive" memories, often forgotten or excluded by the dominant hermeneutics. These are memories, as Metz says, that can "break through the canon of the prevailing structures of plausibility, and have certain subversive features." He explains that, "every utopian concept of liberation which questions and breaks through what is currently held to be plausible is ultimately rooted in this kind of memory."[57] Texts of Christian Story/Vision always have dangerous memories that call ourselves and our world into question, that can empower people in ongoing conversion and social transformation toward God's reign.

I could have situated "dangerous memories" within a hermeneutics of retrieval. I place them here to signal that rediscovering them requires the educator to be suspicious of the dominant version of Story/Vision, to be wary that the "accepted" interpretation does not exhaust the possibilities. They are also "suspicious" in that they can subvert personal and social sinfulness and pose new possibilities of conversion and social transformation. I noted in chapter 7 that "dangerous memories" are of suffering and of resistance to oppression. In movement 3 of shared Christian praxis the most subversive memory the educator can raise up from the Hebrew Bible is the Exodus—its preeminent event when God saw the people's slavery and oppression and brought them out to freedom with "strong hand and outstretched arm" (see Deut. 26:5–10). The most dangerous memory from the New Testament is of Jesus, the Christ, as the crucified and Risen One, who in Christian faith symbolizes all the suffering of humankind and its resistance to every form of oppression with the hope of new life and freedom for all.

For a hermeneutic of suspicion, too, the educators' ecclesial resources and interlocutors are the magisterium of their church, the research of scholars, and the "sense of the faithful." We have ample evidence that the institutional voices of the Christian church are capable of blindness and distortion in hermeneutics of its Story/Vision. But over history and in our time there is evidence too that the church's magisterii are capable of prophetic witness to God's reign, of drawing upon Story/Vision to critique and reform both church and society. The research of scholars can manifest false consciousness in the texts, point out distortions and corruptions in how they have been interpreted and the destructive consequences such interpretations have caused, and can uncover the dangerous memories in the tradition—especially when scholars work with an emancipatory interest. Although often left unspoken or discouraged from being voiced, the "sense of the faithful" can have a Spirit-inspired skepticism toward aspects of the "party line," and a felt conviction that what is not of life in the dominant version of their Story/Vision is also not of God; this too is a resource for the religious educator's hermeneutic of suspicion. We are to note especially the critical consciousness that emerges from communities whose praxis heightens their awareness of distortions in Christian Story/Vision and sharpens their perception of its dangerous memories.

Guideline 6: The educator employs a "hermeneutic of creative commitment" to construct more adequate understandings of Christian Story/Vision and to envision more faithful ways of living it with personal and social transformation. This hermeneutical procedure of movement 3 emphasizes *creativity* and *commitment*. It is creative because, prompted by the needs of the situation and participants, it may well pose "constructions" beyond the present dominant understandings of Story/Vision. As Rahner writes, "The clearest formulations, the most sanctified formulas, the classic condensations of the centuries-long work of the Church in prayer, reflection and struggle concerning God's mysteries; all these derive their life from the fact that they are not end but beginning, not goal but means, truths which open the way to the—ever greater—Truth."[58]

The very historical conditionedness of all symbolic expressions of Story/Vision requires, from era to era, new and more adequate constructs to articulate its meaning and ethic for now. No community of faith can be content with "a rehearsal and translation of the tradition" but must engage it as "a creative activity of the human imagination seeking to provide more adequate orientation for human life."[59] The Israelites were convinced that God could always "do something new" (Isa. 43:19); the Bible often reflects a creative approach to prior tradition, taking older texts and reconstructing them as appropriate to a new context. Matthew's Gospel has Jesus declare, "Every scribe who is learned in the reign of God is like the head of a household who can bring from [the] storeroom both the new and the old" (Matt. 13:52). And Vatican II, in its *Constitution on Divine Revelation,* explains, "This tradition which comes from the apostles develops in the Church with the help of the Holy Spirit," and thus the Christian community is ever moving "toward the fullness of divine truth."[60] The perennial "surplus of meaning" in the classic texts of Christian faith calls for constructive and creative hermeneutics in response to the needs of the time and the "new things" God is doing.

This "constructive" aspect of hermeneutics may at times be more accurately described as acts of "reconstruction." This is writing back into the Story/Vision, from clues and traces that remain in its texts, dimensions that were "written out." Elisabeth Schüssler Fiorenza's work has become a model of such reconstruction; she recreates the history of the first Christian communities to reflect more accurately the "basileia vision of Jesus as the praxis of inclusive wholeness" in a "discipleship of equals" with women as full partners.[61]

The *commitment* aspect of this guideline is not a new emphasis here but reflects the practical and ethical purpose that permeates the whole hermeneutics of movement 3, beginning with its "first" criterion of God's reign. I highlight commitment alongside creativity to emphasize that the educator's intent in "constructions" or "reconstructions" is to move participants to praxis for God's reign in the world. Sharon Welch writes, "The truth of God-language and of all theological claims is measured not by their correspondence to something eternal but by the fulfillment of its claims in history, by the actual creation of communities of peace, justice, and equality."[62]

As with retrieval and suspicion, for hermeneutics of creative commitment, educators should draw upon the resources of and be in dialogue with the "church." The creativity and commitment they encourage in a particular event should reflect the efforts of the magisterium, scholars, and "faithful" to articulate and live the faith of the church in ways appropriate to the tradition and adequate to people's lives in new times and places.

C. *"Marks of Authenticity" for Explanation and Application of Christian Story/Vision*

The previous six guidelines pertain more obviously to *interpreting* texts, although, as noted, Ricoeur emphasizes the dialectical unity of interpretation and explanation, and Gadamer argues that all hermeneutics is undergirded by the practical interest of application. Explanation and application are operative interests in implementing the first six guidelines. However, the very purposes and intended learning outcome of Christian religious education make it imperative that educators attend very deliberately to explanation and application of the communities' texts. Clearly Christian religious educators need authoritative criteria or what Newman called "marks of authenticity"[63] in order to discern between a false and an authentic explanation of the texts of Christian faith.

The "marks of authenticity" I propose here are similar to the criteria for guiding decision making in movement 5 of shared praxis and I reiterate them in chapter 10. Implied already in this chapter, the authenticity of an explanation and/or application of any symbol of Christian Story/Vision is measured by its *continuity, consequences,* and *community.* None is sufficient unto itself; we need all three in concert to guide explanation/application of what is interpreted from texts of Christian tradition. Yet, when all three are honored with the previous six guidelines, with the help of God's Spirit, educators can be confident that they are proposing an authentic (but never exhaustive) explanation/application from Christian Story/Vision.

Guideline 7: Every authentic explanation of a particular text is in continuity *with and appropriate to the constitutive truths and values of the whole Story/Vision.*   An explanation of a particular text should be consistent and compatible with, and conserve the foundational trajectory of beliefs and truths, principles and values, that constitute what is essential to Christian Story/Vision. More plainly, it should be in harmony with what's at the "heart" of Christian faith. Many theologians pose this criterion of continuity for explaining the Christian tradition, albeit in varied terms. McFague speaks of "demonstrable continuities within the Christian paradigm";[64] for Tracy, an explanation is to be "appropriate" to the tradition;[65] for Newman, it must have "dynamic identity" with what has gone before;[66] for Rahner, it should be "in vital contact" with the original sources.[67] In other words, the truths and values that constitute the very identity and particularity of Christian Story/Vision should be reflected in an explanation of a specific symbol of it. These central truths and values belong to the upper echelon of what Vatican II called the "hierarchy of truths" reflected in Christian tradition because of their constitutive "relationship to the foundation of the Christian faith."[68] They have normativity for Christians in that they provide "trustworthy guidance" in interpreting God's revelation— "original" and existential.

Guideline 8: An authentic explanation of a particular text of Christian tradition promotes personal and social consequences *creative of God's reign.*
This guideline echoes the metacriterion of God's reign (number 1) and the guideline of creative commitment (number 6); here, however, it refers to explanation. For clarity about procedures of explanation in movement 3, it helps to set out "consequences" as a particular mark of authenticity. It prompts educators to constantly ask, What is this explanation of this text likely to lead to in these lives?

"Consequences" echoes the Gospel criterion that true disciples of Jesus are known by their "fruits" (see Matt. 7:20). As an authentic explanation is in continuity with the Story, so too it is likely to promote consequences that are the Vision of God's reign. Every explanation/ application is to reflect and promote the practical interest of lived Christian faith by persons and communities, a faith that makes the reign of God present on personal, interpersonal, and social/political levels of reality and "prepares the materials" (Vatican II) for its final completion. Conversely, if an explanation of a text seems likely to prevent the realization of God's "goodwill" for all, it is not authentic.[69]

As educators evaluate an explanation for its potential to promote the love, freedom, peace, justice, wholeness, and fullness of life that God wills for all, they can encounter educational events in which authentic reign of God values have what Hollenbach calls "claims in conflict." Hollenbach offers three helpful "priority principles. When authentic claims are in conflict, "(1) The needs of the poor take priority over the wants of the rich. (2) The freedom of the dominated takes priority over the liberty of the powerful. (3) The participation of marginalized groups takes priority over the preservation of an order that excludes them."[70]

Guideline 9: Community *is a guideline in that authentic explanation of a particular expression of Christian Story/Vision is informed by the understanding of "the church" and is adequate to the praxis of this community of participants.*
By "community" here as a source of authentic explanation, I intend to honor both the catholicity and particularity of a teaching/learning group. When a group uses shared Christian praxis, its explanation of a text for the lives of participants is informed by both its own ecclesial dynamic and by the whole Christian community—the church of which it is a part. Procedurally, this guideline means that an explanation should be *appropriate* to the "church's" understanding of its Story/Vision and adequate to the stories/visions of the immediate group. (See chapter 7 for Tracy's understanding, which I intend here, of appropriateness and adequacy as hermeneutical criteria.) We can call the faith community in its catholicity "church," and in its particularity "group."

Church. I've proposed that in *interpreting* texts, hermeneutics of retrieval, suspicion, and creative commitment are to be done in dialogue with the "church." I elaborate here on what I mean by "church" in this teaching/learning context as a source of authentic *explanation* of texts of Christian faith.

That the "church" has the right and responsibility to carry on Jesus' teaching mission has been the constant tradition of Christianity from the first communities (see, e.g., Matt. 28:16–20) down to the present. Further, when its educators explain and apply the texts of the tradition, as in movement 3, the teaching of the whole "church" in its catholicity should be honored and receptively heard as on "good authority" by the smaller communities that constitute it.

If "church" here is synonymous with what Dulles calls the "institutional model," this guideline would mean simply accepting the official teachings of our church's institutional magisterium. This would exclude any substantive role for the research of scholars and even less for the "sense of the faithful." In the "institutional model" of church, teaching is "juridicized and institutionalized" (Dulles), and the "faithful" are to learn without question what the official magisterium teaches, while scholars prove the official teaching correct[71] (Dulles calls this a "regressive theology").[72] If, however, we understand "church" according to a model more like a community—so clearly the ecclesial paradigm of Vatican II—then to say that an explanation is appropriate to "what the church teaches" means that it is consonant with what the whole "church" teaches and learns together as an inclusive community of discernment. In a community model of the "church," the *ecclesia docens* is also the *ecclesia discens*[73]—all its members teach and learn together.

I favor a communal model of "church" here and identify three overlapping sources of its teaching/learning: the teaching of the official magisterium,[74] the research of theologians, scripture and other religious scholars, and the discernment of the people—the *sensus fidelium*.[75] All three agencies (or what Raymond Brown calls "three organs of teaching and belief")[76] should interrelate in dialogue, support, correction, and affirmation. The official magisterium (and within the churches this may be pope or primate, general assembly, conference, or synod, etc. or simply the faith claims that mark a specific community) performs the service of articulating positions that reflect the communal and identifying faith of a particular Christian people. As Boys writes, and with the "classic text of the divine-human encounter—sacred Scripture" in mind, "not all interpretations, whether from a scholar's vantage point or from 'lived experience,' are equally valid readings—hence the need for a norming body" that can act with authority as "the arbiter of a community's assessment of which traditions are constitutive."[77] This magisterium, however, must constantly interact with and be enriched by the other two "sources" in service to the "church's" faith and witness.

The dynamic between these three "agencies" within the "church," when operative, can be imaged as follows. The effort of all baptized Christians to understand their faith and realize their commitments is informed by the research of the scholars; likewise, the reflections of its scholars are in dialogue with and informed by the living faith of Christian community. The lived faith of members is resourced and guided by the reliable consensus of belief and practice taught by a community's official magisterium; likewise, agencies entrusted with the service of magisterial teaching listen to and are informed by the "sense of the faithful." Between the magisterium and scholars (typically religious but in secular disciplines too when their research is enlightening for "church" teaching), the former does not presume to have a shortcut to the truth; its teaching is informed by the research of the scholarly community.[78] And ecclesial scholars are well served by an official magisterium that articulates a consensus position to reflect "the faith" of the whole church over time as a guideline for their ongoing research and construction.[79] In movement 3 of shared praxis, explaining some texts may warrant particular attention to one of these resources of teaching/learning, but over time our explaining of the comprehensive Story/Vision should reflect what emerges from the interweaving of all three as a catholic consensus of the "church."

Group. The explanation the educator offers in movement 3 is also informed by the discernment of the particular teaching/learning community in the sense that it should be "adequate" to their praxis as expressed in the opening movements. Here "adequacy" is measured by the extent to which participants recognize the resonance between a Christian Story/Vision and their own reflections on present praxis relating to a generative theme or symbol. What participants have talked about (movements 1 and 2) and what is made accessible in movement

3 should be clearly the same "conversation," and participants should see the correlation between these two sources of wisdom in Christian faith. More completely, and drawing again upon Tracy's notes of "adequacy to experience," explanations of texts should be *meaningful* for participants in that they disclose (according to age level, background, context, etc.) the deeper meanings of their own praxis; they should be *coherent* in that they make sense within people's overall understanding of their Story/Vision; and they are to ring *true* to participants' lives and be sources of renewed orthopraxis in Christian faith.

Summary. These guidelines are the hermeneutical procedures of movement 3 of shared Christian praxis. To reiterate, I do not claim that each individual religious educator is personally responsible for the scholarship that many of these guidelines require. In a ministry staffed so widely by volunteers, I would be naive and misleading to so claim. Yet the "church" should see to it that its designated religious educators have the preparation, support, and resources to do responsible hermeneutics in their work, regardless of what approach they are using. But even with the best of curriculum resources reflecting contemporary scholarship and teachings of the "church," educators are always the hermeneutes *in situ;* they cannot presume that someone somewhere else has already done the hermeneutics and they are simply "to ladle it out in doses" (Dewey). I'm convinced that with basic training and reliable resources every religious educator can fulfill the hermeneutical tasks of movement 3. They must, of course, go about them intentionally.

Intentionality, in more personal terms, means that you (1) come to the "texts" of the tradition (remember, this means any expression of Christian faith—liturgy, prayers, practices, etc.—in addition to written texts) convinced that God has total "goodwill" for all humankind and that all aspects of Christian faith should be humanizing and life-giving; (2) remember well what participants said in the opening movements to "pitch" the tradition to their lives so that they can recognize its "familiar ring"; (3) stay aware of your own biases and interests, not letting the bad ones interfere with, but allowing the good ones to enhance, what you teach as Christian faith. As you interpret "texts," deliberately look for (4) what is clearly of God's truth and Christian faith for people's lives; (5) what seems questionable, "off," or life-giving but overlooked; (6) ways you can recast how "it" has been said to these participants before to say it better for them now. In explaining to people what "texts" mean for their lives, remember that your explanations and applications (7) should be faithful to the essentials of Christian faith; (8) encourage people to live as Christians; (9) reflect the "living faith" of the "church" for these lives.

Repeating this summary in more procedural and formal terms, religious educators are to keep the following convictions and questions in mind as they do hermeneutics of any particular "text" of Christian Story/Vision.

For interpretation: (1) Place the reign of God at the center of your consciousness as the constant "first criterion" that guides all interpretation and explanation. Then ask (2) Where am I coming from, and what am I bringing to this text? (3) How do I take account of the stories/visions of participants in my interpretation? 4) What life-giving truths and values does this expression of Christian faith mediate to our lives? (5) Are there possible distortions in the "dominant" interpretation and use of this text? Does it hold "dangerous memories" that can call in question and offer new life to the present? (6) What new and creative possibilities can or should I propose from the text to this context to encourage Christian commitment? *For explanation/application:* (7) Is my explanation in continuity with what is central to and constitutive of Christian Story? (8) Is my explanation likely to encourage these participants to live for God's reign? (9) Does my explanation reflect the teaching/learning of the "church" and respond adequately to the stories/visions of participants in this learning event?

Because many of these guidelines overlap, and all are to coalesce into one's hermeneutical *modus operandi*, educators can summarize them into a ready guide: *Remembering the life-giving purpose of God's reign, and aware of my own perspective and the lives of these participants, what old and new "truths" can I draw from this "text" that encourages people in the praxis of Christian faith?*

4. Developing the Art of Facilitating Movement 3

I draw together my reflections on facilitating movement 3 under three headings: some methods for movement 3 activity, the style of "making accessible" that permeates it, some attitudes movement 3 asks of religious educators.

A. Methods of Movement 3 Activity

We can use a great variety of methodologies to make accessible a Christian Story/Vision, as long as they honor the nature and purpose of movement 3 and reflect the style and commitments outlined below. I have found these methods appropriate and effective, but this is by no means an exhaustive list of the possibilities.

1. lectures, handouts, reading from a common text
2. research projects and reports, group hermeneutics and discussion
3. demonstrations, experiences, panel discussions, colloquies, and symposium dialogues
4. audio and video or film media and artistic presentations
5. group story telling and drama
6. resource people from outside the event or field trips that pro-

vide a praxislike encounter with the Story/Vision of the generative focus

I will comment briefly on each of these loosely grouped genres of teaching methods.

1. Lectures can be presented in a great variety of ways but should honor the canons of clarity and logical sequence that are marks of a coherent statement. I have found the "Advance Organizer Model"[80] of Weil and Joyce very helpful to suggest an overall structure and logical organization for a presentation. Regardless of the lecture model used, its dialogical dimension is enhanced by building into one's language pattern invitations to reflection (see below) and, when feasible, pausing and encouraging comments from participants throughout. (Movement 4 kinds of activities are often interspersed in movement 3; see chapter 9.) When feasible and appropriate to the occasion, making handouts or summaries available promotes participation in that they reduce note-taking and may allow people to enter more actively into dialogue and reflection. With young children in situations using a common text, it can be effective on occasion to have them "read along," perhaps taking turns, and pausing to talk about the meaning and import of what they are reading.

2. A common lament in journals on teaching is that schools do poorly in encouraging students to do research and to be agents of their own access to the disciplines of learning. In movement 3 of shared praxis, research projects, done either individually or in partnership, and perhaps with summary reports to the whole group, can be very effective if the researchers are sent to reliable resources and have good guidance for their hermeneutics.[81] Group hermeneutics, especially of a Scripture passage, can be very effective even with young children; as needed, the educator can serve as resource person with insights from Scripture scholarship and hermeneutical guidelines. One way to suggest appropriate guidelines for participants (especially adults) to approach a text together is to allow the intent of movements 1 and 2, 4 and 5 to suggest engaging questions; for example, What do we hear this text saying to us and why? (movements 1 and 2); What do we say in response to it? (movement 4); and What does it mean for our lives? (movement 5). This style of hermeneutics shifts beyond exegesis and encourages a relationship between people and text, and among participants.

3. Demonstrations, when appropriate to the occasion, can be very effective with participants of any age. (In a fifth-grade class on baptism we simulated a baptismal ceremony at movement 3.) There are also themes that allow or suggest an actual experience of the particular Story/Vision within the event. For example, with adults on "centering prayer" at movement 3 the educator guided participants through an experience of this prayer style. Panel discussions, colloquies,[82] and symposium dialogues can bring variety to making Story/Vision accessible,

especially with adult participants and can build momentum into movement 4.

4. Media and artistic presentations at movement 3 can encourage active and imaginative engagement by participants. In the history of religious education no previous era has had the excellent media resources now readily available; we must use their potential.[83] The graphic arts can also engage participants in a holistic way, and their "stillness" gives time to enter into their "visual understanding."[84] Other forms of art and expressions of the fine arts can also be powerful modes for making accessible some aspects of Christian Story/Vision. For example, I participated in an event on "God's mercy" where movement 3 was built around Francis Thompson's poem "The Hound of Heaven" (it could also have been used as a focusing symbol of the generative theme at the beginning). I have also seen a powerful hermeneutic of Luke 13:10—17 (the woman bent over) presented in dance form.

5. Group story telling can be very effective with both children and adults in movement 3. On a learning occasion focused on healing, the people present were invited at movement 3 to tell their own favorite healing story from the life of Jesus, then they moved into a group hermeneutic of the meaning and import of their stories. Young children can be invited to act out a story they already know and then can be guided in their hermeneutics of it. Employing drama to teach its Story/Vision is an ancient practice of the Christian church (see note 3).

6. Bringing in resource people from outside an educational community is often appropriate at movement 3. This can also be someone whose "expertise" is in the form of living witness to the Story/Vision for attention. In a unit on peacemaking, at movement 3 I've heard a "peace activist" give an inspiring "testimony" on her nuclear protests inspired by Christian faith, including a recent term in jail. "Field trips," when a focused theme lends itself to them, can also be an engaging and praxislike method of making Story/Vision accessible. I use the term *field trip* very broadly for any praxislike encounter with the meaning and import of Christian faith. (Note that this need not be confined to the focusing activity.) I offer these instances of methods for movement 3 only to stimulate the imagination of the reader. There are no limits to educators' creativity in making accessible the community Story/Vision in movement 3; it is for each of us to find the methods best suited to our own talents and to particular occasions.

B. The Style of Movement 3

The "style" of movement 3 activity is well intimated by the phrase "to make accessible"; however, I add a nuance to it here. Mary Boys, who proposes this phrase "as the primary description of religious education,"[85] explains, "Access is given in numerous ways. To provide access means to erect bridges, to make metaphors, to build highways, to provide introductions and commentaries, to translate foreign terms, to remove barriers, to make maps, to demolish blockages, to demonstrate effects, to energize and sustain participation, and to be hospitable."[86] In addition to giving access to tradition, religious education should make manifest "the intrinsic connection between traditions and transformation,"[87] a sentiment I echo with my emphasis on Vision.

I appreciate "making accessible" and its related phrases for the activity of movement 3 because they imply a style of teaching that respects participants as subjects. When participants are given *access* to their Story/Vision of faith, in contradistinction to having it imposed in a doctrinaire or "banking" manner, they are encouraged to have a personal encounter with its texts—a relationship of respect between "knower and known"—and to actively appropriate it to their lives. My nuance is that I do not use "making accessible" to mean a dispassionate activity, free of persuasion. Boys includes affective and persuasive dimensions in it; giving access includes energizing, sustaining participation, and hospitality, and it is to make manifest the "connection between traditions and transformation." However, the phrase has an overtone in common usage of simply rendering something available to someone, who can then "take it or leave it" as far as the access agent is concerned. A little of this meaning is appropriate here, in that the freedom of participants as agent-subjects encountering the tradition must be respected. And yet religious educators' caution to avoid indoctrination (i.e., a thoughtless imposition) should not deter them from persuasive representation of the tradition done in a thoughtful mode of access. In light of its purposes, Christian religious education has aspects of evangelizing— getting people interested in the first place—and of catechizing—"reechoing" the tradition in ways likely to touch people's hearts, form their values, persuade their wills, shape their identities, bring them to worship, and so on. These aspects are not honored by a dispassionate "take it or leave it" access to the tradition but by an affect-laden and persuasive one.

A style of persuasion is not synonymous with homiletic and should not be sermonizing.[88] Instead, I'm proposing that religious educators reclaim some of the ancient but mostly forgotten tradition of rhetoric as eloquence of speech, an art well practiced by many of the great educators of Christendom. As Augustine explained, to be eloquent is to "speak so as to teach, to delight and to persuade."[89] The intent of movement 3 of shared praxis is well served when done with sufficient eloquence to teach, delight, and persuade. This nuance said, "making accessible" suggests three guiding principles for the style of the educator's teaching in movement 3: a *disclosure* manner, a *dialogical* mode, and an *engaging* style.

To illustrate a *disclosure* style it may help to distinguish it from teaching a faith tradition with a style of "closure."[90] The latter presents one hermeneutic of the tradition as unquestionable and final truth, as if this one presentation exhausts the meaning of any symbol. "Closure" forgets the surplus of meaning in every symbol of Christian Story/

Vision and the historical conditionedness and thus relativity of all its interpretations. "Closure" tells people what to "know" and discourages their own imaginative appropriation of their faith tradition. Thus, "closure" tends to arrest people in their faith journeys and confirm them as dependent objects rather than sponsoring them onward as agent-subjects-in-relationship. A disclosure style gives people access in ways that open up the tradition so that they are drawn to intuit, to think, to question, to imagine, to discern, to come to see for themselves, to decide about what this Story/Vision means for their lives now.

A "disclosure" style is enhanced by the educator making evident, as appropriate, one's "principles of selectivity" in interpreting the tradition, thus signaling that this is *one perspective*. It is often appropriate to suggest some alternative perspectives, or at least to make clear to participants that there are various interpretations of every expression of Christian Story/Vision.[91] Even with young children, a presentation can be couched in language that avoids pretending to be exhaustive of Christian Story/Vision and implies that one can continue to grow in understanding and living this faith throughout life. In essence, a disclosure style means making the faith tradition accessible so that people can always build upon and add to what we teach—the antithesis of "closed-mindedness."[92]

Making accessible also suggests a *dialogical style* of teaching in movement 3. Our style should invite participants into active dialogue and conversation with Story/Vision, prompt them to bring their own stories/visions to appropriate their faith tradition. The ideal of a dialogical mode of access in movement 3 is the whole group involved as "educator." But even if movement 3 is enacted by a lecture method, it can be done dialogically if the educator lectures with a language pattern that invites people to recognize and discern, to judge and appropriate for themselves, what is being made accessible. As Freire is wont to say, "Even as I lecture, I am in dialogue with you if I try to put into my speech some challenging content that causes you to reflect."[93] Besides "challenging content," we also encourage conversation by pausing with reflective questions and inviting responses throughout a presentation. A resource person can be dialogical even if he or she does most of the talking; one way of doing this is to insert phrases into a presentation such as "I'll be interested to hear what you think of all this" or "I'm wondering if this is making any sense to you" (i.e., intimations of movement 4) or "Our understanding of this (text, issue, whatever) has varied over the years and continues to develop" or "Take note of your own reactions to what I'm saying."

The third principle, *engagement,* I have elaborated on already as constitutive of a conative pedagogy (chapter 2) and of shared Christian praxis (chapter 4). In movement 3, the religious educator is to make Story/Vision accessible with a style likely to actively engage the lives and interests of participants, in a way that draws them into it with their whole "being" and to take it seriously as something for their lives in faith. Plainly, people are engaged when, metaphorically, they "sit up" and say, "hey—this is about us, for our lives." To actively engage people with the text of Story/Vision should be a conscious interest throughout our hermeneutics in movement 3. It is also enhanced if we use a narrative practical language and if we keep in mind participants' stories/ visions. Engagement highlights too the importance of an image-filled presentation of Christian Story/Vision. Given the role of symbols as modes of God's revelation, it seems imperative that the language world of movement 3 be suffused with engaging and life-giving images from the faith tradition. Sharon Parks advises that "the quality of faith ultimately depends upon the adequacy of the images it employs."[94]

C. Attitudes of the Educator

The drama of a shared Christian praxis event, and especially the dynamic of its third movement, unfolds as an encounter between three dramatis personae: (1) the community of faith, living and dead, represented by its Story/Vision, (2) the other participants with their own stories and visions from present praxis in place and time, and (3) the educator who is responsible to the "others" to see to it that they "meet" in ways both appropriate to the community tradition and adequate to the lives of participants. Developing the art of movement 3 activity invites the educator to some basic commitments or foundational attitudes toward all three "players."

1. Toward Christian Story/Vision.   Christian religious educators are called to commitment that reflects ever deepening attitudes of faith, hope, and love toward the Christian tradition of being religious. We need *faith* in its potential to always be a source of God's revelation again as it is made accessible in *this* teaching/learning event. We need *hope* in the life-giving power of this Story/Vision, that it can be reclaimed from generation to generation as a source of liberating salvation for these lives and for the life of the world. And we need a *love* for the Story/ Vision that cherishes it, even enough to be critical of it, as a gift from God; we are to love it because it represents in very human form the heritage and promise of God's covenant with the community of saints and sinners before us. It can nurture *our* "being" in right relationship with God, self, others, and all creation.

Making such attitudes operative within a particular event has many implications and especially for one's "style" of doing movement 3; here three "procedural" points come to mind. First, these sentiments cannot be developed and maintained by academic study alone. Educators have that responsibility but also need to pray and live their way into ever deepening personal appropriation of the richness of Christian tradition.

Second, commitment to the tradition requires seeing to it that participants have direct access to its symbols and to a well-informed and responsible hermeneutic of them. Since this responsibility belongs first to the "church," I can think of few decisions by a Christian community or school more important than the curriculum resource materials it chooses for its education in faith. Its curriculum resources should always reflect the best of contemporary scholarship, the *sensus fidelium,* and the consensus of the community's magisterium.[95]

Third, I reiterate that the educator should intentionally make accessible both a Story *and* a Vision in movement 3. Because they are symbiotic to each other, I have written of them as one throughout; in a pedagogical event, however, it is imperative that the educator beintentional about proposing Vision as well as giving access to Story. Sometimes if the Story is well explained with practical intent, the Vision is already evident. However, typically the educator teaches the Vision explicitly—proposing to participants what their faith Story promises and demands of our lives.[96]

2. Toward the Other Participants.   In chapter 15 I outline in some detail the anthropological commitments (i.e., understanding of people) that undergird a shared praxis approach. Here I only note the attitude toward other participants suggested by the dynamic of movement 3. Even if the educator is the primary resource person, she or he must never treat other participants as passive "receptacles," as if "they don't know" and need to be filled with the teacher's knowledge. The whole dynamic of movement 3 calls the educator to honor people as agent-subjects-in-relationship who have already encountered God's self-disclosure in their own stories/visions and have an affinity and capacity, by God's grace, to recognize for themselves God's revelation through the symbols of Christian faith. In their dialogue and discernment they can be a community of teachers and learners *with* the educator; she or he should empower rather than control their teaching/learning. This calls especially for the educator to be flexible and open, even after thorough preparation, to adapt a presentation to the comments and needs of the other participants.

3. Toward Oneself as Educator.   The nature and purpose of movement 3 lends special exigency to the educator abandoning the traditional image of teacher as answer-person, as one with "epistemic privilege" who controls the "knowledge." It invites teachers to see themselves, instead, as co-learners who render the service of seeing to it that the Stories and Visions of the faith community are made accessible in ways appropriate to the tradition and adequate to the lives of participants. In movement 3, as throughout shared praxis, we see ourselves best as "leading-learners"—open to learning from Story/Vision and from other participants, even as our leadership serves to facilitate and resource the teaching/learning of the whole community toward wisdom in Christian faith.

Appendix

1. An event with sixth-graders on the creation of humankind used Phyllis Trible's revisionist translation/interpretation of the Adamic myth.[97] The hermeneutics of the story pointed out that Adam means "earth person," not "man" in the gender sense; that when God differentiated the earth person into male and female, God made them as companions and equal partners and not, as usually translated, the woman as "helpmate" to the man. The Vision in movement 3 outlined what it means for us to be "companions" together and with God, highlighted the equality of the sexes, the freedom and responsibility people have to live as stewards of creation, to see themselves and all others as created in God's own image and likeness.[98] I cite this as an instance of drawing upon contemporary biblical and feminist scholarship and of choosing an interpretation precisely because of its reign of God potential for inclusiveness and mutuality. The hope is that young people who learn the Adamic myth this way will never think of it as a legitimation of patriarchy, as it has been so often used in the history of the "church."

2. In a six-week Lenten program with the Altar Society of a Catholic parish, the participants had chosen the generative theme of Women in the Church, with a particular focus on the issue of women's ordination. Apart from myself, the group was of women who were senior members of the congregation. It became evident in the opening movements that they agreed, and I disagreed, with our church's official position of refusing ordination to women. The presentation in movement 3, spread over three meetings and interspersed with much conversation and dialogue, drew upon contemporary scriptural, historical, theological, and magisterial resources. I presented the historical praxis of Jesus as a radical critique of the sexist mores of his time, highlighting his commitment to a "discipleship of equals." We reviewed aspects of the life of the church over its history that have affirmed the equal rights of all people but also ways in which it has been bigoted, discriminatory, and exclusive. We read from and studied together the Vatican document of 1976, "Declaration on the Question of the Admission of Women to the Ministerial Priesthood," and its three main arguments against the ordination of women. We also studied some of the scholarly critiques of those arguments, and especially the one offered by Karl Rahner.[99]

As Vision, we reflected on the text of Galatians 3:28 ("neither male nor female," etc.) and on some of the human rights tradition of Catholicism, to propose a church of mutuality and inclusiveness (i.e., "catholic") for all God's people. Being designated the facilitator and resource person, I made my own "principle of selectivity" and convictions about this issue clear to participants. Movement 4 was a lively dialogue, and movement 5 brought some decisions from participants and facilitator that none had anticipated at the beginning. (See appendix, chapter 10.)

Chapter 9

Movement 4: Dialectical Hermeneutics to Appropriate Story/ Vision to Participants' Stories and Visions

In movement 4 participants place their critical understanding of present praxis around a generative theme or symbol (movements 1 and 2) in dialectical hermeneutics with Christian Story/Vision (movement 3). In the fullest expression of its dynamic, participants ask, How does this Story/Vision affirm, question, and call us beyond present praxis? And, conversely, How does present praxis affirm and critically appropriate the version of Story/Vision made accessible in movement 3, and how are we to live more faithfully toward the vision of God's reign?

Such dialectical hermeneutics between the two sources of Christian faith conation/wisdom (present praxis and Christian Story/ Vision) enable participants to appropriate the community Story/ Vision to their own lives and contexts, to know it for themselves through judgment, and thus to make it their own as agent-subjects in the larger Christian community and in the world.

1. Nature and Purpose of Movement 4

Two general comments may help to introduce the nature and purpose of movement 4. First, because movements 4 and 5 are complementary and proximate activities in a cumulative dynamic, the distinction between them is of emphasis rather than separation; they frequently overlap and trade places in an educational event. Essentially, movement 4 of shared Christian praxis is a dialectical hermeneutics between participants' stories/visions and Christian Story/Vision; movement 5 (chapter 10) is essentially an activity of decision making. This means that the dialectic between participants' visions and a Christian Vision is active in movement 4 but is operative most explicitly in movement 5 as people choose a lived response to the whole process. The dynamic of coming to see for themselves in movement 4 encourages participants into the decision making of movement 5. In some events the transition from movements 4 to 5 is quite subtle. Procedurally, movement 4 usually places emphasis on the dialectic between participants' stories and a Christian Story, whereas the visions-Vision dialectic is emphasized in the decision making of movement 5.

Second, from my attempts over the years to fulfill the intent of movement 4 and to educate others to do likewise, I recognize that this may be the most challenging of the movements of shared praxis to do well. The difficulty may arise not so much from the activity itself as from what we bring to it out of our prior socialization as both "learners" and "teachers." In more traditional models of teaching, the movement after a "presentation" is typically used to establish the "accuracy" with which learners have "absorbed" the material presented, often verified by ability to repeat what the teacher has said. Even the more "liberal" models in my experience do little more than invite participants to raise questions or issues for further clarification. Although movement 4 of shared praxis can well include verifying accuracy of understanding or inviting questions, it also goes beyond these activities to inquire of participants what they are thinking and feeling and "doing" in response to what they have encountered. Beyond inviting questions or points for clarification, it asks if participants have answers or insights, personal sentiments or feelings, disagreements or reservations, or if there are additions they want to make to what was made accessible in movement 3.

The essential purpose of movement 4 is to enable participants to critically appropriate the faith community's Story/Vision to their own lives and contexts. By "appropriation" I mean that participants integrate Christian Story/Vision by personal agency into their own identity and understanding, that they make it their own, judge and come to see for themselves how their lives are to be shaped by it and how they are to be reshapers of its historical realization in their place and time. Movement 4 intends participants to actively appropriate Christian Story/Vision of faith in ways that shape their identity and agency in the world, to personalize and interiorize it as their "ultimate myth" of meaning and ethic of life.

The educator encourages appropriation in many ways and at many levels (according to developmental readiness, etc.). The most complete dynamic activity that undergirds it is that of participants' placing in dialectical encounter their present praxis (as expressed in movements 1 and 2) and the version of Christian Story/Vision made accessible in movement 3. In shared Christian praxis, movement 4 provides occasion for participants to intentionally bring the "praxis" and the "Christian" components of the approach into an explicitly "shared" relationship. Seen as conversation, movement 4 is a dialogue by participants between their own stories/visions and a Christian Story/Vision that is shared and tested in the teaching/learning community. Seen as dialectic, the most complete expression of movement 4 is a two-way hermeneutics between stories/visions and Story/Vision that has moments of affirming and cherishing, questioning or refusing, and "moving beyond."

Movement 4 can often be done quite subtly (e.g., "What are you thinking now?"). Yet the full breadth of its dialectical hermeneutics entails a two-way asking of three questions, to reflect the three aspects of a dialectical encounter. Moving from community faith to participants' lives, they are prompted to ask, (1) In what ways does this symbol of Christian faith affirm present praxis and help us recognize its truth and values? (2) In what ways is present praxis questioned and called into judgment by it? (3) How does this Story call us beyond present praxis to live more faithfully into the Vision of God's reign? Then, moving from present praxis to Christian Story/Vision, participants are prompted to ask, (1) What do we recognize as true and valuable in this symbol of Christian faith? (2) What do we find problematic or perhaps refuse in the version made accessible to us? (3) What do we need to reformulate in our understanding of this Story to live more faithfully into the Vision of God's reign? Stated more obviously, movement 4 is an explicit opportunity for participants to ask and respond to the following questions: How does this aspect of Christian faith affirm, question, and call us beyond present praxis? From our present lives, what do we find true, and what do we question in this symbol of our faith? And from this, how are we to live our Christian faith in the world? Its two-way hermeneutics operates in concert, so rarely will religious educators frame movement 4 questioning activities in such a cumbersome fashion as above.

Some further analogies for movement 4 may help to elaborate its nature and purpose with a view to effecting it in particular events. First, and echoing chapter 3, section 4, on engaging the whole conative structure of participants' "being," movement 4 of shared praxis is analogous to Lonergan's notion of judgment, to Piaget's equilibration between assimilation and accommodation, and to Gadamer's "fusion of horizons" with the intent of practical wisdom.

Movement 4 encourages judgment in the Lonerganian sense, in that the understanding from one's own praxis (movements 1 and 2) enters into dialogue with understanding that has arisen from the faith community over time (movement 3), and by a "critical reasonableness" (Lonergan) both are evaluated in light of each other to discern what is true for one's life. If such judgment is to promote "differentiated consciousness," Lonergan's advice to the educator would be, I believe, to construct questioning activities that prompt participants to consciously attend to, understand, judge, and decide about the adequacy of their appropriation of Story/Vision. In a shared praxis pedagogy, this conscious application of the four transcendentals to one's intentional act of judging is aided by the testing dynamic of the communal dialogue. The educator is also to fashion questioning activities that prompt participants to turn to their own interiority. Procedurally this means asking questions like, What do *you* really think and feel in response to this presentation? Is it true for *you,* and how do you know? What consequences do you perceive, and why do *you* perceive them? That is, questions should bring people to judgment and also to evaluate their own judging activities. Note, however, that movement 4 activity is *analogous* to Lonergan's notion of judgment (i.e., similar but not synonymous) in that the judger in movement 4 is also judged—a two-way relational process. In movement 4 each participant judges the adequacy to present praxis of the version taught of Christian Story/Vision, and that Story/Vision in turn judges the praxis of the participants and of society.

Appropriation in movement 4 is also analogous to Piaget's notion of equilibration—return to a steady state—from the dialectic between assimilation and accommodation. As participants make the faith tradition their own (assimilation) their Christian identity/agency is deepened (accommodation) from their encounter with it. For Piaget, such equilibration is epitomized by the "ah-ha" moment when we "reinvent" the truth that others may have known already but we now see for ourselves.[1] "Equilibration," however, could be a misnomer here, in that the proper outcome of movement 4 is not a state of stasis but an opening onto new horizons and impetus for choice, decision, and action in movement 5. In this regard, Gadamer's "fusion of horizons" with the intent of practical application is a more apt analogy for the activity of movement 4.

Movement 4 intends a "fusion" between the horizon of the "text" of movement 3 and the horizons of participants. In this "fusion" participants recognize their own "horizons" as both reflected in and expanded by the symbols of their faith tradition, and they recognize that the symbols' horizons of meaning and value are "ahead of" or "in front of" the symbols themselves, and ever expanding. Gadamer makes clear that a "fusion of horizons" should never lead to a "closed horizon" but to an ever-expanding one.[2] Such fusing and expanding of horizons has the intent, says Gadamer, of practical wisdom, of the *phronesis* Aristotle described as arising from "a union of desire and intellect."[3] To promote practical wisdom, movement 4 engages the whole "being" of participants as agent-subjects-in-relationship. It is indeed a reasonable activity, but also affect-laden, to prompt the will toward choice (movement 5). Educators pose questions that explicitly invite participants to express their thoughts, their feelings, and their sense of how they *can* respond to what was made accessible in movement 3.[4]

Another perspective on movement 4 is to see it as participants doing to the symbols encountered in movement 3 what they did in movement 2 to their expressions of present praxis in movement 1. As such it is a critical reflection by participants on some form of Christian Story/Vision. As critical reflection, movement 4 engages people's critical reasoning and remembering to evaluate the version of Story/Vision made accessible and its adequacy to their praxis in place and time. But the function of imagination in movement 4 deserves special emphasis. Whatever we come to "see for ourselves" is always perceived through an image. Our poetic and image-making capacity—our poiesis—mediates the dialectical encounter and appropriation between community Story/Vision (movement 3) and present praxis (movements 1 and 2).[5] The more the educator can engage people's imaginations in movement 4, the more likely they are to come to an "owned" faith.

The last perspective on movement 4 worth noting is that rather than an exercise in negativity, it is a creative and hope-filled activity. Its intent is to deepen the Christian identity/agency of participants by enabling them to make the tradition their own in ways that promote commitment and wisdom in Christian faith. Its moments of affirmation and of reservation toward a symbol of Story/Vision both have the positive purpose of uncovering what is true and valuable in the faith handed on. And it separates what is true and life-giving from what is distorted and destructive in order to "move on" with renewed commitment. In this, movement 4 is a moment of "sublation" toward the version of Story/Vision made accessible in movement 3. Lonergan describes such a moment well: "What sublates goes beyond what is sublated, introduces something new and distinct, puts everything on a new basis, yet so far from interfering with the sublated or destroying it, on the contrary needs it, includes it, preserves all its proper features and properties, and carries them forward to a fuller realization within a richer context."[6]

2. Rationale for Movement 4

I offered a philosophical rationale for this movement 4 activity in chapter 3, especially in section 4. I argued that a pedagogy for conation, grounded in an epistemic ontology, must engage the whole dynamic structure of people's "being." Drawing on Lonergan's schema of the dynamics of cognition, I described judgment (for Lonergan, the third transcendental activity) as an activity of dialectical appropriation and proposed it as essential to the cumulative dynamic of a conative pedagogy. Here we need only appropriate this philosophical rationale in the context of movement 4 of shared Christian praxis.

First, the dialectical activity of appropriation in movement 4 is essential for a shared praxis approach to deepen people's Christian identity and educate them as agent-subjects of their faith. If the learning dynamic is structured to bring participants to passively accept the teacher's version of Christian Story/Vision, and if they are not given an opportunity to enter into a dialectical appropriation of it, their own identity and agency as Christian "subjects" is not encouraged; participants will likely repeat what the educator says and "knows" rather than come to their own word and wisdom. On the other hand, when participants actively appropriate, interiorize, and see for themselves what this Story/Vision means for their lives, their own agency and freedom as subjects of their faith are enhanced[7] and they are more likely to come to commitment in movement 5.

Note that the dialogue of movement 4 has two aspects: between each participant's own story/vision and Christian Story/Vision, and between each participant and the whole group as people share their appropriation of the faith tradition to their lives. These dialogues are necessary if participants are to avoid both "objectivism" and "subjectivism" in their discernment and appropriation. Without their own dialogue with community Story/Vision, participants can fall into "objectivism" and deny their perceptions—accepting the version presented as "the last word." Without submitting their dialectical hermeneutics to the testing dynamic of community dialogue, they are prone to "subjectivism" in which they presume to be the sole measure of discernment by themselves, in isolation rather than in "right relationship."

Clearly, then, movement 4 is a crucial moment of transitionfrom the encounter with Story/Vision in movement 3 to the choosing of praxislike decisions and responses in movement 5. It should not be slighted if Christian Story/Vision is to bring participants to new levels of commitment as responsible subjects of Christian faith in the world. Beyond this, it seems appropriate also to make more explicit an aspect of the theology of revelation that undergirds shared Christian praxis and is reflected most evidently in this fourth movement.

The Revelatory Dynamic of Movement 4.   I have already noted the convictions undergirding shared Christian praxis, that both present praxis and faith Story/Vision are sources of symbolic mediation of God's revelation in the existential lives of people and communities of faith. I noted further that critical consciousness about present praxis heightens its revelatory potential and that Christians are to constantly reconstitute their Story/Vision with hermeneutics of retrieval, suspicion, and creative commitment that it may be, as Bernstein says, a "living tradition" rather than a "dead one."[8] This latter conviction flows on into and undergirds the hermeneutical activity of participants in this movement. But movement 4 activity also reflects the conviction that in the encounter between their own stories/visions and a Story/Vision of Christian faith, participants have a "natural" capacity to see the revelatory correlation between the two sources.[9] The revelatory dynamic of movement 4 arises from a basic aptitude or affinity people have to move constantly back and forth between recognizing the truth of God's self-disclosure in their own lives and the resonant truth in "the faith handed on." I emphasize that educators should structure movement 4 activities intentionally in particular events rather than presuming on people's natural ability for correlation, yet I'm convinced that people have an innate capacity and disposition to do what is intended to be done by movement 4—to recognize and appropriate the truths and values of Christian Story/Vision to their own lives.

I note that this conviction is not shared by all; some respond that people have a natural reluctance rather than affinity for the dialectical appropriation intended in movement 4. Undoubtedly, all of us at times prefer being told "the truth" and what to do with it by "authority" rather than having to discern and choose it interdependently in a community of dialogue. In addition, many people are socialized by styles of religious education that discourage dialectical appropriation of their community's Story/Vision; too often the "authority" of a Story/Vision is used to bring people to unquestioning acceptance of its truth rather than to appropriating it as agent-subjects-in-relationship. But according to Kohlberg, Gilligan, Fowler, Parks, and other developmentalists, this style arrests people at a stage of their faith journey (stage 3) where they depend on what "they" (i.e., authority symbols) say. The dynamics of Christian religious education should have the potential to sponsor people (even from the earliest years) beyond a conventional stage toward maturity in lived Christian faith.

I'm convinced that in spite of socialization to the contrary, people always retain at least the seeds of the capacity to place their own life narratives in dialogue and dialectic with Christian Story/Vision. They never lose the ability to recognize the resonance between the truth in each source and to maintain a healthy wonder about both because "mystery" always remains. With an adequate pedagogy, people's natural disposition for dialectical appropriation can blossom and become a permanent *habitus* of their life in faith. In fact, when movement 4 activity is suitably structured and encouraged, I have found that even kindergarten children can begin to participate in an interpersonal appropriation of Christian Story/Vision and to see for themselves what it means for their lives.

Beyond evidence from my own praxis, my warrant for the conviction that people have a native capacity for movement 4 activity reflects the theological anthropology that functions in concert with its undergirding theology of revelation throughout a shared Christian praxis approach. In chapter 5, I drew upon Rahner's notion of the "supernatural existential" in human "being" to buttress the claim that people are capable of encountering and recognizing God's self-disclosure in present praxis. Because the structures of people's "being" are "already graced" by God's original self-communication to them, they are capable of responding to God's loving outreach and revealing presence in their existential lives. Likewise, here I add that by the same "supernatural existential," which is the operative gift of God's Holy Spirit in the depths of human "being," people have the capacity to recognize God's self-disclosure in what Rahner calls "categorical revelation," or what I have been calling throughout Christian Story/Vision.

Rahner's conviction about our inner capacity to recognize God's self-disclosure echoes the biblical sense of the "word" already within us, in our hearts (see Deut. 30:11–14). Augustine had a similar conviction that people have "a truth already within" that enables them to recognize truth symbolically mediated from without. Augustine saw the pedagogical implication of this as a teaching style that encourages people to think and judge for themselves, to recognize and evaluate the truth in a teacher's words and in the narrative of "salvation history."[10] However, in this regard I highlight Thomas Aquinas and his notion of a "connaturality" between human wisdom and divine revelation.

Thomas used the concept of *connaturalitas* in a variety of ways but always to refer a natural affinity or disposition of something for something else. He was convinced that God's loving outreach to humankind (i.e., grace) transforms and works through nature and argued that when the human mind encounters divine revelation, we have a "natural" disposition, by God's grace, to recognize and appropriate its truth. We have a kind of "built in" readiness for the word of God, however it is symbolized to us. Aquinas said our connaturality with divine revelation is guided by the Holy Spirit and functions especially in the activity of judgment (i.e., for shared praxis in movement 4). He wrote, "It belongs to the wisdom that is an intellectual virtue to pronounce right judgment about Divine things after reason has made its inquiry, but it belongs to wisdom as a gift of the Holy Ghost to judge aright about them on account of connaturality with them."[11] For Aquinas, then, God's Spirit in us, working through our natural capacity for reflection, enables us to recognize with connaturality the truth of God's revelation as mediated through Christian Story/Vision. Echoing this sentiment, movement 4 of shared Christian praxis reflects the conviction that as people encounter God's self-disclosure through Christian Story/Vision, they have a "natural" (but graced) ability and affinity to recognize and personally appropriate its truth and values for their lives. Their sharing of such appropriation in a community of dialogue is integral to a curriculum for conation/wisdom in Christian faith.

3. Procedures for Movement 4

Because movement 4 is a participative and dialogical activity among all participants, many of the procedural counsels offered for the opening movements are relevant here too. Ideally, participants have so taken on the dynamic of movement 4 that their comments and questions effect its intent with shared responsibility. But this is the ideal; it takes time and community building and is most likely to emerge with older participants. Meanwhile, the designated educator has primary responsibility for facilitating movement 4. Echoing the procedures of the opening movements, this movement calls educators to maintain an environment of dialogue, to invite people's *own* reflections, to keep the dialogue focused on the intent of movement 4 and typically around a generative theme, to encourage participants to share and test their perceptions and hermeneutics in the group dialogue, to give everyone the opportunity but never force anyone to speak, to ask probing questions without being interrogative, to model the intent of movement 4 if this seems appropriate, to envision questioning activities and to adapt them to the occasion, to maintain active and empathetic listening, to allow time for silent reflection, to be willing to invest their own "self" in the dialectical dynamic of movement 4.

Beyond this general procedural advice (all of which is relevant again in movement 5), to do movement 4 effectively may require a significant shift in style and consciousness of both educator and other participants. It is a big shift for educators to move from asking people to accurately repeat back what they have made accessible to inquiring of them what they really think and feel about it, or from inviting questions to welcoming answers and new insights, including disagreements and additions that participants are coming to see for themselves. Likewise, it is a change for participants from simply accepting and remembering what teachers teach to sharing in dialogue their own dialectical hermeneutics of what teachers or other resources make accessible. As with all the movements of shared praxis, it is important for effective procedures that the educator especially have a clear sense of what is to happen in movement 4. I restate its intent here in more procedural terms.

In shared Christian praxis, movement 4 invites participants to place their naming of and critical reflection on present praxis of a generative theme or symbol (i.e., movements 1 and 2) in dialogue and dialectical hermeneutics with what they have encountered from Christian Story/ Vision (movement 3). They are to evaluate both the version of Story/ Vision as made accessible and the version of present praxis expressed in movements 1 and 2 by bringing these two "sources" to "judge" and be appropriated to each other. This requires participants to turn to their own interiority, to themselves as subjects, to discern how they appropriate community Story/Vision to their own reality, and to test their discernment in dialogue with other participants. Procedurally, then, movement 4 is a self-conscious questioning by which participants share in dialogue their responses to questions like, What are you really thinking, feeling, intuiting, discerning for yourself and of yourself in response to this Story/Vision? What sense or non-sense is emerging for you? What are you recognizing as true, questioning as problematic, negating as false, or adding as new to your own understanding? What are *you* "doing" to this Story/Vision as made accessible, and what is it "doing" to your identity and commitment as a Christian?

As with all the movements of shared praxis, the educator can effect movement 4 by a great variety of different activities and "methods." Its intent, however, calls primarily for questioning activities. The educator's role is to devise questioning activities that are effective in achieving its intent and to adapt them as appropriate to the age level of participants, the time available, the context, the generative theme of the occasion, and so on. As people bring their own stories/visions into dialogue and dialectic with a community Story/Vision, *what* they express can be their sentiments, attitudes, feelings, intuitions, perceptions, evaluations, discernments—whatever reflects their perceived truths, values, meanings, reservations, additions, emerging insights, commitments, and so on. Many procedures used to bring people to expression in movement 2 are also effective here when structured to promote the intent of movement 4. Because of the breadth of *what* people can express, in movement 4 the *how* of their expression is equally broad. I have participated in events that used speaking, writing and sharing, drawing and explaining, creating a symbol or aesthetic expression, journaling, movement, role-playing, a panel followed by general dialogue, a debate, working on a joint appropriation project, and many more.

For example, giving participants opportunity to write their appropriations before inviting dialogue gives them time for clarification and a greater sense of security about sharing with the whole group. The invitation to write may be posed in an understated but nonetheless effective manner; for example, "Continue listening to the dialogue going on inside of you for a few minutes, and perhaps take a few notes on what you're coming to see for yourself." The educator may also pose a series of movement 4 questions, or provide a worksheet with suitable questions, and allow time for silent reflection and responding. A few probing questions are usually sufficient to encourage the group dynamic to test people's expressions.

Role-playing is particularly effective with young children after they have encountered a Bible story or parable in movement 3. When invited to role-play the story "as it might happen today," their appropriation is heightened. Their hermeneutic continues in debriefing after the role-play as they share how they felt in the various roles, what thoughts they had, what the story means for us now, the difficulties in perceiving or living its meaning and values, and so on. These exercises can elicit an amazing level of dialectical hermeneutics and appropriation from even the youngest children.

An example of people working on a common task at movement 4 was a large community engaged in discerning how to renovate their church building according to contemporary standards of liturgical renewal. Movement 3 included a presentation by a liturgical space designer, who articulated some general principles to guide the construction of appropriate worship space. One movement 4 activity invited participants to work in small groups on copies of the floor plan of their present space to apply, but also to adjust, the principles they had heard according to their community needs, resources, and so on (it was in deed a dialectical hermeneutic). With large groups of participants, it can help to have a few designated respondents ready to lead off the dialogue in a panel format. Panelists can be prepared to model a movement 4 response of affirming, questioning, and adding to what they encountered in movement 3. With good modeling, the general dialogue is likely to follow a similar movement 4 dynamic. A debate can also achieve a similar outcome. For a section on social ethics with an undergraduate theology course, I invited four people to prepare brief position papers, two appreciative and two critical, of the U.S. Catholic Bishops' pastoral letter *The Challenge of Peace* (part of their required reading for movement 3). When the dialogue opened to the whole class, a dialectical hermeneutics of the text continued.

Key to the educator's structuring of procedures is that movement 4 is an activity of appropriation enacted through dialogue and dialectic between participants' own perceptions of present praxis and Christian Story/Vision regarding a generative theme or symbol. This may sound complex but can often be done quite subtly. For example, appropriation is encouraged after, or indeed during, movement 3 by such questions as, What are you thinking or feeling now? What are you coming to see for yourself? What insights are emerging for you? What do *you* say about all this? The difference between asking at movement 4, "What are you thinking?" as compared to "Are there any questions?" may appear quite subtle; the pedagogical significance should not be underrated. How often do we hear lecturers say they will "welcome questions" after their presentation? What a different pedagogical dynamic might go on with participants if an educator indicates that she or he will welcome hearing the insights, reservations, and "answers" that are emerging for them. And there are events when it is advisable in movement 4 to emphasize one aspect of the dialectic, for example, what participants would add to what they encountered in movement 3.

A more thorough procedure that honors the fullness of dialectical hermeneutics would ask participants, in one way or another, As you look at your understanding of present praxis regarding (the theme) and at this aspect of Christian Story/Vision that pertains to it, what occurs to you as true and to be affirmed? Is there something that you question or find problematic? What is emerging as your own insight or possible commitment from this dialogue? Such questions are, of course, more feasible for older participants. Yet younger children, when their responses are invited in concrete terms, can enter into activities of dialectical appropriation at their own level of readiness. For example, in an event on God's forgiveness with third-graders, movement 4 was built around such questions as the following:

· Do you really believe God forgives you when you do something wrong? Why or why not?"
· Can it be difficult to believe that God really forgives you? When? Why?

· How does God's forgiveness make you feel about God? What does it tell you about God's love for us?
· How can we respond to God's forgiveness?
· When is it difficult to forgive others?
· What do you think is the most important thing *you* have learned from this lesson?

Teachers often raise the procedural issue about movements 4 and 5—What if participants in their dialectical hermeneutics and decision making reject something that is central to the Story/Vision of their faith community? First, people can and do reject what they are taught in Christian faith education, regardless of the approach used, whether such rejection is explicitly or (more often) implicitly realized. I note too that this question is more often raised as concern for "orthodoxy" than for "orthopraxis." Yet few who claim orthodoxy in Christian faith can also claim consistent orthopraxis; our sins, in a sense, are rejections of something constitutive of "being" in Christian faith. Some of people's refusals or rejections can reflect a healthy skepticism that enables the "sense of the faithful" to detect distortions in the version of Story/Vision presented to them. Some rejection, however, can be of something truly constitutive of the tradition, and the "open" and dialectical dynamics of movement 4 of shared praxis formalizes that possibility. In a sense, encouraging people to express it is an asset of the approach; it is better to address rejection within a teaching/learning event than to allow participants to appear to accept something only to reject it tacitly, or in their lives. Nevertheless, this issue raises understandable concern for the sponsoring community of such a process and for religious educators themselves.

My personal concern with this issue has been relieved by my praxis over the years. I have rarely experienced explicit rejection of something constitutive of Christian faith—on the upper echelon of the hierarchy of truths—within a pedagogical event. A few times it has happened with older participants who had already rejected, at least tacitly, a particular truth or practice before the process began. Often, too, people have refused some aspect of *my* version of Christian Story/Vision, but to accept another possibility more adequate to their experience and perhaps more appropriate to the tradition. Beyond these nuances, however, explicit rejection by participants of something central to Christian Story/Vision is a possibility. It can be rejection of Christian orthodoxy or of orthopraxis. The former is more likely in movement 4 and the latter in movement 5, although the response to each is quite similar. To make the problem concrete, I take an instance of each.

Regarding *orthodoxy* in mainline Christian tradition, it is possible in an event on Christology that someone rejects the dogma that fully human and divine natures existed in hypostatic union in one person, Jesus the Christ. Whether people reject full divinity or full humanity, they place themselves outside the dogmatic definition of Chalcedon (451).[12] What does the educator do?

First, make sure through probing questions and your sense of the circumstances that a person is seriously and knowingly rejecting Chalcedon and not simply your version of its definition or a particular theological interpretation of it. Chalcedon's statement set the parameters within which "orthodox" Christian faith must be confessed about the divinity and humanity of Jesus. These parameters do not exclude diverse explanations and interpretations of its meaning. For example, some scholars now refer to Chalcedon's key words *hypostasis* and *prosopon* (see note 12) other than as "person" (e.g., Rahner's "way of being"). Indeed, a number of different theological schools of thought, all considered orthodox, explain what it means to say that Jesus is fully human and the Son of God. A participant's position may well reflect an acceptable explanation, albeit not the teacher's preferred one. If it is evident, however, that an adult participant rejects the essential meaning of this dogma, a Christian religious educator, out of responsibility to both the person and the faith tradition/community, needs to make clear that such rejection places them at this time in their faith journey outside the professed faith of the Christian community. Unless it is impossible to do so, a statement to this effect should be made in private conversation[13] and must always be handled with great sensitivity. The educator's style in the dialogue should be what Champlin summarizes as "challenge, don't crush."[14] One must avoid all semblance of implication that "outside this church there is no salvation," make clear one's respect for the person's choosing as they best discern, and recognize that in their faith journey they may be in the process of identifying with another faith community.

In matters of belief short of such central dogmatic statements,[15] I find that the normal shared dynamic of group dialogue is sufficient to enable participants to review and test agreements, disagreements, unusual interpretations, and so on. The educator's tasks are (a) to help create an environment conducive to interpersonal discernment and decision making, and (b) to honor in her or his own dialogue the criteria of authentic explanation (continuity, consequences, and "community") outlined in chapter 8. To do more or less than this violates the dynamics of shared Christian praxis and the dignity and religious freedom of participants. Of religious freedom, Vatican II declared, "In spreading religious faith and in introducing religious practices, everyone ought at all times to refrain from any manner of action which might seem to carry a kind of coercion or of a kind of persuasion that would be dishonorable or unworthy."[16]

Regarding Christian orthopraxis, I take up the instance of someone rejecting the mandate of justice. Here again, an educator must make sure that the person is rejecting commitment to the demand of justice and not simply "testing the waters" or challenging the educator's opinion of what it means in particular circumstances to be just. Then, the educator is responsible to both the Christian tradition/community and participants to teach that commitment to justice is not an option for Christians but a mandate of God's reign, that deliberate injustice on any level is sinful. If a participant of sufficient age persists in rejecting commitment to justice as a "constitutive dimension of the . . . Gospel,"[17] then the educator, again with pastoral sensitivity to "challenge, not crush" and preferably in private conversation, must point out that such a stance places that person, at this time in his or her faith journey, outside a central conviction of the Christian community. Beyond that, an educator must respect and encourage a participant's right to choose how to live the mandate of justice.

Jesus is the model for Christian religious educators as they encourage freedom of discernment and decision making. Throughout the Gospels his call to discipleship is in the vocative case—by invitation. When the rich young man refused his invitation "come, and follow me," Jesus was saddened by the refusal but respected his choice (see Luke 18:18–25). After the discourse on the "bread of life" in John's Gospel, we read that "many of his disciples broke away and would not remain in his company any longer" (John 6:66). In response, Jesus turned to the Twelve and explicitly gave them the option, "Do you want to leave me too?" (John 6:67). In the praxis of Jesus, call to discipleship carries with it the right of refusal. God takes the same risk in calling people to covenant and giving them free will. The praxis of Christian religious educators should offer the same call and sense of freedom of response.

4. Developing the Art of Facilitating Movement 4

Most crucial to the art of facilitating both movements 4 and 5 is to grow in genuine "openness" to the discernment and decision making of participants. Otherwise the educator is unlikely to encourage the kind of environment and dynamic that prompts participants to come to their own appropriation and decision making. Ironically, for religious educators, the challenge of genuine "openness" is heightened by the very faith convictions that we bring to our work, as well as by the ordinary human sentiment that prefers people to agree with us. Our faith convictions are evident especially in our hermeneutics of the community Story/Vision; they lead us to propose with particular conviction the personal meaning and ethic we find in Christian faith. For instance, if an educator is strongly committed to peace, she or he will teach the Story/Vision from this perspective and with the hope that participants will become likewise committed. Though educators must honor such hermeneutical guidelines as outlined in chapter 8, I believe their personal convictions should be evident in their teaching, both for its integrity and to encourage conation.

On the other hand, the dynamic of movement 4 asks the educator to sponsor truly open-ended questioning activities that encourage participants to see for themselves and personally own what Christian Story/ Vision means for *their* lives. People are not to repeat our word but to speak their own; that may well be a "new" word for both. "Openness" here will call us to new places in our own faith journeys as participants go beyond where we have ventured, or to where we once were and regressed. The educator needs a kind of "relinquishment" (*kenosis*) that lets go of old patterns of "teacher power" and avoids looking for "right answers" that agree with our expectations. Such authentic "openness" is a journey of lifelong conversion for every religious educator.

My second counsel pertains to the disposition of participants for the dynamic of movement 4. I have claimed that people have a "natural" capacity for it, and their aptitude is encouraged as movement 3 is done with a disclosing, dialogical, and engaging style. Yet participants may be accustomed to didactic pedagogies that dispose them to receive and give back what a teacher teaches. Many at first suspect there is a "right answer" that the teacher expects at movement 4 and search for it instead of listening to themselves and one another. A graduate student told me that it had taken a full semester for him to realize that I really did not have a "right answer" in mind that he was to guess at when I posed movement 4 questions.

Initial hesitancy notwithstanding, participants can engage in the intent of movement 4 if it is done consistently over a period of time and with suitable procedures. I reiterate that the teacher can model movement 4 dialectical activity as a catalyst for reluctant participants. For example, in a lesson I observed with fifth-graders on loving our neighbors as ourselves, the teacher in movement 3 taught the Christian Story/ Vision on the theme with disclosure and dialogical style, and some creativity. When she invited participants to appropriate it to their lives, however, they seemed reluctant to do any more than repeat what she had been teaching. Undaunted, she sat down, looked them in the eye, and said, "Now let me tell you some of the problems I have with loving my neighbor." By the time she finished listing how difficult it can be to truly love one's neighbor as one's self, everyone in the room had something to say. At the end of movement 4, they seemed to know the centrality of the "great commandment" to Christian faith and the challenge it poses, and had their own sense of what it means for their lives.

Educators must encourage all incipient signs of movement 4 activity and proceed with conviction that participants can do the dialectical hermeneutics intended here. We know personally how participants can play the game of telling the teacher what they (we) suspect he or she wants to hear but do their own internal dialogue and dialectic, albeit unnamed. Few of us believed and accepted exactly what our teachers told us, although they may not have suspected as much at the time. Movement 4 of shared praxis provides an environment and dynamic that engages such internal dialogue, welcomes it, and brings it to expression as part of the curriculum for the whole community. By some such dynamic, I'm convinced, they are likely to "make the faith their own."[18]

Appendix

1. On many occasions when the theme of a workshop or seminar has been the shared praxis approach itself, I have built movement 4 activities around asking participants three questions, each representing a leg of the dialectical tripod. The questions can be posed in many ways, as can sharing of responses to them, but usually run something like this: As you encounter the shared praxis approach, and thinking about your own work as a religious educator,

What do you perceive to be its strengths?

What are its weaknesses or difficulties?

What adjustments would you make in the process to use it effectively in your own praxis?

2. In an event with sixth-graders focused on their hopes and dreams, movement 3 was a catechesis on the reign of God in Jesus as an empowerment of people's hopes and dreams, and movement 4 was structured around the following activity:

Looking back at the hopes and dreams you shared at the beginning of class, and having studied how Jesus invites and empowers us to live into the dream of God's reign, what are the hopes and dreams that you now see us being called to live?

Imagine you hear that Jesus is in a nearby city preaching the reign of God. Write Jesus a short letter telling him your greatest hopes for your family, your neighborhood, and for the world.

Now write what Jesus might answer you.

This exercise can invite sixth-graders to appropriate Jesus' call to God's reign and some of what it means for them in their present lives. Movement 5 continued as follows:

Examine Jesus' answer to your letter. Choose some things you will try to do this week to help bring about the reign of God: in your family, in your parish, in your neighborhood.[19]

3. Going back to the earlier example I gave in chapter 7 of shared praxis in farming education, movement 3 makes accessible a great variety of modern techniques and strategies for improving the quality of farming in the particular area. Then movement 4 is typically built around questions such as these:

What strategies or methods seem workable in this community?

What do you think would not be effective here? Why?

What new insights are you having about how we might farm in this community?

These questions flow inevitably into movement 5, which is decision making and corporate strategizing for a renewed farming praxis.

Chapter 10

Movement 5:
Decision/Response for
Lived Christian Faith

Movement 5 offers participants an explicit opportunity for making
decisions about how to live Christian faith in the world. In keeping
with a holistic understanding of Christian faith (chapter 1) and of
conation or wisdom therein that engages people's whole "being" in
"place" and "time" toward "truth" that is cognitive, relational, and
moral (chapter 3), responses chosen by participants, depending on
the generative theme or symbol, context, and so on, can be primarily or variously cognitive, affective, and behavioral and may pertain
to the personal, interpersonal, or social/political levels of their lives.
Decisions too may be personal ones by each participant or be made
by the consensus of the learning community. Whatever the form or
level of response invited, the practical intent of the dialogue in
movement 5 is to enable participants, by God's grace working
through their own discernment and volition, to make historical
choices about the praxis of Christian faith in the world. As long as
they maintain continuity with the central truth claims and values of
Christian Story, reflect the faith of the broader teaching/learning
community—the church—and are creative of the Vision of God's
reign, they are likely to be appropriate decisions for lived Christian
faith.

1. Nature and Purpose of Movement 5

Movement 5 creates a dynamic and dialogue that explicitly invites participants to decision about their response, individual and/or collective,
as the historical outcome of this shared Christian praxis event. Philo-

sophically, movement 5 encourages participants to a decision for knowing, desiring, and doing with others what is humanizing and life-giving
for all; it also provides a community of conversation whose communal
probing and testing dynamic prompts participants to make self-
conscious and intentional decisions. In theological terms, movement 5
reflects and promotes the hope that participants will choose, by God's
grace, a response of renewed Christian praxis, faithful to God's reign.
The process began with the focusing activity that turned participants to
an aspect of present praxis, typically around a generative theme or
symbol, followed with their own expressions of present action (movement 1), their critical reflection upon it (movement 2), their encounter
with a Christian Story/Vision regarding the curriculum focus (movement 3), and their dialectical appropriation of these two sources—
"praxis" and "Christian"—to each other (movement 4). The practical
intent of this cumulative process is that participants might come to
Christian conation or wisdom, to their own "truth" in Christian faith.

Movement 5 not only gives participants explicit opportunity to
make particular praxislike decisions but aims also to form them in the
habit of making decisions conceptually and morally appropriate to
Christian faith. In the context of education in Christian faith, movement 5 intends to influence people's particular actions to be Christian
and to form individual's themselves as "Christian actors." In other
words, its dynamic encourages people to decide and choose both what
to do now in faith regarding this generative theme and who to become
over time.[1] A word about each emphasis may help the educator to
imagine appropriate procedures to facilitate movement 5.

A. "What to Do" Decisions

As intimated by many of the central themes of this book, the decisions the educator invites in movement 5 can be varied, manifold, and
all-embracing. For instance, shared Christian praxis intends the learning outcome of Christian conation, but such wisdom engages every aspect of human "being" in place and time, and Christian faith includes
cognitive, affective, and behavioral activities. Or again, the holistic
understanding of people's own "truth" in Christian faith I proposed
(chapter 3, section 5) should be reflected in the decision making of
movement 5. Likewise, this approach originates with present praxis to
eventuate with renewed praxis in Christian living, but I posed "praxis"
as every intentional human activity. In light of such holistic notions of
Christian conation or wisdom, faith, "truth," and praxis, one readily
recognizes how manifold and comprehensive the decision making of
movement 5 can be. The theme, context, participants' age level, background, and so on can advise a distinct emphasis in the questioning
activities of a particular occasion, but generally any truly human decision whereby people are likely to live their Christian faith is appropriate
to movement 5 of shared Christian praxis.

I can think of at least four categories of appropriate decision-making activity that the educator can encourage in movement 5. There can be many combinations and variations across and within these categories, yet the decisions (1) can emphasize cognitive, affective, or behavioral forms; (2) be invited on personal, interpersonal, or social/political levels; (3) pertain to individual or communal activities; and (4) be effected within the immediate group or outside it.

1. Cognitive, Affective, and Behavioral Decisions.   Participants can give a primarily cognitive or affective or behavioral form to movement 5 decisions, or a decision may engage all three responses in its realization. There can be a primary emphasis in the decisions participants make, but responses from an encounter between present praxis and Christian Story/Vision should not usually be exclusively cognitive, or affective, or behavioral. The particular emphasis usually depends on the generative theme or symbol of the occasion and the context of the event. Doctrinal themes tend to invite a more cognitive decision, spiritual themes a more affective response, and ethical issues elicit a response of overt activity. Likewise, a more "academic" context may advise a more cognitive emphasis in decision making, whereas a congregational or "confessional" context more readily encourages affective and behavioral decisions as well as cognitive ones, and so on. The emphasis may vary from one particular instance to another, but the Christian religious educator should encourage all three in some form to promote wisdom in Christian faith.

Although decision making in movement 5 can have varied emphasis, the Christian educator should structure all questioning activities to encourage the *praxis* of Christian faith. Questioning activities that elicit overt behavioral responses to realize an ethic *of* and *for* life clearly have such practical intent. Less obvious perhaps is that cognitive and affective emphases in decision making at movement 5 should intend the praxis and historical realization of Christian faith in people's lives. This is so because realized Christian faith entails orthodoxy, orthopraxis, and "right relationship"—the latter epitomized in "right worship" (see chapter 12)—in mutually enriching, correcting, and symbiotic unity.

Questioning activities in movement 5 can emphasize cognition; personally I experience this emphasis regularly in my university context with undergraduate theology courses. But from my perspective of a praxis-based pedagogy, even events where the educational dynamic most appropriately intends a cognitive outcome should be structured to elicit not only a chosen insight or understanding of some faith theme but also a sense of *conviction* about and *commitment* to what this means for one's life—that is, people's decisions should move them to practical wisdom with import for their identity and agency in the world. Even in very academic contexts, educators who do less opt for "technical" over "humanizing" rationality, for an epistemology that separates "knowing" from "being," and as Lonergan argues, they stop short of promoting authentic cognition. Certainly to promote conation in Christian faith, educators should invite cognitive decisions that shape people's identity and agency as Christians. For example, if movement 3 is catechesis on the Creed (or, more likely, a tenet of it), movement 5 questioning activities entice decision not only for deepened understanding but also for giving one's heart with intent to live as if one believes it—as if God is truly one's God, and so on. Cognitive decisions chosen with such practical intent and awareness of historical consequences are indeed fitting to movement 5 of shared praxis.

Likewise, when shared praxis is employed specifically to educate in Christian faith the questioning activities of movement 5 can encourage a primarily affective/relational response by participants, for example, inviting them to prayer or worship, to awe, reverence, or wonder, to aesthetic or artistic responses; such decision making should help to form people's identity and agency in "right relationship" with God, self, others, and creation. For instance, if participants choose a response in movement 5 of shared prayer, the prayer should express and dispose them to Christian consciousness and praxis (e.g., instead of "Dear God, please help people who are hungry," pray, "Give us the help we need to be responsible with our possessions and generous to those in need").

In sum, an authentic decision at movement 5 of shared Christian praxis will not typically have an exclusively cognitive, affective, or behavioral emphasis; all should reflect the "practical" interest of realized Christian faith. And there can be themes and occasions when it is fitting to invite decision that reflects all three aspects of faith activity. For example, following a movement 3 catechesis with sixth-graders on the Exodus event and the Ten Commandments, movement 5 presented a worksheet with the following questions, with space left after each one for written responses (parentheses added):

- Choose one of the Commandments that you feel needs your attention at this time. (intuitive/affective)
- *From* what does this commandment set you and others free? (cognitive with practical intent)
- *For* what does it set you free? (ditto)
- What will you do this week to show your respect for this God-given commandment? (behavioral)
- Write a short reflection in which you ask God for the help you feel most in need of right now to live this commandment. (affective)[2]

2. Decisions on Personal, Interpersonal, or Social/Political Levels.   We can make movement 5 decisions on a personal level that pertains to our lives and selves as agent-subjects in Christian faith. Such decisions are not "private," in that they have humanizing consequences for others as well as ourselves. Yet some decisions pertain primarily to one's own subjectivity. They are "personal" in that they bring me to a deeper *understanding* about myself, my Christian identity, convictions, and responsibilities, or to a greater *appreciation* of myself and faith tradition, or to personal experiences of inner healing, freedom, and so on, or to *do* something that reflects authentic love and care for myself as required by the "great commandment." Other decisions may pertain more to the interpersonal level of existence in that they refer to the praxis of our everyday relationships. These decisions can move participants to greater understanding of or right relationship with, or life-giving action toward, others. And movement 5 decisions are often overtly social/political in that they reflect participants' critical consciousness of their social reality, or a deepened feeling of solidarity with victims of unjust social structures, or renewed action for social/ecclesial transformation toward God's reign.

3. Individual or Communal Decisions. Every decision in movement 5 of shared Christian praxis should be made by each participant as agent-subject in interdependence and dialogue with the immediate group and with one's ecclesial community. Yet some decisions are more obviously for one's own praxis, others for a communal praxis by participants together, and still others for praxis that is done both individually and collectively. Clearly there are themes and occasions when participants should make decisions about their own historical praxis. For example, in my graduate courses I often structure movement 5 activity as an essay in which participants write themselves into praxislike clarity and decision about some issue that is foundational for their ministry. There are also themes and occasions that call the whole learning community to choose a common response to do together. Reaching consensus about what this response should be can take time, and effecting it together can require detailed planning. And there are occasions when both individual and communal decisions are invited and made. For example, in a teaching/learning event with a parish study group focused on world hunger (movement 3 included a review of the meaning and responsibilities of Eucharist regarding this generative theme) people made decisions at movement 5 about adjustments in their own personal life-styles, but also the group decided to form a "Bread for the World" committee in the parish.

4. Decisions Realized Within and/or Outside an Event. Some decisions at movement 5 may be effected within the educational community itself, although the consequences will inevitably flow beyond the event as well. An example is when groups choose to do some kind of liturgy at movement 5 to ritualize the wisdom and commitments they have come to from the occasion. Most often, however, movement 5 decisions are realized outside the time and place of the event.

In sum, many praxislike decisions are open to participants in movement 5. My categories for them—form, level, agency, and location—constantly overlap with one another in a variety of combinations. At movement 5 educators should sponsor questioning and discerning activities that invite and prompt participants to decision; decisions can emphasize cognitive/mental, affective/relational, or behavioral/moral forms, may be realized on personal, interpersonal, or social/political levels, within and/or outside the event, and may pertain to individual and/or communal action. Yet the pedagogical dynamic of movement 5 activity of shared *Christian* praxis should be suffused with the practical interest of lived Christian faith for God's Reign.

B. "Who to Become" Decisions

The second emphasis in the practical intent of movement 5 decision making is to nurture participants in the identity and agency of Christian "character," that is, in ongoing Christian conversion and wisdom. At the end of chapter 3, I proposed that a conative pedagogy is a conducive instrument for God's grace to work in people's lives toward conversion. Drawing on Lonergan, I noted that conversion has an *intellectual* aspect whereby one's way of knowing shifts beyond simply "taking a look" to being intentionally and self-consciously attentive, intelligent, reasonable, and responsible in one's cognition; conversion has a *moral* aspect in that people move beyond personal satisfaction toward congruence between the values they claim and how they live their lives; it has a *religious* aspect whereby people grow ever more deeply in love with God. And each aspect of Christian conversion is permeated by a *social* emphasis of ever-growing solidarity and agency in a Christian community, of critical consciousness about one's situation in place and time, of historical commitment to the social/political values of God's reign, of love for God that does justice by one's neighbor. The intent to sponsor such conversion is operative throughout the previous movements of shared Christian praxis but is preeminent here in movement 5.

First, in providing specific opportunity for praxislike decision making, movement 5 honors Aristotle's time-tested insight that virtuous and wise character is formed by repeatedly choosing and doing "right action." As he noted wryly (and with a dig at Plato), "Only an utterly senseless person can fail to know that our characters are the result of our conduct."[3] Second, movement 5 promotes conversion as it brings participants to their interiority as subjects and encourages them to consciously attend to, understand, judge, and decide about the adequacy and appropriateness of their own decision making. Conscious testing of decision making is encouraged by the community dialogue, as each participant is heard by and listens to others. Third, by giving people an experience of dialogue and interdependence in Christian decision making, movement 5 activity helps socialize them in Christian character through the good decisions of others and by the support a "wisdom community" (Braxton) can give its members in being faithful to their decisions.

2. Rationale for Movement 5

Much of Part I of this work and of the previous chapters of Part II has built cumulatively toward the "learning" outcome intended by movement 5 activity; its philosophical, pedagogical, and theological rationales are already well established. But as for previous movements, we can well attend to the theology of revelation that undergirds movement 5 when shared praxis is used in Christian faith education. In gist, it reflects the conviction that renewed engagement in the praxis of doing God's will heightens people's awareness of God's existential revelation in their lives.

To begin a pedagogy for Christian faith with participants' present praxis reflects the conviction that people's "being" and historical reality in the world is an existential source of revelation of Godself and will to them (chapter 5). Movement 5, as a return to praxis, reflects likewise but with the added conviction that people's renewed choice and effort to live their faith in place and time is a heightened source of God's ongoing revelation in their lives and community. As people intentionally choose and realize the fullness of life that God wills for all creation, such praxis brings them "closer to God." The standard Christian perspective is that God's self-disclosure calls for a human response, that revelation leads people to do God's will. But movement 5 of shared Christian praxis reflects this conviction both "forward" and "in reverse"; that is, the process promotes the outcome of lived Christian faith, and renewed Christian praxis leads people more deeply into God's self-disclosure. Conviction about the revelatory potential of doing God's will is strongly reflected in liberation theologies.

The method of liberation theology reflects the assumption that the actual praxis of God's will in the world, especially as realized in social struggles for peace and justice, is a "privileged locus" of God's ongoing self-disclosure to its agents and to the world.[4] That *doing* God's will is a *source* of revelation was expressed most precisely by Jesus in John's Gospel. Reflecting a common conviction of his Hebrew roots and Jewish faith, John has Jesus say, "If you live according to my teaching, you are truly my disciples; then you will know the truth, and the truth will set you free" (John 8:31–32). Note the sequence in what Jesus proposes. Movement 5 of shared Christian praxis reflects a similar conviction that by following Jesus' "way" of life, people can come to the wisdom that sets them free.

3. Procedures for Movement 5

If movement 4 is done properly, the group dynamic already has an impetus for decision making. Moreover, as participants become accustomed to the process they often take on the overall dynamic of shared praxis as a personal disposition and can readily share responsibility for bringing themselves and others to decision in movement 5. However, as throughout all movements, the educator is particularly responsible to render the service of seeing to it that a teaching/learning community is invited to decision making and, as necessary, offers questioning activities suitable to this end.

Rendering this service requires that educators clearly understand the procedural intent of movement 5. Procedurally, movement 5 of shared Christian praxis uses activities structured to elicit participants' own praxislike decisions for lived Christian faith toward God's reign.

Again, because movement 5 is such a dialogical and participative activity, many of the procedural points offered for the opening movements and movement 4 are relevant here. Without repeating them all, I adapt to movement 5 and highlight the following:

· Maintain an open and dialogical environment that welcomes the contributions of all and is conducive to the freedom of choice of participants;
· Invite people's *own* decisions and encourage their testing in the community;
· Respect the readiness of participants for decision making, and never force anyone to make or express a decision;
· Model the intent of movement 5 if this seems likely to encourage others in decision making;
· Imagine procedures to encourage decisions and first test them on yourself;
· Adapt the questioning activities to the age level of participants, context, time available, generative theme or symbol, and so on;
· Facilitate group planning if the whole community reaches a decision for some common action;
· Maintain a presence of empathetic listening and support as decisions emerge;
· Be willing to invest your "self" in the activity and to be called to decision.

Remembering the breadth of the term *praxis,* and the great variety of decisions that are fitting at movement 5, the *content* of what people express as their chosen responses may be their convictions, beliefs, insights, attitudes, sentiments, emotions, resolves, intentions, commitments, strategies, and so on, to be historically realized on personal, interpersonal, and social/political levels, individually and/or as a group, within and/or outside the pedagogical event. Participants can share their decisions through any *form* of human expression—literally, vocally, aesthetically, physically, or by a combination of these.

Beyond the list of counsels above and the ones to come in the next section on facilitation, here I make five procedural points. First, much as in movement 1, educators in movement 5 need to "think praxis" as they construct its participative activities. They offer questions and discerning activities that ask, in one way or another, What are you "doing" or "ready to do" (cognitively, affectively, or behaviorally) in response to this event, and how will you bring your response to expression and realization? Second, it is wise for educators to have prepared a variety of praxislike questioning activities of various forms; if the first one does not engage participants, try another.

Third, in envisioning suitable decision-making activities, educators must remember the generative theme or symbol that began the process, people's dialogue and critical reflection on it, the Christian Story and more especially in movement 5 the Vision made accessible, and participants' appropriation of Story/Vision in dialogue with present praxis. Fourth, educators should emphasize activities that engage the imagination of participants. The underlying dynamic of movement 5 is the dialogue and dialectic between people's own visions and a Christian Vision regarding an aspect of Christian praxis. For this "fusion of horizons" in decision making, people need imagination to both envision what they can or should do and to move their wills by desire to choice.

Fifth, educators are responsible for seeing to it that the criteria of an authentic explanation/application of Christian Story/Vision are operative in the group dialogue. I restate them here for decision making in movement 5. First, the educator should keep before participants the metacriterion of God's reign as the overall horizon of all decisions. Then, within this normative vision, for particular occasions and themes, the community should test its decision making: for *continuity* with the constitutive truths and values of Christian Story of this theme; for likely *consequences* that are consistent with and effect a Christian Vision by these participants now; and make their decisions with their "church" and in *dialogue* with the emerging decisions of other participants. As needed, the educator facilitates such community testing by probing questions; for example, Are these decisions faithful to a Christian perspective? Do they reflect Christian commitment? Do they help us to grow in living our faith?

Two other procedural issues arise frequently about movement 5: memorization and grading.

Memorization. From the beginning, the church's catechesis has had a strong tradition of committing to memory particular Scripture passages and stories, prayer formulas, creedal symbols, doctrinal summaries, and moral codes. The impetus for the church to memorize linguistic symbols of its faith came in part from the social context; before the printing press and widespread literacy, memorization of what seemed important was essential. However, Christians also memorized such symbols of faith to enhance their personal prayer life, to enable participation in community liturgy, as marks of Christian identity, and to be able to share their faith with others.[5] For these same reasons, I'm convinced there is still a place for memorization in Christian religious education, especially with children. People's practice of and witness to their faith, their participation in communal prayer, and indeed their sense of Christian identity are all likely enhanced if they know "by heart" such identifying symbols as the Lord's Prayer, the Nicene Creed, the Ten Commandments, John 3:16, and so on. Memorization is fitting to the dynamics of a shared Christian praxis approach if the form of community Story/Vision in movement 3 would advise it. The general procedural principle I propose is *that educators encourage memorization at the end of movement 5, after participants have come (according to readiness) to understanding, appropriation, and decision.*

This principle is advised by the whole dynamic of shared praxis and particularly by its commitment to promote wisdom through a participative pedagogy. To have participants memorize before—or worse still, without—coming to their own conation of the particular symbol would amount to a banking approach to faith education. On memorization before understanding, Pope John Paul II notes, "We are all aware that this method can present certain disadvantages, not the least of which is that it lends itself to insufficient or at times almost non-existent assimilation, reducing all knowledge to formulas which are repeated without being properly understood."[6] My principle also finds warrant in the traditional phrase for such memorization—*learning by heart*. It has a "subversive" memory for catechesis in a society and church dominated by technical rationality. It lost some meaning in the catechism era when it was used to refer to "learning by rote," with little to do with people's "hearts." But memorization that comes at the end of a process in which participants—according to readiness and as agent-subjects-in-relationship—attend to, understand, appropriate, and decide about the meaning and import of a Christian Story/Vision in dialogue and dialectic with their own praxis, is, we hope, truly memorization "by heart."[7]

Educators can facilitate memorization at the end of movement 5 in a great variety of ways; when it is done creatively, children can even enjoy it. If the symbol for memorization has a set pattern, for example, the Creed, the whole group can recite it a number of times over several occasions, can display it in an art form where it can be read together, can have a personal copy of the text, and so on. After proper pedagogy, a prayer formula can be learned by reciting it at the beginning and/or end of subsequent classes. When what is to be memorized does not have a set form, educators can invite younger children to articulate what they consider the "heart" of the lesson; they can then commit this to memory. A creative teacher I know uses this approach, and when children have decided what is most important to remember, she puts it to rhyme and melody, and they learn to sing it—a very effective way of committing to memory.

Grading. Some religious educators and theologians use a shared praxis approach in a schooling context where grading is required. The question arises, How does one structure course requirements, grade papers, examinations, and so on in ways that are just to participants and fitting to the shared praxis approach? To respond, I take one of the "hardest cases" and one familiar from my own praxis—teaching theology to undergraduates in a university.[8] I first note that at Boston College, as at most Catholic colleges and universities, undergraduate students are required to take at least two three-credit courses in theology; these courses are typically taught with commitment to rigorous academic study and without "confessional" assumption or intent. Students are as concerned about their grades in these as in any courses; theology grades will affect their grade-point average and thus job opportunities and graduate school admission. Also, students have many courses to choose from, but professors can only presume that this course was chosen instead of others (and often for scheduling reasons); one cannot assume that students are taking the course out of personal interest.

My framing of examinations and procedures for grading them in this context reflect three basic principles:

1. Students may be graded only on what Benjamin Bloom called "the cognitive realm of educational objectives"; they should not be graded, even if it were possible, on the affective and behavioral outcomes of their learning. That such "cognitive" evaluation is possible reflects the fact that movement 3 of shared praxis can be as academically rigorous and challenging as any other approach to teaching in such a context.

2. Evaluative instruments should reflect the cognitive processes employed throughout the teaching/learning event. Norris Sanders explains this principle: "An important rule in framing questions is that questions designed for grading should reflect the same kind of thinking used in instruction."[9]

3. To respect and encourage their own cognition as agent-subjects, participants' responses should be evaluated only on their ability to critically analyze, evaluate, and take informed positions on the "cognitive content" made accessible; their ideas are not to be graded against the teacher's preferred theological positions or those of their church.

Combining these three principles, a shared praxis approach calls for examinations that invite (a) an accurate expression of and familiarity with the "cognitive content" made accessible, (b) understanding that reflects students' own analysis and critical thinking about the cognitive content (most reliably evidenced by an ability to express it clearly in their own terms), (c) evaluation and judgment by students of the "cognitive content" they encountered, and (d) their chosen and tested perception of its meaning and import for themselves and others who take it seriously. Although the sequence is different, I note that my "taxonomy" of cognitive criteria is similar to what Bloom and others proposed as evidence of authentic cognition. For Bloom, true cognition in any science includes recalling or recognizing of information, followed by translation, interpretation, application, analysis, synthesis, and evaluation.[10]

4. Developing the Art of Facilitating Movement 5

As is true for the other movements, the art of facilitating movement 5 emerges only from the praxis of it. However, from my own and others' experience over the years, I can think of nine counsels I have learned.

1. In the "behavioral domain" (Bloom), it is important to encourage feasible rather than "fantastic" decisions within the present capacity of participants. Decisions too far out of reach are likely to overwhelm rather than empower people. This does not mean that educators should avoid challenging questions at movement 5 or the prophetic aspects of community Vision. "Without the vision, the people perish" (Prov. 29:18), but people need to begin with what is now possible. As Freire writes, "The best way to accomplish those things that are impossible today is to do today whatever *is* possible."[11]

2. Educators can have a "realistic optimism" about ourselves and others to make and fulfill decisions. Christian theology claims that because of our "fallen" estate, we tend to resist making and living authentic choices for the true and the good, that we have a proclivity for sin. Further, developmental researchers advise that a great majority of adults seem content to remain at a conventional level of faith or moral development; this means that most people make decisions according to social conventions instead of choosing autonomously in dialogue and interdependence with a community of faith and values. Bellah and his colleagues say that in American culture what often looks like personal decision making is a conventional following of the dominant social ethos: rugged and self-sufficient individualism.[12] Developmentalists also claim that the transition from a conventional to a more self-chosen faith is the most difficult and hesitant in a person's faith journey.[13]

We must take such realism seriously but only to temper the overriding optimism that educators need about participants' ability to make and live their own decisions. Christians should have a "realistic optimism" because of their faith. They should not acquiesce in sin or indecision but resist both, with confidence that God's saving deeds in Jesus empower people to follow Jesus' way as disciples. Educators should not take developmentalist *descriptions* as *prescriptions,* as if they are not to invite people to their own decision making until they have reached a postconventional stage of human development. I'm convinced from my work that young children have less difficulty in coming to their own decisions than do typical adults. But even adults who are socialized in a "culture of dependence" about their faith, when encouraged and "permitted" by an approach like shared praxis, can begin making their own decisions.

3. The more effective and fitting movement 5 questioning activities are "open-ended" rather than "yes or no" ones (e.g., What do you think you want to do about x? rather than, Will you *do* x?). Pose all movement 5 questions in an invitational and gentle way, without pressuring people

to decide now or to share their decision with the group. Many partipants may not be ready for decision or to articulate it at this time; their freedom must be respected. Vatican II states, "The Gospel has a sacred reverence for the dignity of conscience and its freedom of choice,"[14] and this must surely be honored by educators in Christian faith. As in movement 4, respecting people's freedom of choice calls educators to a kind of relinquishment and also for patience about "seeing results." John Dewey said wisely, "Perhaps the greatest of all pedagogical fallacies is that people learn the thing they are studying at the time that they are studying it."[15] Open-ended questioning, invitation, respect of choice, and relinquishing of control all highlight the importance of the educator's own maturity and ongoing journey in faith. If we are closed-minded or fossilized in our own faith, we are less likely to encourage participants to new horizons in their decision making.[16]

4. Monitor self and others to resist the temptation to make decisions about what *other* people should do. In a parish group I belonged to for some years, until we "had the habit" of movement 5, we tried to discipline ourselves to avoid saying "I think people should . . . " and to favor statements that begin "I (or we) will . . . " This was effective in prompting us to our own praxislike decisions rather than to "theories" about what "they" (the government, the church, etc.) should be doing.

5. When a community decides on corporate action, they need to make a plan. This entails coming to collective consensus on what action to take, setting common hopes or objectives—short-term and/or long-term—and then concrete pastoral planning of steps to take, by whom, when, and how, to effect the communal decision.[17] Such communal praxis normally presupposes that participants have some level of ongoing commitment to the group.

6. Try to create an environment conducive to decision making, and that supports participants in carrying out their decisions. The goodwill, example, solidarity, and encouragement of a group can empower each of its members to levels of faithfulness far beyond what is attainable by individual effort alone.

7. Communal prayer and liturgy at movement 5 to ritualize and celebrate the wisdom emerging among participants can be a powerful source of deepened support, solidarity, and commitment.[18] Such liturgy not only expresses commitment and community but also becomes a source of them.

8. In one sense movement 5 concludes the dynamics of shared praxis within a formal pedagogical event, but in another it only marks a beginning. There should always be a "sixth" movement—living the decisions made. In an ongoing group the praxis that results from one occasion can be taken up in the focusing activity of the following one.

9. My last counsel here pertains to all the dynamics and movements of the shared Christian praxis approach. Remember that making a decision for lived Christian faith and acting on it always requires the

grace of God. We can never choose or act faithfully by our own efforts alone. Even with our best efforts as religious educators, only the presence and power of the befriending Spirit can "give the increase" (see 1 Cor. 3:6). Whatever approaches we use are no more than "vessels of clay," yet they can carry "treasure" whose "surpassing power comes from God and not from us" (2 Cor. 4:7).

5. Variations and Flexibility of the Movements

I conclude this Part II with some reflections on the flexibility of the process and the variations possible in the sequence of the movements. I first note that a distinct shared praxis event can be spread over a varying length of time. The movements can be done, with adaptation, in a brief encounter or over a whole semester, in a forty-minute class or a weekend seminar, throughout a parish renewal program of extended duration or in a fifteen-minute sermon, and so on. When the movements are separated over time, educators need to provide "linkage" that refocuses the generative theme or symbol and picks up previous dialogue to carry into the movement of the particular meeting.

Regarding age level, faith educators can begin to use shared praxis at least with participants who have reached the onset of concrete operational thinking (about five or six years) and up into old age. From experience I believe that this approach can be used with people from very diverse backgrounds. Its movements unfold differently among kindergarten children, doctoral students, and senior adults, and according to location—congregation, family, school, retreat, and so on. Whether people are poor or wealthy, from the ruling class or marginalized, also shapes the unfolding and outcome. From very limited cross-cultural experience, I'm keenly aware that different cultural backgrounds present their own particular challenges to facilitating a shared praxis approach. Yet I believe there are basic intentions in its dynamics that can be honored, albeit differently, in various contexts.

There is much room for flexibility in the sequence of its movements. The sequence I have outlined from focusing activity to movement 5 reflects the cumulative dynamic of a conative pedagogy. In existential events, however, this dynamic should be an orchestrated process rather than an inflexible sequence. *The movements of shared praxis are dynamic activities and intentions to be consistently honored over time rather than "steps" in a lockstep procedure.* The dynamic among participants often causes the movements to overlap, occur and recur, be recast in many sequences. I use the word *movements* intentionally to signify a free-flowing process orchestrated and choreographed much as are the movements of a symphony or a dance.[19] Educators should remember, as Jesus said of the Sabbath, that the process is made for the participants, not participants for the process. Do not try to "fit them into it";

rather, allow the group dynamic to shape the ebb and flow and sequence of movements.

In general, the proper intention for educators using shared praxis is to honor the dynamic intent of all its movements. But shared praxis is more an attitude, a style, a "way of being with" people that a teacher embodies than a fixed series of pedagogical movements. Due to exigencies of time, size of group, situation, and so on, there are occasions when some movements are done better than others, or when it is not feasible to engage participants in all five of them. For example, in a convention setting with a large audience and fifty minutes to present, the emphasis is likely on Story/Vision, but a lecturer can still at least suggest movement 1 and 2, and 4 and 5 kinds of questions and reflections in her or his presentation.

Educators can combine movements or vary their sequence in a great variety of ways; the following suggestions are meant only to stimulate further creativity. To begin with, the focusing activity and movement 1 can be combined, and it may often be pedagogically more effective to both turn to present praxis and invite participants' own expression of it in the same group activity. Likewise, movements 1 and 2 can be combined into one activity that honors the intent of each, and sometimes with better effect than keeping them separate (e.g., with fifth-graders: What are some of the things you notice about how our society treats people who are nonwhite?—that is, naming and beginning of social analysis of a present praxis). Or the dynamic can proceed from movement 1 to movement 2 and back to movement 1 again as participants share at different levels of expression and critical reflection. There are occasions when a form of movement 2 can be done after the focusing activity, as when participants share memories and hopes regarding a theme before moving to describe present praxis of it (see the appendix in chapter 7). I have also participated in events that began with descriptions by participants of the praxis that emerged from a previous meeting (thus beginning with movement 1); then a generative theme emerged out of this general dialogue (focusing activity) and was followed by a movement 2 dynamic of critical reflection. And as noted in chapter 5, a common focus may emerge only after shared reflection on some aspect of present praxis.

Community Story/Vision of movement 3 can be sequenced both backward and forward from its typical moment in the process. Some summary points from the faith Story can be made as the focusing activity; this can establish a theme and engage people with it. Likewise, it is often apt for the educator to share some Story/Vision during movement 1 and 2 dialogue in response to what emerges from participants. On some occasions there may be no distinct movement 3 because it is intermingled with the dialogue of the opening and closing movements (with the Vision in movement 5 to prompt decision). Even when movement 3 comes in its typical sequence, it can readily refer back to the

stories/visions of the opening movements and may require pause for
further movement 1 or 2 kinds of reflections that are stimulated for
participants by the encounter with Story/Vision. Or, looking ahead
from movement 3, and especially when Christian Story/Vision is made
accessible over a number of meetings, there should often be pause to
raise movement 4 or 5 kinds of questions before returning to movement 3 to unfold it further. Such a sequence may be necessary to maintain the active interest and engagement of participants. I have also
participated in occasions when the more detailed Vision statement was
made prior to movement 5 as a catalyst to decision making.

Movements 4 and 5 can often be combined or flow back and forth
with each other in one group activity that interweaves the intentions of
each. For example, in a history of religious education course, after each
historical period studied I invite participants to draw a "subversive
memory" from it that they want to shape their own praxis in the present and future. Rereading the original sources and notes from class
dialogue and lectures to search for such a life-giving memory engages
participants in a movement 4 activity of dialogue, dialectic, and personal appropriation. However, a "subversive memory" (in contrast to a
theoretical insight) is likely to engender commitment and historical
agency from the one who chooses it.

Educators may give a program the overall structure of a shared
praxis approach, but each movement may be repeated with varying
emphasis within the pedagogy. For instance, the standard edition of the
Coming to Faith curriculum is designed for a school setting where typically there is a religion class each day of the week. Within each five-day
unit, day one (presumably Monday) concentrates on the focusing activity and the first two movements. Days two and three are primarily a
movement 3 emphasis, but each day is introduced with brief movement
1 and 2 activities and concludes with abbreviated movement 4 and 5
activities. Day four begins with a brief movement 1 or 2 activity, has a
movement 3 presentation, usually with a Vision emphasis, and concludes with an extended version of movement 4. Day five (presumably
Friday) is primarily a movement 5 activity followed by a review of the
week's work and some "faith at home" activities.

These are only some variations that educators can give the sequence
of the movements of shared praxis. But as all who have used such a
process well know, there are occasions when the dynamic of the group
provides its own sequence. I have participated in events when a person
at movement 4 shared a reflection that might have been more appropriate in movement 1 or 2 or someone skipped movement 4 and went
to 5, and so on. The fitting response of the educator is to welcome such
interventions whenever they come and whatever their form, while still
maintaining focus on the generative theme or symbol of the occasion
and the general intent of the particular movement.

Appendix

1. In an inner-city church, the focus of the adult study group one Sunday morning was the mission of the church to the inner city. When it came to the fifth movement, the educator invited participants outside to stand facing into the city as they came to their decisions. The change of location seemed to lend them impetus to choose praxislike responses.[20]

2. A fifth-grade event around the theme of ministry and published in the Coming to Faith curriculum is an instance of communal decision making and planning. The opening movements and movement 3 put emphasis on their own praxis of service to others and the call of all the baptized Christians to participate in carrying on the mission of Jesus in the world. I report movement 5 as it appears in the student text; the Teachers' Guide gives suggestions on how the teacher can facilitate the group decision making and planning.

> Choose one of the following ways you and your class will serve or minister to others in your parish, school, or community this week:
>
> · Offer to visit the sick.
> · Offer to help your teacher or catechist in the classroom.
> · Volunteer to participate in any community project for the poor, the handicapped, or those working for peace and justice in the world.
> · Volunteer as a tutor for younger or handicapped children in any topic you are good at.
> · Other suggestions:
>
> Our class chose this project:
>
> Complete your class plan for your project.
>
> · What preparations do you need to make?
> · What will each member of the class do for the project?
> · When will you begin?[21]

3. In the example I cited earlier (chapter 8) of the "altar society" reflecting on "women in the church," movement 5 questions first evoked little praxislike response. However, one of the oldest members finally announced, "I'm going to write to my granddaughter in California and tell her that I think the church is sexist in many ways, and we must all work together to see to it that women are fully included in every aspect of church life, including ordination." Many others seemed to generally agree, but her intervention was a catalyst, and many suggestions emerged about what needs to be changed and how they could help to make the changes. Finally, the group decided to each write a letter to some young woman about whose faith they cared deeply (granddaughter, grandniece, neighbor's child, etc.), telling her of their new hopes for and commitments to an inclusive church.

Appendix to Part II

The Focusing Activity

1. The focusing activity turns people to their own "being" in place and time, to their present praxis, and establishes a focus for the curriculum. Typically, it does this most effectively by engaging participants with shared focus in a generative theme for the teaching/learning event by sponsoring a present action of it or by turning them toward some aspect of their historical reality in the world to recognize the theme as it is operative in present praxis.

2. The focusing activity may also turn participants to present praxis through an engaging symbol so that as people look through it they begin to recognize a particular aspect of their own and/or their society's praxis; from this a specific theme will likely emerge.

3. A generative theme is some historical issue, question, value, belief, concept, event, or situation that has import and meaning for participants' present lives; a generative symbol likewise actively engages participants and turns them to some aspect of their own present praxis. The theme or symbol remains the curriculum focus throughout the subsequent movements.

4. The focusing activity should actively engage the interest and participation of people as agent-subjects in the teaching/learning event.

5. The focusing activity is most effective when it turns people to present praxis in a way that establishes a "shared focus" of attention for this occasion.

6. An overall program can encourage a present action of a theme outside the intentional teaching/learning event, or the actual event can sponsor a communal action around the theme, or it can raise up a symbol/icon that enables people to recall and recognize what they are already "doing" or what is now "going on" regarding the theme or symbol in present praxis.

7. The focusing activity reflects the convictions that God is actively disclosing God's self and will in the everyday history of people's lives and that they are capable of encountering and recognizing this existential revelation through reflection on present praxis.

8. In selecting a generative theme or symbol, the following guidelines should be remembered:

   a. The generative focus should turn to some aspect of present praxis that is likely to engage people's active participation because it is of import and meaning for their lives in the world.
   b. The selection process should be consistent, as far as possible, with the "shared" dynamics of partnership, participation, and dialogue.
   c. Selecting a generative focus in Christian faith education is to attend to both present praxis *and* to Christian Story/Vision.

9. The educator especially is responsible to attend to the psychosocial and physical environments of the teaching/learning event, being attentive to creating an inclusive and dialogical context of intellectual and psychological hospitality, a trustworthy environment of respect and welcome for all, an event in which people have a sense of partnership and shared responsibility for the teaching/learning process.

10. An effective focusing activity within a teaching/learning event is one that

   a. sponsors a praxis of a generative theme or turns people symbolically toward an aspect of present praxis that reflects or suggests a generative focus;

   b. engages participants to elicit their active participation in the teaching/learning dynamic;

   c. establishes a clear and shared sense of the curriculum as it pertains to present praxis;

   d. establishes a focus that is "manageable" for these participants on this occasion.

11. The educator especially has responsibility to clearly understand the theme and maintain focus on it throughout the whole teaching/learning event and to offer it to the community in a style that invites dialogue and reflects respect for participants.

12. In envisioning and constructing a focusing activity, the educator may want to pose the following questions:

   a. Does this activity turn people to an aspect of their own present praxis?

   b. Is it likely to engage participants with what is a generative theme in *their* lives?

   c. Does it establish a common focus that is clear and manageable and around which participants can readily express their present praxis in movement 1?

   d. Does it establish the generative focus in a way that evokes and clearly welcomes dialogue?

Movement 1: Naming/Expressing Present Action

1. Movement 1 invites participants to "name" or express in some form their own and/or society's "present action," typically of a generative theme or around an engaging symbol, as they participate in and experience that praxis in their historical context. Depending on the focused theme, this expression of consciousness of present action varies in both content and form.

2. In content, participants can depict how the theme is being lived or produced, dealt with, realized, "going on" or "being done" in their own or in society's praxis; they can express their sentiments, attitudes, intuitions, or feelings toward it, the operative values, meanings, and

beliefs they see in present praxis of the theme, their perceptions and assessments of it, their commitments regarding it, and so on.

3. In form, present action can be named or expressed through a recognizable activity, in making and describing, in symbolizing, speaking, writing, gesturing, miming, dancing; that is, by any form of human expression. As long as people bring their conscious and historical engagement with the generative theme to expression, the intent of movement 1 is being fulfilled.

4. Note that participants can express (1) their consciousness of their own or (2) of their society's praxis, or (3) their perception of both. Which to invite depends on the theme of the occasion and what seems most likely to engage participants in the dynamic of movement 1.

5. Whether people are expressing their own praxis or that of society around a generative theme or symbol in movement 1, their expressions are to truly be their own. They are to speak their own word about it and express what engagement with the theme prompts in their own consciousness.

6. Movement 1 expressions should not be treated as if they are "objective" or "value-free" reports of present praxis; to do so works against critical reflection in movement 2.

7. Movement 1 can invite an expression of a praxis that is consciously motivated by religious faith or of a human praxis in which the faith dimension is as yet pre-reflective.

8. The expressing of their own consciousness of present praxis is constitutive of people as agent-subjects and an essential step toward responsible freedom and social transformation.

9. The "action" brought to expression in movement 1 can be any intentional human activity or any aspect of what constitutes the participants' "life-world" in their social context, that is, whatever comes into consciousness from what one is "doing" or from what is "being done" regarding the generative theme or symbol.

10. The procedures to effect the dialogue of movement 1 should, (a) insofar as feasible, provide opportunity for all participants to express their consciousness of present praxis to at least one other participant if they so desire and (b) never force anyone to expression.

11. One should not presume that the more silent members are not participating; the educator is to be a catalyst for a hospitable environment that respects the learning style of each participant.

12. Crucial to constructing questioning activities fitting to the dynamics of shared praxis is to keep in mind the specific intent of each movement. The intent of movement 1 is to elicit from participants an expression of their own consciousness of present praxis apropos the generative theme or symbol.

13. In formulating appropriate questioning activities for movement 1, educators should (1) be clear about the generative focus; (2)"think praxis" and imagine what might be elicited from this community regarding their praxis of the theme, without invading people's privacy;

(3) look for open-ended rather than yes-or-no questions; (4) imagine a questioning activity likely to elicit their own consciousness of present praxis, that is, try it first on themselves; (5) adapt the activity to age level, context, time available, and so on.

14. In promoting dialogue, educators (1) are to invite people to expression in a way that reflects the importance of their own word as essential to the curriculum; (2) may ask probing questions but without sounding interrogative; (3) may model the intent of this or any of the movements if it is likely to facilitate dialogue; (4) are to maintain a presence of active and empathetic listening; (5) are to allow time for silent reflection; (6) should be willing to invest their own "selves" in the teaching/learning dynamic.

Movement 2: Critical Reflection on Present Action

1. Movement 2 encourages "critical reflection" by participants on what they expressed as "present action" in movement 1. Critical reflection in movement 2 can engage people in any or all of the activities of critical and social reasoning, analytical and social remembering, creative and social imagining.

2. The intent of movement 2 is to deepen the reflective moment (beyond movement 1) and bring participants to a critical consciousness of present praxis: its reasons, interests, assumptions, prejudices, and ideologies (reason); its social/historical and biographical sources (memory); its intended, likely, and preferred historical consequences (imagination).

3. Movement 2 enables participants to come to a critical appropriation of present praxis in their "place" and "time" and, metaphorically, to share in dialogue their own "stories" and "visions."

4. The most essential activity of movement 2 is critical reflection on present action of the generative theme or symbol that is shared in dialogue. It can also be characterized as a critical and creative hermeneutics of present praxis. The hermeneutics is (a) toward present praxis of the generative focus and (b) by each participant of the dialogue going on within the event itself.

5. As participants critically reflect on present praxis of the theme, interpret it, and test their interpretations, what they come to speak will arise from their own "being" in place and time; this is why the dialogue can be characterized as people's own "stories" and "visions."

6. The critical reflection of movement 2 is warranted (a) so that the process may be "good education" and (b) to heighten through critique and dialogue the revelatory potential of present praxis.

7. In its procedures, the *critical and social reasoning* of movement 2 has two emphases: (a) *personal reasoning,* which questions present praxis with the discerning dynamic of one's own rationality and brings to awareness the sociology of one's own act of thinking about it, and (b) *social analysis,* which thinks systemically about an aspect of present

praxis and how it is shaped by the interrelated "systems" of the whole sociocultural reality.

8. The *analytical and social remembering* of movement 2 has two emphases: (a) on *participants' own biographies* as they have emerged in place and time and now shape their personally initiated praxis and (b) on *social archaeology* by which participants uncover how the history of their sociocultural context over time shapes their society's present praxis relating to the theme or symbol.

9. The *creative and social imagining* of movement 2 has two emphases: for the person (a) to see the consequences, possibilities, and responsibilities of *his or her own present action* and (b) to recognize the likely consequences of *society's praxis,* to imagine what in it can or ought to be refashioned and to envision how to act in solidarity with others as agents of social transformation.

10. Many of the counsels for facilitating the focusing activity and movement 1 are relevant for movement 2 as well:

· Promote an environment that respects and welcomes the contributions of all.
· Maintain the reflection of the group on present praxis of the theme or symbol.
· Invite people's *own* reflections.
· Encourage group dialogue and discernment to test the remembering, reasoning, and imagining of all.
· Provide opportunity for all to speak, but never force anyone in particular to expression.
· Try out envisioned questioning activities on oneself first and note effectiveness.
· Ask probing questions without sounding interrogative or violating people's privacy.
· Model the intent of movement 2 if that is likely to promote critical reflection and dialogue.
· Adapt the questioning activities to the age level of the group, the context, the time available, and other conditions.
· Maintain a presence of active and empathetic listening.
· Allow time for silent reflection.
· Be willing to invest one's "self" in the teaching/learning dynamic.

11. The educator is to be realistic about the challenge that critical reflection on present action poses for all, and especially for people unaccustomed to such a reflective pedagogy in faith education.

12. Questioning activities for movement 2 are best fashioned as open-ended ones that clearly signal to participants that there are no "right answers" that the teacher is waiting to hear.

13. Movement 2 questions should not challenge people to defend what they expressed in movement 1 but invite them to explain to

themselves their consciousness of present praxis relating to the generative focus.

14. Movement 2 is never an exercise in dispassionate analysis, because people's whole "being" is invested in what is expressed as critical reflection on present praxis; likewise, the educator's style of facilitating movement 2 is never "value free."

15. There is often a prophetic aspect to movement 2 activity; there is often overlap between movement 1 and movement 2.

16. Activities that engage imagination can be most effective in making transition from movement 2 to movement 3.

Movement 3: Making Accessible Christian Story and Vision

1. Movement 3 makes accessible expressions of Christian Story and Vision as appropriate to the generative theme or symbol of the learning event.

2. Its Story symbolizes the faith life of the Christian community over history and in the present, as expressed in scriptures, traditions, liturgies, and so on. Its Vision reflects the promises and demands that arise from the Story to empower and mandate Christians to live for the coming of God's reign for all creation.

3. A "mainline Christian" theology of revelation that is fitting to the dynamics of movement 3 of shared praxis is as follows: Christian Story/Vision symbolically mediates through a great variety of forms and with normative import for Christians, the prototype of God's revelation of Godself and will through the events of their history to the Israelite and Christian peoples and primordially in Jesus, the Christ; as people actively engage and personally appropriate, within a community of faith, the inspired scriptures and symbols that reflect and make accessible Christian Story/Vision, they can discern God's self-disclosure and will in their present time and place.

4. In the procedures of movement 3, the hermeneutical responsibilities of "the educator" are (a) to honor the texts of Christian faith in their own right with interpretations appropriate to the tradition and (b) to offer explanations/applications that respond adequately to the praxis of participants as expressed in the opening movements and with a view to appropriation and decision making in movements 4 and 5. The following guidelines pertain to fulfilling these responsibilities.

5. There are three guidelines regarding the pre-understanding the educator brings to Christian Story/Vision.

Guideline 1: The "first criterion" for the hermeneutics of movement 3 is the reign of God.

Guideline 2: Religious educators are to remember the interests and perspectives they bring to every text of Christian Story/Vision from their own "life" in place and time.

Guideline 3: Religious educators are to remember what they bring to the texts of the tradition from the stories and visions of participants.

6. The educator employs hermeneutics of retrieval, suspicion, and commitment regarding the text, using three guidelines.

Guideline 4: The educator employs a "hermeneutic of retrieval" to reclaim and make accessible the truths and values symbolically mediated in the texts of Christian Story/Vision.

Guideline 5: The educator employs a "hermeneutic of suspicion" to uncover mystifications and distortions in the dominant interpretations of Christian Story/Vision and to reclaim its "dangerous memories."

Guideline 6: The educator employs a "hermeneutic of creative commitment" to construct more adequate understandings of Christian Story/Vision and to envision more faithful ways of living it with commitment to personal and social transformation.

7. The following "marks of authenticity" can guide the explanation/application of Christian Story/Vision.

Guideline 7: Every authentic explanation of a particular text is in *continuity* with and appropriate to the constitutive truths and values of the whole Christian Story/Vision.

Guideline 8: An authentic explanation of a particular text of Christian tradition promotes personal and social *consequences* creative of God's reign.

Guideline 9: Community is a guideline in that an authentic explanation of a particular expression of Christian Story/Vision is informed by the understanding of "the church" and is adequate to the praxis of this community of participants.

8. In summary, as a hermeneutical guide, the educator can ask, Remembering the purpose of God's reign, and aware of my own perspective and of the lives of these participants, what old and new "truths" can I draw from this "text" that encourages people in the praxis of Christian faith?

9. Some methodologies that can be used in keeping with the nature and purpose of movement 3 are (a) lectures, handouts, reading from a common text; (b) research projects and reports, group hermeneutics and discussion; (c) demonstrations, experiences, panel discussions, colloquies, and symposium dialogues; (d) audio and video media and artistic presentations; (e) group story telling and drama; (f) resource people or field trips that provide a praxislike encounter with the community Story/Vision of the generative focus.

10. The teaching style of the educator in movement 3 is to make accessible community Story/Vision in a *disclosure* manner, with a *dialogical* mode, and in an *engaging* way.

11. Movement 3 calls Christian religious educators to commitment that reflects ever-deepening attitudes of faith, hope, and love toward the Christian tradition of being religious.

12. Movement 3 calls educators to honor people as agent-subjects-in-relationship who encounter God's self-disclosure in their own stories/visions and have an affinity, by God's grace, to recognize for themselves God's revelation through the symbols of Christian Story/Vision.

13. Movement 3, as for the whole process, invites teachers to see themselves, not as "answer persons" with "epistemic privilege" and knowledge control, but as "leading-learners."

Movement 4: Dialectical Hermeneutics to Appropriate Story/Vision to Participants' Stories and Visions

1. In movement 4, participants place their critical understanding of present praxis around a generative theme or symbol (movements 1 and 2) in dialectical hermeneutics with Christian Story/Vision (movement 3).

2. In the fullest expression of movement 4, participants ask, How does this Story/Vision affirm, question, and call us beyond present praxis? How does present praxis affirm and critically appropriate the Story/Vision made accessible in movement 3, and how are we to live more faithfully into the Vision of God's reign?

3. Such dialectical hermeneutics are to enable participants to appropriate the community Story/Vision to their own lives and contexts, to know it for themselves through judgment, and thus to make it their own as agent-subjects in the larger Christian community and in the world.

4. Beyond establishing accuracy of understanding, movement 4 is to bring participants into dialogue about what they are thinking, feeling, and doing in response to what was made accessible in movement 3, to encourage them to judge and personally appropriate it to their own lives and contexts.

5. Movement 4 activity is analogous to (but not identical with) Lonergan's notion of judgment, to Piaget's equilibration between assimilation and accommodation, and to Gadamer's "fusion of horizons" with the intent of practical wisdom. It is a creative and hope-filled activity.

6. Movement 4 is undergirded by the conviction that participants have a "natural" capacity and affinity to recognize the revelatory correlation between their own stories/visions and Christian community Story/Vision.

7. Echoing the procedures of the opening movements, the educator at movement 4 is to maintain a dialogical environment; invite people's own reflections; keep the group dialogue focused on the intent of movement 4; encourage participants to share and test their perceptions

and hermeneutics in group dialogue; provide opportunity but never force anyone to speak; ask probing questions without being interrogative; model the intent of movement 4 if that seems appropriate; envision questioning activities and adapt them to age level, context, and so on; maintain a presence of active and empathetic listening; allow time for silent reflection; be willing to invest one's "self" in the dialectical dynamic of movement 4.

8. Movement 4 prompts a significant shift in consciousness of both educator and participants—from delivering and accepting to making accessible and personally appropriating the Story/Vision.

9. To facilitate movement 4, the educator needs to have a clear understanding of its intent and allow its purpose to shape all questioning activities with participants. Essentially it is an activity of appropriation by participants that is undergirded by a dialogue and dialectic between their own perceptions of present praxis and Christian Story/Vision regarding the generative focus.

10. *What* participants express in movement 4, as they place their own stories/visions in dialectic with community Story/Vision, can be their sentiments, attitudes, feelings, intuitions, perceptions, evaluations, and discernments that reflect their perceived truths, values, meanings, reservations, additions, emerging insights, and commitments.

11. *How* participants express themselves in movement 4 can be as varied as in the opening movements: speaking, drawing and explaining, creating a symbol or aesthetic expression, journaling, movement, role-playing, and many other methods.

12. The educator is to respect the freedom and discernment of participants in movements 4 and 5. If some participants of sufficient age appear to reject something that is constitutive of Christian orthodoxy or orthopraxis, the educator has responsibility to (a) witness to what is essential to Christian faith and (b) remind them of the limits beyond which they place themselves at this time in their faith journey outside the professed faith of this community.

13. For movements 4 and 5, the educator is to maintain an environment of openness to the discernment and decision making of participants and expect to be "led out" by them in her or his own faith journey.

14. The dynamic of movement 4 is enhanced if movement 3 is done with disclosure and in a dialogical manner. Developing the art of facilitating movement 4 takes time and patience (as it does for all the movements), and all incipient signs of its activity should be encouraged.

Movement 5: Decision/Response for Lived Christian Faith

1. Movement 5 offers participants an explicit opportunity for decision making about how to live Christian faith in the world.

2. Decisions made in movement 5 are to maintain continuity with the central truth claims and values of Christian Story, reflect the faith

of the broader teaching/learning community—"the church"—and be creative of the Vision of God's reign.

3. The intent of movement 5 is twofold and practical: to make a particular choice for a faith-filled Christian praxis and to form participants' identity and character as agents of God's reign; that is, to promote conation, wisdom, and ongoing conversion in Christian faith.

4. Particular decisions at movement 5 should not typically be of only one "type" but (1) can emphasize cognitive, affective, or behavioral forms; (2) be invited on personal, interpersonal, or social/political levels; (3) pertain to individual and/or communal activities; and (4) result in responses within the immediate group or outside it.

5. In nurturing participants in Christian "character," movement 5 decision-making activities are to encourage ongoing Christian conversion that is intellectual, moral, religious, and social.

6. The theology of revelation undergirding movement 5 is the conviction that renewed engagement in the actual praxis of doing God's will heightens people's awareness of God's continuing self-disclosure in their lives.

7. As a pedagogical procedure, movement 5 is to bring people into dialogue and partnership to respond to questioning activities structured to elicit their own praxislike decisions for lived Christian faith toward God's reign.

8. Many of the procedural points and counsels offered for the opening movements and movement 4 are to be operative here, structured to achieve the purpose of movement 5. Adapted to movement 5, the following deserve emphasis: maintain an open dialogical environment that is conducive to the freedom of choice of all; invite people's *own* decisions and encourage their testing in the whole community; respect the readiness of participants for decision making; model the intent of movement 5 if that seems appropriate; imagine fitting procedures to elicit decisions and first test them on oneself; adapt questioning activities to age level, context, time, theme, and so on; facilitate group planning if a decision is reached for common action; maintain a presence of empathetic listening and support for decision making; invest oneself, and be open to one's own decision making.

9. It is important for the educator at movement 5 to formulate praxislike decision-making activities; to have a variety of such activities ready at hand; to raise questions that emerge from the dialogue and dynamic of the previous movements; to create questions that particularly engage people's imaginations; to see to it that decision making reflects the criteria of continuity, consequences, and "church."

10. Depending on the theme and occasion, memorization can be an appropriate activity in movement 5; the procedural principle here is that memorization be encouraged after participants have come, according to readiness, to understanding, appropriation, and decision.

11. If "grading" is required by the context, it should be limited to the "cognitive realm" of educational objectives; the evaluative instru-

ments should reflect the cognitive processes employed throughout the event; participants' responses are to be evaluated only on their ability to critically analyze, evaluate, and take informed positions on the "cognitive content" made accessible and not be measured against the grader's preferred positions.

12. In the "behavioral domain" especially it is important to encourage feasible decisions and to maintain a realistic optimism in our expectations of others and ourselves.

13. Movement 5 questioning activities should be open-ended and presented with an invitational style, without pressure either to decide now or to share one's decision with participants.

14. When a communal decision is made for corporate action of some kind, there is need for group planning. The group is to be a community of support to participants in living out their decisions.

15. Communal prayer and liturgy at movement 5 to ritualize and celebrate what is emerging among participants can be a powerful source of deepened support, solidarity, and commitment.

16. In an ongoing group the praxis that results from one learning occasion can be taken up again in the focusing activity of the following one.

17. The movements of shared praxis can be effected over varying lengths of time, with participants who have reached the onset of concrete operational thinking (about five or six years old), with people of different cultural backgrounds, and in various contexts.

18. The movements of shared praxis are dynamic activities and intentions to be consistently honored over time rather than "steps" in a lockstep procedure. There can be great variety and flexibility in the sequence of the movements.

PART III

SHARED CHRISTIAN PRAXIS AS AN APPROACH TO OTHER FUNCTIONS OF MINISTRY

Prologue

SHARED PRAXIS is an appropriate way to structure what are readily recognized as intentional events of Christian religious education. It has its roots in religious education and is now used primarily for this purpose. However, my own first deliberate attempt with a shared praxis approach was a high school retreat. I employed it subsequently and so did others in functions of pastoral ministry other than religious education: in community renewal programs and retreat work, in liturgical planning and preaching, in counseling and spiritual direction, for peace and justice work, for discernment in congregational assemblies or decision-making bodies, and for many occasions that are now being described as "doing theology in a pastoral context."[1] I am convinced that the commitments and dynamics of a shared praxis approach suggest an appropriate style for Christian ministry in general and for many particular functions of ministry. I begin this Part III by placing the shared praxis approach in dialogue with the general ministry of the church (chapter 11). I reflect on its potential for liturgical planning and preaching (chapter 12), for justice and peace ministry (chapter 13), and for pastoral counseling (chapter 14).

Shared praxis has potential for many functions of Christian ministry because it is more an *approach*, or "way of being with people," than a pedagogical method. Shared praxis should not be reduced to the mechanics of the movements; it is more essentially a style of human encounter that honors and engages people as historical agent-subjects in partnership and dialogue about their lives in the world. In Christian faith, it prompts people to reflect critically on present praxis to discern God's self-disclosure therein; it mediates a Christian Story/Vision to the historical situation; it attempts to cultivate people's identity as agent-subjects of a realized Christian faith that is emancipatory and responsible on all levels of existence toward the reign of God. Such a style seems fitting to the overall intent of Christian ministry. All Christian ministry, in one way or another, is a service that mediates between the human condition and God's saving will for the world, between present praxis and Christian Story/Vision. Shared Christian praxis is an intentional procedure designed precisely to facilitate such mediation. It can provide a framework through which a minister can develop her or his own consistent approach.

In addition to its potential as a style of ministry in general and to enhance the fulfillment of the formal intent of various functions of ministry—to counsel and guide, to facilitate community discernment, to preach, and so on—shared praxis can also help ministers to be intentional and responsible about the educational aspect of all ministry. To appreciate that all functions of ministry educate people in faith one must abandon the typical mind-set that education is synonymous with schooling and that school is a place where children go to receive information.[2] Among other false assumptions, this naïveté separates "knowing" from "being."[3] The fact is, though church-sponsored schools—Sunday schools, parochial schools, and others—are the most obvious expressions of its educational ministry, the church also carries on a whole world of educating for Christian faith around and beyond them. In fact, when one understands the intended learning outcome as conation/wisdom in Christian faith and sees religious education as an enterprise of *informing* people's beliefs and convictions, *forming* their values, identity, and ethic, and empowering them as *transformers* of themselves and their world toward God's reign, then one readily recognizes that *the church's whole way of "being" in the world has faith education consequences*.[4] As Maria Harris states well, "The church does not *have* an educational program; it *is* an educational program."[5]

The *whole life* of a Christian community functions as its primary curriculum because of the formative power of the symbolic world it constitutes for its people. Everything the church is and does, every aspect of its shared life, every ministry it carries on creates a public symbolic world that proposes to its people a self-understanding, a pattern of meaning, and a system of values. As people are socialized into and appropriate those symbols as their own, they are informed, formed, and (we hope) transformed by them in Christian identity, conviction, and agency. Everything about the church as a community is a source of socialization and thus of education, broadly defined. How and what it preaches and teaches or fails to preach and teach, how it assembles and enacts its liturgical symbols in worship, its communal structures and how it administers its assets, its institutional rules and regulations, its ways of being with people in ministries of peace and justice, counseling, and spiritual direction, the human services it renders, the causes it espouses and the values it gives witness to, and so on—all educate the identity, convictions, and agency of its members.

Each function of Christian ministry has its formal purpose but how it is carried on has faith education consequences. This means that all ministers, regardless of their specific function, need a keen "educational consciousness." They must attend, not only to the distinctive purpose of a particular service, but also to its educational consequences in people's lives—what it is likely to "teach" them and what they are likely to "learn" from it. An approach like shared praxis to functions of ministry has the advantage of encouraging attention to faith education consequences because of its dynamics and commitments.

A note on terms before proceeding: In the subsequent chapters I use the terms *function, form,* and *style* in referring to ministry. By a "function" of ministry I mean the service it renders—*what* gets done. By "form" I mean the criteria for participation in a function of ministry and the formal structures of it—*who* gets to do it. By "style" I mean the way of approaching it—*how* it gets done intentionally.

Chapter 11

Christian Ministry:
An Overview

This chapter reflects on Christian ministry in general and places its emerging functions, forms, and style in dialogue with the commitments and dynamics of a shared praxis approach. To propose and test the potential of any style of Christian ministry, at least four considerations should be taken into account: (1) the purpose and tasks that Christian ministry is to serve, (2) the style of the historical Jesus, (3) the historical evolution of ministry that shapes both its present and future, and (4) the ecclesial structures and social realities through and in which contemporary ministry takes place.

I attend to its purpose because our way of doing ministry should serve what is to be done. We should take account of the style of the historical Jesus, insofar as it can be discerned, not as a "blueprint" for very different times and contexts from his, but as indicating what is appropriate to carrying on his mission today. The history of ministry is important to understand the "givens" of present ministerial praxis and to envision new possibilities. As always, history both "roots and relativizes"; it enables Christians to think faithfully and creatively about ministry today. And all approaches to ministry should be adequate to the historical context in which it takes place and be appropriate to the nature and mission of the Christian community—the church, the designated sponsor of specifically Christian ministry. My brief review of these four considerations is from the perspective of my own Catholic community, with an eye to the developments and tensions around ministry therein. This limit seems advisable because of the varied history of ministry among Christian denominations; I hope my comments and proposals will find resonance in other Christian communities as well.

1. The Purpose and Tasks of Christian Ministry

All Christian ministry has its historical origin and purpose in the life of Jesus of Nazareth; it is to carry on the mission that he had from God to the world. Thus the metapurpose of all Christian ministry is to serve the reign of God as portrayed and catalyzed in history by Jesus the Christ. Christian ministry must carry on Jesus' mission of doing and bringing others to do God's will "on earth as it is in heaven" (Matt. 6:10). Ministry is to help realize the fullness of life that God wills for all and the values of God's reign in every arena of life, on every level of existence, for here and hereafter.

Beyond the metapurpose of God's reign, there have been many attempts to schematize the central functions of Jesus' ministry.[1] A favorite listing that emerged in later Christian tradition (perhaps crystallized first by Calvin)[2] is of Jesus as *priest, prophet,* and *king* (or, as now preferred, *pastor*); this threefold designation, however, is nowhere explicitly stated in the New Testament to sum up the ministry of Jesus. A thorough study of the Gospels' portrayal of the functions of Jesus' ministry is far beyond the scope of this work. I point only to Luke 4:18–21 as particularly suggestive of Jesus' own understanding of his ministry.

Luke places the incident of Jesus in the synagogue at Nazareth as the immediate sequel to what looks like heightened preparation to begin his public ministry. Luke 3 reports Jesus' baptism by John in the Jordan, followed by a theophany in which "the Holy Spirit descended on him in a visible form like a dove. And a voice came from heaven, 'You are my beloved Son; with you I am well pleased'" (Luke 3:22). Luke continues with his account of Jesus' "temptations in the desert," where he refused to succumb to the powers of evil. Thereafter, Jesus returned to Galilee "in the power of the Spirit." These events indicate that his ministry was by God's Spirit and to defeat the rule of sin in the world.[3] Jesus then came to Nazareth, and, at least by Luke's account, launched his public ministry in the "basic community" of his home village. Jesus stood up to read in the synagogue on the Sabbath; he searched for and found the passage of Isaiah, 61:1ff. He first read, "The Spirit of the Lord is upon me, because [God] has anointed me to bring glad tidings to the poor. [God] has sent me to proclaim liberty to captives and recovery of sight to the blind, to let the oppressed go free, and to proclaim a year acceptable to the Lord" (Luke 4:18–19). He then announced that this promise of a messianic era "is fulfilled this day in your hearing" (4:21).

In claiming that God's Spirit was upon him, Jesus indicated his conviction that his ministry was from God; all subsequent Christian ministry is likewise.[4] He summed up his purpose as effecting now a year of Jubilee (a fiftieth year at the end of seven sabbatical cycles in which all land was returned to its original owners and all slaves freed; see, e.g., Lev. 25:8–17). This incident presents the basic functions of Jesus' ministry as (1) *to preach the healing and prophetic word of God to all,* (2) *to tend with love and justice to human suffering and alienation,* (3) *to call people into a community of free and right relationship with God, self, others, and creation,* and (4) *to live as if God rules in their lives.*

Throughout his ministry, Jesus called together "an inclusive discipleship of equals" to participate in his mission and to carry it on after him. The first Christian communities believed that they were incorporated by baptism into the Body of Christ, and that Jesus' ministry of "at-one-ment" among and between humankind and God was passed on to them as disciples (see 2 Cor. 5:18). Ever after the church exists to be an effective sign in history—a sacrament—of God's reign in Jesus.[5] Through the Christian community, any act of human service by a baptized person can be called Christian ministry when it is prompted by and consonant with Christian faith. McBrien uses the term "Christian/universal" to name this ministry of all Christians by baptism. Within "Christian/universal" ministry, we can distinguish particular functions of service that are rendered with ecclesial designation and specifically in the name of a Christian community. McBrien refers to these formal functions of service as "Christian/specific" ministries;[6] I also call them "designated ministries."

In continuity with the ministerial functions of Jesus, and beginning with the first Christian communities, the church over time has understood its overarching purpose of carrying on the mission of God's reign in Jesus as requiring four more particular tasks or historical activities. I later propose an adapted version for our time, but any listing of the functions of Christian ministry should subsume these four tasks. From the earliest days, they have been identified by their Greek terms: *kerygma, koinonia, leitourgia,* and *diakonia.*[7] They refer to the ministries of word, community, worship, and human service.

1. Ministry of the Word. From the beginning, the church understood itself to have the kerygmatic task (from *keryx,* meaning herald) of *evangelizing, preaching,* and *teaching* the "good news" *of* Jesus and *about* Jesus to the ends of the earth. Of the first Christians we read that, "Day after day both in the temple and at home, they never stopped teaching and proclaiming the good news of Jesus the Messiah" (Acts 5:42). The New Testament uses separate terms for evangelizing, preaching, and teaching, but they clearly overlap, never exclude one another, and constitute together "the ministry of the word." Over time *evangelizing* came to refer to announcing the core of the "good news" to would-be Christian converts, *preaching* to designate a spiritual reflection on scripture and especially in a liturgical context with people already Christians or with catechumens becoming Christians, and *teaching* to describe the in-depth instruction and formation of people in the way of life and wisdom that is lived Christian faith.

In addition to the "good news" of and about Jesus, before long the question was raised, prompted especially by the right-wing heretic Marcion (d. 160), about the Hebrew Scriptures. The church came to recognize that they too mediate the inspired word of God and included them in the Christian canon of sacred scripture to be preached and taught alongside the New Testament, which confirms and reinterprets them in light of Jesus. With the years, and growth in the church's understanding of its scriptures and the meaning of the Jesus event, the task of kerygma came to include sharing not only the biblical word but also the tradition of Christian faith. In sum the kerygmatic task of Christian ministry includes any activity—evangelizing, preaching, teaching—that makes accessible Christian Story/Vision. This kerygmatic task is a constitutive and permanent aspect of the church's ministry in the world.

2. *Ministry of Community Witness.*   In its task of *koinonia,* the church is to be a witnessing community of faith, hope, and love, bonded together "in right relationship" with Christ and each other by the "koinonia of the Holy Spirit" (see 2 Cor.13:13). This task of community witness means that the church should be an effective symbol and source of what it heralds, preaches, and teaches. Through its public praxis and structures, it should be for all people a welcoming and believable community of prophetic witness to God's reign; for its own members, it is to be a community of solidarity that empowers them to live the way of Jesus and to inherit new life in Christ. So great was the bonding in partnership of the first Christians that, we read, "Those who believed shared all things in common; they would sell their property and goods, dividing everything on the basis of each one's need" (Acts 2:44–45). The church always has the task of being a community of disciples that is a credible symbol and effective agent (a sacrament) of God's reign in Jesus.

3. *Ministry of Worship.*   The church's task of *leitourgia* is to assemble its people to worship God in public and communal rituals. In Greek society, liturgy referred to service in the body politic—a public work, but it was used in the Septuagint to mean an act of public worship. The new Christian community used *liturgy* to name its task of assembling together to worship God, to keep alive with hope the memory of Jesus, to celebrate the presence of the Risen One in the community, and to build up the Body of Christ as it anticipated Christ's final coming in glory. Among first-generation Christians the two central liturgical acts were assembling "for the breaking of the bread" (see, e.g., Acts 2:46), and the baptism of new members into the community (see, e.g., Acts 2:38). Other expressions of public worship, some designated as sacraments, were added over the years. The Christian community is always to fulfill the liturgical function of publicly worshiping God, of expressing its faith in Jesus, and of renewing its members by symbolic encounter through the Holy Spirit with the Risen Christ in their efforts for God's reign.

4. *Ministry of Service.*   The term used to designate this task from the beginning, *diakonia,* in Greek society meant a penal or menial service rendered in submission. The New Testament, however, used it to describe human service to one's neighbor out of love. Today the

church's task of "deaconing" is perceived as a call to promote human welfare and to tend to human needs. A Christian community, toward both itself and *all* neighbors without limits, is to minister to human suffering and alienation—*physical, emotional,* and *spiritual,* to challenge social structures that deny fullness of life to anyone, and to help create social, political, and ecclesial arrangements that promote freedom, peace, and justice for all and the integrity of creation. The first Christians remembered Jesus as "the one who serves" (*diakonon,* Luke 22:27), who had washed his disciples' feet with the bidding "I have given you a model to follow, so that as I have done for you, you should also do" (John 13:15). The church always has the task of serving human needs and of redressing the personal, interpersonal, and social/political causes of suffering, violence, injustice, and ecological destruction.

2. Jesus' Style of Ministry

Kenan Osborne writes, "Jesus' own ministry remains the abiding source, model and dynamism of all Christian ministry."[8] Whatever approach Christians take to any function of ministry—word, witness, worship, welfare—should be at least consistent with how Jesus went about fulfilling his mission. In his historical praxis, I believe we can detect a consistent style and dynamic, a particular way of "being with" people that marked his ministry. It is evident in many Gospel incidents but is even more noticeable if we stand back from particular examples to get the overall impression of how he went about it. No interpreter can claim to present an exhaustive or unbiased description of something as nebulous as the ministerial style of Jesus; clearly the "lens" I bring to it is the *commitments* and *dynamics* of a shared praxis approach. Of the overall commitments reflected in the style of Jesus, three in particular stand out for me: (1) he took the initiative for a personal "presence with" people without exception; (2) he empowered people to act out of their own truth and freedom as agent-subjects; (3) he called people into partnership and community.

1. Jesus' style of ministry is marked by initiative and inclusion that was unusual for a religious leader in his culture. Grassi explains that "in those days, it was customary for a disciple to choose his [*sic*] own teacher. However, Jesus reversed the process and went out to choose his own."[9] His initiative was amazingly inclusive, seeking out the ordinary people, and with a special outreach to sinners, the physically and psychologically sick, the marginalized, and those who suffered from any kind of social or cultural oppression. Perkins notes that typically teachers "had a limited audience. They spoke to educated persons, most often men, who were seeking some higher insight into interpreting the Law or 'wisdom' about divine things or the teachings of a philosophical school." Even "the prophets usually directed their preaching to the priests, kings, and aristocratic leaders of society." In contrast, "Jesus'

teaching is not addressed to an elite, but to 'all persons, sinners, the outcasts, even women and children.'"10 His outreach and care for people was marked by a style of personal "presence with" them. It was certainly not a being "over" or "under" people, and his service "to" and "for" them showed respect for their personal dignity. Jesus entered into an I/Thou relationship *with* people.

The early church condemned as heresy the movement called Docetism (from the Greek word "to pretend"), which claimed that the humanity of Jesus was apparent rather than real, that Jesus only seemed to be human. The incarnation of God's "real presence" in Jesus is a central tenet of Christian faith, but Christians often show a docetic reluctance to recognize the historicity of "the Incarnation" in time and place. Jesus, the Second Person of the divine Trinity, was as fully and bodily present as any human being could be present in the familial, cultural, religious, and social realities of his world. Far from being above the fray of life, Jesus was present with people to rejoice at weddings and to weep at wakes, to share food with friends and to feed the hungry, to alleviate sadness and suffering and to rejoice in the goodness and beauty of creation, to encourage people to reject the ways of hatred and death, and to choose the fullness of life that comes from loving God and one's neighbor as oneself. Jesus Christ, the Son of God, was so fully "present with" and incarnate in human "being" that at the end of his life, bystanders could jeer, "He saved others but he cannot save himself" (Mark 15:31).

2. Jesus' style of ministry empowered people as agent-subjects in history, to be free to live their truth in response to their awareness of God's will and presence. He repudiated the social mores that objectified and discriminated against people on any basis, and invited all to "fullness of life" (John 10:10). His way of treating the poor, the hungry, the sick, the oppressed, the sinners, the excluded, welcoming them into his community of disciples, reflects a radical commitment that all people might live as subjects in right relationship. Likewise, the way he encouraged disciples to avoid dependency and paternalism—calling no one "Father" (see Matt. 23:9) and not "lording it over" others (see Mark 10:42)—reflects a commitment that his disciples live as agent-subjects of their faith. He empowered people to see and hear for themselves, to reflect on their lives in the world, and to make decisions to live as if God reigns.

3. Jesus' style of ministry called people into partnership with him and one another, invited them to bond together in an inclusive community of equal disciples. This commitment is evident from the beginning of his public life when he called disciples to be partners in his ministry. On one occasion he commissioned some seventy of them and sent them out "two by two" (i.e., in partnership; see Luke 10:1 ff.). The inclusiveness of his table fellowship is a powerful symbol of his egalitarian and community-building style.11 It would seem that present approaches to Christian ministry should reflect initiative and personal

"presence with" people, empower them as agent-subjects of their faith, and build communities of inclusion and partnership.

I also recognize a dynamics in Jesus' style of ministry, and especially in his interaction with people, that is not unlike the movements of a shared praxis approach. To begin with, Jesus constantly invited people to recognize their present historical reality and praxis in the world. He turned them to their feelings, thoughts, and values, to creation around them, to the beliefs, practices, attitudes, and mores of their religious tradition and culture, to their work and social arrangements, to their joys and sorrows, fears and hopes, sins and goodness. Turning people to their historical praxis is evident throughout Jesus' ministry but most compellingly so in his parables. As stories taken from the everyday, the parables served as icons through which hearers could look to see themselves, their beliefs, practices, values—to recognize their own praxis. Perkins notes that because they direct attention to the "everyday," "the parables imply that our destiny is at stake in ordinary domestic, economic and social existence."[12]

Second, throughout his ministry, Jesus assumed a kind of threefold dialectical stance toward his social/cultural world and invited disciples to do likewise. He affirmed and blessed what was of God's reign—God's truth in "the Law and the Prophets," the innocence of children, the widow's mite, the prayer of the publican, the honesty of the Samaritan woman, the repentance of Zaccheus, and so on. He condemned hypocrisy and the shallowness of ritual without doing God's will; he said no to physical, spiritual, and psychological sickness by healing them; he pushed back against sexist and racist mores and all forms of social oppression. And Jesus invited people into a new covenant of "being" in the world, into a new sense of identity and of living for God's reign.

This critical consciousness to which Jesus led people is also exemplified in his use of parables, with their dialectical moments of orientation, disorientation, and reorientation. They begin by orienting toward the familiar, but typically do not confirm people in their present praxis and ways of looking at life. Jesus often gave unexpected twists to his stories that disoriented people by calling them and their praxis into question and that could reorient them to more life-giving possibilities. None of his hearers would have expected the Samaritan to be neighbor to the one beset by robbers, or the father to welcome home the prodigal, or the prostitutes and tax collectors to enter the reign of God before priests and elders. Such subversive twists were his way of inviting people to critically reflect on their lives, to come to a new consciousness and way of living as a people of God. As Perkins explains, "The parable does not present factual information that a person can receive and remain neutral." Rather, it engages us as active participants in the kind of wisdom "that is to reshape the whole life of the disciple." In the parables, "Jesus was struggling for the social imagination of his audience."[13]

Third, we can recognize in the dynamics of Jesus' ministry an authority that was life-giving. He used his power against evil, suffering, and ignorance and to empower others to live for God's reign. His authority was not the kind that comes from rank or social position but from personal integrity and the life-giving nature of his ministry. (See e.g., Luke 7:18–23; Matt. 11:2–6.) The authority he proposed to disciples was the right to serve others (see Mark 10:42–45). In his preaching and praxis, Jesus affirmed and cherished the tradition of his people, obeyed its precepts, quoted its scriptures, and said that he had come not to abolish the Law and the Prophets but "to make their teachings come true" (Matt. 5:17). And yet, he also felt free to reinterpret the tradition, to point to inadequacies in people's understanding and living of the spirit of the Law, and he had a new word and Vision for them, which he taught "with authority" (Mark 1:22). Matthew has him say: "Every scribe who is learned in the reign of God is like the head of a household who can bring from [the] storeroom both the new and the old" (Matt. 13:52).

Fourth, his call to discipleship had a profound respect for people's own discernment and decision making. It is clear he wanted people to open their eyes and ears, to know and see for themselves the meaning of God's reign for their lives. But nowhere is there any hint of control or attempt to have people simply repeat his words.[14] Notice, for example, the style of discourse between him and the Samaritan woman (John 4). The interchange brings her *to see for herself* that he "could possibly be the Messiah?" (John 4:29), and eventually her whole village said they came to recognize him "for ourselves" (John 4:42). Notice too that his saving deeds were gifts freely given, but he expected the recipients to be partners with him through their own acts of faith. On the one hand, we read "Courage, my daughter, your faith has restored you to health" (Matt. 9:22), but also, "He did not work many miracles there because of their lack of faith" (Matt. 13:58).

And fifth, though he respected people's freedom of choice (see the rich young man of Luke 18 or the doubting disciples in John 6), he constantly invited people to decision in response to him. He had a note of apocalyptic urgency in his call to metanoia—to change one's life, to live now for the reign of God. Nowhere do we get the impression that his interest was in philosophical constructs or ideational clarity for his hearers; never did he say, "This is my idea." But he did say, "This is my body . . . this is my blood" (e.g., Mark 14:23–24); "As I have done, so you must do" (John 13:15); and, "Love one another as I have loved you" (John 15:12). He wanted people to live this "way" as disciples and invited them to so decide.

I see these commitments and dynamics in Jesus' general style of ministry, but they are epitomized in the story of the Risen Christ and the two disciples on the road to Emmaus (Luke 24:13–35). Ministerially, this incident can be interpreted with an educational[15] perspective or from a liturgical one,[16] but it reflects a general style of ministry of any function.

The event begins as the Risen Jesus, perceived only as another traveler, takes the initiative and inserts himself into the company of two disciples on the road from Jerusualem to Emmaus that first Easter day. Rather than pointing to himself or distracting them from their reality, he prompts them to focus on it more deliberately by asking, "What are you discussing as you go your way?" (Luke 24:17). When they give an easy answer ("the things that went on in Jerusalem these past few days," v. 18), he invites them to name with detail by asking, "What things?" (v. 19). We must surely recognize the irony of this question—no one knew better than he what had just happened in Jerusalem. Clearly he respects them as agent-subjects in the encounter and invites them to speak their own word and truth, as best they know it. They become partners in his act of ministry as they express their story and vision about the things that went on in Jerusalem. They recount their version of what befell "Jesus of Nazareth, a prophet powerful in word and deed" (v. 19), lament their now-shattered vision of how they had hoped "he was the one who would set Israel free" (v. 21), and express their confusion and disbelief at the report of the women from the tomb that "he was alive" (v. 24).

Jesus respects them and their word by inviting and listening to them, but now confronts them with their blindness and lack of faith. He invites them to a new perspective by raising up relevant aspects of their faith Story ("Beginning then with Moses and all the prophets, he interpreted for them every passage of scripture which referred to himself," v. 27) and the community Vision that the Messiah "had to undergo all this so as to enter into his glory" (v. 26). He must have taught them with a felt sense of authority; they later report that their hearts were "burning" during the discourse on the road. Yet, they still do not "see for themselves," *nor does he tell them what to see.*

His commitment to personal presence is reflected again in his acceptance of their invitation to stay the night and have supper with them. And again, he takes the initiative, unusual for a guest: "He took bread, pronounced the blessing, then broke the bread and began to distribute it to them" (v. 30; echoes of Luke 9:16, loaves and fishes, and Luke 22:19, the Last Supper). In this simple but profound act of service—feeding others—they came to recognize "the stranger" for themselves: "Their eyes were opened and they recognized him, whereupon he vanished from their sight" (v. 31). The verb translated "recognize" here is *epiginoskein,* but it "embraces every organ and mode of knowledge" and had taken on "a technical meaning of conversion to Christianity."[17] They had come to "know" him in a way that leads to discipleship, and so they respond and act with renewed faith. Although it would have been a hazardous journey by night, they return to Jerusalem immediately to proclaim Jesus' resurrection. When they arrive, they find the community already assembled and hear its kerygmatic witness that the Lord "has appeared to Simon." Then they tell their story of "what had happened on the road and how they had come to know him in the breaking of the bread" (v. 35). I believe the commitments and dynamics reflected here offer a model of ministry for Christians today.

3. Ministry Evolves: A Brief Historical Review

A. The First Christian Communities

Like every social group, the Christian church has a "giveness" in its structural arrangements that shape the life of the community long after the era of their origin has passed. This means that ministry in any age is influenced not simply by the choices of individuals or by theological ideas but by its community structures that have emerged over history. All recommendations for a ministerial style in our time must be in dialogue with these historical structures. The broad historical strokes that follow are meant to indicate the origins of the ecclesial context in which contemporary styles of ministry are realized.[18]

It is surely significant to ministerial style that the first Christian communities chose to refer to themselves as an *ekklesia,* a word taken over from Greek politics that designated "an assembly of equal citizens" (also used in the Septuagint to render the Hebrew *kahal*). Clearly there were leadership functions in the Christian communities from the beginning, yet self-identification as "church" reflected a basic sense of inclusion and co-responsibility for carrying on the mission of Jesus. It is evident too that first Christians used the term *church* to refer to local Christian communities and to the community of disciples everywhere (see, e.g., 1 Cor. 1:2 and Eph.1:22–23 respectively). Likewise, it seems, they saw ministry as both local and universal in its origins and concerns.

After the event of Pentecost, the first Christians were convinced that the Holy Spirit was present to all "born again of water and the Holy Spirit" (see John 3:5). Through baptism and its completion by anointing in the Spirit they were to "change their lives" (see Mark 1:15) and were empowered to carry on the mission and ministry of Jesus in history. They perceived their call to ministry as from God, who in response to the Jesus event had poured out the gifts of the Holy Spirit upon the people for the service of all. Thus all ministries are as one, because although there are "different gifts," it is "the same Spirit" that is given "to each person . . . for the common good" (see 1 Cor. 12:4–7). It is clear that the first Christians had a radical understanding of Christian initiation as expecting a transformation of life and as giving all Christians the mandate to participate, according to their gifts, in the mission of the church to the world.

Beyond this "Christian/universal" ministry, it is also evident that the first Christian communities publicly designated particular people for distinct functions of leadership and service. These "designated" functions were marked by much variety and overlap, both within the communities and from one to another. Scholars often contrast the functions that grew up in the Palestinian church with those that emerged in Pauline communities, or compare Jewish and Hellenistic Christianity. Significant for our own time is "that the present ministerial structure of the Catholic Church, or of any of the Christian churches, is not to be found as such in the New Testament itself." Instead, we find "a variety of ministries, a variety of combinations of ministries, and a variety of ministerial structures."[19] Because of this diversity, "studies of ministry in the New Testament seem to indicate that it is next to impossible to give a clear factual description of the state of ministries in that era."[20] Remembering this diversity at the beginning of the church has, as Schillebeeckx notes, "a power to open up the future of ministry."[21]

As gifts of the Holy Spirit, the many specific ministries in the New Testament church seems to have emerged from the existential situations and needs of the first Christian communities. As communities grew and became self-conscious about their mission, they came to two related realizations. One was that the ministerial tasks of word, of community building, of service to human need, and of communal worship required particular gifts and functions of service to fulfill them. Some people were needed to preside at worship, others to preach, to teach, or to bring the "good news" to neighboring villages, others to care for the institutional well-being of the community itself, others to minister to people in need, and so on. Second, as the needs became evident, communities came to a corresponding awareness that certain members had received the requisite gifts of the Holy Spirit that readied them to render the specific services. Thus the communities began to designate people to fulfill functions of service, corresponding to their particular gifts from God, in the name of the church. They did not understand the commissioning to confer a sacral status, but rather appointed people to specific functions in service to the apostolic mandate of the community "to build up the Body of Christ" (Eph. 4:12). Designation called one to a function of service but not apart from the rest of the community.[22]

When reviewing the variety of what came to be recognized as designated ministerial functions among different communities, Scripture scholars count as many as twelve; but many of them clearly overlap, and the same functions may have had different names from place to place. They include apostle, prophet, evangelist, teacher, pastor, miracle worker, healer, helper, administrator, deacon, elder, and overseer. (See, e.g., Eph. 4:11–13; 1 Cor. 12:4–11; 12:28–31; Rom. 12:4–8; 16:3–5; 1 Tim. 3:8–13; Acts 20:28.)[23] Some designations were borrowed from Scripture (e.g., pastor and servant) and others from the surrounding culture (e.g., elder and overseer).[24] It appears that the ministry of the word was served primarily by the functions of apostle,[25] prophet, evangelist, and teacher. The more institutional ministry of building up the witnessing community was served by pastor, administrator, elder, and overseer. The ministry of service to human welfare would have been by deacon, healer, helper, and miracle worker. What then of the task of communal worship and especially of presiding at Eucharist?

That the first Christian communities celebrated Eucharist seems beyond doubt, but who presided is far from clear. Brown writes:

> There is simply no compelling evidence for the classic thesis that the members of the Twelve always presided when they were present, and that there was a chain of ordination passing the power of presiding at the Eucharist from the Twelve to missionary apostles to presbyter-bishops. How one got the right to preside and whether it endured beyond a single instance we do not know; but a more plausible substitute for the chain theory is the thesis that sacramental 'powers' were part of the mission of the church and that there were diverse ways in which the church (or the communities) designated individuals to exercise those powers.[26]

Brown is proposing, and his thesis now seems generally accepted,[27] that the first Christians did not see the confecting of Eucharist as a personal and ontological power invested in one person who rendered Eucharist for the community. Instead, through the presence of the Holy Spirit, the "sacramental powers" resided in the whole community[28] and in its enacting of the sacred symbols that made manifest God's saving presence; the community chose certain people to preside at divine worship for the sake of "holy order." Usually, but not invariably, this designation fell to the community leader, not because of a sacral power, but by her or his function of leadership.[29] Power to celebrate Eucharist did not lead to community leadership, but rather leadership led to presiding at Eucharist.[30] There is also evidence in the *Didache*, for example, that "itinerant prophets" presided at Eucharist, and so too did the *didaskaloi*—the teachers.[31] In fact, the notion that presiding at Eucharist is an exclusively priestly function did not become widespread until the beginning of the third century. The association of priesthood with Eucharist emerged as later Christians began to allegorize the sacrifices of the Hebrew covenant, which were offered by priests. As Christianity became separated from Judaism and thus from Jewish priesthood, Eucharist was perceived as replacing the sacrifices no longer offered in the now destroyed temple, and thus requiring the sacerdotal function of a priest.[32]

The interrelation between the various designated functions of ministry seems to have been more like a circle than a pyramid, a communal stewardship for mission rather than levels of command.[33] For designation by the community to a particular function, there seems to be no clear-cut practice. In imitation of Jewish custom, there was a laying on of hands by the local leaders in the Pauline communities (see 1 Tim. 4:14 and 5:22) or by Paul himself (see 2 Tim. 1:6). Such a ritual is mentioned also in Acts 6:6 and Acts 13:3. By the third century, this rite became the practice for designating bishops, presbyters, and deacons, at least in the church at Rome, as evidenced in the Decree of Hippolytus (c. 215). It increased in significance by way of designation in subsequent centuries. In the first century, however, laying on of hands for ministerial commissioning was not practiced in all the communities, and where it was used, it designated people for a variety of ministries (not only sacerdotal) or was simply a symbol of blessing. This early practice, then, is too fluid to be taken as synonymous with what we mean today by "ordination." Osborne summarizes: "Only around 200 do we have an ordination ritual which can be verified. Installation from 90 to Hippolytus remains a matter of hypothesis, with no historical data for verification."[34]

By way of "form" for such ministries, that is, the criteria for designation to them, the first communities seem to have had a general principle that form follows from function; that is, what needs to be done is the first consideration in who is chosen to do it. Who to call to any particular ministry was decided by the needs of the church to fulfill its apostolic mission from Jesus and the gifts present in the community. The criteria for admission to designated functions seem to have been (1) that the person have received from the Spirit the charism or ability for the particular task and (2) that she or he be called and designated for the service by an apostolic Christian community.[35]

Coming away from the first century of Christianity, McBrien offers a helpful summary of "four constants" regarding ministry that can be discerned amidst all the diversity: "(1) Ministry is rooted in the Holy Spirit; (2) there is a distinction between general and particular ministry; (3) all ministry is functional, that is, for the benefit of others, not primarily for the benefit of the minister; and (4) ultimately all ministry is for the sake of the Kingdom of God."[36] We now turn to sketch even more briefly some of the developments that emerged thereafter.

B. From Second Century to Second Vatican Council

To appreciate the developments, tensions, crises, and new possibilities around the issue of ministry that have emerged in the Catholic communion, catalyzed by the Second Vatican Council (1962–65), it helps to recall how "ministry" was typically perceived in Catholic consciousness in the era between the Council of Trent (1545–63) and Vatican II. Much of it continues in Catholic understanding of ministry, but momentous developments are also taking place.

In a Tridentine perspective, Catholics rarely use the term *ministry* (perceived as Protestant), preferring instead, and significantly, the term *priesthood.* Ministry is synonymous with priesthood, which entails the hierarchical "degrees" of bishop, priest, and deacon. It is entered by ordination to Holy Orders, which also designates its recipients as "clergy," set aside from the "laity"; the clergy are considered to possess in and of themselves the awesome power to consecrate Eucharist and forgive sins. The pope possesses the fullest and highest degree of Holy Order and is the successor of Peter as the bishop of Rome in a direct line of succession; he is the universal pontiff with a primacy of rule invested in him by reason of his Petrine office. Bishops are like "arch-priests" and are the direct successors to the apostles (apostle and sac-erdotal ministry seen as synonymous); canonically bishops also function as the representatives of the pope in an area and owe their elevated status to the Petrine office. By ordination, priests are the bishops' help-ers, and priesthood is nigh synonymous with sacramental power. Prior to Vatican II the diaconate was seen as a stepping-stone to priestly ordination. There were other "minor orders" (acolyte, porter, lector, exorcist, and subdeacon), but they too were preparatory stages for priesthood. All the above functions are reserved to men and, since the twelfth century in the Roman Rite, to celibate men. Other vowed but nonordained women and men (nuns and brothers) participate with ser-vice in the mission of the church, but their work is typically named an "apostolate" rather than ministry.[37] In this Tridentine perspective, uni-versal ministry by which all baptized Christians participate in the church's mission is largely absent; the laity are only recipients of min-istry. Prompted by scriptural and historical scholarship and by con-temporary pastoral theology, there are now significant developments beyond this mind-set.

Undoubtedly, the ordained and those in the "apostolate" have faithfully carried on ministry through the Tridentine structures, forms, and functions. They preached and taught the Scriptures and traditions, celebrated the sacraments, built up community, and often rendered extraordinary service to human need. I'm convinced that the Holy Spirit has been operative in and through such structures, as I am like-wise of the Spirit's presence in contemporary developments. And, as indicated by the New Testament communities, the church can designate people for particular functions of ministry in its name.[38] Yet New Tes-tament evidence suggests this crucial insight: the Tridentine perception of ministry outlined above is much more the product of history and of the sociocultural contexts in which the church found itself than of any blueprint to be found in the New Testament communities.

Many historical influences caused the demise of the universal min-istry of all Christians. Most significant, perhaps, was that as Christianity received preferred status in society, baptism and confirmation lost their radical meaning of a call to holiness of life and to participate in the apostolic mission and thus the ministry of the church. Infant baptism became the ecclesial norm and expected cultural practice, with children submitted for baptism more to wash away "the stain of original sin" than to incorporate them into the Body of Christ, its mission and min-istry. As the formal functions of ministry became increasingly clerical-ized and hierarchalized, laypeople were seen not as agents of ministry but only its recipients.

The diversity of ministerial functions in the first communities was gradually replaced by the "degrees" of priesthood, with emphasis on its "sacramental powers." This tendency gained impetus as the church began to emphasize Eucharist as a sacrifice and thus, by association, requiring a priest to preside at it. By the beginning of the third century, roles previously distinct—presiding at Eucharist, and the more institutional functions of elder (*presbyteros*) and overseer (*episkopos*)—are being united in one sacerdotal function[39] and identified as *priest* (a term not used in the New Testament). At first, "priest" was used only of bishops, not of presbyters.[40] But as the church grew and it became impossible for the bishop-priest to preside at all liturgies, then, as Dix points out, "a presbyter was the obvious delegate for the bishop's liturgical functions at the minor eucharists . . . though the first explicit mention of a presbyter celebrating apart from the bishop is found only in the middle of the third century in the Decian persecution at Carthage." Dix adds, "The presbyter only acquires liturgical functions by degrees and then . . . as the bishop's representative." Not until the middle of the fourth century do we find widespread "change in the language used about the presbyter. He is referred to no longer as an 'elder' but as a 'priest.'"[41] Even then the bishop-priest still had the fullness of priesthood as a "high priest," whereas the presbyter-priest shared in priesthood to a lesser degree and to help the bishop in carrying out his functions.[42]

The *Apostolic Tradition of Hippolytus* (c. 215) indicates that at least the church at Rome, by the early third century, had the practice of ordaining bishops, presbyters, and deacons, with emphasis on the function of bishop for celebrating Eucharist and for the presbyter to be helper to the bishop (the ordination prayer over presbyters makes no mention of them presiding at Eucharist). Noting that "ordination is for the clergy on account of their ministry," the *Tradition* states that deacons are "not ordained to the priesthood but to serve the bishop and to carry out the bishop's commands."[43] The central symbol in the rite of ordination was the laying on of hands by bishops on candidates for bishop, by bishops on presbyters, with other presbyters present allowed "to touch" the candidate, and by bishops alone on candidates for deacon.[44] Yet, even in the *Tradition,* seen by many scholars as a more institutional document that may have reflected only the church at Rome, there is latitude in the procedures for coming into ordained ministry. It directs that people who have given heroic witness to their faith thereby have the status of presbyter. "On a confessor, if he has been in bonds for the name of the Lord, hands shall not be laid for the diaconate or the presbyterate, for he has the honor of the presbyterate by his confession."[45] In general practice thereafter, ordination emerged as the mode of designation for ministry, and ministry was perceived as "degrees" of priesthood, with liturgical ministry, and particularly presiding at Eucharist, as its central function. As this arrangement became established, other designated functions that had been distinct in the New Testament communities were subsumed into priesthood. As Brown summarizes, "The priesthood represents the combination or distillation of several distinct roles and special ministries in the N.T. church."[46]

Of the presumed correlation and direct lineage between apostles and bishops in Tridentine ministry, Brown writes, "The affirmation that all the bishops of the early Christian church could trace their appointments or ordinations to the apostles is simply without proof."[47] Osborne is even more emphatic: "Nowhere in the New Testament does it say that the apostles were episkopoi. . . . If one says that the apostles were the first 'bishops,' one is clearly going beyond New Testament evidence. The apostles were the first chief leaders of the Christian community, but they did not have the name 'episkopos' (bishop), nor did they function in the way later episkopoi (bishops) functioned."[48] On the other hand, it seems that many of the pastoral functions of the first "Twelve" (see note 25) were taken over by the bishops. We should note too that the consistent attitude of the church over its history has been that all ministry carries on the apostolic mandate given by Jesus; in that sense "all ministry in the church is of apostolic succession, in one way or another."[49] The *Tradition of Hippolytus* also advises, "Let the bishop be ordained after he has been chosen by all the people."[50] People continued to choose their bishops at least into the early Middle Ages.[51]

The traditional Catholic assertion that there is a direct historical line of succession between the present pope and Peter, presumed to be the first bishop of Rome, must also be nuanced. That the New Testament indicates a special leadership role for Peter seems clear, as does the intent of the first Christian communities to preserve the Petrine office.[52] Peter is listed first among the Twelve (see, e.g., Mark 3:16–19), is frequently their spokesperson (see, e.g., Mark 8:29), is the "rock" on which Matthew has Jesus promise to build the church (Matt. 16:18), is the first of "the Twelve" to witness the Risen Christ (see, e.g., Luke 24:34), continued to be prominent in the original Jerusalem community and is well known to many other churches (Acts 1:15–26), and so on. In my Catholicism I'm also convinced that the continued exercise of the Petrine office in a special way by the bishop of Rome has been a grace for the whole church. However, in light of New Testament scholarship, we cannot presume a line of direct succession between pope and Peter. As Brown points out, "The two roles of primate and of bishop of Rome, separate at the beginning, were subsequently joined."[53] As already noted, the function of bishop as we might recognize it today did not begin until the second century. Equating apostle with bishop (and indeed, apostle with sacerdotal function, see note 27) is not in the first century; nowhere in the New Testament is Peter referred to as a bishop. In light of this, "the supposition that, when Peter did come to Rome (presumably in the 60's), he took over and became the first bishop represents a retrojection of later church order."[54]

A long and fruitful ministry has been carried on over the centuries in the Catholic communion by these ministerial structures and degrees of an ordained priesthood. To presume, however, that limiting designated ministry to the ordained is normative for all time and adequate to our time is indeed problematic. My purpose here is not to argue against the functions of pope, bishop, and priest but to nuance old assertions so that Catholics can imagine and create in continuity with our past a fuller and more inclusive expression of ministry, both "designated" and "Christian/universal." In first-century practice, ministry was integral to the identity of all the baptized, and there was diversity in functions and more openness in form of designated ministry. The story of ministry took many twists and turns thereafter, but the shrinkage to priesthood and its degrees as the equivalent of all ministry, that began in the second to fourth centuries, was to increase. O'Meara writes, "The later history of ministry strikes one as a diminution. Ministry shrinks. Ministry is institutionalized. Ministry becomes priesthood and is grafted onto canonical posts from charismatic roots."[55] Four aspects are summarized here: designated ministry became increasingly *clericalized, sacralized, hierarchized,* and *exclusive.*

1. Clerical. In Catholic ideology, "clericalism" presumes that people in ordained ministry (a) are of an elevated and more divine quality of "being" than people who are "only baptized," (b) are preferred in the eyes of God and should have preferred social/ecclesial status, (c) are to form a caste group called "clergy" that is distinct and separated from other Christians (especially by life-style), typically called "laity."[56] Undoubtedly there have always been ordained ministers who resisted the preferential status of clericalism and opted for the service of priesthood. Yet clearly social/ecclesial structures emerged within Christendom that clericalized ministry, and clericalism as a pernicious ideology can still debilitate the ministry of the baptized and of those also ordained.

It is clear that there were leadership roles in the first Christian communities, and a keen sense that all Christians are "a holy priesthood" (1 Pet. 2:5) who participate in the church's ministry of carrying on God's mission in Jesus Christ to the world. But before long, a gap widened between leadership as clergy and membership as laity. Osborne writes, "A clericalization process is already in full swing at the beginning of the third century."[57] Subsuming all functions of designated ministry into the role of bishop-priest contributed to the clericalizing of ministry. Another contributing factor was the breakdown of the careful catechumenal process of the first centuries. As Christianity became a sociocultural expectation, the church lost its catechumenal understanding of baptism as calling all Christians to transformation of life, to participation in its mission and ministry. And as the importance of ordained ministers increased, the status of the laity decreased.

The sociocultural context of the early Middle Ages also encouraged the clericalizing of ministry. The old pagan priesthood played a significant civic and political role in the empire; it often functioned as part of the local civil service. As Christianity became the established religion,

Christian priesthood was given social privileges and expected to fill the
civic roles of the old pagan priesthood. McBrien writes, "A division
between clergy and laity began to develop with the establishment of
Christianity as the state religion in the fourth century and with the
transformation of the clergy into a kind of civil service, with all the
political and economic privileges of rank and status."[58] As clergy were
set apart from laity by preferred status in the social realm, the emerging
notion of celibacy for the ordained tended to set them apart by life-
style. Eventually, a clear distinction between clergy and laity was institutionalized in church law.[59]

   2. Sacral. The church came to perceive priesthood/ministry as a
sacral state, that is, as a sacred and divine power possessed by the
individual priest qua individual. Instead of a function of service
exercised through, with, and in the name of a Christian community,
priesthood was posed as the *sacra potestas* of the ordained, sacred power
especially for consecrating of Eucharist and absolving in the sacrament
of penance. This reflected a subtle but significant shift by the church
from a valid expectation of holiness of life for its designated ministers
to presuming that their sacred function and holiness also made them
ontologically different from and closer to God than other baptized
Christians. It was epitomized in the Catholic practice of referring to the
ordained alone with the revered title of *alter Christi,* ignoring the fact
that the call to "put on Christ" (Gal. 3:27) and to be "ambassadors"
(*presbeuo*) of Christ (2 Cor. 5:20) is addressed to all the baptized.
   For the first Christians "sacramental power" comes from the presence of the Holy Spirit in the community; then they select and designate someone with the appropriate charism to act in their name. The
Council of Chalcedon (451) in its Sixth Canon condemned the practice
of "ordination at large . . . unless the person ordained is particularly
appointed to a church."[60] This gradually changed, and priestly power
was seen as belonging to a priest independent of any community, and
as establishing a sacral character. Thereafter, as Boff notes, "a priest
can celebrate the Eucharist without the community, but the community
cannot 'celebrate' the Eucharist without the priest."[61]
   Again, historical factors contributed to this sacralizing of priesthood. Schillebeeckx notes two in particular. First, in the feudal system,
many local overlords moved to have priests and bishops ordained to
care for their own personal needs and private chapels. Because they
were neither called forth by nor assigned to a faith community, the
assumption grew that they had priesthood as a personal power that
they could exercise independently of a community.[62] Second, in its institutional structures and canon law, the church gradually came to accept the Roman notion that power is invested in a ruler independent of
"territoriality." As Schillebeeckx summarizes, this encouraged "authority as value-in-itself apart from the community"; then "the old relationship . . . between ministry and church shifts to a relationship between

potestas and eucharista," and "ordination became the bestowal of special power to be able to perform the consecration in the eucharist."[63]

These medieval influences for the sacralizing of priesthood were augmented for Catholicism by the polemics of the Reformation era, with perhaps both sides taking more extreme positions than originally intended. As Reformers rejected the ontic power of priesthood and emphasized the "priesthood of all believers," Catholicism placed increased emphasis on the sacral nature of priesthood, on "absolute ordination," and on the qualitative difference between laity and priest. This, however, must be interpreted in the context of the time. Against the Reformers, the Council of Trent insisted that the sacraments of baptism, confirmation, and holy orders are nonrepeatable because they confer a "sacramental character." Osborne writes, "By the use of the term sacramental character, the bishops of Trent stood firmly with the hard-won position that these sacraments were not to be repeated. There is no description, definition, discussion on 'what' this character might be. Only the fact that these three sacraments confer a character has been promulgated; the exact make-up of such a character is an open question."[64]

Osborne may be correct on this point, but the *Catechism of the Council of Trent* (first published in 1566 and also called *The Roman Catechism*), reflects a total sacralizing of priesthood. In that the Tridentine Catechism was the effective promulgation of Trent's positions and became a primary text and doctrinal norm for priests in preparing their sermons for much of the next four hundred years, it had incomparable influence on Catholic consciousness. The *Catechism* states, "Priests and bishops are, as it were, the interpreters and messengers of God, commissioned in his name to teach men [sic] the divine law. They act in this world as the very person of God. It is evident that no office greater than theirs can be imagined. Rightly have they been called angels (Mic. 2:7), even gods (Exod. 22:28), holding as they do among us the very name and power of the living God." It continues, "The power of the Christian priesthood is literally heavenly; it surpasses the very power of the angels."[65] With that, the sacralizing of priesthood would seem to have triumphed completely.[66]

3. Hierarchical.   Ministry became hierarchized not only in the sense of concern for "holy order" (suggested by the etymology of *hierarchy*) but in the sense of descending levels of canonical authority and sacramental power. Priesthood came to include both "the power of the keys" (i.e., juridical) and "sacramental power," and one's level of authority and power depended on one's "degree" of priesthood. The *Catechism of Trent* well summarizes this hierarchizing of ministry.

The *Catechism* counts "the various degrees of the sacred ministry" as "seven in number, according to a long-standing tradition of the Catholic Church." It lists them as "Porter, Lector, Exorcist, Acolyte, Subdeacon, Deacon and Priest" and notes that all derive their function from "the consecration and administration of the Holy Eucharist, for which they were principally instituted." It describes the first four listed as minor orders and subdeacon, deacon, and priest as major orders. Among the major orders there is further gradation, the subdeacon is the lowest level, the deacon second highest, and priesthood "the third and highest degree of all Holy Orders." Since the minor orders and the first two of major orders were stepping-stones to priesthood, only the *Catechism*'s understanding of the last need concern us here. Within priesthood it distinguished five "different degrees of dignity and power" and reviews them in ascending order. The first and lowest is priest, the second bishop, the third archbishop, the fourth patriarch— "the first and supreme Fathers in the episcopal order." Then the *Catechism* adds, "Superior to all of these and venerated by the Catholic Church as supreme is the Bishop of Rome."[67]

As the historical notes above made clear, one does not find in the New Testament or early church the hierarchical arrangement of ministry as reflected in the Tridentine Catechism. It arose, in large part, from the influences of history and from the social contexts in which the church found itself. To say this is not to judge its efficacy over the years but to recognize its historicity and thus its potential for adjustment in other times. Historically, the social model most available to the church as it moved to institutionalization was the Roman Empire, with its vertical lines of command. As might be expected, the structure of the clergy "assumed a physiognomy very similar to that of the civil service. Ascent in the ranks was designed to develop worthy ministers, but the process was very like that used by the state, even down to the vocabulary."[68] With the rise of the feudal system and the marriage of throne and altar in the world of Christendom, "bishops . . . came to adopt and imitate the political trappings of the secular princes and became themselves prince-bishops, with rings, croziers and other insignia of office."[69]

The social influences to make ministry hierarchical found theological legitimation in the writings of Pseudo-Dionysius.[70] This unknown author, writing about 500 C.E. and heavily influenced by Neoplatonism, had immense influence on both Eastern and Western Christianity. The author argues that the hierarchical arrangement of ministry is of divine origin. There is a heavenly hierarchy of divine beings (nine degrees of angels!) that communicate divinity to people in a descending scale. Thus, the divine hierarchy is reflected in the earthly one and institutionally in the degrees of priesthood—pope, bishop, priest, and deacon. The "hierarch" at the head of the church takes on "a likeness to God"; through him, power is "imparted to those below him according to their merit."[71] As Power explains, "When the work of the Pseudo-Dionysius was assimilated into a later medieval vision of the church and sacrament, . . . the vision of the universe as hierarchical provided strong support for a hierarchical vision of the church, and of the sacraments as actions performed by the clergy for the other members."[72] Now people believed that divine authority and power is not through the whole church by the indwelling of the Holy Spirit, but from God to the pope, to archbishops and so on, down the descending hierarchy.

4. Exclusive.   First, and most obviously, ministry became exclusive when made equivalent to ordained ministry. Vowed religious women and vowed nonordained men forged what were in fact authentic ministries, but their work was not so designated and was deemed of lesser status than ordained ministry. Because access to juridical as well as sacramental power in Catholicism was through ordination, people in "the apostolate" were excluded from ecclesial decision making. And until the "lay apostolate" of the twentieth century, laity who did not choose the vowed religious life were excluded from all ecclesially recognized ministry.

Beyond reserving designated ministry to the ordained, the Catholic church made priesthood itself exclusive by requiring that its candidates be male and celibate. We already noted the openness of form for designated functions of ministry in the New Testament communities. Nowhere are maleness or celibacy indicated as preconditions of formal ministry; the only requirements seem to have been that a candidate have the requisite charism from God for a particular function and be called to it by a Christian community.

Elisabeth Schüssler Fiorenza, probably more than any other New Testament theologian, has established the inclusive praxis of Jesus toward women and the "inclusive discipleship of equals" he intended for his community.[73] The consensus among Scripture and patristic scholars is that women participated actively in the designated ministries of the early church and shared in functions later subsumed into priesthood; likewise, there is no warrant in the scriptural evidence to exclude women from any expression of ordained ministry.[74] Historically, it seems that as priesthood subsumed all functions of ministry, maleness as a precondition for it was a product of the patriarchy and the sexist mores of the church's cultural surroundings.

In the early church an "inclusive discipleship of equals" was soon replaced by the metaphor of *pater familias.* Borrowed from Roman culture, in which the "father of the household" was considered sole owner of wife, children, and slaves, it became the model for church leadership and ministry.[75] The pater familias model prompted the assumption, soon made explicit, that women could not participate equally with men in the church community, and as ministry became synonymous with priesthood, they were gradually excluded from ordination,[76] and not only from priesthood but from the lives of priests. As late as the seventeenth century when women like Mary Ward (d. 1645) were struggling to found vowed religious communities of women to take part in the public mission of the church (outside of contemplative religious life), they were refused permission on the grounds that it was inappropriate for women to work alongside priests.[77]

Of celibacy, from the Synod of Elvira (c. 309) the church made many unsuccessful attempts in the first millennium to establish it as a precondition for ordination. The first decisive step was taken at the Second Lateran Council (1139), which declared that marriages of priests were not only unlawful but invalid. Thereafter celibacy for priests has been an established law in the Western church, albeit never declared an absolute requirement for ordination.[78]

The practice of the Western church to require celibacy of its ordained ministers reflects a long and complex history. It was certainly influenced by the monastic movement. Monasticism gained ground in the West as baptism became a sociocultural expectation; it was at first a "lay" movement to take baptism seriously. It left a rich spiritual legacy, but the baptismal call to holiness, once perceived as the vocation of all Christians, became a life set apart from the world and under the vows of poverty, chastity, and obedience. Because of the church's valid sentiment that people in its designated ministry should be marked by holiness of life and have spiritual as well as institutional authority, it began to choose at least its bishops from the monasteries. As the monastic way of life became the paradigm of holiness, there was strong sentiment that the priest should at least approximate the life of the monk. O'Meara writes, "From the fourth century on, certain bishops such as Martin of Tours, Paulinus of Nola, and Augustine of Hippo had favored a monastic life for their priests. By 814 Councils were urging the spirit and life of the monk upon the diocesan clergy." O'Meara adds, "Since celibacy appeared as essential to monastic life, there was an inevitable drive ... to nourish celibacy" for diocesan clergy.[79]

From the Middle Ages on, the church was also concerned to prevent the alienation of its property that might otherwise pass into the possession of priests' families. Another root of mandatory celibacy was a dubious and at first Manichaean-influenced theology of human sexuality and marriage.[80] In fairness to the church's record here, I note that Manichaeism, and other movements that disparaged the human body and sexuality, were condemned by the church as heresy. But it seems some of their negative attitudes "rubbed off" and influenced official sentiments and policy. Bainton summarizes the historical evidence well when he writes, "The campaign for clerical celibacy had been waged with a general disparagement of marriage and of woman, who was portrayed as the gateway to hell."[81]

Schillebeeckx contends that negative attitudes toward marriage and sexuality encourage the pious sentiment that priests should abstain from intercourse before celebrating Eucharist. This was also influenced by Stoic philosophy and some statements from the Hebrew Scriptures that after the emission of seed the Levitical priesthood had to be rendered "clean" before making the sacred offerings (see e.g., Lev. 22:4). Schillebeeckx contends that when daily celebration of Eucharist became common practice, the law of sexual abstinence, hitherto considered required of priests before the sabbath, was extended to every day of the week and soon became the law of celibacy.[82]

Whatever the origins of the celibacy law, like the exclusion of women, it was the product of cultural influences and not a mandate of Christian scriptures. Without negating the value of the vowed life of chastity when freely embraced as one's call to holiness, it is self-evident that legislating celibacy as a precondition for ordination excludes people from priesthood who do not have such a charism. The requirements of both maleness and celibacy for priesthood are unfortunate diminutions that maintain the exclusiveness of ordained ministry. All four "diminutions" reviewed had serious implications for the mission and ministry of the church. They coalesce in their influences, but I note some particular consequences of each.

A. The *clericalizing* of ministry discouraged the laity's awareness and initiative to fulfill their vocation in the mission and ministry of the church in the world. It negates the rights and responsibilities that come with baptism by literally taking ministry out of the hands of the church as the whole community of Jesus' disciples and assigning it to an elite caste group to be done "for" or "to" the people. Clericalism disempowers the laity. For the ordained, clericalism inhibits a priesthood of service modeled on Jesus. By encouraging priests to see themselves as the sole providers of ministry, a clericalized structure can be physically, emotionally, and spiritually destructive of priests.

B. The *sacralizing* of ministry gave people the impression that the quest for holiness through Christian service is the exclusive preserve of a chosen few, that priests are more favored by God than "laity," who depend entirely on them for access to God's grace and blessings. Conversely, it gives the ordained a pedestalized self-understanding and an exaggerated sense of their "power" apart from and independent of their faith community. A sacralized self-image leads priests to presume that they control people's access to God rather than recognizing that God is always already present in the community through and with whom they are to minister.

C. The *hierarchalizing* of ministry created a "top-down" model of ministry in which goods and services are in the hands of the hierarchy and the people are dependent recipients. When "hierarchy" means that the people have no significant part in choosing their ministers, in holding them accountable, and in exercising their own gifts for service through a Christian community, then it encourages at best a paternalistic style of ministry—*for* the people—or at worst an autocratic one— *over* the people. Again, rather than empowering people in their ministry, a top-down model maintains them in dependence.[83]

D. The *exclusiveness* of designated ministry as ordained, male, and celibate has prevented people with special gifts for ecclesial service from being so designated and engaged by the community and has robbed the church of a countless number of fine candidates for priesthood. Maleness and mandatory celibacy as preconditions are countersigns to the sacramental function of priesthood and, I believe, are related expressions of sexism in the church.

4. Post–Vatican II Developments for Ministry to "The Modern World"[84]

Here I attend to some developments in patterns of Christian ministry and to the social/political contexts in and to which this ministry is carried on. Again, my ecclesial focus is on the Catholic community, and socially I reflect from the context of the United States but, I hope, with a global consciousness.

A. The Ecclesial Context of Ministry

A "ministry explosion"[85] is now occurring in the Catholic church, a repatterning in function, form, and style that could be called a *new* paradigm if it were not so much in continuity with the patterns of ministry in the first Christian communities. The watershed was undoubtedly the Second Vatican Council (1962–65). The Council's primary focus was the nature and mission of the church, and developments in ecclesiology were likely to bring adjustments in the structures, functions, and styles of ministry. The Council clearly advanced a more communal understanding of the church. Summarizing, Dulles writes, "The principal paradigm of the church in the documents of Vatican II is that of the People of God."[86] McBrien notes that even the drafts through which the Council's *Constitution on the Church* came to its present form, "disclose the extraordinary development which occurred in the council's self-understanding. Whereas at the beginning the emphasis was on the institutional, hierarchical, and juridical aspects of the Church, with special importance assigned to the papal office, the finally approved and promulgated constitution speaks of the Church as the People of God and of its authority as collegial in nature and exercise."[87]

This *Constitution* opens with a chapter, "The Mystery of the Church" and then moves, significantly, in chapter 2, to "The People of God," before addressing "The Hierarchical Structure of the Church" in chapter 3. Vatican II and contemporary ecclesiology reflect other ecclesial models, such as institution, servant, herald, and sacrament of God's reign, but all complement a primary understanding of the church as "the community of Jesus' disciples."[88] This paradigm shift in Catholic ecclesiology has been a concerted challenge to the clerical, hierarchical, and exclusive model of Tridentine ministry.

The shift to a more communal understanding of church notwithstanding, the Council documents did not immediately herald significant structural developments in the forms and functions of ministry. In fact, the Council was quite tentative and at times ambiguous about a new ministerial paradigm. But by affirming the rights and responsibilities of all Christians to participate in the mission of the church, the Council clearly reestablished the universal ministry of all the baptized; by recognizing a "variety of ministries" the Council signaled that formally designated ministry is broader than the episcopal/priestly functions.

To begin with, Vatican II gave clear affirmation to "the priesthood of all believers," strongly resisted heretofore as a Protestant notion; at least, this marked the beginning of a more "ascending" paradigm of ministry, through the God-given charisms of the baptized. The *Constitution on the Church* declared, "The baptized, by regeneration and the anointing of the Holy Spirit are consecrated into a spiritual house and a holy priesthood" (par. 10). Having summarized the mission of the church in the world, the *Constitution* went on, "Everything which has been said so far concerning the People of God applies equally to the laity, religious and clergy" (par. 30). It explained that "the laity" are "by baptism made one body with Christ" and therefore share "in the priestly, prophetic and kingly functions of Christ" (par. 31). Likewise, "through their baptism and confirmation, all are commissioned" to "a participation in the saving mission of the Church" (par. 33). It explained further that because all Christians "share a common dignity from their rebirth in Christ, . . . there is in Christ and in the Church no inequality on the basis of race or nationality, social condition or sex. . . . All share a true equality with regard to the dignity and to the activity common to all the faithful for the building up of the Body of Christ" (par. 32).[89]

More significant perhaps for the "priesthood of the laity" than such verbal statements were the changes in the liturgy that Catholics experienced as a result of Vatican II, and especially their increased participation in the Mass. The *Constitution on the Liturgy* called "all the faithful . . . to that full, conscious and active participation in liturgical celebrations which is demanded by the very nature of the liturgy."[90] The transformation that followed in the symbolic world of Catholics and especially through the central liturgical symbols of their weekly lives, had the pervasive conscious and subconscious effect on lay Catholics of reclaiming their "priesthood." In post–Vatican II renewal, the liturgy is becoming the public work of all the people, a celebration by the whole community at which the priest presides.[91]

Since the tentative beginnings of Vatican II, Catholicism has had much momentum for what two commentators describe as "a return from exile" by ministry and church leadership; what was previously held as exclusive to a few is being reclaimed by the whole community of faith.[92] There is growing awareness that the alleged "shortage of vocations" is at best false, if not a refusal to recognize the vocations/gifts blossoming in the community and to adjust the structures of ministry to nurture and engage them. O'Meara points out that "the present 'expansion,' 'alteration' or 'explosion' in ministry . . . was not mandated by universal or local churches, nor by bishops or curia in Geneva or Rome." Rather, "Church ministry expanding throughout the world suggests that the Holy Spirit is intent upon a wider service, a more diverse ministry for a church life that will be broader in quantity and richer in quality."[93]

Regarding "Christian/universal" ministry, Catholics are becoming convinced that ministry is the prerogative and responsibility of everyone initiated into the Body of Christ. Begun in baptism, affirmed in confirmation, and constantly nurtured through Eucharist, this initiation designates people for ministry within and through the Christian community *and* in their daily lives in society. Recalling the purpose and tasks of Christian ministry, this means that all Christians are formally designated to participate in realizing God's reign in the world. Motivated by Christian faith and in solidarity with a faith community, every Christian is to contribute in their place and time so that, to quote Vatican II, "God's Kingdom can be everywhere proclaimed and established."[94]

Every Christian is to participate as an active agent in the church's functions of kerygma, koinonia, leitourgia, and diakonia. In every arena of life, Christians are to share by word, as appropriate, and always by example the kerygma of God's love for all humankind and what it means to live as disciples of Jesus. In the apt words of *Evangelii Nuntiandi*, this means, "bringing the Good News into all the strata of humanity, and through its influence transforming humanity from within and making it new."[95] They are to help build communities of witness and "right relationship," not only in church but in workplace, family, neighborhood, nation, and world. Their daily lives should be suffused with a consciousness of the sacramentality of life though which God is present and to be praised, by commitment to personal prayer and to participation in the public worship of their church. And Christians are to render service to human welfare with a love that demands justice and the "integral liberation" of humankind.

In summary: *"Christian/universal" ministry is the baptismal vocation from the Holy Spirit to all Christians that they employ their God-given talents with the conscious commitment of Christian faith, to work as a community for the realization of God's reign in Jesus; this vocation includes the tasks of sharing God's word, building community, worshiping God, and serving human welfare.*

Concerning *designated functions of ministry,* including the ordained, I note first the sentiments of Vatican II. It claimed there is a difference not only "in degree" but "in essence" between the common priesthood of all and ordained priesthood. Though this reflects the present "mind of the church" (historical circumstances and critical scholarship may yet nuance it), commentators have made too much of the Council's distinction; in its context (*Constitution on Church,* par. 10) the primary intent was to affirm the close relationship between the two and their common ground in the priesthood of Christ, and their distinction seems more parenthetical. "Though they differ from one another in essence and not only in degree, the common priesthood of the faithful and the ministerial or hierarchical priesthood are nonetheless interrelated. Each of them in its own special way is a participation in the one priesthood of Christ."[96] And the Council made clear that whatever "sacred power" the priest has should be used only for service and to enable the "faithful" to fulfill their "various charisms" effectively.[97]

The Council recognized that designated ministry is not synonymous with priesthood. It specifically stated, "For the nurturing and constant growth of the People of God, Christ the Lord instituted in His Church a variety of ministries which work for the good of the whole body."[98] The church expanded this openness to recognize diverse functions of designated ministry in postconciliar church documents.[99] In pastoral practice, however, since Vatican II, the line of demarcation between ordained and otherwise designated ministries has at least become faded at the edges as increasing numbers of nonordained people participate in officially commissioned functions of ministry (giving rise to the anomalous language of "lay ministry").[100]

Designation is sometimes for full-time careers in "Christian/specific" ministries, for example, religious educators, liturgists, pastoral leaders, church administrators, spiritual directors, and peace and justice ministers. There are also the general ministries carried on by vowed women and men. The church also designates people for more occasional or part-time ministries. The most obvious are for liturgical functions like readers, eucharistic ministers, song leaders, music ministers. Part-time designated ministries also include regular service in religious education or in any other function occasionally rendered in the name of a Christian community.

In pastoral practice, designation for both full-time and part-time "Christian/specific" ministries can be with or without ecclesial ceremony. A special and traditional instance now recognized as designation for formal ministry are the ceremonies of commitment of religious sisters and brothers. For laity who do not enter vowed life, designation at times is as simple as being hired (e.g., as D.R.E.) or recruited (e.g., as a lector) by a parish but increasingly is given communal expression in liturgical rite. As long as there is clear awareness on the part of a sponsoring community and a particular minister that she or he is rendering a Christian service in their name, then the person has designation for that function.

For all designated "Christian/specific" ministries, full-time and part-time, ordained and otherwise commissioned, there is growing recognition of diversity in functions and openness in form, with priesthood increasingly seen as one designated function among others. And for form of priesthood there are serious challenges, on both theological and pastoral grounds, to the criteria of maleness and celibacy. The *functions* the church now widely recognizes as designated ministries include the following:

- Evangelizing and preaching the kerygma of Christian faith
- Leading, coordinating, and serving the community at worship and in celebrating the sacraments
- Education in Christian faith and formation of Christian community
- Care for the psychological and spiritual needs of people in the functions of pastoral counseling and spiritual direction
- Care for immediate human needs in social services
- Engagement in social/political work for peace and justice
- Administration and stewardship of the community's material assets
- Biblical and theological scholarship that researches and renews the community's spiritual assets
- Nurture and coordination of all the charisms of a faith community to work together in the church's mission, that is, with "holy order"

Reflecting openness in *form*, contemporary practice does not require maleness, or the celibate or vowed religious life, as preconditions for full-time designated ministries other than priesthood. The vowed religious life continues to be cherished in Catholic consciousness and spirituality as a unique call to holiness and ministry. And married and nonvowed single people are also entering careers in full-time designated ministry with a unique sense of vocation to service and holiness of life. The "church" seems to have growing conviction that the criteria for admission to any designated function of ministry are threefold: *inclination* (have the gifts needed for the function and the personal readiness to so serve), *preparation* (be adequately prepared, theologically, pastorally, and spiritually to render the service), and *designation* (be somehow recognized and commissioned for this service by a Christian community).

In summary: *Designated Christian ministry is any specific function of service and empowerment rendered by a baptized follower of Jesus who, gifted with the requisite charism by the Holy Spirit, is called and commissioned to do it by, with, and on behalf of a Christian community to make God's reign present in the world.*

What now of priesthood? Given our past—the central role of Eucharist and the sacraments to Catholic identity, of uniting authority and holy orders—I believe ordained ministry now fulfills a pivotal function in Catholic faith life and ministry and, in continuity with tradition, will continue to do so. Yet clearly the "church" at large is rethinking the forms and functions of ordained ministry. Hussey writes, "The Council deprived the priest of his traditional identity and clear self-image."[101] Osborne says that "the scholastic approach to priesthood which defined the priest in terms of his relationship to the eucharist . . . was set aside, changed, or modified by Vatican II."[102] Vatican II also posed shifts in the Tridentine understanding of bishop and deacon.

Regarding the "degrees" of bishop, priest, and deacon, the Council said they do not point to one function of Eucharist, but each has its own service to render. It made clear again that bishops have a proper ministry in their own right, that episcopacy is not simply an office added to priesthood by the pope's delegation. Rather, "by episcopal consecration is conferred the fullness of the sacrament of orders . . . the high priesthood, the apex of the sacred ministry."[103] It added, "Bishops in an eminent and visible way undertake Christ's own role as Teacher, Shepherd and High Priest . . . they act in His person."[104]

Of priests, the Council taught that they too share in the ministry of Jesus and the apostles. The apostles' "ministerial role has been handed down to priests in a limited degree. . . . they are co-workers of the episcopal order."[105] The *Constitution on the Church* says that, "although priests do not possess the highest degree of the priesthood, and although they are dependent on the bishops in the exercise of their power, they are nevertheless united with the bishops in sacerdotal dignity." Like the bishops they participate in Jesus' functions of preaching, pastoring, and "celebrat[ing] divine worship."[106] Osborne notes, "In what way bishop and priest differ in this participation might not be totally clear; but the identifying of priest to this threefold mission and ministry is quite clear."[107]

Of deacons, the Council made some significant, albeit limited, statements. It declared, "At a lower level of the hierarchy are deacons, upon whom hands are imposed, 'not unto the priesthood, but unto a ministry of service.' For strengthened by sacramental grace, in communion with the bishop and his group of priests, they serve the People of God in the ministry of the liturgy, of the word, and of charity."[108] The Council reaffirmed a diaconate transitional to priesthood but decreed that "the diaconate can in the future be restored as a proper and permanent rank of the hierarchy" and can be "conferred upon men of more mature age, even upon those living in the married state."[109]

Concerning ordained ministry, the Council tried but did not succeed in quieting the debate about maleness and celibacy as criteria for bishop and priest, and maleness for deacon. And although it intimated that ordained ministries do not subsume all functions of designated ministry, it proposed no blueprint for what should emerge. Clearly this is a moment of great opportunity; the "church" will draw new life if it has the courage now to rethink and restructure its ordained ministry, while continuing to develop and diversify its other functions of designated ministry. What follows are some directions I discern and recommend.

Regarding function, pastoral practice reflects growing clarity that the services of ordained ministers are specific rather than all-inclusive, that we can no longer presume or expect priests to have every ministerial charism (all twelve?). Regardless of priest shortage or supply, it seems wise to limit priestly function in order to encourage and give scope to the other charisms present in every Christian community. In continuity with historical roots and respecting the functions of other ministries, the function of priest in a local Catholic community is constituted by a threefold service:

- To preside with the community at worship and in celebrating its sacramental life
- To preach the Scriptures and tradition of Christian faith, especially when the community assembles for worship
- To coordinate and enable the other functions of ministry in the parish for "holy order"

Regarding form of priesthood, both celibacy and maleness continue to be challenged—and for good reasons. Contemporary scholarship and pastoral practice pose serious dissent to both requirements. Celibacy *can* be the most appropriate life-style for a particular person's call to holiness if he or she has this charism,[110] but there is neither theological nor pastoral warrant for continuing to make it a precondition for honoring a call to priesthood—a distinct charism of service. Boff writes, "To deprive thousands upon thousands of communities of the sacrament of the Eucharist, and of the incomparable benefits of having an ordained minister, through inflexibility in maintaining a tradition that has bound a necessary service (namely that of priesthood) to a free charism (that of celibacy) is tantamount to an unlawful violation of the rights of the faithful."[111]

Confining ordained ministry to men is rightly challenged as the creation of a patriarchal culture and without biblical warrant (see note 74). Official Catholic declarations typically offer three arguments against ordination of women: that there were no women among "the twelve"; that it is contrary to the tradition; that to represent Jesus, a priest must be male (the "iconic" argument).[112] From a scholarly perspective these arguments are widely viewed as seriously inadequate:[113] (a) "the twelve" *then* cannot be equated with priesthood *now,* nor can the "chain theory" (Brown) from "the twelve" to priests as currently understood be historically substantiated (see note 32); (b) the "tradition" of excluding women from ordained ministry must be evaluated in light of the broader social context in which the practice emerged and the inferior position socially assigned to women generally; (c) it was not the maleness of Jesus that effectively "represented" humankind before God but his humanity, thus any human being can represent the Risen Christ in the sacramental moment of Eucharist. It seems that the exclusion of women from ordained ministry is the result of a patriarchal mind-set and culture and is not of Christian faith. The injustice of excluding women from priesthood[114] debilitates the church's sacramentality in the world; it is a countersign to God's reign. In sum, the criteria for admission to ordained ministry should be no more and no less than for other designated functions of ministry—*inclination, preparation,* and *designation.*

B. The Social Context of Ministry

All Christian ministry, in every time and place, carries on the church's mission of word and witness, worship and welfare. Because it is to serve God's reign in human history, Christian ministry must be realized and turned toward its social context. Each situation calls for a style of Christian ministry that is adequate to its traditions and cultures, needs and opportunities. An appropriate style for our "modern world" calls ministers to keen awareness of the *global,* the *public,* and the *local* contexts of their ministry—all are intertwined.

Christians must recognize the *global* context of their ministry, be concerned with the needs of the whole human family, and the well-being of all creation. We live now in a "global village"; all of life is a web of interrelations—ecological and social, economic and political. The well-being of our ecosociopolitical system depends on the well-being of all its parts and members; the welfare of all human beings is so inter-twined that we must care for one another if for no other reason than our "common good." With the developments in communication and transportation of the past century, we cannot pretend ignorance of the "main dangers" (Foucault) that face the human family. The most ulti-mate is the nuclear sword of Damocles that hangs over our heads, threatening, if dropped, to annihilate us. Kaufman writes that for the first time in history "humankind has in its own hands the means to obliterate itself." We face "a possible calamity the consequences of which we have no adequate means of evaluating . . . a catastrophe for which we would be exclusively responsible."[115] Ministry for God's reign must help rid the world of the threat of nuclear catastrophe.

With equal urgency Christians must care for people living in des-perate poverty and oppression, for whom annihilation and death are an immediate threat each day. The U.S. Catholic Bishops state in their pastoral letter *Economic Justice for All* that "beyond our own shores, the reality of 800 million people living in absolute poverty and 450 million malnourished or facing starvation casts an ominous shadow . . . at home."[116] Styles of Christian ministry should empower people to alle-viate poverty and all forms of social, economic, and political injustice, wherever they occur.

The well-being of humanity is inextricably bound up with the pres-ervation of the environment and the integrity of creation. We are vi-olating the biblical mandate to be good caretakers of God's creation by causing pollution, contamination, despoliation, deforestation, depletion of the ozone layer—with the threat of terrible consequences for all humankind and generations yet unborn. Christian ministry should be in the forefront of responding to the ecological crisis of our planet. It should reflect and encourage a "green consciousness," with leadership and commitment to the integrity God wills for all creation.

Christians should have global concern in ministry because of the tenet of our faith that God's love is universal. This was never entirely lost in Christian tradition, but some of our hegemonous faith claims (e.g., "Outside of the church there is no salvation," or, "Error has no rights") caused Christians to often forget it. Vatican II frequently referred to the universality of God's love and the "universal design of God for the salvation of the human race."[117] The Council's *Pastoral Constitution* states, "The joys and the hopes, the griefs and the anxieties of the [people] of this age, especially those who are poor or in any way afflicted, these too are the joys and hopes, the griefs and anxieties of the followers of Christ" (par. 1). Later, the *Constitution* points out that the Christian community is to be "a leaven . . . for human society" (par. 40), a community whose "pilgrimage toward the heavenly city" increases rather than decreases "the weight of their obligation to work with all [people] in constructing a more human world" (par. 57).[118]

Closely related to a global focus there must be a *public* aspect to Christian ministry. For Christian faith, the age-old separations between private and public, secular and sacred, faith and life are debilitating and reflect a denial of monotheism. We cannot have different Gods for private and public; there is but one and very same God for all times, places, and levels of existence. A purely "private" religion is impossible, and a privatized Christianity is a contradiction in terms. Far from being confined to a "private" and "apolitical" sphere, the church is a public institution in society whose *raison d'être* is to promote the eminently social values of God's reign in the world. As its life and symbols are publicly realized in "the company of strangers," [119] it has significant power in the public arena to promote or prevent fullness of life for all. Christian ministry is to be carried on with styles and structures that enable it to fulfill its "public" responsibilities.

Third, in ministry Christians must attend to their local context. They need a keen awareness of the cultural patterns, social structures, human needs, and historical opportunities that are present in their given context. This varies, of course, from one neighborhood to another. However, U.S. Christians share a common "local" context; our ministry should engage it in ways locally adequate (see the brief section on inculturation in chapter 4) and globally responsible.

To begin with, it is important for Christians in the United States to realize that their locus of ministry is the richest, most privileged, and most powerful nation on the face of God's earth and a nation founded on the reign-of-God principles of "liberty and justice for all." We should recognize and be grateful that its people enjoy a goodly measure of both liberty and justice, and that the United States has often been an influence for the same throughout the world. There is, however, a pervasive underside to the "American" reality that is contrary to God's reign and against which Christian ministry should be a countercultural influence. This underside is not easy to pinpoint, but one way to name it is as the product and producer of a "thingification" of people. This malaise expresses itself in what Kavanaugh calls a "commodity form" of culture, an ethos in which "things" are the measure of meaning and the nexus of relationship. When what we euphemistically call "goods" and their possession become the driving force of the culture, products are viewed as "subjects," as makers of meaning, and the true subjects— people—become "objects" over against them. Then, Kavanaugh explains, "We begin to worship things, to relate to them as if they were persons; and we relate to other persons as if they were things."[120] The "commodity form" of culture, Kavanaugh claims, "sustains and legitimates the entire fabric of dehumanization."[121] Though the causes of injustice and oppression are more than economic, in a nation that consumes 40 percent of the earth's resources annually but numbers only 6 percent of its population, critique of our "commodity form" seems especially to the point.

"Thingification" takes various forms—sexism, racism, class bias, age bias, and so on; all are, at root, refusals to treat some people as persons. Within the local context of U.S. society, Christian ministry should avoid and oppose all social structures and cultural mores that "thingify" people. Christians are to carry on ministry that is an antidote: against the rampant consumerism of American society and the unbridled capitalism we so readily practice that makes profit the only norm; against sexism and patriarchy that denies women their equal rights and dignity and diminishes the humanity of men as well; against racism that continues to divide us and to discriminate against anyone other than the white majority; against age bias that treats the elderly as voiceless and worthless and victimizes children through abuse, neglect, and malnutrition; against unconscionable destruction and diminishment of human life at any stage; against the environmental damage caused by industrial expansion, waste, and greed; against militarism that encourages the arms race and military superiority. While avoiding a "manifest destiny" kind of American chauvinism, as citizens of this most influential nation, members of the worldwide Christian community and brothers and sisters to all humankind, American Christians have unique opportunity to help realize the values of God's reign for people here and everywhere. Our social sins help keep millions of people in the Third and Fourth Worlds in abject poverty and oppression. Their struggles for liberation will bear little fruit without a revolution in the American way of life. American Christians have a historically unsurpassed and urgent opportunity to effect such a revolution. (I return to this theme in chapter 13—"The Church's Ministry of Justice and Peace".)

5. Shared Praxis as a Style of Ministry

The foregoing reflections on Christian ministry in general provide a backdrop for the remainder of Part III. For now, this review indicates that the *modus operandi* of Christian ministry should be appropriate to the overarching purpose of God's reign and effective in the tasks of evangelizing, preaching, and teaching Christian Story/Vision; in building up inclusive and witnessing communities of Jesus' disciples; of enabling communities to worship God and to celebrate the sacraments of encounter with the Risen Christ; and of rendering personal and social/political service for the welfare of all and the integrity of creation. The ministerial style of Jesus suggests that Christian ministry initiate a personal "presence with" people, empower them as agent-subjects of their faith, and call them into partnership and community. The early historical roots of Christian ministry and contemporary developments pose the possibility of a style of ministry that subsumes and surpasses the Tridentine paradigm. Beyond the style of clerical/sacral structures, ministry is to be a partnership that empowers Christians to work together and with all people of goodwill in using their gifts and talents to realize what they understand to be the reign of God in the world; it is to express and enhance the whole Christian community in fulfilling the mission of Jesus. Beyond an exclusive and hierarchical model, the style of Christian ministry is to honor the baptismal calling of all Christians; it should be marked by dialogue and co-responsibility and exclude no one from designation to a particular function who has the necessary inclination and preparation, when the community needs the service to be rendered. Christian ministry is to be carried on in a way that is adequate to the culture, needs, and gifts of its local context and responsible to its public and global aspects. Christian ministry requires an approach that engages and nurtures the universal ministry of all Christians for God's reign and likewise the work of designated ministries that are diverse in function and inclusive in form.[122] Such "new" wine will burst old wineskins!

Clearly the "church" needs many different styles of ministry and each particular minister a "style" that is uniquely their own. Without overclaiming for it, I believe the commitments and dynamics of a shared praxis approach suggest one fitting and effective style that can be adapted to various functions and many occasions of Christian ministry. It reflects commitments to engage and empower people in their whole "being" as agent-subjects-in-relationship in the world, to honor the tradition and community of Christian faith and their import for life, to bring people to partnership, mutuality, and dialogue in an inclusive community of participants. Its dynamics suggest a style of ministry that engages and enables people to express and reflect on their lives, that renders them access to the life-giving resources of Christian faith and community, that intends to empower them in holy and humanizing ways, and, should it be their tradition, to renew them in Christian living. Its commitments and dynamics suggest a general perspective through which ministers and communities can fittingly review and imagine their ministry.

In more detail, honoring the dynamics intended by the focusing activity and movement 1 of shared Christian praxis encourages a style of ministry that turns with people to their present existential lives, to praxis, whatever it may be, to engaging this situation and these people to *work with them* to render the ministry as needed. It means empowering people to take on the issues and needs of their lives and to respond to them together out of Christian faith. Such style is the antithesis of being aloof from the situation, or elitist toward people, as if "they need me to do this for them," or of waiting for people to come looking for precisely what the "church" thinks it has to offer and presumes they need. Instead of "gazing heavenward" (Acts 1:11), the focusing activity and movement 1 mean to attend to, engage, and care for the whole human condition, in *this* time and place, confident that this is where God is actively present with saving intent and where people, by God's grace, can participate in "the work of [their] salvation" (Phil. 2:12). The focusing activity advises a style of ministry that takes the initiative to reach out to people whatever their need or potential may be, that enables people to take on the real issues that face them. Movement 1 likewise suggests a style of ministry in which people work in partnership to use their talents, share their gifts, speak their word, name their reality, in service to and with others. It shifts beyond service to empowerment; it prompts us to see no one exclusively as provider or receiver but encourages all to be engaged as agent-subjects to render and receive ministry.

The dynamic of movement 2 of shared praxis suggests a style of ministry marked by "thoughtfulness," both as sensitive to other people's needs and enabling of their gifts, and as encouraging people to reason and remember about what is and to imagine what can and should be for the reign of God. I believe all Christian ministry, even of direct service to immediate human need, is to have some dimension that intentionally promotes with people their critical consciousness of historical reality, a life-giving perspective for self and others. In Freire's term, Christian ministry should be "conscienticizing," that is, enable people "to see" what they should see—good and bad—and to act accordingly. In Matthew 25, Jesus says that on Judgment Day, the "goats" will offer the defense that they never "saw"—never saw the hungry, the thirsty, the homeless, the oppressed; but it will not be an acceptable defense. Movement 2 of shared praxis and its dynamic of critical reflection suggest a style of ministry that enables people "to see" and to act.

Movement 3 suggests a style of Christian ministry that repeatedly realizes through deeds, words, and symbols the life-giving resources of Christian faith in this community and in the world. It suggests that ministry be made available rather than imposed; that it have a deep respect for and sensitivity to the people whom it serves and calls into service; that ministry be constantly reviewed for its appropriateness to the tradition and to the Vision of God's reign. Regardless of its function, the meaning, values, and ethic of Christian Story/Vision should suffuse the style and substance of the ministry rendered and give credible witness to Christian faith. Movement 3 reminds that Christian ministers are to embody in deed and make accessible in word and sacrament the reality of God's saving presence and intentions of fullness of life for all humankind, with special preference for people whose life and well-being is most denied.

The dialectical appropriation of movement 4 of shared praxis suggests a style of ministry in which all participants are agent-subjects in the encounter, that all "make it their own," with their personal styles of giving and receiving, and with authentic exchange and interchange between "givers" and "receivers." It reminds ministers to "be themselves" in the encounter, to do the ministry by their own style and as their own, to be alert and open to receive from the others to whom and with whom they minister. Movement 4 indicates a style that encourages even recipients of direct human service to actively appropriate what is rendered, retaining their dignity and discernment rather than being reduced to passive recipients, transcending their needs enough to find and share their own gifts.

Much of what movement 5 suggests for a style of ministry has been indicated already, especially by the focusing activity and movement 1. Yet it poses the specific emphasis for Christian ministry: that it must primarily intend the empowerment of people as agent-subjects, humanly and in faith—whatever their faith may be—that people may come to act and be actors in humanizing and faith-filled ways. Even in situations of direct service, it should never encourage people in dependence but reflect that there is always something people can choose to do for themselves and others, if only to pray. It suggests a style of ministry committed to improving rather than simply meeting the needs of a situation. Existentially, of course, there can be situations where Christian ministry does well to alleviate immediate human need and suffering. However, it is always to be suffused as well with intent to change the situation, to help people to help themselves and others.

Two Instances

Shared praxis is only one suggestive framework for fashioning a fitting style of Christian ministry; many other suitable ones are possible, and elements of many styles can combine as appropriate in different functions, cultures, contexts, and so on. The three chapters that follow place a shared praxis approach in dialogue with liturgy and preaching (chapter 12), justice and peace ministry (chapter 13), and pastoral counseling (chapter 14).[123] Here, to stimulate imagination about a shared praxis style of ministry, I offer brief descriptions of using it for a community meeting, and for the outreach of evangelization.

For Communal Discernment. The discernment process of any community or committee meeting can be readily facilitated by the movements of shared praxis. First, it is best to focus a particular and "generative" agenda item so that participants have common perception about the substance of the issue for attention and its parameters. Then participants can be invited to state their own positions, actions, attitudes, perspectives, sentiments, or whatever seems most relevant in response to the focused agenda (movement 1). Thereafter, a facilitator can prompt participants to deeper critical reflection on present praxis by inviting them to think critically about present action, sentiments, attitudes, and so on, regarding the agenda, to remember the sources and contexts that shape this present praxis, and to imagine the likely and preferred consequences of any potential decision (movement 2). Movement 3 of shared Christian praxis reminds that at some point (I'm presuming the movements overlap and vary in sequence) there is to be explicit attention to the beliefs, values, and ethics suggested by Christian Story/Vision as relevant to this issue—what Christian faith advises here. The facilitator can encourage a free-flowing dialogue that invites participants to weigh the "pros and cons" of various perspectives, to evaluate their likely consequences, to judge what is appropriate to Christian faith for this issue, adequate to this context, at this time, and so on (movement 4). Finally, after such "weighing" of the issue, the facilitator can encourage the group to decision making that reflects the consensus of participants and to planning, if necessary, to carry out their decision (movement 5).[124]

For Evangelization.   I limit this to an occasion when a Christian "believer" has an opportunity for outreach to a would-be Christian "inquirer"—someone who shows interest in Christianity. The movements undoubtedly overlap in such an encounter but can suggest a framework. The focusing activity can vary but most obviously is the initial evangelizing outreach. At times this can be quite overt but often as subtle as a passing word to a friend or co-worker that turns them to think about the "ultimacies" of their life. Movement 1 could be an invitation to the inquirer to talk descriptively about life and especially about how she or he deals with ultimate questions of meaning and issues of value; that is, to express the inquirer's own present faith praxis. Movement 2 suggests that evangelists also pose questions that invite inquirers to remember and review the influences and assumptions that are shaping their present praxis, to question what they may be accepting as "givens," to recognize dissatisfactions, to imagine what might be more life-giving for themselves and others. Movement 3 reminds the evangelizer to make accessible (i.e., not to impose) the central kerygma of Christian faith and especially what seems relevant to the life questions and ultimate issues the inquirer may have already raised. It also implies that this is done best after the person has reflected on his or her own faith praxis and has indicated openness to hearing a Christian Story/Vision. Movement 4 demands an attitude of deep respect for the inquirers; questions posed should invite them to see for themselves the meaning and possibilities the Christian tradition and community may or may not have for their own life. This questioning must be totally free of any manipulation, coercion, or argument for agreement with the evangelizer. God's grace draws people to Godself in a myriad of different ways; the *kairos* time and unique response to that allurement must be respected. For example, if a person was reared in another rich religious tradition but has become lax in practicing that faith, then the evangelizer will be eminently "successful" if the person chooses to turn more self-consciously to God by renewing commitment to his or her own religious tradition. (Surely God also uses Christian evangelizers to help people become better Jews, Moslems, Buddhists, etc. or simply "better people.") Movement 5 suggests that the evangelizer invite the inquirer to decision, but this must be carefully discerned in the context of each encounter. The invitation may be as tentative as "to think some more about it and talk again," or "to learn some more about your own religious tradition," or, if the inquirer expresses interest, to investigate the catechumenate program or whatever is available for Christian inquirers in the local parish or congregation.[125]

Chapter 12

Liturgy and Preaching

My general theme in this chapter is the liturgical life and preaching of the Christian church; my perspective is that of a religious educator; my pastoral interest is the sacramental adequacy of the church's liturgy and the effectiveness of its preaching. Liturgists can suspect that a religious educator's perspective on liturgy means to treat it as a didactic tool. But I consider that debilitating to the true function of liturgy and thus, ironically, to its educational power. My intention instead is to honor the liturgy in its primary function of worshiping God, convinced that when liturgy is so "sacramentally adequate," it is also a source of nurture and ongoing conversion for the faith life of a Christian community. For now, I note that a liturgy's "sacramental adequacy" is measured according to how effectively its symbols draw people into an intensified experience that God's life is mediated to them in love, that they express their own lives to God, and that they are empowered for God's reign in the world. I'm convinced that a religious education perspective, albeit a limited one, can enhance the sacramental adequacy of a community's liturgical actions and preaching. My focus, then, is not the role of religious education in preparing people to participate in liturgy (a worthy though unilateral topic) but rather how an educational perspective can enhance *the liturgical event itself*.

My reflections on preaching and the possibility of a shared praxis style in homiletics are offered in the closing section; the body of the chapter attends to liturgy. For manageability, however, I limit the scope to a particular focus. I already noted that my theme is *Christian* liturgy; this, however, includes any and every public act of communal prayer enacted by a Christian community. The understanding and praxis of liturgy varies significantly from one Christian denomination to another, and worship can be given different expressions within the same community. Exigencies of space alone prohibit reflection on "liturgy in general." I focus, then, on the particular I am best qualified to reflect on, my Catholic tradition of worship and sacramental celebration. But even this I must limit further.

Catholicism has a rich variety of liturgical forms—liturgy of the hours that sanctifies the time of the day, celebration of seven sacraments, and nonsacramental but communal prayer events. My reflections pertain at times to all Catholic liturgy, but my particular focus is its Sunday worship service, the liturgy of word and Eucharist that constitute "the Mass." I use this particular instance because it is the central paradigm of Catholic liturgy and the liturgical event in which Catholics most often participate. Though limited, it is an appropriate focus for my pastoral interest; attention to sacramental adequacy in this central instance is likely to permeate the whole liturgical life of the church.[1] I also hope that insights gleaned are resonant for other Christian communions and their Sunday worship.

Section 1 discusses the traditional relationship between liturgy and catechesis. Sections 2, 3, and 4 focus on the functions, forms, and effectiveness of the liturgy. Section 5 offers a shared praxis perspective on enacting the various activities of the Mass and how such an approach can enhance attention to its sacramental adequacy. The concluding section 6 is on preaching with a style of shared praxis.

1. Liturgy and Religious Education: An Old Partnership

Leading authors offer many definitions of liturgy, and there is significant diversity in Catholic church documents concerning its function. I attempt my own statement of its function below (section 2) but for now note the summary statement of Vatican II: "The sacred liturgy is above all things the worship of the divine Majesty."[2] The Council makes clear that this worship is offered as a common prayer action by the whole church, and the church can do so because of the presence of the Risen Christ through the indwelling Spirit to the community. In Christian faith, then, fitting worship is by the grace of God's Spirit in Jesus Christ; it is human participation in a divine initiative. "Christ indeed always associates the Church with Himself in the truly great work of giving perfect praise to God and making [people] holy . . . the liturgy is considered an exercise of the priestly office of Jesus Christ. . . . in the liturgy full public worship is performed by the Mystical Body of Jesus Christ, that is, by the Head and His members."[3]

To its summary statement that liturgy is to worship God, the Council adds, "It likewise contains abundant instruction for the faithful."[4] I add that liturgy is educational in a holistic sense (i.e, beyond "instruction"). As an expression of communal faith, it can inform, form, and transform participants in renewed Christian faith as well. Like lovemaking in marriage, liturgy in the life of Christians should be both an *expression* and a *source* of faith, hope, and love. From this perspective, we recognize the "educational" power of liturgy. To nurture people and communities in Christian identity and living is the learning outcome for Christian religious education. But as I substantiate below (section 4), nothing that the church does in the world has more consequence for the faith identity and agency of its people than its "public work" of liturgy. Though the primary intent of liturgy is to worship God, it always has existential impact on the lives of participants that is profoundly educational.[5]

Awareness that liturgy "instructs" is as old as the people of Israel. Israel had summary statements that reflected, in story form, its identity in faith (e.g., Deut. 6:20–25; 26:5–9; Josh. 24:2–13). Commentators note, however, that the formal context of those creedal stories and the occasions on which the people would hear them repeatedly was the liturgical life of Israel.[6] Through their communal worship the Israelites reminded themselves and taught their children who they were as a people of God. Likewise, the first Christians expressed their kerygma of faith in liturgy, and especially at baptism. The early formulae of belief were amplified and emerged later as the creeds of the church. At first, the creeds were used only to test the faith of catechumens. But by the fifth century the practice began to emerge of regularly reciting the Nicene Creed at Sunday worship as a norm of the faith of those already within the church.[7] Christians were well aware that their Sunday worship was a source of instruction and a norm of faith. In the controversy with the Pelagians, Prosper of Aquitaine (d. c.462) and Augustine (d. 430) popularized the phrase *lex orandi, lex credendi* (literally, "the law of prayer is the law of faith"), meaning that the church's liturgy is the normative expression of its faith. In fact, the faith norm implied was the Christian tradition, but they were assuming that it is most vitally expressed in the liturgy.

The Eastern Orthodox tradition seems to have remembered *lex orandi, lex credendi* better than the West, although the latter never lost it entirely, and its reality was clearly recognized by Vatican II in its *Constitution on the Liturgy*. I already noted its comment that the liturgy offers "abundant instruction" (par. 33). Later, in commenting on the sacraments, the *Constitution* states, "Because they are signs they also instruct. They not only presuppose faith, but by words and objects they also nourish, strengthen, and express it."[8] Present religious education literature reflects growing awareness of the educational import of liturgy, that its symbols engage participants in their whole "being" and are powerfully formative for them and their communities. As Maria Harris summarizes well, "We are educated by prayer."[9] One should never "use" the liturgy to educate, but how communities worship together is, of itself, profoundly educational.

As liturgy educates, so too the Christian community must educate itself for its liturgical "work." Again, Vatican II reemphasized the importance of such catechesis: "That all the faithful be led to the full, conscious and active participation in liturgical celebration which is demanded by the very nature of the liturgy," the church must provide "the needed program of instruction."[10] A glance at any of the published curricula since Vatican II immediately indicates the centrality of liturgical/sacramental catechesis in Catholic religious education. In addition, many parishes engage parents and guardians in the sacramental catechesis of their children, especially in preparing for the sacraments of initiation and reconciliation. These parental programs have been among the most successful ventures in adult faith education and in renewing the liturgical life of the Catholic community. Now some liturgists encourage a type of regular catechumenate to prepare the community to celebrate the great events of the liturgical year (especially during Advent and Lent).[11]

Beyond the traditional appreciation of their reciprocity, I believe we need a deeper analysis of the relationship between religious education and liturgy that focuses on how liturgy functions as educational in a holistic way for its community of participants and how an educational perspective can help to enhance liturgy's sacramental adequacy.[12] It seems tautological yet important to say that there is nothing inevitable about liturgy being sacramentally adequate to participants' lives. There is a strong Catholic tradition of presuming that if liturgical rites are enacted according to prescribed form, they inevitably have the intended effects of God's transforming grace for people. But our own experiences of liturgies poorly enacted belies this. Alves summarizes the warning of the prophets of Israel that the sacred symbols of worship "could be used to illuminate or to blind, to make one soar or to paralyze, to give courage or to make afraid, to liberate or to enslave."[13] When its symbols are abused, misused, or inadequate to liturgy's proper function in people's lives, its consequences can be the second in each of Alves's couplets. Annette Honan, a student with me, wrote in a term paper, "Sacramental and liturgical life as I experience it in the institutional church either excludes, alienates, and angers me or anesthetizes and tranquilizes, leaving me unmoved, or unchallenged or unchanged." What a sad indictment, but how true it rings for too much of the church's liturgical praxis.

Undoubtedly, as Mary Kay Oosdyke writes, "The Christian community lives and works in a cultural milieu which militates against some of the essential features of liturgy."[14] This only means, however, that there is urgent need, especially in the dominant cultures, for Christian communities to care for the sacramental adequacy of their liturgical praxis. I'm convinced that to bring an educational perspective to how liturgy is prepared and enacted helps to prompt such care. By this, I mean a constant posture of asking, *What will this symbolic action say to and cause in the existential lives of this community of participants?* In this way, concern for what a liturgy expresses to God (its first function) is accompanied by concern for the existential experience and consequences of that expression in people's lives.[15] To elaborate on the symbiotic relationship between liturgy and faith education, and on how an educational perspective can enhance attention to sacramental adequacy, I turn with more detail to the functions, forms, and effectiveness of liturgy.

2. The Functions of Liturgy

As a profoundly symbolic and mystical activity, liturgy's functions, forms, and consequences are inevitably polyvalent and existentially are never separated. With the paradigm of the Mass particularly in mind, I propose the following as one description of the functions of liturgy. *By the grace of God's Holy Spirit, Christian liturgy is an intensified symbolic mediation of covenant and encounter between God and a Christian community in the Risen Christ; as such it is to symbolically express "in Spirit and truth" (John 4:23) God's life in love to its community of participants and their life in faith to God, to empower people for God's reign in the world.* Some aspects of this statement need elaboration here, and some I explain in later sections where they are more to the point.

First, as Christian faith is always a gift of God, so too people are brought to its expression in liturgy by the initiative of God's grace. Referring to the sacraments, Schillebeeckx writes, "Communion with God is possible only in and through God's own generous initiative in coming to meet us in grace."[16] In more existential language, the strong impetus in humankind to recognize and worship God, and if not God then some ultimate center of perceived value, is itself by the design of God in us. In Christian terms, though never negating the freedom and responsibility of the human partners in the encounter, liturgy's true functions and effects are realized always by the power of the Holy Spirit who works through the symbolic action of the community assembled around word and sacrament.

Second, all Christian liturgy is an encounter between God and a Christian community in the Risen Christ. I already noted Vatican II on the liturgy as "an exercise of the priestly office of Jesus Christ." This means that the community exercises its priesthood with and through the presence of the Risen Christ; "full public worship is performed by the mystical Body of Jesus Christ, that is by the Head and His members" (see note 3). Vatican II explains that the Risen Christ is sacramentally present in the community assembled, in the word proclaimed, and "especially under the Eucharistic species."[17] By symbolically mediating the presence of the Risen Christ in the community, the liturgy is an intensified experience of the encounter between God and humankind in their covenant relationship. As the historical Jesus united perfectly and completely in one person both divinity and humanity, so the symbolic presence of the Risen Christ in liturgical event brings God and humankind into the "at-one-ment" of the new covenant in Jesus.

Schillebeeckx, in his work with the apt title *Christ, the Sacrament of the Encounter with God,* was the first in modern times to pose this understanding of the liturgy. Affirming Chalcedon's Christological doctrine that in the one person Jesus, divine and human natures were perfectly united, and echoing the traditional Catholic understanding of a sacrament as a visible sign that effects the grace it signifies,[18] Schillebeeckx writes, "Because the saving acts of the man Jesus are performed by a divine person, they have a divine power to save, but because this divine power to save appears to us in visible form, the saving activity of Jesus is sacramental."[19] Positing that "mutual human availability is possible only in and through (human) bodiliness,"[20] what then, asks Schillebeeckx, of the sacramentality of Jesus now that the historical person is no longer physically present in the community? His response is that the Risen Christ is "visibly" present through the symbols of the sacraments. He writes, "If Christ did not make his heavenly bodiliness visible in some way in our earthly sphere, his redemption would after all no longer be for us."[21] Thus, Christ "makes himself visibly present to and for us earthbound [people] . . . by taking up earthly non-glorified realities into his glorified saving activity. . . . This is precisely what the sacraments are: the face of redemption turned visibly toward us so that in them we are truly able to encounter the living Christ."[22]

Since Schillebeeckx first proposed this position (Dutch edition, 1960), Vatican II, as noted, has renewed Catholic understanding of the liturgical presence of the Risen Christ as sacramentally mediated in word proclaimed and community assembled, as well as in sacraments celebrated. Our understanding of the power of symbols "to effect what they signify" has also deepened, and I return to this in section 4. For now, suffice it to say that all the symbols and actions that constitute a liturgical event are to work together to mediate a historical experience of encounter between divine and human praxis. This does not mean that human symbols control God's grace or "deliver" God's presence, but only that God mediates Godself to us in ways appropriate to our human condition. Our task is to see to it that liturgical events are existentially appropriate to people's lives. A document from the U.S. Catholic bishops summarizes this point well: "Liturgy has special significance as a means of relating to God, or responding to God's relating to us. This does not mean that we have 'captured' God in our symbols. It means only that God has graciously loved us on our own terms, in ways corresponding to our condition. Our response must be one of depth and totality, of authenticity, genuineness, *and care with respect to everything we use and do in liturgical celebration.*"[23] In the second part of my statement of function, I say that liturgy should express people's lives in faith to God and mediate God's life in love to them, and that this encounter between divine and human praxis is always "for the life of the world."[24]

A. "Our Lives in Faith to God"

Through its symbols and symbolic actions the liturgy is to express the corporate faith life of its community of participants as an act of worship to God. I first highlight that it is lives *in faith* that people bring to God in liturgy; true worship is a response to God's prior gracious initiative. But the event engages participants in an act of encounter, and thus their human mode of expression. In liturgy we express symbolically our very "selves," our individual and corporate life, our whole "being," personal and communal. No aspect, dimension, or sphere of our lives in the world should be excluded from what we present to God in liturgy. In keeping with the ancient Christian formula that all things human were assumed and redeemed in Jesus, our whole existence can and should be brought to expression in liturgy as our "lives in faith to God."

In Christian liturgy the symbolic self-expression of the people to God is made in union with the Risen Christ, whose priestly activity continues in the community through the Holy Spirit. People's lives are brought into encounter with God through the presence of the Risen Christ that is mediated in a "tangible" mode through the sacred symbols of the event. In the words of the ancient doxology, it is "through Christ, with Christ, in Christ, in the unity of the Holy Spirit" that Christians offer honor and praise to God.

The primary intent of our personal and communal "self-" presentation is to worship God, to symbolically express our recognition of who our God is and our dependence on how God is for us, who we recognize ourselves to be in God's presence and how we are to live as a people of God. For participants, liturgy is always a *re-membering* of the covenant and the "right relationship" into which God calls them. In liturgy, then, we express as worship to God sentiments of *adoration* and *praise* to recognize who our God is, *thanksgiving* and *petition* as we recognize how God is *for* us, *repentance* and *renewed commitment* as we recognize who we are and how we are to live as a people of God.

Christians believe that because they express their lives in faith in union with Jesus Christ, they can become "an acceptable offering" and "a holy priesthood" (see 1 Pet. 2:5).[25] And yet, people symbolically express their *own* lives in liturgy. Jesus is our representative to God, but he is not our substitute or replacement.[26] We come to God in worship as we are—with our joys and sorrows, health and brokenness, faithfulness and sins, love and apathy, hope and fears; a measure of the "truth" of any liturgical event is how adequately its symbols reflect and express the "real" life of participants.

Of course, Christians never have perfect lives to express to God in liturgy and indeed come there in part for the grace of forgiveness and renewed commitment. As I discuss in more detail presently, a key function of liturgy is to transform people's lives and to empower them as transformers "for the life of the world." And yet to bring lives that have acquiesced in sin and expect the representation of Christ to make them acceptable before God is, as the prophets of Israel named it, a blasphemy. They had perennial concern for the kind of lives people must live to offer true worship to God; they placed central emphasis on justice and peace and on living the "right relationship" demanded by the covenant. First Isaiah teaches that worship is "worthless" before God, unless the people "learn to do good, make justice [their] aim, redress the wronged, hear the orphans' plea, defend the widow . . . set things right" (see Isa. 1:13, 17–18). Amos has God say to the House of Israel about their worship, "I hate, I spurn your feasts, I take no pleasure in your solemnities. . . . But if you would offer me holocausts, then let justice surge like water and goodness like an unfailing stream" (Amos 5:21–24). Of the temple and its worship, Jeremiah has God warn the people, "Only if you thoroughly reform your ways and your deeds; if each of you deals justly with their neighbor, if you no longer oppress the resident alien, the orphan, and the widow, if you no longer shed innocent blood in this place, or follow strange gods to your own harm, will I remain with you in this place" (Jer. 7:5–7). And Third Isaiah warns the people in God's name that their fasting, rituals of repentance, and Sabbath observance are acceptable to God only if they engage in "releasing those bound unjustly, untying the thongs of the yoke; setting free the oppressed, breaking every yoke; sharing your bread with the hungry, sheltering the oppressed and the homeless; clothing the naked when you see them, and not turning your back on your own" (Isa. 58:6–7).

In the New Testament, we hear Jesus echo the lament of Isaiah, "This people honors me with their lips but their hearts are far from me" (Matt. 15:8). When a scribe replies to Jesus' statement of the great law of love by saying that to love God and neighbor "is worth more than all burnt offerings and sacrifices," Jesus responds by telling him, "You are not far from the reign of God" (see Mark 12:28–34). For lives to truly worship God, then, they are to be lived "in faith," that is, committed to struggle against all forms of idolatry, injustice, and oppression and to living in "right relationship" with God, self, others, and all creation as demanded by the covenant. Hughes writes, "Worship is an expression of right relationship or it is worse than worthless; it is an abomination to the Lord."[27] Albeit never perfectly successful, yet the measure of our efforts to live for the reign of God also measures the "truth" of our worship, at least from our side of the covenant.

Regarding the sacramental adequacy of this first named function of liturgy, a liturgical event should express to God the "real" lives of its community of participants' and in such a way that they can experience their "selves" being so expressed. Such adequacy would seem more likely, first, if the whole community is engaged in the liturgical event; an action of and by the participants would seem more adequate than an event that they only observe. Second, the symbols employed and how they are enacted should enable *all* the community to express their lives as worship to God; symbols that alienate or dominate people, that exclude their historical praxis, or with which they simply cannot identify are not likely to be sacramentally adequate in this regard. Third, in presenting people's lives to God, the symbols should also bring them into bold relief for themselves as well. Liturgy should enable participants to perceive their lives as they are, to recognize God's goodness to them, to examine their consciences and consciousness, to become aware of their sins and complicity in sinfulness, to recognize their need for repentance and renewal in their efforts to live as disciples of Jesus. Symbols and symbolic actions that conceal people's lives from themselves or cover them over with false legitimation are not sacramentally adequate.

Obviously, there is nothing inevitable about the adequacy of liturgy to give participants an existential experience of expressing their lives to God. For people formed in the Christian tradition, the ancient symbols likely have a sacramental adequacy they would not have for people from other communities. Though the "core" symbols of the liturgy (bread, wine, water, oil, light, assembled people, and so on) have more potential to be transhistorical and transcultural, the less essential ones are less likely to "travel well" and may be experienced as problematic by people in some historical and cultural contexts.[28] Even for people socialized to appreciate them, the "core" symbols cannot be presumed existentially adequate because of a theological principle that announces they are "effective." The witness of people who experience in the liturgy sexism, racism, militarism, clericalism, and so on warns against presuming the adequacy of its symbols on the basis of a formal principle.[29]

B. "God's Life to Us in Love"

Central to Christian faith is the conviction that because of God's saving action in Jesus Christ, God's life in love—that is, God's grace—is always and irrevocably turned toward and available to humankind. In faith, Christians believe that from God's side of the covenant, God's Holy Spirit is active in history, enabling people to encounter and experience God's grace. And yet, from our side of the covenant, we existentially experience and recognize the mediation of God's life in love typically according to our mode of encountering the relationship and appropriating the goodwill of any "other" toward us. As we express ourselves to God through symbols, so we experience the mediation of God's grace to us in a tangible mode as befits our human condition. I reiterate, this does not mean that liturgical symbols per se "cause" God's grace for people; rather, they symbolically and thus effectively mediate an intensified and tangible moment of encounter with God's ever present love and goodwill for them. The hug of a parent and child is a heightened experience for both of the love already present between them; likewise, liturgy can mediate for participants a heightened experience of God's grace and dispose them to welcome and respond to God's life in love that is ever turned toward them.[30]

Rahner writes, "The world is constantly and ceaselessly possessed by grace from its innermost roots, from the innermost personal center of the spiritual subject. It is constantly and ceaselessly sustained and moved by God's self-bestowal even prior to the question (admittedly always crucial) of how creaturely freedom reacts to this 'engracing.'"[31]

Catholicism and other Christian traditions that reject the notion of the total depravity of creation and human nature and agree with a sentiment like Rahner's, hold that any aspect of existence or creation can be a symbol of God's self-mediation to humankind—people, events, nature, words, and so on. All of life can be "sacramental." McBrien defines this general "principle of sacramentality" as "the fundamentally Catholic notion that all reality is potentially and in fact the bearer of God's presence and the instrument of divine action on our behalf."[32] This means that there is no line of demarcation between God's presence to us in life and in liturgy; rather, liturgy is a climactic expression of the sacramentality of life. For Christian faith, the mediation is intensified in liturgy because of the presence of the Risen Christ in the community as it assembles for public prayer, proclamation of the word of Scripture, and celebration of the sacraments. Liturgy should be an intensified experience of God's grace for its participants—grace to sustain and nurture, to heal and forgive, to console and affirm, to confront and invite to the praxis of Christian faith. As Kavanagh writes, "Christian tradition knows that God is not restricted to a sacramental order or to a rite, but [God] has nevertheless willed to work through these media regularly as nowhere else in creation."[33]

The symbolic effectiveness of liturgy to mediate God's grace to humankind is intimated in the traditional "catholic" understanding of sacraments as sacred signs that effect the grace they signify. Augustine described sacraments as "visible signs of invisible grace," and Aquinas added the emphasis that they are "efficacious signs." The Council of Trent described the sacraments as effective signs of God's grace that "confer the grace which they signify." Trent went on to state that the sacraments are effective *"ex opere operato"* (literally, "from the work worked," and meaning "by the rite itself") and intended to say that their effectiveness is by the gift of God's grace rather than by the worthiness of their ministers.[34] Trent did not intend to teach, as the *ex opere operato* tenet was sometimes interpreted, that the sacraments confer grace automatically. In fact, influenced by Aquinas, Trent said that the sacraments are "occasions" of grace insofar as they clearly signify it,[35] and they require the right "disposition and cooperation" from participants.[36] Thus the adequacy of its symbolization, the dispositions people bring to them, and the lived response we make are "conditions" for liturgy's effectiveness in people's lives.[37]

This second named function of liturgy brings again into bold relief the responsibility of communities and their liturgists to see to it that liturgy is symbolically adequate to mediate to participants an intensified experience of God's loving outreach to them. To presume that the liturgy inevitably says to and means for people what it is supposed to say and mean, regardless of the quality of its symbolic actions, reduces liturgy to magic. The symbolic actions should give people a deep sense of who their God is and how God is turned toward them in never ending love. Stated negatively, failure to engage the assembly as a com-

munity of participants, an inaudible, slipshod, or nonengaging proclamation of the Scriptures, a rambling, irrelevant, poorly prepared sermon, a banal, irreverent, nonparticipative enactment of the eucharistic
action, or the effecting of any of its symbols to seem alien, excluding,
or oppressive to participants makes liturgy less likely to mediate for
people an experience of God's saving grace in their lives.

C. "For the Life of the World"

The encounter between divine and human praxis in liturgy should
be a source of ongoing conversion for its participants and empower
them as a community of transformation "for the life of the world." As
the epitome of the "public work" (the etymological root of *liturgy*) of the
church in the world, liturgy is to reflect the whole mission of the church
for God's reign and empower every aspect of the church's ministry to
the human condition.

From the beginning, and in continuity with their Hebrew roots,
Christians have known that they are to worship God through liturgy
(see Acts 2:47) and that such action has historical consequences for
participants. In reenacting the Last Supper in eucharistic liturgy, they
remembered Jesus to have declared his body as "given for you" and
blood as "shed for you" (see Luke 22:19–20). Throughout history, the
church maintained some sense that baptism calls people to holiness of
life, that confirmation strengthens people for Christian witness, that
Eucharist is an ongoing source of nurture in Christian living, that penance offers the grace of forgiveness and *metanoia*, and so on. But the
sacraments became cultural expectations and salvation became limited
to saving one's soul after death, so people perceived the consequences
of liturgy in a privatized and otherworldly sense.

Liturgy should always give people hope for fullness of life, even in
the face of death. I affirm the ancient and rich tradition of understanding the eucharistic liturgy especially as an eschatological sign and
foretaste of the heavenly banquet. The *Constitution on the Sacred Liturgy*
states, "In the earthly liturgy, by way of foretaste, we share in the heavenly liturgy which is celebrated in the holy city of Jerusalem toward
which we journey as pilgrims."[38] But as the church dehistoricized the
symbol of God's reign to refer only to the afterlife of heaven, so too the
notion that liturgy is to have intrahistorical consequences on all levels of
human existence found little emphasis. Lost especially was the profound linkage forged by the Hebrew prophets between worship and the
works of justice and peace, between liturgy and living the covenant
demand of "right relationship" with God, self, others, and creation.

During the early days of the renewal movement, liturgists showed
a strong sense of the historical import of liturgy but then seemed to lose
their social consciousness.[39] Kathleen Hughes, a fine liturgist, laments
that the movements for liturgical renewal and for social justice have
tended to see their concerns as unrelated.[40] Himes summarizes the

opinion of many: "Even Vatican II was disappointing on this matter of connecting liturgy and social justice."[41] Now, however, there is evidence of renewed awareness that the historical consequences of liturgy are to be "for the life of the world," that liturgy should express and resource all the "public work" of the church.[42] One rationale for this claim might be as follows.

God's Spirit of life reaches out in love to our human condition. Divine grace always has the intent and power to save and free, to forgive and heal, to empower and renew people in living for God's reign. Analogous to human love, God's love as true love sets us free, even while it empowers and disposes us to respond. As we choose a faithful response, the consequences of God's grace are salvation, freedom, forgiveness, renewal, for ourselves and for the world. The doctrine of the Trinity reflects that even within Godself (the immanent Trinity) God's life is a "right relationship" of love; thus God's life in love to humankind (the economic Trinity) has the intent and, with our free but graced cooperation, can have the consequence of "right relationship," the biblical understanding of both justice and holiness of life. As Robert Imbelli writes, "God's own being is 'political.' The Triune God of Christian faith shares a common life; and it is this life which constitutes the city of God. . . . Christian Trinitarianism fosters the transformation of the political, just as it summons us to the transformation of every dimension of human existence."[43] The liturgy, which so eminently mediates an encounter with God's Trinitarian life turned toward humankind, should have historical consequences "for the life of the world." It is to be a source (a) of "holiness" of life for participants, (b) of renewal in mission for the church, (c) of peace and justice in its social context.

A. Vatican II echoes an ancient tradition when it says that the liturgy is to "make people holy" (note 3). It should nurture and sustain its community of participants in the holiness and thus "wholeness" of life that is realized as Christians live their covenant with God in Jesus. It should help people to live free of idolatry and with God consciously at the center of their lives, to realize their own deepest truth as disciples of Jesus, to care for the neighbor and especially those most in need, to heighten their sense of the sacramentality of all life and creation, and to live with the responsibility that comes from consciousness of God's gracious presence therein. B. The liturgy should renew both its immediate community and the universal church in its mission of God's reign in Jesus. It can empower the church to be itself a sacrament of what God wills for all. In its identity and agency, the church is called to be "one, holy, catholic and apostolic," so its liturgy is to both reflect and resource its deepening unity in faith and witness, the holiness and "right relationship" within the church's own life and structures, the inclusiveness and mutuality of its *modus operandi*, and its faithfulness to the apostolic mandate to live and promote the way of Jesus. C. As the church's most "public work," the liturgy, through its communities of participants, should be a resource for peace and justice in its immediate

context and incrementally in the world. Its liturgy is to constantly empower the church in reviewing its own life and structures, in harnessing
its resources, in employing its good offices, in using every means of
moral persuasion, including its own good example, to be an effective
agent of peace, justice, and fullness of life in society.

That liturgy is "for the life of the world" highlights again the need
for communities and their liturgists to attend to its sacramental adequacy. Our own experiences remind us that liturgy is not inevitably a
source of conversion and transformation; in fact, it is too often the
contrary.[44] It would be historically naive, of course, to expect every
liturgy to be a transforming event for its community of participants, in
the sense of a Damascus road experience. The enactment of liturgy
should never exclude such potential, but its effects are typically more
"ordinary" and "everyday." People often need liturgy to be an experience of stability and continuity in Christian identity, to reassure them
with a sense of meaning in the midst of chaos, hope in the midst of
heavy burdens. As liturgy provides such authentic maintenance and
nurture it indeed functions "for the life of the world." And all of us
have times when our own disposition makes it difficult to actively engage in liturgy, in times of spiritual desert, distraction, pain, and so on;
we then rely on the community to pray for us until better times. Likewise, for social or historical reasons, a whole community's disposition
may not be conducive to being challenged or changed by its liturgy.
Even when people come to liturgy with the best of dispositions, its
transforming influence is typically by gradual nurture in ongoing conversion. On the other hand, to be sacramentally adequate a liturgical
event should be likely to nurture and renew the life of its community
of participants in Christian living for God's reign. This does not mean
that the liturgy is "planned" with utilitarian purpose—for example, to
raise consciousness of social sin—that is an abuse of the liturgy. What
needs deliberate attention is precisely its sacramental adequacy to function "for the life of the world"; then it will, of itself, have such potential.

I will note ways to attend to the life-giving function of liturgy in
ensuing sections; some of the counsel already offered for attending to
the other two functions is relevant here too. Clearly it requires enacting
liturgy in ways which reflect the inclusiveness of the Body of Christ in
those assembled. When liturgy is truly a shared prayer action by an
assembly of Christians, it can serve as an antidote to self-seeking individualism and prompt an experience of the solidarity needed to work
for peace and justice (see note 39 and Virgil Michel on this point).
Second, a community needs to monitor its liturgical symbols, both to
avoid legitimation of sinful practices, personal and/or social, and to help
empower people to avoid and act against them.[45] Third, a community
should enact its liturgy in ways that encourage participants to reflect
critically on their lives and world, that raise up life-giving and empowering expressions of Christian Story/Vision through action, word, and
sacrament, and that prompt renewed commitment in Christian praxis.

3. The Form of Liturgy

By the "form" of liturgy I mean the typical symbolic actions and existential dynamics that constitute a Christian liturgy and are to be enacted and experienced by its community of participants. As a historical event, the form of Christian Sunday liturgy of word and sacrament is constituted by the following activities: (a) people assemble as a Christian community for the symbolic action of public prayer, (b) with a sense of sacred time and place, and (c) employ both continuity and creativity in sacred ritual, (d) to proclaim and hear God's word mediated through Scripture, (e) to celebrate the Eucharist together, and (f) to be sent forth renewed and recommitted to live for God's reign in the world.

A. Assembling as Community

The first activity of liturgy is that people assemble as a Christian community in which all are to actively participate in the symbolic action of public prayer. There cannot be a Christian liturgy without a Christian community as its historical agent; it is not the action of an "I" but of a "we"—of the church, a term whose etymological roots mean an assembly (Hebrew, *quahal*) and an inclusive assembly of "citizens" (i.e, of equal voice; Greek, *ekklesia*). The act of gathering, then, is not simply to bring people into attendance as spectators, but to establish them as a self-recognized community in solidarity and participation with each other, and indeed with the whole church throughout the world. Dom Gregory Dix says that liturgy "as primarily something *done*" by the whole assembly was central in the church's liturgical consciousness of the first three centuries, but subsequently lost.[46] A primary commitment of the renewal movement has been to restore the liturgy as a communal action "performed by the Mystical Body of Jesus Christ, that is, by the Head and His members." In another central statement, Vatican II urged "that all the faithful be led to the full, conscious and active participation in liturgical celebration which is demanded by the very nature of the liturgy. Such participation by the Christian people as 'a chosen race, a royal priesthood, a holy nation, a purchased people' (1 Pet. 2:9; cf. 2:4–5) is their right and duty by reason of their baptism."[47]

Designated members have particular functions in the assembly for "holy order," but the liturgy is the action of the whole assembly as an inclusive discipleship of equals. As the U.S. bishops note, "Different ministries in such an assembly do not imply 'superiority' or 'inferiority.'" Rather, all particular roles are "to facilitate worship" and "those who perform such ministries are indeed servants of the assembly."[48] Kavanagh finds it significant that Jesus celebrated the original event of Eucharist in the context of a traditional Passover seder—"to give concrete and perennial form to the new relationship he had come to establish between God and our race—a relationship not of a deity to devotees, nor of sovereign to subjects, nor of general to troops, but a relationship between friends at dinner."[49]

The symbolic action of gathering should be sacramentally adequate to enable people to recognize and experience a sense of themselves as a community and to ready them for active participation. Further, the gathering rite is to mediate an ethos of hospitality and inclusion to people, and the designation of those for particular functions should reflect the diversity of the community. Again to quote the U.S. bishops, "Among the symbols with which liturgy deals, none is more important than the assembly of believers. . . . Because liturgical celebration is the worship action of the entire church, it is desirable that persons representing the diversity of ages, sexes, ethnic and cultural groups in the congregation should be involved in planning and ministering in the liturgies of the community."[50] The very worship space should help establish a sense of community and be conducive to corporate action. Ideally it is to be "a space in which people are seated together, with mobility, in view of one another as well as the focal points of the rite, involved as participants and not as spectators."[51] The presiding minister and other ministers should be "conveniently situated for the exercise of their respective offices," but they are to be "clearly part of the one assembly," and their location "should not suggest either domination or remoteness."[52] (These directives from the U.S. Catholic bishops interpreting Vatican II clearly pose a significant challenge for the reconstruction of much of present worship space in Catholic church buildings.)[53]

B. In Sacred Time and Place

Through its symbolic world, the liturgy is to induct people into an experience of sacred time and place. This means that its dynamics are to give participants a heightened sense of the presence of God in ordinary time and place, of the sacramentality of life. Liturgy is not to "bring people to God" but to deepen their awareness that they are already in God's presence, a reality now intensified because the community is assembled for public prayer. To deepen the sense that *this* time and place are sacred, liturgy should engage people's emotions and elicit sentiments such as awe, wonder, reverence, celebration, thanksgiving, and praise. By intensifying those feelings, liturgy encourages an experience of *kyros* time,[54] a felt sense that this is a holy time and a privileged place for experiencing the presence of God.

Christian faith is that where "two or three are gathered" for prayer, God's Holy Spirit and the Risen Christ are present in the community assembled. But it is far from inevitable that participants experience a sense of God's presence in liturgy. All of us have been to liturgies where one had to struggle to remember the presence of God. That liturgy be adequate to mediate an experience of sacred time and place requires that the whole symbolic action be marked by a clear sense of reverence in its gestures and movements and an aesthetic quality in its context, words, music, and physical furnishings (vestments, decor, art pieces, and so on).

C. With Continuity and Creativity in Sacred Ritual

I understand ritual as a physically formalized and patterned structure of symbolic action. By this I mean that ritual engages people to establish an "acted out" framework of expression, within which other symbols, both verbal and nonverbal, are enacted and assigned a fitting or proper place. As an embodied structure of expression, ritual is more primary than language (the impetus to ritualize is present before words); apparently it is closely related to the "original" disposition for play. Christian liturgy is a form of *sacred* ritual in that it provides a framework of expression toward "the holy"; its symbols are invested by participants with a consecrated status.

In its dynamic as sacred ritual, liturgy should reflect both continuity and creativity. People need a pattern of continuity to epitomize the faithfulness of God's everlasting love, to assure that their faith has a firm foundation (see Isa. 28:16), that there is meaning in the midst of the chaos of life, that its burdens can be managed. A stable pattern in liturgy gives this community a sense of continuity with its faith Story/Vision over time and with the pilgrims that came before it and will come after. A familiar pattern can also engender in participants a feeling of being "at home," of belonging to the community.

On the other hand, because it symbolizes people's lives to God and God's life to them for the life of the world, the dynamic of liturgy should maintain a dialectic between stable pattern and imaginative creativity. Our lives and world are ever changing. Jesus constantly calls disciples to metanoia—to ongoing conversion and social transformation. A stable pattern simply repeated could become deadening and cause participants to presume that the status quo is to be maintained. The dynamic of liturgy needs to reflect creativity and novelty to actively engage, surprise, and pose new possibilities for participants.

The ordinances of the Roman Rite clearly provide for a stable pattern of continuity but also for creativity in the public prayer of the Catholic church. As the liturgical year unfolds, with the constancy of repetition, it offers a variety of themes, readings, prayers, songs, symbols, actions, and so on. As White points out, the "ordinary" parts (e.g., creed) "provide a necessary constancy," whereas the "propers" (what changes daily or weekly) "supply variety and interest."[55] But again, sacramental adequacy requires that communities and their liturgists attend to the delicate balance between continuity and creativity in their liturgy. Too much novelty from the familiar pattern can make the liturgy seem strange and alienating; routinized repetition of ritual that does not make full use of the scope for creativity is less likely to renew the faith of participants for the life of the world.

D. To Proclaim and Hear God's Word Mediated Through Scripture

We tend to take for granted why the Scriptures are proclaimed at liturgy. Christians believe that the Bible symbolically mediates God's revelation in history through the Hebrew people, in Jesus, and through the first Christian communities. In its sacred Scriptures they find their primordial Story/Vision of faith and can have access to "God's word" for their own lives now. But why are they proclaimed at liturgy specifically? Surely it is so that the whole community, and as an assembly, can have access to "God's word" together. We need to hear *our* holy Scriptures with the community of faith because only together can we live them. We need a sense that "we're all in this together" if we are to take them on as our overarching myth of meaning and value, if we are to live what they disclose to us about God and God's will, about ourselves and how we are to live as a people of God. The very act of proclaiming and hearing them together bonds us in solidarity as a people of God. For this reason, at no time are our Scriptures more like our "lifeline" to God, and at no time can they be more life-giving for all, than at liturgy. To paraphrase the words of Isaiah, just as the rain and snow water the earth, making it fertile and fruitful, so God's word—especially as proclaimed and heard by a faith community assembled at liturgy—is to achieve the life-giving end for which God sent it and is not to return to God empty-handed (see Isa. 55:11). We cannot, however, take its "effectiveness" for granted as if this is a "magic word."

For sacramental adequacy, it is crucial that the Scriptures be proclaimed (a) in a way that makes them accessible to all and (b) in life-giving ways. I amplify on this below (movement 3 of shared praxis); clearly it requires proclaiming the Scriptures with a style that encourages people to listen and hear them, to enter into them as participants rather than letting them "pass by," to feel and be touched by them as if they are their own. Here I highlight that because Scripture is encountered as word—the medium is an aspect of the message—its very language pattern should be life-giving and likely to effect God's will for the world. This principle ought to be operative throughout the whole language world created by liturgy, so I enunciate it here apropos liturgy's most powerful linguistic symbol—the Scriptures. Throughout the liturgy's verbal world of preaching and proclaiming, praying and singing, and without violating the original intention of the scriptural texts, all discriminatory and excluding language should be avoided and "inclusive" language used instead. Inclusive language reflects that all people are full human beings with equal value and dignity; it avoids excluding, demeaning, or stereotyping anyone on any basis; its personal images for God reflect analogously all humanity, without favor to any.[56]

E. To Celebrate Eucharist Together

Contrary to so much of how we have been catechized, the best Catholic theology of the event of Eucharist seems to be that it is first and foremost an action by "the Mystical Body of Jesus Christ, that is, by the Head and His members" (Vatican II, see note 3). From the human side of the covenant, it is the work of the whole community. By the power and presence of the Holy Spirit in the community, the assembly acts in union with Christ to realize again the Risen One's eucharistic presence in its midst. The priest is designated by the community for "holy order" and ordained by God to enact the community's *sacra potestas* of Eucharist. This does not take from the priesthood of the people, however, but helps them realize themselves most eminently as a "priestly people" (1 Pet. 2:9). The priest symbolizes their participation in the priestly office of Jesus Christ as the whole church, head and members, engage in "the truly great work of giving perfect praise to God and making [people] holy" (*C.S.L.* 7).

The action of Eucharist most apparently symbolizes the liturgical dynamic of people's lives to God and God's life to them for the life of the world; it is a powerful symbolic moment of encounter between divine and human praxis. In the Preparation of the Gifts (traditionally called the Offertory), the community express their life and praise to God by coming to the common table with gifts of bread and wine. Their praise continues in the words and actions of the eucharistic prayer where it is united with "the sacrifice of praise" (Eucharistic Prayer I) made to God by Jesus. The community remembers and does what Jesus did at the Last Supper. Christian faith is that the Holy Spirit works through this act of remembrance so that the Risen Christ is truly and uniquely present, that through the consecrated bread and wine Christ's body and blood presence is realized and extended into this time and place. In Holy Communion, participants share together the "bread of life" and the "cup of salvation." Shared communion with the Risen Christ and one another is to sustain and nurture participants in Christian living, to bond them as Christ's Body, to enable them to become and live what they have "received"—the Body of Christ.

In Catholic tradition, probably no action of liturgy has been more invested with a "substantialist" perspective than the liturgy of Eucharist. This is the notion that as long as a priest fulfills the rubrics of the eucharistic prayer, the bread and wine become the body and blood of Jesus Christ, and there is no need to consider how this action is existentially experienced by participants. But a substantialist perspective fails to take account of how symbols function in people's lives and neglects the significance of how people experience the phenomenon of liturgy (section 4). A community, and especially its presider, must deliberately attend to the sacramental adequacy of the eucharistic action to provide for participants an existential experience that this is an ac tion by God's Spirit through the community that symbolizes "their lives to God, and God's life to them for the life of the world."

F. To Be Sent Forth

Having been agents and recipients in word and sacrament together, participants are "sent forth" (*missa*) renewed and recommitted to the peace and justice, love and freedom, and "right relationship" that is God's reign in the world. As such, the dynamic action of "sending forth" is the decision-making symbol, a moment of choice and commitment for participants in response to the historical and ethical intent of the whole liturgy. Throughout its action, consciences are to be examined, sins repented of and forgiven, and consciousness deepened of the historical responsibilities that true worship places on participants. Bernard Haring is convinced that the liturgy is "a privileged school" for Christian moral formation.[57] Bernard Cooke writes, "if eucharistic liturgy is celebrated genuinely and humanly, . . . it is an act of deciding to live, or not to live, according to the meanings and demands of the gospel. Eucharist should be the focal act of Christian decision-making . . . the key to the formation of Christian conscience."[58] This "sending forth" time is preeminently the moment of decision for ongoing conversion as disciples of Jesus. It needs to be symbolically structured to prompt such an action by participants. Too often the "concluding rite" (as the Roman *Sacramentary* calls it) is enacted and experienced as a termination, an act of closure rather than an opening up to living what has been enacted.

4. The Effectiveness of Liturgy

A. How Effective?

My opening claim that the sacramental adequacy of liturgy to be what it should be in people's lives is also the measure of its educational adequacy has been a subtheme in the previous sections, but here it is our explicit focus. I propose that *liturgy can be powerfully effective in informing, forming, and transforming its community of participants in Christian faith if it is sacramentally adequate to enable them to express their lives in faith to God and to experience God's life in love to them for the life of the world.*

The church has always had a sense that liturgy is to effectively express its communal and public prayer as worship to God, and that its historical effectiveness should be evident in people's lives. But beginning at about the emergence of scholasticism (c. 1000 C.E.), the Catholic church has been concerned with the "effectiveness" of liturgy and sacraments to "cause" grace. The general outcome, often forged in reaction to counterpositions, was a "substantialist" perspective. This presumes that if liturgical rites are fulfilled according to the required rubrics and forms, then they are inevitably effective by their very performance in causing for participants the grace and consequences intended.

This perspective correctly emphasizes, I believe, the graciousness of God's action in the liturgy, the unconditional nature of God's faithful love for humankind, and that "grace" is always God's free gift (*gratis*). But it can neglect the human side of the covenant and can encourage neglect of how liturgy is actually experienced by its participants. What has emerged of late, and with significant ecumenical consensus, is renewed emphasis that the symbols of liturgy should be adequate to enable people to personally experience the functions of liturgy. Browning and Reed explain that this "phenomenological perspective" focuses on "what happens in people's lives" as they experience and participate in liturgy.[59] It attends more deliberately to the existential adequacy of liturgy's symbols to help people experience "their lives to God, and God's life to them, for the life of the world." A phenomenological perspective has the dual emphasis proposed by the U.S. Catholic bishops of "sacramental signification" and fulfillment of "rubrical form."[60] Joseph Powers summarizes well this shift in perspective:

> The power of sacraments, granted it is divine power, operates within the dynamics of the symbolic function of the believing community. We cannot, therefore, put blind faith in traditional ritual with the confidence that 'God will take care of it.' Rather than relying on the legalistic tradition of the 'validity' of sacraments, we would do far better to return to the older tradition of the 'truth' of the sacramental sign. For this approach is not simply concerned with legal acceptability of sacraments, but goes further to take into consideration how sacraments really function in the relationship of the believer with God (grace). In this context, the power of sacramental action corresponds to the truth of the sign-act.[61]

We also find echoes of concern for the phenomenological adequacy of liturgical symbols in Vatican II. The Council states, "In the liturgy the sanctification of [people] is manifested by signs perceptible to the senses, and is effected in a way which is proper to each of these signs." The Council adds, "It is . . . of capital importance that the faithful easily understand the sacramental signs."[62] This bodes well for attention to the educational power of liturgy because whatever people experience and do there is how it educates.

To appreciate the effectiveness of sacramentally adequate liturgy to inform, form, and transform people (i.e, to educate) in Christian faith, I offer a brief reflection on symbols, drawing especially from cultural anthropology. Heretofore we have reflected more on the "manifest" functions and forms of the liturgy, that is, the community's public understanding of how to enact it and with what intent. But attention to the ontic-forming power of symbols brings into relief what Robert Merton calls their "latent effect."[63] They have a "latent" effect in that symbols operate primarily at a subconscious level that people may not readily recognize; nonetheless, they are powerfully formative for them. Merton clarifies with the instance of a Hopi rain dance. The tribe knows how to do the dance ("manifest" form) and has the shared purpose to bring rain ("manifest" function). But by providing opportunity for scattered members to assemble and to engage in a common sacred activity, the dance's "latent" consequence, effected whether rain comes or not, is to renew the tribe's sense of solidarity and each one's identity within it. Liturgists must be keenly conscious of the "latent effects" of symbols if they are to attend to the sacramental and thus educational adequacy of liturgy.

B. Persons: Formers of and Formed by Symbols

It is not possible to speak precisely about signs and symbols because we are using them (i.e, words) to reflect on what they are. To think about them, however, is to recognize how we express ourselves as human beings and thus how we come to be the persons that we are. Stated most broadly, "sign" is the generic category for any and every form of human representation and communication, for anything that expresses ourselves and names our world. Symbols can be identified first as a species of sign; they are a form of representation and communication. But they are signs that have potential to express a deeper level of meaning and communication than other more functional signs do; they propose a meaning and "world" beyond their immediate or obvious signification.[64] For example, a sign that says "stop" has one meaning only, whereas a symbol like the American flag is a sign of the United States of America but also communicates and evokes from people a whole world of meaning beyond its functional designation. Recognizing that symbols are a form of sign, social scientists find it helpful to distinguish between them, especially in analyzing the role of symbols in a culture.

Typically, sign is used of any word, act, or thing that has a precise meaning and an unambiguous designating function; symbol is a word, act, or thing that evokes many meanings and points to a world of meaning behind or in front of itself rather than simply fulfilling a functional service.[65] It may be most helpful to think of a sign as an unambiguous indication or communication of one specific meaning, in a one-to-one correlation.[66] (A sign that says "do not enter" indicates one thing and one thing only.) Symbols can be identified as signs that are more representations of meaning than indications of function. They are things, words, or actions that point not so much *to* as *through* themselves to a whole world of meaning and value that they represent[67] and "draw together" for our consideration.[68]

The primary power of symbols lies, says Langer, in "their power of formulating experience and presenting it objectively for contemplation, logical intuition, recognition, understanding."[69] Symbols carry a perspective on the meaning and value of human "being," and as we encounter them they readily engage our whole "being"—physically, mentally, and emotionally.[70] They invite us to personally appropriate the world of meaning and ethic that they reflect "from life," and they lure us into the experience of them in our own lives. And though symbols are shaped by and express the worldview of a particular culture, they invariably have more than one meaning; they have what Ricoeur calls a "surplus of signification."[71] Michael Fuchs offers a helpful description of symbol that brings out its engaging, its holistic, its praxis-based and multivalent characteristics: "Symbol makes present not only an idea or state of mind or body, but renders present an experience"; it is "that particular form of human interchange that has the ability to call forth reality and render it present in an enigmatic or multivalent manner with the explicit call to existentially engage ourselves in its reality."[72]

Human beings are distinguished from the rest of God's creation by our ability to make symbols to re-present the meaning, value, and self-identity we discern in the praxis of our lives. As agent-subjects-in-relationship who are capable of and intent on making meaning out of life, we are and must be symbol makers.[73] We use symbols to help us choose and interpret our life praxis, to represent and communicate with others what is most essential to us, to preserve over time the measure of meaning that we find in our lives, the ethics and values with which we think we should live them, and indeed the sense we have of our own identity, both individually and as a people.[74] We build our very "world" with symbols.

In chapter 3, section 2, I gave a description of the process of "socialization"; a brief review here helps us focus the role of symbols in "enculturation." Culture is the sum total of the symbols through which a particular people express and find a common form of life together with shared patterns of meaning, attitudes, and values. People are always born into and reared in a cultural context that mediates to us through symbols its particular schema of meaning, value, and self-identity. The cultural life of our context and its symbols that we inherit carry a set of meanings, attitudes, and values for us, and the power of symbols disposes us to make them our own. Thus, symbols shape the lives and identity of their participants. We find meaning, values, and self-identity through our culture's symbols, and in consequence these symbols shape our very "being." This is the process of enculturation; the meaning, values, and attitudes proposed by the symbols of a particular culture do not remain outside us; we interiorize them and make them our own. We tend to become "people of our culture," or as Sullivan states it, "human beings partly become the symbols they behold."[75]

Sullivan's word "partly" reflects the dialectical relationship that exists between ourselves and our symbols. All the social sciences now recognize that symbols can both form their participants in "an established version of reality" and also "render articulate the shape and rhythms of a new emergent vision."[76] I also argued in chapter 3, section 2, that we need not be determined by our cultural context; in fact, education can encourage a dialectic with it so that its symbols, rather than being only a limit, can also be a constant source of new possibilities for us. In faith terms, symbols can be sources of both nurture and conversion, and we need them to be both. But there is nothing inevitable about people appropriating their symbols in a dialectical way. They can be as readily used to legitimate oppressive cultural mores and social structures and to domesticate people within them as to call the status quo in question and empower people to be transformers of it. Fuchs wisely notes the "ever-present possibilities for misuse and destructiveness within the symbol."[77] It seems that the need for caution is heightened by the power of "sacred" symbols.

C. Religious Symbols: Effective Sources of Ultimate Meaning and Purpose

The social sciences portray religion as a system of sacred symbols that represent and propose an ultimate basis of meaning, ethic, and identity for its adherents. Symbols are "religious" when they represent for people an ultimate ground or transcendent backdrop for interpreting, making sense out of, and engaging in life.[78] The sacred symbols of any religion function in powerfully formative ways to shape people's perspectives and commitments according to their ultimate view of existence. In the face of the threat that life is absurd and devoid of reliable commitment or worthwhile purpose, religious symbols propose that there is a trustworthy "ground" to our "being."[79] Like other symbols, then, religious ones express *from us, create for us,* and *shape in us* a sense of meaning, purpose, and self-identity, but their "aura of ultimacy" makes their formative and potentially transformative power second to none.[80]

Geertz and other anthropologists contend that *the* most formative and potentially transformative symbols in people's lives are the religious symbols they encounter regularly in liturgy and sacred ritual.[81] Liturgy, the moment when a faith community expresses the very heart of its life in faith before God and the world, is without equal in its effectiveness to form the "being" of its community of participants. It would seem that even from a social science perspective, Vatican II was accurate in its statement of the efficacy of liturgy: "No other action of the Church can match its claim to efficacy, nor equal the degree of it."[82]

Vatican II repeats in various ways that the liturgy is the moment when the church most fully realizes its nature and mission. This does not mean that the liturgy is "the entire activity of the church,"[83] but rather it gathers up and expresses to God all the church's "public work" in the world and is to constantly renew it as a community of witness and praxis of God's reign. Again, it is analogous to lovemaking in marriage—a climatic expression and source of love from and for the everyday. Vatican II uses other imagery: "The liturgy is the summit toward which the activity of the Church is directed; at the same time it is the fountain from which [its] power flows."[84] The old formula—*lex orandi, lex credendi*—is existentially true for us because liturgy is expression, source, and measure of what is, in fact, our Christian faith. Michael Warren writes, "If one wishes to find out the lived belief of a particular church, examine the prayers, hymns, and rituals they use."[85] I add that to discern what a faith community is *teaching* most effectively, do likewise.[86] At no time is the church more "educational" than in the liturgy. Every liturgist must constantly ask of the liturgy, What do these symbols effect for these participants in this place and time about life, about themselves, about God?

D. Worship "in Spirit and in Truth"

My reflections on the functions, forms, and effectiveness of liturgy have had a constant concern for its sacramental adequacy and the accompanying conviction that to attend to the latter is to enhance its educational adequacy as well. From the previous section, we can say that a liturgy is symbolically adequate and thus effective in people's lives, both sacramentally and educationally, when it is an experience of "true worship." In many ways, then, my concern for adequacy throughout this chapter is not unlike the church's traditional concern for "validity." There is an ancient tradition in the church that for liturgy, and especially sacramental liturgy, to be effective, its enactment must be "valid." But I note again Joseph Powers's advice that in establishing validity, instead of turning to the more recent "legalistic tradition," we should "return to the older tradition of *the 'truth' of the sacramental sign*" because "the power of sacramental action corresponds to the truth of the sign-act."[87]

Every effective Christian community, every community that is truly a sacrament of God's reign in Jesus, is marked by orthodoxy, orthopraxis, and "true worship" in faith; the three features are symbiotic to one another, with "true worship" probably the most "original" requirement in that it is so normative for the other two. To intimate the measure of "true worship" I first recall the evocative phrase that John places on the lips of Jesus in his discourse with the Samaritan woman, that "authentic worshipers will worship the Father *in Spirit and truth*" (John 4:23). "In Spirit and truth" cannot be heard as separate concerns for worshipers, because as a Scripture commentator notes of the phrase, "the two words actually signify a single idea";[88] in Christian faith the Spirit is "the Spirit of truth" (John 14:17). Because liturgy is an encounter between divine and human praxis, however, it should be symbolically adequate to mediate both sides of the covenant encounter in the experience of its participants. I will take the phrase "in Spirit" to refer to God's life-giving activity (as it always so refers throughout Scripture) and "in truth" as a guideline for what to express from the human side.

To mediate worship "in Spirit," a liturgy should (1) symbolize to participants that this action is of God and by God's grace of faith, which moves them to worship; (2) be enacted as the work of the whole "Body of Christ . . . head and members" and as an exercise of the priestly office of Christ; (3) mediate to participants a faithful (i.e, to Story/Vision) sense of who their God is and of God's never ending and unconditional love turned toward them. Conversely, liturgy is not "worship in Spirit," for example, (1) if it reflects undue confidence in human initiative and agency (e.g., in the "power" of the priest) or allows people to forget their dependence on God, even for the activity of divine worship; (2) if it excludes participation by any part of the whole Body of Christ there assembled; (3) if the symbolic action mediates to participants a distorted image of God (e.g., as approving injustice, as exclusively male, as untrustworthy, etc.).

To worship "in truth" a liturgy should (1) engage the whole community as active participants, physically, emotionally, and mentally and enable them to express their lives in faith to God, making conscious both their sins and graces; (2) symbolize to people that their lives have ultimate meaning and purpose, that they have dignity and equality before God; (3) empower their ongoing conversion in Christian discipleship by reiterating their co-responsibility for God's reign, deepening their consciousness of personal and social sin, and renewing their commitment to live their faith "for the life of the world." Conversely, liturgy is not worship "in truth," for example, (1) if it is not adequate to engage the community of participants, and in a holistic manner, or if it conceals people's own praxis or the praxis of society; (2) if it fails to give people a sense of ultimate worth and meaning or proposes a distorted identity to participants by favoring some while putting down others; (3) if it hides God's intentions for the life of the world, deadens people's consciousness of sin or of the historical tasks to be done, or fails to challenge and empower people to live as disciples of Jesus for God's reign.[89]

5. A Shared Praxis Perspective for Attending to the Sacramental Adequacy of Liturgy

For liturgy to be sacramentally adequate, as Vatican II says, "more is required than the mere observance of the laws governing valid and licit celebrations."[90] The urgency of attending to liturgy's sacramental adequacy is heightened by the realization that its fittingness to worship God "in Spirit and truth" is likely the measure of how well or poorly it "educates" people in Christian orthodoxy and orthopraxis.

Caring for liturgy is particularly the responsibility of liturgists, and they include all who resource and enable a Christian community to realize its public worship of God. To responsibly fulfill their ministry, liturgists need to have a clear understanding of the essential functions and forms of liturgy. In addition, I believe their work is enhanced if they have some overall perspective or approach that can help them remember and imagine how each aspect of liturgy, and the overall event, is to be existentially enacted with participants. I propose that the commitments and dynamics of a shared praxis approach suggest *one* such overarching perspective. It is not equally illuminating for all forms of liturgy nor exclusive of other perspectives; in fact, it needs to be complemented by other outlooks and styles. But it can heighten sensitivity regarding the adequacy with which a community enacts its liturgy.

The undergirding commitments of shared Christian praxis—for example, to create communities of inclusion, participation, and dialogue, to engage people with their own lives in place and time, to bring their praxis to encounter the Christian Story/Vision of God's praxis in human history, to invite people to make choices and decisions for lived Christian faith—all seem appropriate to liturgy's essential functions. Likewise, the constitutive functions of liturgy are at least resonant with the dynamics of a shared Christian praxis event. Its movements can be discerned, approximately and with varying sequence, in the liturgical pattern of both word and sacrament. For the present mass of the Roman rite, the focusing activity and movement 1 are reflected in the assembling, in the call to worship, in the invitation to participants to bring themselves and their lives into the conscious presence of God. The examination of conscience, general confession, and "Lord, have mercy," reflect a movement 2 dynamic of critical reflection on present praxis to recognize its graces and repent of its sins. The readings from Scripture reflect God's Story/Vision to participants (movement 3), and the sermon can enable them to appropriate it as their own (movement 4). In the creed, participants affirm their faith, and asking God's help in the prayers of the faithful implies the praxis to which they are also committed (movement 5). The same basic dynamic is repeated, again approximately, in the liturgy of Eucharist. Through the offertory gifts, participants raise up their lives before God and unite them as an act of praise with the offering of Jesus (a semblance of movements 1 and 2). The Eucharistic Prayer is the community reminding both God and themselves of the Story/Vision effected in Jesus and especially in his death and resurrection (movement 3). Holy Communion reflects the dynamic of coming "to know him in the breaking of the bread" (Luke 24:35; movement 4) and the sending forth is a call to decision for renewed Christian faith (movement 5).

It seems appropriate, then, to bring a shared praxis perspective to the preparation and enactment of Christian liturgy. Being much more suggestive than exhaustive, I indicate how it can foster attention to sacramental and educational adequacy, or, subsuming both concerns and their reciprocity, to the *symbolic adequacy* of liturgy's principal actions. Clearly, Christian communities that enact a less rubrically regulated form of liturgy have more room for creativity if they choose to structure their Sunday worship from the perspective of shared praxis.

A. *Liturgy of the Word*

1. Assembling of Community.   The purpose of the opening acts of the Sunday liturgy is to establish for participants a sense of themselves as a Christian faith community, assembled in sacred time and space. As the *General Instruction of the Roman Missal* (hereafter *G.I.*) states, "The purpose of these rites is to make the assembled people a unified community and to prepare them properly to listen to God's word and celebrate the eucharist."[91] Typically the liturgy begins as a liturgical procession of the primary ministers while the congregation sings an accompanying "entrance" song, then a veneration of the altar, a greeting of the assembly, and a call to worship.

To be symbolically adequate, these introductory words and actions should reflect that here begins a corporate act of public worship by the whole community, an event in which everyone is invited to be engaged as an active participant—a focusing and engaging activity. Attention, then, should not be placed on the presider but on the assembly and on God's presence in which they are assembled. For example, for the cantor to say, "Let us stand to greet our celebrant, Fr. (giving his name) with hymn number six" (a too-common opening greeting), is already a poor beginning. People stand and sing the opening song as a corporate expression of common faith and to remind themselves that they are assembled, as a community, with the Risen Christ to worship God together. *Who* the primary ministers are and *how* they enter the sanctuary is to reflect the "catholicity" of the community (both women and men, and its age, race, ethnic, class, etc. makeup) and the corporate nature of the action now beginning. To symbolize that they are *of* the community, it seems most fitting that the primary ministers come through the congregation to the sanctuary/altar, and their positioning during the celebration should visibly indicate that they are part of rather than apart from the assembly.

The focusing activity of shared praxis suggests that this opening rite turn people to the praxis of their lives in faith by assembling them as a Christian community and clearly establishing in the consciousness of all that their "present praxis" is to publicly worship God together. Its songs, words, gestures, actions, artifact, etc. should give people a sense that their lives are being gathered up together here, that they are bringing with them their lives in the world. On occasion, this "turning to present praxis" may be done around a particular theme, especially when the season suggests one (e.g. Lent, Easter). For "ordinary" Sundays the Sacramentary now leaves focusing on a theme optional.[92] This seems wise given the diversity of sentiments, gifts, and needs that a congregation may bring together on any Sunday. If a theme is raised up (by words, symbols, actions, colors, graphics, things such as advent wreaths, and so on), it should truly be a generative one for this assembly and be general enough to likely engage all. And remembering the function of liturgy as a mediation between divine and human praxis, if a theme is focused on, it should reflect both; for example, "On this Easter Sunday, we celebrate God's raising of Jesus from the dead, and rejoice in the possibility of new life that the paschal mystery means for all humankind."

2. Penitential Rite and Kyrie, Gloria (in season), Opening Prayer, or Collect. These actions complete the introductory rite of the Mass. One way of viewing them is as participants' turning to their own historical praxis with critical discernment before God, followed by acts of repentance, praise, and petition. The dynamics of movement 1 and especially movement 2 of shared praxis may suggest how to effect them with symbolic adequacy. Because the Gloria is a fixed formula, and the collect prayer one of two alternative "propers" of the day from the *Sacramentary,* some creativity seems most permissible in the penitential rite (the *Sacramentary* offers many options and notes that the priest "may use these or similar words");[93] here too, I believe, creativity is most needed.

Presiders frequently appear awkward or uncomfortable with the call to repentance. Often it appears hurried or is reduced to a pious or legitimating platitude (e.g., "Let us pause and be thankful for God's blessings"), as if we and our society are in no need of repentance today. A shared praxis perspective suggests that the penitential rite be enacted in a way that, by God's grace, helps people recognize their own historical praxis, enables them to critically reflect on it, to repent of personal sins and participation in social sinfulness, and to become aware of the changes they can or should make. This activity can go beyond the traditional "examination of conscience" and invite participants to an "examination of consciousness" about their lives in faith and thus become consciousness-raising. For instance, a shared praxis kind of penitential rite (suggested by a recent personal experience) might first invite participants to look at their lives of the past week. After a pause to recognize for themselves some of their praxis, the celebrant then invites them to a deeper level of critical reflection and discernment (these movements could, of course, be combined). For example, "Let us try to recognize the ways we failed to respond to God's grace, to look at our personal sins, to become aware of the ways we may have been accomplices in sinful social structures, and to see what in our lives and situations God is calling us to change." After some substantial time for reflection, the prayer of repentance and the "Lord, have mercy" could be prefaced by a call to conversion that reflects both the personal and social dimensions of metanoia. For example, "As we ask for God's mercy, let us also pray for the grace to avoid greed in our lives and to push back against the consumerist ethos of our society."

The *kyrie* could be followed by an exchange of a sign of reconciliation among participants. In small, bonded communities with a goodly trust level, I can imagine some dialogue among participants at this time, especially about their discernment of the social realities they should help to change. This kind of penitential rite would take more time than it is usually given at Sunday worship. Yet it would surely heighten the effectiveness of liturgy to enable participants to bring their lives to God with consciousness of both their grace and their sinfulness.[94] When participants repent, they are also disposed to pray the Gloria as a song of praise, thanksgiving, and recommitment to God as their only God and to Jesus as their only Lord. The typical petition format of the collect prayer reflects both our dependence on God's goodness and our responsibility to live our faith. There can be a pause between its invitation, "Let us pray," and saying the collect to encourage participants to recognize what they need God's help to do—their own visions.

3. *The Scripture Readings.*   The three designated Scripture readings and psalm response, and the alleluia or chant before the Gospel, can be viewed as making accessible some aspects of Christian Story/Vision to the assembly for each particular occasion (movement 3). This shared praxis perspective suggests a style of reading the Scriptures that gives participants ready access to them, in contrast, perhaps, to the traditional emphasis on "proclamation." "Making accessible" prompts that the Scriptures be read in a manner likely to actively engage the whole assembly, with a style that invites people into dialogue with them and to come to see for themselves the "life" they bring to their lives.

Here I can only note the challenge of making the Scripture readings accessible to small children. Some parishes have a special assembly of the smaller children for the liturgy of word, beginning after the opening rites, and then they rejoin the main assembly for the liturgy of Eucharist.[95] If a community is serious about *all* having access to the Scriptures at liturgy, then it needs to devise such creative ways to include children in this. I also believe small children can "hear" some of the Scriptures if they are presented with a fitting style within the main assembly. The following may help encourage such a style.

First, the assembly can be readied to hear the readings by some symbolic action that expresses reverence for the Scriptures. Readiness can also be enhanced by the lector inviting participants to listen with open hearts, to expect that these Scriptures will be revelatory for them as they have been for countless generations before. An adequate pause after each reading symbolizes that participants are to continue thinking about it and appropriating its meaning for their lives.

Second, the Scriptures are to be heard communally—why they are read at liturgy in the first place—as an act of common access to the assembly's original shared Story/Vision. This advises communal listening rather than individual "reading along" with the lector. In a literate culture, people often find this listening difficult to do, but it is easier if the public reading is done well. Martin Marty counsels against "the hearing . . . [being] done by people whose noses are buried in the text" and adds, "look, listen: this reading is for the assembly, not for the private person in the library carrel."[96] When a text lends itself to it, and this is most often true of a Gospel story, communal hearing is enhanced by a dramatic presentation.

Third, the whole style of the reader is to invite people to actively engage the text—in a sense, to step into its symbolic world of meaning, ethic, and value. It is difficult to describe this style on paper, yet all of us have likely had the experience of being left outside the text, because it was read as if it were not for us. On the other hand, there have been times when we could not but listen to the readings, because they were made accessible in a way that invited us to actively engage them, that "touched" us personally. This style is usually marked by clarity of articulation, by a tone of voice that invites easy listening, by proper emphasis to highlight the key words of the text, by appropriate modulation to intimate its meaning (as the reader understands it, at least), and by well-placed pauses for emphasis and reflection. Lectors need to be confident in public reading and to spend time rehearsing a particular text. It is best that they be familiar with it to the point that they can maintain eye contact with the assembly, rather than being turned down to the book. If they are to make it accessible "from the heart" and in the style of a heart-to-heart conversation with the assembly, lectors need to have prayed through their reading and made its meaning their own.

4. The Homily. I earlier portrayed the homily in the overall dynamic of the liturgy of Word as akin to movement 4 of shared praxis—congregants appropriating Christian Story/Vision to their own reality. The *G.I.* describes "the homily" as "a necessary source of nourishment of the Christian life" and adds that the "homilist should keep in mind the mystery that is being celebrated and the needs of the particular community."[97] Resonant with this, from a shared praxis perspective, the homily or sermon places people's own stories/visions in dialogue and dialectic with the Story/Vision of the Scripture readings. As such, it should "develop some point of the readings" (*G.I.*)[98] with a view to the present praxis of participants and in a mode likely to enhance their appropriation and decision making (section 6 below is on a shared praxis style of preaching).

5. The Creed and General Intercessions. These actions conclude the liturgy of the Word, with the assembly standing for both. Effecting them as resonant with the intentions of movement 4, and especially movement 5, of shared praxis can enhance their symbolic adequacy.

Throughout history, the creed has served as a powerful symbol of the Christian community's shared faith; in fact, in the early catechumenate it was referred to simply as "the symbol." (See note 68.) At liturgy, it provides Christians with an opportunity to express together the faith commitment to which they "give their hearts" (*cor dare* is the etymological root of *credere*, "to believe," and thus of *creed*).

The *G.I.* states, "In the profession of faith or creed the people have the opportunity to respond and give assent to the word of God which they have heard in the readings and the homily."[99] In shared praxis terms, the creed is an opportunity for people to publicly choose and claim the faith of the church as their own. But participants are not likely to so experience the creed if it is recited in a routinized manner; it needs to be intentionally posed as a moment of decision and recommitment. I once participated in a liturgy when the presider prefaced the creed along the following lines: "The creed is an opportunity to reaffirm our faith as a Christian community. Let us pause for a few moments after each article to reflect on the commitments we are making together." This helped me to recognize again that the creed reflects the very heart of the church's Trinitarian faith as its ground of meaning and identity. In it, Christians should experience an ultimate symbol of our covenant with God and of the right relationship into which the covenant calls us. (In this light, its adoption of inclusive language seems pressing for the creed.)

A shared praxis perspective on the general intercessions, more often called the "prayers of the faithful," highlights that as prayers of petition they also offer opportunity for decision making (movement 5). A community often needs to make petitions that reflect our total dependency on God's grace (e.g., for a miracle of healing, safety from natural disaster), but typically the old adage "Pray for what you are willing to work for" is eminently wise and theologically sound here. This means that the prayers of the faithful should (a) reflect a good theology of the nature-grace relationship and (b) ideally be "of the faithful." A. They are to express both petition for God's help *and* willingness to act as historical agents of God's grace to achieve the intention prayed for. For example, in praying for the homeless, people should also ask for the grace they need to help the homeless. B. The *G.I.* states, "As a rule the sequence of intentions is: (a) for the needs of the Church, (b) for the public authorities and the salvation of the world, (c) for those oppressed by any need, (d) for the local community."[100] It would seem that the prayer action of the assembly is best honored when petitions in *c* and *d* at least are articulated or suggested (e.g., submitted before the liturgy) by people from the congregation. They should at least be structured to reflect both the hopes and needs and the commitments of this congregation.

B. Liturgy of the Eucharist

In the Roman rite, the liturgy of Eucharist is constituted by four primary actions—preparation of the gifts, Eucharistic prayer, Communion rite, and concluding rite. The liturgy itself has traditionally imaged the life-giving encounter in Eucharist between God and participants as an "exchange of gifts." In a mass of the Christmas season, the church says in the "prayer over the gifts," "Lord, receive our gifts *in this wonderful exchange:* from all you have given us we bring you these gifts, and in return, you give us yourself"[101] (emphases added). It can enhance its symbolic adequacy to review the encounter it mediates between divine and human praxis through the "lens" of shared Christian praxis.

1. Preparation of the Gifts. Here the whole assembly begins the action of offering their lives in praise to God, symbolized through the principal gifts of bread and wine. This act is completed as their offerings are united with the gift of Christ in the eucharistic prayer and presented to God as a "perfect offering " (E.P. III) and "a living sacrifice of praise" (E.P. IV). The prayer formula that accompanies the offering of bread recognizes it as an expression of human praxis; it is a blessing from God's "goodness" and what "human hands have made." Likewise, God is praised for the gift of wine, but it too is from "work of human hands." That both are raised up to God as symbols of the assembly and of their human work on God's creation is also reflected in the summary prayer, "God we ask you to receive *us* and be pleased with the sacrifice we offer you with humble and contrite hearts" (emphasis added). Schmemann writes of the offertory, "The time has come now to offer to God the totality of all our lives, of ourselves, of the world in which we live. This is the first meaning of our bringing to the altar the elements of our food."[102] The *Sacramentary* states, "It is desirable that the participation of the faithful be expressed by members of the congregation bringing up the bread and wine for the celebration of the eucharist, or other gifts for the needs of the Church and the poor."[103]

From a shared praxis perspective this offertory action recapitulates movements 1 and 2 in that it presents the "stories" of people's lives to God as gift and expresses their hopes that, united with the life of Jesus by the power of the Holy Spirit, their offerings will "become for us the bread of life" and "our spiritual drink." This suggests that the whole action, beginning with the preparation of the table, should be enacted in a way that symbolizes to participants that this assembly is beginning to offer as an act of praise the praxis of its corporate life to God, that all its "work" is being represented in this "public work" of worship.[104] The gift bearers should be representative of those assembled and come from among them. The bread is to be clearly recognizable as bread and with the wine be visible to the assembly (e.g., a glass container in preference to an opaque one). Throughout, the bread and wine should be handled "with dignity" (*G.I.* 22), not simply because of what they become, by God's grace, but also because they represent the lives of the people present. In addition to bread and wine, money from the collection and other gifts of food are to be offered in a mode that reminds the assembly of its material responsibilities to the poor and to the work of God's reign in the world.[105] This perspective would also encourage the carrying to the altar at this time of other symbols that represent the historical praxis of the community.

2. *The Eucharistic Prayer.* The *G.I.* states that, "The eucharistic prayer, a prayer of thanksgiving and sanctification, is the center and high point of the entire celebration." It adds, "The meaning of the prayer is that *the whole congregation joins Christ* in acknowledging the works of God and *in offering the sacrifice*"[106] (emphases added). Beginning with divine thanksgiving (in the preface) and acclamation (in the Sanctus), the prayer continues with the *epiclesis* in which, the *G.I.* notes, "the Church calls on God's power and asks that the gifts offered . . . may become the body and blood of Christ." There follows a "narrative of the institution and consecration" of the Eucharist and the "proclamation of the mystery of faith" by the congregation. Then the anamnesis recalls Christ's death and resurrection, makes the offering of praise and thanksgiving and intercessions for the living and the dead, and concludes with a doxology of praise and "the acclamation of the people."[107]

One suggestive perspective on the eucharistic prayer is to see it as symbolizing the core of Christian Story/Vision in Jesus, the Christ. It reenacts especially the Story of his symbolic action the night before he died, of his subsequent crucifixion and resurrection, and it prays that the whole church and all humankind, living and dead, may come to enjoy the Vision this Story promises. The paschal event and promise of Jesus is retold for the community assembled but also on behalf of the community so that God may "hear" it again. Through the eucharistic prayer the community reminds God of what God has done to save humankind, throughout history and especially in Jesus, and of the Vision of liberation this promises to all creation. Here the assembly is doing what Moses advised the people of Israel to do when they offered the firstfruits of the promised land to God. In presenting their gifts, they were to tell God the Story of God's liberating deeds for them in the past (see Deut. 26:1–11). Uniting gift with saving narrative reflected faith that God would be moved by the Story to accept the people's offering, and the effects of God's liberating deeds in the Story would be experienced again in the present. Likewise, with the eucharistic prayer: in telling God this Story, Jesus' life of commitment to God's reign is raised up again as a "sacrifice of praise" before God, and its liberating effect is renewed. The conviction of Christian faith is that by this action, through the power of the Holy Spirit, Jesus becomes as body and blood present in life-giving bread and saving cup.

This shared praxis perspective (movement 3) on the eucharistic prayer suggests at least two recommendations for how it is enacted and especially for those privileged to pray it in the name of the community. First, its symbolic effectiveness may be heightened for participants if the presider prays it with the tone and modulation of a story. The ancient structure reflected in all the eucharistic prayers lends itself to being prayed in such a narrative mode. Second, though present rubrics regulate that it be prayed by the presider as sole voice rather than by the whole assembly together, the priest's prayer, gestures, tone, and speaking emphases (e.g., on its first person plural—"we," "our," etc.) should symbolize that this is the action of the whole community, not something done for them but by the assembly together.

3. *The Communion Rite.*   As a dynamic whole, the actions here of the Lord's Prayer, the prayer for and exchange of peace, the breaking of bread accompanied by the threefold "Lamb of God" petition for mercy, the Communion, pause for meditation, and post-Communion prayer together constitute a deep interpersonal encounter between the Risen Christ, present through the symbols of bread and wine, and the assembled people. The Communion rite can help bond participants as the Body of Christ in the world, and, as on the Emmaus road, it can prompt the kind of "knowing" of the Risen Christ that empowers conversion and decision making for Christian living. The intentions of movement 4 of shared praxis clearly are resonant with the Communion rite. This perspective suggests that it be effected in a mode likely to enable people to experience and see for themselves how they are to live as disciples of Jesus in the world.

From this perspective of personal appropriation, the Lord's Prayer is best prayed in unison by the whole assembly. Because the import of its words for people's lives can be missed in routine recitation, it helps to pray it slowly, phrase by phrase, for reflection on its meaning. Dix points out that the sign of peace, traditionally called "the kiss," was introduced into the liturgy to symbolize "the necessity of reconciling any fellow-Christians who might be at variance with each other before they could attend the eucharist together." In the early church, "the greatest pains were taken to see that this . . . did not degenerate into a formality"; it was to be a "weekly test" of "the charity and good living of Christians."[108] Its restoration for the whole community in the liturgical reforms of Vatican II reclaimed the ancient meaning and potential effect of this symbol. It ought not be done as a formality but in a way that encourages personal appropriation of its meaning. Its introduction and form of exchange can make it a clear symbol of the "right relationship" with which the people are to live; it can remind of God's peace that demands the work of justice (see Isa. 32:17).

The breaking of the bread "signifies," as the *G.I.* states, "that in communion we who are many are made one body in the one bread of life which is Christ."[109] Clearly, then, the bread is to be "breakable," and appreciation of its fragmentation is enhanced if at least the opening gesture of it is done in a pronounced way that can be seen by the whole assembly. Personal appropriation suggests that how the assembly comes to receive Holy Communion be marked by reverence and decorum and by a meditative, reflective mood; this pertains too to the kind of "communion song" during this action. Insofar as possible, the action should reflect that the assembly is sharing in a community meal of bread and wine to symbolize the covenant that eating together implies. Their covenant unity is also symbolized by participants' receiving the same bread consecrated at the particular mass and from the same chalice (unless prohibited by numbers). The *G.I.* points out, "It is most desirable that the faithful should receive the body of the Lord in hosts consecrated at the same Mass and should share the cup when it is permitted. Communion is thus a clearer sign of sharing in the sacrifice that is actually being celebrated."[110] Likewise, personal appropriation can be more adequately symbolized by people taking the eucharistic bread and cup in their own hands.

Movement 4 of shared praxis recommends that the post-Communion time of reflection be substantive rather than perfunctory. It can be explicitly introduced, at least on occasion, as a time of thanksgiving and reflection so that people may come to personally "know" the Risen Christ in this "breaking of the bread" (see Luke 24:30–35). An opportunity for those who wish to do so to share with others the fruits of their reflections would seem apt here, at least among "basic Christian communities." Of the post-Communion prayer, the *G.I.* says that here "the priest petitions for the effects of the mystery just celebrated, and by their acclamation, Amen, the people make the prayer their own."[111] The intent of the instruction suggests that if the prayer appointed in the *Sacramentary* does not encourage such appropriation and decision for this community, the celebrant can construct one more fitting to the occasion.

4. Concluding Rite.   The action of "dismissal," very brief and too often done in a perfunctory way, consists of a greeting to and then a blessing over the people, a commissioning of them with such words as, "The Mass is ended, go in peace to love and serve the Lord," to which the congregation responds, "Thanks be to God." The primary ministers reverence the altar and process out during a closing hymn by all. The *G.I.* states that the dismissal "sends each member of the congregation to do good works, praising and blessing the Lord."[112] From the perspective of movement 5 of shared praxis, such intent is more effectively symbolized if the assembly is offered specific opportunity for decision making, and they experience the rite as a commissioning for Christian praxis in the world. For example, after the post-Communion prayer, there could be a brief pause here, prefaced by an invitation to participants to look to the week ahead and recognize how God calls and graces them to live what they have celebrated together "for the life of the world." (This could also be posed before the post-Communion meditation). If an opportunity for people to share their decisions/responses with others is not provided within the liturgy, they can be encouraged to do so soon thereafter (at postworship refreshments, on the way home with family, at the Sunday meal, etc.). Kathleen Hughes writes, "Participation in liturgy demands decision."[113] Why not provide a specific opportunity for decision making within its dynamic, and the concluding rite is an obvious time for it. Whether or not such an explicit opportunity is provided, the whole style of effecting the concluding rite and its closing song should clearly symbolize for the community that what they have celebrated in the liturgy they are to "historicize" in the world.

6. A Shared Praxis Approach to Preaching

I have already identified the homily or sermon as fulfilling a movement 4 interest of appropriation following the readings from Scripture. However, it is also a bridge between liturgy of Word and Eucharist,[114] and the dynamics of the homily can be structured to reflect the commitments and all five movements of shared praxis. Our concern here is liturgical preaching from this perspective.

In the Sunday assembly, the general purpose of preaching is to place in dialogue some aspect of participants' present historical reality and some aspect of Christian Story/Vision from the Scripture readings, so that people can come to see for themselves what their Christian faith means for their lives and renew commitment to living it.[115] The intentions of liturgical preaching are ongoing nurture and conversion of participants in Christian faith. In this light, one can readily recognize how the commitments and dynamics of a shared praxis approach are suggestive of what Buttrick calls a general "mode" and particular "moves" for preaching.[116] It may not be equally apt for all themes and times, preachers and places, but it can suggest an effective style of preaching that is fitting to the general purpose of the homily within Sunday liturgy.

Regarding "mode," a shared praxis approach to preaching suggests the following principle: *The sermon is a dialogue that actively engages the assembly.*

To create this dialogue, the preacher needs to draw upon four sources of reflection and perspective: (1) the preacher's story/vision, (2) the stories/visions of the congregation, (3) the social and ecclesial context of the community's life in place and time, and (4) a Story/Vision of the faith community, especially as reflected through the Scripture readings of the day.[117] The preacher especially has to "listen" to and honor each component and weave them into a conversation that engages the active participation of the whole assembly.[118] Claiming that good preaching is an event in which "preacher, listener, the message and the impinging social environment all come together" Steimle et al. recommend the image of preacher as "story-teller" and of preaching as "shared story."[119]

In the immediate aftermath of Vatican II, Catholic preachers made a concerted effort to promote what were then called "dialogue homilies"; the style was a group discussion around the readings of the day.

This approach can be effective when conditions are conducive—small congregation, adequate space, time available, and so on. But I'm convinced that every sermon can and should be a dialogue that engages the whole community—even when only the preacher speaks, and even in large churches with hundreds of congregants who have typical expectations about the length of a Sunday sermon. The style and content of every sermon can be dialogical if it gives people access, and in a disclosure manner, to images, metaphors, examples, anecdotes, analogies, parables, exegesis, questions, statements, invitations, and so on that prompt them to actively engage in recognizing, in imagining, remembering, and reasoning, in judging, discerning, and deciding what the Scriptures mean for their lives now.[120] Such personal dialogue, engaging especially peoples' imaginations, can be generated even in staid mainline congregations where participants typically have no opportunity to express their response to the sermon.[121] It happens when, to use Marty's phrase, the preacher "preaches with" rather than "preaches at" the assembly.[122]

The monologues that can be heard in too many churches on Sunday are ready evidence that the sermon is not inevitably dialogical. In fact, I wager that most of us, both preachers and hearers, have been socialized to think of sermons as "telling" people what the Scriptures mean for them. I'm convinced that a dialogical mode of preaching is prompted if the preacher imagines and approaches the sermon *as a conversation*. I have a traditional affection for the term *sermon*, and it is probably too time-honored a name to be replaced, but the word *homily* may be more indicative of the proper approach to liturgical preaching. Its etymological root is *homilein*, meaning to have a conversation. *Fulfilled in Your Hearing* (hereafter *F.I.Y.H;* see note 114) states, "The New Testament usage suggests that a homily should sound more like a personal conversation, albeit a conversation on matters of utmost importance, than like a speech or a classroom lecture."[123]

Baumer explains that as a conversation, a homily is an exercise in transactional rather than transmissive speech.[124] Transmissive speech uses language as a conduit or delivery system for "ready-made" truths to the minds of others who receive them. Baumer notes that most of the literature on preaching presumes that the homily is an act of transmissive speech. Transmissive speech sermons are monologues—"banking" sermons. Transactional speech, on the other hand, creates a language world that gives access to truths and invites people to discern and discover meaning for themselves; it engages people as agent-subjects, as partners in the quest, and evokes meaning from them rather than transmitting it to them. In the homily, says Baumer, preachers should not "transmit meaning in messages" but rather create conversations "that evoke meaning."[125] They do this by creating a conversation that invites the assembly into discourse, at least in their own heads and hearts, to see for themselves the import of these Scriptures for their lives.

Preaching as conversation requires that the preachers attend to the pattern of their language as well as to its image-filled substance. It should be invitational, specific, graphic, evocative, questioning, and nuanced and filled with images, metaphors, pauses for reflection, and so on; it is to avoid absolute pronouncements, final interpretations, and closure statements, remembering that there is always a "surplus of meaning" in every Scripture text, even after the most brilliant exegesis. *F.I.Y.H.* states, "The Word of God which we are called to proclaim is a divinely inspired Word, and therefore an authoritative and unfailing Word. But we who are limited and fallible possess no guarantee that our understanding of this Word—or of the human situation—is without error and therefore relevant and binding."[126] Preachers are also encouraged in transactional language if they consciously remember that this "language event" is a conversation with a Spirit-filled assembly. By baptism, participants have the presence of the Holy Spirit to them, a gift that must surely be allowed to function when they assemble to worship God. Preachers can create a language world that is an adequate instrument of the Spirit; they are not to act as the Spirit's replacement.

Preaching with the Movements of Shared Praxis

Buttrick portrays the sermon as "a series of rhetorical units or moves" and advises preachers to stop thinking in the typical mind-set of "points to be made" and develop instead a basic structure of "moves for speaking."[127] *F.I.Y.H.* warns, however,

> Many homilies seem to fall into the same three-part pattern: "In today's readings. . . . This reminds us. . . . Therefore let us. . . . " The very structure of such homilies gives the impression that the preacher's principal purpose is to interpret scriptural texts rather than communicate with real people, and that he [or she] interprets these texts primarily to extract ethical demands to impose on a congregation.

It recognizes that "there is no one correct form for the homily" but recommends that

> another way of structuring the homily . . . is to begin with a description of a contemporary human situation which is evoked by the scriptural texts, rather than with an interpretation or reiteration of the text. After the human situation has been addressed, the homilist can turn to the Scriptures to interpret this situation, showing how the God described therein is also present and active in our lives today. The conclusion of the homily can then be an invitation to praise this God who wills to be lovingly and powerfully present in the lives of [God's] people.[128]

The movements of shared praxis are clearly resonant with such a dynamic; they suggest one structure of moves for preaching dialogically.

A shared praxis approach to preaching advises the homilist to structure the sermon around a clearly established focus that is a generative theme for this assembly. This point should not be taken for granted; too often preachers preach what is of no life import for their hearers or attempt to take on too many themes for the scope of one homily. An appropriate generative theme for a homily emerges as the preacher "listens" to the texts of the day, to the lives of the people in this assembly, to the broader social and ecclesial context of the time, and to her or his own story. Such listening is essential, because the homily is to "help people make connections between the realities of their lives and the realities of the Gospel."[129]

Attentive listening to the Scriptures is essential because, "unless the Word of God in the scriptures is interiorized through prayerful study, it cannot possibly sustain the life-giving, love generating words that preachers want to offer their people."[130] Preachers listen to the assembly to discern the existential life issues, needs, feelings, and questions that people are bringing to their dialogue with the text and homily. They listen to the historical context to recognize its praxis and to remember the social responsibilities that God's word places on its hearers. They listen to their own life to recognize the story through which their preaching is filtered; this is necessary (a) to avoid undue subjectivism and (b) to preach with integrity from truth that is owned as one's own. From dialogue among these four "sermon sources," the preacher can discern a generative theme for this occasion that honors the text, the assembly, the context, and that the preacher can preach with integrity. Ideally, discernment of a generative theme is done best in "attentive listening" with representatives of the congregation.[131]

The sermon's *focusing activity* should establish the generative theme in a way that engages the assembly with it. *F.I.Y.H.* notes wisely: "Beginning the homily with 'in today's Gospel . . . ,' or words to that effect, risks losing the attention of the congregation right at the beginning, for they will not have been given any indication of why they should be interested in what was said in today's Gospel." Rather, the bishops advise that the opening move is "to show how and where the mystery of our faith, focused upon by that day's Scripture readings, is occurring in our lives."[132] In a shared praxis style, the focusing act raises up a symbol or icon for participants that brings them to attend to the sermon's life-theme as it is operative in their own context and praxis. A story, a news item, a poem, a line from a song, an example from history, literature, or mass media, a repeated verse from the readings—even a simple statement followed by a praxislike question (i.e, flowing into movement 1)—can all be effective to establish the theme and turn participants toward present praxis of it. For example, the sermon at a liturgy I participated in on a Monday of one Holy Week began with a simple statement, "Today we begin a week called holy. Perhaps it can be a special moment of God's grace for us to intensify our attempts to lead holy lives." It then flowed into movement 1 with the questions, pausing after each one: "But what does it mean to be holy? What do you imagine when you think about yourself being holy? What signs of holiness do you already recognize in your own life?" Typically the focusing activity is done verbally, but it can also be done effectively, especially in children's sermons, with a "visual aid."

Movement 1 can take many forms in preaching. Its essential task is to offer an expression of present praxis of the theme, so that participants can perceive what is going on and being done regarding this issue in their lives. Clearly, one way to do this is by a series of questions, with pauses, that evoke for attention people's own consciousness of present praxis. It can also be done by the preacher "naming," in a suggestive rather than absolute or definitive way, what she or he perceives as identifying present praxis of the theme. Here the preacher is helping the congregation to name what should be named—what is "going on," or what they need to name—joys and sorrows, hopes and fears, and so on. However movement 1 is done, it is to evoke from participants their own recognition of present praxis around the generative theme.[133] The cumulative effect of the focusing activity and movement 1 should be some felt sense by participants that "this is about my life—this preacher is talking with me."

Movement 2 in a sermon brings participants beyond recognition to some level of critical reflection (according to age, readiness, etc.) regarding present praxis of the theme. It reflects questioningly and analytically, as befitting the theme, on the personal, ecclesial, and social causes of present praxis, the memories and histories behind it, its consequences, liabilities, and possibilities. Rather than announcing a definitive analysis to be accepted, movement 2 again calls for transactional speech, for a language pattern that prompts the congregation to personal discernment of the causes and consequences of present praxis. Movement 2 can also be done by reflective questioning or by the preacher posing an analysis, both personal and social as appropriate, for people's consideration. For example, in the Holy Week sermon, the preacher reflected on what he presumed to be the typical socialization of the people present, which encouraged the attitude that holiness is something very removed from real life, associated with being "churchy," dull, and no fun and exclusive to a chosen few. He followed with his perception of how our society typically views holiness as something impractical and nonutilitarian—a bit of a joke—and how these personal and social influences combine to tell us that holiness of life is not a worthy pursuit for contemporary people. Throughout he was asking the congregation if they could identify with such sentiments. These opening movements, of course, typically overlap. Their intent is to enable people to come to recognize their own stories/visions of the generative theme that they now bring into dialogue with the preacher's hermeneutics of the Scriptures.

Movement 3 is typically the preacher's hermeneutic of the assigned Scripture texts or of a particular reading as advised by the generative theme. In a shared praxis style, the preacher's hermeneutics of the texts seeks their practical wisdom, is done with practical intent for these people's lives. It also should be raised up with a disclosure style, that is, with a language pattern that invites people to think about the texts for themselves, to have their own discernment of their meaning for their lives. Such interpretive activity promotes what Gadamer calls "a fusion of horizons" between the participants' stories/visions and the Story/ Vision of the text. In other words, the text should be honored in its own right and the tools of critical biblical scholarship employed to interpret it, but the preacher's task is not a disinterested or "objective" exegesis of the text (even if possible) but a hermeneutic consciously suffused with the practical intent of people's wisdom in faith. *Disclosure* rather than closure of the texts' wisdom can be prompted as simply as the preacher's prefacing their exploration with some comment like, "Let me share some thoughts that today's Scripture readings prompt for me and invite you to think about what sense they make for *your* life."

Scripture hermeneutics in a sermon calls into play the principles of interpretation and explanation I outlined in chapter 8. With the metacriterion of God's reign as a foundational perspective, preachers are to remember what they bring to the text from themselves, from the congregants, and from the present historical context. Then, employing hermeneutics of retrieval, suspicion, and creativity, they are to search out the truth and life-giving memories in the text, indicate and critique, as appropriate, distortions or destructive interpretations that have been drawn from it over history, and suggest some creative possibilities it holds for this congregation, in continuity with its Story, responsibility to its Vision, and solidarity with the "church" (see chapter 8, section 3).

A more usable guideline for sermon preparation is that the preaching raise up the world *of, behind,* and *before* the text. Analyzing the world *of* the text allows it to speak for itself, to express the meaning it discloses in and of itself. Attending to the world *behind* the text uncovers its historical context and what it might have meant for its first hearers— the literary form of it, the meaning suggested when read in context of the book from which it is taken, the probable intent of its author, and so on. Raising up the world *before* the text, or as Ricoeur says, "in front of the text," explores its wisdom for present hearers in this time and context, and what it asks of people's lives now. *F.I.Y.H.* states realistically that "exegesis for preaching need not always be done at the highest professional level," yet it insists that preachers have access to the scholarly resources that can accurately inform and enrich their preaching.[134]

For *movement 4,* if the preacher makes the exegesis accessible in a disclosure manner and with practical intent, congregants are already engaged throughout in activities of personal appropriation. It is helpful, however, to have a specific "move" after attention to the text that promotes such conversation and dialectic in the consciousness of participants. The preacher can invite them to recognize what they are seeing for themselves as they think about its meaning for their own situations, to discern what wisdom this Scripture may have for their lives, and so on. Again, this can be done by a series of reflective questions that ask, in one way or another, What do you perceive this to mean for your life? The preacher may also offer some reflections that model a dialectical appropriation of the exegesis and invite participants to do likewise. For example, in the Holy Week sermon, at movement 3 the preacher raised up from the Scripture readings an understanding of holiness as "right relationship" with God, self, others, and creation and what this might ask in this time and place. Then for movement 4 he reflected on how difficult it can be to live a life of holiness as "right relationship," the social/political obstacles to the works of peace and justice and his personal concern about the courage needed for such holiness of life. He twice repeated the question, What do *you* think such holiness requires of *your* life? Again, modeling of movement 4 should be done with a suggestive and transactional rather than a definitive and transmissive language pattern, inviting congregants to identify and discern for themselves the historical implications of these Scriptures now.

Movement 5 may often be combined with movement 4. But a shared praxis style of preaching suggests that the preacher specifically invite the "co-preachers" to make decisions around the generative theme. It is important here not to lapse into what might be called "sermon as salad"—with a lot of "let us," as in moralizing exhortations. More appropriate instead is to pose questions that invite participants' own praxislike decisions and responses. In our recurring example, the preacher asked the people, "What will you ask God to help you do to make this week holy? What will you try to change in your life to grow in holiness as wholeness for yourself and others?" The preacher may also suggest some possible decisions for people's consideration, and I have heard movement 5 done effectively by using an example of a historical person who models a faith-filled response to the theme. If a specific time for dialogue with one another is not provided at the end of the sermon, participants can at least be encouraged to share their insights and decisions from the sermon with someone after the service.

Chapter 13

The Church's Ministry
of Justice and Peace

The primary focus of this chapter is the church's social ministry of peace and justice. To highlight their unity, so emphasized in the Bible, I also use the phrases *peace through justice* or *justice for peace*. Section 1 proposes the kind of peace through justice essential to the church's ministry and why it has emerged with urgency and deepened clarity in present consciousness. Section 2 reviews the general mission of the church in light of the social obligations of Christian faith and makes explicit that the whole life of the church in the world ought to be an effective symbol, a sacrament, of peace through justice. Section 3 reflects more particularly on the religious education ministry of the church from a social perspective and claims that all its educating, in both content and process, should be suffused with commitment to justice for peace. Section 4 reflects on the need in every Christian congregation for specific programs and projects that engage in particular forms of social service and reconstruction. It places this social ministry in dialogue with shared praxis as one action/reflection approach that can be effective and fitting to the purposes of "social ministry." I conclude with a postscript on resources needed by all Christians to "keep on" in the struggle for justice and peace.

1. What God Asks of Us

Justice and peace are difficult realities to describe and even more difficult to define; perhaps we know their meaning most readily in their absence. Contemporary Christian understanding of both have deep roots in the Bible and the church's traditions. We cannot describe those roots exhaustively here but can indicate how and why peace and justice are currently understood as responsibilities of Christian faith.

A. From the Hebrew Scriptures

The term most often used for justice in the Hebrew Scriptures is *sedaquah,* and less frequently *mishpat;* the former is usually translated "righteousness" (not in the sense of "self-righteous" but as in "doing what is right"), and the latter as "right judgment," as in just exercise of the law. The two words are also used synonymously.[1] Together, Heschel writes, they represent "an a priori of biblical faith," in the sense that *justice is essential to God* and thus for how people in covenant with God are to live.[2] Brueggemann says that, "in biblical faith, the doing of justice is the primary expectation of God."[3]

That "the Lord is a God of justice" (Isa. 30:18), who "secures justice and the rights of all the oppressed" (Ps. 130:6), delights in it (Jer. 9:24), loves it (Ps. 99:4), and hates injustice (Isa. 61:8), is a constant theme, perhaps the most central one, in the Hebrew Scriptures.[4] This God of justice calls the people into covenant to live as God's own people with the promise, "I will set my dwelling among you. . . . Ever present in your midst, I will be your God and you will be my people" (Lev. 26:11–12). The covenant, however, brings a law, a way the people should live if they are to be faithful partners in it. Because God is just, God's law and presence cannot but demand justice by the people, and the kind of justice that is of God. To be in covenant as a people with God is to be in a bonded relationship with God and one another; it means to live in "right relationship." Donahue writes, "In general terms, the biblical idea of justice can be described as *fidelity to the demands of a relationship";* it is the "harmony which comes from a right relationship to the covenant Lord and to the neighbor to whom a person is related by covenant bond."[5]

If the people are to live the law of this kind of covenant with this kind of God, then "justice and justice alone shall be [their] aim" (Deut. 16:20). By doing justice toward "the weak and the poor" people come to truly "know" God (Jer. 22:15–16) in the holistic sense of "right relationship." In the Hebrew Scriptures, "knowledge of Yahweh absolutely cannot be understood if we do not realize that it is a strict synonym for the realization of justice."[6] Conversely, people do not "know" God (at least not in the wisdom sense) unless they do justice; they do not keep the covenant without living in "right relationship" with God, self, others, and all creation, the latter they are to "govern . . . in holiness and justice" (Wis. 9:3).

What, then, characterizes such "right relationship"; how do people know what is "right" for justice' sake? In the Hebrew Scriptures, the model and measure of rightness (righteousness) in people's relationships is God's relationship with humankind. How God relates with all people is the standard by which we are to relate to others and creation. People are to behave as God does toward all; the way of God's justice is to mark a people of God as well. And God relates with us, not as a blindfolded judge who balances a scales to measure our legal deserts, but with compassion, mercy, and loving-kindness, with largess, munificence, and profound favor for our life and well-being. Donahue writes, "The justice of Yahweh is not in contrast to other covenant qualities such as steadfast love (*hesed*), mercy (*rahamin*) or faithfulness (*emunah*) but, in many texts, is virtually equated with them."[7] Yahweh has "espoused" the people of Israel "in right and in justice, in love and in mercy" (Hos. 2:21), and to be faithful partners, they must live those values and ethic in their own relationships.[8]

The covenant, then, demands that the people live according to a law of right relationship. But God's law, rather than being an arbitrary whim of God to test their faithfulness, is guidance to wisdom and freedom, to wholeness of life that is shalom. The law is a powerful sign of God's love for humankind in that our own best interests are realized by living the law of right relationship with God, self, others, and creation. Given God's loving relationship with humankind, the demands and effects of God's law could not be otherwise for us. The Decalogue, for example, is announced within the memory of what God has done to free the people (see Exod. 19:1–6). It is prefaced with the reminder that "I, the Lord, am your God, who brought you out of the land of Egypt, that place of slavery" (Exod. 20:2). The code that follows calls the people into "right relationship" with God, self, and others. The Israelites clearly understood that God set them free and now gave them the Decalogue that they might continue in true freedom as a people of God.

The Hebrew Scriptures reflect a clear awareness that sin, as a willful transgression of the covenant and thus a choosing of wrong relationship (a "missing the mark"), is indeed a real possibility. But though God calls people to account when they break the law of "right relationship," Yahweh is never vindictive or vengeful toward the sinner. God is always "a merciful and gracious God, slow to anger and rich in kindness and fidelity" (Exod. 34:6). Donahue explains that "Yahweh's justice is saving justice where punishment of the sinner is an integral part of restoration."[9] Unlike other legal codes of the ancient Near East, the covenant code of Israel mixed justice, even for the wrongdoer, with mercy.

Central to the emancipatory, munificent, and life-giving mode of God's relating with humankind, that is, God's justice, is what Heschel calls God's "burning compassion for the oppressed,"[10] God's special favor and largess for those whose lives are threatened—the poor, the widow, the orphan, and the alien in the land. God hears their cry (see Exod. 22:22), comes to their aid (see Ps. 113:7), and "renders justice to the afflicted, judgment to the poor" (Ps. 140:13). God's justice endures forever and includes a "lavishness" toward those most in need (Ps. 112:9). God sides with the poor and oppressed because God wills fullness of life for all and so must favor most those to whom fullness of life is most denied.

Again, the people of the covenant are to imitate God's "option" for the poor and oppressed; as God does, so should they (see Dan. 4:24). The justice of the community is measured, ultimately, by its treatment of the powerless and poor in its midst. Because the poor are those from whom their just deserts have been taken, the community is to help them not simply out of charity but out of justice. As Brueggemann writes, from a biblical perspective "justice is to sort out what belongs to whom, and to return it to them."[11] The prophets speak for Yahweh on behalf of the poor—"those who have no voice."[12] They remind the people that to offer true worship to God, they must do justice by and favor those whom God favors. "The marginal groups in society—the poor, the widows, the orphans, the aliens—become the scale on which the justice of the whole society is weighed. When they are exploited or forgotten neither worship of God nor knowledge of [God] can result in true religion."[13]

By adding widows, orphans, and aliens to "the poor" as having God's favor, the Hebrew Scriptures intimate an inclusive definition embracing all whose lives are threatened. Undoubtedly, economic poverty is the defining note in the Hebrew Scriptures for who "the poor" are; yet by specifying concern for the young who are poor, women who are poor, and people of other races who are poor, they intimate that age bias, sexism, and racism are also condemned by an "option for the poor," and likewise, we can presume, all forms of injustice on any basis. I return to this note below.

In the Hebrew Scriptures the consequence of living in right relationship, of doing justice, is shalom. Conversely, shalom is the rule of justice as right relationship. This frequently used Hebrew word is so rich in content that the English "peace" is not adequate to translate it. Its overarching meaning is more completely rendered as "well-being," "completeness," "essential happiness," or better still "wholeness." Von Rad notes that "shalom always finds external manifestation, and in its most common use it is a social rather than an individual term."[14] Scripture scholars say that the Hebrew understanding of "peace" developed from meaning a sense of personal well-being to a more complete and social meaning of public harmony marked by the absence of war and by the presence of right relationship among the people, with other peoples, and with creation. The Israelites recognized peace as a great blessing of God and that its realization depended on keeping their covenant. (See Lev. 26:3–13, esp. v. 6.) Thus, shalom represents the flowering of the relationship that is to exist between God and the people, and the social relationship that should prevail among the people, with other peoples, and with all creation. The covenant is a "covenant of peace" (Isa. 54:10). There is, then, a symbiosis between justice and shalom; true peace is the work of justice (see Isa. 32:17). Isaiah has Yahweh say, "I will appoint peace your governor and justice your ruler" (60:17). On the other hand, "There is no peace for the wicked" (Isa. 48:22). Ezekiel condemns the false prophets who said there was peace in the land when idolatry and injustice were rife (Ezek. 13:16), and Jeremiah berates those who overlook injustice and cry, "Peace, peace," where there is no peace (see, e.g., Jer. 6:14). For the biblical tradition, peace comes through justice, and justice is realized in peace.

Throughout the Hebrew Scriptures runs a promise of a messianic time when "kindness and truth shall meet; justice and peace shall kiss" (Ps. 85:11). Then justice will be "secure" and peace without end. (See Isa. 9:6–7.) Meanwhile, the covenant places urgent "within history" responsibilities upon its adherents. The classic summary of what Yahweh asks in covenant of all humankind is found in Micah 6:8; a passage that King refers to as "the Magna Carta of prophetic religion."[15] God asks "only this, to act justly, to love tenderly and to walk humbly with your God" (Mic. 6:8, JB). The three mandates cannot be separated; as people do justice with loving-kindness, their faith as right relationship with God is realized.

B. From the New Testament

Christian faith recognizes Jesus as the promised Messiah, as the ultimate sacrament of God's justice, peace, and loving-kindness to the world. The summary foundation for a specifically Christian commitment to justice and peace is Jesus' commitment to the reign of God. Viviano claims that the reign of God in the preaching of Jesus is "the best New Testament basis" for commitment to peace and justice, because "it points to a realm of divine justice here on earth."[16] Given all I've said already on the symbol of God's reign, it is repetitious to comment further here. Within the ambit of it as Jesus' stated purpose for his life, I only highlight his special favor for the poor and oppressed, his commitment to peace, and his radicalizing of the law of "right relationship."

According to Luke's Gospel, before Jesus was born, his mother Mary praised God for doing "great things" in her conceiving—deposing the mighty, raising up the lowly, and feeding the hungry as promised (see Luke 1:46–55, the Magnificat). A "heavenly host" proclaimed "peace on earth" (see Luke 2:13–14) as the salvation to come from his birth. Toward the end of his life Jesus presented an account of God's judgment as rewarding "the just" (Matt. 25:37) because of their care for the poor, the alien, the imprisoned, and all in need and condemning those who have failed in such right relationship. "Peace" was Jesus' farewell gift to the disciples (see John 14:27) and the first gift of the Risen Christ to them (see John 20:19).

In between, Jesus' whole life was one of right and loving relationship with God, self, others, and creation, with a special outreach to the poor, oppressed, and marginalized. His care for the poor was accompanied by "hard sayings" regarding money and possessions (see, e.g., Mark 10:25, "easier for the camel . . . ") and by public opposition to all forms of "thingification." His praxis was a countersign to sexism, racism, and to all social/religious structures and cultural mores of discrimination. He presented his life and mission as fulfillment of the Jubilee Year promise of Isaiah 61:1–2, of bringing "glad tidings to the poor," "liberty to captives," "sight to the blind," and "release to prisoners" (see Luke 4:18–19). In the Beatitudes he said that the reign of God belongs to the poor; he promised satisfaction to those who work for justice; and declared peacemakers to be God's own people (see Matt. 5:3–10). Disciples should seek God's reign and justice first (see Matt. 6:33); no longer is it "an eye for an eye and a tooth for a tooth" but even enemies are to be loved and persecutors prayed for, because Jesus' disciples should be as God is (see Matt. 5:38–45).

His great commandment of radical love engages a disciple's whole heart, soul, mind, and strength (see Mark 12:30) and unites as one, love of God, self, and "neighbor" without limit; this is the strongest possible statement of the "rightness" demanded by the covenant relationship. Jesus made clearer than perhaps any prophet before him that people should live in right and loving relationship with God by loving even their enemies as they love themselves. Interpreting his meaning for their lives, disciples came to see that the reign of God in Jesus is a way of justice, peace, and joy (see Rom. 14:17), that they must "put on justice" to preach his "gospel of peace" (see Eph. 6:15). They recognized that Jesus is "our peace" among humankind and between us and God (Eph. 2:14–18), that God has reconciled the world to Godself in Jesus and "has entrusted the ministry of reconciliation to us" (2 Cor. 5:17).

If the New Testament adds anything to the traditional Hebrew understanding of justice as "right relationship," it is its emphasis on agapic love, that the covenant be fulfilled with munificent love that includes but also goes beyond justice in relationship with others, even one's enemies. This radical love was suggested by the life and preaching of Jesus, whom disciples perceived as the embodied "truth" of their covenant with God. Now the mandate of justice and peace was subsumed into the whole task of "doing the truth [i.e., keeping the covenant] with love." (See chapter 3, section 5 for the biblical notion of "truth.")

That the new covenant calls people to "do the truth with love" is evident across a wide range of New Testament literature, indicating how pervasive the notion was in early Christian consciousness. From the Pauline corpus we read, "If we live by the truth and in love, we shall grow in all ways into Christ" (Eph. 4:15, JB). In 1 Peter 1:22 we read, "By obedience to the truth you have purified yourselves for a genuine love. . . . Love one another constantly from the heart." And 1 John 3:18 has "Let us love in deed and truth and not merely talk about it." As "right relationship" is an evocative summary of the way of justice/peace in the Hebrew Scriptures, so "doing the truth with love" is likewise for the New Testament. All this and more has led the church to recognize that "Action on behalf of justice and participation in the transformation of the world fully appear to us a constitutive dimension of the preaching of the Gospel, or, in other words, of the church's mission for the redemption of the human race and its liberation from every oppressive situation."[17] And for Christians, "Peacemaking is not an optional commitment. It is a requirement of our faith."[18] In sum, the Bible calls people to "faith that does justice for peace." This requires that we live "the truth through right and loving relationship."

C. From the Tradition

Awareness and understanding of the social responsibilities of Christian faith have varied greatly over the church's history; Christian traditions, East and West, Protestant and Catholic, have come to particular perspectives and emphases in this regard. But one can recognize, dimly at times, a consistent and common conviction that Christians should live the virtues of justice and peace, at least in the form of honesty and truth telling, and not resort to violence or war without just cause. As with all mandates of the gospel, the evidence of history indicates that our record has been mixed, at best. Yet the "subversive memory" of the biblical covenants, and of the "right and loving relationships" they demand, has never been totally lost. There have always been prophetic voices and communities within the church who have called Christians to repentance, justice, and peace and to oppose all "thingification" on any basis. I cannot review this long and complex story of both faithful witness and miserable failure, of common and particular perspectives among our various communities over history; I can only highlight a few significant emphases. With hope for "shared service that unites" beyond the diversity of our traditions, I raise up three central clusters of emphases that mark the Catholic appropriation of a faith that does justice for peace. These characteristics are shared in various ways by other Christian churches, but their configuration in the Catholic tradition makes for one rich perspective on the social responsibilities of Christian faith.

1. In addition to the biblical sources already noted, Catholic social teaching has grounded itself consistently in the *imago Dei* tenet of Jewish and Christian faith, in the Genesis conviction that humankind is created in the image and likeness of God. Because we are made in God's image and participate in God's own life, we have a certain God-given dignity and value by birth—by "copyright." And Catholicism has a particular perspective on the *imago Dei* tenet. Holding to a more positive anthropology than the radical Reformers, the Catholic tradition has insisted that the first biblical word about us as "very good" (Gen. 1:31) remains, that the divine image was never completely lost to humankind by "original sin"; though "fallen," the human condition is not totally depraved. Our tarnished but still present image in God's likeness gives people both the right to be treated with dignity and justice and the responsibility, because still capable of freedom and agency, to respect

and promote the rights and dignity of others. Further, we can still recognize, embedded in our own "being," a "natural law" that reflects God's intentions for us and is consonant with God's revealed law in Scripture. We are able to rationally discern the dictates of this law because our "being" participates in God's Being, and thus we have a "co-naturality" (Aquinas; see chapter 9, section 2) for knowing God's will; empowered by God's grace, we can freely choose to do it. Because it is implanted in all humankind by God, a natural law perspective can provide a common basis for discussing moral norms in the public forum. This is an important advantage in a pluralist society,[19] and with many Christians divided in their interpretations of biblical ethics.

From a natural law perspective, Catholicism argues that God has given all humanity inalienable rights and historical responsibilities for one another. The most thorough listing of universal human rights was by Pope John XXIII in the encyclical *Pacem in Terris*. In summary they are (1) "the right to life" and to the means necessary "for the proper development of life . . . food, clothing, shelter, rest, medical care and . . . the necessary social services"; (2) "the right . . . to freedom in searching for truth" and expressing it; (3) "the right to a basic education"; (4) the right to worship God freely; (5) the right "to choose freely a state of life"; (6) "the right to free initiative in the economic field and the right to work"; (7) the right to decent working conditions; (8) "the right to a wage determined according to criteria of justice"; (9) the right to private property; (10) "the right of assembly and association"; (11) "the right to freedom of movement and of residence"; (12) "the right to take an active part in public affairs and to contribute one's part to the common good of the citizens."[20] The encyclical adds that these natural rights "are inseparably connected in the very person who is their subject, with just as many respective duties."[21] Every right, then, brings its own duty to exercise it responsibly and to promote its realization for all humankind.

In exercising rights and fulfilling responsibilities, the effectiveness of human agency by way of influencing the course of history has a distinct emphasis in Catholicism, one also shaped by its positive anthropology already noted and by its concomitant theology of grace. Catholicism contends that God's grace can work through "nature" (i.e., human agency and the created order) because it effects an inner transformation in nature. This means that human agency is significant in realizing God's intentions for history. By God's grace, we can be God's covenant partners, and our cooperation can influence the quality and outcome of human history. Grace empowers people to act as free and responsible agents of God's will; God holds us accountable for our actions, and our efforts can improve our common well-being. Because grace transforms and works through nature, there are not "two kingdoms"—one of God and one of humankind, one of grace and one of human effort—that oppose each other. Rather, God's reign is a task to be done now within history and through free human cooperation, empowered by God's grace. As noted repeatedly, the reign of God is always God's gift, but the gift comes now as grace that, as Vatican II states, makes possible the efforts "by which the human family strives to make its life more human." God's grace empowers people now "to make ready the materials" for the final completion of God's reign, and our historical efforts have "enduring" significance in bringing about "a kingdom of truth and life, of holiness and grace, of justice, love and peace."[22]

2. Another mark of a Catholic perspective on justice for peace is dual commitment to the dignity of the human person *and* to the common good of all. Justice requires attention to the well-being of individuals and to the welfare of the community and social/political structures in which people's rights and responsibilities are historically realized. Vatican II says that Christians are to oppose "whatever violates the integrity of the human person"[23] and work for "the common good," which "embraces the sum of those conditions of social life by which individuals, families, and groups can achieve their own fulfillment in a relatively thorough and ready way."[24] The Council adds there must be a balance "between socialization on the one hand and personal independence and development on the other."[25] Rather than subsuming individuals into the social group as in totalitarian communism, or championing the personal rights of individuals over the welfare of others as in unbridled capitalism, Catholicism takes a both/and approach that intends to balance personal and communal well-being in a fruitful dialectic. (This dialectic is well imaged for the church itself as a social institution in its self-image as the Body of Christ.)

The dialectic between individual well-being and the common good is reflected in Catholic social teaching by its distinguishing of three essential dimensions of "basic justice": commutative, distributive, and social. The pastoral letter of the United States bishops *Economic Justice for All,* states, "Biblical justice is the goal we strive for. . . . On their path through history, however, sinful human beings need more specific guidance on how to move toward the realization of this great vision of God's kingdom. . . . Catholic social teaching, like much philosophical reflection, distinguishes three dimensions of basic justice: commutative justice, distributive justice, and social justice."[26]

The pastoral gives a helpful description of each. First, "*Commutative justice* calls for fundamental fairness in all agreements and exchanges between individuals or private social groups."[27] In other words, justice as "right relationship" is demanded in every interpersonal human exchange, in all one-on-one, one with group, or group-to-group activities. Then, "*Distributive justice* requires that the allocation of income, wealth and power in society be evaluated in light of its effects on persons whose basic material needs are unmet."[28] Hollenbach makes the holistic nature of such justice (i.e., including but beyond "material needs") more specific: "The function of distributive justice . . . is to ensure that the rights of all are guaranteed in social, economic, political and cultural interaction."[29] Thus, society has a responsibility to distribute its common resources so that all have access to what is necessary for a decent quality of life. The pastoral, quoting Vatican II, adds as a special emphasis that "we are obliged to come to the relief of the poor and to do so not merely out of our superfluous goods."[30] *"Social justice,"* as a distinctive dimension of "basic justice," "implies that persons have an obligation to be active and productive participants in the life of society and that society has a duty to enable them to participate in this way."[31] Social justice, then, pertains to the responsibility of society and of the individuals within it to create social structures through which "people can contribute to society in ways that respect their freedom and the dignity of their labor."[32]

In these three dimensions, each constitutive of "basic justice," we see the dialectic between individual and social well-being. Justice is realized in all interpersonal relationships; society is to care for the common good of all; society must see to it that all can contribute to the common good according to their full capacity.[33]

3. Contemporary Catholic social teaching has a deepened consciousness and new commitment concerning peace and peacemaking. I note only two related aspects: (a) a sense of the "new moment" presented by the threat of nuclear war and (b) the ecclesial responsibility to help eradicate "institutionalized violence."

A. The U.S. Catholic bishops wrote their pastoral *The Challenge of Peace* from the perspective of "bishops and pastors ministering in one of the major nuclear nations."[34] Their context of reflection gives it significant credibility in the universal church, and particular urgency not only for Catholics but for all Americans—"citizens of the nation which was first to produce atomic weapons, . . . the only one to use them and . . . capable of decisively influencing the course of the nuclear age."[35] Here I take the bishops' core positions as indicative of a new peace consciousness in mainline Catholicism.

The peace pastoral recognizes that the threat of nuclear war has presented "a new moment" for a tradition that has heretofore rendered moral opinions about war on the basis of the "just war" theory. It points to the strong tradition of pacifism in Christianity since its very beginning and notes Vatican II's encouragement of pacifism and conscientious objection to all war as a praiseworthy option for Catholics.[36] But it also recognizes that pacifism has been a minor tradition in Catholicism. More typically, the "presumption against war" has been tempered by "the principle of legitimate self-defense,"[37] when the mandate to love even one's enemies is considered outweighed by love for innocent victims who are threatened. From the principle of self-defense, there arose, beginning with Augustine, the "just war theory." It recognizes that when certain stringent conditions are fulfilled regarding both when and how to conduct war, then the "presumption [against war] may be overridden,"[38] and war can be justified as the lesser of two evils.[39]

Now, however, "both the just war teaching and non-violence are confronted with a unique challenge by nuclear warfare"; humankind finds itself with the destructive potential of nuclear weapons so great that their use would "threaten the entire planet."[40] Essentially, the bishops state that initiating a nuclear conflict could never fulfill the criteria of a "just war" (see note 39). "We do not perceive any situation in which the deliberate initiation of nuclear warfare, on however restricted a scale, could be morally justified."[41] Even the use of nuclear weapons to repel either a conventional or nuclear attack would "cause destruction which goes far beyond 'legitimate defense.' Such use of nuclear weapons would not be justified."[42] And about holding nuclear weapons as "deterrents," the bishops take "a strictly conditioned moral acceptance" of it, adding "we cannot consider it adequate as a long-term basis for peace."[43]

These positions have been recognized by commentators as a significant development in Catholic consciousness; they have brought the urgency of peacemaking and of opposing the nuclear arms race to the forefront of Catholic social responsibility. The bishops also call on "every diocese and parish to implement balanced and objective educational programs" of peace education, using the pastoral as a guide and framework.[44] They challenge all religious educators to "creatively rise to the challenge of peace."[45]

B. Recognition of the reality of "institutionalized violence"[46] has deepened the church's consciousness of the symbiotic relationship between injustice and violence and thus between the work of justice and the quest for peace. Injustice is already a form of violence; beyond open warfare, violence is present whenever social structures and cultural arrangements deny people their God-given rights. Only as injustice of every kind is eradicated can "that harmony built into human society by its divine Founder"[47] be realized. The peace pastoral gives a suggestive summary of the institutionalized violence that Christians should help eradicate for peace to prevail. "Violence has many faces: oppression of the poor, deprivation of basic human rights, economic exploitation, sexual exploitation and pornography, neglect or abuse of the aged and the helpless, and innumerable other acts of inhumanity. Abortion in particular blunts a sense of the sacredness of human life."[48] I add to this list "domestic violence." The peacemaking of Christians must eradicate violence from our own and others' homes, and especially violence against women, children, and the aged. The pastoral adds that the arms race is not only a threat to peace but also "an act of aggression against the poor, and a folly which does not provide the security it promises."[49] Awareness of how injustice and violence are intertwined in social and interpersonal structures has deepened the church's consciousness of the old biblical insight that only "justice will bring peace" (Isa. 32:17).

D. Catalysts of Contemporary Christian Social Consciousness

With such roots in Bible and tradition, one wonders why justice and peace have emerged as urgent issues in our time and what, if anything, is new about contemporary Christian social consciousness. Clearly, it is prompted and informed by a variety of social/political movements and influences in the wider society—by various struggles for liberation from political and economic oppression, from sexism and racism, by heightened awareness of the growing gap between wealthy and poor nations, by the existential danger of nuclear annihilation, by the emergence of a "green" consciousness and political movement, to name a few. Here I highlight three intra-ecclesial catalysts of a deepened Christian social consciousness: from theology, from attention by the church to a sociological perspective, and from a more "inclusive" spirituality.

1. From Theology.   Contemporary theology is marked by pluralism of perspectives unparalleled in the history of the church; nevertheless, some common features are evident that contribute to a Christian social consciousness. Many of them are shifts in theological method and foundations. The following seem most significant for a social consciousness: (a) recognition that present praxis and historical context are not simply points of application for theological insight but crucial theological sources for interpreting the Christian foundations of Scripture and tradition; (b) the emergence of theological reflection from existential situations of human suffering and from struggles to overcome injustice and oppression (Third World, feminist, black, etc. theologies); (c) a critical perspective that is, among other things, aware of the "historicity" of all "ideas" and of the need to uncover their "constitutive interests," that is committed to a hermeneutics of retrieval of what is life-giving in Christian tradition and of suspicion for what has been used to legitimate injustice; (d) the transcending of old polemics about anthropology and the "nature/grace" relationship and replacing them with perspectives that are not naive about the reality of human sinfulness, personal and social, yet are convinced of the possibility, by God's grace, for human agency to act responsibly.

These developments have encouraged: awareness of the social/ political sources and consequences of theological reflection and of the duty of Christian theology to have a pastoral and humanizing influence on the human condition; greater consciousness of the liberating and political tasks of Christian faith; dissolving of "reified" theological ideas that legitimate oppressive social arrangements and the reclaiming of subversive memories that prompt personal and social transformation; recognition that Christian theology is to empower people's living as disciples of Jesus.

Critical Scripture scholarship has contributed to these theological developments and is pertinent of itself to deepened social consciousness. In particular, the "new quest" for the historical Jesus (see chapter 15, note 12) offers a clearer picture of the social values that Jesus preached and lived. It especially highlights the centrality of the reign of God to Jesus' purpose and ministry. As noted many times, this symbol, a profoundly social one, establishes an intrahistorical eschatology toward peace and justice, love and freedom, wholeness and fullness of life as God's intentions in Jesus for humankind and all creation. Moving away from totally "futurist" eschatology, as if the reign of God is to be realized only in a future life, and beyond a totally "realized" eschatology, as if God's reign has already come fully in Jesus, a consensus Christian opinion understands God's reign as inaugurated in Jesus, as promised in completion at the end-time but placing personal, interpersonal, and social/political responsibilities on people now to be co-partners with God in realizing God's will within history. (See chapter 1.) Contemporary Christian theology recognizes that this symbol, or some more adequate synonym that carries its equivalent meaning, must be taken seriously to shape the intent of the whole theological enterprise. To take the reign of God seriously is to recognize that peace and justice are mandates of Christian faith.

2. From Sociology.   In mediating and interpreting the relationship between faith and culture, the church has been increasingly informed by the social sciences. The insights of sociology have been significant for a deepened peace and justice consciousness. It has helped Christians to think sociologically about their faith, "to see the wider picture," with its structures, linkages, divisions, levels, and so on and what one's context and culture asks of living one's faith commitments. Social analysis has deepened awareness of the structural dimensions of both sin and salvation. There is always a human choice involved in sin, but the sins of a social group over time become reified in sinful social structures that, in turn, dispose people to sinfulness. Likewise, repentance and salvation require not only a personal change of heart but opposition to sinful structures of oppression and injustice. A social perspective on Matthew 25:31–46, for example, readily recognizes that the "works of mercy" are in fact works of justice, that they cannot be fulfilled by personal "charity" alone but demand that Christians struggle to change the structures that cause people to be hungry, homeless, oppressed, in the first place. Likewise, a social perspective on the great commandment has helped Christians to retrieve what was in fact an old consciousness in the church: "Christian love of neighbor and justice cannot be separated. For love implies an absolute demand for justice, namely a recognition of the dignity and rights of one's neighbor."[50]

3. From an "Inclusive" Spirituality.   A third catalyst that lends both impetus and form to contemporary Christian social consciousness is a renewed spirituality that reflects the biblical sense of both justice and holiness as "right relationship," as two sides of the same coin. In particular, a social consciousness is augmented by the emergence of an "inclusive spirituality" or what is also being called "a holistic Christian spirituality."[51] This emerging spirituality is inclusive/holistic in at least two socially significant ways. First, it is marked by awareness that *all*

Christians are called by baptism to holiness of life that "embraces the totality of a person's existence, including one's relationship with others, with one's work, and with the material world."[52] Historically, the monastic life and later the vowed apostolic communities of men and women "religious" encouraged an assumption, at least in Catholic consciousness, that holiness of life is exclusive to an elite few, that the basis of the Christian call to holiness is something other than baptism. In contrast, contemporary Catholicism has a spiritual awakening in which, as Vatican II states, "it is evident to everyone that all the faithful of Christ of whatever rank or status are called to the fullness of the Christian life and to the perfection of charity. By this holiness a more human way of life is promoted even in this earthly society."[53] The very title of the chapter in which this statement occurs is significant: "The Call of the Whole Church to Holiness."[54] As Wilkie Au explains, Vatican II's reaffirmation "that the call to holiness is universal" has led to "a gradual shedding of elitist interpretations of religious profession" and to the recognition "that one can be deeply religious without being a religious."[55]

Second, this emerging spirituality includes, as the quotation from Vatican II indicates, promoting a "more human way of life" for all "in this earthly society." Rather than being a way apart from the ordinary and the historical, it demands that Christians' whole way of life and the world in which they live be made holy and acceptable to God. This "historicized" spirituality highlights again the unity of justice and holiness. In the "holiness code" of Leviticus 19, God says to the people through Moses, "Be holy, for I, the Lord, your God, am holy" (19:2). The code that follows makes it clear that to be holy like God requires the work of justice. We are not to "stand idly by when [our] neighbor's life is at stake" (v. 16); we are to have the same love for the poor as for ourselves (v. 34). Later, Jesus reechoes this sentiment by calling disciples to the holiness of God with, "You must therefore be perfect [one translation has 'complete in righteousness' for *teleios* here] as your heavenly Father is perfect" (Matt. 5:48). And 1 Peter 1:15–16, quoting Leviticus 19:2, says, "Become holy yourselves in every aspect of your conduct, after the likeness of the holy One who called you; remember, Scripture says 'Be holy, for I am holy.'" From a biblical view, holiness and justice are as one. To be holy, as to be just, is to live in right and loving relationship with God, self, others, and all creation.

Because Christians are called to be holy/just as their God is holy/just, they are to make a "preferential option for the poor,"[56] that is, to always side with those whose well-being is most threatened and denied. The U.S. Catholic bishops state in their pastoral *Economic Justice for All:* "As followers of Christ, we are challenged to make a fundamental 'option for the poor'—to speak for the voiceless, to defend the defenseless, to assess lifestyles, policies and social institutions in terms of their impact on the poor."[57] It is important to be clear about who are "the poor." In keeping with the Bible, economic poverty is the first defining note. But, consonant with the Hebrew Scriptures and the praxis of Jesus, "the poor" also include all who are "thingified" or treated as less than full human subjects by discrimination on any basis. All who are demeaned, violated, exploited, oppressed, or excluded from what they need for fullness of life, or from full participation in the life of society or church, are among "the poor" for whom Christians must make a "preferential option."[58] In sum, an option for the poor and for justice should be "a seamless garment."[59]

2. "Church" in Dialectic with "World" as Effective Symbol of Justice and Peace

As the communal context of nurture and support for Christian living, the church as a community is eminently under the mandate of justice/ peace and its whole ministry should be structured to reflect and empower a faith that does justice for peace. First, however, I should make explicit two points: (a) the Christian community is to be a "church" and (b) should be in dialectic with "the world."

A. In terms of the categories of Ernst Troeltsch, the community of Jesus' disciples is to be a "church" in the world. In his classic work *The Social Teaching of the Christian Churches,* Troeltsch classified the social forms of Christianity into three predominant "types"—"church," "sect," and "mysticism," each one with significant roots in the New Testament. The "church" type sees itself as an inclusive community that welcomes all, saints and sinners alike, and attempts to realize itself within its historical situation. It affirms the power of God's grace to enable the Christian community to be a transforming influence in the world, to be a leaven within its cultural context. The "sect" type consists of a voluntary association of strict and definite adherents who maintain radical commitment to Christian values but do so over against or apart from "the world," convinced that it is too sinful to be improved, except from without. The "mystical" type consists of an informal group without structures of worship, doctrine, or organization that places emphasis on inner spiritual experiences and the dispositions of the individual person.[60]

My conviction is that the whole community of the disciples of Jesus is to be a "church" as Troeltsch defines it, a community that welcomes all and both realizes itself in ways indigenous to its cultural context and acts as a leaven for its transformation. It may have "sects" within it that take a more radical stance toward the world (e.g., religious orders, the peace churches) and must always honor and nurture the spiritual experiences of its members, but its overall form is of a "church" in the world. The implication is that the whole "church" and all who claim to be Christians, rather than only small dedicated groups within it, are called by baptism to a faith that does justice for peace.

B. The church's way of life should be a dialectic with its "world" that works for its own renewal and for social transformation. Rather than being "against the world" as if the world were inherently evil, or "of the world" as if the church were to be no more than a reflection of its social context, it enters into a dialectical relationship of affirming, refusing, and transforming its historical situation and thereby also maintains its own ongoing reformation.[61] The church is to affirm and defend what is of God's reign of peace and justice; as Vatican II stated, the church has "the task to uncover, cherish and ennoble all that is true, good and beautiful in the human community."[62] The church must place itself over against sinful structures and arrangements that "poison human society"[63] and constantly review the justice of its own structures. In transformation, the church works for "the renewal of the whole temporal order" and to "perfect the temporal sphere with the spirit of the Gospel."[64] Through such dialectic, the church becomes a sacrament of God's reign of justice and peace.

The Church as Sacrament of God's Reign

The church's whole *raison d'être* is to be a symbol of God's reign in Jesus. It is not the reign of God, but exists to be a community of Jesus' disciples that is a visible, credible, and effective agency of the fullness of life that God wills for all. The church often fails to be such a sacrament; at times it has been and is a countersign of God's reign. But rather than acquiescing in its sinfulness or presuming on its holiness, a committed ecclesial faith calls Christians to be ever reforming their own community (*semper reformanda*, as Augustine put it). To delineate some implications of the church as sacrament of God's reign, I return to its fourfold tasks but interpret each from a justice and peace perspective.

A. *Kerygma.*   In every activity to fulfill its kerygmatic mission, the church should self-consciously remember that God's word through Scripture is a word of justice. Whether preaching, teaching, or evangelizing, the commitment to justice ought to be constitutive of interpretation and explanation of every aspect of Story/Vision. We have already reflected on preaching (chapter 12), and section 3 of this chapter is on commitment to justice/peace in the church's educational ministry. Here I focus on evangelization from a justice/peace perspective. Evangelization is any activity whereby the church proclaims the Good News (*euangelion*) through every possible means (missionary outreach, media, renewal movements, personal contact, etc.) to people who have not heard it before and to all who need to have Christian faith enlivened by hearing it again. One of the richest statements on it, especially as it relates to justice, is the statement of Pope Paul VI *On Evangelization in the Modern World,* usually referred to by its Latin title, *Evangelii Nuntiandi (E.N.).*

E.N. often uses the terms *salvation* and *liberation* interchangeably and speaks of "liberating salvation" to portray a holistic understanding of what the gospel is to effect in the world. It is careful not to reduce "liberating salvation" to "a simply temporal project" or only "to material well-being."[65] Liberating evangelization is to open people to "the divine absolute" and include "the prophetic proclamation of a hereafter, [humankind's] profound and definitive calling."[66] But the document also insists on the immanent purpose of evangelization. It is to promote an "integral salvation" that begins within history, to empower people to engage in the struggle for justice and liberation. The church must proclaim the gospel in a way that promotes "liberation from everything that oppresses [humanity]" and has "the duty of assisting the birth of this liberation, of giving witness to it, of ensuring that it is complete."[67] In a powerful summary, *E.N.* states,

> For the Church, evangelizing means bringing the Good News into all the strata of humanity, and through its influence transforming humanity from within and making it new. . . . The purpose of evangelization is therefore precisely this interior change, and if it had to be expressed in one sentence, the best way of stating it would be to say that the Church evangelizes when she seeks to convert . . . both the personal and collective consciences of people, the activities in which they engage, and the lives and concrete milieus which are theirs.[68]

The Gospel, then, is to permeate all strata of society, to help liberate humanity from within, and to transform the contexts of people's lives. To evangelize is to create in people, both individually and collectively, a deepened social/political consciousness and commitment to justice. As *E.N.* asks rhetorically, "How in fact can one proclaim the new commandment without promoting in justice and in peace the true, authentic advancement of [humankind]."[69]

B. Koinonia. For the sacramentality of its mission and the credibility of its kerygma, the church is itself to be a just community; all its structures (of governance, canon law, public worship, forms and functions of ministry, education, etc.) should be marked by and witness to justice. Nothing is more crucial to the sacramentality of the church than the evident justice of its own koinonia. To whatever extent a Christian community practices, or is seen to practice and legitimate (for sacramentality, appearances *do* matter) consumerism and undue attachment to money and possessions, patriarchy and sexism, racism and ethnic discrimination, a lack of true care and appreciation for the old and the young, destructive practices or uncaring attitudes toward the environment—to that extent it is not a sacrament of God's reign and fails at the very heart of its mission. The document "Justice in the World" of the Second General Synod of Catholic Bishops (1971) declared, "While the Church is bound to give witness to justice, [it] recognizes that anyone who ventures to speak to people about justice must first be just in their eyes. Hence we must undertake an examination of the modes of acting and of the possessions and lifestyle found within the Church [it]self."[70]

Hearkening back to the threefold dimensions of "basic justice" outlined above, the mandate to be just requires of the church itself (a) that it be a community of "right relationship," partnership, and mutual respect among its members. All forms of clericalism are antithetical to this *commutative* justice. (b) As a social entity, the church is to honor the rights of all its members to have access to what they need for fullness of life in faith, with a special care for the poor and marginalized in faith and for those whose faith is most threatened. Knowledge control and sacramental control are antithetical to this *distributive* justice. (c) The church is to promote the responsibilities and rights of all the baptized to contribute to the church's mission, welcoming and nurturing the gifts of its members and especially those whose gifts have typically been denied or refused. Sexism and racism are surely the most evident countersigns to such *social* justice in the church.

As a koinonia of justice and peace, the Christian church must embrace the "new moment" of ecumenism and work for reconciliation within its own communions. Beyond that, as Vatican II stated in its "Declaration on Non-Christian Religions," the church is to be in "dialogue and collaboration with the followers of other religions," with special appreciation for the "spiritual patrimony common to Christians and Jews."[71] It must be committed to "mutual understanding and respect" for "the people of God of the Old Covenant, which has never been revoked"[72] (Pope John Paul II).

C. Leitourgia.   In chapter 12 I argued that liturgy should be sacramentally adequate in people's lives "for the life of the world." From the time of the prophets to the present, the faith community has known, although often forgotten, that "right worship" should arise from and enhance the work of peace through justice; worshiping God "in Spirit and truth" forms people to fulfill the social responsibilities of their faith.

D. Diakonia.   From the beginning, the Christian community has been marked by its direct service to the needy. It has a distinguished tradition of performing the corporal and spiritual works of mercy— educating, feeding, sheltering, healing, visiting, releasing, clothing, comforting, and reconciling those so in need. Contemporary understanding of the social responsibilities of Christian faith clarifies that the "works of mercy" require the church to engage in challenging and helping to reconstruct the social structures and cultural arrangements that cause hunger, oppression, and suffering in the first place. The Christian community should always give direct service to immediate human needs *and* work at a political/structural level for distributive and social justice for all. "We can no longer pretend that the inequalities and injustices of our world must be borne as part of the inevitable order of things"; rather, the church is to oppose the "institutionalized injustice" that is "built into economic, social, and political structures that dominate the life of nations and the international community."[73]

In the mainline Christian churches of North America the political aspect of diakonia is reflected in the signs of a "public church." (See chapter 4, section 3B, and chapter 11, section 4B). Martin Marty defines the "public church" as a "family of Christian Churches" that are "especially sensitive to the *res publica,* the public order that surrounds and includes people of faith."[74] In the Third and Fourth Worlds, and in North America too, there is a more radical and liberationist praxis of political diakonia, and there are many basic Christian communities committed to direct political action. Yet the emergence of a "public church" consciousness among mainline congregations in America is significant. In its founding, religion and especially Christianity played a primary role in shaping "the American experiment." Then, with independence, the promulgation of the United States Constitution and especially the First Amendment, a structural separation emerged between church and state. Be the separation a "wall" (Jefferson) or a "line" (Madison),[75] it came to imply a *division* between faith and life, between religious values and politics. It is commonly accepted that the churches have no role in the economic and political life of the country. The "public church" movement is an antidote to such historical naïveté and dichotomous thinking. It recognizes that the church, as a public institution within society (see chapter 1, note 4) must oppose structures of injustice and violence and promote peace and justice for all. It is to harness every institutional resource at its disposal and educate its individual members to engage in the public realm "for service to the advancement of the common good" (Vatican II).[76] It should take sides with the poor and oppressed of society and engage in all public debates about social morality.[77]

3. Justice and Peace as Constitutive in Religious Education

The understanding of Christian religious education I propose throughout this book—its nature, purposes, intended learning outcome, and approach—implies that every instance of it is to educate for a faith that does justice and peace. In this section, then, I make more explicit, however briefly, that *every aspect of the church's religious education curriculum, both its content and its process, should be intentionally structured to form people's character in a faith that does justice for peace.*

A. *Every Aspect of the Church's Curriculum.*   That justice and peace are integral to Christian faith is becoming established in the consciousness of the church. There is a tendency, however, especially in curriculum materials, to present justice/peace as a distinct topic (sometimes even as an "elective") alongside other topics like Christology, ecclesiology, sacraments, and so on. Social responsibility certainly deserves explicit attention as a particular topic in the curriculum, but if it is dealt with only as one among many others, the danger is that justice can be perceived, to quote Gabriel Moran, "as a peripheral bit of content" rather than as "the center of the process"[78] of religious education. Every aspect of the curriculum, its content and process, is to be suffused with commitment to a faith that does justice for peace.

B. *Justice in Content.*   There is no theme from Christian Story/Vision that does not present curriculum choices for whether or not we educate for a socially responsible faith. This is most evidently true, of course, when the curriculum is focused on ethical issues, on social questions, on Christian values and virtues. But Padraic O'Hare contends insightfully that "the chief tool of peace and justice education is classical doctrine, ethically retrieved."[79] He advises such retrieval especially in a "gradualist" approach to peace and justice education with the "conventionally religious."[80] We need to interpret old familiar doctrinal symbols from a justice/peace perspective if it is to permeate the content of the whole curriculum and find a hearing among people who cherish those symbols but have not, perhaps, seen their ethical import.[81] Some examples may illustrate; I present them as either/or choices to highlight the "politics" of *what* we choose to teach.

God can be presented and imaged to people as distant from "ordinary" people and everyday life, as a God for the "heavens" who cares only about "souls," as exclusively male; or God can be presented and imaged as an inclusive God who is active in history on behalf of justice, peace, and freedom for all and brings humankind into a covenant to live in "right relationship" toward what God wills in every arena and level of their existence. *Jesus* can be presented as "nice," "pious," and "churchy," as preaching a kind of "private" religion, with no relevance for people's politics; or he can be presented as Jesus the Liberator who lived and gave his life for God's reign of fullness of life for all, whose "good news" of radical love was reflected especially in outreach to the poor and oppressed, who preached judgment in which love of God is synonymous with care for the needy. *Sin* can be presented solely as a personal affair between oneself and God whose effects are taken away when we tell God we are sorry; or we can also teach that sin is a refusal of "right relationship" and an injury to our social well-being, as promoting and perpetuating itself in sinful social structures. *Salvation* can be presented only as an otherworldly hope for souls later, or as a this worldly responsibility to live as disciples of Jesus toward liberation that is to begin now for ourselves, society, and all creation. *Church* can be presented solely as a hierarchical institution that controls God's word and sacrament, a salvation club for getting souls to heaven, or as an inclusive discipleship of partners who carry on Jesus' mission as an effective symbol of God's reign in the world. The *sacraments* can be presented as automatic channels of God's grace for our own-sanctification alone, or as effective mediations of God's saving presence that require our participation "for the life of the world." And so it can go on with every doctrinal symbol of Christian faith. Similar "politics" are reflected in our hermeneutics of the great life-themes from Scripture. Religious educators are to draw from their Scriptures and traditions what is likely to educate in faith that does justice for peace.

C. *Justice in Process.*   All religious education should be done justly and by a process that is itself peaceful. Stated negatively, "banking education" (Freire), even if its content is for justice/peace, is a form of injustice and violence to participants because it robs them of their own "word" and tries to control what they are to think, do, value.[82] Clearly, and after all I've already said, I'm not proposing a false liberalism here in which the educator simply tries to make people feel good, with no thorough testing of positions, no critical reflection on present praxis, no dialectical aspect, no making tough decisions. On the contrary, those dynamics must be present precisely to serve justice and peace; as with love, they often demand honest confrontation and "hard sayings."

My own bias, of course, is that a process of educating for justice/ peace is well facilitated by a process of participation and dialogue in which people are prompted to focus on an aspect of their own and their society's praxis, to name and express that praxis for themselves. Present praxis as a source of conscientization is enhanced if participants reflect critically on it and "decode" it with critical analysis. Christian Story/ Vision should be interpreted and explained with the practical interest of faith that does justice, and a "justice process" is enhanced when Story/Vision is made accessible by a style that invites people to personally appropriate it to their own reality rather than having it imposed in a doctrinaire way. To motivate actions and actors for justice/peace, the process should encourage people to decisions that realize the values of God's reign.

D. *Forming People's Character.*   Justice and peace are values to be lived, commitments to be historicized, actions to be done by "agent-subjects-in-relationship." Educating for a faith that does justice, then, is more than informing people *about* the social responsibilities of Christian faith; it requires forming their character in the *habitus* of justice, that is, in the consciousness, dispositions, and commitments needed to live justly for peace. Teachers are indeed to teach clearly the ideas of justice, peace, liberation, compassion, and so on, and participants are to understand them as integral to "orthodox" faith of the Christian churches. But people's characters are to be formed for the orthopraxis of them as well—*to live* justly, *to be* peacemakers, *to act* with compassion, and so forth, in the personal, interpersonal, and social/political arenas. The task is to form actors as well as to inform action for a faith that does justice, albeit recognizing that the latter (i.e., the praxis) is the surest way to the former (i.e., the character; see Aristotle). I am convinced that this can begin from the first days of intentional religious education[83] and that it is greatly enhanced by an approach that originates with reflection on present praxis and has renewed Christian praxis as its intended outcome.

The reflections above have focused on the church's religious education. Beyond this, however, the church is also a significant agent of general education. Many Christian denominations sponsor or have much influence on a vast number of schools, colleges, and universities throughout the world. The role of such schools in educating for justice/peace is a major topic; here I can only make a note in passing. The church must recognize the political nature of *all* its educational activity (chapter 1, section 1) and strive to shape the politics of its schools toward justice and peace. This does not mean teaching a particular political party line but rather educating in ways that are consciousness-raising, teaching people to read critically their own reality and to think for themselves, informing them about traditions and perspectives, and forming in values that encourage them to fulfill their social/political responsibilities, to claim their own human rights and promote the rights of others. In this way their whole curriculum in every discipline of learning can be "infused" with commitment to justice and peace.[84] Likewise, the public postures of such institutions and how they are administered internally should reflect commitment to the social values of God's reign. The church needs to see and do all its educational work as a "social ministry."

4. A Shared Praxis Approach to Social Ministries

People often assume that to work for justice and peace one must be directly involved in some form of social action that is readily identified as "social ministry." The import of this chapter is that justice and peace are to suffuse the life praxis of every Christian and all expressions of the church's ministry in the world. In every arena of life and level of human existence, every Christian and every Christian community is responsible for living in "right relationship" by "doing the truth in love" and helping create social structures in which others can do likewise.

This section 4 attends specifically to what would be readily identified as "social ministry" and to the potential of a shared praxis approach for doing it. All functions of Christian ministry should reflect and contribute to a faith that does justice, but *every congregation needs particular programs and groupings of people whose shared purpose is to engage in some particular aspect of the work of justice and peace.* For example, the community to which I belong in Boston has a peacemakers' group, a women's issues group, a community meals program, a Central America group, a hunger and housing action group, an economic justice group, an environmental concerns group, to name only a few.[85]

The formal purpose and praxis of social ministry programs varies in any congregation. They may deal with the results or the causes of injustice or both; they may provide direct service to people in need, be consciousness-raising and empowering groups that address the structural aspects of injustice and/or violence, engage in political action for social reconstruction, attend deliberately to the sacramental adequacy of the church as a koinonia of justice and peace, and so on; and any one may reflect a combination of many such purposes. Every Christian community needs to sponsor such social ministries not only out of a faith-inspired sense of responsibility "for the life of the world" but also for deepening the faith life of the community itself. As the prophet Jeremiah witnessed, doing what is "right and just" (see Jer. 22:15–16) is a privileged locus of God's presence and self-disclosure. A community's participation in the work of justice/peace and in service to "the poor" is a powerful source of its own conversion and renewal in Christian faith. Is it not possible for a Christian community to nurture and renew its members in Christian faith without such Christian praxis.

To be effective in addressing particular issues and to be a source of deepened faith for the community, social ministries can be enhanced by some general style or approach to them that is adequate and appropriate to the purposes of such ministry. Clearly, *how* they are done should reflect justice/peace, and their dynamics should be likely to empower all participants, be they primarily sponsors, beneficiaries, or both (as is always the case to some extent) as "agent-subjects-in-right-relationship." Beyond this, it is difficult to be more specific, given the variety of contexts and issues these programs may address. But I propose as a general and adaptable principal *that Christian social ministry function as an action/reflection process, that it engage all participants as agent-subjects, that it reflect the ethics, values, and spiritualities of Christian Story/ Vision, that it be a source of empowerment for all participants.* Action alone soon becomes activism and dies, and reflection alone soon becomes verbalism that is ineffective. To see some participants solely as providers and others exclusively as recipients encourages a subject-object division instead of "right relationship" (especially in programs of direct service). Christian Story/Vision is needed as source of the commitments that nurture and guide the service and for a spirituality to sustain it as an expression of Christian faith. And such ministry should never intend dependency, nor even service alone, but empowerment of all.

In light of this general principle, the commitments and dynamics of shared Christian praxis suggest one fitting, adaptable, and readily usable *modus operandi* for many forms and occasions of social ministry. Its commitments to participation, partnership, and dialogue, to engage in present praxis with critical reflection upon it, of attending to the resources of Christian faith, and to empower people as agent-subjects of renewed historical praxis could prompt people in social ministries to do things they might not remember to do otherwise. The dynamics of its movements need to be complemented by other approaches and are not equally relevant for all programs of social ministry. Its movements will rarely unfold in sequence, yet the intent of each one can be suggestive of the appropriate dynamics for such programs. Here again, I can only sketch the movements as they might emerge.

In a social ministry, what I call the *focusing activity* of shared praxis is typically the essential praxis of the program—the historical activity that it invites from participants or enables them to do together. As such it runs throughout, and the program typically begins with such action. This may be some direct service with the poor, the homeless, the abused, and so on, or participation in some political action to challenge structures of injustice and/or violence. I say that such praxis is "typically" called for from the beginning because it is needed more by groups that have no such prior praxis than by people who are already engaged in it. For example, middle-class people becoming involved in issues of hunger or homelessness do well to begin with direct work with people who so suffer.[86] On the other hand, there are programs that focus on a particular form of social discrimination (sexism, racism, ageism, etc.) whose participants may know firsthand the pain of such oppression and are already involved in resisting it. Even there, a group's solidarity may be established more effectively if they engage from the beginning in some common praxis for justice and peace around their shared purpose.

As participants continue in the praxis of the ministry, movements 1 and 2 suggest that there be intentional moments, either formal or informal, when participants have an opportunity to name for themselves and reflect critically on their work together. In programs of direct service, this advises, at a minimum, inviting the thoughts, sentiments, and ideas of those served by the ministry and, insofar as feasible, encouraging them to reflect critically on their social situation.[87] For the sponsors of direct service ministry and especially in programs of social reform and/or consciousness-raising, movement 2 suggests a dynamic that questions the political, social, economic, legal, educational, and ecclesial structures, and the cultural mores and divisions related to class, gender, race, and age that are roots of injustice and violence. As participants engage in their "shared praxis," they can look at who is making the decisions that shape this present reality, who is benefiting, who is suffering, and why.[88]

Movement 3 of shared praxis suggests that social ministry have intentional moments when participants turn to Christian Story/Vision for inspiration, motivation, and direction and to draw upon its prayer and liturgy traditions for spiritual sustenance. The Story is a catalyst for such ministry because through it people can find, as Butkus says, "the remembrance of God's redemptive activity on behalf of suffering humanity,"[89] and the dangerous memory of the suffering and resistance of Christian people to injustice over time, beginning with the suffering and resistance of Jesus. The Vision suggests ethical norms and values to guide discernment and decision making. And participants are sustained in commitment and can avoid burnout by turning, personally and com-

munally, to the spiritual and liturgical traditions of Christian faith.
Moran writes, "The greater the injustice, the greater is the need for
prayerful quiet in the midst of passionate activity."[90]

Movements 4 and 5 of shared Christian praxis suggest that social
ministry programs have intentional dynamics that encourage participants, through a dialectic between action/reflection and their faith
Story/Vision, to come to deeper consciousness of injustice, of violence,
and of their causes, and to ever deepen and renew their commitment
to the praxis of justice and peace. When programs build in opportunities "to take stock" and to discern the direction of future praxis, they
are likely to be more effective and a source of ongoing conversion for
participants. Even old decisions give new life as they are made again.

5. Keeping On in the Work of Justice and Peace

People need resources to "keep on keeping on" (Letty Russell's phrase)
in the work of justice and peace. My list of "resources," which I frame
as "counsels," is only suggestive and intended to stimulate readers' own
discernment of their needs in this regard. I have discovered their truth
from my own praxis, but I recognize them as much more my vision
than my story. *Nor* should they be seen as preconditions before one can
begin the work of justice; they are realized and renewed by our praxis,
even as they sustain it.

1. Remember that human agency is empowered by the grace of God.   In
the Christian life, but particularly in working for justice and peace,
there are two eminent heresies to avoid: the typically Catholic heresy of
"works righteousness," also called "Pelagianism," and the typically
Protestant heresy of "cheap grace" (Bonhoeffer). The first presumes
that human effort unaided can do God's will and achieve "salvation." In
the work of peace and justice, its likely consequences are burnout or
paralysis from the enormity of the task. The "cheap grace" heresy
presumes that (a) human effort can contribute nothing to the
realization of God's reign, and (b) God's grace in Jesus has already
achieved both our justification and sanctification, and we only need to
accept this in faith (i.e., we have nothing "to do" historically in
response). For the work of justice, its likely consequence is indifference,
at least about human effort, because it assumes that God's grace alone,
without human cooperation, can improve social conditions *if* they can
be improved at all. Both "heresies" deny the nature of our covenant
with God that requires the agency of its "partners." A more balanced
and historically responsible position recognizes that the reign of God
and its presence/coming is always by the gift of God's grace. Yet God
has taken humankind into a covenant of co-partnership. From "this
side" of the covenant, God's grace empowers people to be responsible
agents of God's activity and will in the world. Truly, "we are God's

co-workers" (1 Cor. 3:9). The praxis of justice/peace requires such spirituality and perspective to avoid a destructive despair or a dangerous presumption.

   2. Seek support in a community of shared faith.   One is not likely to sustain commitment to justice/peace without the solidarity and support of a committed faith community. Mainline Christian tradition has always recognized an ecclesial context as necessary to lived Christian faith; its urgency is intensified, I believe, by the demands of a faith that does justice. As people cannot do the work of justice/peace without God's help, we cannot do it without the help of other people either; in fact, they are a primary mediation of God's grace to us. If we do not find or cannot build such a community in our formal parish or congregation, we do well to seek it out in other contexts.

   3. Redefine "success" and be convinced that there is always something one can do.   American culture has a pervasive ideology that equates "success" with "solving the problem." Consequently, when people see that the *whole* problem cannot be "solved" soon (e.g., world hunger), we tend to give up, to presume that there is really nothing we can do. In the work of peace and justice, it is wise to redefine success and move beyond expecting any "quick fix" or easy solution. We need to think of success in small portions and with a gospel sense of hope and reversal: mustard seeds can grow into large trees; grains of wheat that fall to the ground bring new life; the last can become first and the first last; even a cup of water given in the name of Christ is rewarded; some people plant, others water, and it is always God who gives the increase. Regardless of who or where we are, we can always make a "significant" contribution to peace and justice. I once met a retired octogenarian Jesuit who told me that a deepened commitment to a faith that does justice had significantly changed his prayer life (how he prays and what he prays for), and the kind of letters he writes to nieces, nephews, and friends ("Now I always find a way to mention the needs of the poor"). Paulo Freire has said that "we must do what we can today so that we can do something more tomorrow."[91] Michel Foucault insists that people can always find points and places in structures of domination where resistance is possible, if not already going on, and we can help augment it.[92] Paul advises Christians to remember that hope is most a virtue when its object is not seen and yet aspired to "with patient endurance" (see Rom. 8:24–25).

   4. Encounter "the poor" in praxis, and remember personal oppression and suffering.   The first point of this counsel is likely more relevant for people not directly involved in "social ministry." Many times I have described working with "the poor" and works of justice as privileged places of God's presence and self-disclosure. When one's daily life does not readily lend such relationship and opportunity, it is wise to create the occasion (e.g., volunteer work in a soup kitchen). Volunteer occasions should not be equated with fulfilling the social responsibilities of Christian faith; rather, they can serve as a personal source of empathy and of critical consciousness that can permeate one's life and sustain commitment to a faith that does justice.

Some have raised the question whether people who have no felt sense of the "crisis" of injustice and violence can have sufficient empathy to work for justice and peace.[93] The question highlights the need for persuasive teaching and preaching for a faith that does justice in the local community; access to Christian Story/Vision should prompt empathy for the poor and critical consciousness of injustice. However, I am convinced that for middle- and upper-income Christians, or other people of social privilege, it also helps to recall personal experiences of some form of poverty, injustice, or violence; surely everyone has had such experiences. From the "dangerous memories" of personal suffering people can draw empathy for others whose lives are more threatened than theirs. For example, if the wealthy and well-fed do not recognize some form of deprivation or "hunger" (albeit a more privileged one than physical hunger) in their lives, the physical hunger of the poor is less likely to move them to empathy and action.

5. *Avoid elitism and debilitating guilt.* Both of these counsels seem more relevant for neophytes than for those who have "borne the heat of the day" in the works of justice and peace; all, however, need to guard against them. To avoid elitism it helps to recognize one's personal sins and complicity in social sinfulness, to remember that a faith that does justice is a lifelong conversion for all. "Let the one among you who has not sinned be the first to cast a stone" (John 8:8) reflects Jesus' recognition of the "democracy" of sin. None can afford an "us versus them" stance; all participate, often to our benefit, in structures of injustice. Objectifying evil in others and subjectifying good in ourselves is never a Christian approach to the reality of sin, and such "puritanism" seems unlikely to be effective. The task is to struggle on, by God's grace, in faithfulness to the justice and peace that God wills, to oppose sin but always to love the sinner, in self and other—albeit with confronting love.

Foisting a debilitating guilt on self or others is also unlikely to sustain commitment to justice. There is a "healthy" guilt we need about our own sins and about the injustices, violence, and destruction in and of our world. But people can also feel a debilitating guilt that overpowers and paralyzes instead of empowering them to act. For example, there can be injustice in our use of food, but justice for the hungry does not mean that people so committed should feel guilty about eating; rather they must work to see to it that everyone has enough to eat.

6. *Let action be informed by reflection and study and regularly brought to prayer.* The whole notion of praxis throughout this work has emphasized action and reflection as constitutive of Christian religious education and ministry. The need for critical reflection seems augmented

by the challenge of "keeping on" in the work of justice. We need research and study to know the context and culture in which we work; we need the insights of the social sciences to do personal and social analysis and to unmask the debilitating myths that legitimate oppression and warmongering; and we need to listen to the "subjugated knowledges" of those who suffer and are excluded by the "dominant rationality" (Foucault).

Last, and a fitting note with which to conclude this chapter, we need to bring our social praxis to prayer *and* our prayer to social praxis. Here I reiterate the symbiosis between justice and holiness of life. Christian spirituality is to be historicized in a faith that does justice and peace, but there is also a time-tested wisdom in the tradition that one needs to set aside specific times for prayer, lest one lose sight of the Source of one's efforts in Christian living. Such times are opportunities to review one's praxis before God, to endeavor to see it as God sees it, and to be sustained, guided, and renewed by God's Spirit in fulfilling the social responsibilities of Christian faith.

Chapter 14

Pastoral Counseling

The focus of this chapter is the "everyday" pastoral counseling that the church carries on as part of its general ministry to human well-being, often called pastoral care.[1] As in previous chapters of Part III, I place this function of ministry in dialogue with a shared Christian praxis approach and indicate the potential its commitments and dynamics may have for facilitating an event of pastoral counseling. It offers a "model" with particular sensitivity to the religious education aspect of pastoral counseling, something typically present but not always attended to in counseling events. It seems wise at first to indicate the limitations and parameters of these reflections and to give an example of a counseling event facilitated along the lines of shared praxis; first, the limitations and parameters.

I am not a professionally trained pastoral psychotherapist, nor would pastoral counseling be readily recognized as a significant aspect of my work. I have great respect and appreciation for the competence of colleagues who are professionally trained and designated as pastoral counselors. They are well educated in their discipline and have years of supervised training in various models of depth psychotherapies; they are equipped to handle serious human psychoses and neuroses with healing effect. They are the people to whom I refer my own counselees when they struggle with emotional disorders beyond my limited competence to assist. I do not pretend, then, to dialogue with the clinical practice of advanced forms of pastoral psychotherapy. People so trained would have to discern whether or not a shared praxis "model" might be useful in their work.

On the other hand, short of in-depth clinical therapy carried on by extensively trained and accredited pastoral counselors, there is in every parish and community a wide range of opportunity and need for what I call, for lack of a better term, "everyday" pastoral counseling. It is an integral part of most ministers' work and frequently of my own. A Christian community should create an ethos of pastoral care, and people have a right to expect that they can approach the community, and especially its ministers, for competent counseling from a faith perspective. They may be in need of emotional healing for life's hurts, support in a time of crisis, guidance in decision making or times of confusion, reconciliation of alienation and brokenness, or spiritual sponsorship in their faith journey. All ministers should be prepared by their ministerial training and by ongoing education to be "everyday pastoral counselors" for people in such need.

Undoubtedly, the more professional training ministers have, the better equipped they are to handle even everyday needs. But lack of in-depth psychotherapeutic training should not deter ministers from offering an everyday kind of pastoral counseling. It would be a sad capitulation to the myth of professionalism, and indeed a serious default by a Christian community, if, for example, a pastoral minister were to routinely refer people mourning the death of a loved one to a professional counselor.[2] The inclusiveness that Seward Hiltner intended with the subtitle of his classic book of many years ago—*Pastoral Counseling: How Every Pastor Can Help People to Help Themselves* (first published 1949)[3]—is an important affirmation not to be lost to professionalization. My reflections here, then, are on the pastoral counseling that most ministers do every day regardless of designated function, and are informed by many hours as both counselor and counselee over the years, in both parish and university settings, with individuals and in groups. I also draw insights from some significant authors who share Hiltner's conviction that pastoral counseling is an aspect of the work of every pastoral minister.[4]

First, my example. Some time ago, a young woman came to talk with me. She was a first-year undergraduate student in a theology course I was teaching; I will call her Mary (not her real name). Mary did not make an appointment but simply knocked on my door; when seated after initial greetings she began to cry in a very heartrending way. As the tears subsided, she asked if she could talk to me as a friend, not as her theology professor. I, of course, agreed. Mary's first statement was that she felt totally overwhelmed by her problems and had decided to drop out of school but could not "go home," and so felt totally "lost." She seemed so troubled that, aware of my limits to offer the in-depth therapy she might need, I assured Mary I was happy to talk with her but strongly encouraged her to talk with a professional counselor and offered to make arrangements for her to see one immediately at the university health services. She adamantly resisted this, saying that it had been very difficult to get up the courage to talk to me; if I would not talk with her, she had no interest in seeing "a real counselor." With that, we proceeded. After an extended first session we had three subsequent meetings over the following ten days. I took a shared praxis approach to facilitate our dialogue because it seemed suitable; it was also the model I knew best. As to be expected, there was a great deal of overlap, adaptation, and repetition among the movements; however, I outline the pattern of our conversations according to their numbered sequence.

Since the generative theme and focus was already set—Mary's sense of feeling overwhelmed and "lost" (a word she often repeated)—and she had already expressed some trust in me, I invited her to portray a detailed picture of the state of her life as she saw it (movement 1). As Mary "expressed her present reality," the situation indeed seemed dismal. A straight-A student in high school, she now had failing grades in college and felt totally alienated from her family and friends and from the personal values with which she had been raised. My main response throughout this movement was to assure her of my empathy and understanding. I asked questions aimed at eliciting as complete a description as possible of her "lostness" and her life in general. Only when both of us had some sense of the issues and pain with which she was struggling did I begin to invite Mary to reflect on some of the personal and contextual causes of her "lostness."

Toward the end of our first session, and for most of the second one, I encouraged Mary in critical reflection on her present situation (movement 2). Here my questions and comments were to enable her to "see" some of the sources of her pain and confusion. I encouraged her to trace the history of when and why she began to feel overburdened, to uncover contributing factors, personal, familial, and social. I invited her to imagine ways she could alleviate some of the sense of lostness but with little effect. Mary felt overwhelmed and saw no way to tackle the problems in her life beyond being willing to continue talking with me. But she was beginning to be more aware of the familial and contextual influences shaping her present reality; for example, she recognized that some of her behavior was similar to the dysfunction in her family caused by alcoholism, and she also "remembered" that this was her first time living away from home and, at one point, commented, "Maybe I shouldn't be so down on myself for the mess I'm in."

In our third session, after some review of our conversations thus far, I introduced the parable of the prodigal son into our dialogue (movement 3). I prepared to do so ahead of time and for two reasons. First, Mary had said in an earlier conversation that in one crisis moment she had tried "to read the Bible" but had been disappointed. This, as well as that she had come to talk to someone identified with Christian theology and ministry, indicated that Mary was at least not closed to considering a religious source of help for her pain. Second, as I reflected on our first two conversations, the parable kept coming back to me as paradigmatic of Mary's situation; perhaps it might offer some hope in the midst of her own "far country" experience.

We spent our third meeting on the text (Luke 15:11–32), reading it through line by line, I inviting Mary to express the thoughts and feelings the story elicited from her. When it seemed apt, I shared information about the context of the text: how totally the prodigal had left home; how complete his sense of being lost and alienated must have been; how unusual it was in that cultural context for the father to welcome home and forgive him after what he had done; that the robe, ring, and shoes upon return were symbols of elevated status in the family, and so on. Mary readily identified with the "far country" experience of the prodigal, and what I recognized as a breakthrough was when she fastened on the line "when he came to himself" (Luke 15:17; we were using the RSV). Mary commented that maybe being lost could be an opportunity to begin to find her own true self. She also recognized that doing so would entail changing some of the social circumstances of her life. In this third conversation, movements 3 and 4 frequently overlapped and, though I offered some exegesis of the passage for consideration, her own hermeneutics and appropriation of it was primary. I encouraged her to return to it often before our next meeting.

At the beginning of our fourth session, I invited Mary to tell me her thoughts and feelings about her situation and about the Scripture reading since our last conversation (movement 4). The gloom seemed to have lifted a bit, but she was apprehensive and unclear about what it would mean for her to "come home." She was adamant that she did not want to go back to her "old home" (in the sense both of how she perceived her life even before the present crisis, *and* that she did not wish to function in her family as heretofore). She also felt she could take some steps to move out of her present sense of "lostness." I asked her what might be "one first step" in order to "come home" to herself, to a different life-style (movement 5). One was to join an A.C.O.A. group (Adult Children of Alcoholics) that I had mentioned previously (my vision statement). A second was that she felt ready for ongoing counseling; we decided together that it would be best for her to do this with a clinical psychologist I recommended in the counseling services of the university; she called from my office to make her first appointment. I invited her to drop in any time for "a chat with a friend" if she felt like it.

I saw Mary many times over the years until she graduated. It was clear that she benefited significantly from membership in the A.C.O.A. group and from her work with the professional counselor. Our subsequent conversations tended to focus more on the faith dimensions of her life, and eventually she declared me her "spiritual director." More professionally trained counselors may discern a lack of expertise in my work with Mary. Yet it exemplifies an encounter in which the style of counseling used reflects the dynamics of shared Christian praxis.

The Nature, Purpose, and Resources of Pastoral Counseling

Nature.   The standard pattern in the literature of the field is to see pastoral counseling as a particular function within a broader enterprise, typically called "pastoral care" (see note 1). Authors disagree on precisely what services pastoral care includes or excludes It appears that most use it as a generic term for the functions of service offered by designated ministers to particular persons in particular situations. Fowler, for example, writes that "pastoral care consists of all the ways a community of faith, under pastoral leadership, intentionally sponsors the awakening, shaping, rectifying, healing and ongoing growth in vocation of Christian persons and community, under the pressure and power of the in-breaking kingdom of God."[5] Gerkin is equally inclusive and describes pastoral care as "the pastoral facilitation of the Christian life in the world."[6]

The tasks of *kerygma, koinonia, diakonia,* and *leitourgia* are expressions of "pastoral care" in this generic sense. More particularly, pastoral counseling is a specific function of pastoral care. Its distinctive nature is that it is a conversational activity with intent to enable particular persons to handle the crisis or opportune moments of life in a growthful way and from a faith perspective (i.e., pastoral). It may be done in a group setting as well as one-on-one, but typically each participant is attending to a particular personal issue. Clinebell writes, "Pastoral counseling, one dimension of pastoral care, is the utilization of a variety of healing (therapeutic) methods to help people handle their problems and crises more growthfully and thus experience healing of their brokenness."[7] Note Clinebell's emphasis on both crisis management and growth, a point I return to under the discussion of purpose.

Like many authors, Clinebell distinguishes pastoral counseling from "pastoral psychotherapy," or its synonym "depth pastoral counseling." The latter is "a long-term helping process aimed at effecting fundamental changes in the counselee's personality"; it uses "psychotherapeutic methods to enable people to change basic aspects of their personality and behavior patterns to make them more constructive and creative."[8] Following these distinctions that seem to have wide acceptance in the literature, hereafter I use the term *pastoral counseling* to refer what I described earlier as "everyday" counseling, as distinct from in-depth pastoral psychotherapy.

Purpose.   Pastoral counseling can have any or all of five primary purposes. It may intend to *heal* people in their brokenness from the hurts of life and from personality disorders; to *sustain* people to live faithfully in life's struggles and to support them in times of crisis (death, divorce, illness, etc.); to offer *guidance* in times of confusion and decision making; to *reconcile* people with themselves, others, and God and to assure them of God's never-ending mercy;[9] to offer *nurture* and companionship in people's spiritual journey.[10] This latter function is more often called "spiritual direction" in my Catholic tradition. It is not typically identified as a form of pastoral counseling because it builds on opportune moments and issues for spiritual growth, but I believe the work of pastoral counselors is enhanced if they see spiritual direction as an aspect of their ministry.[11] I appreciate Clinebell's insistence that pastoral counseling should not focus exclusively on alleviating crises—a tendency in much of the literature—but should also promote growth toward "spiritual and ethical wholeness."[12]

All these functions can overlap, and they have the common purpose of enabling people to realize their Christian faith in humanizing and life-giving ways in their particular circumstances. In this sense, I'm convinced that all pastoral counseling has a religious education dimension; it is difficult to imagine fulfilling its purposes without helping to inform, form, and transform people in Christian identity and agency.

Resources. What now of procedures and resources? Pastoral counseling uses a great variety of methods and procedures—typically called "models"—depending on the occasion, the background and personality of the counselee(s), the training, perspective, and natural ability of the counselor, and so on. In general, however, all procedures employed should be processes of empowerment, that is, ways of "helping people to help themselves." The counselor is not to play an authoritarian or benevolent role that encourages, as Hiltner puts it, the counselee's issue to be "shoved over to the pastor for solution." Rather, counselors should use procedures likely to bring people to their own agency without "reinforcing the illusion that the way to solve a problem is to get an authority to do it for us." Hiltner adds, "By proceeding on the assumption that the creative dynamic forces which can produce needed change are potentially present within the individual already and do not have to be 'poured in,' the only lasting results are achieved."[13] (Note again the educational aspect; *e-ducare* means to draw or lead out.)

I'm convinced that to be a catalyst of empowerment for the person or group toward their own agency and growth, *the counselor's procedure is primarily to listen to and act as co-interpreter of people's stories, drawing as appropriate upon professional counseling competencies to do so, and because it is pastoral counseling, to make accessible and co-interpret the Christian community's Story/Vision a propos the person's life issues.* My position also reflects what Gerkin poses as the foundation of counseling procedures, namely, "the notion that the self, in the particularity of its experiences of living from birth, develops a narrative or 'story of the self' that, at the deepest levels, is connected to the larger narratives and their metaphors of the context into which the individual has been born."[14] Elsewhere he explains, "Pastoral counselors are, more than anything else, listeners to and interpreters of stories. Persons seek out a pastoral counselor because they need someone to listen to their story."[15] Pastoral counseling is to proceed as "a hermeneutical dialogue"[16] in which the story/vision of the counselee(s) is shared and interpreted in mutual dialogue with the counselor. Though the primary agenda is the historical praxis of the counselee(s), in addition to her or his own story/vision the pastoral counselor draws upon three sources of interpretation and explanation to aid the hermeneutical process: psychology, sociology, and Christian Story/Vision.

Psychology. According to their level of training and competence, pastoral counselors draw from scientific study of the human psyche perspectives and procedures for interpreting human behavior that can have a clarifying, healing, and empowering effect. There are many schools of such "applied psychology" with various approaches to interpreting and reshaping emotional/mental states, attitudes, and behavior. All of them, however, focus with therapeutic intent on what Anton Boisen called "the living human document":[17] the historical person as an interpreter of her or his own life praxis. All of them take seriously both conscious actions, thoughts, and feelings and the inner dynamic forces of the psyche that influence personality and agency without being consciously recognized. Pastoral counselors can draw upon psychology to enable counselees to interpret their conscious life and to probe the unconscious sources of their praxis as well. We can generally expect that the more training one has in such therapeutic resources, the more effective one's pastoral counseling is likely to be.

Sociology. Pastoral counseling heretofore has been unduly caught in a psychological paradigm—and a rather individualized one at that. This imbalance is now widely recognized by authors in the field. Gerkin notes critically, "As practiced by its practitioners, pastoral psychotherapy in its methodology has come to rest its primary work of decision making and action on psychological and psychotherapeutic criteria."[18] And Clinebell writes, "The weakness of much pastoral care has been its hyperindividualism. Privatized pastoral care and counseling (along with privatized religion in general) ignore the pervasive ways in which racism, sexism, ageism, speciesism, nationalism, militarism, economic exploitation and political oppression cripple human wholeness on a massive scale in all societies."[19] An exclusively psychological paradigm for pastoral counseling plays into one of the most irresponsible aspects of the modern Western ethos—a rugged individualism whose *modus operandi* is to "take care of number one." Pastoral counseling must draw upon the insights of sociology and social analysis if it is to be an antidote to "hyperindividualism" and a catalyst for "self-other-society wholeness" (Clinebell), or of "a faith that does justice for peace" (chapter 13).

Ironically, a sociological perspective is essential even to promote the authentic well-"being" of an individual counselee. An exclusively psychological paradigm is more likely to enable people to "cope" with problems in a privatized way than to question and change the immediate and public structures of their lives that help cause their problems in the first place. Such pastoral counseling, to use Freire's educational language, tends to "fit" people into their sociocultural context as it is, rather than empowering them to deal with it critically and creatively. Then even their own personal well-"being" is not well served. Clinebell writes wisely, "Since wholeness is always relational, self-fulfillment is a psychological impossibility. Growth pursued egocentrically, for its own sake, becomes a cul-de-sac."[20]

Pastoral counselors are to enable counselees to see "the wider picture" of their historical reality, to analyze its social "linkages," its cultural "dimensions," its interrelated "levels" (Holland and Henriot), to recognize the social causes and consequences of their present praxis, to realize that "the personal is also political." When the counselor engages people in social as well as personal reasoning, remembering, and imagining, they can address both the inner and outer causes of crisis (which typically are a dialectical unity). Likewise, the internal healing, growth, and liberation that emerge for people are more likely to be externalized and turned toward transforming the contexts of their pain. The more informed and aware counselors are about the "social construction of reality," and the more trained they are to bring people to social consciousness and decision making, the more "effective" their pastoral counseling is likely to be.

Christian Story/Vision. The third resource pastoral counselors draw upon is the practical wisdom in faith that the Christian community has inherited and come to over time. The resource of Christian Story/Vision is what qualifies counseling as "pastoral," and shapes its uniqueness as counseling. In *Christian* pastoral counseling the community Story/Vision should be interpreted by and brought to interpret, heal, and lend new possibilities to the lives of counselees.

From the time "pastoral" counseling emerged as a ministerial art to be studied in North American seminaries, the word *pastoral* (used of a ministerial activity in a particular situation) was intended to signify precisely its faith resource and intent. Gerkin notes, however, that as pastoral counseling "borrowed from secular theories and therapies," there was a weakening of its faith perspective and a concomitant confusion about how and if "pastoral" qualifies "counseling." This loss of a faith perspective is now widely recognized; summarizing a prevalent trend in the current literature, Gerkin writes,

> Happily, as recognition of the identity problems within pastoral care and counseling has increased, there has come a strong call for recovery of pastoral care and counseling's theological rootage. This move toward reconsideration of rootage is a significant one in more than simply the obvious sense that theology is central to all forms of ministry. Hermeneutically speaking, it signals an awareness that identity is linked to origins, most particularly origins that supply the deep metaphors and meanings that tell us who we are.[21]

In addition to any faith convictions about Christian Story/Vision as a symbolic mediation of God's self-disclosure and of the practical wisdom in faith that this community has come to over time, there are typically three existential reasons why it is to be an interpretive resource in *pastoral* counseling: (1) the faith context, (2) the expectation of the counselee(s), (3) the identity of the pastoral counselor.

First, the context is usually some kind of Christian community to which a person comes for counseling. The counseling takes place within the ambit of the community's overall function of pastoral care.[22] Second, people who come to a Christian community for counseling can be presumed to have some expectation that the help offered is from a Christian faith perspective. It seems reasonable to presume, unless they clearly indicate otherwise, that they expect to have some access to the tradition of meaning and ethic in this faith community. Further, Gerkin implies that it is for more than reasons of faith and piety that pastoral counselors should draw upon Christian Story/Vision as an interpretive resource for people's present reality. If Christians are to analyze their historical praxis with any reliability, then turning to their "religious origins," which supply their deepest sources of meaning, ethic, and identity is an imperative. An educational perspective on pastoral counseling suggests that to be healed, sustained, guided, reconciled, and nurtured, Christians are often in significant need of education (sometimes "remedial") about the primary symbols, beliefs, practices, and so forth of their faith tradition. Third, pastoral counselors are typically designated (somehow) representatives of a Christian community and are presumed to be such by their counselees. Their ministerial vocation and the expectation of their designating community call upon them to make accessible the paradigms of meaning and ethics of Christian Story/Vision in their counseling ministry.

Nor should the *pastoral* counselor's "faith perspective" be limited to drawing upon the faith tradition as a hermeneutical resource or as lending an appropriate story, metaphor, or image on occasion when there is obvious correlation between it and the life issues of counselees (as in my opening example). The whole encounter and its procedures are to be suffused with a faith perspective and purpose. It should reflect the conviction that the "health" to be promoted is ultimately a spiritual wholeness,[23] that human brokenness can be healed and the quest for meaning satisfied by right relationships with God, self, others, and creation. A faith perspective is to shape the questions pastoral counselors ask, the issues they raise, the myths and metaphors, stories and symbols they make accessible as resources of interpretation and explanation, the images and hopes they raise up, and the criteria they propose to people for decision making in their lives. Maintaining a faith perspective throughout the dynamic of a pastoral counseling event while also avoiding moralizing and sermonizing is difficult and challenging. I can think of three cautions that may help to avoid these pitfalls.

First, like all pastoral ministers, counselors draw upon Christian Story/Vision (and especially its Story dimension) as a paradigmatic source of meaning, truth, and value. As I have indicated many times, the underlying conviction in doing so is that these paradigms of and for life from the community's tradition can be personally appropriated by counselees as sources of life, healing and insight, consolation and hope, in the present. But counselors should never pose Christian Story as a shortcut to wholeness or a source of easy answers to life's problems. In fact, the tradition is a source of insight and healing, consolation and hope precisely because it is a mirror of the existential pains, struggles, confusions, and problems of everyday life. But it does not explain these away or banish the threat of chaos or the reality of suffering and death. On the contrary, Christian tradition should insert some "hard realities" or "facts of life" into a pastoral counseling event. Clinebell writes, "A variety of biblical images make it clear that, though wholeness is a gift of God, it takes effort, intentionality, and often painful struggle to receive this gift by developing our potentials. Images of taking up one's cross (Matt. 16:24); of dying and being born again (John 3:3; Rom. 6:6); of the narrow gate and strait way leading to the new age; of a radical transformation or conversion (metanoia)—all communicate this truth."[24] Precisely because it reflects hard-won wisdom from the realities of life, "the biblical view offers a healthy corrective to the superficial optimism that sometimes appears in humanistic psychologies."[25]

Second, and emphasizing the Vision aspect, pastoral counselors draw upon Christian Story/Vision to challenge people with new possibilities for action and to offer guidelines for decision making. But the Vision they propose should also seem "warranted" to counselees, in that through their own process of discernment they come to see for themselves the practical wisdom of its counsels and ethical criteria. To present Christian Vision as ethical norms whose authority is based solely on faith is not likely to be therapeutic or empowering. Though pastoral counselors are to draw upon Christian Story/Vision for ethical guidelines, counselees need to see for themselves that these guidelines are wise, not because "they are in the Bible" (or "the church says so," etc.), but rather that they are in the Bible because they are wise.

On Christian Story/Vision as source of ethical guidelines for pastoral counseling, I particularly appreciate the work of Don Browning. He has been most influential in helping ministers recognize that pastoral counseling is a form of ethical discourse and that the Christian tradition provides "the moral context of pastoral care."[26] Browning is concerned that as pastoral counselors draw insights from psychology and sociology, they never feign value neutrality in their use, and that they draw their ethical guidelines from Christian tradition. Pastoral counseling should enable people to discern *what* they are to do (deontic issues) and *who* they are to be and become (aretic or character identity issues). Christian Story/Vision can suggest ethical guidelines from the most general level, an overarching vision or metaphor (e.g., reign of God), down to specific "rules and roles" (see chapter 10, note 1). Browning says it can do so with philosophical warrant because a Christian ethic reflects a universal structure of practical moral reasoning, and such warrant is needed because of the pluralism both within and outside the churches.[27] Here again, an educational perspective can help pastoral counselors to give people access to Christian Story/Vision in a way that enables them to recognize and choose for themselves what they are to do and who they are to become.

My third caution is that explicitly religious language and guidelines and the encouraging of religious practices like prayer, Bible reading, and worship, should be introduced in a counseling context with great care and sensitivity. As Clinebell warns, "Such symbols and practices mean many things to many people. For some they carry heavy negative, emotional freight. They can be used in rigid, legalistic ways that arouse inappropriate guilt feelings and block creative dialogue and spiritual growth in counseling." He suggests nine guidelines for the pastoral counselor; the first three deserve to be highlighted: "(1) Use religious words and resources only after one has some awareness of persons' problems and their background, their feelings and attitudes regarding religion. . . . (2) Before using resources such as prayer or scripture in care or counseling, ask if this would be meaningful. . . . (3) After using a traditional religious resource, give persons an opportunity to discuss the thoughts, feelings and fantasies they had during the experience."[28]

To summarize by way of procedure, pastoral counselors help people to help themselves through a dialogical hermeneutic of the praxis of their own lives. As "a guide . . . to the interpretive process of God's people,"[29] pastoral counselors draw upon and make accessible the healing and life-giving resources of psychology, sociology, and the faith tradition. The primary "language world" is that of the counselees as they name and reflect critically on their life praxis. Their life praxis is placed in dialectic with the language worlds of psychology, sociology, and Christian Story/Vision as both counselor and counselee(s) engage in interpreting and explaining the latter's life to promote well-being and wholeness for self, others, and society.

A Shared Praxis Style of Pastoral Counseling

Before placing shared Christian praxis in dialogue with my understanding of pastoral counseling, I first note that there is a fundamental affinity between Christian religious education and pastoral counseling. Although they are discreet functions of ministry, both contribute to the general purpose of enabling people to appropriate Christian tradition to their life contexts, and their intended outcomes can be variously described as wholeness, holiness, conversion, conation or wisdom in Christian faith, and so on. Among other things, they are both modes of "doing theology," or at least of doing what is presently understood as "practical" or "pastoral" theology,[30] in that they enable people to interpret and live their lives with the practical wisdom of Christian faith. I agree with Clinebell when he claims that religious education and pastoral counseling are "natural allies."[31]

I'm convinced that there is always a pastoral counseling dimension to religious education and a religious education dimension to pastoral counseling.[32] Yet as distinct ventures with their own assets, each one can contribute to the other. Religious educators can learn much from pastoral counselors about listening, about how to elicit people's own inner truth, feelings, and attitudes, about facilitating group dialogue, this last being essential for participative approaches to religious education. Greater conversance with the literature of pastoral counseling could help religious educators draw insights from a wider body of psychological tradition than is typically our wont; our praxis has been significantly informed by developmental psychology, but we have largely ignored the more psychoanalytic traditions. Likewise, the praxis of pastoral counselors is enhanced if they have a religious education perspective in their work. It could make them more alert to "teachable moments" and more adept at resourcing them to counselees' advantage. So much pastoral counseling calls for what is, in fact, religious education (or what Hiltner calls "religious re-education") if symbols, beliefs, and practices of the Christian tradition are to be life-giving for people. Religious education procedures can help pastoral counselors to help people confront and correct the consequences of miseducation in their religious background and can suggest styles and guidelines for making the faith tradition accessible in life-giving ways.

I'm convinced that shared Christian praxis can suggest one appropriate model for facilitating a pastoral counseling event in either a one-on-one or a group context. I recognize that there are a great variety of approaches favored by different "schools" of pastoral counseling. Steckel writes, "Not many years ago the Rogerians and the Freudians contended for the theoretical souls of the pastoral counseling movement. Then came the Jungians, the neo-Adlerians, Gestalt, Transactional Analysis, Logotherapy, Reality Therapy, Rational-Emotive Therapy, Behavioral Methods, and a host of others."[33] Shared praxis can suggest a schema for facilitating a counseling event that is sufficiently adaptable to be used with many of the perspectives of the "schools" just listed. Without becoming a straitjacket, its movements can prompt pastoral counselors to weave together a hermeneutical dialogue around counselees' praxis and draw upon the resources of psychology, sociology, and Christian Story/Vision to enable them to come to greater wholeness and holiness of life. Beyond this, I can think of two other assets that a shared praxis approach can have for pastoral counseling.

1. Because of its educational sensitivity, shared Christian praxis can help counselors to give counselees access to Christian Story/Vision of faith. It can make them more alert to counselees' need in this regard and enable them to give access in life-giving ways—dialogically, in partnership, in a disclosure manner, without imposing. Further, the approach can offer hermeneutical guidelines of interpretation and explanation (see chapter 8) to enable pastoral counselors to make Christian Story/Vision accessible in ways likely to be heard and personally appropriated by people to their own lives.

2. The emphasis in shared praxis on critical reflection, and especially on social analysis in movement 2, could serve as an antidote to privatizing tendencies in pastoral counseling. It suggests ways to con-

sistently include a sociological perspective. Its emphasis on critical reflection that is both personal and social has the potential to be both
healing and emancipatory for participants themselves and socially
transforming for their situations. If pastoral counseling includes critical
and social reasoning, analytical and social remembering, creative and
social imagining, it helps to release repressed dialogue, debunk oppressive social myths and controlling ideologies, uncover "forgotten"
memories—personal and social—that hold people bound to their influence, and activate imagination for new possibilities on all levels of existence, personal, interpersonal, social/political, and cosmic.[34] A shared
praxis model of pastoral counseling can enable people to move beyond
"coping" in their present context to both change themselves and reconstruct their situation.

For each movement, I indicate its possible form and function in the
dynamics of a pastoral counseling event. The approach can be used in
a context of group counseling,[35] but for focus I fashion these reflections around a one-on-one counseling occasion. Obviously, the movements overlap a great deal, especially in an ongoing counseling relationship, sometimes begin one place and then another, and get varied
emphasis. Nevertheless, the movements can be "markers" to remind the
counselor of activities to be attended to.

The Focusing Activity and Movement 1.   In the literature, I have yet
to find an author who does not emphasize the importance of the quality
of the "counseling relationship." Emphasis on a positive emotional
environment in a counseling event is to be expected. By the very nature
and purpose of pastoral counseling, healing and empowerment are to
begin in the actual event; the quality of the relationship is crucial to the
therapy. The focusing activity in a shared praxis approach suggests a
concerted effort, and from the beginning, to establish a subject-to-
subject partnership of dialogue in which each is willing to speak his or
her own word and to hear the word of the other. A very detached and
aloof relationship on the counselor's part, for example, or posing one's
function as solely to ask questions and listen without affect, would not
be congruent with a shared praxis style of counseling.

Undoubtedly, a counseling event is a service to the counselee, and
the integrity of this purpose must be honored. Counselors should not
use the occasion to focus on their own pains or crises. Yet counselors
using this model *are* co-interpreters of a person's "being" in place and
time and cannot participate in such hermeneutics without engaging as
agent-subjects willing to share their own story as well. Counselees
should experience their pastoral counselor as a "soul friend,"[36] a companion "pilgrim in time" who has deep empathy and goodwill for them
on their journey. Whether the encounter is a single session, a first of
many, or one in an ongoing relationship, it is crucial for the counselor
to establish or reestablish at the beginning and then nurture throughout an I/Thou relationship of mutuality and dialogue. This also entails

encouraging an environment of hospitality and respect, trust and open-ness, one in which the counselee feels "safe" and "at home" enough to take the risk of honest conversation.

Beyond the "focusing activity" of attending to the quality of the relationship and emotional environment, in my experience, establishing a specific focus or generative theme for the dialogue is usually done by the counselee by a statement of the issue that prompted him or her to seek counseling. In some situations the counselor may need to pose an opening question that invites a person to establish the theme for a particular occasion, especially with more reticent people (e.g., "What is it that seems most important for us to talk about today?"). If a counselor has very good reason to suggest a theme (e.g., knows that the person is pained by some recent loss), it should be posed as an invitation, with openness for the counselee to choose another focus (e.g., "Well, shall we talk about your recent bereavement, or is there something else you would prefer to talk about?").

When a generative theme has emerged, movement 1 of shared praxis suggests that counselors invite counselees to articulate as clearly and completely as possible their own praxis around the issue, and how they are "dealing" with it—their behaviors, beliefs, feelings, emotions, pains, fears, anxieties, attitudes, and so on. The intent here is to enable people to name and begin to interpret their own reality. It is crucial that counselees do the naming/expressing here; counselors should never presume that they "know already what the problem is." A counselor may be familiar with recurring patterns of crisis and opportunity in the human journey, but every person's context is unique, and therapy be-gins by people naming it for themselves. To personally name one's present praxis is always the first step to healing and growth. The coun-selor has a twofold role in movement 1: to ask, with gentleness, probing questions that help elicit as complete an expression of present praxis as the person can venture at this time; and to listen in a way that conveys understanding, identification with, and empathy for the counselee. For the latter, one's body language may be as significant as what is said out loud.

Movement 2. The second movement prompts counselors to facilitate critical reflection on the causes and consequences, as the counselee sees them, of present praxis around the topic of conversation. Critical reflection recurs frequently throughout an event; however, it is particularly fitting immediately *after* or even *as* the counselee names present praxis. In facilitating in-depth personal and socially critical reflection, counselors can draw upon the resources of both psychology and sociology.

Freud was the first to establish that human behavior, thoughts, and feelings are shaped by dynamic forces that operate at a deep level in the psyche beyond purview of consciousness. The counselor's service, to the extent that training and competence allow, is to fashion questions and make suggestions that enable the person to bring into consciousness and probe those deeper levels of the psyche, to uncover the repressed dialogue, forgotten memories, and neglected images around the issue at hand. The intent here is to bring the interior sources and elements of the issue to recognition and to loosen images of new possibility for it. The healing and emancipatory potential of a counseling event depends significantly on this "un-covering" and "dis-covering" activity.

In movement 2 dynamic, counselors can also raise fitting questions and insights as suggested by sociological resources and from their own social consciousness. Even obvious questions that invite counselees to describe the social, cultural, political, and economic situation of their lives, how they perceive the influence of those factors on their present behaviors, worries, fears, and how they can or should change them may be effective to encourage a social consciousness. If systemic analysis is not encouraged, the social causes of conflict, pain, or lack of growth may be left hidden, and thus their consequences for self and others fatalistically accepted as inevitable "givens." Counselors should help counselees to engage the "context" as well as the "text" of themselves as "living human documents," to uncover the relativity (i.e., always related to a context) of what appears to be and to pose new images of what might be or ought to be.[37] According to competence, counselors can prompt the fullest expression of critical reflection—critical and social reasoning, analytical and social remembering, creative and social imagining (see chapter 7, section 3).

In movement 2 the counselor also has a dual role: to listen in a way that conveys understanding, empathy, and support; to pose the kinds of probing questions and, as relevant, to make available the insights from sociology and psychology that prompt the counselee to critical reflection on present praxis. Such insights must be presented as catalysts for the counselee's critical reflection, not as "answers" to be accepted. There may be occasions when it is fitting for the counselor to propose an interpretive response to the counselee's movement 1 conversation (e.g., "Could it be that your sense of being exploited and unappreciated at work is causing tension in your marriage at home?"), but, again, it must be offered only to deepen the person's own critical reflection rather than as a definitive pronouncement.[38] From a shared praxis movement 2 perspective, the counselor is to bring the counselee to a dialectical hermeneutic of present praxis, that is, to see its possible assets, its liabilities, and how it might be or should be changed. On occasion, there will also be a dialectic present in the dialogue between counselor and counselee. Or, as Clinebell puts it more patently, the counselor is to offer "both accepting love and honest confrontation."[39]

Movement 3. This prompts pastoral counselors to honor Christian Story/Vision as a source of practical wisdom in faith, but I reiterate that, like the other movements, movement 3 can be intertwined throughout the whole encounter. A Christian faith perspective can shape the questions and interpretations posed in the opening movements and offer hope and guidance in the closing ones. But making Christian Story/Vision accessible as a symbolic source of meaning, ethic, and value seems most appropriate in response to the counselee's critical reflection on present praxis—at least, it would not typically be done at the beginning or after new decisions are already made.

I reiterate the need for caution here, especially by the counselor. Clinebell warns that for many people who seek pastoral counseling "their religion is pathogenic—sickness-producing and growth-blocking." The last thing they need is to have their religious stories, symbols, and practices raised up again "in rigid, authoritarian, reality-denying, idolatrous ways."[40] It is important then for the counselor to honor the hermeneutical guidelines and the style of making accessible I outlined in chapter 8 as essential to a shared praxis model. Adapting a summary of the guidelines there to a pastoral counseling event here, they place the following responsibilities on the counselor. In general, all biblical, theological, and spiritual resources should be interpreted in ways most likely to empower the realization of the values of God's reign—love, freedom, peace, justice, healing, right relationship, faithfulness, forgiveness, hope, and so on—in this person's life and, through him or her, in the world. More particular guidelines: (1) being cognizant of one's own perspective and of the needs of the counselee, help the person to uncover the life-giving truths and values in Christian Story/Vision; (2) be alert for distortions ("pathogens") in the person's present faith understanding and confront them if present; (3) raise up the "dangerous memories" from the tradition that call into question perspectives and arrangements that are taken for granted and propose imaginative possibilities for the person's healing and growth in wholeness. As the counselee appropriates the resources of Christian tradition, the counselor encourages the person to consider continuity with what is essential to Christian Story, to imagine consequences that are creative of God's reign for self and others, and to take seriously the present corporate wisdom of the "church." This style of making accessible is done in a dialogical, disclosure, and engaging way for the counselee, preferably in a "co-hermeneutics," with access (movement 3) and appropriation (movement 4) constantly overlapping.

Movement 4. All the activities suggested by the movements of shared praxis are essential when used as a model of pastoral counseling, but perhaps none is more crucial than the movement 4 dynamic of appropriation. A "dialectical hermeneutics" is present already in movement 2 activity of interpreting the counselee's praxis. But movement 4 reminds counselors that they are to deliberately structure into the counseling event opportunities to recognize and "make one's own" the insights that are emerging, be they from psychology, sociology, the faith tradition, or their mutual exchange. Coercion, manipulation, or authoritarianism are all foreign to the spirit of a shared praxis approach wherever it is used, but nowhere are they more alien and worthless than in pastoral counseling. Without a movement 4 activity the purpose of helping people to help themselves is vitiated. The most brilliant insights of the counselor and of the social sciences and the most life-giving paradigms from the faith tradition are of little avail for health and wholeness unless counselees come to recognize them for themselves, to personally appropriate them and make them their own.

A pastoral counseling event using a shared praxis model allows ample opportunity for the participant to enter into a dialectical hermeneutics that places her or his own critical reflection on praxis in dialectic and dialogue with the insights of psychology, sociology, and the faith tradition. Counselors can prompt counselees to discern what is or is not making sense, what is or is not ringing true from those resources, and what they want to take as life-giving into their own context. The counselor poses questions that prompt such personal appropriation, creates an emotional environment to foster it, and maintains presence to the person as an empathetic and understanding listener.

Movement 5.   Whether the primary intent of a pastoral counseling event is to help heal, sustain, guide, reconcile, or nurture in holiness, or a combination of these purposes, it is to have humanizing consequences for people's identity and agency (their "being"), and the fruits should be evident in a new or renewed praxis by counselees. Its dynamic should be likely to bring people to act in more healthful, "whole," and holy ways for themselves and for others. Movement 5 of shared praxis reminds counselors to regularly provide an opportunity for such decision making. Decisions may reflect an affective, a cognitive, or a behavioral adjustment by the person and may pertain to the personal, interpersonal, or contextual levels of one's life. The pastoral counselor is to formulate questions that invite praxislike decisions, provide support as they emerge, and at times suggest possible modes of action, but always in an open-ended and invitational way. (e.g., "Would you want to talk over this issue with your spouse?"). Counselors should avoid all semblance of pressure for decision making; their service is to provide the opportunity/dynamic for it but then to remember that the healing and growth is more likely to come in the *kyros* of God's time than in the *chronos* of the counseling hour.

PART IV

POSTSCRIPT:
THE SPIRITUALITY OF
SHARED CHRISTIAN PRAXIS

Prologue

PART IV is a *postscript* in that I could write it only after the work was completed; it draws together many of the book's themes and proposals in summary form. But like most postscripts it adds a new thought too, or one that could be missed otherwise. It makes more explicit and weaves together in a new configuration two foci implicit throughout: (1) the *theological* convictions that I propose as foundational to a shared *Christian* praxis approach and (2) the *spiritual* commitments that I perceive the approach asks of and encourages in the "hearts" of people who use it. I present them as one statement: "My Pedagogical Creed as a Christian Religious Educator" (chapter 15). As in Parts I and II, my language pattern is again educational, although one can readily make the correlation with other functions of ministry. First, in this prologue, I explain my perspective here and why I weave theological and spiritual foundations together as "my pedagogical creed."

Like every educational approach, shared praxis reflects responses to foundational issues that can be articulated philosophically—an understanding of the person, of human history, of what it means to know, of the meaning of truth, and so on; some of these I addressed in Part I within my general proposal of an "epistemic ontology." The foundations of shared praxis could also be stated in distinctly pedagogical terms, as I have often done throughout. Likewise, the approach reflects claims and convictions that need warrant from the social sciences; I have left much to be said in this regard but have also drawn from them here. But beyond its foundations in philosophy, pedagogy, and the social sciences, when shared praxis is employed as shared *Christian* praxis, when it is sponsored by a Christian community and used to educate for conation/wisdom in Christian faith, the commitments and dynamics of the process are complemented and qualified by its faith context and purpose. This warrants a statement of its *theological* and *spiritual* foundations. They have practical import because they shape what is taught through both the content and process of shared Christian praxis.

I first note that my statement of *theological foundations* is a personal one, shaped by my faith community and by my own identity as a Catholic Christian. It is *my* theology, what *I* propose as adequate to the process itself and appropriate to a mainline Christian perspective. People of other or of no theological persuasion could well have fitting foundations that are other than mine for a shared praxis approach to education in their context. People are now using a shared praxis approach to other forms of education and to religious education in traditions other than Christian. It is employed in Christian churches by congregations that span a broad spectrum of theological opinion. Clearly the approach can find fitting foundations in many philosophical and religious traditions, and in Christian traditions other than mainline Trinitarian Christianity. My intent, then, is to propose theological foundations that are resonant and clarifying for religious educators that share my mainline Christian perspective and especially for those committed to an approach like shared praxis.

My second and companion focus is the *spiritual commitments* that *I* perceive this approach asks of and nurtures in the hearts of its educators. Shared Christian praxis apart from its agents is an ideational construct. If its foundations are to be realized in history, they must be the owned and operative commitments of the people who employ it, and the heart-held commitments that are operative in a religious educator's praxis constitute her or his spirituality as a religious educator.[1]

Karl Rahner writes, "Spirituality is a mysterious and tender thing about which we can speak only with great difficulty."[2] This caution is especially to the point for religious educators. "Things spiritual" are our stock-in-trade, and we readily fall into the easy talk of salespeople. We are more prone to speak about it for others, however, and less likely to reflect on the kind of holiness asked of ourselves by the very service we render as religious educators. Yet our attempts to be spiritual guides must surely be grounded in and a resource for our own spiritual journeys.

The distinctive spirituality asked of Christian religious educators can only be appreciated within the more general notion of Christian spirituality, of which it is a particular instance. As I understand it, *Christian spirituality is people's conscious attending to God's loving initiative and saving presence in their lives and their response to the movement of God's Spirit, who moves their spirits to freely commit themselves through a Christian community to God's reign of fullness of life for all, by living in right and loving relationship with God, self, others, and creation, according to the way of Jesus.*[3]

The time-honored conviction of Christian tradition is that the grace of "conscious attending" to God's presence and discernment of the movement of God's Spirit is sustained by prayer, personal and communal. The "spirit" in Christian *spirit*uality refers to both the Holy

Spirit and our own, with the former empowering the latter to commitment, without violating our freedom. There is always an ecclesial dimension to Christian spirituality; it is realized through and sustained within a Christian faith community. And Christian spirituality is a life lived in the right and loving relationship of God's reign following the model and enabled by God's grace in Jesus. All Christians are called by baptism to this holiness and wholeness of life.

Because it is historicized in life, the particularity of people's praxis lends distinction to their spirituality. This is why we can speak of a spirituality of the Christian religious educator. It is made particular by our educational praxis, which in turn is both an expression of and a resource for our own growth in holiness. For example, all Christians are called to live in "right and loving relationship," and religious educators are to realize this particularly in how and what they teach; all are to attend to God's loving initiative and saving presence in their lives, and Christian religious educators are to teach in a way that prompts people to do so, and so. Even more specifically, it is possible to propose a spirituality that is needed and nurtured by a particular approach to religious education, like shared Christian praxis.

In Christian tradition creeds have symbolized both the theological convictions and the spiritual commitments to which Christians are called to "give their hearts." It seems fitting then to weave my version of the theological and spiritual foundations for shared Christian praxis into a creedal statement; combining them also reflects my conviction that the "heart" of such an approach is the "heart" of the religious educator or minister who would use it.[4] The convictions and commitments reflected in shared Christian praxis are "of my heart"; they are my "creed" as a Christian religious educator.[5] I claim their normativity and vision for no one other than myself, but I hope my statement prompts others of both similar and dissimilar approaches to clarify their own.

I gather the articles of my creedal statement around the following central themes for the hearts of Christian religious educators: the human person, God the Father/Mother,[6] Jesus the Christ, the Holy Spirit, the church, one's attitude toward Christian Story/Vision, and one's self-understanding as a religious educator. Some of my creedal statements inevitably overlap, and my treatment of each is from the perspective of the pedagogy of Christian religious educators. For these reasons I state each article and its commentary in narrative practical language and then follow with what I perceive it to ask of our hearts to be realized in our pedagogy.

Chapter 15

My Pedagogical Creed as a Christian Religious Educator

About the Person

Article 1: Agent-Subjects-in-Relationship

> I believe Christian religious educators are to promote an understanding of persons as "agent-subjects-in-relationship" who reflect the image of God by whose self-communication they have their very "being,"[1] and our pedagogy should help to realize this understanding by educating people to be free and responsible historical agents of their own becoming "fully alive" to the glory of God.

As physical/personal reflections of God in history, we are embodied beings, located and related in time and place. This means that we are finite, limited, and contingent; we cannot take our existence for granted. Yet God's own life in us constitutes us as affective, rational, creative, and decision-making people, as historical agents. Being, then, "like the beasts that perish" (Ps. 49:12) but also "a little less than a 'god'" (Ps. 8:16), we are limited and at the same time endowed with limitless potential for becoming authentic subjects who reflect the image and grow in the likeness of God. Becoming such fully alive "agent-subjects" (i.e., avoiding "objectivism") and "in relationship" (i.e., avoiding "subjectivism"), does not come to us as a "nature" already complete but presents us the historical task of engaging as agents in our own becoming.

For Our Hearts. This conviction asks of Christian religious educators, first, that our way of being present with people, and our whole curriculum, reflect the conviction that this work is ontological, that we are teaching people—educating—their very "being." Second, we are to create teaching/learning events that are humanizing for people, that teach them that and as if they are both already made in the image of God and are constantly challenged to become agent-subjects who grow in God's likeness as "fully alive" in the world. This especially requires that we honor and engage participants as agent-subjects-in-relationship rather than treating them as dependent-objects-in-isolation, that the curriculum (environment, process, and content) be humanizing for them for "fullness of life" (John 10:10), that it be free of manipulation, domination, and indoctrination. Our pedagogy is to actively engage people's whole "being" in place and time—their physical, mental, and volitional capacities, their head, heart, and action, their intellect, desire, and will, their reason, memory, and imagination, and enable them to reclaim their past, embrace their present, and take responsibility for their own and others' future.

Article 2: Communal Subjects in Right and Loving Relationship

> Christian religious educators are to teach persons as communal beings who are to grow in right and loving relationship with God, self, others, and creation. Our pedagogy should honor and help realize the conviction that at the heart of us there is a transcendent disposition that leads us out of ourselves into relationship and interdependence; that ultimately our reach for relationship is to return us to eternal union with the relational God (Trinity) whence we came.

Made *in* the image and likeness of right and loving Relationship, we are made *for* such relationship with God, others, and creation; we are to grow and realize our "selves" as communal and interdependent subjects. This existential disposition for right and loving relationship is like God's "original grace" in us; it is intrinsic to all human existence and can be experienced in every aspect of life. We can refuse it, but our potential for it is never entirely lost. By this "breath" of God's own life in us, we can freely reach out of ourselves for interdependence and with true care for others. This "communal grace" enables us to transcend self-centered narcissism and disposes us to love our God by loving others as we love ourselves. Our relational disposition is also realized through interdependence with and care for God's creation. And by living our potential for right and loving relationship with all, we begin to realize and experience now the "salvation" that is foretaste of our eternal destiny of complete union with God.

For Our Hearts.   The communal disposition of people asks Christian religious educators to create teaching/learning events that promote people's realization of themselves as relational beings, to educate them for and in right and loving relationship with self, God, others, and creation. Our pedagogy should model and reflect relationships of love, peace, and justice toward all participants. It is to invite people out of themselves into participation, partnership, and interdependence, into a community of inclusiveness and mutuality. The whole curriculum is to teach people that and as if they have a transcendent destiny that they are to begin to realize now through their relationships, and that their lives have ultimate meaning, value, and significance.

Article 3: Both Capable of Sin and Graced

> The praxis of Christian religious educators is to reflect a realistic understanding of persons as capable of and prone to sin *and* an optimistic image of ourselves and others as more capable, by God's grace, of freely choosing to do the good and true and of contributing within history to the coming of God's reign.

There is an inherited dynamism toward sin in humankind and in our social milieu that we have not brought about by our own choosing alone—traditionally symbolized as "original sin." It disposes us toward self-sufficiency and separation from God and others and can alienate us from our own true selves. To deny the social reality of sin, or of our own disposition for personal sin and for participation in sinful social structures, is the ultimate historical naïveté. On the other hand, it is a lack of faith in both God and ourselves to deny that by the power of God's creating, redeeming, and sanctifying love, there is also present in us a greater dynamism for doing God's will than for sin. In our "originally" sinful but also fundamentally graced existence, humankind has a transcendental freedom to choose between good and evil, that is, a freedom that is prior to and precedes all particular choices. By this transcendental freedom, and for Christian faith by the grace of God in Jesus,[2] we can decide about and actualize our selves as "agent-subjects in right and loving relationship," and can help transform historical structures toward God's reign. This potential for freedom, of course, is no freedom at all unless realized in the midst of historical reality, and that our human efforts are both essential and significant. God's grace that empowers human agency does not lessen our freedom or responsibility as God's co-partners in the covenant. In fact, God's gifts of grace and freedom make us responsible to be makers of history, and our efforts have consequences for ourselves, others, and creation.

For Our Hearts. The sin and grace dimensions of human existence call Christian religious educators, first, to recognize our own capacity for both good and evil and that doing what is right, even in our pedagogical praxis, cannot be taken for granted. Choosing and doing an appropriate pedagogy demands our deliberate efforts and heartfelt prayer for God's help. Second, regarding our co-learners, our pedagogy is to take with great seriousness the structural influences that dispose people to sin and the personal proclivity for sin in all. In content and process, our pedagogy should promote critical consciousness of personal and social sin, help people to uncover the inner and outer sources of sin and the consequences of it, and help form the character of ourselves and others in the priestly work of rectifying its results and the prophetic work of struggling against all sin, personal and social. The work of Christian religious educators is to reflect to participants a profound confidence in their potential goodness. It should affirm and nurture their ability to know and choose the peace and justice, love and freedom, and fullness of life that God wills for all, and their ability to help transform their social structures accordingly, with significant consequences for their own and others well-being.

About God the Creator

Article 4. Transcendent Mystery and Immanent Love

> I believe the praxis of Christian religious educators is to reflect and promote understanding and images of God: as Ultimate Mystery and Transcendent "Ground of Being"; as Immanent One of absolute closeness who lovingly sustains and cares for all that is and who is present to our favor in the depths of existence, in creation, in history, in the everyday; as unconditional Love, both within Godself and toward all humankind; as the only God we are to honor and worship as the "center" of our lives.

God is Ultimate Mystery and Transcendent Creator on whom we depend for "being," the one we can neither comprehend nor control to our own ends, the one "than which nothing greater can be imagined" (Anselm). Realizing this is crucial if we are to avoid the deception and destructiveness of self-idolatry, have faith without self-made certainty, and be religious without resorting to magic. But God is not only Transcendent Mystery or a distant originator—a removed "first mover." God is immanent to us and the care-full sustainer of all with God's own life and love, immediately in the depths of our "being" and mediately through creation, through personal and communal praxis, through relationships, and especially through a faith community. In biblical terms, God is God "of the heavens" *and* "of the earth," God is "very God," "living" and "true," and God is "with us" and "for us." In Christian faith, God is like Love both within Godself in a Trinity of loving relationships and as never ending love toward all humankind. Out of love, God calls us to live free of idols who enslave us; only a "god" who loves us as God does, deserves and can be trusted with our first allegiance in life.

For Our Hearts. God as transcendent mystery and ground of "being" calls for a pedagogy that reflects and invites people to heartfelt conviction that God *is*, and is an ultimate and gracious mystery who radically favors the well-being of all. We are to educate people in a "God consciousness," with a sense of awe and reverence at all that is and a sense that their own horizon of life is never closed, not even by death. Our "God talk" and imagery should be free of idolatry—our images are not "equal to God"—and avoid arrogance or intolerance toward God language and faith that is different from ours. We should always "teach God" in a way that is life-giving for all and never in a way that encourages domination by some or deprecation of others. God as immanent and unconditional Love calls for pedagogy that through content and process educates people in trusting and loving relationship with God, encourages them to cherish themselves and others as being of unqualified dignity and worth, and to make their lived response to God's love the central commitment of their lives.

Article 5: God Reveals Godself

In both content and process, the pedagogy of Christian religious educators is to reflect the conviction that God has revealed and continues to reveal Godself to humankind in history, and that we are capable of encountering, recognizing, and appropriating God's revelation as our normative source of meaning and ethic of life. Our pedagogy is to make accessible the saving truths of God's primordial revelation that began for this community with the people of Israel, reached its high point for Christian faith in the event of Jesus Christ, and has continued over time as a living tradition in the community of Jesus' disciples, the church. Our pedagogy is also to enable people to discern and appropriate God's disclosure of Godself and will that they existentially encounter in present historical praxis.

The reflections on revelation throughout chapters 5–10 are a more complete commentary than my remarks here. This article reaffirms that God reveals Godself in history and fittingly for us. Though God remains mystery, God has taken and continues to take initiative to reveal God's own self and will to humankind, and we are capable, by God's grace, of encountering, recognizing, and appropriating God's self-disclosure, at least enough to know who our God is and how God is for us, who we are and how we are to live as a people of God. By God's originating grace, we have an a priori capacity to receive God's self-disclosure, and God's ongoing grace enables us to recognize it in our lives (see note 2). However, God's grace never violates but improves our natural capacities and agency in events of divine revelation. Existentially, revelation emerges from events of divine-human encounter, and we recognize it according to our human capacity for knowing truth and meaning in our lives.

The special locus of divine self-disclosure is history, where revelatory encounter with God takes place in ordinary, extraordinary, and sometimes disruptive events. Christian faith is that God's primordial revelation originated in the life of the people of Israel and reached its apex "with the fullness of time" (Heb. 1:3) in the historical event of Jesus. The inspired symbolic mediation of this revelation is through the Hebrew Scriptures and the New Testament. Though the Bible is in human language and reflects the cultural mores in which it first emerged, it is an inspired and normative source of God's word for this faith community; access to it *can be* a revelatory event of divine-human encounter for people in the present.

The church as a community of faith indwelt by the Holy Spirit (see art. 10 below), and its "tradition" that has emerged from reflection on and living of its biblical faith in different times and contexts, provides a community of ready access, testing discernment, and guiding perspective for interpreting God's original revelation as a living tradition in the present. But God's revelation symbolically mediated through Scripture and tradition is not a shortcut to divine truths to be passively and uncritically accepted. Scripture and tradition can occasion divine-human encounters that are revelatory in the context and consciousness of people's history.[3] Because God has not abandoned human history but is still present and disclosing Godself in people's lives, each generation of Christians must uncover God's existential revelation in their own praxis, and especially in their efforts to do God's will. People can appropriate the symbolic mediation of God's self-disclosure in Scripture and tradition by placing them in dialogue and dialectic with the "present revelation" (Moran) of their lives.

That God's revelation occurs through history, past and present, does not mean that we should canonize historical praxis as inevitably reflecting God's intentions for humankind. The reality of both sin and grace in the human condition calls for an "epistemological realism" about history past and present, and for critical reflection on it in a community of faith and dialogue, to test what is of God and for God's reign and what is not.

For Our Hearts.　　Faith in God's original *and* existential revelation asks numerous commitments from the hearts of Christian religious educators. Many emerge again around the themes of Spirit, church, and Story/Vision; here I highlight two in particular.

First, and most obviously, Christian religious educators must give its participants access to "the faith handed on" through Scripture and tradition and as faithfully and critically understood by the "church" (people, scholars, and magisterium). Our style of making Scripture and tradition accessible should reflect respect for participants as agent-subjects in divine-human encounter and confidence in their God-given ability and affinity to recognize God's word to their lives and to make it their own. The symbolic forms of Scripture and tradition, their historical conditionedness, and their "surplus of meaning" call for education that enables people to critically and creatively reclaim them in the present, and that prevents biblical or doctrinal fundamentalism, closed-mindedness, or stasis in people's faith journeys.

Second, we are to employ a pedagogy that encourages a sacramental consciousness toward life, an awareness in people that God is present and revealing Godself in their own reality and in their "everyday." Our curriculum should honor and engage this existential encounter with God's revelation and create communities that encourage people to name present praxis and to critically reflect upon it in dialogue to discern the meaning of God's self-disclosure over time and how they are to live faithfully now as a people of God in this time and place.

Article 6: God as Life-giving and Faithful Partner in Covenant

> Christian religious educators are to teach that and as if God completely favors humankind and wills justice and peace, love and freedom, wholeness and fullness of life for all (God's reign); that God is active through human history opposing all that denies life and promoting the realization of God's intentions; that God calls all humankind into partnership (covenant) with Godself and one another to live according to what God wills—shalom.

That God so favors humankind, is active in history on behalf of God's intentions, and calls us into partnership thereto is profound affirmation of human existence and source of hope and responsibility for our historical agency. God's favor and intentions affirm our unqualified worth and fundamental rights as human beings. God as faithful partner in the covenant gives grace and hope that none of our efforts for God's reign can be lost or come to naught. Our partnership in the covenant brings profound historical responsibilities. God's faithfulness neither diminishes these nor lessens the significance of our efforts. We are to avoid the dichotomous view of a "city of God" and a "city of sin" as separate worlds. Through human cooperation, the structures of grace are to transform the structures of sin to make human history coextensive with salvation history. If we refuse our part in the covenant—if we choose alienation instead of right and loving relationship, death instead of life (Deut. 30:19)—God does not rescind our freedom to choose. We cannot act irresponsibly to the covenant and presume that God intervenes to save us from the consequences of our evil actions, even should that be our own annihilation.

For Our Hearts. This article calls for at least three significant commitments in the pedagogy of Christian religious educators. First, we are to teach of God, not as an "idea" to be known about (a favorite idol of educators), nor as a privatized "god" for individual souls (a favorite idol of Western society), but as God active among us, with us, politically involved in history on our behalf, as God of all levels of human existence, as opposed to injustice and violence, as the One who leads people out of slavery and raises up innocent victims of sinful principalities and powers—even from death. Second, we are to teach by content and process that all people have ultimate self-worth and are called to fullness of life. This too requires us to create humanizing teaching/learning environments that are dialogical, participative, respectful, and empowering so that participants may come to value themselves. Participants are to be convinced of their dignity and rights and encouraged to embrace their lives as gifts of God and live them to the full. Third, our pedagogy should inform and form people in their noble and historically significant purpose, to be, by God's grace, co-partners and effective agents of God's reign in history, to accept their personal and corporate responsibilities for the well-being of all. Our pedagogy is part of God's saving activity in people's lives and through them in the world; it should enable them to participate in "the work of our salvation" (see Phil. 2:12).

About Jesus

Article 7: Divine and Human

> The praxis of Christian religious educators should reflect and encourage the conviction that Jesus, the Christ, is the fully God and fully human One who, made flesh in time and place, is God's irrevocable promise and our hope that humankind can come into at-one-ment with God, ourselves, others, and creation; that in Jesus we encounter the summit of God's self-disclosure to us and of us to ourselves.

This article points to Jesus as the person in whom God and humanity are truly at one, that Jesus is at once the human face of God and the divine face of humanity. Jesus is God's sacrament of right and loving relationship between God and humankind because, consubstantial with God, he embodied God's saving presence in human history and, consubstantial with humanity, he was the perfect human response to God's intentions; Jesus Christ now empowers the fulfillment of the deepest quest of humankind—to be in right relationship with all and with God.[4]

As divine and human, Jesus is the decisive revelation of both who God is for us and the meaning and potential of human existence. He reveals God as like a loving, kind, and gentle parent, as a God of closeness, great compassion, mercy, and faithful love for all, and especially for the poor, for sinners, the outcast, the victimized, and those whose life is threatened. Jesus reveals us to ourselves because we can see in him what it means to be fully human, what our dignity and vocation is when we say yes to God's love and to our own deepest truth. He reveals the truth of our own humanity, not that he brought us new information about ourselves "from the outside, in," but because he lived "from the inside, out" the full potential embedded, by God's love, in human existence. As we come to know Jesus, we discover the truth about ourselves, the potential of our own "divinization" through right and loving relationship with God and what it means for us to "have life, and have it to the full" (John 10:10).

As divine and human, Jesus is especially a sacrament of hope for humankind—hope that our lives are meaningful and that the deepest longings of our hearts can be fulfilled. Jesus is God's irrevocable pledge of divine love for humankind, and because Jesus responded from humanity with perfect faithfulness to God's love, now all humanity is permeated by the hope of at-one-ment with God, with ourselves, with each other, and with all.

For Our Hearts. This article requires commitment to teach the central Christological affirmations of the church as expressed in its creedal statements, and most particularly its understanding of the divinity and humanity of Jesus. We should present this foundational doctrine (see note 4, and chapter 9, note 12) as an effective symbol of ultimate and unshakeable hope for humankind, for our humanization and our "divinization," as our abiding hope that longing for union with God and longing to be our own best selves in interdependence with others can be realized. We can address this doctrine to people's hearts and hopes because only through the deepest patterns and longings of our lives can faith in a God-person have meaning and be life-giving for us. Our teaching of this aspect of Christology should inform, form, and transform people as "hopers," to know that the power of sin need never defeat them nor structures of alienation finally triumph; rather, by the grace of God in Jesus, we can join in solidarity with others to make our best hopes come true for all humankind.

Article 8: Model and Liberator

> The pedagogy of Christian religious educators should enable people to symbolically encounter the historical Jesus in his life, death, and resurrection as the model of Christian discipleship and as the liberating Christ of faith—God's anointed and effective agent of "liberating salvation"[5] in history, who empowers people to live as disciples for God's reign.

This article reflects two key convictions about Jesus the Christ that I note immediately. First, our perception and understanding of who we confess as God's anointed One, the Christ of faith, should be in radical

continuity with the identity and praxis of the historical Jesus. To accept
Jesus in faith as "Lord and Savior" requires allegiance to the values,
commitments, and purpose reflected in his life; his praxis is the first
norm of what we teach about the meaning and implications of Jesus' life
for disciples now.[6] Second, this article reflects the conviction that Jesus
is both the *model* of how we are to live in Christian faith, *and* God's
anointed one who "saves" and "frees" us to so live. Jesus both shows
people the way of God's reign and is the historical catalyst of God's
grace that empowers people to participate in the struggle for liberating
salvation—*from* personal sin and sinful social structures and *for* undoing
the consequences of sin and contributing to fullness of life for all, here
and hereafter. In Christian faith, Jesus is both model of how we are to
live, and the effective historical catalyst of God's saving grace, through
his (a) life, (b) death, and (c) resurrection.

A. *Jesus' life* is both model and effective symbol (sacrament) of God's
reign because of the integrity with which he lived it. I recall some obvious examples of congruence between his preaching and praxis. God's
reign was the central theme of his preaching and his personally perceived purpose; he lived it with such integrity that he could say to
people, "Come follow me," and they recognized they would be living
for God's reign. Jesus radicalized its law of love by explicitly uniting
love of God, neighbor, and self, with neighbor including even one's
enemies; he lived such love that he could tell disciples, "Love others as
I have loved you" (John 13:34). Jesus urged people to change their lives
and to live as if God's reign is at hand (see Mark 1:15); he performed
immediate and visible services that people recognized as signs of God's
saving presence in him—enabling the blind to see, cripples to walk,
lepers to be cured, raising the dead to life, and preaching good news to
the poor (see Matt. 11:5). Jesus perceived and presented his public
ministry as bringing liberty to captives, sight to the blind, emancipation
to the oppressed, and inclusion to the marginalized; he lived his life for
others with a special outreach to the suffering, the poor, sinners, the
excluded, victimized, and oppressed and welcomed all into an "inclusive
discipleship of equals." Jesus preached simplicity of life to disciples,
eschewing of needless possessions, both respect for and freedom in
living the spirit of the law, placing of God at the center of their lives;
he had "nowhere to lay his head" (Matt. 8:20), fulfilled and reinterpreted the law, and resisted all temptations to idolatry. Jesus taught his
disciples to pray; he prayed frequently. This congruence between
preaching and praxis brought the first disciples, and Christians ever
since, to recognize in Jesus both model and effective catalyst of living
for God's reign.

B. In *Jesus' passion and death* we find a model of how to live in
faithfulness to one's deep inner truth and, in Christian faith, an effective source for people to so live. It was Jesus' lived integrity for the
reign of God that threatened political and religious forces and brought
him to his death. Yet in faith Christians believe that he went to his

death "for the forgiveness of sins" and that his cross is powerful for human salvation (see 1 Cor. 1:18). By his helplessness and refusal to use coercive power to achieve his goals, and because it resulted from the integrity of his life, Jesus' cross gave new meaning to human suffering by making possible a great reversal that turns its destructive potential into life-giving power. His passion and cross invite and can enable disciples to see life from the perspective of the poor, the outcast, the maltreated, the powerless, the oppressed, the enslaved, the reviled, and all who suffer. It at once challenges Christians to act on their behalf and empowers them to so act.

C. *Jesus' resurrection,* and faith "that God raised him from the dead" (Rom. 10:9), is the primary Christian symbol of how God affirms the lives of people who live for God's reign. The resurrection is God's endorsement of all that Jesus lived for in his pre-Easter existence. Christians believe that by baptism into union with him, "just as Christ was raised from the dead . . . we too might live a new life . . . and be slaves to sin no longer" (from Rom. 6:5, 6). Through the paschal event of his life, and because of his at-one-ment with humankind and with God, Jesus has permeated the whole human condition, as a leaven permeates dough, and has radically augmented the human capacity to say yes to God, to rise above the power of sin, personal and social, to be empowered to oppose it, to heal its consequences, and to live for the fullness of life God intends for all people. In his living, dying, and rising, Jesus the Christ is both model and empowerment of humankind's "liberating salvation."

I indicated in chapter 1 my reasons for using the language of liberation and freedom to name for contemporary consciousness the historical consequences of Jesus, the Christ. When the positive faith affirmations reflected in the traditional soteriological titles (Savior, Redeemer, Divinizer) are interpreted in light of a contemporary understanding of the historical Jesus, when Jesus' praxis is the first norm for what we teach of the Christ of faith, when sin is recognized as both personal and social and salvation as a this-worldly task as well as an otherworldly promise, then Christians can truly confess and express the historical meaning of Jesus with the symbol of Liberator. But to repeat the caveats of chapter 1, Jesus as Liberator does not mean an easy license or a freedom that is taken for granted; rather, he empowers disciples in the historical task of living now with and for true freedom for all. Jesus' emancipatory work is not a substitute for human efforts but a catalyst that calls and empowers people to produce an abundant harvest of personal, interpersonal, and social/political freedom and for "creation that groans and is in agony" to be set free (see Rom. 8:22). To neglect our historical responsibilities for the freedoms yet to be realized denies the historical significance of the living, dying, and rising of Jesus, the Liberator.

For Our Hearts. The affirmation that Jesus is both model and liberator to human existence, so constitutive of Christian faith, calls for many commitments in the praxis of Christian religious educators. Some already indicated around previous articles could be reechoed from a Christological perspective, and some that follow could be anticipated. But three seem particularly appropriate to note here.

First, our pedagogy should enable people to encounter through the primary symbols of Christian faith the person of the historical Jesus, to come to know him for themselves as their model and liberator. In Christian faith, the central Christological affirmations of the church in its creedal statements serve as an interpretive framework for the encounter. But the heart of Christian faith is not a dogma but this "person"; Christians are to come to "know" him in the relational sense of knowing. We encourage this encounter by giving people direct access to the Christian Scriptures, by bringing them to participate in the worship of a Christian community and to personal prayer. From the earliest age (with adjustment for language level) participants should have access to the Jesus of history in his cultural setting and faith tradition, to the stories of him and by him, to how the first generation of Christians perceived him in faith. They need to have access to the "whole story" of the "whole Jesus" (not only a Liberator, not only a spiritual leader, etc.)[7]—how he lived and what he lived for, how he died and why, that he was raised up and from and for what. We should educate people for and through "full, conscious and active participation in liturgical celebrations" (Vatican II) to encounter the presence of Christ through the assembled community, in the Scriptures proclaimed, and especially in the constant sacrament of Eucharist that continues the "visible bodiliness" (Schillebeeckx) of Jesus to Christians now. Likewise, people are to be educated as "pray-ers" with Jesus, and from the rich spiritual tradition of the community, offered a variety of prayer forms—dialogue, meditation, contemplation, traditional prayers, body prayer—to develop their own preferred mode.

Second, this article highlights again the formative task of our pedagogy; by God's grace, it is to form the "characters" of people for ongoing conversion as disciples of Jesus. This formation needs the supporting context of a Christian community (see article 12). It also advises a "modeling" principle to ourselves as educators that should be most readily evident in how we teach and in our relationships with participants. But in formation of Christian character, I refer again to the ancient wisdom of Aristotle: "Our characters are the result of our conduct."[8] It is most appropriate to the curriculum, then, that participants recognize and critique their own and society's present praxis, that they be invited to make decisions, and that they have explicit opportunities through the teaching/learning community for renewed praxis of Christian faith.

Third, our teaching is to nurture people to have faith in Jesus as their liberator and to trust his empowerment of them to live for God's reign. Avoiding the heresies of both "cheap grace" and "works righteousness," we are to educate disciples to take on his mission, commitments, and values, confident that by God's grace in Jesus the Liberator, their efforts can have significant historical consequences for their own and others well-"being." Both the content and processes of our pedagogy should educate people in a Christology that challenges them to live responsibly as disciples of Jesus and gives them a realistic optimism in their historical agency for God's reign. Jesus as Liberator calls for faith education with an emancipatory dynamic; our pedagogy is to be consciousness-raising and empowering of people as agent-subjects; it should enable them "to see" who and what should be seen (see Matt. 25:31–46) and to act for the "liberating salvation" of themselves, others, and God's creation.

About the Holy Spirit

Article 9: Source of Our Faith

> Christian religious educators are to employ pedagogical processes that reflect the conviction that the Holy Spirit is the dynamic source of people's faith, the One who enables people to recognize and faithfully respond to God's offer of grace, and to God's self-disclosure in Scripture and tradition and existentially in their present praxis.[9]

In the farewell discourse of the Fourth Gospel, Jesus promised, "I will ask the Father and he will give you another Paraclete to be with you always; the Spirit of truth" (John 14:16). The Spirit, "sent" as promised in Christian faith on the first Pentecost, continues to instruct "in everything," to "remind" of all that Jesus revealed lest we forget (see John 14:20), bears witness to Jesus in history, and enables disciples to be witnesses to Jesus as well (see John 15:26–27). In the phrase of Irenaeus, Jesus and the Holy Spirit are "the two hands of God" to the world. Now that the historical Jesus is no longer physically with us, it is by the Spirit that Christians continue to encounter God's presence and the presence of the Risen Christ in their lives and are empowered to respond as disciples of Jesus.

From the perspective of the "economic Trinity" (i.e., how God acts toward us), it is as if God is the Giver, Jesus is the Gift, and the Spirit is the Giving and Receiving. We experience the power of God's Spirit in our lives as original grace in the depths of our "being" that disposes us to welcome God's outreach in love and revelation to us and as the source of "created grace" (see note 2) that empowers people to respond freely and faithfully to what God wills.

The Spirit is the power of God's ongoing creative and saving activity in history and continues the liberating work of Jesus. The Spirit comes into human history from God the Mother/Father and (or through)[10] God the Liberating Christ; by "baptism in the Holy Spirit"

(Matt. 3:11, e.g.) Christians are empowered as disciples for Jesus' mission in the world. The Spirit makes possible our freedom as a people of God in Jesus (see Romans 8). The Spirit enlivens us in faith, making us temples of God (1 Cor. 3:16); the Spirit gives the community the gifts of service needed for the upbuilding of the Body of Christ (see 1 Cor. 12, e.g.). The Spirit enables Jesus' disciples to "live in the Spirit" (Gal. 5:25, e.g.) with understanding, wisdom, knowledge, counsel, piety, fortitude, and reverence for God.[11] The fruits of living in the Spirit are "love, joy, peace, patience, kindness, goodness, truthfulness, gentleness and self-control" (Gal. 5:22–23).

For Our Hearts. This article calls Christian religious educators to teach Christian faith in the Holy Spirit with the practical interest of what the Spirit can mean for people's lives. This "content," however, is to be reflected in the processes we employ. *How* we teach should reflect trust in the Spirit's presence within and between participants, in the church, and in the world. Trust in the presence of the Holy Spirit in participants' lives calls for a pedagogy: (a) that enables people to critically reflect on their own historical reality to discern God's presence therein and to come to a critical consciousness about it (both are by the grace of the Holy Spirit), (b) that makes accessible the Story/Vision of Christian faith, with confidence that by the Spirit it can be a revelatory source for people in the present, (c) that trusts the Spirit to guide and enable people's appropriation of "the faith handed on" and their own faith decisions/responses. Any kind of "banking education" is a denial of the presence of the Holy Spirit in people's lives.

Faith in the Spirit's presence does not alleviate the educator's responsibility for thorough preparation and careful sponsorship. As Paul advises, "The Spirit . . . gives witness with our spirit" (Rom. 8:16); the Spirit works through our praxis, and we are responsible, with the help of the same Spirit, to provide a fitting instrument. In fulfilling our responsibility, we are wise to preface preparation and the event itself with prayer to the Spirit to "fill the hearts of the faithful" and to "enkindle in us the fire of God's love" (a traditional prayer to the Holy Spirit).

Article 10: Source of Communion and Mission

> The pedagogy of Christian religious educators is to reflect and teach the conviction that the Holy Spirit calls and empowers people to authentic community and to right and loving relationship with God and one another, and that the Holy Spirit is the genesis and animator of the Christian community that is to carry on Jesus' mission of "liberating salvation" in the world.

One traditional (since Augustine) imaging of the inner life of the Trinity poses the Holy Spirit as the Love between God the Father/

Mother and the Second Person, revealed in Jesus Christ. As the Loving Relationship between the Lover and the Beloved within Godself, so too, toward us, the Spirit is the source of our loving communion with one another and with God. The Spirit is the "between" of love within the Godhead, among us, and of God with humankind.

We can, then, image the Spirit as the source of loving communion, solidarity, and right relationship among humankind, and of humankind with God. But remembering that "right relationship" is a central biblical understanding of both holiness and justice/peace, one recognizes both the sanctifying role of the Spirit as the source of holiness *and* that to live "in the Spirit" empowers and demands the works of justice and peace. The Spirit calls to holiness *and* wholeness of life; God's Spirit intends to be the transforming power of both our prayers and our politics.[12] The Spirit is "to renew the face of the earth."

Anticipating the theme of ecclesiology (articles 11 and 12) from a pneumatological perspective, Christians recognize that the Holy Spirit originates the life of the church and bonds it in community as the Body of Christ in the world. By the "fellowship of the Holy Spirit" (2 Cor. 13:13) Christians form an ecclesial communion of faith to realize their covenant relationship through Jesus with God and one another. Paul writes, "It was in one Spirit that all of us, whether Jew or Greek, slave or free, were baptized into one body" (1 Cor. 12:13). Echoing Paul's imagery, Aquinas portrayed the Spirit as the Soul that animates the church as the Body of Christ in the world. And Christian communion in the Spirit is always for mission—for sending into the world to carry on God's saving work begun in Jesus—the Spirit empowers the church to participate in God's cosmic "saving liberation" (see 2 Cor. 3:17–18).

For Our Hearts. To be "in the Spirit," our pedagogy should be fitting in content and process to educate people in holiness and in the works of justice and peace. The discernment and decision making we encourage with participants and in our faith communities should enable people to recognize and respond to the movement of God's Spirit in their lives *and* come to a critical social consciousness whereby they recognize sins and sinful social structures and commit themselves to reconciliation and transformation. To teach "in the Spirit" means to nurture both ongoing conversion and what Freire calls "conscientization."

Regarding the Spirit as animator of the church, here I highlight that pedagogy "in the Spirit" is to have both a genuine hospitality and an "outward-bound" orientation. Clearly, it is possible to bond people into a closed or elitist group that has a sense of communal identity but is turned in on itself. The pedagogy of Christian religious educators should never encourage any kind of sectarianism; it is to help create a welcoming and inclusive community and "lead them out" into solidarity with any human community in which God's Spirit is moving to bring about God's reign for all creation.

About the Church

Article 11: Inclusive Community of Partnership

> Christian religious educators are to teach that and as if the church
> is to be a community of partnership and fundamental equality that
> welcomes all people to full participation as disciples of Jesus; we are
> to educate for "church" so that through the ministry of all its mem-
> bers, according to their gifts, the community will be an effective
> symbol of God's reign by teaching the faith handed on (kerygma),
> by worshiping God for the life of the world (leitourgia), by witness-
> ing in its communal life to the kerygma it teaches and the hope it
> celebrates (koinonia), and by serving on all levels for fullness of life
> for humankind and the integrity of creation (diakonia).

Note first that the community of Jesus' disciples is to be a "church"
(in the Troeltschian sense): a community inculturated in its context that
welcomes all as bona fide members, saints and sinners alike, where
there are "strangers and aliens no longer" (Eph. 2:19). This catholicity
of the church is reflected in each local community and in their maintaining communion with other local churches and with the whole
church throughout the world. It is to be an inclusive community of
partnership and participation in which all members are nurtured as
agent-subjects-in-relationship to own their own faith identity and
agency and to be interdependent with others for the well-being and
mission of the whole community.

Concerning the "nature" of the church, we first recognize that it is
"a reality imbued with the hidden presence of God"; as Vatican II
added, it is a "mystery" that cannot be fully expressed in human language.[13] Yet the tradition suggests many rich images that illuminate the
church's polyvalent nature. In its self-portrayal as *Body of Christ*, the
Christian community can find an antidote to both the subordination of
the individual to the group and the canonization of individual self-
interest at the expense of community well-being. In its self-image as a
People of God the church is reminded that its first allegiance is to God
and that it should be an egalitarian community. The church as a *Community of Disciples*[14] seems particularly apt to our educational interest
(*discipulus* means learner). It points to the Christian community as people called by God to learn and teach together through "shared" praxis,
dialogue, and discernment how to live the way of Jesus. It reminds each
member and the whole community, as Vatican II says, "that the Church
constantly moves forward toward the fullness of divine truth";[15] we are
never more than "becoming" Christians through ongoing conversion
and reform. The church as *Sacrament of God's Reign* is a comprehensive
"model" that subsumes many of the assets of the others. It reminds
Christians of the church's inner spiritual life *and* that its visible and

structured reality should be an effective historical symbol of God's intentions for the world—the purpose for which the church exists.

In serving its "first purpose" of God's reign, we refer again to the time-honored fourfold listing of its historical tasks. (1) The church is to make accessible in every time and place its living faith handed on through the symbols of Scripture and its traditions (kerygma); for this, it engages in the reciprocal activities of evangelizing, preaching, and teaching. The intent of its kerygmatic ministry is humanization and salvation; the church is "to bring the Good News into every strata of humanity . . . transforming humanity from within and making it new."[16] This requires that the church make its Story/Vision accessible in ways consoling and confronting, that prompt healing and judgment, promise and demand, sound doctrine and prophecy. (2) The church is to be a witnessing community of faith, hope, and love (*koinonia*). With unity in the midst of diversity, it is to realize in its communal life relationships of respect, partnership, and justice; it ought to be free of sexism, racism, classism, ageism, clericalism, and every form of discrimination. (3) The church is to carry on the "public work" of worshiping God as a community (*leitourgia*). This work is to effectively symbolize a communal offering of people's lives in faith to God and the gift of God's life to this community for the life of the world. (4) As servant (*diakonia*) the church is to carry on the "liberating salvation" of God in Jesus by caring for the human needs of its own members, and of all people, and caring for the integrity of creation; it is to live a faith that does justice for peace. It is called to "curative diakonia" of helping and healing those who suffer or are victimized; to "preventive diakonia" that challenges social structures that threaten, deny, or destroy human life or creation; and to "prospective diakonia" to create social structures and arrangements that ensure well-"being" and justice for all.[17]

For Our Hearts.   This article calls religious educators to a pedagogy that in content and process teaches *about* the church—its nature and mission—and teaches *for* the church—to "build up the Body of Christ" (Eph. 4:12). Regarding content, teaching "about" and "for" the church means (a) that we teach the kerygma in a way that "leads out" to an inclusive community of partnership for God's reign; (b) that we inform and form people for partnership and participation in an ecclesial koinonia; (c) that we educate people for "full, conscious, and active participation" (Vatican II, *C.S.L.* 14) in the church's liturgy and for their contribution to its sacramental adequacy in this community; (d) that we inform people and form their characters to participate in the church's ministry of welfare that demands justice for humankind and creation. In process, our pedagogy should be radically communal in its dynamic, and thus likely to encourage human and Christian community among participants and to form them as members of the local and universal church. Such a process calls for a dynamic of active participation, dialogue, inclusiveness, partnership, mutuality, respect, and hospitality for all participants.

Article 12. A "Mixed Body"

> Christian religious educators are to educate people in ecclesial identity with a "realistic" faith in the church: as constituted by divine *and* human partners; as called to continuity with its apostolic roots *and* to change its ways toward greater faithfulness to God's reign; as capable of nurturing people in Christian faith *and* as constantly in need of education and reformation.

That there is a "divine partner" in the life of the church recognizes it as more than a human construction or product of history; it is the Body of Christ animated by the Holy Spirit. Its original impetus came from Jesus' gathering of a community of disciples and from the outpouring of the Holy Spirit on that community. Since then, the Spirit has sustained the church to mediate God's ongoing saving activity in Jesus, the Risen Christ. Because it is "a reality imbued with the hidden presence of God," the church can always be a source of true holiness and wholeness for Christians, and through them for others. On the other hand, the church is also constituted in history by human partners: people like ourselves. It is, then, marked by human goodness and sinfulness and by structures of sin and grace. Because the church is realized in history, it reflects the social, cultural, and political influences of its contexts in place and time. The church walks a fine line between indiginization as an effective symbol of God's reign in a particular situation and domestication by its context to be no more than a reflection of it. In this effort its success is often mixed with failure.

As a venture of divine and human partners,[18] the church can be an effective mediation of God's saving grace to the world but is also a *corpus mixtum* (Augustine's phrase)—a "mixed body" that reflects human goodness and sinfulness in its individual members and in its corporate structures. For this reason its members are called to ongoing conversion and as a community to constant reformation (*semper reformanda*, Augustine). The church is to constantly return to its "foundation of the apostles and prophets" (Eph. 2:20) to renew its fidelity to and continuity with its primordial roots. And as it critically reclaims its heritage of truths and values, the church must also create and propose new possibilities in faith for its members, for its own reformation, and for its contribution to social transformation. The church should never settle for its own or any status quo until the final coming of God's reign.

Human identity is formed in a social context, and Christian faith identity requires the socialization of a Christian community. As a public community that shapes social consciousness and a socializing community that nurtures people's identity in faith, every aspect of the church's life in the world has "educational" import.[19] But because it is a *corpus mixtum,* it can both educate and miseducate. It is not enough then to simply socialize people into ecclesial communities as they are and expect the outcome to be authentic identity and agency in Christian faith. The church as educator is itself ever in need of critical and self-reforming religious education.

For Our Hearts.   This article calls Christian religious educators to be faithful "church educators." Our whole curriculum should help educate people in ecclesial identity by which they truly know themselves as Christians and know what it means to be Christian, to be "realistic" about what the church is and is not, and to be committed to its constant reform. Such ecclesial pedagogy reflects at least four particular commitments.

First, our teaching should be likely to sponsor people in lifelong conversion, to open them to ongoing possibilities of faithfulness and maturity of faith. Religious education that closes people's minds and hearts and brings them to stasis in their faith journey, albeit giving them a sense of Christian identity, is a disservice to them and to the church. Second, we are to educate people in an ecclesial faith, to actively participate in a Christian community, drawing life from it and contributing to its holiness and sacramentality in the world. Third, we are to educate people in a critical ecclesial consciousness, to enter into a dialectical relationship with the church from within, preserving and drawing life from its resources, refusing to acquiesce in its shortcomings and sinfulness, and contributing to its reformation. Fourth, Christian religious educators are to bring a critical educational consciousness to every dimension and aspect of the church's life in the world. We are to render the constant service of enabling our particular ecclesial community to review how its communal life and ministry is educating the minds and hearts of members and witnessing to its wider social community.

About Christian Story/Vision

Article 13: A Stance of Faith, Hope, and Love

> Christian religious educators are called to reflect and promote in their pedagogy *cherishing* of Christian Story/Vision as gift and challenge that comes out of the rich heritage bequeathed by God's activity among our mothers and fathers in faith; *faith* in its possibilities to reveal God and ourselves to us and thus to be a reliable framework of meaning and ethical norms for our lives; *hope* that its life-giving memories can be constantly rediscovered, critically appropriated, and developed by ongoing generations of Christians as a source of new life in every age.

Regardless of the particular approach we use in Christian religious education, the Story of the faith community is to be faithfully made accessible and its Vision proposed as sources of meaning and ethic for Christian living. To fulfill our commission from the Christian community in whose name we educate, we must teach what is constitutive of the community's faith. By teaching both Story and Vision we fulfill a priestly service of conservation and a prophetic function of liberation for the community apropos its tradition. Truly, Christian religious educators are to be "learned in the reign of God," which means taking from "the storeroom" both the old and the new (see Matt. 13:52). Here I characterize as *faith, hope, and love* the general attitude toward Story/Vision asked of Christian religious educators.

We need a *love* for Christian Story/Vision if we are to educate people to embrace it joyfully as their "ultimate myth" of meaning and ethic. When we ourselves cherish it as the heritage and promise of the communion of saints and sinners before us and around us, we are less likely to present it as a hardened ideology beyond critique that controls people's lives. We can teach it instead as a life-giving "friend" that gives roots and wings, direction, and a sense of being "at home." We need to *trust* that this Story/Vision is a reliable source of God's self-disclosure if we are to present it with integrity to shape people's identity and agency in faith. Undoubtedly it should be interpreted and explained with the best of critical scholarship, in dialogue and dialectic with contemporary consciousness and communities of faithful Christian witness, and have no version canonized as a final hermeneutic. Yet, to mistrust what is constitutive of the tradition means that God has led astray the Christian people before us and could be doing the same now. Faith in its revelatory potential does not mean that we encourage people in a sectarian or elitist attitude that ours is the only tradition of faith that reflects God's truth for people's lives. Rather, we should present it as our particular home in God's family, which can open us to God's universal revelation through all the great religious traditions of humankind. And Christian educators need a *hopeful* and open attitude toward their community Story/Vision, or they will present it to people as if it is a reified and dead tradition. They need hope that it can be constantly reclaimed as a source of "liberating salvation," of new possibilities and surprises for themselves and for the life of the world. Our present version of it is certainly not "perfect" or "finished," but we need hope that people can draw from it what they need to live as fully alive, free, and faithful people of God in this time and place.

For Our Hearts. Faith, hope, and love toward Christian Story/Vision calls Christian religious educators to the following commitments. We are to study and pray our way into its richness to nurture our ongoing conversion in living it. Second, we are to assiduously prepare ourselves to teach it and have available competent resources that enable us to make accessible a life-giving understanding and an informed version of it from the research of the scholars, the *sensus fidelium,* and the consensus teaching of our faith community's magisterium. Third, we are to faithfully make Story/Vision accessible with a style that engages the whole identity and agency of participants, a style that gives access without authoritarianism and enables people to make it their own with practical and life-giving consequences. Fourth, we are to bring hermeneutics of retrieval, suspicion, and creativity to our interpretation of its symbols; we are to evaluate our explanations for continuity with what is constitutive of it, for likely consequences that are of God's reign, and we are to discern its meaning now in this historical context and in dialogue with the whole "church."

About Ourselves as Christian Religious Educators

Article 14: "Leading Learners"

> Christian religious educators are to be "leading learners" in the pedagogy of Christian faith, people who enter subject-to-subject relationships with other participants in faith education events and communities and who render the art of enabling such events and communities but always as learning participants.

This article about "ourselves" is a fitting way to bring this work to a close, but needs little comment. The persistence of the stereotype of educators as answer people and the established division between teachers and learners mean that Christian religious educators need to often review their self-image to continue as "leading learners" in Christian faith. When we cease to learn, our faith can die, if only from boredom at the hands of our own "teaching."

Note that this article poses the work of Christian religious educators as a form of art. I have referred to it as a ministry throughout, and this is true; it is a specific function of ministry that should be so designated by the church. But it is also illuminating to see it as an art, especially as realized in the dynamics of a teaching/learning event. At a minimum, this can prevent us approaching its praxis as a technique or even a "method." Good artistry engages people's whole "being" in a sensible encounter marked by good taste and good judgment and enables them to experience with heightened awareness their world as it is or might be, to see the "more" in the ordinary, the ultimate in the immediate. Surely an event of Christian religious education should do as much.

For Our Hearts.   The art of being "*leading*-learners" calls Christian religious educators to sponsor events that engage the whole "being" of participants in ways that are adequate to people as agent-subjects-in-relationship and appropriate to the humanizing and saving potential of Christian Story/Vision. Educational events should reflect good taste and good judgment in how and when the educator enables people to express their own stories/visions; in how, when, and what to make accessible from the community Story/Vision; in how and when to encourage appropriation and to invite decision making. In short, the whole curriculum—environment, process, content—should be marked by an aesthetic quality.

The art of leading-*learner* calls Christian religious educators to participate in every event as co-learners. We are to invest our "being" and remain open to be led out by our co-learners to greater holiness and wholeness in Christian living. Every word we address to them is addressed to ourselves as well; every word they speak, question they raise, insight they reach, or decision they make can be an occasion of ongoing conversion for us.

Such good art never comes easily but is a lifelong challenge for all religious educators. It is enhanced by trying to do it and by critical reflection on our efforts. We are motivated to continue developing this noble art by remembering that our teaching can have significant historical consequences for our own and other lives, and for the life of the world. We should approach it with the discipline, preparation, self-investment, and imagination required of any fine artist. Yet we are always to remember that we are never more or less than artists in the work of another Creator—the One who gives the increase from our "sharing faith."

Notes

Preface

1. Hereafter I refer to this work as *C.R.E.*

2. The *God with Us* and *Coming to Faith* curricula are published by W. H. Sadlier, 11 Park Place, New York, NY 10007. They have both parochial school and parish program editions with teachers' guides to accompany all nine grade texts. All have the ecclesial imprimatur for use in Catholic schools and parishes. They are overtly Catholic in their language, scope, and sequence, but ecumenical in spirit; many Sunday school teachers in mainline Protestant congregations have found helpful especially the teachers' guides for lesson planning along the lines of shared praxis.

I note my indebtedness to Ralph Fletcher, who first had the courage to realize shared Christian praxis in a major catechetical series. As president of Sadlier, in 1981 he convinced me to be the principal author of a K–8 curriculum that would reflect a shared praxis approach. In creating the *God with Us* curriculum, we adapted the scope and sequence of Sadlier's previous *Lord of Life* series for grades 1–5. Though I was responsible for creating the first draft of each manuscript, for grades 1–6, I benefited much from working with the text and authors of the *Lord of Life* series, Sr. Maria de la Cruz Aymes, S.H., and Rev. Francis Buckely, S.J. For grades 7 and 8 my partners on the authorship team were John Nelson, Catherine Zates Nelson, and Msgr. John Barry, and for the kindergarten, Audrey M. Munoz. Throughout the writing of the *God with Us* program I especially benefited from the help of the series catechist, Dr. Eleanor Ann Brownell.

Coming to Faith is a totally new program, with a different scope and sequence from all previous Sadlier series. With myself as principal author, it was created with a revised and expanded authorship/editorial team. Uniquely, Dr. Elinor R. Ford, then president of Sadlier, is the originator and designer of the *Coming to Faith* series. She constantly brought to its editing and publishing her great expertise and wide experience from a long and distinguished career in Catholic education. It profoundly reflects her "story and vision" for Catholic catechesis. I especially recommend *Coming to Faith* for instances of the movements of shared Christian praxis at its grade levels.

These two curricula have been well received by their clientele. So too have a number of new and revised series from other publishers that have been deliberately fashioned in the style and spirit of shared Christian praxis as I understand it. Such "empirical" evidence indicates that with proper resources, a shared praxis approach can be used successfully by both trained teachers and volunteers. This is an important point in light of the sometimes complex explanations that follow here.

3. In *C.R.E.*, chap. 2, I explain why I use this term in preference to *catechesis, Christian education,* etc. See also chap. 7, note 15 here.

4. Grimmitt distinguishes between learning about religion and learning from religion. Cited in Moran, *Religious Education as a Second Language,* p. 98. Moran footnotes Grimmitt, *Religious Education and Human Development.*

5. In *Second Language,* Moran states, "Religious education has to do with the religious life of the human race and with bringing people within the influence of that life" (p. 218). He presents a helpful schema for conceptualizing what he poses as the constitutive activities of religious education, namely: (a) "teaching people to be religious in a particular way" (takes place in family, religious community, and other institutions, including schools); and (b) "academic instruction in religion," or what he also calls "teaching religion" (takes place in state school classrooms, e.g., in the United Kingdom and in classrooms of religiously affiliated schools). See fig. 7, p. 85. In this schema, parish-based activity (a) intends "formation in being religious," whereas school-based and academic activity (b) is to enable people "to understand religion." See fig. 2, p. 218.

I find Moran's schema clarifying but also limited, in that it presumes a separation between "being" and "knowing," a dichotomy that Part I of this work attempts to transcend.

6. The First Amendment to the U.S. Constitution reads: "Congress shall make no law respecting an establishment of religion, or prohibiting the free exercise thereof."

7. In the *Abington v. Schempp* case (1963), the Supreme Court declared that the reading of the Bible as a religious act in public schools is unconstitutional. But the comment on the decision also stated, "Nothing we have said here indicates that such study of the Bible or of religion, when presented objectively as a part of a secular program of education, may not be effected consistently with the First Amendment" (quoted in Nelson, *How Faith Matures*, p. 35).

Part I. Prologue

1. I was reluctant at first to begin with this quotation from Yeats's "A Prayer for Old Age" because of its exclusive language. On reflection, however, I realized that his language can serve to remind us that the undue confidence in the "mind alone" is identified, in large part, as a male syndrome in the history of Western epistemology.

2. Paul Nash writes in an excellent *Encyclopedia Britannica* essay, "Although there is wide agreement that the assimilation of knowledge by the learner is a principal goal of education, this agreement is more apparent than real, because there is much disagreement about what constitutes knowledge" (*Encyclopedia Britannica* [1983], "Philosophy of Education," Macropaedia 6:411).

3. Williamson's *Language and Concept in Christian Education* has an insightful chapter on epistemology and Christian education (chap. 4). Although written in 1970, his call for "an immediate and wide-scale discussion on the relations between epistemology and Christian education" (pp. 55–56) has largely gone unheeded.

4. My awareness of the need for an "ontological turn" in the praxis of Christian religious education has been growing for some time, but I footnote a 1985 conversation with Harold Daly Horell, then an M.T.S. student at Harvard Divinity School, as particularly clarifying. See also Charles Taylor's essay "Overcoming Epistemology." Taylor argues that the move beyond epistemology must lead to analysis of human agency, or to what he calls a philosophical anthropology. With this, one realizes that "ways of knowing" arise from "ways of being," not simply from "ways of thinking."

Only when the manuscript was completed did I come upon the work of Donald W. Oliver on "ontological knowing" and the distinction he makes between it and "technical knowing." I wish I had found it sooner, and I recommend it highly. See especially *Education, Modernity and Fractured Meaning*.

My call for an "ontological turn" has clear resonance, I believe, with the biblical notion of "knowing." In the Hebrew Scriptures, the verb *yada*, "to know," implies a personally engaging, relational, and obediential activity; the same verb is used for human lovemaking. Likewise, for the New Testament, "to know God in Jesus Christ" (see John 17:3) clearly implies entering a relationship that demands one's whole "being."

For an overview of the Old Testament usage of the verb *yada*, see *Theological Dictionary of the Old Testament*, 5:448–81. See also "ginosko," by Rudolf Bultmann, 1:689–714, esp. pp. 696–701.

5. From the Greek *ontos-logos*, literally "science of being," *ontology* was first coined by 17th-c. Scholastic philosophers, at first as synonymous with all of metaphysics but then as a subdivision alongside cosmology and psychology. For Christian Wolff (1679–1754), the first to popularize the term, *ontology* referred to the study of being as such, i.e., of the necessary truths about the essence of what exists. That, of course, had been an issue for early philosophy as well, but it was not called ontology. In Aristotle, e.g., dealing with "the being of beings" is called "first philosophy," the deducing of the ultimate nature of reality and its properties—substance, quantity, quality, relation, place, time, position, state, action, and affection.

The 18th-c. emergence of the study of "being as such" however, was dealt a serious blow by Kant, who was interpreted (some would say misinterpreted) by Western philosophy to be claiming that we can never know "being as such," never the noumena of being but only the phenomena—its appearances. Thus, ontology as a distinct field of study became somewhat disparaged. It was revived by the existentialists, however, and especially by Heidegger, for whom ontology basically means the study of the being of the beings who can reflect on and question their own being, of the beings for whom "being" is a question—ourselves in the world.

Chapter 1. Educating for Conation in Christian Faith

1. My prologue claim that Christian religious education requires an epistemic ontology as its foundation and is to engage the whole "being" of people clearly reflects my understanding of the nature and purposes of Christian religious education. I have already written about both at some length. (See *C.R.E.*, chaps. 1–5.) Here, however, I restate what I perceive to be the nature and purposes of Christian religious education and for three reasons: that this work may stand as a complete statement in its own right; to deepen my rationale for claiming that education in Christian faith requires an "epistemic ontology" as its philosophical foundation; and to clarify the particularity of Christian faith conation or wisdom as the intended learning outcome of Christian religious education.

2. Burnet summarizes the position of both when he writes, "The theory of education is treated by Plato and Aristotle as a part of politics" (Burnet, *Aristotle on Education*, p. 131).

3. Huebner, "Curricular Language," p. 37.

4. "Pastoral Constitution on the Church," Abbott, *Documents*, p. 242. My position here should not be heard to claim that the church is like a political party or lobby. In the words of Vatican II, "Christ, to be sure, gave His Church no proper mission in the political, economic or social order. The purpose which He set before her is a religious one. But out of this religious mission itself comes a function, a light and an energy which can serve to structure and consolidate the human community according to the divine law" (ibid., p. 241).

John Courtney Murray made a helpful distinction between "political" and "social" to describe the relationship between church and state. For Murray, both church and state are social institutions within any society. The church is properly concerned with the religious and the state with the political. Yet the church as a social institution has political influence in that it is never separated from its social world and through the life of its members is to influence the structures and quality of sociopolitical life, even while not being tied to any particular political party or government system. See Murray, *We Hold These Truths*. My position here, then, is that *how* the church educates its members to live in society inevitably has political consequences. (A comment by Harold Daly Horell helped to clarify this position.)

5. I take these distinctions from Elliot Eisner, who insists that "schools provide not one curriculum to students, but three" (*The Educational Imagination*, p. 74). Eisner names the three curricula the *explicit*, the *implicit*, and the *null*. (See ibid., chap. 5.) The explicit is the stated content and observable procedures used to teach. The implicit is what is taught through the ethos and socializing influence of the school and its educational procedures. The null curriculum is what is taught, ironically, by what is *not* taught. "It is my thesis that what schools do not teach may be as important as what they do teach . . . because ignorance is not simply a neutral word" (ibid., p. 83).

6. Sonya Quitslund summarizes many critiques of the term *kingdom of God* when she writes, "At least three objections to the image come immediately to mind: it is obsolete, sexist and misleading" ("A Feminist Perspective on Kings and Kingdom," p. 134). Of the power implied by *kingdom,* she writes, "For the most part, the Christian experience of this power has been through a hierarchical, male and, in the case of Roman Catholics, celibate caste system that appears to use its power more to dominate than to serve, clinging tenaciously to the status quo" (p. 135). After an insightful review of its problematics, Quitslund finally concludes that *reign of God* "is an image that is salvageable only if we take the trouble to bring out its true essence of justice, peace and love, making clear that that essence is derived from the divine nature, not from a human, political concept, and only if we allow the feminine dimension of that divine essence to achieve its proper complementary role" (pp. 138–39).

7. McFague, *Models of God,* p. 23.

8. Writing of the use of metaphor in theology, McFague says that "metaphor always has the character of 'is' and 'is not': one assertion is made but as likely account rather than a definition" (ibid., p. 33).

9. See Perrin, *Language of the Kingdom,* p. 31.

10. I recognize that I may not share the same lack of ease with the term *reign of God* as people who write out of the Reformed tradition (e.g., McFague), because my Catholic roots have never emphasized the sovereignty of God to the exclusion of human agency. In fact, the emphasis on human responsibility for "good works" has been a central emphasis—some would say to a fault—in the Catholic understanding of Christian faith.

11. There are a number of tensions in Jesus' preaching of the reign that were also evident in his Jewish tradition but were heightened by him and bequeathed to Christians thereafter. These tensions have at least three related but distinct expressions: "already realized" or "yet to be fulfilled," coming solely by the gift of God's grace or requiring human agency, and an eschatological event promised outside of history or an intrahistorical task that places personal and social responsibility on people now.

12. Viviano gives a helpful historical view of "four main currents of interpretation . . . of the Kingdom of God in the history of Christianity . . . down to modern times" (*Kingdom of God in History,* p. 32). He lists them as (1) the eschatological, (2) the spiritual-mystical, (3) the political, and (4) the ecclesial emphases. See ibid., chap. 2.

13. Here, as my language suggests, I am thinking of the possibility of nuclear destruction. Gordon Kaufman argues that the possibility of nuclear destruction alters our traditional sense of eschatology in which we typically presumed that God would never allow us to completely fail in the covenant. The nuclear issue forces us instead into a much more radical awareness that the covenant really does mean that we *can* refuse our side of the partnership, with terrible consequences for all human life—even the possibility of its total destruction. Kaufman writes "Devotion to God today means . . . that we resolve to make ourselves fully accountable for the continuance of life on earth" (*Theology for a Nuclear Age,* p. 46). The whole book proposes a contemporary consciousness regarding eschatology and thus the reign of God.

14. Judy Chicago gives a moving expression of this universal myth when she writes of the human yearning for an "Eden" existence once again (*The Dinner Party,* [New York: Doubleday, 1979] p. 256):

> And then all that has divided us will merge
> And then compassion will be wedded to power
> And then softness will come to a world that is harsh and unkind
> And then both men and women will be gentle
> And then both women and men will be strong
> And then no person will be subject to another's will
> And then all will be rich and free and varied
> And then the greed of some will give way to the needs of many
> And then all will share equally in the Earth's abundance
> And then all will care for the sick and the weak and the old
> And then all will nourish the young
> And then all will cherish life's creatures
> And then all will live in harmony with each other and the Earth
> And then everywhere will be called Eden once again

15. Rahner uses the terms *a priori* and *a posteriori* to describe, respectively, the relationship between faith as the gift of God and the expressed faith of the community that acts as the bearer of God's "categorical revelation." Though faith always begins from inner illumination through "the light of faith" that is God's self-revelation by grace, it is actualized and consciously appropriated only by encountering what Rahner calls the "a posteriori proposition of verbal revelation." For Christians the latter is carried within a historical context by a community of Christian faith. (See, e.g., *Foundations,* p. 150.)

16. "Decree on Ecumenism," Abbott, *Documents,* p. 354.

17. A. W. Whitehead, *Aims,* p. 1.

18. I do not deal with the issue of "readiness" in this work, because I dealt with it at length in *C.R.E.* (see pp. 235–57). In summary, my position on the issue of readiness

for critical reflection is that a form of concrete reflection is possible and should be encouraged at least from the beginning of formal education. As the tree is in the seed, so the potential for critical reflection in children should be encouraged if they are to do mature critical reflection (critiquing ideologies, unmasking social assumptions and interests, social analysis, etc.) later on as adults.

19. As W. C. Smith points out, the roots of the Latin *credere*, "to believe," are in the words *cor-dare*, literally, "to give one's heart." Smith also notes that the Old English word *bileve* had a similar meaning of pledging one's loyalty and commitment to God's service. See *Belief and History*, p. 42.

20. Little has a very helpful fourfold summary of the functions of "belief" in the life of Christian faith. She describes its functions as follows (*Heart*, pp. 18–21):

To help a person make sense of the world and have a frame of reference for understanding, caring, deciding, and doing.

To aid a community—in our case, specifically the religious community called the church—to achieve and maintain continuity.

To link human experience and the Christian tradition through an interpretation that internalizes meaning and gives direction to life.

To link lives of individuals and communities to larger, ultimate realities and purposes.

21. Aquinas writes, "The act of faith is directed to the object of the will, i.e., the good, as to its end: and this good that is the end of faith, viz., the Divine Good, is the proper object of charity. Therefore charity is called the form of faith in so far as the act of faith is perfected and formed by charity" (*Summa Theologica*, II–II, 4, 3; vol. 3, p. 1186).

22. Bonhoeffer wrote well of this: "Faith is only real when there is obedience, never without it, and faith only becomes faith in the act of obedience"(*Cost of Discipleship*, p. 55).

23. For this identification of the cognitive emphasis with Catholicism and the fiducial emphasis with Protestantism, see Dulles, "The Meaning of Faith."

24. Tillich, *Dynamics of Faith*, p. 4.

25. For a highly respected and oft-cited explanation of "the three main types of the idea of the atonement," see Gustaf Aulen, *Christus Victor*.

26. See McFague, *Models of God*, p. 64, for an insightful critique of the "satisfaction model."

27. For an insightful differentiation between Christ as substitute and Christ as representative, see Dorothee Sölle, *Christ the Representative*.

28. Denial of the resurrection of Jesus is not done simply by those who doubt the empty tomb story or who contend that the resurrection happened only in the hearts of the disciples. To deny the intrahistorical and political implications of the resurrection as a source of freedom and new life for all is the most dangerous denial of the resurrection of Jesus.

29. Hough and Cobb, *Education*, p. 58.

30. On the rationale and need for church-sponsored schools to function as communities of Christian faith, I highly recommend the excellent work of Marcellin Flynn. See Bibliography.

I deliberately nuance my claims here about fostering a Christian faith community in a schooling context because of the diversity of social/political contexts in which church-related schools function. To cite one instance from personal experience, in Pakistan there is a large and very influential network of church-sponsored schools, financed by the government, whose student population is typically 95 percent Moslem. The government strictly forbids any Christian evangelizing of the Muslim students, which makes giving an overtly Christian ethos to the school environment very problematic. However, even in that context there are significant ways in which the environment of church-sponsored schools reflects a distinctly Christian value system and worldview, albeit implicit, with significant consequences for the character formation of their students.

31. I borrow these terms from Locke Bowman and use them here much as he intends them. See *Teaching for Christian Hearts, Souls and Minds*, esp. chaps. 2, 3. I appreciate Bowman's work because he begins by raising the question of "knowing" for Christian education (his preferred term) and proposes a "holistic" understanding of it

that is "more than cognition" (p. 27). Drawing especially from the work of Rabbi Max Kadushin, he proposes that people be taught cognitive concepts and value concepts, clustered around "maxi-concepts" (e.g., God's love) in a way that informs and forms people's "hearts, souls and minds."

32. My previous writings have been consistently misinterpreted by James Michael Lee on this point. Lee constantly refers to the shared praxis approach as "cognitivist" and sees it as engaging people in a narrowly cognitive activity. See, e.g., Lee, *Religious Instruction,* pp. 76–77.

In almost fifteen years of using the approach I have never experienced shared praxis as a "cognitivist" process. There is indeed a cognitive dimension to it, as I believe there must be to all education worthy of the name, but in its dynamics, it is affect laden and praxislike in both origin and outcome. In fairness to Lee's critique I recognize that I have previously written about a praxis-based epistemology as "a way of knowing." It is my hope that these opening chapters will clarify that a shared-praxis approach educates for conation or wisdom rather than simply cognition and engages the whole of human "being" rather than the intellect alone in a "cognitivist" process.

Though Lee's critique has helped me to clarify what I am not saying, and thus to state more adequately what I intend, I also note with regret the vitriolic and *ad hominem* manner in which he has presented it in his writings. In a review of a collection of essays that includes one by Lee, Charles Melchert writes of Lee's piece as follows: "It is sad that an author of such brilliant potential seems driven to mount such harsh and petty personal attacks on others in the field, rather than simply making his own worthwhile critical contributions. His bitter tirades often make it hard to hear his legitimate insights" (Review of *Does the Church Really Want Religious Education?* p. 477). I agree!

33. The possibilities of the word *conation* were first suggested to me by a written comment of Sarah Little. Little uses *conative* to describe the knowledge outcome that emerges from Paulo Freire's praxis-based process of educating. She writes, "The knowledge that resulted might be called conative, with will and desire united in action that in turn developed the freedom of sense, power, and understanding" (*Heart,* p. 82).

34. See Cicero's *De Natura Deorum Academica* II:58; pp. 178–79, for his use of *conatus* to translate the Greek *hormae,* a term the Stoics used for desire or appetite.

35. See, e.g., E. R. Hilgard, "The Trilogy of Mind."

36. See, e.g., Kolbe, *The Conative Connection,* p. 16. Late in my research for this book I discovered the fascinating work of Kathe Kolbe on conation and what she proposes as "the conative connection." Her primary audience seems to be the world of management, and her intent is to revive attention to conation and to the conative characteristics of people as a crucial strategy for promoting creativity and productivity. Though she proposes a rather holistic understanding of conation, much as I do here, we diverge in that she settles for the traditional understanding of conation as the third—to cognitive and affective—of the "three faculties." See ibid, p. 9.

37. Plato, *The Republic,* book 4, 435E–444E; pp. 235–45.

38. Plato, *Theaetetus,* 153A; pp. 44–45.

39. Aristotle writes, "We can now define motion or change (*kinesis*) as the progress of the realizing of a potentiality, qua potentiality" (*Physics* III, 201a; vol. 1, pp. 194–95).

40. Aristotle, *Metaphysics,* 1072b; pp. 150–51.

41. From my research, it seems that scholars disagree on how Aristotle used the term *kinesis,* and it appears most accurate to say that he used the term variously. I have already given what seems to be his classic definition from the *Physics* (see note 39). However, also in the *Physics,* Aristotle limits *kinesis* to three of the "accidents," quality, quantity, and change of place; i.e., he excludes *kinesis* from what happens on the level of substance (*ousia*), action, and passion (see *Physics,* V, 225b5–226b17; vol. 2, pp. 19–33). It is also clear that in *De Anima* Aristotle limits *kinesis* to one of the four main functions of the *psyche,* the others being nutrition, sensation, and thought (see *On the Soul,* 413a–b; pp. 71–77), and he resolves *kinesis* into the operation of desire (*orexis*) in conjunction with what is perceived as a real or apparent good. In fact his use of the term *orexis* (desire) as the active reaching out for whatever the animal or human perceives as good for it (and for which Liddel and Scott give *conation* as one translation) may well be closer at times in his writings to what I intend here by conation.

42. Aristotle, *De Anima* III, 429a–431a, 433a–b; pp. 162–77, 185–91.

43. Spinoza used *conatus* as Cicero had used it, to translate the Stoic term *hormae,* their word for the "first appetite" that moves the soul to action.

44. Cicero insisted that "every natural organism aims at being its own preserver" (*De Finibus Bonorum et Malorum,* IV, 7, 16; pp. 318–19).

45. Augustine devotes a chapter (book 11, chap. 27) in *The City of God* to how all things in nature wish to exist and to conserve their existence: "Merely to exist is so pleasant that in itself it is enough to make even the wretched unwilling to die." (*City of God,* p. 236).

46. Aquinas writes that "everything has a natural desire to be kept in existence" (*On the Power of God,* 5, 1, 13; p. 85).

47. Spinoza, *Ethics,* part 4, prop. 22; p. 167.

48. Ibid., part 3, prop. 7; p. 109.

49. See ibid., part 3, prop. 28; p. 121.

50. "Desire is the very essence of man [*sic*], that is, the conatus whereby man endeavors to persist in his own being" (ibid., part 4, prop. 18; p. 164).

51. "This conatus of the mind wherewith the mind, insofar as it exercises reason, endeavors to preserve its own being is nothing else but a conatus to understand" (ibid., part 4, prop. 26; p. 168).

52. Aquinas's use of *conatus* is usually translated "effort" or "endeavor"; he uses it as the active dynamic of life that causes historical agency toward the good. For example, he writes, "Everything by its own operation and effort [*conatu*] tends to good only for no one acts intending evil" (*Summa Theologica,* I, 103, 8; vol. 1, p. 510).

53. *Encyclopaedia Britannica* (1983), "Conation," Micropaedia 3:60.

54. Baldwin, *Dictionary,* vol. 1, p. 206.

55. That the term appears in Baldwin's dictionary, which includes psychological terms, was no accident, however; by the beginning of the 20th c. its usage was largely confined to psychology. In the work of two British psychologists, William McDougall (1871–1938) and George Frederick Stout (1860–1944), conation was given a central place and used with a holistic meaning. McDougall described his work as "conative psychology" and referred to the "conatives" as the primary dispositions and dynamics that initiate and sustain all human activities—cognitive, affective, and behavioral. Stout used "conative activity" to describe all the psychophysical processes that enable human engagement in the world. Conation, then, is the consciousness that emerges from such engagement. Though he distinguished two categories of conative activity, namely, practical and theoretical, with the former moving us to the production of change and the latter to a clearer apprehension of our life in the world, Stout insisted that his conative theory of human agency was an attempt to unite mind and body in the one consciousness of the embodied self.

See McDougall, *Physiological Psychology* (1905) and *An Introduction to Social Psychology* (1908); and Stout, *A Manual of Psychology* (1899).

56. See *A Catechism of Christian Doctrine* (commonly called The Baltimore Catechism), 1885 edition, p. 5. (Emphasis added.)

57. Murphy, "Concept of Old Testament Wisdom," p. 492.

58. For some fine reviews of "wisdom" in the Hebrew Scriptures see *"CHAKHAM"* in *Theological Dictionary of the Old Testament,* vol. 4, pp. 364–91, and *"BIN,"* vol. 2, pp. 99–107.

59. See Blanchard, "Wisdom," pp. 322–24.

60. Braxton, in *The Wisdom Community,* proposes this as "a descriptive image" of the church.

61. Heidegger wrote, "To work out the question of Being adequately, we must make an entity—the inquirer—transparent in his own Being. This entity that each of us is himself and that includes inquiring as one of the possibilities of its Being, we shall denote by the term 'Dasein'" (*Being and Time,* p. 27). In *Being and Time* Heidegger proposed this shift to the "Being" of the inquirer as essential if epistemology and ontology are to be united. He took Dasein as his starting point in his effort to think "Being" (*Sein*) as such and set out to delineate a phenomenological understanding by analyzing the aspects of our "Being" that immediately appear in our consciousness—the characteristics of Dasein. For Heidegger, the true subject of ontology is Dasein, because it "is ontically distinguished by the fact that, in its very Being, that Being is an issue for it." He adds, "It is peculiar

to this entity that with and through its Being, this Being is disclosed to it. Understanding of Being is itself a definite characteristic of Dasein's Being" (ibid., p. 32). I should note, however, that he never completed the project proposed for *Being and Time*. His later work abandoned the effort to think "Being" by beginning with *Dasein* and favored less metaphysical approaches instead.

62. I take this rendering from the translators' (Macquarrie and Robinson) footnote on p. 27 of *Being and Time*.

63. Heidegger, *Being and Time*, p. 67. Sartre, for one, read Heidegger to claim that existence is all we are, that existence precedes essence. (See *Existentialism and Human Emotions*, p. 15.) Heidegger, however, rejected this as a misinterpretation. (See his "Letter on Humanism," *Basic Writings*, pp. 205ff.) I am indebted to Raymond Devettere for alerting me to this essay and its point.

64. This is the theme of Heidegger's opening statement in *Being and Time*. See pp. 21–24. Many critics of Heidegger who are familiar with Thomas Aquinas reject Heidegger's claim as certainly untrue of Aquinas. In reply to Heidegger, Mondin writes, "Not only did St. Thomas not lose sight of being, but on the contrary he made it the basis, the center and the crown of his entire philosophical system" (*St. Thomas Aquinas' Philosophy*, p. 35).

65. Though Heidegger often wrote of Dasein as co-Dasein, his critics generally agree that the relational (and thus the political) dimension of human existence was more linguistic than real in his thought. In addition, in his writings "authentic existence" always reads as if it is forged through a rugged individualism by oneself and for oneself alone.

Chapter 2. Epistemology Re-visioned

1. With this typical usage of the term *epistemology*, and even in my very employing of the term, I am reading something retroactively back into the history of Western philosophy. It appears that the first person to actually use the word *epistemology* (from *episteme*, meaning "knowledge," and *logos*, an "account") was the Scottish philosopher J. F. Ferrier (1808–1864) in his *Institutes of Metaphysic*, first published in 1854. Ferrier distinguished two branches of philosophy: ontology and epistemology, thus formalizing a dichotomy that had long been operative in Western philosophy. Thereafter the word gained common currency and was used to describe the concern for knowledge and knowing that had characterized philosophy long before Ferrier coined the word. How it is understood at present is not, however, the same as how many of the ancients might have understood it. Plato, e.g., saw *episteme* as "scientific knowledge" alone and scientific knowledge as the only form of reliable knowledge. Aristotle, by contrast, had a broader notion of knowledge than *episteme*, including knowledge of how to live a practical ethical life. Thus, in referring, e.g., to Aristotle's praxis epistemology I am using the term with its present understanding and not as he would have understood it.

2. See Ackermann, *Knowledge*, p. 4.

3. The origin of Skepticism is usually traced to the philosophers of the Eleatic school (5th c. B.C.E.) who questioned the reality of the sensory world and raised doubts about our human ability to know from experience. A more thorough form of Skepticism, questioning the ability of both reason and experience to engender reliable knowledge, emerged with Pyrrho of Ellis (365?–?275 B.C.E.) and Timon of Phlius (c. 320–c. 230 B.C.E.).

4. Aquinas popularized this phrase but claimed to have learned it from Aristotle. See Aquinas, *Truth*, 2, 3, Diff. 19; vol. 1, p. 69.

5. Harding, *The Science Question*, p. 136.

6. See Fox-Keller, *Gender and Science*, esp. chaps. 3, 4.

7. One way to appreciate Plato's position here is to understand him as attempting to build upon but also to correct the error in two opposing positions that were prevalent before his time. Heraclitus had claimed that everything is in a state of constant change ("We cannot step into the same river twice," was his famous metaphor) and that we can only have opinion through sense experience of the ever-changing (thus unreliable) world of "becoming." On the other hand, against Heraclitus, Parmenides insisted that reality is unchanging (the saying "The more things change, the more they remain the same," is

often cited as a pithy summary of his thought) and that by reason we can have sure ideas of the unchanging world of "being." Essentially, Plato subsumed both of those positions, shaping them into a dualistic and hierarchical metaphysics.

8. Fox-Keller, *Gender and Science,* p. 22.

9. Found in bk. 7 of Plato's *The Republic,* pp. 312ff.

10. Ibid., bk. 6, 509; p. 309.

11. Plato writes, "By images I mean first of all shadows, then reflections in water and in surfaces which are of close texture, smooth and shiny, and everything of that kind" (ibid.).

12. See Plato, *Phaedo,* 66; Jowett trans., p. 449.

13. Plato writes, "In the first part [CD] the soul in its search is compelled to use as images the things imitated—the realities of the former part [BC]—and from things taken for granted passes not to a new beginning, a first principle, but to an end, a conclusion" (*The Republic,* bk. 6, 510B; p. 310). See also the *Meno;* 79C–81A; pp. 41–42.

14. See Plato, *The Republic,* bk. 6, 511B; p. 311.

15. See ibid., bk. 7, 517C–519C; pp. 316–17.

16. In the *Timaeus,* Plato himself posits the existence of God as the divine Creator who patterns the universe in space and time according to the world of forms. See *Timaeus,* 29E–30; pp. 54–57.

17. It is true that Plato argued in favor of women being educated on a par with men. (See *The Republic,* bk. 5, 453–35; pp. 251–53.) He left no doubt, however, that the philosophers to rule the rest are to be men. (See ibid., bk. 7, 518; p. 318).

18. Aristotle writes, "Scientific Knowledge is a mode of conception dealing with universals and things that are of necessity; and demonstrated truths and all scientific knowledge (since this involves reasoning) are derived from first principles" (*Nicomachean Ethics,* bk. 6, chap. 6: 1; p. 341).

19. Ibid., bk. 6, chap. 7: 3 and 5; pp. 343, 345.

20. Aristotle defined the good as "that for the sake of which everything is done" (ibid., bk. 1, chap. 7: 1; p. 25). He described the good life as "the active exercise of the soul's faculties in conformity with excellence or virtue, or if there be several excellences or virtues, in conformity with the best and most perfect among them" (ibid., bk. 1, chap. 7: 15; p. 33).

21. Ibid., bk. 7, chap. 7: 5; p. 345.

22. Aristotle's notion of contemplation, however, is not quite the same as what emerged in Christian monasteries as the contemplative life. The latter was reflection on God as manifested in the visible world. For Aristotle, contemplation meant removing oneself from the physical world to interior introspection on things eternal.

23. Ibid., bk. 10, chap. 7: 8; p. 617.

24. Ibid., bk. 10, chap. 8: 7; p. 623.

25. On occasion Aristotle spoke of the praxis of animals (see Aristotle, *Parts of Animals,* bk. 2, chap. 1, 646B; pp. 109 ff.). This, however, was more of a colloquial use. Strictly speaking, animals cannot perform praxis, because it always requires reflection and choice.

26. It is not easy to render in English what Aristotle meant by praxis. Clearly it is the root of our word *practice.* But for Aristotle, it meant more than what we typically mean by "practice" (as in "theory applied to practice"). In contemporary theological and pedagogical literature, where praxis typically refers to reflection on and in action, or, conversely, activity done reflectively, the tendency is to leave the term untranslated. I do likewise throughout this work. On occasion I use *action/reflection* as a synonym for praxis.

27. Aristotle, *Nicomachean Ethics,* bk. 6, chap. 2: 1; pp. 327–29.

28. See ibid., bk. 6, chap. 1: 5–6; p. 327.

29. See ibid., bk. 3, chap. 12: 8; p. 187.

30. Ibid., bk. 6, chap. 2: 3–4; p. 329.

31. Ibid., bk. 6, chap. 5: 4; p. 337.

32. See ibid., bk. 1, chap. 13: 20; pp. 67–69.

33. See ibid., bk. 6, chap. 11: 7; pp. 345–47. Aristotle later writes, "But when we . . . *judge* . . . about matters that are in the sphere of Prudence, we are said to *understand* (that is, to judge rightly, for *right* judgment is the same as *good* understanding)" (ibid., bk. 6, chap. 10: 3; p. 359).

34. "[O]nly an utterly senseless person can fail to know that our characters are the result of our conduct" (ibid., bk. 3, chap. 5: 12; p. 147). Here Aristotle was pushing back against Plato's notion that knowledge is virtue. He writes, "For it is our choice of good or evil that determines our character, not our opinion about good or evil" (ibid., bk. 3, chap. 2: 11; p. 133). Thus, "our moral dispositions are formed as a result of the corresponding activities" (ibid., bk. 2, chap. 1: 7; p. 75).

35. Aristotle wrote, "Art, being concerned with making, is not concerned with doing" (ibid., bk. 6, chap. 4: 5; p. 335). Of the distinction between praxis and poiesis, Lobkowicz writes, "The distinction is not easily rendered in English; what comes closest to it is the difference between 'doing' and 'making.' We *do* sports or business or politics, and we *make* ships or houses or statues" (*Theory and Practice,* p. 9). Interestingly, and perhaps wisely, Aristotle did not distinguish between the artistic and the productive; for him, both belonged within the life of poiesis. Up to the "modern" era, skilled craftspeople continued to be called "artisans"; what remains of their work has come, when compared to the artifacts of later mass production, to be often recognized as "art." With the industrial revolution, however, art and technics were not only distinguished but separated. Art came to refer to expressions of the inner and subjective life, and technics, as Mumford describes it, to the attempt "to control the forces of nature and to expand the power and mechanical efficiency of man's [*sic*] own natural organs, on their practical and operational side" (*Art and Technics,* p. 32). In consequence, laments Mumford (and I concur), "Technics is steadily becoming more automatic, more impersonal, more 'objective'; while art, in reaction, shows signs of becoming more neurotic and self-destructive, regressing into primitive or infantile symbolism, to babble and mud pies and formless scrawls" (ibid).

36. Aristotle, *Nicomachean Ethics,* bk. 6, chap. 4: 6; pp. 335–37.

37. Aristotle, *Metaphysics,* bk. 1, chap. 1: 9; p. 5.

38. Aristotle, *De Anima,* bk. 3, 7, p. 177. And Aquinas, footnoting Aristotle, argued that the role of imagination in reasoning is especially evident if one grants that knowing begins, not as the Platonists claim from a world of separate forms, but from "sensible things." (See *Summa Theologica* 1.84.7; vol. 1, pp. 429–30.

39. Aristotle, *De Anima,* bk. 3, 10, p. 191.

40. "It is obvious, then, that memory belongs to that part of the soul to which imagination belongs; all things which are imaginable are essentially objects of memory, and those which necessarily involve imagination are objects of memory only incidentally" (Aristotle, *Parva Naturalia,* p. 293).

41. Comparing the historian who depends on memory to the poet, Aristotle wrote, "The real difference is this, that one tells what happened and the other what might happen" (*Poetics,* bk. 8, 4; p. 35). See also p. 15.

42. See Aristotle, *Rhetoric,* bk. 1, 5, 1361a 6; pp. 50–51.

43. Hartsock, "The Feminist Standpoint," p. 293. Hartsock explains that the activity of "women as mothers . . . is far more complex than the instrumental working with others to transform objects. . . . The female experience in reproduction represents a unity with nature which goes beyond the proletarian experience of interchange with nature" (ibid.).

44. Hilary Rose, quoted in Harding, *The Science Question,* p. 142.

45. My position here reflects the common interpretation that though Aristotle saw all three lives as valid ways of knowing, he separated and opposed them to each other, poiesis to praxis and praxis to theoria. (See Lobkowicz, *Theory and Practice,* pp. 9, 17.) The basis of this interpretation can certainly be found in Aristotle. For example, he opposed theoria and praxis because theoria attends to that which is unchangeable, whereas "matters of conduct [*praxis*] admit of variation" (*Nicomachean Ethics,* bk. 6, chap. 5: 3; p. 337).

Then, though poiesis and praxis pertain to "things of variation," yet "the rational quality concerned with doing is different from the rational quality concerned with making; nor is one of them a part of the other, for doing is not a form of making, nor making a form of doing" (ibid., bk. 6, chap. 4: 2; p. 335).

46. "Let it be assumed that there are five qualities through which the mind achieves truth in affirmation or denial, namely Art or technical skill, Scientific Knowledge, Prudence, Wisdom, and Intelligence" (ibid., bk. 6, chap. 3: 1; pp. 331–33).

47. Ibid., bk. 10, chap. 7: 8; p. 617.

48. See Maria Harris, "Art and Religious Education: A Conversation," for an insightful review of the "elements" of "the mystical, numinous and mystery" in religious education.

49. I extrapolate this point from my overall reading of Aristotle. For example, in *De Anima* he explained that *kinesis* (human "movement") is produced by "appetitive and practical thought," but he spoke similarly of the source of praxis throughout the *Ethics*. See *On the Soul*, bk. 3, chap. 40, pp. 186–91.

50. It is interesting to note that in the Septuagint, the verb used for God's creative activity of both heaven and earth is *poieo* (Gen. 1:1 ff.) and likewise for God's creation of humanity (Gen. 1:27, etc.). God is named as the Creator (*ho poiesas,* Prov. 14:31) and as the Creator of the chosen people (Isa. 43:1). *Poiesis* is used to denote either God's creating (Ps. 19:2) or what God has created (Sir. 16:24). Not only does the Septuagint use both *praxis* and *poiesis* when speaking of God's activity, but it does not make the clear distinction between the two activities that Aristotle made. For example, *poiemata* is used to describe God's actions in history as well as God's creation (Eccles. 1:14) and is used of God's saving deeds, e.g., in bringing the people out of slavery (Exod. 13:8). See *Theological Dictionary of the New Testament* (abridged ed.), *"poiemata,"* by H. Braun, pp. 895 ff.

51. I take this phrase from Elisabeth Schüssler Fiorenza, *In Memory of Her*. It is her description of the community called forth by Jesus. See, e.g., p. 154. I will use the phrase frequently throughout this work.

52. Lobkowicz, *Theory and Practice*, pp. 60–61.

53. See *The Didache*.

54. Irenaeus wrote, "There is now no need to seek among others the truth which we can easily obtain from the Church. For the Apostles have lodged all that there is of the truth with her. . . . And so anyone that wishes can draw from her the draught of life" (*Adversus Haereses* 3.4.1, in Bettenson, ed., *Documents*, pp. 69–70).

55. Tertullian wrote, "What is there in common between Athens and Jerusalem? What between the Academy and the Church? . . . Away with all projects for a 'Stoic,' a 'Platonic' or a 'dialectic Christianity!' After Christ Jesus we desire no subtle theories, no acute enquiries after the gospel" (Tertullian, *De Praescriptione Haereticorum* 7, in Bettenson, ed., *Documents*, p. 6).

56. The beginnings of Neoplatonism are difficult to pinpoint. Historians place its origins sometime in the 2d c. C.E. and say it became a formal school in Alexandria under Ammonius Saccas (died c. 241). Ammonius was a contemporary of Clement of Alexandria and the reputed teacher of both Plotinus (see following note) and Origen. Alexandria was a crossroads between East and West, which explains some of the varied religious and philosophical components that influenced Neoplatonism.

57. Plotinus studied under Ammonius Saccas (see note above) at Alexandria. He also studied in India and was influenced by mystical religious thought encountered there. He taught in Rome from 245 to 268. For ready access to his most important writings, see *The Essential Plotinus*.

58. See Viviano, *Kingdom of God in History*, pp. 9–10.

59. Lobkowicz writes of this Neoplatonist position, "Nothing opposed to contemplation was any longer a perfection in its own right; only contemplative life truly counted and everything else was either its radical absence or a path leading toward it. Virtue and human perfection were now divorced from all socio-political context" (*Theory and Practice*, p. 55).

60. See *New Catholic Encyclopedia*, "Paideia, Christian," by T. P. Halton, 10:862–64.

61. The Catechetical School at Alexandria was founded by Pantaenus (died c. 190), who was well schooled in Neoplatonism.

62. See Bonino, *Christians and Marxists*, esp. chap. 2.

63. Clement has been referred to as "the creator of the first grand synthesis of speculative theology" (Congar, *A History of Theology*, p. 42) but also as "a slightly Christianized version" of Neoplatonism (Lobkowicz, *Theory and Practice*, p. 69). For Clement, the most virtuous Christian life is contemplation, because it brings one to mystical union with God. Epistemologically, this communion is achieved by inner illumination whose source is Christ the Logos, the fullness of reason and truth. The life of Christian praxis is useful for Clement, but as Lobkowicz summarizes his position, "only insofar as it leads to a cognitive and eventually contemplative, even mystical, union with God" (ibid.).

If Clement was the first systematic theologian in the church, Origen can be called the first great scripture scholar and proponent of textual criticism. Origen's best known scripture commentary was the *Hexapla,* an allegorical interpretation of the Old Testament to show Christians its fulfillment in the New. (See *The Jerome Biblical Commentary,* "Modern New Testament Criticism," by John S. Kselman, 41:3, and "Hermeneutics," by Raymond E. Brown, 71:38.) Origen seemed to fare no better than Clement, however, in attempting to construct a theoretical system to balance the practical demands of Christianity with the mystical and rationalist traditions of Greek philosophy. Unduly influenced by the Neoplatonism of Ammonius Saccas (see note 56), whose lectures he attended in Alexandria, Origen said that the active life is only "the stirrup to contemplation" (quoted in Lobkowicz, *Theory and Practice,* p. 60). In consequence, Origen concluded, there are two classes of Christians: the simple people who must be satisfied with unquestioning faith in Christ crucified, and "the purified," an elite group of scholars, all men, who ascend by contemplation to union with God in Christ.

64. Augustine, *The Trinity,* bk. 9, chap. 1; p. 270.

65. See Augustine, "On Free Will," bk. 1, chap.2, in *Augustine: Earlier Works,* p. 115. In his *Homilies on the Gospel of John,* Augustine wrote, "For understanding is the reward of faith. Therefore do not seek to understand in order to believe, but believe that thou mayest understand" (tract 29, no. 6; p. 184).

66. Manicheaism, founded by a Persian monk, Manes (c.216–c.276), was an amalgam of Gnosticism and dualism. It posited a Good Spirit of Light reflected in the mind and soul and a Spirit of Darkness that is reflected in the body (and thus in women, they said) and in the created order. Salvation was to be found by transcending bodily existence and the physical order. Augustine became a Manichaean at about the age of twenty and remained one for approximately ten years. In Tillich's opinion, "Augustine always remained under the influence of Manichaeism" (*History of Christian Thought,* p. 106).

67. Augustine approvingly quoted Plato's position that "there are two worlds, an intelligible world where truth itself dwells, and the sensible world which we perceive by sight and touch" (*Answer to Skeptics* 3.17.37; p. 213).

68. See Augustine, "The Magnitude of the Soul," p. 83.

69. Augustine, "The Catholic and Manichaean Ways of Life" 1.27.52; p. 41.

70. In his treatise *The Trinity,* Augustine posed the unity and distinctions of reason, memory, and will as an analogy of the Trinity. Concerning their unity, he wrote, "Since these three, the memory, the understanding, and the will, are therefore not three lives but one life, not three minds but one mind it follows that they are certainly not three substances but one. . . . Therefore, these three are one in that they are one life, one mind, and one essence. And whatever else they are called in respect to themselves, they are called together, not in the plural but in the singular" (*The Trinity,* bk. 10, chap. 11: 18; p. 311).

71. Augustine writes, "If, then, this is the correct distinction between wisdom and science [i.e., knowledge], that to wisdom belongs the intellectual cognition of eternal things, but to science [i.e., knowledge] the reasonable cognition of temporal things, it is not difficult to decide which is to be preferred" (ibid., bk. 12, chap. 15: 25; p. 367).

72. Ibid., bk. 15, chap. 12: 21; p. 482.

73. Augustine wrote of "the light by which the soul is illumined, in order that it may see and truly understand everything . . . the light is God Himself [*sic*] . . . since [the soul] is rational and intellectual, it is made in His image" (*The Literal Meaning of Genesis,* vol. 2, p. 222).

74. See Augustine, *The Trinity,* bk. 15, chap. 12: 22; p. 483.

75. See Augustine, *The Confessions,* bk. 10, chap. 10; pp. 239–40.

76. See Augustine, *The Teacher,* chap. 12: 40; p. 180. Augustine explains further, "Regarding, however, all those things which we understand, it is not a speaker who utters sounds exteriorly whom we consult, but it is truth that presides within over the mind itself; though it may have been words that prompted us to make such consultation. And He who is consulted, He who is said to dwell in the inner man [*sic*], he it is who teaches— Christ—that is, the unchangeable Power of God and everlasting Wisdom. This Wisdom every rational soul does, in fact, consult" (ibid., chap. 11: 38; p. 177).

77. See Augustine, *The Confessions,* bk. 10, chap. 8; pp. 236–37.

78. "With the eye of the mind, therefore, we perceive in that eternal truth, from which all temporal things have been made, the form according to which we are, and by which we effect something either in ourselves or in bodies with a true and right reason" (Augustine, *The Trinity,* bk. 9, chap. 7: 12; pp. 281–82).

79. See Augustine, *The Enchiridion on Faith, Hope and Love,* pp. 124–25.

80. See Augustine, *The Confessions,* bk. 10, chap. 21: 30; p. 250.

81. See ibid., bk. 10, chap. 23: 33; p. 252.

82. Augustine sometimes spoke of unity between the "three lives." As the following quote indicates he did not understand the three ways of life as Aristotle did (or perhaps he misread Aristotle) but was convinced that the contemplative life and Christian praxis should never be totally separated. "Or take the three modes of life, the contemplative, the active, the contemplative-active. A man [*sic*] can live the life of faith in any of these three and get to heaven. What is not indifferent is that he love truth and do what charity demands. No man must be so committed to contemplation as, in his contemplation, to give no thought to his neighbor's needs nor so absorbed in action as to dispense with the contemplation of God" (*City of God,* bk. 19, chap. 19; p. 467).

83. See Augustine, *The Teacher,* chap. 12: 40; p. 160. See also chaps. 11 and 12 generally.

84. Ibid., chap. 14; p. 185.

85. See Augustine, *The Confessions,* bk. 10, chap. 11: 18; pp. 240–41.

86. Augustine, *Divine Providence,* bk. 2, chap. 9: 26; p. 303.

87. The intent of spiritual wisdom was clearly more evident in the work of Augustine and in the theological method of prayerful reflection (aided by divine illumination) on the sacred pages of Scripture that was generally practiced throughout the first millennium. See Gustavo Gutierrez, *A Theology of Liberation,* pp. 4–6, for a fine delineation of the historical distinction between theology as spiritual wisdom and theology as rational knowledge and the Scholastic preference for the latter. Though he does not use the same categories as Gutierrez, see also Edward Farley, *Theologia,* esp. chaps. 2, 3, and 4, for the historical evolution of theology from *theologia* as a "*habitus . . .* of practical knowledge having the primary character of wisdom" (p. 81) to theology as an encyclopedia of sciences.

88. Aquinas was familiar with Stoicism and Neoplatonism, with Augustine and with Boethius, had read the Islamic Aristotelians (Avicenna and Averroës) and the great Jewish Aristotelian philosopher Maimonides.

89. For Aquinas's understanding of the unity and interdependence of body and soul, see "Disputed Questions on the Soul" 8, in *The Soul,* pp. 98–102.

90. See Aquinas, *Summa Theologica* 1.85.1; vol. 1, p. 432.

91. See *Summa Theologica* 1.79.4 ad 4; vol. 1, p. 400.

92. Aquinas explained that the "passive" or "sensitive" intellect has "four interior powers." First, there is a general or what he called *common sense* power by which we perceive and grasp what is seen, heard, touched, etc. We have a sense power of *imagination* that is "a storehouse of forms received through the senses" that acts to retain these forms long after their stimulus has passed. We have a *memory* sense power that associates objects of sense perception with past experience. And we have a *cogitative* or *estimative* power (he also called it "particular reason") that collates sense impressions and comes to discern the meaning of things. See *Summa Theologica* 1.78.4; vol. 1, pp. 394–96.

93. Aquinas writes, "The higher and more noble agent . . . the active intellect . . . causes the phantasms received from the senses to be actually intelligible, by a process of abstraction. According to this opinion, then, on the part of the phantasms, intellectual knowledge is caused by the senses. But since the phantasms cannot of themselves affect the passive intellect, and require to be made actually intelligible by the active intellect, it cannot be said that sensible knowledge is the total and perfect cause of intellectual knowledge, but rather that it is in a way the material cause" (*Summa Theologica* 1.84.6; vol. 1, p. 428).

94. See *Summa Theologica* 1–2.57.1; vol. 2, pp. 827–28; and 2–2.47.2; vol. 3, p. 1384.

95. *Summa Theologica* 1.79.11; vol. 1, p. 406.

96. See *Summa Theologica* 1–2.57.3; vol. 2, pp. 829–30.

97. For Aquinas, "God's essence" is "existence" (*esse*). (See *Summa Theologica* 1.3.4; vol. 1, p. 17.) To summarize some of Aquinas's central themes that may be relevant

background here, first, this "existence" of God is very much as an active "Being." In an agential and creative sense—God is fully noun and fully verb (to use the language of chap. 1)—or "fully Act"—to use Aquinas's language. Human beings participate in God's "Being" because our soul is the divine presence of God's "Being" within us, so that what God is in Act, we share in potency. Our potencies are to be realized according to the will of God, and we are drawn to realize them because we have a natural desire for "Being." We are lured to become who we ought to become because we are turned toward the "Being" of God. Because our "being" is a participation in divine "Being," there is a "natural law" in us by which we can rationally know God's providential design for the world and can choose to act in conformity with what we know to be God's will. As the true, the good, and the beautiful are perfectly realized in God, so we can move toward knowing the truth, doing the good, and creating the beautiful. In our historical agency we are empowered by God's grace, but we are also responsible historical subjects. God's grace works through nature, perfecting and empowering human agency rather than replacing it.

98. For this insight I am indebted to the research of my spouse, Colleen Griffith.

99. This is an important point for me to make, especially as a Catholic religious educator. As a tradition, Catholicism is prone to draw upon Aquinas as a primary theological authority. Yet Aquinas has often been misinterpreted, especially in Catholic catechesis, as if he were opposed to people's thinking for themselves in matters of faith. A more faithful interpretation of Aquinas's epistemology would point to the contrary. The critical role of reason was certainly expanded by the Enlightenment and by later awareness of the sociology of knowledge. Nevertheless, I believe Aquinas would very much approve of the present emphasis on critical reflection and consciousness-raising in religious education to uncover the distortions in present social praxis—sexism, racism, militarism, age bias, etc.

100. I draw heavily from Lonergan's work in chap. 3 to outline the functional dynamics of a conative process, but we must remember where he first found his "insight," and Lonergan would be first to footnote Aquinas for it.

101. I think of the emergence of the Catholic Counter-Reformation catechisms of Canisius, Trent, and Bellarmine as epitomizing the triumph of objectified and metaphysically stated "truths" in Catholic catechesis.

102. Aquinas, Summa Theologica 1.92.1; vol. 1, pp. 466–67. His patriarchal bias was also epitomized in a now oft-quoted passage just prior to the one cited. It reads, "As regards the individual nature, woman is defective and misbegotten, for the active force in the male seed tends to the production of a perfect likeness in the masculine sex; while the production of woman comes from defect in the active force or from some material indisposition, or even from some external influence; such as that of a south wind, which is moist, as the Philosopher observes" (ibid., p. 466).

103. In De Magistro (The Teacher) Aquinas argued strongly against the discovery method, claiming it to be inferior to the didactic one. He said that the most effective, expeditious, and reliable pedagogy, especially in educating the "ignorant," is instruction by a teacher, because the learner's own experience is not a reliable source of knowing. See The Teacher, esp. 2, 4; p. 118.

104. The Catechetical Instructions were probably delivered as a series of Lenten sermons at Naples in 1272; thus they may not reflect what his actual pedagogy was in an educational setting. Throughout the sermons, however, the articles of the Creed, the Commandments, the Sacraments, the Lord's Prayer, and the Hail Mary (a sequence that later became the classic version of Catholic catechisms as creed, code, cult) are presented in a very didactic and objectified way with no apparent attempt to address the lives or engage the reflection of the congregation.

105. John Duns Scotus (c.1265–1308) argued strongly that theology ought to be a quest for right living rather than for knowledge about God. For Scotus, because God is love, blessedness for the Christian is obtained by active loving. Faith is grounded in the will, not in assent of the intellect as Aquinas contended. Scotus was the only one of the medievalists to even retain the term praxis and propose it as a way of coming to faith knowledge. He wrote, "God is the 'doable knowable' [cognoscibile operabile], that is, that object of knowledge which may be reached by a doing which is true praxis" (quoted in Lobkowicz, Theory and Practice, p. 74). William of Occam (1285–1347), very much persona

non grata with the papal and ecclesiastical authorities of his time, was tried for heresy and had fifty-one propositions from his work censured. A critic of both the papacy and the dominant relationship between philosophy and theology among the Scholastics, Occam was much more in favor of intuition over abstraction and induction over deduction. Thus he prepared the way for a more "scientific" (by which he meant experimental) approach to knowing reality.

106. Luther railed against the decadent rationalism of the theology of his time, but alas, when he came to recommend a process of religious instruction, Luther wrote his *Short Catechism,* followed by the *Larger Catechism* (1529), in a question-and-answer format and very conceptual language mode. In the preface to his *Short Catechism,* Luther ordered pastors and parents to "take these tables and forms, and instruct the people in them word for word" (*Short Catechism,* p. 88).

Calvin too opted for a catechism approach, writing what became known as *Instructions in the Christian Faith* or simply *Instruction in Faith* (1537) as a catechism version of his *Institutes of the Christian Religion.* He followed with "The Catechism of the Church of Geneva" (1542) in a question-and-answer format that was to be committed to memory.

107. In the intervening years, a challenge to the unduly speculative mode of traditional metaphysics was launched by Francis Bacon (1561–1626), the English statesman and philosopher of science. Bacon had little time for speculative philosophy, because, he believed, it had proved to be so useless in practical matters. What is needed, argued Bacon, is a *novum organum* (1620)—a whole new beginning and a method of procuring knowledge that would give humankind mastery over nature. Thus Bacon proposed an empirical mode of knowing as the basic method of scientific inquiry. Instead of theorizing about the world of ideas, the way to knowledge is by experimentation and induction from the facts of experience to fundamental principles. By gathering empirical data through sense experience, by judicious interpretation, and by further experimentation to verify emerging hypotheses, the world of nature could be known for human benefit, and science would issue in practical results. See Bacon, *Novum Organum.*

108. The work of the Skeptic philosopher Michel de Montaigne has not survived the test of time in its own right; he is remembered only as the philosophical foil who drove Descartes to seek rational certainty. A fideist in philosophy, for de Montaigne, faith alone, a gift of God's grace, was the reliable guide and source of knowledge. Did Descartes overreact to such skepticism, as Plato and Aristotle had done before him? See Curley, *Descartes Against the Skeptics.*

109. Descartes, *Meditations on First Philosophy* (hereafter, *Meditations*), p. 16.

110. Descartes wrote, "I call a perception 'clear' when it is present and accessible to the attentive mind. . . . I call a perception 'distinct' if, as well as being clear, it is so sharply separated from all other perceptions that it contains within itself only what is clear" (*Principles of First Philosophy* [hereafter *Principles*], pp. 207–8).

111. Descartes wrote about "resolving to seek no knowledge other than that which could be found in myself or else in the great book of the world" but then proceeded to eliminate the reliability of what could be known by sense perception from the world. Thus, the mind alone was his only reliable source of certainty. See Descartes, *Discourse on Method* (hereafter *Discourse*), p. 115.

112. Having established such a complete dualism between mind and body, a chasm remained for Descartes between the physical world of nature and the social world of human beings on the one hand, and the rational world of certain ideas on the other. Yet he knew that he had to avoid the solipsism of claiming that his own reasoning and its thoughts are all that are real. He granted that material things must exist in order for us to have ideas of them. But he claimed that the world is a "clockwork universe" which functions according to mechanical and rational principles implanted in it by God, the first mover of the machine. Its primary qualities—size, shape, and motion—are known by reason, especially by mathematics, physics and other sciences that measure and quantify reality. The rational structure of the world reflects the rational ideas we have of it—not from our senses but from our mind alone.

This still begs the question of how reason and reality encounter each other, of how the body and mind interact. For this Descartes was forced to offer perhaps the weakest aspect of his grandiose rational construct. He said that the interaction is possible because the soul is located in the pineal gland of the brain. There it both performs its reasoning functions and receives its sense data from the body. Thus the pineal gland is the cross-roads between reason and body. See Descartes, *The Passions of the Soul,* pp. 340-48 passim.

113. Descartes wrote, "even bodies are not strictly perceived by the senses or the faculty of imagination but by the intellect alone, and that this perception derives not from their being touched or seen but from their being understood . . ." (*Meditations,* p. 22).

114. Descartes, *Rules for the Directions of the Mind* (hereafter "Rules"), p. 43. (Inserts added.)

115. Descartes, *Meditations,* p. 16. In the *Discourse,* Descartes explained the workings of his method of doubt in detail, building it around four basic rules: "The first was never to accept anything as true if I did not have evident knowledge of its truth. . . . The second, to divide each of the difficulties I examined into as many parts as possible and as may be required in order to resolve them better. The third, to direct my thoughts in an orderly manner, by beginning with the simplest and most easily known objects in order to ascend . . . to knowledge of the most complex. . . . And the last, throughout to make enumerations so complete, and reviews so comprehensive, that I could be sure of leaving nothing out" (p. 120).

116. Descartes's classic statement of the cogito argument is as follows:

> I resolved to pretend that all the things that had ever entered my mind were no more true than the illusions of my dreams. But immediately I noticed that while I was trying thus to think everything false, it was necessary that I, who was thinking this, was something. And observing that this truth 'I am thinking, therefore I exist' (*cogito ergo sum*) was so firm and sure that all the most extravagant suppositions of the sceptics were incapable of shaking it, I decided that I would accept it without scruple as the first principle of the philosophy I was seeking. (*Discourse,* p. 127)

It is interesting to note that Augustine offered a similar argument for the certainty of human existence. Instead of *cogito ergo sum,* however, Augustine argued *si fallor sum*—"even if I'm mistaken in my thinking, I still know that I exist." See Augustine, *The Trinity,* bk. 15, chap. 12: 21–22; pp. 480–83.

117. Descartes, *Meditations,* p. 18.

118. Descartes classified ideas into three categories: innate, known by the light of our reason alone; fictitious, invented by human imagination; and adventitious, which appear to come from outside us and despite our will, e.g., hearing a noise. See ibid., p. 26.

119. I give his cosmological argument here. He did, however, give two other "proofs," one a variation of this argument from "the cogito," and the other an "onto-logical" argument that ran thus: (a) God in God's essence must possess all positive attributes of perfection; (b) existence is a positive attribute; (c) hence, God must exist (ibid., no. 5; pp. 44–47).

120. Descartes summarized his conclusion thus: "By the word 'God' I understand a substance that is infinite (eternal, immutable), independent, supremely intelligent, supremely powerful, and which created both myself and everything else (if anything else there be) that exists. All these attributes are such that, the more carefully I concentrate on them, the less possible it seems that they could have originated from me alone. So from what has been said it must be concluded that God necessarily exists" (ibid., no. 3, p. 31).

Descartes later explained that this clear and distinct idea of God is "innate in me, just as the idea of myself is innate in me" (ibid., p. 135).

121. In *Discourse,* Descartes stated, "Our ideas or notions, being real things and coming from God, cannot be anything but true, in every respect in which they are clear and distinct" (p. 130). Notice that here Descartes has set up what came to be known later as "the Cartesian circle"; i.e., God guarantees our clear and distinct ideas, but our clear and distinct ideas are what guarantee the existence of God.

122. Descartes wrote, "The privation which constitutes the essence of error . . . lies in the operation of the will" (*Meditations,* p. 41). He goes on: "For it is surely no imperfection in God that he [*sic*] has given me the freedom to assent or not to assent in those cases where he did not endow my intellect with a clear and distinct perception; but it is undoubtedly an imperfection in me to misuse that freedom and make judgments about matters which I do not fully understand" (ibid., p. 42). See the whole "Fourth Meditation" for his notion of truth and error and the role of the will in both.

123. Griffith, "Does Matter Matter?" p. 3.

124. Bracken writes, "Berkeley is neither British nor empiricist. If he must be labelled, he might more accurately be called an Irish Cartesian" (*Berkeley*, p. 18). I am indebted to Liam Wegimont for alerting me to this point in Bracken.

125. Russell's best-known work is his *Principia Mathematica*, which he wrote with Alfred North Whitehead. Russell claimed that mathematics and natural science are the only scientific, thus reliable, forms of thought. Philosophy is only a temporary study for now of problems that we do not yet know how to treat mathematically or empirically.

126. See note 7 on Parmenides and Heraclitus as "original" rationalists and empiricists, respectively. Though Aristotle could not be called an empiricist in the strict sense, because he claimed that reason alone can provide necessary truths about the world, yet his pushing back against Plato's undue rationalism and his posing sense perception (*emperia*) as the source of data from which the mind abstracts universal ideas demonstrated empirical sympathies. Aquinas believed he had Aristotle's endorsement for the view that "nothing is ever in the mind that was not first in the senses" and is sometimes pointed to as a forerunner of modern empiricism. However, for Aquinas, knowledge is not derived *immediately* from sense experience; the latter is more of an original source, a "material cause" (see note 93) than an efficient cause of knowledge. For modern empiricists, sense experience is an efficient cause of knowledge, and we know nothing that does not come from experience. The new empiricists, however, were still metaphysical dualists, only reversing the hierarchy in Plato's dualism. (Remember the perpendicular line!) For Plato, the "real world" is the world of ideas and forms, with the physical world mere shadow and source of unreliable opinion. For modern empiricists, the material world *is* the real world, and the task is to make sure that our ideas accurately reflect it.

127. Locke's reflections on the "law of nature" led him to conclude that all human beings have the same natural rights to life, liberty, and property and the same obligations to respect the rights of others. See, e.g., the *Second Treatise of Government* (first published 1690), p. 8. Such sentiments had a profound effect on the American Declaration of Independence and on the writing of the U.S. Constitution.

128. See Locke, *An Essay Concerning Human Understanding* (hereafter, *Understanding*), pp. 261–67.

129. See ibid., pp. 344–55.

130. See Aristotle, *On the Soul*, 3, 4; p. 169.

131. Locke, *Understanding*, p. 42.

132. See ibid., pp. 73–79. For Locke, then, unlike Aquinas, sense data is the "efficient cause" of cognition and not simply the "material cause" (see notes 93 and 126).

133. See ibid., p. 66.

134. See ibid., p. 64.

135. Of primary qualities, Locke wrote, "These I call *original* or *primary qualities* of body, which I think we may observe to produce simple ideas in us, viz., solidity, extension, figure, motion or rest, and number" (ibid., p. 67).

Then, of secondary qualities, he added, "Secondly, such qualities which in truth are nothing in the objects themselves, but powers to produce various sensations in us by their primary qualities, i.e., by the bulk, figure, texture, and motion of their insensible parts, as colours, sounds, tastes, etc.; these I call *secondary qualities*."

136. Berkeley believed that to admit the real existence of a physical world would lead to materialism and/or atheism. For him, the ideas of things exist in us, but the things themselves exist only in the mind of God. His summary dictum—*esse est percipi*, "to be is to be perceived"—expressed this central tenet of his epistemology, that things exist only in their being perceived and that the physical aspects of the world are reducible to mental phenomena. Berkeley's construct is most often referred to as subjective idealism. See Berkeley, *A Treatise Concerning the Principles of Human Knowledge*, (first published 1710).

137. For Hume, all knowledge begins and ends with the basic units of sensory experience—what he called "impressions." (Locke called them "sensations.") Impressions give rise to our ideas through the activities of memory or imagination, but as ideas they lose the initial vivid impression they had on the senses. The mind, however, is no more than a passive receptacle of impressions and has no agency in constructing or judging the knowledge that we actually achieve. This conviction led Hume to reject metaphysical

thinking (the best way of dealing with philosophical problems is by inattention to them) and the very existence of a personal identity. See Hume, *Treatise of Human Nature.*

138. Locke, *Understanding,* p. 343.

139. Kant was raised in a puritan and pietist home, which may have explained his anxiety to defend religion against the attacks of rationalism. His methodicalness was so complete, the story goes, that the people of Königsberg (then in East Prussia, now in the Soviet Union and renamed Kaliningrad) could set their clocks by the regularity of his afternoon walk. As a philosopher, Kant was a "late bloomer"; he published his first magnum opus, *Critique of Pure Reason* (hereafter *Pure*) (1781), at fifty-seven years old. His thinking was complex and his style of writing beclouded by intricate terminology.

140. Kant, "Fundamental Principles of the Metaphysics of Morals," in *Kant's Critique,* p. 7.

141. Kant delineated four different kinds of judgment of truth that reason can make. (His most precise statement can be found in *Pure,* pp. 48–51.) Kant began with a twofold distinction between a priori and a posteriori judgments. A priori judgments are judgments in which the truth is recognized independent of experience or of empirical investigation. Such judgments are made by capacities present in the mind apart from any perceptions of sensibilia. A posteriori judgments are based on sense experience. Kant further distinguished between analytic and synthetic judgments. Analytic judgments give no further information about the thing judged, in that the predicate is already contained in the concept of the subject. For example, to say that "a bald man is a man" adds nothing to our knowledge. Synthetic judgments do give further information about a thing, in that the predicate is not included in the subject but is synthesized from experience. To say that "the day was cold and wet" tells us something about the day we could not have known apart from experience. So far, so good!

Kant went on to combine the two pairs of distinctions into four categories of possible judgments and thus, in a sense, four different kinds of "truth" that can be "known." First, it is evident that there are such things as *analytic a priori* judgments—e.g., a circle is round. It is analytic in that roundness is implied by circle, and Kant would say that it is *a priori* in that the concept of circle is something innate to us, known independent of experience. Then clearly there are *synthetic a posteriori* judgments. These are the everyday judgments we make when we predicate something of a subject that is not necessary but evident to us from experience. Third, we can imagine *analytic a posteriori* judgments, but we rarely make them because they amount to tautologies. They are judgments about our experience that add nothing to our knowledge of those experiences, such as "I know from experience that red apples are red."

A key development occurs, however, with Kant's notion of *synthetic a priori* judgments. Here the connection between the subject and the predicate is not knowable by the mere analysis of the subject. Instead, it is synthetic, in that it is a judgment influenced by our experience. But there is an *a priori* dimension to it as well, i.e., something that was in the mind prior to all experience. Kant gave the example "everything that happens has its cause" (*Pure,* pp. 124–25). We experience the truth of that judgment; it reflects something of our experience. And yet, says Kant, we know it because of an a priori category (causality) that was already in the mind before we ever experienced it in reality. His analysis of theoretical reason is a review of how we come to such *synthetic a priori* judgments; his review of practical reason is an analysis of how we come to *analytic a priori* judgments, i.e., truths that do not depend on experience at all.

	JUDGMENTS→	SYNTHETIC	ANALYTIC
TRUTHS	A PRIORI	e.g. "everything that happens has its cause"	e.g. "a circle is round"
TRUTHS	A POSTERIORI	e.g. "I see the big red balloon"	e.g. "red apples are red"

(I am indebted to Harold Daly Horell for suggesting this diagram.)

142. By "critique," Kant means not criticism but analysis. He calls it "pure" reason because he delineates the knowing capacities in the mind *a priori*, i.e., prior to all experience—the categories of understanding that in fact make experience of sensibilia possible.

143. Hereafter referred to as *Practical*. Kant wrote a third critique, *The Critique of Judgment* (1790) concerned primarily with aesthetics. (Do we still hear echoes of Aristotle's divisions of theoria, praxis, and poiesis, albeit with very different analyses?) Kant's intent in the third critique was to recognize and harmonize the subjective and objective bases of aesthetic judgment. It could be said that his intention was to unify the sensible and supersensible, which he had distinguished and separated in the first two critiques. However, by way of influence on Western epistemology, his first two were by far the most significant, and his attempt to unite the theoretical and practical was considered limited to the aesthetic realm. For this reason, in this already lengthy section, I have chosen not to review his *Critique of Judgment*.

144. See *Pure,* pp. 22–25.

145. For his distinction between perceptions and concepts, see ibid., pp. 105–6.

146. Kant writes, "Categories are concepts which prescribe laws a priori to appearances, and therefore to nature, the sum of all appearances" (ibid., p. 172).

147. Ibid., p. 41.

148. Kant wrote: "The capacity (receptivity) for receiving representation through the mode in which we are affected by objects, is entitled *sensibility*. Objects are *given* to us by means of sensibility, and it alone yields us *intuitions;* they are *thought* through the understanding, and from the understanding arise *concepts*. But all thought must, directly or indirectly, by way of certain characters, relate ultimately to intuitions, and therefore, with us, to sensibility, because in no other way can an object be given to us" (ibid., p. 65).

149. "By way of introduction or anticipation we need only say that there are two stems of human knowledge, namely, *sensibility* and *understanding*, which perhaps spring from a common, but to us unknown, root. Through the former, objects are given to us; through the latter, they are thought" (ibid., pp. 61–62).

150. For Kant, a priori categories have four common features: (1) they are logically prior to experience and presupposed in our very ability to have experience; (2) they remain independent from experience, in that experience does not alter them; (3) they are universal, in that they are part of the structure of every human mind; (4) they are necessary, in that without them there could be no theoretical knowledge of reality.

I am extrapolating these four characteristics out of Kant's overall work. His own most precise description of the meaning of the term a priori is in *Pure,* pp. 43–45, where

he highlights the conditions of universality and necessity.

151. For his understanding of space and time, see ibid., pp. 67–82.

152. Kant wrote: "Space and time contain a manifold of pure a priori intuition, but at the same time are conditions of the receptivity of our mind—conditions under which alone it can receive representations of objects, and which therefore must also always affect the concept of these objects" (ibid., p. 111).

153. I first came across this aspect of Kant's thought in the work of Sharon Parks. See *Critical Years,* p. 113. I should note, however, that for Kant the imagination is "a blind but indispensable function of the soul" (*Pure,* p. 112). In theoretical reason he seems to give no creative function to it beyond preparing the data from sensation for appropriation by understanding. Parks poses a more creative and critical role for imagination. For Kant's understanding of the synthesizing role of imagination, see ibid., pp. 132–33.

154. See ibid., p. 113, for his Table of Categories, and pp. 113–19 for his elaboration of them.

155. See ibid., pp. 124–25.

156. "The understanding is an object for reason, just as sensibility is for the understanding. It is the business of reason to render the unity of all possible empirical acts of the understanding systematic; just as it is of the understanding to connect the manifold of the appearances by means of concepts, and to bring it under empirical laws" (ibid., p. 546).

157. Ibid., p. 304. Kant later explained: "For pure reason leaves everything to the understanding—the understanding (alone) applying immediately to the objects of intuition, or rather to their synthesis in the imagination. Reason concerns itself exclusively

with absolute totality in the employment of the concepts of the understanding, and endeavors to carry the synthetic unity, which is thought in the category, up to the completely unconditioned" (ibid., p. 318).

158. "Practical principles are propositions which contain a general determination of the will, having under it several practical rules. They are subjective, or maxims, when the condition is regarded by the subject as valid only for his [sic] own will. They are objective, or practical laws, when the condition is recognized as objective, i.e., as valid for the will of every rational being" (Practical, p. 17).

159. It is not easy to identify the dimension of ourselves to which Kant referred when he spoke of the faculty of pure practical reason. One could be tempted to call it our natural moral "feelings" about right and wrong, but Kant was too much of a rationalist to say this. He wrote instead, "The practical rule is always a product of reason, because it prescribes action as a means to an effect which is its purpose" (ibid., p. 18). It is so reasonable, in fact, that it never takes feelings into account. See ibid., p. 24.

160. Ibid., p. 25.

161. Ibid., p. 17.

162. Ibid., p. 30.

163. Ibid., p. 38. Kant explained that the categorical imperative is "natural" to us. It is "the object of our will as pure rational beings . . . as though through our will a natural order must arise" (ibid., p. 45). He added, "The moral law thus defines that which speculative philosophy had to leave undefined" (ibid., p. 49).

164. Kant maintained that because theoretical knowledge begins with sensible perceptions, we can never know "the thing in itself"—the noumena, but only the phenomena of it, i.e., how it appears to our senses (see Pure, p. 82). Lonergan offers a helpful rebuttal to Kant on this point when he writes, "A thing is a concrete unity—identity—whole grasped in data as individual. Describe it, and it is a thing-itself" (Insight, p. 339). See ibid., pp. 339–42, for Lonergan's differentiation of his position from Kant's.

165. Flax, "Patriarchal Unconsciousness," p. 248. Flax continues, "Furthermore, it [i.e., Kant's division] has blinded philosophers and their interpreters to the possibility that apparently insoluble dilemmas within philosophy are not the product of the immanent structure of the human mind and/or nature but rather reflect distorted or frozen social relations" (ibid.).

166. The standard assumption is that Marx worked in collaboration with Friedrich Engels to create the revolutionary movement of social and economic theory that bears his name. Revisionist scholars, however, now claim that his spouse, Jenny von Westphalen, also made a significant contribution to his theoretical work.

167. In Paris (1843–45) Marx wrote a series of essays, The Economic and Philosophical Manuscripts, often referred to as the early Marx because of their humanistic tone and concern for the alienation of the individual person. But they contain the beginnings of Marx's economic interpretation of history, which achieved mature expression in the later Marx as a "scientific" analysis of the economic laws (class struggle, class consciousness, etc.) that govern all historical evolution. The best-known works of the later Marx include The German Ideology (1846) and The Communist Manifesto (1848), both written in Brussels; The Critique of Political Economy (1859) and Capital (vol. 1 published in 1867 and vols. 2 and 3 edited by Engels and published posthumously in 1885 and 1894), Marx wrote in London, where he lived with his spouse, Jenny, from 1849 until his death in 1883.

168. See C.R.E., pp. 165–69.

169. See Berger and Luckmann, Reality, p. 5.

170. Marx, Critique of Political Economy, p. 220.

171. Davaney, "Problems with Feminist Theory," p. 82.

172. See Viviano, The Kingdom of God, p. 116.

173. See Kearney, Modern Movements, p. 15.

174. Husserl's notions of individual and essential intuition is most succinctly expressed in his work Ideas. See esp. pp. 48–49.

175. See ibid, pp. 97–98, and all of chap. 5, pp. 133–54.

176. Paulo Freire cites Husserl as a source of his understanding of the process of conscientization. See Pedagogy of the Oppressed, p. 70.

177. Without being exhaustive, this list includes Kierkegaard, Heidegger, Marcel, Buber, Berdyayev, Sartre, de Beauvoir, Ortega y Gasset, Unamuno, Camus, Jaspers, and Merleau-Ponty.

178. Here I draw exclusively from *Being and Time* (1927), Heidegger's major philosophical work. *Being and Time* represents the first two parts of an intended six-part work that Heidegger intentionally never completed. He became convinced that it was not possible to "think Being as such" by beginning with Dasein and thus abandoned the project begun in the first two parts. In his later works he favored a less metaphysical approach. Nevertheless, *Being and Time* remained his most influential work.

179. Heidegger described such activities as "having to do with something, producing something, attending to something and looking after it, making use of something, giving something up and letting it go, undertaking, accomplishing, evincing, interrogating, considering, discussing, determining . . ." (*Being and Time,* p. 83).

180. All the themes summarized here were gleaned from my reading of *Being and Time,* part 1. In part 2 of *Being and Time* Heidegger analyzed *time* as the ground of Dasein's unity; I discuss his understanding of time in chap. 3.

181. Dewey actually resisted the appellation pragmatism, preferring instead to call his work instrumentalism or experimentalism. He was, however, perceived as the leading pragmatist of his day. Dewey's particular influence will be evident in the constructive work of chap. 3.

182. Charles S. Peirce, quoted in *Dictionary of Philosophy,* "Pragmatism," by V. J. McGill, p. 201.

183. James, *Pragmatism,* p. 45.

184. Dewey, *Reconstruction in Philosophy,* pp. 156–57.

185. Metz argues convincingly that the Christian understanding of God and of Christ are eminently "practical." See *History,* pp. 51 and 67.

186. Flax, "Patriarchal Consciousness," pp. 269–70.

187. Ibid, p. 248.

188. Horkheimer writes, "Modern science . . . refers essentially to statements about facts, and therefore presupposes the reification of life in general and of perception in particular" (*Eclipse of Reason,* p. 81).

189. Ibid, p. 94.

190. In a now classic statement Horkheimer and Adorno write, "The loss of memory is a transcendental condition for science. All objectification is a forgetting" (*Dialectic of Enlightenment,* p. 230).

191. Horkheimer, *Critique of Instrumental Reason,* p. 22.

192. Horkheimer, *Eclipse of Reason,* p. 103. By "speculative thought," I hear him to mean what I intend by "critical reason."

193. Horkheimer, *Critique of Instrumental Reason,* p. 26. For some of the research in this section on Horkheimer, I am indebted to an unpublished paper given by Russell Butkus at the annual Association of Professors and Researchers in Religious Education (APPRE) convention, New York City, November 3, 1989.

194. Another powerful critique of "technocracy" and technical rationality is presented by Mary Daly. Daly claims that such rationality has brought us to the brink of nuclear destruction and is the logical outcome of patriarchy. See, e.g., *Gyn/Ecology,* pp. 89–105.

195. Welch, *Solidarity,* p. 9.

A central theme in Foucault's work is development of the insight (first articulated by Bacon) that "power and knowledge are joined together" (*History of Sexuality,* p. 100). See also *Power/Knowledge.*

196. Foucault, *Power/Knowledge,* pp. 81–82, quoted in Welch, *Solidarity,* p. 19.

197. Recognizing the diversity of voices in "women's studies," Mary Boys offers a helpful summary view. She writes, "I think it is possible to generalize that the following five fundamental activities are characteristic of feminist theory: questioning conventional wisdom—the concepts, conclusions, and principles deeply rooted in scholarship; reexamining sources; searching for information overlooked or previously inaccessible; attending to methodology; and stimulating new theories" (*Educating in Faith,* p. 159).

198. As in feminist theory, there is much diversity in feminist epistemology. See Sandra Harding, *The Science Question,* pp. 24–29, for "A Guide to Feminist Epistemologies," in which she describes three different approaches: (1) "feminist empiricism," (2) "the feminist standpoint," (3) "feminist postmodernism."

The books I have found most helpful on feminist epistemologies are Fox Keller, *Reflections on Gender and Science;* Harding and Hinitikka, eds., *Discovering Reality;* Harding,

The Science Question in Feminism; Harding, ed., *Feminism and Methodology;* Josephine Donovan, *Feminist Theory.*

199. Fox Keller, *Gender and Science,* p. 9.

200. See Flax, "Patriarchal Consciousness," pp. 269–71. See also Parker Palmer, "The Violence of Our Knowledge," for a similar conclusion but one not reached from an explicitly feminist perspective.

201. Flax writes, "Ways of thinking and thinking about thinking must be developed which do justice to the multiplicity of experience, the many layers of any instant in time and space" ("Patriarchal Consciousness," pp. 270–71).

202. See Harding, *Feminism and Methodology,* pp. 181–90, for a discussion of the various rationales offered "for why we all—men as well as women—should prefer women's experience to men's as reliable bases of knowledge claims" (ibid, p. 10).

203. Donovan, *Feminist Theory,* p. 172.

204. Ibid., pp. 172–73.

205. The now classic expression of this ethic is found in Carol Gilligan's book *In a Different Voice.* The point I make here, echoing Donovan (see *Feminist Theory,* pp. 176–78), is that such an ethic is integral to and constitutive of a "feminist epistemology."

206. Mary Field Belenky and three colleagues, after extensive interviews with women from varied backgrounds,

> grouped women's perspectives on knowing into five major epistemological categories: *silence,* a position in which women experience themselves as mindless and voiceless and subject to the whims of external authority; *received knowledge,* a perspective from which women conceive of themselves as capable of receiving, even reproducing, knowledge from the all-knowing external authorities but not capable of creating knowledge on their own; *subjective knowledge,* a perspective from which truth and knowledge are conceived of as personal, private, and subjectively known or intuited; *procedural knowledge,* a position in which women are invested in learning and applying objective procedures for obtaining and communicating knowledge; and *constructed knowledge,* a position in which women view all knowledge as contextual, experience themselves as creators of knowledge, and value both subjective and objective strategies for knowing.(*Women's Ways of Knowing,* p. 15)

Belenky et al. are careful not to make universalist claims for their categories and note that "similar categories can be found in men's thinking" (ibid.).

Chapter 3. The Dimensions and Dynamics of "Being" Engaged

1. Erikson describes identity as what "provides the ability to experience one's self as something that has continuity and sameness, and to act accordingly" (*Childhood and Society,* p. 42).

2. See Merleau-Ponty, *Phenomenology of Perception.*

3. Richard Kearney writes, "Language as gesture precedes language as word"(*Modern Movements,* p. 79).

4. Ibid., pp. 73–74.

5. See Colleen Griffith, "Bodiliness," p. 8.

6. See Montessori, *Montessori Method.* Although she does not use terms like *body wisdom,* the pedagogy of Sylvia Ashton Warner reflects the foundational conviction that the body is our first source of learning. Her "organic" approach begins by drawing out of people the words that they see by their "inner vision" as part of their very "being" and arise from the "organic dynamic of life" (*Teacher,* pp. 31–35).

7. Sears, in forward to Campbell and McMahon, *Bio-Spirituality,* p. vii.

8. Derrida, *Dissemination,* p. 35.

9. Ibid., p. 108, for both citations.

10. Alasdair MacIntyre writes, "I can only answer the question 'What am I to do?' if I can answer the prior question of 'What story or stories do I find myself a part?'" (*After Virtue*, p. 201).

11. Frankl, remembering his concentration camp experience, wrote, "Even though conditions such as lack of sleep, insufficient food and various mental stresses may suggest that the inmates were bound to react in certain ways, in the final analysis it becomes clear that the sort of person the prisoner became was the result of an inner decision, and not the result of camp influences alone. Fundamentally, therefore, any man [*sic*] can, even under such circumstances, decide what shall become of him—mentally and spiritually. He may retain his human dignity even in a concentration camp" (*Man's Search for Meaning*, p. 105).

12. See Campbell and McMahon, *Bio-Spirituality*, pp. 14–15. Campbell and McMahon footnote their indebtedness to the work of Eugene T. Gendlin for what they call "bodily knowing." Gendlin has pioneered a form of psychotherapy that draws upon the felt wisdom of the body. See Gendlin, *Focusing*.

13. See Leech, *Experiencing God*, p. 25. Leech adds, "Without . . . creative doubt, religion becomes hard and cruel, degenerating into the spurious security which breeds intolerance and persecution" (ibid.).

14. My technical use of the terms *I* and *me* here is suggested by the work of George Herbert Mead. For Mead, the "I" is the sense we have of ourselves over time as self-identified selves; our "me" is the identity proposed to us over time by the role modeling and social attitudes of others toward us. Mead proposes that self-identity arises from the inner dialectic between the "I" and the "me." See *Mind, Self and Society*.

15. My list here is a slightly adapted one from the listing of "intentional feelings" offered by Lonergan (*Method*, p. 31). Lonergan notes that by our intentional feelings "we are oriented massively and dynamically in a world mediated by meaning" (ibid.).

16. Griffith, "Bodiliness," p. 8. A general note: The work of my spouse, Colleen Griffith, on a "theology of the body," has had a significant influence on my thinking about the corporeal aspect of conation.

17. For this insight, I am indebted to a comment made by Liam Wegimont, a reader of an early draft of this manuscript.

18. Kearney, *Wake of Imagination*, p. 370.

19. Ibid., p. 364.

20. See ibid., p. 370. Kearney is careful to point out that "the postmodern imagination is as much in need of poeisis as of ethos" (ibid., p. 367), and in fact the poetical and ethical impetes of imagination "are . . . two different but complementary ways in which imagination can open us to the otherness of the other" (ibid., p. 370).

21. Huebner, "Practicing the Presence of God," p. 571.

22. A socialization approach to Christian formation is certainly not new in the church; the early catechumenate was a process of socialization. Horace Bushnell (1802–1876), however, is seen as the grandfather of the modern theorists of a socialization approach to Christian formation. See Bushnell, *Christian Nurture*. Among the leading socialization theorists since then have been George Albert Coe (see *A Social Theory of Religious Education*), Harrison Elliott (see *Can Religious Education Be Christian?*), C. Ellis Nelson (see *Where Faith Begins*), and John Westerhoff (see especially *Will Our Children Have Faith?*). There has been a growing appreciation of the socialization model of catechesis within the Catholic tradition, especially since Vatican II. Many recent universal and national Catholic church documents have emphasized the role of the whole community in catechesis. For fine articulations from a Catholic perspective, see Berard Marthaler, "Socialization as a Model for Catechetics," and Maria Harris, *Fashion Me a People*.

23. Geertz, *Cultures*, p. 89. Or, as Lonergan puts it more pithily, "A culture is a set of meanings and values informing a common way of life" (*Method*, p. 301). Browning's definition of culture is also insightful. He describes culture as "a set of symbols, stories (myths), and norms for conduct that orient a society or group cognitively, affectively, and behaviorally to the world in which it lives" (*Moral Context of Pastoral Care*, p. 73). Anthropology is the science that studies the origins, development, and characteristics of culture.

24. Here I echo Tonnies's distinction between a *gesellschaft*, i.e., social structures based on rational choice, and a *gemeinschaft*, i.e., a natural group or community of some

kind. Tonnies's classic work *Gemeinschaft und Gesellschaft* (1887) was translated into English as *Community and Society* (1963). *Sociology*, a term first coined by the French social philosopher Auguste Comte (1798–1857), is the science or group of sciences that studies society.

25. This idea is in Hegel's *The Phenomenology of Mind*, and it may well predate him. However, Durkheim is the social scientist who gave it central emphasis in sociology. See *The Rules of Sociological Method*, pp. 1–13.

26. Weber pointed out that one can come into "authority" by "traditional," "legal," or "charismatic" modes. *Traditional authority* is grounded in the rules and customs of a commonly held tradition. It reflects the mores of a people that have been sanctified by time and are powerful enough to dispose people to conform to them. *Legal authority* does not replace traditional authority but emerges when traditional authority is challenged. Legal ordinances are based on some agreed-upon rational basis and made by people appointed to legislate. Their authority is "by virtue of the belief in the validity of legal statue and functional 'competence' based on rationally created rules." *Charismatic authority* is based on "extraordinary and personal gift" and exercised by a great demagogue or prophet whose authority is grounded in the strength of personal charisma (Weber, *From Max Weber*, pp. 77–79).

27. Berger, *Invitation to Sociology*, p. 71.

28. A "system of legitimation" is a stable social arrangement that serves to explain and justify social expectations as they currently exist. A "plausibility structure" is the theoretical base a society gives its present arrangements so that they appear reasonable and for the best.

29. Berger explains that "ideology both justifies what is done by the group . . . and interprets social reality in such a way that the justification is made plausible" (*Invitation to Sociology*, p. 122).

30. This is Berger's phrase, and the title of one of his most insightful books.

31. This is a key insight to which we will return. In contemporary sociology, Mannheim is usually footnoted for it. For example, he pointed out that a religious tenet like love of neighbor can be a legitimating ideology that encourages acquiescence to some form of "serf-dom," or a source of utopian impulse that calls present social arrangements into question and empowers people to create alternatives where love of neighbor is more likely to be approximated. See *Ideology and Utopia*, esp. pp. 194–96.

32. Social scientists seem to agree that primary socialization is the most determining of us; it is the formative process of early childhood by which children come to their self-concept, value system, and worldview by interiorizing the implicit or explicit expectations, value systems, and worldviews of their primary nurturing adults. Secondary socialization is "any subsequent process that inducts an already socialized individual into new sections of the objective world of his [*sic*] society" (Berger and Luckmann, *Reality*, p. 130).

33. Drawing especially from Mead, Berger, and Luckmann, I give one summary description of how the process of socialization effects itself through externalization, objectification, and internalization in *C.R.E.*, pp. 110–13.

34. In Westerhoff and Neville, *Generation to Generation*, p. 39. I should note that Westerhoff now prefers the language of enculturation instead of socialization, seeing the former as more dialectical than the latter. See *Will Our Children Have Faith?*, p. 79.

35. Max Scheler was a German phenomenologist and social philosopher who coined the term and first took up the formal study of "the sociology of knowledge." Interesting to note that it was Scheler's conviction about the sociology of the person that brought him to analyze the sociology of knowledge.

36. Durkheim and Mannheim see the social context as a determining force in human knowledge. They understand the individual as the most likely source of error and the society as the most reliable source of truth. Thus, society is the test for the validity of any belief, and "the true" is what works effectively in a particular social system. This, however, reduces truth to mere convention and, given the variety of societies, to total relativism. Scheler and Weber, on the other hand, contend that the social influence on mental activity is merely directional. Society is neither a destroyer nor a guarantor of truth but gives direction to what knowledge will be sought and found in a particular context, a position radicalized by Foucault. Among contemporary authors on the sociology of knowledge, there is a consensus position that sees a functional relationship between a society

and knowledge within it; the context shapes consciousness, but the consciousness and thought of its members also shape the society. The critical theorists, however, have a sobering warning, especially for educators, that in this functional relationship society has a particular interest in controlling its members' thinking, and it harnesses its educational agencies to serve that end. See Giroux, *Theory,* pp. 23ff.

37. Davaney, "Feminist Theory," p. 82.

38. For Hegel, the cause of historical dialectics is the world of ideas. In brief, from the Greek *dialektikis,* meaning discourse or conversation, dialectics first emerged in classical thinking as the art of debate based on logical argumentation. Educationally, it was recognized as the art of teaching through questioning, epitomized in the Socratic dialogues of Plato. Thereafter, and up to the late Middle Ages, dialectics was listed as one of the trivium, i.e., the arts of discourse, the others being rhetoric and grammar, with dialectics as the discipline of formal logic. Hegel (1770–1831), however, proposed a more detailed understanding of the dialectical process of thinking. For Hegel, dialectic is the distinguishing characteristic of speculative thought by which an idea passes over into its own problematic or negation because of contradictions inherent within it and then passes on to subsume the insights of both the first and second moment into a new synthesis of understanding. Marx accepted Hegel's threefold understanding of the dialectic and applied it to his interpretation not only of ideas but of economic and social/historical processes as well. In addition, Marx intensified its second movement as one of inevitable negation and posed the whole dialectical dynamic as conflictual and a violent struggle between social classes. Contemporary Hegelian scholarship recognizes this as an exaggeration of Hegel's position, that the second moment is not necessarily an antithesis to the first as thesis. (See Bernstein, *Praxis and Action,* p. 20.) My own conviction and use of dialectic here is that while the second moment may be one of negation, it can also be a discerning one that perceives a problematic or alternative perspective and with dialogue can be a moment of peace rather than conflict.

39. Those who admit little possibility for individuals to refuse the determining power of society are often associated with the school of thought established by Durkheim. Theorists who give more weight to the subjective side of the dialectic have traditionally been aligned with a Weberian school of thought.

40. We already drew upon some of this work in chap. 2 with Horkheimer's critique of "technical rationality." The "critical theorists," sometimes referred to as the Frankfurt School because of their concentration at one time or other around the Frankfurt Institute for Social Research, are a group of social commentators committed to creating a "critical" theory of social reality that is capable through ideological critique of re-creating rather than maintaining present sociocultural arrangements. Its members have included such major thinkers as Horkheimer, Adorno, Fromm, Marcuse, and Habermas. For scholarly analysis of the overall contribution of the school, see Wellmer, *The Critical Theory of Society;* Jay, *The Dialectical Imagination;* Schroyer, *The Critique of Domination;* David Held, *Introduction to Critical Thinking: Horkheimer to Habermas;* Raymond Geuss, *The Idea of a Critical Theory: Habermas and the Frankfurt School.* For a collection of key essays tracing the historical evolution of the Frankfurt School, see Connerton, *Critical Sociology.* For a critical review of Habermas, see McCarthy, *The Critical Theory of Jurgen Habermas.*

41. By "interest" Habermas means a basic perspective and sense of purpose we bring to our praxis as human beings in history. It is "interest" that links our theory and praxis, allowing our knowing to shape our doing and our doing to shape our knowing. Note, however, that as both perspective and purpose, "interest" is Habermas's way of pushing back against the presumed disinterested rationalism of the Enlightenment and reuniting reason with desire as Aristotle had done in *phronesis.* His notion of "knowledge constitutive interests" is very similar, I believe, to Gadamer's notion of "justified prejudices productive of knowledge." See Gadamer, *Truth and Method,* pp. 245–53.

42. Habermas speaks of "constitutive interests" as "quasi-transcendental" in the sense that though they are universal to all humankind, they are also shaped by both the conditions of a given society and by the sedimented history or personality structure of individuals themselves.

43. See Habermas, *Knowledge and Human Interests,* pp. 308–9. Habermas describes the sciences that arise from labor, with its interest of "technical control," as "empirical analytical."

44. See ibid., p. 176.

45. Habermas describes the sciences that arise from symbolic interaction, with its interest of "practical control," as "historical hermeneutical." He argues that historical hermeneutical activity always remains "within the walls of tradition" (Habermas quoted in Gadamer, "On the Scope," p. 87). Habermas's rationale is that the reflective moment in the hermeneutical sciences is not sufficiently critical to be emancipatory. They interpret "what is there" in the tradition and in culture/society rather than uncovering and questioning the geneses—the constitutive interests—that produced reality as it appears to be or posing an alternative beyond the walls of a given tradition. Habermas's analysis of the hermeneutical sciences has been rightly challenged, most obviously by Gadamer. I side with Gadamer and disagree with Habermas in his undue criticism of the hermeneutical sciences. I believe a dialectical hermeneutic that is authentically critical is capable of more than mere maintenance. In fact, it can be emancipatory. The work of Elisabeth Schüssler Fiorenza, e.g., is an instance of hermeneutics being done with a radical and emancipatory interest. See *Bread Not Stone* and *In Memory of Her*.

46. Habermas says that the praxis of social power, when marked by an emancipatory interest, gives rise to the "critical sciences." He uses psychoanalysis as his central example of such a science, but, when sufficiently critical, these sciences can include any of "the sciences of social action that attempt a critique of ideology" (*Interests*, p. 310).

47. See ibid, pp. 18–19.

48. Clearly Habermas is proposing the "theoretical," not as separated from politics (as in Aristotle) but as its constitutive interest and capable (in the manner of the Enlightenment confidence in critical reason) of promoting human emancipation. His work, however, is also in a dialectic with the Enlightenment notion of disinterested and ahistorical reasoning, being well aware of its potential to promote destruction rather than emancipation.

Habermas is simply convinced that only critical reflection on present social praxis can prevent people's "life world" from being "colonized" by the systemic rationalization of productive and practical interests.

49. See *C.R.E.*, pp. 121–27, for further elaboration.

50. When people bring reason, memory, and imagination to reflect critically (i.e. socially) on their own conative activities, the dynamic can be set out schematically something as follows: they remember the context of their own memorative activities, as well as the context of their corporeal/maintaining and volitional/inheriting; they recognize how their "place" shapes their reasoning activities and their corporeal/engaging and volitional/relating; they direct their imagining activities toward their social context and to imagining the sociocultural implications of their corporeal/regenerating and volitional/committing.

51. This emancipatory function of social remembering is surely reflected in the existential life of the people of Israel. As the Hebrew Scriptures make clear, when the Israelites "remembered" their social identity and genesis as a people, they lived faithfully as God's people; when they "forgot," they returned, metaphorically, to the "slavery" of Egypt again.

52. See Kearney, *Wake of Imagination*, p. 387.

53. The point I am making here will be more obvious after section 4 of this chapter, where I explain Lonergan's four transcendental imperatives and the need to consciously apply the transcendental activities to our own performance of each transcendental activity.

54. See Heidegger, "Letter on Humanism," *Basic Writings*, p. 213. Likewise, Ricoeur, referring to "discourse" as "the event of language" argues for "the ontological priority of discourse." See *Interpretation Theory*, p. 9.

55. Chauvinist language is coming to be readily recognized and avoided by religious educators. Its most obvious form is sexist language, but there are also language patterns that are exclusive and oppressive on the basis of race, age, class, etc. (See my *Inclusive Language*.) By mechanistic here I refer to a language pattern that implies that people are like machines. This awareness has brought a shift in my own teaching language. For example, I have moved away from talking about giving some *input* on the *subject* and asking for *feedback*, to making accessible some resources on the topic and inviting people to share their insights.

56. This is what Ricoeur calls "the event of discourse." See *Interpretation Theory*, pp. 9–10.

57. This should not be understood to exclude the use of "lecturing" at a particular moment in a conative pedagogy. As I will clarify in chap. 8, it is possible, I believe, to lecture "dialogically."

58. Western philosophy was diminished when it began to act as if the dialectics of thought should be performed by oneself alone; we lost the central dimension of dialectics as reflected in its original meaning of "conversation." And even if the dialectics of thought can be performed alone, dialogue is the appropriate context for the dialectics of "being." As Lonergan points out, when "there is . . . dialectic in which human subjects are concerned with themselves and with one another . . . dialectic becomes dialogue" ("The Ongoing Genesis of Methods," *Third Collection*, p. 159).

59. I use "conversation" as an activity within the more generic category of "dialogue"; dialogue is the relational context within which true conversation can take place. Describing the "hard rules" of conversation, Tracy writes: "say only what you mean; say it as accurately as you can; listen to and respect what the other says, however different or other; be willing to correct or defend your opinions if challenged by the conversation partner; be willing to argue if necessary, to confront if demanded, to endure necessary conflict, to change your mind if the evidence suggests." *Plurality and Ambiguity*, p. 19. See also Cowan and Lee, *Dangerous Memories*, chap. 5 (Conversations with Michael Cowan and Christopher Murphy promoted me to include "conversation" here.)

60. Buber's existentialism, unlike Heidegger's, was grounded in a profound faith in God. For Buber, all true community is built around an "Eternal Thou" who is the "Living Center" to which all people are related. Being so related, ultimately, when people relate to each other there exists among them what he called "the between," a reflection of "The Living Center" that is the presence of God. Only by going out of and beyond one's private sphere and interests does one encounter "the between." This is the "real place" in which people enter into a genuine I/Thou relationship. See *Between Man and Man*, (sic) passim and esp. p. 203.

61. Buber writes, "Individualism understands only a part of man [*sic*], collectivism understands man only as a part; neither advances to the wholeness of man, to man as a whole" (ibid., p. 200).

62. See ibid., p. 32.

63. He wrote, "Without 'IT' a human being cannot live. But whoever lives only with that is not a human" (Buber, *I and Thou*, pp. 85).

64. Buber writes, "[Person] becomes an I through a You" (*I and Thou*, p. 80).

65. I have extrapolated these characteristics from *I and Thou*, in which they are scattered throughout. Paulo Freire also has a powerful and confronting listing of the requirements for dialogue, which complements Buber. For Freire, dialogue requires profound love, humility, intense faith, hope, and critical thinking. See *Oppressed*, pp. 77–81.

66. Habermas, "Toward a Theory," p. 367.

67. Constructing a theory of "communicative action" has been the primary focus of Habermas's most recent work. He distinguishes *communicative* action from *strategic* action. "We call an action oriented to success *strategic* when we consider it under the aspect of following rules of rational choice and assess the efficacy of influencing the decisions of a rational opponent. . . . By contrast, I shall speak of *communicative* action whenever the actions of the agents involved are coordinated not through egocentric calculations of success but through acts of reaching understanding (*Theory of Communicative Action*, vol. 1, pp. 285–86).

Communicative action is marked by an illocutionary use of language and strategic action by a perlocutionary one. Illocutionary acts of language are grounded in rationality and mutuality and are openly expressed in conversation directed to intersubjectivity and understanding; it is undistorted by individual, group, or social bias. Perlocutionary acts are an instrumental use of language designed for manipulation; it is when "one subject inconspicuously harnesses another for his [*sic*] own purposes, that is, induces him to behave in a desired way by manipulatively employing linguistic means and thereby instrumentalizes him for his own success" (ibid., p. 288).

68. Habermas has clearly moved beyond Marx's concern for economic control of the means of production and sees the emancipatory task in our technological society as critique of the ideological control of the means of communication. (For Habermas, "ideology" represents a "false consciousness" that reifies meaning, represses dialogue, distorts

communication, and conceals domination.) Habermas is confident that by authentically critical reflection, ideological control of communication can be uncovered and challenged. Such reflection, however, calls for a situation of "communicative competence."

69. He lists validity claims (i.e., criteria of truth) as "comprehensibility, truth, truthfulness and rightness." As I understand him, by "comprehensibility" Habermas means that the language pattern be understood by all, by "truth" that the utterance express what is true, by "truthfulness" that the speaker be sincere in what he or she speaks, and by "rightness" that the speech act be according to existing speech norms, i.e., properly stated.

70. Kearney gives a helpful summary of Habermas's notion of "an ideal speech situation." He writes: "This regulative ideal represents a democratic system of communication where there would exist a symmetrical distribution of chances to choose and apply speech-acts in an undistorted manner. It would be fulfilled when all possible participants in discourse possess an equal opportunity to initiate communication and become transparent by their words and actions" (*Modern Movements*, p. 227).

71. The "Mud Flower Collective" offers an engaing description of dialogue as "a sharing of our lives that seeks justice-based relation" (*God's Fierce Whimsy*, p. 64).

72. See Habermas, *Toward a Theory*, p. 372, and *Communicative Action*, vol. 1, p. 134.

73. Habermas offers little specific critique of the structures of sexism, racism, and class bias that prevent "communicative action." I also pointed out in *C.R.E.*, p. 175, that Habermas seems to overstate the importance of such communicative competence as if it were an end in itself. It cannot be so, but it *is* a constitutive component to the struggle to transform the world—the real end of authentic dialogue. Giroux, drawing upon Marcuse, reiterates this same critique of Habermas. See *Theory*, pp. 26–27.

74. In Part II, we return many times to how such dialogue can be intentionally fostered in a pedagogical process. Here, we can anticipate a key insight of those reflections: authentic dialogue emerges in the praxis of trying to intentionally do it. We cannot wait until there are perfect conditions of trust, openness, noncoercion, mutuality, respect, commitment to consensus, etc., before beginning. We forge ahead with intentionality about dialogue and firm commitment to its ideal, and true dialogue emerges in that praxis.

75. Gerkin, *Widening the Horizons*, p. 52.

76. In chap. 4 I dwell at some length on the appropriateness of the metaphors Story and Vision to our pedagogical purposes and their adequacy to reflect the faith tradition that arises from the narrative practical history of Christianity over time.

77. Instead of writing "Story *and* Vision" I will often use this construct of Story/Vision to highlight their unity. The Story is of what has been and is, and the Vision is of the demands and eschatological promises that the Story brings to our lives; thus they are two expressions of the same reality—the unfolding of God's reign in history. Further, I typically do not refer to *the* Christian Story/Vision to avoid the impression that Christian faith is one monolithic Story and a univocal Vision; there are many stories within Christian Story, and many visions within its Vision.

78. Augustine, *The Confessions*, book 11, chap. 14; p. 287.

79. See especially, Aristotle's *Physics*, book 6, 231a20—231b20. Aristotle uses the image of a continuous line for both time and motion. He argues, "It is manifest that any continuum is divisible into parts that are divisible without limit." He adds, "Now the same argument applies to spatial magnitude and time and motion" (*Physics*, book 6, 231b15–20; vol. 2, pp. 96–97).

80. Augustine wrote: "If any point of time is conceived that can no longer be divided into even the most minute parts of a moment, that alone is it which may be called the present. It flies with such speed from the future into the past that it cannot be extended by even a trifling amount. For if it is extended, it is divided into past and future. The present has no space" (*The Confessions*, book 11, chap. 15; p. 289).

81. Ibid., chap. 18; p. 291.

82. Ibid., chap. 20; p. 293.

83. See Aquinas, *Commentary on Aristotle's Physics*, book 4, lect. 17: 580, where he states, "Time is nothing else than the number of motion in respect to before and after" (p. 259).

84. See *The Encyclopedia of Philosophy*, "Time," by J. J. C. Smart, 8:126–34.

85. In *Being and Time*, Heidegger proposed "time" as the primordial and unifying foundation of Dasein's "being in the world" and Dasein as the unifier of time. "Temporality makes possible the unity of existence, facticity, and falling, and in this way, constitutes primordially the totality of the structure of Care" (*Being and Time*, p. 375). ("Care" is Heidegger's overarching concept for the whole structure of Dasein.) In his later work, Heidegger abandoned his attempt at "finding a concept of time" by a fundamental ontology of Dasein. (See *On Time and Being*, p. 32.) Instead, he argued, time has to be conceptualized by thinking *sein*, not by a phenomenology of Dasein. (I am indebted to a comment by Raymond Devettere for this footnote.)

86. In my emphasis on "present time," I am more influenced by Augustine than Heidegger. Although Augustine's point is not contrary to Heidegger's, Heidegger preferred to emphasize the future as the primary influence upon our existential experience of time. Because Dasein's possibility is always what causes us to reach out beyond ourselves in anticipation toward the totality of what we can become, time, for Heidegger, is primarily futural. He wrote, "The character of 'having been' arises from the future, and in such a way that the future which 'has been' (or better, which 'is in the process of having been') releases from itself the Present. This phenomenon has the unity of a future which makes present in the process of having been; we designate it as 'temporality'" (*Being and Time*, p. 374). Thus he concludes, "The primary phenomenon of primordial and authentic temporality is the future" (ibid., p. 378).

87. A. N. Whitehead, *Aims*, pp. 3, 14.

88. This heading is suggested by the title of one of Dwayne Huebner's essays, "Curriculum as Concern for Man's Temporality." I should also note here that Huebner (my major advisor in doctoral studies) first introduced me to a holistic understanding of time. For example, "Human life is not futural; nor is it past, but, rather, a present made up of a past and future brought into the moment. . . . The point is that [person] is temporal; or if you wish, historical. There is no such 'thing' as a past or a future. They exist only through [a person's] existence as a temporal being. This means that human life is never fixed but is always emergent as the past and future become horizons of a present" ("Curriculum as Concern," p. 244).

89. "Curriculum field" typically refers to the study of curriculum as a formal specialization within education. In North America, curriculum began to receive special attention in the 1890s, with the work of brothers Frank and Charles McMurray, who had been trained in Herbartianism at the University of Jena. The "curriculum field" became a recognized specialization in schools of education in the 1940s. See Mary Louise Seguel, *The Curriculum Field*. However, the three points of emphasis I refer to in curriculum construction have been operative throughout the history of education, long before curriculum became a formal field of study.

90. A particularly helpful schema is offered by Michael Schiro in *Curriculum for Better Schools*. Schiro identifies four "curriculum ideologies": (1) "the social efficiency ideology," which places emphasis on "the functioning of society by preparing the individual child to lead a meaningful adult life within society" (p. 9); (2) the "scholar academic ideology," which emphasizes the academic disciplines of learning in curriculum construction; (3) "the child study ideology," which emphasizes "the child's innate nature . . . the needs and concerns of the individual child" (p. 11); and (4) "the social reconstruction ideology," which designs curriculum "to educate students to understand the nature of their society in such a way that they will develop a vision of a better society, and then act so as to bring that vision into existence" (p. 12).

Elliot Eisner offers a fivefold schema, four points of which closely resemble Schiro's "ideologies"; Eisner's fifth one emphasizes developing the ability of students to think cognitively, an emphasis at least implied in Schiro's "scholar academic" approach. See *The Educational Imagination*, chap. 4. As indicated in what follows, I believe both schemas can be reduced to three points of emphasis—on the disciplines of learning, the learners, and the society.

91. For helpful overviews of this threefold schema, see Arnold Bellack, "History of Curriculum Thought and Practice"; and Ole Sand, "Curriculum Change."

92. Dewey, "Creed," p. 19.

93. Hough and Cobb write insightfully, "Israel was remarkable in its ability to depict its own history realistically, giving an honest account of the sins of its heroes and of its collective failures. Christians have yielded more often than Jews to the temptation to exalt the greatness of their historical achievements, but this has been checked by the scriptures and the awareness of the need for repentance" (*Education*, p. 47).

94. Both the Christian and Jewish traditions have a definite concern for the future. They are eschatological and marked by a strong note of anticipation; the Jewish tradition awaits a messiah to come, while the Christian tradition expects the messiah to come again with the fullness of God's reign. But neither tradition understands its anticipatory stance as passive waiting. Rather, the waiting should be a creative leaning forward into the future to co-create, as covenant partners with each other and God, the promised reign.

95. Lonergan, *Method*, p. xii.

96. Ibid., p. 13.

97. Lonergan writes, "Self-transcendence is the achievement of conscious intentionality" (ibid., p. 35). He adds, "I have conceived being in love with God as an ultimate fulfillment of man's [*sic*] capacity for self-transcendence" (ibid., p. 111).

98. Lonergan writes, "The ascent from the darkness of the cave to the light of day is a movement from a world of immediacy that is already out there now to a world mediated by the meaningfulness of intelligent, reasonable, responsible answers to questions" ("Theology and Praxis," in *Third Collection*, p. 193).

99. "The transcendentals are comprehensive in connotation, unrestricted in denotation, invariant over cultural change. While categories are needed to put determinate questions and give determinate answers, the transcendentals are contained in questions prior to the answers" (Lonergan, *Method*, p. 11).

100. Lonergan, *Method*, p. 25. This question is a favorite of Lonergan's, and he notes that the answer to it provides a cognitional theory. When one asks, Why is doing that knowing? one moves to articulate an epistemology (ibid.).

101. Ibid., p. 4, 20.

102. Ibid., p. 9 (emphasis added). Note here that Lonergan has followed a pattern similar to Kant's dynamics of cognition, in that it flows from sense data, to understanding, to reason. He differs significantly, however, in that he sees "decision"—Kant's practical reason—not as separated from the other three activities of theoretical reason but as logically flowing out of them in the life of the existential subject. I agree with Lonergan.

103. See ibid., pp. 54–55.

104. Ibid., p. 213.

105. Note that Lonergan's use of the term *reason* pertains more to judgment than to how I have used it heretofore as a particular activity (reasoning) within critical reflection.

106. Lonergan writes, "So intelligence takes us beyond experiencing to ask what and why and how and what for. Reasonableness takes us beyond the answers of intelligence to ask whether the answers are true and whether what they mean really is so. Responsibility goes beyond fact and desire and possibility to discern between what truly is good and what only apparently is good" (*Method*, p. 11).

107. See ibid., p. 120.

108. Lonergan writes, "Judgments of value differ in content but not in structure from judgments of fact . . . inasmuch as in both there is the distinction between criterion and meaning" (ibid., p. 37).

109. See ibid., p. 76.

110. Ibid., p. 20, passim.

111. Lonergan writes, "So the proper achievement and end of the first level, experiencing, is the apprehension of data; that of the second level, understanding, is insight into the apprehended data; that of the third level, judgment, is the acceptance or rejection of the hypotheses and theories put forward by understanding to account for the data; that of the fourth level, decision, the acknowledgment of values and the selection of the methods or other means that lead to their realization" (ibid., p. 133).

112. Lonergan, *Method*, p. 9.

113. Lonergan writes, "But the presence of the subject resides in the gazing, the attending, the intending. For this reason the subject can be conscious, as attending, and

yet give his [sic] whole attention to the object as attended to" (Method, p. 8). He writes elsewhere that "where knowing is a structure, knowing knowing must be a reduplication of the structure" ("Cognitional Structure," in Collection, p. 224).

114. At times, however, I find Lonergan overclaims for the power of conscious intentionality to bring people to their authentic subjectivity in history. Real historical subjects also need sociocultural contexts that are just and life-giving in order to live into their subjectivity. Lonergan does recognize the reality of "individual," "group," and "general" biases (see Insight, pp. 218–62). He notes that "the sundry aspects of this threefold bias, . . . can arise not only in the sphere of economics but also in that of government, not only in politics but in any of the areas into which political benevolence may extend, not only in things secular but also in things sacred" ("Emerging Religious Consciousness of Our Time," in Third Collection, pp. 62–63). However, he seems to place unbounded confidence in the intentional and conscious performance of the transcendental imperatives as the solution to personal alienation and social decline. (See Method, p. 55.) He often seems to imply that this reach for authenticity is by a self-sufficient kind of rugged individualism. He pays little explicit attention to the need for historical struggle against oppressive political, economic, and cultural arrangements (sexism, racism, class bias, etc.) that rob people of their historical subjectivity, regardless of how intentional they are about the activities of their own consciousness. He also pays little attention to the need for a community of dialogue as a context and catalyst for one performing the transcendental activities intentionally and self-consciously. Lonergan would still seem to be caught with the transcendental subject that he found in Kant.

115. In the Third Collection Lonergan writes, "In fact I have argued for the possibility of some thirty-one distinct differentiations of consciousness" ("Theology and Praxis," in Third Collection, p. 186). He adds in a footnote that "a succinct presentation of the pieces that may be combined in various ways may be found in my Method in Theology, 1972, pp. 302–5." In that reference, Lonergan's "succinct presentation" distinguishes ten differentiations of consciousness.

116. Writing about this process, Lonergan says, "It is a matter of applying the operations as intentional to the operations as conscious" (Method, p. 14). See also note 113.

117. Ibid., p. 19.

118. As I noted, Lonergan has an insightful delineation of our individual, group, and general biases. (See Insight, pp. 218–42.) It seems to me, however, that in his call for the conscious and intentional performance of the four transcendental activities as the antidote to all bias, Lonergan fails to make central a critical awareness of the sociology of knowledge, or of the constitutive cognitive interests (Habermas), so shaped by our sociocultural context, with which we perform the four transcendentals. Nor does there appear to be any conscious attention to the need to test one's cognition in a community of dialogue. Consequently, the performance of the transcendental activities as he outlines them do not seem likely to bring people to a socially critical consciousness that can be a source of transformation toward one's social structures as well as for oneself. I believe my own posing of the necessity to attend to and engage people with critical reflection upon their whole "place" and "time" in a community of dialogue is a corrective to Lonergan's oversight, at least for our interest in a pedagogical process for conation. (See also note 19, chapter 4.)

119. See Lonergan, "Theology and Praxis," in Third Collection, p. 186.

120. Method, p. 13.

121. Method, p. 74.

122. See ibid., pp. 76–81.

123. In fully differentiated consciousness, according to Lonergan, there are four realms of meaning: the realm of common sense, of theory, of interiority, and of transcendence. In the latter, "the subject is related to divinity in the language of prayer and of prayerful silence" (ibid., p. 257). For his basic explanation of the four realms of meaning see ibid., pp. 81–85.

124. Piaget explains that "a truth is never truly assimilated as a truth except in so far as it has first been reconstructed or rediscovered by means of some activity adequate to that task" (To Understand, p. 26). He adds that "it is clear that an education which is an

active discovery of reality is superior to one that consists merely in providing the young with ready-made wills to will with and ready-made truths to know with" (ibid.).

125. Piaget, *Child*, p. 6.

126. In making good judgments that promote oneself as "an authentic human being" Lonergan says that "knowledge alone is not enough . . . moral feelings have to be cultivated, enlightened, strengthened, refined, criticized and pruned of oddities" (*Method*, p. 38).

127. See Lonergan, "The Subject," in *Second Collection*, pp. 70ff.

128. Lonergan observes, correctly I believe, that "insistence on objective truth and the same neglect of its subjective conditions informed the old catechetics" ("The Subject," in *Second Collection*, p. 72).

129. In Lonergan's schema we noted that the transcendental values that are the "active potency" of judging and deciding are "the true" and "the good," respectively. This distinction seems more appropriate, however, when a prior distinction is made between speculative and practical reasoning, the traditional Scholastic designations, the speculative intending "the true" and the practical "the good." However, when a pedagogy reflects an "epistemic ontology," a separation of theoretical from practical reasoning is inappropriate and misleading. Concern for both "the true" and "the good" is integral to and combined within its decision making dynamic.

Aquinas wisely recognized that "truth and goodness include one another" and that "the practical intellect knows truth just as the speculative but it directs the known truth to operation" (*Summa Theologica*. I, 79.II; vol. 1, p. 406).

130. Contemporary literature speaks of a fourth major understanding, "the semantic theory of truth." For this, much influenced by linguistic philosophy, "truth" is expressed and shaped by language because it is language that picks up the "facts" and describes the world. Here I include the semantic within the correspondence theory.

131. See Thomas Aquinas, *Summa Contra Gentiles* I, 59. See Mondin, *Aquinas' Philosophy*, pp. 20–35, for an insightful discussion of Aquinas on this point.

132. Woozley explains the correspondence theory thus: "a judgment is correct or a proposition judged as true if there is a fact corresponding to it, false if there is not" (*Knowledge*, p. 129).

133. Solomon gives a good summary of the critiques when he writes, "against the 'correspondence theory of truth' there are three telling arguments: (1) it is, at best, limited. All cases of necessary truth, and perhaps some others, cannot be accounted for by it at all; (2) there is no such thing as a statement of a belief which, by itself, is capable of 'corresponding' to anything; (3) there is no such thing as a 'fact' which can be picked out independently of the language used to describe it" (*Philosophy*, p. 172).

134. "According to the coherence theory, the truth of a judgment consists in its coherence within a system of judgments" (Woozley, *Knowledge*, p. 29).

135. Solomon explains the pragmatic theory: "a statement or belief is true if and only if 'it works,' that is if it allows us to predict certain results, functions effectively in everyday life, and encourages further inquiry and helps us lead better lives" (*Philosophy*, p. 189).

136. *Theological Dictionary*, abridged, p. 37. See also pp. 37–39 for a good summary statement.

137. See Couturier, "Jeremiah" in *Jerome Biblical Commentary*, vol. 1, p. 307.

138. Dewey, "Truth," *Harper's Bible Dictionary*, p. 1100.

139. Parker Palmer, *Known*, p.59.

140. Metz writes: "It is quite clear . . . that the crisis of Christianity today is not primarily a crisis of the content of faith and its promises, but a crisis of subjects and institutions which do not measure up to the demands made by faith" (*History*, p. 76).

Welch makes a similar point when she writes of "an inability to claim that Christianity is true in any significant sense outside the realm of its becoming actually true in history" (*Solidarity*, p. 14).

141. Lonergan writes, "One not only chooses . . . but also thereby makes oneself an authentic human being or an unauthentic one" (*Method*, p. 38).

142. In Christian religious education, and especially since the publication of Horace Bushnell's *Christian Nurture* (1847), there has been a debate over whether we are educating for conversion or nurture. Of late, a more centrist position has emerged that

recognizes the need both for people's nurture and ongoing conversion in Christian faith. See Westerhoff, *Will Our Children Have Faith?*, and my own article "Conversion, Nurture and Educators."

143. For a very helpful summary of the meaning of *habitus*, see *Sacramentum Mundi*, "Habitus," by Oswald Schwemmer, 3:1–3.

144. See, e.g., Lonergan, *Method*, pp. 268–69.

145. Lonergan writes, "Conversion is a change of direction . . . one frees oneself from the unauthentic. One grows in authenticity. Harmful, dangerous, misleading satisfactions are dropped. Fears of discomfort, pain, privation have less power to deflect one from one's course. Values are apprehended where before they were overlooked. Scales of preference shift. Errors, rationalizations, ideologies fall and shatter to leave one open to things as they are and to man [or woman] as he [or she] should be" (*Method*, p. 52). In describing the process of conversion Lonergan writes, "Conversion . . . is total surrender to the demands of the human spirit: be attentive, be intelligent, be responsible, be in love" (ibid., p. 268). As such, conversion is a self-conscious turning toward the given, the intelligible, the true, and the good, with a total openness and self-transcendence in the quest for those intentions. But, as noted, for Lonergan authenticity and self-transcendence require a consciousness of oneself being intentionally faithful to the transcendental activities. Thus, "conversion," Lonergan writes, "is finding out for oneself and in oneself what it is to be intelligent, to be reasonable, to be responsible, to love" (*Method*, p. 253).

146. Ibid., pp. 238, 130. Lonergan explains that "Normally it is a prolonged process though its explicit acknowledgement may be concentrated in a few momentous judgments and decisions. Still it is not just a development or even a series of developments. Rather it is a resultant change of course and direction. It is as if one's eyes were opened and one's former world faded and fell away. There emerges something new that fructifies in inter-locking, cumulative sequences of development on all levels and in all departments of human living" (*Method*, p. 130).

147. Ibid., p. 237.

148. See ibid., p. 238.

149. Ibid., p. 241.

150. Ibid., p. 240.

151. See ibid., p. 241.

152. Ibid., p. 240.

153. Lonergan writes, "Religious conversion is a total being in love as the efficacious ground of all self-transcendence," and "I have conceived being in love with God as the ultimate fulfillment of man's [*sic*] capacity for self-transcendence" (*Method*, pp. 241, 111).

154. Here Lonergan is insisting on and balancing divine grace and human agency in religious conversion. To clarify their relationship, he turns to the Augustinian distinction between operative and cooperative grace. "Religious conversion . . . is interpreted differently in the context of different religious traditions. For Christians it is God's love flooding our hearts through the Holy Spirit. It is the gift of grace . . . operative grace is the replacement of the heart of stone by a heart of flesh, a replacement beyond the horizon of the heart of stone. Cooperative grace is the heart of flesh becoming effective in good works through human freedom" (*Method*, p. 241).

155. Regarding religious conversion, Braxton, working out of the Lonergan construct, makes a helpful distinction from a Christian perspective between theistic and Christian religious conversion. Theistic conversion is coming explicitly to accept "God" as one's "ultimate concern." "Theistic conversion makes explicit the referent, source or object of the feelings of awe and reverence that characterize conversion" (*Community*, p. 76). "'Christian conversion' then is the specification of that orientation of humankind and that outreach of God by means of the focal reality of Jesus exalted as the Christ" (ibid., p.79).

156. Concerning the relationship of the three aspects of conversion, Lonergan seems to opt for no hard-and-fast sequence. He writes, "A changed relation to God brings or follows changes that are personal, social, moral, and intellectual. But there is no fixed rule of antecedence and consequence, no necessity of simultaneity, no prescribed magnitude of change" ("Theology in its New Context," p. 13). Their relationship is typically one of "sublation" i.e., moral conversion takes up and goes beyond intellectual conversion, and religious conversion takes up and goes beyond both of them. Again, however, this does

not imply a necessary sequence. "Though religious conversion sublates moral, and moral conversion sublates intellectual, one must not infer that intellectual comes first, then moral, and finally religious. On the contrary, from a causal viewpoint, one would say that first there is God's gift of his [sic] love (Method, p. 243).

Chapter 4. An Overview of Shared Christian Praxis

1. Paulo Freire is the contemporary author most responsible for developing a praxis-based approach to education as a systematically understood option for educators—especially for those intending liberation and humanization. See Pedagogy of the Oppressed; Education for Critical Consciousness; Pedagogy in Process; and The Politics of Education.

2. My work has been criticized too for diverging not only from Aristotle's notion of praxis but from Freire's as well. This may well be the case (although Freire is never quite precise in what he means by praxis), given that Freire's focus is to teach literacy, whereas my intent is to fashion an approach to Christian religious education that is usable for all age levels, in all contexts (e.g., schools), and for all themes of life in Christian faith and of Christian faith in life. I also note that in Freire's praxis-based approach to literacy education, the "codifications" represent people's ordinary lives and everyday realities. A sociopolitical consciousness emerges in the process of decodification and decision making. This can happen similarly in the shared praxis approach to faith education.

3. Browning makes a helpful distinction when he writes, "The difference between practice and praxis is that in the latter the theory has been made self-conscious and reflected upon critically" (Practical Theology, p. 13).

4. Marx made this point about praxis but then tended to limit its active moment to production.

5. There is, of course, a "theoretical" dimension to Christian tradition. As a systematic attempt to bring faith to understanding, Christian theology has given rise to doctrines, dogmas, creeds, and teachings that are most often expressed in theoretical and metaphysical language. However, its doctrines, dogmas, and creeds are symbols of the meaning that the Christian community has come to by reflecting on the faith life of its pilgrim journey through history. Religious educators are to teach them as symbolic expressions and summary statements of the practical wisdom that emerges from the narrative of the Christian community over time.

6. Aristotle, De Anima, III, 11, 434 A; pp. 191–95.

7. For this insight I am indebted to the work of Ann Louise Gilligan. See The Feminist Imagination, pp. 273–305.

8. To speak of people reflecting on their praxis is a somewhat imprecise use of the word praxis, in that praxis already entails a reflective moment. However, in point of fact a praxis-based pedagogy that honors the cumulative dynamic of conation is structured to deepen the reflective moment and to bring participants to do critical reflection intentionally and consciously (Lonergan).

9. Tracy writes, "What the 'essence of Christianity' might be after Christians seriously acknowledge first the plurality within their own traditions, second, the import of the many other religious traditions for Christian self-understanding and third, the profound cognitive, moral, and religious ambiguity of Christianity itself is, to put it mildly, a very difficult question . . ." Plurality and Ambiguity. p. x.

10. Fowler writes, "The dynamic character of narrative, as opposed to ontological categories inherited from preprocess metaphysical perspectives, is one of the reasons for the growing interest in theology as 'story' and in explorations of the return to narrative as the primary mode of theological work. . . . It reflects a hunger to recover a sense of meaning as being connected with history, a sense of disclosure and depth as being connected with experience" (Becoming Adult, p. 81). By way of example of this shift to narrative language, a statement like "the church is the sacrament of God's reign," although theologically "accurate," reflects an ideational language pattern. In more narrative language, its truth and meaning would run something as follows: "As the community of Jesus' disciples in the world, Christians have a historical responsibility to be effective agents of peace and justice, love and freedom, and fullness of life for all. At times the

church has been and is so effective, but we also have failed and do fail miserably in this task, and we are always challenged to be such a community."

11. Metz, *History,* p. 161.

12. Some of the reflections in this section were first suggested by work with my colleague Mary Boys for a joint presentation, "The Role of Story in Religious Education," given at the Los Angeles Religious Education Congress, March 24, 1984.

13. A central theme of Elisabeth Schüssler Fiorenza, *In Memory of Her,* is that in his historical praxis, Jesus intended to liberate from patriarchal structures and to call people into a "discipleship of equals." She writes,"The woman-identified man, Jesus, called forth a discipleship of equals that still needs to be discovered and realized by women and men today" (ibid., p. 154). She points out, however, that this central characteristic of the Jesus movement was "written out" of the New Testament and must now be reconstructed.

14. Partnership has been an implicit theme in Russell's work since *Christian Education in Mission* (1967), a book that had profound influence on my early work. It became a central theme, however, in *The Future of Partnership* (1979) and in *Growth in Partnership* (1981).

15. See Russell, *Future,* p. 18.

16. Russell, *Growth,* pp. 39, 12.

17. In shared Christian praxis this especially requires becoming convinced that God is revealing Godself in one's own life and in the lives of co-learners; only thus is one likely to truly value one's own word and the word of others as constitutive of the curriculum. We return to this theme as an aspect of the theology of revelation that undergirds the approach.

18. I say this with confidence. Many times in shared praxis groups I have experienced how people who had little value for their own word or for the word of other participants and expected only a teacher-centered didactic process have moved into partnership through the dynamics of such an approach.

19. Recalling chap. 3, section 4, a more philosophical warrant for my claim that the dynamics of a shared praxis approach are "natural" to people can be found in Lonergan's description of the structure of cognition. Fred Crowe, one of the best interpreters of Lonergan, writes as follows about the dynamic structure: "We have been talking about human nature. . . . We have noticed a dynamism at work, unfolding in successive activities that reveal a structure and are exercised with the kind of regularity and inevitability that belong to a 'nature' " (*Old,* p. 12).

Placing the shared Christian praxis approach in dialogue with Lonergan's insight about the four transcendental activities that cumulatively result in cognition, we notice a profound resonance between the two schemata. I noted in chapter 3, section 4 that as a conscious and intentional process, all four transcendental activities are operative in all five movements of shared praxis, and then each particular transcendental has a distinct resonance with one of the movements. Using Lonergan's terms, the focusing activity and the first movement attend to the data (transcendental activity 1); movement 2 is the attempt to "understand" (transcendental activity 2); movement 3 draws upon the understanding of the community over time to aid understanding (transcendental activity 2) and moves to judgment/appropriation (transcendental activity 3, movement 4) in order to make responsible decisions (transcendental activity 4, movement 5). Assuming that Lonergan is correct in posing the transcendental activities (attending, understanding, judging, deciding) as a natural dynamic, then the shared praxis approach is correspondingly a "natural" approach to education in Christian faith. And given its engagement of the whole "being" of participants as agent-subjects-in-relationship, it is also a conative pedagogy.

There are also, however, significant ways in which the shared praxis approach differs from and is a critique of Lonergan's construct. In notes 114 and 118 of chap. 3, I critique Lonergan for (a) appearing not to take seriously the sociology of knowledge and the constitutive cognitive interests with which people perform the four transcendentals (his nod to biases notwithstanding) and (b) his lack of attention to a community of dialogue to encourage people to perform the transcendental activities both self-consciously and intentionally. Within a conative dynamic I emphasized social and critical reflection in a community of dialogue as responses to these lacunae in Lonergan's thought. Now, from the perspective of a shared praxis approach to religious education, I add the following to my critique of Lonergan.

When Lonergan applies the four transcendentals to theological method, he outlines eight "functional specialties" to which they give rise, namely: (1) research, (2) interpretation, (3) history, (4) dialectic, (5) foundations, (6) doctrines, (7) systematics, and (8) communications. (See *Method,* chap. 5 and p. 355 for a summary.) The research begins with attending to the original sources and texts of the tradition and then moves to understanding in hermeneutics, judging in historical studies, etc., in a cumulative effort going up and then back down the transcendental activities to end in communication. Though all four transcendentals are always operative in every functional specialty, each functional specialty is the end proper to a particular transcendental in an ascending and descending order. A diagram of the specialties as related to the transcendentals may help!

Transcendentals		*Functional specialties*		
Deciding	to	Dialectic	→	Foundations
↕		↑		↓
Judging	to	History		Doctrines
↕		↑		↓
Understanding	to	Interpretation		Systematics
↕		↑		↓
Attending	to	Research		Communications

Notice that communications, under which Lonergan categorizes education, is simply the cumulative outcome of the other specialties and amounts to "the task of finding the appropriate approach and procedure to convey the message to people of different classes and cultures" (*Method,* p. 142). He speaks of "systematics fixing the kernel of the message to be communicated" and then adds, but more as an afterthought, "questions for systematics can arise from communications" (ibid.).

In other words, the data attended to in Lonergan's schema seem to be exclusively the data of the original sources and texts of the tradition. That data from people's own praxis in the world are a primary existential source of faith knowing is totally undeveloped in Lonergan's construct. Nowhere does he recognize that religious education is any more than a delivery system for the findings of the "scholars"—an unfortunate and debilitating stereotype for both theology and religious education.

20. See David Tracy, *The Analogical Imagination,* and "The Foundations of Practical Theology"; Martin E. Marty, *Public Church;* Parker Palmer, *The Company of Strangers.* Parallel to this "public" theology is the emergence of a North American political theology, again, not from situations or particular struggles with oppression, as in liberation theologies, but from among "mainline" Christians.

The statements by the U.S. National Conference of Catholic Bishops on the nuclear issue and on the economy are powerful examples of an attempt by the institutional structures of a "mainline" church to shape the discourse about public policy. See *The Challenge of Peace* and *Economic Justice for All.*

21. See esp. Seymour, O'Gorman, and Foster, *The Church in the Education of the Public;* see also Boys, ed., *Education for Citizenship and Discipleship;* Moran, *No Ladder to the Sky: Education and Morality,* esp. part 3; Maureen O'Brien, *Religious Education and the Public;* Toton, "The Public and Political Responsibility of Christian Education"; Schmidt, "Toward a Strategy for Public Christian Education." A focus on "public" church and religious education has also been central to James Fowler's recent work.

22. Seymour et al., *Public,* p. 11.

23. Ibid., p. 19.

24. Ibid., pp. 128, 129.

25. On the Communidades de Base movement in Latin America, see Sergio Torres and John Eagleson, eds., *The Challenge of Basic Christian Communities;* and O'Halloron, *Signs of Hope.* For creating such communities in North America, see Lee and Cowan, *Dangerous Memories;* Baronowski, *Creating Small Faith Communities*; and Kleissler et al., *Small Christian Communities.*

26. Harvey Cox writes, "The origins of the base communities will probably always be shrouded in legend and dispute" (*Religion in the Secular City,* p. 117).

27. Undoubtedly the work of Paulo Freire has had a major impact on the base community movement, first in Latin America, and later in Africa. However, Freire would be first to insist that his work is more a source of practical clarity for the movement than the cause of it. In fact, his own work emerged out of a grassroots literacy movement in Brazil.

28. See *The Rite of Christian Initiation of Adults: Study Edition* (1988). This is the final version of what was originally published (1972) as a provisional text. The actual document recommends a series of liturgical rites to mark the steps of initiation into active church membership. It did not suggest a pedagogical process to facilitate faith formation. James Dunning is the primary author of a very creative and widely used process for implementing the pedagogical component of the RCIA. Though I believe he had worked out a similar approach before my own first published essays, he often graciously footnotes the influence of the shared praxis approach on his implementation of the RCIA. See James Dunning, "Method Is the Medium is the Message: Catechetical Method in the RCIA."

A large amount of material is available on how to implement the RCIA in a congregation from W. H. Sadlier, Paulist Press, and other publishers. For more information, write The North American Forum on the Catechumenate, 5510 Columbia Pike, Arlington, VA 22204.

29. For details, write National Office of Renew, Archdiocese of Newark, 499 Belgrove Drive, Kearney, NJ 07030. The Renew Program Materials are published by Paulist Press, 545 Island Road, Ramsey, NJ 07446.

30. The following are only a few of many instances: Gilbert Ostdiek, *Catechesis for Liturgy,* which uses the shared praxis approach in liturgical catechesis; Richard M. Gula, *To Walk Together Again: The Sacrament of Reconciliation,* focused on the sacrament of reconciliation and structured entirely and most creatively around the five movements of shared praxis; Neil A. Parent, ed., *Adult Learning and the Parish,* which uses the shared praxis approach and reflects it in the basic structure of the book as a model of adult learning.

In addition, a number of doctoral dissertations completed at Boston College have pushed the shared praxis approach beyond where I left it in *C.R.E.* (1980). See especially Russell Butkus, *Dangerous Memory;* Katherine Zappone, *Restructuring Relationality;* Ann Louise Gilligan, *The Feminist Imagination;* Deidre Palmer, *A Discipleship of Equals.* Two dissertations of which I am aware from other schools are Joe F. Stewart, *Shared Praxis: A Therapeutic Approach* (Perkins School of Theology, Dallas, Texas, 1986), a creative attempt to use shared praxis in group counseling; and William F. Sutherland, *A Critical Examination of Shared Praxis in Religious Education* (University of Pittsburgh, 1984).

31. There are many other authors whose work is very much consonant with what I would describe in general as a praxis approach to faith education and "development." I think especially of Mary Elizabeth Moore, *Continuity and Change;* Letty Russell, *Growth in Partnership* and *Future of Partnership;* D. Campbell Wyckoff, see especially "Understanding Your Church Curriculum." Maurice L. Monette's book *The Supper Table* is an adult education program for community spirituality—very much a participative, praxis-based, and consciousness-raising approach. Donald E. Miller, *Story and Context,* reviews the field and its many approaches, but his emphasis on community, Story, and narrative places the approach Miller recommends, I believe, in the praxis-based school. In *Working Out Your Own Beliefs,* Douglas Wingeier offers a reflective dynamic resonant with the movements of a shared praxis approach. In addition, the faith development researchers who have written explicitly about religious education seem to favor a praxis approach. See, e.g., Sharon Parks, *The Critical Years;* James Fowler, *Becoming Adult.*

There is also a growing awareness among theological educators that their present educational praxis is inadequate, especially for preparing people for ministry, and a growing tendency to recommend a praxis approach, at least for ministerial education. For example, without delineating the actual pedagogy to effect his proposal, Edward Farley names four components that should be engaged in order to form people in the *habitus* of *theologia*, i.e., the ability to do theology in a pastoral situation. They are (1) beginning with the contemporary situation and praxis, (2) using the faith tradition to bring a herme-neutic of suspicion to present praxis, (3) using the present situation to interpret the faith tradition, and (4) returning to the historical situation with a more "theonomous inter-pretation." See *Theologia*, pp. 165–68. The resonance with the components of a shared praxis approach is obvious. The significant work of Don Browning on a method for doing "practical theology" also recommends a praxis-based approach. See his five levels for practical theological thinking in *Religious Ethics and Pastoral Care*, esp. chaps. 5 and 6, and his essay "Pastoral Theology in a Pluralistic Age."

Lastly, the copious literature on theological method reveals a growing awareness that both present praxis and the Christian tradition must be engaged, critiqued, and placed in a dialectical hermeneutic with each other. For example, David Tracy has proposed a method of critical correlation between "the meanings present in common human expe-rience and language" and "the meanings present in the Christian fact" (*Rage*, p. 43).

32. I do not imply that a praxis-based approach is new to religious education. In *C.R.E.* (1980) I tried to footnote, insofar as I knew them, the many shoulders on which I stand. Two obvious examples in the recent history of religious education that have resonance with a praxis approach are the Munich Method in Catholicism and the teach-ing process developed by William Clayton Bower in Protestantism.

The Munich Method emerged at the beginning of the twentieth century. It was influenced by the "activity school" of pedagogy, which in turn was shaped by Herbar-tianism. It had variations but in general organized the teaching/learning act into five moments, namely, preparation (a participative activity), presentation, explanation, sum-mary, and application. The exponent of the Munich Method best known to American readers was R. G. Bandas. See, e.g., his *Catechetical Methods*.

Seymour, O'Gorman, and Foster summarize Bower's teaching method in five steps: "(1) Assist persons to reflect objectively on the actual situations they face in life experi-ence; (2) help persons reconstruct and understand the experience in terms of their own past experience; (3) guide persons to understand the experience in terms of the cultural heritage of the religious group and the society; (4) engage these reflections with one another, searching for meanings, values, possible responses, and outcomes; and (5) de-cide upon the action or behavior that should be adopted" (*Public*, pp. 117–18). They footnote William Clayton Bower, "A Curriculum for Character and Religious Education in a Changing Culture."

33. James and Evelyn Eaton Whitehead, *Method in Ministry*, p. 1.

34. Ibid., pp. 12–13.

35. They describe these in graphic summary as follows:

"I. Attending: Seek out the information on a particular pastoral concern that is available in personal experience, Christian Tradition, and cultural sources.

"II. Assertion: Engage the information from these three sources in a process of mutual clarification and challenge in order to expand and deepen religious insight.

"III. Decision: Move from insight through decision to concrete pastoral action" (ibid., p. 22).

36. By way of dialogue with them, their use of "experience" does not seem to point as readily to the historical *actions* of agent-subjects as does the term *praxis*. In addition, shared praxis makes more explicit the dimension of critical reflection in what they call "attending" and the dialectical hermeneutic needed in "assertion."

37. Holland and Henriot, *Social Analysis*, p. 7.

38. Ibid., pp. 8–9. Placing their pastoral circle in dialogue with shared Christian praxis, I first note that they are not attempting to propose, as I am, an overarching approach suitable to all intentional religious education. For example, their commitment to pastoral planning is essential when a social ethical issue is the focused theme but might not be as immediately appropriate with a more doctrinal issue. Yet there is very obvious resonance between "insertion" and movement 1; social analysis is very much a part of movement 2; "theological reflection" correlates with movement 3; and "pastoral plan-ning," when the theme is a social issue, is certainly an aspect of movement 5. If shared

praxis adds anything to the "pastoral circle" model, it does so in its potential to move beyond specifically justice issues and in the deliberateness of the dialectic in the fourth movement as an intermediate step between theological reflection and decision making. Their social analysis model, however, highlights the need for group pastoral planning, especially when required by a particular social issue.

39. Tillich, *Theology and Culture,* p. 42.

40. Quoted in Schreiter, "Faith and Cultures," p. 752.

41. Pastoral Constitution, in Abbott, *Documents,* p. 242.

42. Ibid, p. 246.

43. See Rahner, "Toward a Fundamental Interpretation of Vatican II." Rahner poses this shift as a third era in the church; the first was its "Jewish moment," centered in Jerusalem, and the second was Western Christianity.

44. See Schineller, *Handbook on Inculturation,* pp. 14–17.

45. See Schreiter, *Local Theologies,* p. 2; and Schineller, *Handbook,* pp. 18–24. Schineller writes that inculturation "moves beyond imposition, translation, and adaptation toward the reorientation, renewal, and transformation of culture from within in light of the gospel message" (ibid., p. 23).

46. "'Inculturation' is now the most widely used term in Roman Catholic circles to describe the proper relation between faith and cultures" (Schreiter, "Faith and Cultures," p. 747). It is distinct from *enculturation,* the learning of a new culture, and *acculturation,* contact between two different cultures.

47. See esp., Shorter, *Toward a Theology of Inculturation;* Schreiter, *Constructing Local Theologies;* Luzbetak, *The Church and Cultures;* and Schineller, *A Handbook on Inculturation.* Schreiter, "Faith and Cultures," includes a helpful review of the literature.

48. See Schreiter, "Faith and Cultures," p. 753, for the very fine definition of A. A. Roest Crollius; Schineller quotes the definition of Pedro Arrupe, *Inculturation,* p. 6.

49. Reflecting these three aspects, Pope John Paul II said to the Kenyan church, "Inculturation, which you rightly promote, will truly be a reflection of the incarnation of the word, when a culture, transformed and regenerated by the gospel, brings forth from its own living tradition original expressions of Christian life, celebration, and thought" (quoted in Schineller, *Inculturation,* p. 43).

50. Charles Kraft uses this phrase. Borrowing from Bible translation but recognizing that univocal translation is not possible from one culture to another, by "dynamic equivalence" Kraft means finding what is "core" to Christian faith and translating it in terms indigenous to another culture. See *Christianity in Culture.* See Schreiter, "Faith and Cultures" for a helpful review of Kraft's proposal.

51. Drawing on the work of Stephen Bevans, Schreiter reviews six models. See "Faith and Cultures," pp. 756–57. I much appreciate the model Schineller offers; it proposes a dynamic interaction between "three poles"—the situation, the Christian message, and the agent of inculturation. See *Inculturation,* chap. 5.

Chapter 5. The Focusing Activity in Shared Praxis

1. See Freire, *Oppressed,* esp. chap. 3, for his understanding of "generative theme." Freire also uses the language of "problem posing" (see ibid., chap. 2) to describe the pedagogical activity of establishing the generative theme. I choose not to use that phrase, however, because all the themes entailed in lived Christian faith cannot be reduced to "problems to be solved." There are joys to be celebrated, mysteries to be embraced, and gifts to be accepted as well.

2. Cavalletti, *Child,* p. 98. She explains that whatever is presented thereafter should be "contained in the linking point as a tree is contained in the seed" (ibid.). I do not favor making this an absolute principle, but, when possible, it is certainly an asset to the learning process.

3. In his book *Models of Revelation,* Dulles renders an extraordinary service by drawing together and summarizing the major authors and principal understandings of revelation, past and present, into five recognizable "models." Because I often draw upon and refer to his various models throughout these chapters, it will help to have a summary of them at the outset. He reviews the five as follows:

a. Revelation as Doctrine. According to this view revelation is principally found in clear propositional statements attributed to God as authoritative teacher. . . .

b. Revelation as History. This type of theory, proposed in conscious opposition to the preceding, maintains that God reveals himself [sic] primarily in his great deeds, especially those which form the major themes of biblical history. . . .

c. Revelation as Inner Experience. For some modern theologians, both Protestant and Catholic, revelation is neither an impersonal body of objective truths nor a series of external, historical events. Rather it is a privileged experience of grace or communion with God. . . .

d. Revelation as Dialectical Presence. . . . Utterly transcendent, God encounters the human subject when it pleases him by means of a word in which faith recognizes him to be present. The word of God simultaneously reveals and conceals the divine presence.

e. Revelation as New Awareness. . . . These thinkers hold that revelation takes place as an expansion of consciousness or shift of perspective when people join in the movements of secular history. God, for them, is not a direct object of experience but is mysteriously present as the transcendent dimension of human engagement in creative tasks (ibid., pp. 27–28).

Later, Dulles offers a pithy summary of how each of the five models would define revelation:

From the models we have considered one could distill different and competing definitions of revelation, such as the following five:

· Revelation is divinely authoritative doctrine inerrantly proposed as God's word by the Bible or by official church teaching.
· Revelation is the manifestation of God's saving power by his (sic) great deeds in history.
· Revelation is the self-manifestation of God by his intimate presence in the depths of the human spirit.
· Revelation is God's address to those whom he encounters with his word in Scripture and Christian proclamation.
· Revelation is a breakthrough to a higher level of consciousness as humanity is drawn to a fuller participation in the divine creativity.

(Ibid., p. 115)

4. Ibid., p. 53.
5. Ibid., p. 60.
6. Rahner, *Belief Today*, p. 4. In this statement, Rahner is echoing the poetic lines of a brother Jesuit that "the world is charged with the grandeur of God. It will flame out, like shining from shook foil" (Gerard Manley Hopkins, *Poems and Prose*, p. 27).

Macquarrie explains this ongoingness of revelation beyond the "classic" or "primordial" revelation on which communities of faith get founded as "repetitive" revelation (*Principles*, p. 90).

7. Dulles is correct, I believe, when he critiques the *experiential model* of revelation (his model 3) for "its excessively narrow concept of experience" (*Revelation*, p. 81).

8. Leech, *Experiencing God*, p. 47. Bultmann writes of the Hebrew sense of knowing God: "Knowledge has an element of acknowledgement. But it also has an element of emotion, or better, of movement of will, so that ignorance means guilt as well as error. . . . To know Him [sic] or His name is to confess or to acknowledge, to give Him honor and to obey His will" (*Theological Dictionary of the New Testament*, "ginosko," 1:698).

9. Barr, *Bible and the Modern World*, p. 29.

10. Cooke, *Sacramentality*, p. 32.

11. See, e.g., Rahner, *Foundations*, chap. 1. Rahner uses the terms *experience* and *existence* but intends by them together what I have described as "being."

12. Ibid., p. 116.

13. Rahner explains the "supernatural existential" in chap. 3 of *Foundations*, pp. 126–32. A good, concise summary can also be found in his (with Vorgrimler) *Dictionary of Theology*, pp. 163–64.

14. "God's self-revelation in the depths of the spiritual person is an a priori deter-mination coming from grace and is in itself unreflexive. It is not in itself an objective, thematic expression: it is not something known objectively, but something within the realm of consciousness" (Rahner, *Foundations*, p. 172).

15. Ibid., p. 21. In explaining the transcendental experience, Rahner writes, "We shall call *transcendental experience* the subjective, unthematic, necessary and unfailing con-sciousness of the knowing subject that is co-present in every spiritual act of knowledge, and the subject's openness to the unlimited expanse of all possible reality" (ibid., p. 20).

16. Rahner explains, "From a theological point of view, the *concrete* process of the so-called natural knowledge of God in either its acceptance or its rejection is always more than a merely natural knowledge of God. This is true when the knowing takes place unthematically in the basic and original self-interpretation of human existence as well as when it is reflexive, thematic knowledge" (ibid., p. 57).

O'Leary and Salinow, much influenced by a Rahnerian anthropology, explain the consequence of this insight for religious education as follows: "The so-called 'natural knowledge' of the child becomes the *sine qua non* of the entire process, the original gift of vision which is further enlightened and deepened by what we specifically offer the child by way of Scripture, doctrine, liturgy and all other media employed to illuminate the total spectrum of his experience" (*Love and Meaning*, pp. 82–83).

17. Explaining this historical groundedness of Rahner's position, Ann Carr writes, "In stressing the intrinsic and reciprocal relationship between transcendence and history, Rahner notes that any aspect of human history may be the carrier of transcendence; the particular experiences, actions, and aspects of our various histories together form the prism through which our transcendent natures are realized" (Carr, "Starting with the Human," p. 27).

18. For a classic statement of the *sensus fidelium* tradition that also indicates some of the controversy that surrounds it, see John Henry Newman, *On Consulting the Faithful in Matters of Doctrine:* "The body of the faithful is one of the witnesses to the fact of the tradition of revealed doctrine and . . . their *consensus* through Christendom is the voice of the Infallible Church" (p. 63). Newman goes on to enumerate five characteristics of the *sensus fidelium*, the second of which is "a sort of instinct . . . deep in the bosom of the mystical body of Christ" (p. 73) that is a source and measure of truth.

19. See Tyler, *Basic Principles*, p. 26.

20. See O'Hare, "Hospitality as a Paradigm for Youth Ministry." O'Hare, writing in the context of youth ministry, adds a third category of "ecclesial hospitality."

21. Ibid., p. 5.

22. Maria Harris writes, "To dwell as a teacher with other human beings is to dwell in the area of *mystery*, not because subject matter is dense, but because we humans as the *Imago Dei* are ourselves mysteries and interaction between us always takes place on holy ground, the only kind of ground there is" (*Imagination*, p. 16).

23. Any one of Lyman Coleman's books offers many imaginative ways to begin forming or enhancing community in a group context. See, e.g., the Leader's Guides for his Serendipity Personal Growth Programs. These programs include *Come Fly: Discovering a New Life Style* and *Destiny: Discovering Your Call.*

24. See, e.g., Doyle, "Learning and the Classroom Environment"; Moos, *Evaluating Educational Environments;* David and Wright, eds., *Learning Environments;* Loughlin and Suirna, *The Learning Environment.*

25. It is regrettable that educators are rarely consulted in the design of educational buildings; usually they are presumed to be simply an architectural issue. Consequently, the buildings, especially classrooms and lecture halls, usually reflect the epistemological assumption that the teacher has all the knowledge and wisdom and students have nothing to learn from one another.

26. Freire describes a "codification" of present praxis as a "representation of the existential situations of the learners" (*Politics*, p. 51). He explains further: "Codification thus transforms what was a way of life in the real context into 'objectum' in the theoretical context. The learners, rather than receive information about this or that fact, analyze aspects of their own existential experience represented in the codification" (ibid., p. 52). Movement 1 in shared praxis corresponds to the beginning of what Freire calls "decod-ification."

27. See Dewey, *Art as Experience*.

28. This is also a foundational claim of Maria Montessori. See *Montessori Method*, esp. pp. 168–223.

29. My instance here does not imply that on such a learning occasion the official church's position would not be made accessible to the community. That would likely be appropriate in movement 3. It certainly should not be presented as a "closed" position in the focusing activity.

30. This lesson was later published in the *God with Us* religion series, grade eight, *Growing with the Catholic Church*, lesson 13 (standard edition).

31. See Lawrence Waddy, "God's Tumbler." (The event referred to was with the Sisters of Saint Joseph of Philadelphia, Oct. 18, 1986.)

Chapter 6. Movement 1

1. Freire, *Politics*, p. 54.

2. Later published in the *God with Us* religion series, grade 7, *Growing with the Catholic Faith*, lesson 12 (standard edition).

3. Francis Schüssler Fiorenza writes insightfully on this point. Though he uses the language of experience, we can also read "praxis" in his statement:

> Contrary to popular understanding, experience is primarily an act of interpretation. Experience is not an immediate act of consciousness or some feeling underlying human thoughts and concepts. Instead, experience takes place within the context of memory, the memory of previous examples and similar cases. Moreover, experience is embedded within a cultural tradition and a network of social interaction and mutual interpretation. Memory, tradition, and interpretation are as much a part of experience and as determinative of experience as are the acts of consciousness, sensation, or feeling. (*Foundational Theology*, p. 296)

He later adds, "Experience is therefore not merely a perception of something immediate, but rather an interpretation dependent upon knowledge and memory" (ibid., p. 298).

4. See Gadamer, *Truth and Method*, pp. 245–74.

5. Comenius (1592–1670), Rousseau (1712–1778), Pestalozzi (1746–1827), Herbart (1776–1841), and Froebel (1782–1852) have held this as a common basic position. Dewey (1859–1952) was the greatest champion of the conviction that "knowing" must always arise from the knower's reconstruction of present experience. His classic definition of education says that "education is that reconstruction or reorganization of experience which adds to the meaning of experience, and which increases ability to direct the course of subsequent experience" (*Democracy and Education*, pp. 89–90). Shared praxis honors Dewey's conviction by beginning with present praxis in this first movement and then proceeding to critical reflection on it (i.e., its "reconstruction" in Deweyian terms) in movement 2.

6. This language is unfortunate and to be avoided by educators committed to an approach like shared praxis, yet in fact, so often it reflects educational praxis. As teachers we can "cover" rather than "un-cover" or "dis-cover" what we intend to teach. Likewise, the "subject" is often presumed to be the "thing" being taught, which, of course, implies that the people are the "objects"—an unfortunate reversal.

7. Freire, *Politics*, pp. 49, 21.

8. See Belenky et al., *Women's Ways of Knowing*, pp. 25–34.

9. This is a central theme in Freire's work. See, e.g., *Politics*, pp. 51ff.

10. See Howe, *The Miracle of Dialogue*, p. 4.

11. I learned this mode of bringing people to expression from the literature on synectics as an educational method. See W. J. Gordon and T. Poze, *The Metaphorical Way*. One evening with undergraduates in a unit on the church (not a favorite topic) I began the first movement by asking them to complete the sentence "For me, the church is like an automobile because . . . " I was amazed at the amount of their own ecclesiological praxis that it elicited. See also McKeon, "Synectics in Shared Christian Praxis."

12. Although we call this exercise an "association of *ideas*," in fact, it can be effective in eliciting an expression of people's praxis or a description of their society's praxis regarding the theme of a learning event. In a unit on the theme of hunger, e.g., the movement 1 exercise invited people to write down their most immediate associations with the words *world hunger*. Some expressed their own sentiments or attitudes, others their values or commitments; others described their participation in the struggle to address the problem—i.e., the exercise seemed to elicit a praxis response from them.

13. A description of this learning occasion was later published in *Adult Learning and the Parish*, Neil A. Parent, ed., "Theme 4: Leadership," pp. 97–123.

14. When my spouse, Colleen Griffith, and I were teaching 5th-grade CCD at St. Agnes Parish, Niantic, Connecticut, in 1989–90, we invited students to keep a personal notebook and when appropriate to write their responses to movements 1, 2, 4, and 5 questioning activities in it. (They called them their "freebies," because we gave the notebooks out "free" at the beginning of the year.) We invited people to leave their notebooks with us for written comment, or a "chat," and typically they did so. We found that the more comments we made on their notebooks, the more deliberately the students seemed to engage the questioning activities we posed in class.

15. Asking praxislike questions instead of "theoria" questions is crucial to the first movement; however, this does not obviate fashioning movement 1 activity to invite an expression of people's ideas about a theme. But thought questions must be formulated in a praxis manner. St. Mary on the Hill parish, Augusta, Georgia, used a shared praxis approach to communal discernment about how to renovate their church building (spring 1989). In movement 1, participants named "the kind of Christian community we are to be in this place and at this time." Then, their statement of their own ecclesiology as a parish became a resource for people in movement 2 as they imagined the kind of worship space needed by such a community.

16. Cavalletti writes, "Listening is the leaning toward others, the opening of ourselves in a receptive attitude toward the reality around us; it is only the capacity to listen that prevents us from revolving around ourselves" (*Child*, p. 49).

17. Buber, "The Education of Character," in *Between Man*, pp. 105, 114.

18. This lesson was published in the *God with Us* series, grade 5, *Growing with God's Life*, lesson 17, (standard edition).

19. This lesson was written by Peter Mann and Edward Mahoney as part of a high school religion curriculum.

Chapter 7. Movement 2

1. In chap. 11 of *C.R.E.* I draw upon Piaget's research especially to make the argument that a form of critical reflection that remembers, reasons about, and anticipates the outcome of present praxis can begin with the onset of concrete operational thinking. Given this potential for critical reflection, at least in a rudimentary form, and remembering that "the tree is in the seed," I believe young children ought to be encouraged to engage in critical reflection, thus forming the disposition and capacity for it that makes full critical reflection more likely in adult life. The findings of the more scientific research of Piaget have also been borne out in my own praxis with kindergarten children; I have been amazed at their ability for critical reflection as long as the questioning activities are posed in concrete operational terms. For examples of how shared praxis and its second movement can be used effectively with young children, see the kindergarten and grade 1 books of both the *God with Us* and the *Coming to Faith* religion series.

I also note that for people capable of formal operational thinking, there probably are "stages" in the emergence of critical consciousness. Gaylor and Fitzpatrick offer a very helpful analysis of "stages of consciousness raising." They outline six in all: (1) Perplexity, (2) Contact, (3) Seesaw, (4) Ownership, (5) Anger, and (6) Resolution. See "The Stages of Consciousness Raising," pp. 6–11.

2. "Prejudice" here has a negative connotation, in the sense that a "blind prejudice" has a controlling and distorting influence on present praxis. Its "blindness" must be brought to light by critical reason. I also appreciate, however, Gadamer's use of "prejudice" that is more neutral, something akin to Habermas's word *interest*. In this more

positive sense, prejudices are what motivate and give shape to people's participation in the world; without them, we would be reduced to passivity. Gadamer writes, "In fact, the historicity of our existence entails that prejudices, in the literal sense of the word, constitute the initial directedness of our whole ability to experience. Prejudices are biases of our openness to the world" ("The Universality of the Hermeneutical Problem," in *Philosophical Hermeneutics,* p. 9). See also *Truth and Method,* pp. 241–52.

Commenting on Gadamer's use of the word *prejudice,* Bernstein writes, "It is clear, however, that Gadamer does want to make the all-important distinction between *blind* prejudices and 'justified [*berechtigte*] prejudices productive of knowledge'" (*Beyond Objectivism,* p. 128).

3. Mannheim writes, "The concept 'ideology' reflects the one discovery which emerged from political conflict, namely, that ruling groups can in their thinking become so intensively interest-bound to a certain situation that they are simply no longer able to see certain facts which would undermine their sense of domination. There is implicit in the word 'ideology' the insight that in certain situations the *collective unconscious of certain groups obscures the real condition of society both to itself and others and thereby stabilizes it* (*Ideology and Utopia,* p. 40; emphasis added).

Through critical analysis of one's social ideologies, movement 2 is a process of ideological critique of the "collective unconscious" and of the "facts" that undermine forms of domination.

4. Freire writes, "Education of a liberating character is a process by which the educator invites learners to recognize and unveil reality critically" (*Politics,* p. 102).

5. David Tracy, echoing Habermas, writes, "We need, therefore, some form of a critique of ideologies that can perform a critically emancipatory function on a societal level by unmasking those ideological distortions in the same way psychoanalysis unmasks the distortions and illusions of any individual" (*Imagination,* p. 74).

6. I say that it "can be" emancipatory because critical reflection alone is not sufficient to bring about personal and social emancipation. (I do not have the same confidence in critical reason as do some of its proponents, e.g., Habermas.) It also requires a community of solidarity, involved in actual historical struggles for justice and emancipation.

7. Tracy's method for doing theology interprets and critically correlates "the meaning present in our own common human experience and the meaning present in the Christian fact" (*Rage,* p. 64). For this he developed three criteria for "interpreting common human experience and language" (ibid., p. 43).

8. Ibid., p. 69.

9. Ibid., p. 70.

10. See ibid., p. 71.

11. This is John Westerhoff's distinction, made first, I believe, in *Will Our Children Have Faith?* Although the theorists I refer to here do not all use Westerhoff's categories, I find them helpful to identify the arenas in which they see critical reflection as either necessary (instructional paradigm) or not central (enculturation paradigm).

12. See Rossiter, "Change in Catholic Religious Education," pp. 268–69.

13. Moran, see *Religious Education as a Second Language,* pp. 85, 218.

14. For Moran, see ibid. For Rossiter, see "The Need for a 'Creative Divorce' Between Catechesis and Religious Education in Catholic Schools." Rossiter sees catechesis as a process of "socialization into faith" (ibid., p. 24) that is more appropriately and effectively carried on by family and parish community than by a school. Religious education, on the other hand, "provides young people with information about religion and an experience of intellectual searching" (Crawford and Rossiter, *Teaching Religion in the Secondary School,* p. 2). Here the focus for the students will be "on intellectual knowledge" (ibid., p. 3) and on "learning how to think critically" (ibid., p. 13).

Elsewhere Rossiter argues that school-based "classroom religious education" is not to engage students "at a personal level." Yet he intends the intellectual study that leads to knowledge and understanding of religion to "also show how the education of the emotions, reflection on faith, development of critical skills for analysis, evaluation and decision making are integral parts of the process" ("Change in Catholic Religious Education," p. 269). It is not possible to achieve the latter, however, unless participants are engaged as agent-subjects (i.e., "personally") in the process. I empathize with Rossiter's intent to undo the "'poor' image for religion as a school subject that does not 'count'" (ibid., p.

276). However, his notion of "intellectual study" and its separation from "the personal" seems to reflect the traditional but debilitating dichotomy between knowing and "being." I believe that academically rigorous "religious education" in a school classroom should reflect a humanizing rather than a technical rationality; this requires engaging people qua "persons" in the teaching/learning dynamic. Or, in terms of Lonergan's description of cognitional structure, to promote authentic cognition, an academic study of religion must promote not simply attention to and understanding of data but judgment and decision as well. To honor these activities both engages and influences students qua persons.

Moran's position is more nuanced, and probably accurate in describing what in fact is "going on" regarding critical reflection in religious education, at least in a Catholic context. In an essay on the question, Does the church really want religious education? (a question first posed by Chuck Melchert's landmark essay of 1974), Moran takes the approach more of a reportor than an advocate:

> My answer, therefore, to whether the church really wants education is that nearly all elements of the church want the kind of education that preserves, continues, and expands what is valued from the past. The catechizing of children in the Roman Catholic Church gets widespread approval as an idea and some support in practice. A slightly fuller meaning of religious education that includes the catechizing of adults gets nodding approval but not much practice. A religious education that critically challenges the church in relation to other religious and nonreligious interpretations of life has little approval (outside of the university), and it is implicitly opposed by church officials in their typical pronouncements on teaching ("Of a Kind and to a Degree," p. 31).

See also Kieran Scott, "Communicative Competence and Religious Education" and "Collapsing the Tensions."

15. The question of what to call this enterprise becomes particularly significant around an issue like the one raised here. Personally I am still content with the position I took in C.R.E. (1980) that "Christian religious education," though a cumbersome title, is the most adequate name for what I do and what I perceive a great host of others doing by way of education in Christian faith. I also recognize, however, that my position is shaped by my social/political context in the United States, and its adequacy may be limited to this situation. Here intentional education in Christian faith takes place primarily in congregation-based programs or in church-sponsored or -affiliated schools that receive no direct state funding and typically are still committed to educating their students in Christian faith (if that is their religious tradition). For this activity, I find Christian religious education appropriate and adequate because (1) it affirms the educational aspect of the enterprise; (2) as "religious," it is located within and thus can be in partnership and dialogue with the universal human effort to live in right relationship as a response to what is perceived as ultimate in life; and (3) "Christian" signifies its particularity within the religious universal, and that it is to inform, form, and transform people in Christian identity and agency.

16. David Tracy writes, "Western history alone provides ample evidence for the complicity of the churches, Catholic, Protestant, and Orthodox, in the sheer indecencies, the thoughtless injustices, the careless mystifications of our blood-drenched history as a civilization" (Analogical Imagination, p. 50).

17. My reference is to Bushnell's Christian Nurture. For the position that Christian schools are to socialize people in Christian faith, I particularly appreciate the work of Marcellin Flynn. See Some Catholic Schools in Action (1975); Catholic Schools and the Communication of Faith (1979); The Effectiveness of Catholic Schools (1985).

18. See Giroux, Theory, p. 115. Giroux insists that critical education is essential if "students [are to] come to grips with what a given society has made of them, how it has incorporated them ideologically and materially into its rules and logic, and what it is that they need to affirm and reject in their own histories in order to begin the process of struggling for the conditions that will give them opportunities to lead a self-managed existence" (ibid., p. 38).

19. See Cavalier and Loewe, "Socialization and Shared Praxis."

20. The question has been raised, and for historical reasons, whether or not the church really wants a truly educational activity, in the sense of a process of rigorous

investigation. See, e.g., Melchert's classic essay, "Does the Church Really Want Religious Education?" Moran writes, "For anyone who claims to have the final answers to life, education poses a threat. This is a fact which the Christian churches do not acknowledge, namely that religion and education are in conflict" (*Religious Body*, p. 148). See also note 14.

Undoubtedly, there are times when our churches act as if they are more interested in "knowledge control" (Foucault) than open inquiry. It is to be hoped, however, that this defensive posture can be recognized for what it is—a lack of real faith and a sinful form of ideological self-maintenance. MacQuarrie writes insightfully, "The ideal of a *rational* religion, in the sense of one founded on a *rational* metaphysic, may be an impossible and perhaps an undesirable one, but we should never relinquish the ideal of a *reasonable* religion, in the sense of one whose content has been subjected to the scrutinizing and corrective exercise of critical reason" (*Principles*, p. 17).

I also note here a point that is especially important, I believe, in the context of my own Catholic community. Beginning at least with Aquinas, the Catholic tradition has argued for the rightful place of reason in matters of faith. Aquinas's summary statement—"Faith is a habit of the mind, whereby eternal life is begun in us, making the intellect assent to what is non-apparent" (*Summa Theologica*, II–II, 4, 1; vol. 3, p. 1184)—recognized both the role of human reason and the gift of God's grace in coming to faith. Likewise, Vatican I (1869–70) in its "Constitution on Faith" declared,"Faith and reason can never disagree; but more than that, they are even mutually advantageous. For right reason demonstrates the foundations of faith and, enlightened by the light of faith, it pursues the science of divine things; faith, on the other hand, sets reason free and guards it from errors and furnishes it with extensive knowledge" (*The Church Teaches*, p. 34).

21. Melchert has a very helpful listing of six criteria that should mark good education: that it (1) be intentional; (2) be "of value," in that its participants are "changed for the better"; (3) promote "knowing and understanding in depth and breadth"; (4) take place over a period of time; (5) be an interpersonal interaction; and (6) promote "wholeness" in that it affects a person's relationships "with self, with others, and with things" ("Does the Church Really Want Religious Education?" pp. 15–16). Here I am obviously emphasizing Melchert's second, third, fifth, and sixth criteria for good education.

22. Dewey defined education as "that reconstruction or reorganization of experience which adds to the meaning of experience, and which increases ability to direct the course of subsequent experiences" (*Democracy and Education*, pp. 89–90).

23. Dewey, *How We Think*, p. 58.

24. In her book *The Life of the Mind*, Arendt commented to the effect that what struck her most at the Eichmann trial was "the manifest shallowness of the doer, not the demonic nature of his motives but rather his thoughtlessness." This summary of Arendt's insight is quoted from Little, *Heart*, pp. 6–7.

25. There are promising signs that imagination and "right brain" activity in faith education is being reclaimed, deepened, and expanded as never before. I recognize as pioneers in this endeavor Gloria Durka and Joan Marie Smith (see esp. their *Aesthetic Dimensions of Religious Education*). My own awareness of the role of imagination in religious education was first significantly influenced by the work of Sharon Parks (see *The Critical Years*) and later by the dissertation work of Ann Louise Gilligan (see *The Feminist Imagination*). The work of Maria Harris (see esp. her *Teaching and Religious Imagination*) has brought this attention specifically into teaching. See also Kathleen Fischer, *The Inner Rainbow;* Richard Kearney, *The Wake of Imagination;* James Mackey, ed., *Religious Imagination;* and Mary Warnock, *Imagination*.

26. Craig Dykstra makes a significant contribution to the role of imagination in moral formation. He contends that moral formation has been too dependent on a "juridical" understanding of ethics and too preoccupied with a deontological emphasis on doing one's duty according to the law. Consequently, Christian moral education has concentrated on instructing people in moral precepts, presuming that knowing the law moves them to fulfill it out of duty. In contrast, Dykstra proposes a "visional" ethics based on character formation in the virtues of Christian life; the crucial strategy in character formation is to engage the imagination. He writes, "The transformation of the moral life, the transformation of character, is a transformation of the imagination." He explains further

that "The process of moral growth through the transformation of the imagination is not the only way we make moral progress, but it is one very basic and important one. . . . The imagination is foundational to all our seeing, believing, feeling, and acting; and any shift of its contours is also a transformation of ourselves as moral beings" (*Vision and Character,* pp. 78, 87; see passim).

There is truth in Dykstra's claim that moral education has typically placed too much emphasis on teaching precepts and duties; this finds ready evidence in a review of most of the standard curricula being used in Christian churches. One finds little formation in the virtues but much emphasis on instruction in the law—especially the Ten Commandments. My own hesitancy about embracing Dykstra's position completely is that he seems to lay out the issue too much as an either/or proposition, to forget that "vision" needs "law" as much as law needs vision.

For a concrete attempt to forge a unity and do both instruction in law and formation in virtues and vision of Christian living, see my own textbooks, *Growing with the Catholic Church,* in the *God with Us* curriculum, esp. chaps. 13–24, (Standard Edition); and *Coming to the Catholic Church,* in the *Coming to Faith* curriculum, esp. chaps. 18–31 (Catholic School Edition).

27. Fischer, *Rainbow,* pp. 24, 130. Fischer explains,"The imagination loosens and dissolves past images in order to recombine them in new forms for the future. . . . The imagination is not simply a passive or reproductive power, imitating the realities of our experienced world. It is a rainbow spanning the distance between past and future. From the world we know, we produce a vision of the world we want to build" (ibid., pp. 23–24).

28. Paul Ricoeur, "The Image of God and the Epic of Man," quoted in Harris, *Imagination,* p. 3. And Kearney writes, "Resisting the pervasive sense of social paralysis, the poetic imagination would nourish the conviction that things *can be changed.* The first and most effective step in this direction is to begin to *imagine* that the world as it is could be *otherwise* (*Wake of Imagination,* p. 370).

29. My claim here is resonant with Dulles's fifth model of "revelation as new awareness" or "fuller consciousness." Dulles writes, "According to this approach, revelation is a transcendent fulfillment of the inner drive of the human spirit toward fuller consciousness" (*Revelation,* p. 98); it is a "breakthrough into a more advanced stage of human consciousness" (ibid., p. 109). Dulles also notes, "A theology of revelation following these general lines has been developed by a variety of English-speaking theologians such as Gregory Baum, Leslie Dewart, Gabriel Moran, Ray L. Hart, and William M. Thompson. Elements of this approach may be found in eminent theologians such as Paul Tillich and Karl Rahner, although each of them combines elements belonging to several different models" (ibid., pp. 88–99). See ibid., esp. chap. 7, for Dulles's description and evaluation of this fifth model of revelation.

30. Ibid., pp. ix, 131. See esp. chap. 9 for further elaboration.

31. Warnock, "Religious Imagination," pp. 148, 150.

32. Fischer, *Rainbow,* p. 7.

33. Ibid., p. 10.

34. George Bernard Shaw, *Saint Joan,* p. 66.

35. Holland and Henriot, *Social Analysis,* p. 13.

36. Ibid., p. 3. They later add, "Social analysis can be defined as the effort to obtain a more complete picture of a social situation by exploring its historical and structural relationships" (ibid., p. 14).

37. Ibid., p. 21. (Emphasis added.)

38. In the *Ah-hah!* text by Gatt-Fly, there is a good instance of a group doing social analysis that attends to "the multiple levels of the issues involved":

A memorable seminar with the Working Women's Alliance in London, Ontario, started by drawing the doughnut shop where one of the women worked. Before long, we had drawn linkages to Columbia and Peru where the coffee and sugar came from, as well as to the Canadian farmers who grew the wheat for the doughnuts. Then we listened to her talk about her experiences in the shop and pooled the knowledge of others in the group about the owners of the shop. In the end we had drawn a comprehensive picture of the city's ruling establishments and trade union movement and their connections to the world economy. (ibid., p. 49)

39. Here, Holland and Henriot's distinction between an "academic" and a "pastoral" approach to social analysis is helpful. They write, "The academic approach studies a particular social situation in a detached, fairly abstract manner, dissecting its elements for the purpose of understanding. The pastoral approach, on the other hand, looks at the reality from an involved, historically committed stance, discerning the situation for the purpose of action" (*Social Analysis,* p. 7).

Later, they add, "Social analysis is not value-free. This point is extremely important. Social analysis is not a neutral approach, a purely 'scientific' and 'objective' view of reality. Of course, we should try to be clear, precise, reasoned, and logical. However, in our very choice of topics, in our manner of approach, in our questions, in our openness to the results of our analysis, we reveal our values and biases" (ibid., p. 16).

40. The insights of these social sciences cannot be glibly accepted as value free or beyond ideological critique. They should be evaluated with an emancipatory interest and critically appropriated in a mode that promotes critical consciousness rather than legitimation of present praxis. That is why I refer to the "critical" social sciences. Taking psychology as an example, E. V. Sullivan writes, "Critical psychology pays specific attention to how the personal world of individual and groups is affected by stabilization of unjust social structures" (*Psychology,* p. 108).

41. For Holland and Henriot's extensive list of questions to facilitate people through a process of social analysis, see *Social Analysis,* p. 102.

42. Ibid., p. 14.

43. Russell Jacoby writes that "the loss of social memory is a type of reification— better, it is the primal form of reification" (*Social Amnesia,* p. 4).

44. Benjamin, *Illuminations,* p. 262. Russell Butkus, to whose research I am much indebted here, presents Benjamin as the greatest exponent of "dangerous memory" among the Critical Theorists of the Frankfurt School, and traces a similar theme in Horkheimer, Adorno, Marcuse, and Habermas. For all of them, "memory" as subversive social remembering is a category of practical reason and the primary source of an emancipatory dynamic in the quest for human liberation. Butkus points to Metz especially, but also to Schillebeeckx, as theologians for whom "dangerous memory" is a central hermeneutical tool and practical category. See Butkus, *Dangerous Memory,* part 3.

45. Butkus explains that this dimension of dangerous memory entails "the remembrance of those stories, symbols and personal/collective voices which stood to alleviate injustice in the name of compassion and human freedom" (ibid., p. 295).

46. Kearney, *Wake of Imagination,* p. 393.

47. Butkus, *Dangerous Memory,* p. xiii. In his dissertation, Butkus argues convincingly that if middle-class American Catholics would remember their social history of discrimination and exploitation, they would find impetus for the struggle against discrimination and for social justice in present-day America; if they forget, they repeat oppression similar to what they suffered toward others now located socially where they once were.

48. An adapted version of this unit was published in the *God with Us* series, grade 7, *Growing with the Catholic Faith,* lesson 13, (Standard Edition). See also the Seventh-Grade Teacher's Guide for recommended participative activities.

49. Gilligan argues, correctly, "Creative imagination permeates critical reflection at all times, whether we are engaged in critical reason to evaluate the present or critical memory to uncover the past. To vision a liberative future, creative imagination must be present at each step of the critical process" (*The Feminist Imagination,* p. 281).

50. Freire, *Cultural Action,* p. 42.

51. A version of this unit was published in the *Coming to Faith* religion series, grade 8. See *Coming to the Catholic Church,* lesson 26 (Catholic School Edition).

52. Sharon Parks, drawing from her own research and in dialogue with the work of James Loder (see esp. *The Transforming Moment,* pp. 31–35), describes five recognizable "moments" within an act of imagination. The first she calls "conscious conflict"—the initial awareness, often discomforting, that "something is not fitting." This highlights the necessity of critical questions by the educator to promote imagination—to create a little "discomfort." The second moment is "pause," which is an "interlude for scanning"—a time for incubation of the needed image. This is a reminder that the process cannot be hurried; it requires patience and can be enhanced by silence in a teaching/learning event. In the third moment, imagination begins to unify what hitherto seemed disparate and in

conflict—"shaping it into one" with new and life-giving possibilities. A fourth moment of "repatterning" follows, when "the whole of one's knowing and being is reordered." Moments three and four call for a profound sensitivity from the educator, who must respect people's agency for their own insights, remembering that the image maker is the one most likely to be changed by the image. Last, there should be a moment of submitting one's new pattern of meaning to the test of public scrutiny, to be confirmed or challenged by others in a community of discernment. (See *Critical Years,* pp. 117–32.)

Maria Harris delineates three types of imagination—*confrontative, distancing,* and *compositive.* It seems that Parks's description of the functioning of imagination in general subsumes all these types as Harris outlines them. The confrontive imagination is engaged in the first moment of "conscious conflict," the distancing in the second moment of "pause," and the compositive in the third, fourth, and fifth moments of "shaping into one," "repatterning," and "testing." See *Imagination,* pp. 16–22.

53. An adapted version of this lesson was published in the kindergarten text of the Sadlier religion series. See *Growing in God's World,* lesson 19 (Standard Edition). See also the kindergarten Teacher's Guide for recommended activities.

54. Shor, *Critical Teaching,* see p. 66, passim.

55. Holland and Henriot, *Social Analysis,* p. 17.

56. I do not mean to imply that the Christian Scriptures or traditions are merely a collection of experiences or only a human record, but rather to say that there is a correlation and "natural affinity" between present praxis and the Story/Vision of the faith community. The Whiteheads write insightfully on this point: "When we recognize Scripture and Tradition as rooted in experience, as recalling specific human experiences, we do not reduce the Scriptures to *mere* experience or suggest they are *only* a human record. We can continue to believe in the divine inspiration of these texts and to affirm that these accounts are the core of revelation for Christians, and yet recognize the events recorded in Scripture as not so distant from our own lives" (*Method,* p. 35).

57. An adapted version of this lesson was published in the Sadlier *Coming to Faith* religion series. See *Coming to God's Love,* chap. 1 (Catholic School Edition).

58. See grade 8 of Sadlier's *Coming to Faith* religion series (by Groome et al.), *Coming to the Catholic Church,* lesson 27 (Catholic School Edition).

Chapter 8. Movement 3

1. Dwayne Huebner, my advisor in doctoral studies at Columbia, was the first I heard using the imagery of "making accessible" regarding curriculum. He introduced the notion with a 1970 essay "Curriculum as the Accessibility of Knowledge"; see also "Curriculum as Concern." My colleague Mary C. Boys significantly developed this imagery for religious education and established it with central currency in the field. A consistent theme in her work over the years, in *Biblical Interpretation* (1980) she wrote, "Religious education is the making accessible of the traditions of religious communities and the making manifest of the intrinsic connection between tradition and transformation" (p. 282). See also her *Educating in Faith,* chap. 8, for a more recent commentary on this definition.

2. By "language patterns" here I mean expressions of "classic" religious language that are like code words of identity in different Christian churches, e.g., holy communion, Blessed Trinity, testimony.

3. Drama as an expression of Christian Story is rarely used. Throughout the history of the church, however, and especially in the Middle Ages, the Story of faith was often taught by passion, mystery, miracle, and morality plays.

4. "Artifacts" as expressions of the communal faith Story are more common in the Catholic, Orthodox, and Episcopal than in other traditions of the Christian church, e.g., statues, vestments.

5. See Anderson, *The Living Word of the Bible,* pp. 48–61.

6. Macquarrie, *Principles,* p. 160.

7. Vatican II, "Declaration on Non-Christian Religions," Abbott, *Documents,* p. 661.

8. Vatican II, "Decree on Missions," Abbott, *Documents,* p. 595, and "Declaration on Non-Christian Religions," ibid., p. 662.

9. See Goldberg, *Theology and Narrative*, p. 41.

10. Gordon Kaufman writes, "To interpret it in that way is to make it into one more idol which will only deepen our difficulties" (*Nuclear*, p. 61). He goes on, "What the Christian tradition can give us is a vision of the overall character and shape which human life must assume if it is to find salvation or fulfillment—indeed, if it is to survive: an orientation (in both individuals and groups) of radical self-denial for the sake of wider communities, ultimately for the universal community that includes all beings (the 'kingdom of God')."

And Don Browning explains that beyond the story of Jesus Christ, there "must be added more specific principles, rules, and value judgments for the purpose of guiding and shaping our concrete moral thinking. Some of these may be derivable from the Christian story, but never without difficulty, and never without special effort to examine them for their universal validity" (*Care*, p. 63).

11. "A community of faith must shape its identity in relation to a corporately held narrative structure" Fowler, *Becoming Adult*, p. 114.

12. Dulles, *Revelation*, p. 115.

13. Ibid., p. 27.

14. Ibid., p. 42.

15. See ibid., pp. 46–52 for Dulles's review of the merits and criticisms of this model.

16. E. Schüssler Fiorenza, *Stone*, p. 10. Schüssler Fiorenza explains further: "For instance, many scriptural texts speak of God as a male, patriarchal, all-powerful ruler. Therefore, it is argued, feminists have to accept the patriarchal male language and God of the Bible, or they have to reject the Bible and leave behind biblical religion" (ibid.).

17. See Tracy, *Rage*, p. 68, and *Imagination*, p. 108.

18. Dulles, *Revelation*, p. 27.

19. Ibid., p. 55. (At the end of that citation Dulles is quoting from G. E. Wright, *God Who Acts*, p. 57.)

20. See Barr, *Bible and the Modern World*, p. 29.

21. See E. Schüssler Fiorenza, *Stone*, pp. 10–15, 61.

22. Dulles, *Revelation*, p. 131.

23. Ibid., p. 132.

24. Ibid., pp. 136–37.

25. Ibid., p. 138.

26. This point highlights the scholarly responsibilities of curriculum publishers, upon whom individual parishes and congregations so often depend for reliable resources. The procedures and guidelines I outline should be faithfully honored, I believe, in all curriculum materials for every age level and situation of Christian faith education. From my experience of writing the *God with Us* and *Coming to Faith* grade school religion curricula, I am convinced that the guidelines I outline here can be honored, even in kindergarten curricula.

27. R. Palmer, *Hermeneutics*, p. 121.

28. Ricoeur, *Interpretation*, pp. 74, 91.

29. Ibid., pp. 87, 30.

30. See Ricoeur, "The Model of the Text," p. 536.

31. See Gadamer, *Truth and Method*, pp. 274ff.

32. See Ibid., pp. 267ff.

33. Citing Gadamer's point here, Tracy explains that "the primary meaning of the text does not lie 'behind' it (in the mind of the author, in the original social setting, in the original audience) nor even 'in' the text itself. Rather, the meaning of the text lies *in front of* the text—in the now *common* question, the now common subject matter of both text and interpreter. . . . Interpreters seek, in Gadamer's often misunderstood phrase, to 'fuse the horizon' of the text (the horizon of meaning in front of the text) with our own horizon" (Grant, with Tracy, *Short History of the Interpretation of the Bible*, pp. 159–60).

34. Gadamer, *Truth and Method*, p. 289.

35. See Dewey, *Experience and Education*, pp. 46, 82.

36. Bernstein, *Beyond Objectivism*, pp. 174, 150.

37. Tracy, *Imagination*, p. 154.

38. Sanders, *Story*, p. 5. Throughout this work Sanders argues that the very authority of the canon comes from both its stability and its flexibility, its continuity and its creativity.

Even within the Bible itself we have this dual phenomenon as the Bible continually uses the Bible to reinterpret the Bible—taking older texts and restating them in a new form for a new context.

39. These principles of stability and adaptability with hermeneutics as a "mid-term" between them may appear problematic, at first sight, especially as they affect the creeds, dogmas, and doctrines of the church in more doctrinally identified traditions of Christianity. On the contrary, however, hermeneutics of such symbols of meaning and value that have arisen from the encounter between God and the community of faith over time is essential if people are to appropriate their revelatory potential in the present time. Simply to repeat them without interpretation robs them of their meaning for people now. As Lonergan writes of all church teachings, "But one has only to peruse such a collection of conciliar and pontifical pronouncements as Denzinger's *Enchiridion symbolorum* to observe that each is a product of its place and time and that each meets the questions of the day for the people of the day" (*Method,* p. 296). Braxton advises insightfully, "Just as the church has gradually overcome biblical fundamentalism, it must now overcome a dogmatic fundamentalism that does not fully explore the historical and cultural context of magisterial statements" (*Community,* p. 8).

40. Pelikan, *The Vindication of Tradition,* p. 65.

41. Brueggemann, *Word,* p. 6.

42. Only thus is the hermeneute likely to establish what Evelyn Fox Keller calls "dynamic objectivity" toward the text. She explains this as a mode of interpretation that honors the "independent integrity" of the text and yet recognizes and draws upon one's "connectivity" with the text through one's own subjective experiences. Fox Keller distinguishes this "dynamic" from "static objectivity"; the latter is "the pursuit of knowledge that begins with the severence of subject from object." She explains further that "dynamic objectivity is not unlike empathy," a sentiment that echoes Gadamer's posing of the hermeneutical encounter as a conversation. See Keller, *Gender and Science,* pp. 116–17.

43. Lonergan, *Method,* pp. 208–9.

44. Elisabeth Schüssler Fiorenza writes, "If we claim that oppressive patriarchal texts are the Word of God then we proclaim God as a God of oppression and dehumanization" (*Stone,* p. xii). But as we reject interpretations of texts used to legitimate patriarchal oppression, we must also decry interpretations of Story/Vision that legitimate racism, ageism, militarism, anti-Semitism, destruction of the environment, economic oppression, and all the other forms of social sinfulness that continue to bedevil our lives, societies, and churches. Why? Because such injustices are contrary to God's reign; using the Story/Vision for their legitimation is to say that God is an oppressor. Blasphemy!

45. See Grant, with Tracy, *History of Interpretation,* pp. 155–57. Tracy explains further: "There does not exist any exegete or historian as purely autonomous as the Enlightenment model promised. This recognition of the inevitable presence of tradition in all preunderstanding, moreover, does not require that the interpreter share the tradition to which the text to be interpreted belongs" (ibid., p. 156). For Gadamer on how "effective-history" shapes our hermeneutics, see *Truth and Method,* pp. 267ff.

46. If we need empirical evidence of the importance for hermeneutes of Christian tradition to critically remember their social context, we need only contrast the interpretations from various historical struggles for freedom as expressed in liberation theologies with interpretations more legitimating of the status quo offered by theologians in the dominant political/cultural matrix. I believe Hough and Cobb are correct when they write,

> The bourgeoisie have dominated the church as well as society since the Enlightenment. Thus the Christian tradition has been controlled by the interests of those who live well, or at least relatively well. The interests of persons like these are, of course, not to be ignored. However, the middle and upper classes have so dominated Christianity that its institutional forms and even its theology reflect those interests almost to the exclusion of the large masses of the poor and dispossessed. Even the powerful theological virtue of charity did not survive the dominance of bourgeois mentality. It was domesticated and in practice reduced to the giving of alms. (*Education,* p. 36)

On the other hand, when people read the texts of the tradition from the contexts of historical struggles for freedom and justice, there seems to be a constant uncovering of emancipatory dimensions that were not seen before by the traditionally white, male, upper-class interpreters of the Story/Vision.

47. Lonergan writes insightfully, "If the interpreter is to know, not merely what his [*sic*] author meant, but also what is so, then he has to be critical not merely of his author but also of the tradition that has formed his own mind" (*Method*, p. 162).

48. In *Freud and Philosophy*, Ricoeur refers to these two dialectical dimensions or "poles" as "the manifestation and restoration" of meaning (p. 27), on the one hand, and as a "demystification" or "an exercise of suspicion," on the other. He writes, "Over against interpretation as restoration of meaning we shall oppose interpretation according to what I collectively call the school of suspicion" (p. 32). See ibid., esp. pp. 28–36.

49. This conviction is common to much of liberation theology. See for example, Schüssler Fiorenza, *Stone*, p. 50. My point here does not mean that such critical consciousness be accepted unquestioningly: it can also have its "blind spots." For example, the confronting insights of Latin American and black liberation theologies that emerge from economic and racial oppression are not equally attentive to the oppression of sexism; likewise, all Christian feminist theology is not equally attentive to economic and racial oppression. Lack of the latter has prompted the emerging literature on "womanist theology."

50. There is a serious critical position among some feminist scholars that rejects Christian tradition as inherently patriarchal and instead of seeing it as life-giving poses it as antithetical to the emancipatory struggle of women in the present. (See, e.g., Mary Daly, *Gyn/Ecology*.) This, quite obviously, is not my position here. I reject it because it is equivalent to saying that God has been totally untrustworthy and has completely misled this faith community in the past, thus implying that God cannot be trusted in the present or future either.

51. Tracy, *Rage*, p. 12.

52. My point here is clarified by Francis Schüssler Fiorenza's notion of "retroductive warrants" for interpretations. He explains that a "retroductive warrant . . . is neither deductive nor inductive" but reflects an interpretation's "fertility . . . its explanatory and pragmatic success." An interpretation is "arranged retroductively" according to its "ability to illumine" the text and its "potential for further developments" and "to the degree that it can guide praxis." See *Foundational Theology*, pp. 306–7.

53. Farley, *Theologia*, p. 167.

54. Lamb points out, "Theologies have abounded attempting to rationalize imperialism, colonialism, racism, sexism, capitalism, militarism, totalitarianism, communism, sacralism, atheistic secularism, consumerism, multinationalism, fascism, anti-Semitism, Nazism, chauvinism, technocratic elitism, clerical authoritarianism, etc. It is difficult to think that theology was ever considered more than a dumping ground of biases" (*Solidarity*, p. 14).

55. Hough and Cobb, *Education*, p. 27. Here Christians should be inspired by the example of the people of Israel. As Hough and Cobb write, "A peculiar greatness of Israel lay in its refusal to deceive itself about its own history. The Jewish scriptures record the sins and failures of even the greatest heroes. They record also the people's refusal to follow God at crucial points in their history" (ibid., p. 98).

This hermeneutic of suspicion is essential, if the interpretive activity of religious education is to avoid Habermas's criticism of the hermeneutical sciences. As noted in chap. 3, he claims that hermeneutics has the interest of "practical control" and thus tends to maintain people "within the walls" of a tradition by forgetting the social interests that gave rise to the original expressions of the tradition and who it was intended to benefit. Habermas's critique is valid, I believe, if the hermeneutics employed are of simple retrieval and avoid a hermeneutics of suspicion and creative commitment.

56. Capps, citing Ricoeur, writes, "The hermeneutics of suspicion uncovers the false consciousness of a text not in the interests of destroying but for the purpose of recovering true consciousness. Or, as Ricoeur puts it, 'Destruction . . . is a moment in every new foundation. The destruction of hidden worlds is a positive task'" (*Pastoral Care and Hermeneutics*, pp. 31–32).

57. Metz, *History*, pp. 110, 56.

58. Rahner, *Theological Investigations*, vol. 1, p. 149. Gadamer also points to the need for ongoing construction in interpreting all classical texts. He writes, "But the discovery of the true meaning of a text or a work of art is never finished; it is in fact an infinite

process. Not only are fresh sources of error constantly excluded, so that the true meaning has filtered out of it all kinds of things that obscure it, but there emerge continually new sources of understanding, which reveal unsuspected elements of meaning" (*Truth and Method*, pp. 265–66).

59. Kaufman, *Nuclear,* p. 20.

60. Abbott, *Documents,* p. 116.

61. This is the central project of Elizabeth Schüssler Fiorenza's work *In Memory of Her*.

62. Welch, *Solidarity,* p. 7.

63. I take this term from Newman's work on the development of doctrine; it has greatly influenced my own search for criteria to guide both explanation in the third movement and decision making in the fifth of a shared praxis approach. Shared praxis is concerned with more than "doctrinal" explanation; yet orthopraxis should always reflect orthodoxy; and Newman's classic statement *An Essay on the Development of Christian Doctrine* (first published 1845) has proved most helpful.

Having established from the evidence of church history that doctrines can and do develop, Newman attempted to set out "marks of authenticity" by which "faithful developments" could be discerned from "corruptions." He arrived at "seven Notes of varying cogency, independence and applicability, to discriminate healthy developments of an idea from its state of corruption and decay" (p. 169). Newman's seven notes were (1) "Preservation of Type," by which he meant that "the parts and proportions of the developed form, however altered, correspond to those which belong to its rudiments" (p. 171); (2) "Continuity of Principles," by which he meant that a true development must be in accordance with the basic principles of the original teaching (pp. 178–80); (3) "Power of Assimilation," by which he meant that a true development must have a "unitive power" of incorporating rather than fragmenting the previous body of teaching (pp. 186–88); (4) "Logical Sequence" by which he meant that a doctrine is a true development "in proportion as it seems to be the logical issue of its original teaching" (p. 195); (5) "Anticipation of Its Future," by which he meant that there must have been intimations and an anticipation of the development in the original teaching (pp. 196–99); (6) "Conservative Action upon Its Past," which means (stating it negatively) that ideas that "contradict and reverse the course of doctrine which has been developed before them, and out of which they spring, are certainly corrupt" (p. 199); (7) "Chronic Vigor," by which he meant that a true development will stand the test of time (pp. 205–6).

64. See McFague, *Models of God,* pp. 31ff. She footnotes Cobb for this phrase (ibid., pp. 193–94).

65. See Tracy, *Rage,* pp. 72–79.

66. Newman drew all seven "marks of authenticity" (reviewed in note 63) together and proposed "dynamic identity" as his overarching principle for the development of doctrines. By this he meant that whereas doctrines must necessarily develop (i.e., be dynamic), they must also retain identity and continuity with what has gone before.

67. See Rahner, *Theological Investigations,* vol. 1, p. 56.

68. Vatican II's *Decree on Ecumenism.* Paragraph 11 states that "in Catholic teaching there exists an order or 'hierarchy' of truths, since they vary in their relationship to the foundation of the Christian faith" (Abbott, *Documents,* p. 354).

69. In discussing the likely historical consequences of an explanation, the hermeneute can again employ Francis Schüssler Fiorenza's test of "retroductive warrants." In assessing an explanation's likely "fertility" and its ability to "guide praxis," it is well to remember the historical consequences that similar explanations have had in the past and whether or not they have promoted the "fruits" of God's reign.

However, I diverge a little from his position as I understand it. An explanation's "fertility" cannot be established simply on the grounds "that it is more successful than others in explaining more data"; it should also promote the prophetic fruits of denouncing structures and arrangements that are dehumanizing and of announcing the social responsibilities of Christian faith. See F. Schüssler Fiorenza, *Foundational Theology,* p. 307.

70. Hollenbach, *Claims in Conflict,* p. 204.

71. See Dulles, *Models of the Church,* esp. chap. 2. Dulles explains that when the church is viewed solely under the institutional model, then,

from the point of view of its teaching function, it resembles a school in which the masters, as sacred teachers, hand down the doctrine of Christ. Because the bishops are considered to possess a special 'charism of truth' . . . it is held that the faithful are in conscience bound to believe what the bishops declare. The church is therefore a unique type of school—one in which the teachers have the power to impose their doctrine with juridical and spiritual sanctions. Thus teaching is juridicized and institutionalized. (Ibid., pp. 34–35)

72. Dulles describes the "regressive method" of doing theology as "utilizing the latest teaching of the magisterium as an indication of what must have been present from the beginning" and "defending what the magisterium had already said" (*Church*, p. 37).

73. Raymond Brown writes, "At one time or another and in some way, everyone in the Church is part of the *ecclesia docens*, . . . and, at one time or another and in some way, everyone in the church is also part of the *ecclesia discens*, including Pope and bishops. Again the words of our Master are almost a reproach: 'You have only one Teacher—all the rest of you are brothers and sisters' (Mt. 23:8)" ("Bishops and Theologians," p. 675).

74. I use the term *official magisterium* here to refer to the recognized teaching agency in any denomination of Christianity. For Roman Catholics this obviously means the pope in communion with the bishops of the world. The general assemblies of the World Council of Churches are coming to occupy a somewhat magisterial role in the faith life of many Protestant Christians. I note, however, that *magisterium* has not always been understood in this restricted way. Yves Congar points out that "until the 1820s and 30s magisterium simply means the function or activity of any teacher (magister)—any authority in a given domain" ("The Magisterium and Theologians," p. 17). Congar then draws attention to Aquinas's distinction between two magisteria—"'the magisterium of the pastoral or episcopal chair' and the 'magisterium of the teaching chair.' The first enjoyed an excellence of power, the second a publicly recognized personal competence" (ibid., p. 16). The second magisterium certainly included the theologians. This leads Dulles to conclude, "In a certain sense, then, we may speak of two magisteria—that of the pastors and that of the theologians" ("What Is Magisterium?" p. 36).

75. In chap. 5, note 18, I referred to Newman's statement regarding the *sensus fidelium:* that "their *consensus* through Christendom is the voice of the infallible Church" (*On Consulting the Faithful*, p. 63). Pedagogically, however, we must recognize that the discernment that emerges from the lived faith of people who belong neither to the class of scholars nor to the official magisterium has often been forgotten as a source of teaching in the church. Yet, by baptism "the faithful" have the presence of the Holy Spirit to guide them in faith. Jesus promised the Paraclete to anyone who loves him and keeps his commandments (John 14:15–16). To deny the value and validity of the faithful's discernment is to claim that the Holy Spirit inspires only the hierarchy and/or the scholars. Vatican II, however, in its *Dogmatic Constitution on the Church*, paragraph 12, declared, "The body of the faithful as a whole, annointed as they are by the Holy One (cf. John 2:20, 27), cannot err in matters of belief" (Abbott, *Documents*, p. 29). Consistent with this position, Dulles writes about "the interior guidance of the Holy Spirit, who implants in the hearts of the faithful an instinctive sense of what is, and what is not, a valid expression of revealed truth" (*Resilient Church*, p. 50).

76. Brown, "Bishops and Theologians," p. 675.

77. Boys, *Educating in Faith*, p. 197.

78. Writing from a Catholic perspective, Raymond Brown explains, "I recognize fully that the office of Pope and bishop is a charism that involves divine help; but, as far as I know, in good Catholic theology grace is thought to cooperate with nature. To use properly the teaching role that is theirs by the charism of their office bishops must take the step of learning about what they are teaching—that is not only common sense; it is the age-old understanding of the church" ("Bishops and Theologians," p. 676).

79. Concerning the interrelationships between these two sources, or what he calls the "pastoral magisterium" and the "magisterium of the scholars," Dulles writes,

Neither of these two magisteria, however, is self-sufficient. Rather, they are complementary and mutually corrective. Were it not for the theologians, bishops might settle issues by the sole criterion of administrative convenience, without regard to scholarship and theory. In their zeal for uniformity, they might attempt to impose assent by sheer decree, overlooking the values of Christian freedom and maturity. The theologians, on the other hand, would suffer the opposite temptation. They would want unlimited freedom for discussion without regard to the demands of fidelity to Christian revelation. For the unity of the Church as a community of faith and witness, and for its perseverance in its assigned task, the pastoral magisterium is indispensable. ("What Is Magisterium?" p. 86)

Congar has a threefold arrangement somewhat similar to the one I have outlined. He writes, "One must put truth, the apostolic faith which has been handed down, confessed, preached and celebrated, at the top. And under it, at its service, we must place the magisterium of apostolic ministry and the research and teaching of theologians, together with the belief of the faithful" ("The Magisterium and Theologians," p. 20).

80. See Weil and Joyce, *Information Processing Models of Teaching*, pp. 197–275. Briefly, the "advance organizer" model is structured around three phases. The first presents an "advance organizer" of the whole topic, something akin to a summary of the central theme of the presentation and a skeletal outline of how the theme will be elaborated. The second phase is the actual presentation, following the structural outline. Phase three returns to the central theme to promote its active and critical appropriation by the learners and to help people integrate the new material into what they already knew. (This third phase is more obviously done in movement 4 of a shared praxis approach.)

81. For "group hermeutics" I have found William F. Hill's Learning Through Discussion a suggestive model for organizing systematic interpretation of a text by a group of older participants. Hill's approach outlines nine clearly delineated steps for group hermeneutics of a text and is well informed by the literature on group dynamics.

82. Martha Leypoldt describes a colloquy thus: "Three or four persons selected from a group present various aspects of a problem to three or four resource people who respond to them" (*40 Ways to Teach in Groups*, p. 51). Many of the other "ways" that Leypoldt suggests are effective in this third movement. See esp. numbers 1, 5, 7, 12–14, 16, 18, 20, 22, 24, 26–27, 30–31, 33–35, 37.

83. For an excellent "vision" of how the church can employ modern communication media, see Peter Mann, *Through Words and Images*.

84. See Margaret Miles, *Image as Insight*, for an excellent review of "visual understanding" in the history of Western Christianity and culture.

85. Boys, "Access to Traditions and Transformation," p. 15.

86. Boys, *Educating in Faith*, p. 209.

87. Ibid., p. 193.

88. Gabriel Moran gives an insightful review of "a homiletic use of speech" in teaching. He poses the "conditions" of homiletic as "a community freely gathered, an agreed upon text, a speaker designated by the community to inspire the rest" (*Religious Education as a Second Language*, p. 70). He argues "that the homiletic form of speech in teaching is inescapable," but adds, "when the classroom teacher is engaged in instruction, the homily has almost no part to play" (ibid., p. 72). From my perspective, Moran stops short of recognizing a place for persuasive rhetoric in religious education as classroom instruction.

89. Augustine was citing Cicero, from whom he had learned much about rhetoric. The Latin here is: *Ita discere ut debere, loquentem ut doceat, ut delectat, ut flectat* (*On Christian Doctrine*, IV, 12, par. 27). The translation I use here is from William Harmless, S.J.; his dissertation first brought this quote to my attention. For this whole nuance to the phrase *make accessible* and the need for persuasive eloquence in Christian faith education, I am indebted to Harmless's work. See his dissertation, *Augustine and the Ancient Catechumenate*.

90. These terms were first suggested to me by Ian Ramsey. See *Models and Mystery*, pp. 10–21.

91. Parker Palmer writes well: "The teacher who offers a single body of data and omits competing evidence closes the learning space. The teacher who gives a single interpretation of the data rather than suggesting alternate theories fails to open a space in which students are challenged to learn" (*Known*, pp. 77–78).

92. This is another way of saying that movement 3 of shared Christian praxis should reflect good theology and Scripture scholarship on all occasions, even with young children. For example, it is pedagogically ill-advised to present the Bible story of creation to

young children as an accurate factual account (six days, etc.) of *how* God created the world and humankind. Someone later will have to deny this before they can expand upon the meaning of God's agency in the creation story.

93. Paulo Freire, Summer School, Boston College, 1982. A course entitled "Education for Critical Consciousness," co-taught by Freire, Regina Coll, and myself.

94. Parks, *Critical Years*, p. 110. Ann Louise Gilligan writes, "I believe that the imagination should be the midwife if the delivery of our tradition is to be life giving in our age" (*Feminist Imagination*, p. 287).

95. My awareness of the importance and the possibility of providing both pedagogically adequate and well-informed resource materials has been heightened by my work in creating the *God with Us* and *Coming to Faith* curricula. In both series we tried assiduously to see to it that the content of movement 3 faithfully makes accessible the teachings/learnings of the "church." We also paid particular attention to the "Catechists' Resource Pages" in the Teacher's Guide for each grade as an additional source of well-informed theological and spiritual resource for the teacher's own faith development.

96. One of my primary critiques of much published and standardized curricula for Christian religious education is their lack of specific attention to this Vision dimension. Even texts that do a fine job of making present Christian Story often leave the Vision implicit, or take for granted that participants will make the link between their own lives and what the Story asks of them. The Vision is to be intentionally proposed, albeit never in a "final" or hardened form.

97. Trible, *God and the Rhetoric of Sexuality*, chap. 4.

98. An edited version of this lesson was published in the *God with Us* series. See grade 6, *Growing with God's Word*, Lesson 4 (Standard Edition). See also the *Coming to Faith* series, grade 6, *Coming to God's Word*, Lesson 4 (Catholic School Edition).

99. See, e.g., Rahner, *Concern for the Church*, esp. chap. 3, "Women and the Priesthood."

Chapter 9. Movement 4

1. See Piaget, *To Understand*.

2. See, e.g., Gadamer, *Truth and Method*, p. 267–74.

3. Aristotle, *Nicomachean Ethics*, p. 331.

4. Throughout the *God with Us* and the *Coming to Faith* textbooks we often use a How *can* you . . . ? question in movement 4, as distinct from a How *will* you . . . ? question in movement 5.

5. Ann Louise Gilligan captures imagination's mediating role in dialectical appropriation when she writes, "Here the image anticipates fulfillment as it holds sameness and difference in union. Here the image is connected with that movement towards emergent meaning rather than being the static residue of past thought" (*Feminist Imagination*, p. 185).

Drawing upon Gadamer's notion of the "fusion of horizons," Baumer offers the insightful image of a "water lock" to capture the imaginative moment of correlation between the horizon of the text and the horizons of participants as I intend it to be effected in movement 4. He writes, "The imagination in which these horizons are fused to create transformation can be conceived as the lock between two bodies of water. The lock is the channel which allows the two bodies of water to flow together. The imagination is the channel where the fusion of horizons takes place. It simply is the function that interweaves two other realities" (*Homiletic as Rhetorical Genre*, p. 242).

6. Lonergan, *Method*, p. 241.

7. In this regard, Michael Fahy, citing Karl Rahner, writes, "Freedom is preserved by consistent conscious attempts to appropriate personally one's faith commitment" ("On Being Christian Together," p. 135).

8. Bernstein writes, "There has been a deformation of the concept of tradition when we think of it as the 'dead weight' of the past. A living tradition not only informs and shapes what we are but is always in the process of reconstitution. When tradition is no longer open in this manner, we can speak of it as 'dead,' or as no longer a tradition" (*Beyond Objectivism*, p. 131).

9. Francis Schüssler Fiorenza writes, "The method of correlation between human experience and Christian belief affirms a basic coherence between the two because of a more original disclosure of the meaning and truth of each" (*Foundational Theology,* p. 281).

10. See esp. Part 1 of Augustine's "The First Catechetical Instruction." Augustine's claim is also borne out by Edward Robinson's research on people's "original vision." Robinson, after many interviews with people concerning their earliest religious experiences, contends that people are born with an "original" and religious "inner authority." He writes that "no Church God can ultimately be acknowledged unless He [*sic*] is acceptable to this inner authority" (*Original Vision,* p. 96).

11. Thomas Aquinas, *Summa Theologica,* II-II, 45, 2; vol. 3, p. 1374.

12. The central dogmatic definition of the Council of Chalcedon (named after the city in Asia Minor where it was held in 451) confesses that Jesus Christ "is perfect both in his divinity and in his humanity, truly God and truly man . . . cosubstantial with the Father in his divinity, cosubstantial with us in his humanity. . . . We declare that the one self-same Christ . . . must be acknowledged in two natures without any commingling or change or division or separation . . . that the specific character of each nature is preserved and they are united in one person (*prosopon*) and one hypostasis" (*The Church Teaches,* p. 172).

13. In more than fifteen years of using this approach, I have had one such conversation.

14. See Champlin, *The Marginal Catholic.* This sensitive pastoral guide insists that it is risky and ill advised for anyone to evaluate another person's faith, yet suggests how ministers can follow the maxim "challenge, don't crush" toward "the marginal" churchperson.

15. Richard P. McBrien, writing from a Catholic perspective, is helpful on the issue of "dissent" from official church teachings. First, McBrien distinguishes between a dogma and a doctrine:

A belief that receives the official approval of the Church, whether through a pronouncement of an ecumenical council (literally, a council drawn from 'the whole wide world'), a pope, or a body of bishops in union with the pope (as at an international synod or at a general council, i.e., representative of segments of the Church universal), is called a *doctrine.* A doctrine that is taught with the fullest solemnity, i.e., so that its rejection is heresy, is called a dogma (literally, "what seems right"). (*Catholicism,* vol. 1, p. 67)

McBrien recognizes that

the determination of what constitutes a dogma is always a theological problem. Surprising though it may seem to many, there is no list of dogmas to which all Catholic theologians or even pastoral leaders would agree. Some criteria for determining what constitutes a dogma are: (1) The teaching is explicitly identified with the essence of Christian faith. (2) It is the clear intent of the teaching Church to bind the whole Church on the matter. (3) The teaching is contained in Sacred Scripture and/or is unmistakably present in the various doctrinal pronouncements of the Church through the centuries. (Ibid., p. 71)

McBrien then explains,

Dissent is never possible against a dogma, assuming that the preceding criteria have been taken into account—in other words, if there is no question that it is a dogma, and if its meaning is clear to all. To reject such a dogma, however sincere or well-intentioned the act, places one outside the Catholic Church and technically makes one a heretic. (Ibid.)

Then, concerning doctrines, McBrien explains,

Dissent against a non-dogmatic teaching (doctrine) is always a possibility . . . if (1) the teaching did not seem to make sense (even if one is wrong, one cannot pretend to see truth where none seems present); (2) the teaching seems to conflict with other clearly established truths of faith; (3) the teaching conflicts with one's own Christian experience regarding the matter in question; or (4) the teaching generates dissent from other members of the Church who merit respect by reason of their scholarly competence, pastoral experience, or personal integrity and prudence. (Ibid., p. 72)

See also Ladislas Orsy, *The Church: Learning and Teaching,* esp. pp. 98–101. Orsy's is a fine essay on the issues of magisterium, assent, dissent, and academic freedom. Unfortunately, nowhere does he even mention the *sensus fidelium* as a source of "teaching."

16. "Declaration on Religious Freedom," in Abbott, *Documents,* p. 682.

17. This is the often-quoted phrase from the decree *Justice in the World,* issued by the Second General Synod of Catholic Bishops at Rome, 1971. See "Justice in the World" in Gremillion, ed., *The Gospel of Peace and Justice,* p. 514.

18. This is the apt title of movement 4 in the children's texts of the *God with Us* curriculum (Groome et al.).

19. An adapted version of this event was published in the *Coming to Faith* series, grade 6, *Coming to God's Word,* lesson 27 (Catholic School Edition).

Chapter 10. Movement 5

1. Don Browning makes a similar distinction, calling them "deontic" and "aretic" decisions. The first responds to "the question of what we are obligated to do," and the "aretic" to the "characterological" questions "which try to identify the nature of the good person and the morally proper character, motivation and virtue" ("Practical Theology," p. 81). In this essay Browning summarizes a proposal he has developed over the years and published in detail in *Religious Ethics and Pastoral Care* concerning "the levels" of moral decision making. He proposes that there are five such levels: (1) "A visional or meta-phorical level" that asks "the most fundamental question . . . what kind of world do we live in" and in response "must necessarily resort to metaphors and narratives which sym-bolically and dramatically represent the ultimate context of our experience"; (2) "an obligational level" that asks "what must we do" and resorts "to some general principle which tells us rather abstractly but comprehensively what we are morally justified in doing"; (3) "a tendency-need level" that asks "what are the basic tendencies, needs, and values which humans . . . seek to satisfy"; (4) "a contextual level" that asks "what is the present cultural, sociological, or ecological context, and what constraints does it place on our actions"; and (5) "a rule-role level" that asks "what should be the concrete rules and roles that we should follow?" ("Practical Theology," pp. 88–89).

Browning identifies those questions as "deontic" and then delineates a correspond-ing set of levels for the "aretic" dimension of moral formation with the (1) visional or metaphoric calling for faith development, (2) the obligational calling for moral develop-ment, (3) the tendency-need level calling for emotional development, (4) the contextual calling for perceptual or ego development, and (5) the rule-role level calling for what Browning names "rule-role development" (ibid., p. 92).

Browning also critiques the shared Christian praxis approach for its lack of "an explicit theological ethic" and identifies his five levels of ethical decision making as, among other things, "an ethical refinement of Groome's shared praxis approach" (ibid., pp. 88 ff.). I have learned from his critique and attempt to incorporate his insights more deliberately in this chap. 10, but I also believe shared Christian praxis honors, at least implicitly, the five levels that Browning outlines. The "visional" level of shared praxis is reflected in its overarching Vision of God's reign; the "obligational" level in its third movement that explicitly makes present the demands of the Christian Story upon our lives. The "tendency-need" level is brought to expression by participants in movement 1; the "contextual" level is attended to in the critical reflection of movement 2; and the "rule-role" level is present in this fifth movement.

2. See *Coming to God's Word,* lesson 12 (Catholic School Edition), in the *Coming to Faith* curriculum. (The Teachers' Guide suggests various ways in which the participants' deci-sion making can be shared and tested in dialogue.)

3. Aristotle, *Nicomachean Ethics,* book 3, chap. 5. 2; p. 147.

4. This position reflects Dulles's fifth model of revelation in which revelation is the "new consciousness" that emerges from historical praxis toward the horizon of God's reign. See *Revelation,* chap. 7.

5. In the catechumenate of the early church, teaching and learning the Creed by heart had a special symbolic significance by way of Christian identity. As Marthaler explains: "In Lent, as the day of baptism approached, the bishop 'handed over' the Creed (the *traditio symboli*) and proceeded to comment on it phrase by phrase. The catechumens in turn were expected to learn it by heart so as to be able to 'give it back' (the *redditio symboli*); that is, they were asked to recite it publicly to demonstrate that they were sufficiently grounded in the faith" (*The Creed*, p. 9). The latter practice has been restored in the *Rite of Christian Initiation of Adults* in the Catholic church.

6. Pope John Paul II, "Catechesi Tradendae," no. 55, pp. 75–76.

7. A very insightful essay on memorization in religious education is Paul Philibert's "The Promise and Perils of Memorization," pp. 299–310. On the appropriateness of memorization for children, Philibert writes: "If we deal with textual materials which are truly important for the child, related to real questions and possibilities for growth in the life of the child, then the use of repetition, imitation, and even memorization can both simplify the adults' task of transmitting social knowledge and prove an attractive activity to the child as well" (ibid., p. 302). On the other hand, Philibert says, "It is not very productive to propose rote memorization of something a child does not understand" (ibid.).

8. Throughout grades K–8 of the *God with Us* and *Coming to Faith* curricula there is a "Review," or "Review Test" at the end of each chapter. They pose a variety of questions but typically one cognitive, one affective, and one behavioral. For example, in the grade 1 text, *Growing with God*, Lesson 6, the review questions are

· What are some of the things we have learned about God's world?
· How do you feel about the beautiful things in God's world?
· How can we take care of what God has made?

The first question could be "graded" if necessary, but it was certainly never this author's intention that responses to the other two be graded. In both the *God with Us* and *Coming to Faith* series, however, the Teacher's Guide and the end of each unit have Unit Reviews with questioning activities that lend themselves more readily to grading, if necessary.

9. Sanders, *Classroom Questions*, p. 162.

10. See Bloom, *Taxonomy of Educational Objectives*, passim. An example of such an exam question follows; it was posed in the final "blue book" exam of a course in which one month-long unit had focused on a Catholic theological anthropology.

"Grace works through nature" is an often-cited summary of a Catholic anthropology. Reflect on it and express in your own terms:

A) The questions to which the statement is a response.
B) The Catholic position, compared to other classic positions that it summarizes.
C) Your own assessment of its value and truth.
D) To demonstrate the practical implications it has for people who subscribe to it, take a particular life issue (e.g., human well-being, evil, responsibility, etc.) and show how the principle that "grace works through nature" applies in that instance.

11. Freire, *Process*, p. 64.

12. In *Habits of the Heart*, Bellah et al. point out that American society encourages a self-reliant individualism and a utilitarian form of decision making. They warn that our common assumption about the "independence" of such decision making is a fiction: "The irony is that . . . just where we think we are most free, we are most coerced by the dominant beliefs of our culture. For it is a powerful cultural fiction that we not only can, but must, make up our deepest beliefs in the isolation of our private selves" (p. 65). Such "rugged individualism" is not the kind of autonomy intended by movement 5 of shared praxis. It seeks to promote decisions chosen by participants as agent-subjects but always in dialogue and dialectic with a Story/Vision and in a community of discourse.

13. See Parks, *Critical Years*, esp. pp. 73–75.

14. *Pastoral Constitution*, Abbott, *Documents*, p. 240.

15. Dewey, quoted in Harris, *Imagination*, p. 37. Harris also has helpful insights on the need for the educator at this moment to practice "release," to be able to say to

participants, "It is no longer mine, it is now yours . . . a fine time to learn humility" (ibid., pp. 38–39).

16. This point emphasizes the importance of the ongoing faith development of religious educators. In terms of Fowler's "stages," it would seem unlikely that a teacher at stage three will be likely to sponsor others toward stage four or five. Of course the dynamic of a group process like shared praxis can be a powerful source of ongoing development for the educator.

17. An excellent resource for corporate decision-making processes is Gerard Egan's *Change Agent Skills in Helping and Human Service Settings*.

18. Zappone writes of ritualization at the end of such a process: "Prayers and rituals enable the educational community to express, in symbolic form, the truths discovered throughout the educational process. They capture the meaning and truth of present experience and precious memory. Fashioning prayers and creating rituals invite each member to tell the future story, to express a hope for new relationships and the insight and courage needed for more accurate emancipatory praxis" (*Reconstructing Relationality*, p. 328). See also Zappone, *Hope for Wholeness*.

19. Writing of teaching as a "work of creation," Maria Harris outlines "five movements, or steps." She adds, "The steps envisioned, however, are not like steps of a staircase, progressing upwards. Rather, they are like steps in a dance, where movement is both backward and forward, around and through, and where turns, returns, rhythm, and movement are essential" (*Imagination*, p. 25; Harris footnotes Judith Dorney for this insight).

20. This took place at First and Second Church in Boston. The religious educator was Rev. Lawrence X. Peers.

21. See *Coming to God's Life* (Catholic School Edition), p. 184, in the *Coming to Faith* curriculum.

Part III. Prologue

1. One of the first concerted efforts to use shared praxis in other than formal moments of teaching was initiated by the Sisters of the Sacred Heart (RSCJ) for school evaluation. They used it for a number of years in their nineteen schools throughout the United States, and a very effective program emerged for engaging a whole school community (students, administrators, parents, alumnae) in self-evaluation of their school. They begin by looking at and describing their present school reality (movement 1), then critically reflect upon that reality (movement 2), encounter a statement of "goals and objectives" that the Society, out of a long and rich educational tradition, proposes for its schools (movement 3), and come to dialectical appropriation (movement 4) and decision for school renewal (movement 5). The process seems to have particular appeal to the school community under evaluation because it engages them in self-critique rather than subjecting them to being judged by outside evaluators.

2. Moran writes, "During recent centuries, especially the last, we have placed nearly all our educational eggs in the basket of the school. Our system was built on a simple premise: People of a certain age (children) should go to a certain place (school) to receive a certain package of information (education)" (*Religious Education Development*, p. 157).

3. Gabriel Moran provides a valuable insight for religious educators by highlighting the fact that "education" is far broader than "schooling"; "education" takes place through all the "life forms" in which people participate. He proposes a fourfold schema of such "life forms" and of their "universal values" as family/community, schooling/knowledge, job/work, and leisure/wisdom. Moran notes that all of them are constantly interrelated in the process of education—a sentiment that recognizes the unity of "knowing" and "being." See ibid., chap. 8, and *Religious Education as a Second Language*, chap. 2, for a more recent summary statement.

4. This has been a common insight in the writings of the "social theorists" of religious education for some time. Maria Harris has recently offered a very helpful summary statement on the educational dimensions of the whole life of the church in the world. In gist, she reviews the "forms" of ecclesial ministry under the traditional categories: "*kerygma*, proclaiming the word of Jesus' resurrection; *didache*, the activity of teaching;

leiturgia, coming together to pray and to re-present Jesus in the breaking of bread; *koinonia,* or community; and *diakonia,* caring for those in need" (*Fashion Me a People,* p. 16). She proposes "that the forms themselves are the primary curriculum of the church, . . . and that in these forms we fashion the church. And because *we* are the church, the fashioning of the forms becomes the fashioning of us" (ibid., p. 17). For Harris, the curriculum of Christian religious education is "the entire course of the church's life"; all its forms have faith education consequences, especially when such education is understood as an empowering of people "on behalf of the church and the gospel." (See ibid., p. 48.)

  5. Ibid., p. 48.

Chapter 11. Christian Ministry: An Overview

  1. See Osborne, *Priesthood,* pp. 2–15, for one helpful listing.

  2. See Calvin, *Institutes of the Christian Religion,* book 2, chap. 15.

  3. Drawing upon Jeremias's attempt to pinpoint the core of Jesus' message, Osborne first notes, "the return of the quenched Spirit" and "overcoming the rule of Satan." He adds also, "the dawn of the Kingdom of God" and "the poor have the Good News preached to them" (*Priesthood,* pp. 16–24).

  4. See ibid., pp. 4–7, and passim.

  5. This understanding of the church's purpose is well stated by Vatican II's *Pastoral Constitution.* "The Church has a single intention: that God's kingdom may come, and that the salvation of the whole human race may come to pass" (Abbott, *Documents,* p. 247).

  6. McBrien proposes a fourfold categorizing of ministry. His distinctions are clarifying and also help to remind us that ministry is not synonymous with Christian ministry. First, he refers to "general/universal ministry"; this is "any service (which is the root meaning of the word *ministry*) rendered to another person or group of people who happen to be in need of that service. . . . In this sense ministry has nothing intrinsically to do with religion." Second, he refers to "general/specific ministry"; that is the "special service rendered by people specifically called to serve others in the so-called helping professions—e.g., nursing, social work, etc." Third, there is "Christian/universal ministry," which "is rooted in our baptism and confirmation" and "is any general service rendered to others in Christ and because of Christ." Lastly, there is "Christian/specific ministry," which is "any general service rendered to others in Christ and because of Christ *in the name of the Church and for the sake of helping the Church fulfill its mission.*" McBrien adds, "The call to ministry in this fourth and most specific sense is rooted in some form or act of designation by the Church itself" (*Ministry,* pp. 11–13).

  7. In the Eastern tradition of Christianity especially there was also a fifth task— *marturia* or witness. I have subsumed it, as the Western tradition has tended to do, under *koinonia,* seeing it as part of the church's task to be a community of Christian witness.

  8. Osborne, *Priesthood,* p. 3.

  9. Grassi, *The Teacher,* p. 22.

  10. Perkins, *Jesus as Teacher,* pp. 30, 37, and 87.

  11. Sawicki writes, "There was a custom in Jesus' day for groups of friends to meet regularly for formal dinners at which the Law and the destiny of Israel would be discussed. Ordinarily only observant Jews would be included in the circle. Jesus, however, welcomed tax collectors to his table and held his gatherings in the homes of people outside the Law" (*The Gospel in History,* p. 86).

  12. Perkins, *Hearing the Parables of Jesus,* p. 16.

  13. Ibid., pp. 9, 16. Elsewhere Perkins writes "Much of Jesus' teaching challenges the imagination to look at the world and others differently." *Jesus as Teacher,* p. 60.

  14. Grassi explains, "Rabbinic teaching in those days depended mainly on careful and constant repetition of the master's words. It was the duty of the pupil to repeat exactly the words of his [*sic*] teacher" (*The Teacher,* p. 45).

  15. This story has become paradigmatic for people committed to a shared praxis approach to religious education; the movements are clearly reflected in the dynamics of the event on the Emmaus road. The focusing activity is Jesus, now the Risen One, inserting himself into the company of the two disciples. He turns them toward their own

reality by asking, "What are you discussing as you go your way?" (v. 17; movement 1). They tell their story of the events in Jerusalem and what their hopes and vision had been (movement 2). He responds by reminding them of the broader Story and Vision of their people (movement 3). He allows them to come to see for themselves in the breaking of the bread (movement 4); then they act on their faith by returning to Jerusalem to share the good news of his resurrection (movement 5).

16. The story clearly witnesses to the faith of Luke's community that the Risen Christ is encountered in word and sacrament and may reflect the earliest pattern of eucharistic liturgy in the church. See Fitzmyer, *Luke,* in Anchor Bible, vol. 28a: p. 1560; and Dillon, *Eye-Witnesses,* pp. 75, 79.

17. *Theological Dictionary,* abridged, p. 121.

18. For this overview, I have drawn especially upon the following works: Cooke, *Ministry to Word and Sacraments,* esp. chaps. 1, 8, 15, 20, 27; Schillebeeckx, *Ministry* (now revised and republished as *The Church with a Human Face*); O'Meara, *Theology of Ministry;* Power, *Gifts That Differ;* Brown, *Priest and Bishop;* and Osborne, *Priesthood.* I have also found two more popular works to be helpful and clarifying: Bausch, *Traditions, Tensions and Transitions in Ministry;* and McBrien, *Ministry.*

19. McBrien, *Ministry,* pp. 28, 30.

20. Power, *Gifts That Differ,* pp. 88–89.

21. See Schillebeeckx, *Ministry,* p. 3.

22. Schillebeeckx writes:

> There is no mention in the New Testament of an essential distinction between "laity" and "ministers." The particular character of the ministry is set against the background of many different, non-ministerial services in the church. In this sense the ministry is not a status, but in fact a function, though it is rightly called "a gift of the Spirit" by the community *qua* assembly of God. For the New Testament, the essential apostolic structure of the community and therefore of the ministry of its leaders has nothing to do with what is called the "hierarchical" structure of the church (on the basis of later Roman models in the Roman empire, and even later of feudal structures). (*Ministry,* p. 31)

23. O'Meara writes of such a listing, "Actually, the lists tell us more about the theology of ministry than they do about its precise structure. It is easier to conclude that ministry was active, diverse and flexible than to derive a job description of the ministries listed" (*Theology of Ministry,* p. 80). Writing of the era up to 110 C.E., Osborne summarizes, "At the conclusion of this period, there is still no set pattern to the names for Christian ministers, and there is also no common pattern which is historically verifiable of specific functions for any of these various titles of ministry" (*Priesthood,* p. 40).

24. Writing of overseer and presbyter (elder), respectively, Osborne notes, "Both episkopos and presbyter are non-liturgical, and non-priestly in origin and usage. Leadership is the primary aspect of these two titles. Applied to members of the early Church, they indicate community leadership rather than 'priestly,' i.e., liturgical, ministry" (*Priesthood,* p. 52).

25. Scripture and patristic scholars now insist on a distinction between "the Twelve" who were apostles and "the apostles". The latter were a much wider category than the original "Twelve" listed (variously) in the Gospels. Brown argues for "the historicity of the Twelve as apostles," but adds, "the thesis that there were only Twelve apostles is certainly a later simplification. There were many apostles in the early days, but the Twelve had a special place in the apostolate not so much because of their missionary activities but because they had been the intimate companions of Jesus" (*Priest and Bishop,* p. 49). (Note: In the above, Brown is commenting on "apostles" in the Lucan community. In Pauline communities the "apostles" did participate more actively in missionary and administrative activity. See ibid., pp. 59–73. See also Power, *Gifts That Differ,* pp. 92–93.)

26. Brown, *Priest and Bishop,* p. 41.

27. Of the traditional Catholic notion that the apostles were commissioned at the Last Supper to preside at Eucharist, Osborne writes, "In spite of the long tradition of this view, contemporary scholars find no basis for such an interpretation. In other words, Jesus did not ordain the apostles (disciples) at this final supper to be 'priests,' giving them thereby the power to celebrate the eucharist" (*Priesthood,* p. 79).

28. This conviction is reflected in the church's insistence throughout history that any Christian can conduct a valid baptism, even though the mandate to baptize was clearly given by the Risen Christ to "the eleven." Even as late as the 3d c., Tertullian could write, "Are not we laity priests also? . . . Where there is no bench of clergy, you offer and baptize and are your own sole priest. For where there are three there is a church, though they be laity" ("De Exhortatione Castitatis," 7; p. 71).

29. This open process of designating the community leader as presider at Eucharist is reflected in the writings of Justin Martyr (d. c.165) (see Justin Martyr, "Apology I:65," p. 66.) and Irenaeus (d. c.202; see "Against Heresies," in *Ante-Nicene Fathers*, pp. 484–86), indicating that the practice continued at least into the 3d c. In fact, not until the Fourth Lateran Council (1215) did the church declare that Eucharist could be celebrated "only (by) a priest who has been rightly ordained according to the keys of the Church" (Denzinger, *Sources of Catholic Dogma*, p. 170). In light of such evidence, Schillebeeckx concludes that "the modern situation in which a community might not be able to celebrate the eucharist because no priest is present is theologically inconceivable in the early church; the community chooses a president for itself and has hands laid on him [*sic*] so that they can also be a community which celebrates the eucharist, i.e., a 'community of God'" (*Ministry*, p. 41).

30. See Osborne, *Priesthood*, p. 80.

31. Regarding Eucharist, the *Didache* states, "Accordingly, elect for yourselves bishops and deacons . . . for they too render you the sacred service (*leitourgeo*) of the prophets and teachers" ("The Didache," p. 24).

32. See Brown, *Priest and Bishop*, pp. 17–20. Brown states, "Such a picture of the development of the Christian priesthood must of necessity modify our understanding of the claim that historically Jesus instituted the priesthood at the Last Supper" (ibid., p. 19). Summarizing the evidence from the pre-Nicene church, Legrand writes, "The perception of the president of the Eucharist as an explicitly sacerdotal figure is not attested before the beginning of the third century" ("The Presidency of the Eucharist," p. 407).

33. Commentators often make much of the fact that a tension emerged between the more evangelical and charismatic functions and the functions that cared for the well-being of the community. By the late 2d c., this tension emerged as between prophet/evangelist/teacher and bishop/priest/deacon, the latter the "institutional" functions and the former the "charismatic." For the first Christian communities, however, all ministry was seen as a charism/gift of the Holy Spirit; 1 Cor. 12:28, e.g., refers to "the charism of administration." (See Brown, *Priest and Bishop*, p. 36.)

34. Osborne, *Priesthood*, p. 129. See also Power, *Gifts that Differ*, pp. 94–96.

35. As I note on the issue of women in ministry below, there is no evidence that maleness was a specific criterion for any designated function of ministry. In fact, the New Testament offers ample evidence that women served in the designated functions. (See, e.g., 1 Tim. 3:11; Rom. 16:1–2.)

36. McBrien, *Ministry*, p. 11.

37. Though "apostolate" was considered to be something qualitatively less than priesthood, I believe it has a "subversive memory" that might advise its retention. It clearly refers to work that carries on the apostolic mandate Jesus gave to the first disciples.

38. Brown writes, "If the sacramental power resides in the Church, it can be given to those whom the Church designates or acknowledges, without a lineal connection to the Twelve" (*Priest and Bishop*, p. 55).

39. Brown explains, "About the turn of the century (or a little earlier) the roles that once may have been separated had been joined: the role of the presbyter-bishop and the role of the celebrant of the Eucharist" (ibid., p. 42).

40. See ibid., p. 43. For further comment, see Mohler, *The Origin and Evolution of the Priesthood*, esp. chap. 4.

41. Dix, *Liturgy*, pp. 33–34.

42. The arrangement of a bishop presiding over a college of presbyters was in place in some communities as early as Ignatius of Antioch (d. c.110), although it is not clear how widespread the practice was. (See Brown, *Priest and Bishop*, p. 38.)

43. *Apostolic Tradition of Hippolytus*, pp. 38, 40.

44. See ibid., p. 33 #2, p. 37 #8, p. 38 #9.

45. Ibid., p. 39 #10. This point clearly has significance for Catholic communities today that are left without regular celebration of Eucharist because of a shortage of ordained priests. Leonardo Boff, citing this "exception" from Hippolytus, argues in favor of the "coordinator" of a "basic Christian community" being allowed to function as an "extraordinary minister of the sacrament of the Eucharist" (*Ecclesiogenesis*, p. 73; see all of chap. 6).

46. Brown, *Priest and Bishop*, p. 20.

47. Ibid., p. 73.

48. Osborne, *Priesthood*, p. 49.

49. Ibid., p. 138.

50. *Apostolic Tradition of Hippolytus*, p. 33. Thus, the bishops ordain but the people choose.

51. Pope Leo the Great (d. 461) declared, "No one, of course, is to be consecrated [bishop] against the wishes of the people and without their requesting it" ("Letter 14," *Fathers of the Church*, vol. 34, p. 63).

52. See Brown, *Priest and Bishop*, p. 79. I recognize that my reading of the New Testament on this point is indeed from a Catholic perspective; other Christians of good-will read it differently. I am not claiming, however, that the New Testament clearly establishes a blueprint for how the Petrine office is to be exercised. McBrien writes, "The terms primacy and jurisdiction are best avoided when describing Peter's role in the New Testament. They reflect a post-biblical development" (*Catholicism*, vol. 2, p. 831).

53. Ibid., p. 54.

54. Ibid., p. 53.

55. O'Meara, *Theology of Ministry*, p. 77.

56. For further reflections on clericalism, see my essay "From Chauvinism and Clericalism to Priesthood."

57. Osborne, *Priesthood*, p. 146.

58. McBrien, *Ministry*, p. 38.

59. In the first Code of Canon Law compiled by Gratian (1142) we read, "There are two classes of Christians. One class is given to divine worship and is dedicated to contemplation and prayer—cut off from all temporal distractions. To this class belong clerics and those devoted to God. There is another sort of Christian, called lay folk. *Laos* means people. To these it is allowed to possess goods, to marry, to till the earth, to pay their tithes; and so they can be saved, if they do good and avoid evil" (quoted in Dosh, "Clericalism," p. 21).

60. "Canons of Chalcedon," in Percival, ed., *Seven Ecumenical Councils*, p. 271.

61. Boff, *Ecclesiogenesis*, p. 63.

62. Schillebeeckx notes, "This view (i.e., of absolute ordination) opens up the way to practices which would have been unthinkable to earlier Christians, above all the private mass. If a man has been personally ordained priest, he has the 'power of the eucharist' and can therefore celebrate it on his own. For the early church this was quite simply inconceivable" (*Ministry*, p. 57).

63. Ibid., pp. 56–57. Schillebeeckx then adds, "As a logical consequence of this, the Fourth Lateran Council went on to say that only a validly ordained priest can speak the words of consecration" (ibid., p. 58).

64. Osborne, *Priesthood*, p. 258.

65. *The Roman Catechism*, Daughters of St. Paul edition, pp. 308, 312. Note: This new edition of the *Catechism of Trent*, more commonly known as *The Roman Catechism*, was published in 1985. I quote it here because it is in more contemporary language as well as being a fine translation of the original.

66. By identifying the sacralizing of priesthood as a diminution, I certainly do not argue against the validity and rightful place of the sacrament of Holy Order in the sacramental and ministerial life of the church; as does my Catholic tradition, I cherish Holy Orders as one of the seven sacraments. Through it, the church continues to maintain its sense of apostolic identity, to exercise its sacramental ministry as a community, and to recognize its dependence on the gifts of God's Holy Spirit for all functions of ministry. I resonate with David Power's notion that "ordination is a recognition of the gifts and spiritual authority of the person whom the community deems fit for leadership . . . a sacramental and formal institution of social authority which aggregates the freely given

power of the Spirit to the sacramental and institutional structures of the Church," thus giving the ordained person "a formal authority within the community" ("The Basis for Official Ministry," pp. 80, 82). I understand ordination to constitute a permanent function, guaranteed by the church as it exercises its sacramental ministry by the power of the Holy Spirit. Of rendering priestly services of word, sacrament, and "holy order" through the faith community for the upbuilding of the Body of Christ (see Eph. 4:12).

67. *The Roman Catechism*, pp. 313–14, 319, 321–23.

68. Power, *Gifts That Differ*, p. 71.

69. McBrien, *Ministry*, p. 39.

70. See *Pseudo-Dionysius: The Complete Works*, esp. "The Ecclesiastical Hierarchy."

71. See ibid., pp. 201, 196. See also Miles, *Practicing Christianity*, chap. 4, for an insightful commentary on the influence of Pseudo-Dionysius on the hierarchizing of ministry.

72. Power, *Unsearchable Riches*, p. 50.

73. See E. S. Fiorenza, *Her*, esp. chaps. 4, 5.

74. The Pontifical Commission set up by the Vatican to evaluate biblical evidence on the question of ordination of women declared in its final draft, "The Bible does not contain a ready answer to the question of the role of women in the Church or in society" and went on to say that it found no biblical evidence to justify their continued exclusion from priesthood (Pontifical Biblical Commission, "Can Women Be Priests?" pp. 92–96).

A second significant statement from a biblical perspective is the U.S. Catholic Biblical Association's report by its Task Force on the Role of Women in Early Christianity. Their conclusion deserves to be quoted in full:

An examination of the biblical evidence shows the following: that there is positive evidence in the N.T. that ministries were shared by various groups and that women did in fact exercise roles and functions later associated with priestly ministry; that the arguments against the admission of women to priestly ministry based on the praxis of Jesus and the apostles, disciplinary regulations, and the created order cannot be sustained. The conclusion we draw, then, is that the N.T. evidence, while not decisive by itself, points toward the admission of women to priestly ministry. (Catholic Biblical Association Task Force on the Role of Women in Early Christianity, "Women and Priestly Ministry: The New Testament Evidence," pp. 612–13)

Arguments in favor of women's ordination have also been advanced in position papers by the Canon Law Society of America and the Catholic Theological Society of America. (See Canon Law Society of America, "Consensus Statement from the Symposium on Women and Church Law"; and Catholic Theological Society of America, *Research Report: Women in Church and Society*.)

75. See E. S. Fiorenza, *Her*, esp. chap. 7.

76. I say "gradually excluded" because the early church ordained women as deacons. See Osborne, *Priesthood*, p. 199.

77. See Grisar, *Mary Ward*, pp. 12–13.

78. This is an important point for the possibility of change in the legislation of the Roman Rite regarding celibacy. Osborne summarizes the historical record as follows: "Throughout the historical material on the celibate clergy, the Church has never officially declared that celibacy is an essential element of deacon, priest or bishop. In other words, marriage is not per se an invalidating impediment to ordination" (*Priesthood*, pp. 146–47).

79. O'Meara, *Theology of Ministry*, pp. 105, 108.

80. This is taking it that the requirement of celibacy was first formally discussed at the Council of Elvira (a Spanish council about 309) where there was a significant Manichaean influence. See Laeuchli, *Power and Sexuality*, p. 104.

81. Bainton, *Christianity*, p. 176. For example, the recommendation of the *Catechism of Trent* to married people of "abstinence from the marital act . . . for three days prior to their receiving Holy Communion and also for the duration of the Lenten fast" does not reflect a positive theology of sexuality as integral to a married couple's call to holiness of life (*The Roman Catechism*, p. 343).

82. See Schillebeeckx, *Ministry*, pp. 85–94.

83. I do not share the opinion that an episcopal hierarchy necessarily must be rejected if the church is to exercise the fullness of its ministry. Hierarchy, in the sense of

ordained leadership (see note 66) that coordinates the ministries of the whole church and renders the service of nurturing its "holy order" (i.e., right relationship within the community and of the community with God and all creation), can in fact bring the church to the fullness of its ministry. Such a structure, however, can scarcely come "from the top down" but could arise "from the bottom up," i.e., from and through the community by the grace of God. It should promote partnership in ministry by the whole community, empower the gifts of all for service, and provide structures by which those gifts can be used and nurtured.

84. This phrase is suggested by one of Vatican II's most significant documents—*The Pastoral Constitution on the Church in the Modern World* (also known by its Latin title, *Gaudium et Spes* and referred to throughout this work as *Pastoral Constitution;* see Abbott, *Documents*). In its more technical meaning "the modern period" usually refers to the era in the West from Descartes to the recent past. Now, commentators say, we are in a "post-modern" period that is marked by a critique of the individualism and undue confidence in reason of the Enlightenment era, by a chastened admiration for technology, by a new awareness of the threat of nuclear destruction, and by commitment to social/political struggles for liberation.

85. Hater, *The Ministry Explosion.* Note, however, that the "explosion" was prepared for by the movement variously called the "lay apostolate" and "Catholic action," first encouraged by Pope Pius XI in the 1920s.

86. Dulles, *Models of the Church,* p. 48.

87. McBrien, *Catholicism,* vol. 2, p. 671.

88. Dulles, *A Church to Believe In,* chap. 1.

89. Abbott, *Documents,* pp. 27, 56–59.

90. Ibid., p. 144.

91. One insightful priest commentator writes, "No longer could I be a priest so that others did not have to be priests; but I had to be a priest in order to enable the entire community to be a priestly people, a worshipping church, a eucharistic community. No longer could I say Mass which others heard or even celebrate Mass at which others assisted. Rather, the entire community must now celebrate a liturgy at which I would preside" (Hussey, "Needed: A Theology of Priesthood," p. 579).

92. See James and Evelyn Eaton Whitehead, *The Emerging Laity,* passim. Elsewhere they write with hope that

> a quiet revolution is occurring in the land. Ancient distinctions between clergy and laity are giving way. A time-honored separation between Christians who "have vocations" and those who do not is being bridged. . . . This is a revolution of the *imagination:* new visions of Christian life—of adult faith, of ministry, of community— are being born. . . . Every Christian is called. . . . It is when the sacrament of Baptism takes root that a vocation is begun. . . . This nonelitist vision of Christian vocations arises from a more vigorous sense of adult faith and will, in time, give new shape to the structures of Christian ministry. (*Seasons of Strength,* p. 9)

93. O'Meara, *Theology of Ministry,* p. 5.

94. *Decree on the Missionary Activity of the Church,* in Abbott, *Documents,* p. 584. Robert Reber writes, "Often we have taken a simplistic view of the ministry of the laity, seeing it as limited to 'church' work, support of the clergy or use of religious language on appropriate occasion. If ministry does not involve those areas of life where we spend our time and energy, surely we relegate it to the periphery of our lives and deny what the Gospel is all about" ("Vocation and Vision," p. 1).

95. Pope Paul VI, *Evangelization,* p. 15.

96. Abbott, *Documents,* p. 27. Rather than emphasizing their difference, Hussey writes, "I would suggest that the principal affirmation of that sentence in *Lumen Gentium,* the interrelatedness of the priesthood of the faithful and the hierarchical priesthood, might be a better starting point. It might then be easier to see that the ordained priesthood does not intrude between God and the priesthood common to all the faithful, but rather enables the priesthood of the faithful to be fulfilled and effective" ("Needed: A Theology of Priesthood," p. 581).

97. See "Decree on the Ministry and Life of Priests," in Abbott, *Documents,* pp. 534, 553.

98. Abbott, *Documents,* p. 37.

99. For example, Pope Paul VI in his apostolic letter *Ministeria Quaedam* (1972) designated the roles of lector and acolyte as ministries in their own right, said that they are to be conferred by installation, and left open the possibility of recognizing other forms of "lay" ministry.

Further openness to diversity was reflected in Pope Paul VI's *On Evangelization in the Modern World* (*Evangelii Nuntiandi,* 1975) which states,

> These ministries, apparently new but closely tied up with the Church's living experience down the centuries—such as catechists, directors of prayer and chant, Christians devoted to the service of God's Word or to assisting their brethren [*sic*] in need, the heads of small communities, or other persons charged with the responsibility of apostolic movements—these ministries are valuable for the establishment, life, and growth of the Church, and for her capacity to influence her surroundings and reach those who are remote from her. (p. 53)

100. O'Meara makes the interesting proposal that all "public commissioning" for any function of ministry be called "ordination." He is also convinced that "every Christian at times would be involved in such services." *Theology of Ministry,* p. 147.

101. Hussey, "Needed: A Theology of Priesthood," p. 580.

102. Osborne, *Priesthood,* p. 315.

103. *Constitution on the Church,* in Abbott, *Documents,* p. 41.

104. Ibid., p. 42.This reclaiming of the function of bishop lent impetus to the ancient notion, championed by Vatican II, of episcopal collegiality, i.e., that the bishops in union with the pope are to function, nationally and/or internationally, as a collegium of discernment and decision making rather than being seen as individuals who are no more than representatives of the pope in a particular diocese.

105. *Decree on Priests,* in Abbott, *Documents,* p. 534.

106. See Abbott, *Documents,* p. 53.

107. Osborne, *Priesthood,* p. 320.

108. *Constitution on the Church,* in Abbott, *Documents,* p. 55.

109. Ibid., p. 56.

110. The Whiteheads write, "The contemporary challenge to celibacy as a requirement for community leadership does not question the *gift* of this life-style, which has continuously demonstrated its gracefulness and fruitfulness in Christian history. It does question the *bonding* of a particular life-style to the ministry of a sacramental community leader" (*Laity,* p. 146).

111. Boff, *Ecclesiogenesis,* p. 63. Note that Boff also argues strongly in favor of the ordination of women.

The urgency of the challenge to mandatory celibacy for priests has probably been fueled more by pastoral exigencies than by theology, since it is typically blamed for the significant drop in the number of available priests, especially in Europe and the Americas. It is to be hoped, however, that the theological challenge to mandatory celibacy will be equally compelling when the requirement is finally changed. The very positive understanding of marriage and sexuality that emerged from Vatican II is an antidote to at least some of the reasons why celibacy was introduced as a law for priests in the first place. In addition, feminist critique has heightened consciousness that such a requirement reflects a sexist mentality; as a public symbol it implies that conjugal love and marriage could never enhance but would only detract from a priest's ministry.

112. Most recently, the official Catholic church refusal of ordination to women was stated (but more in passing) in *Ministeria Quaedam* (see note 99). Its position was amplified in "Declaration on the Question of the Admission of Women to the Ministerial Priesthood," issued in 1976 by the Sacred Congregation for the Doctrine of the Faith, which, significantly, was not signed by the then pope, Paul VI (published in *Origins* 6:3 [Feb. 1977]:517–24).

113. For a fine, balanced, and scholarly refutation of the three standard arguments, see Rahner, *Concern for the Church,* esp. chap. 3. See also Leonard and Arlene Swidler, eds., *Women Priests.*

114. I am convinced that the exclusion of women from ordination reflects injustice in at least three significant ways. (1) It is an injustice to women who recognize themselves

as gifted and called by God to serve the church in ordained ministry; (2) it is an injustice to the church and its people, who could be served so significantly by ordained women; and (3) such exclusion functions as a legitimating sign for patriarchy and sexism—thus doing spiritual and moral harm in society.

115. Kaufman, *Nuclear,* pp. 16, 6.

116. National Conference of Catholic Bishops, *Economic Justice,* p. 3.

117. *Decree on the Church's Missionary Activity,* in Abbott, *Documents,* p. 586.

118. Abbott, *Documents,* pp. 199–200, 239, 262.

119. This is P. Palmer's descriptive phrase for "the public." See *Company of Strangers,* p. 22 and passim.

120. Kavanaugh, *Consumer Society,* p. 6.

121. Ibid., p. 10.

122. There is pressing need in the Catholic church for institutional structures that ensure a decent quality of life for people in nonordained but full-time ministries (insurance, pension, job security beyond the goodwill of the bishop or pastor, etc.) if they are to live their vocation as a lifelong calling.

123. I'm convinced from my own work that a shared praxis approach can be used in ministerial formation in a seminary or pastoral institute and has possibilities as an approach to teaching theology in a university or graduate school of theology. See my essay "Theology on Our Feet."

124. One personal experience in using the shared praxis approach for communal discernment took place at St. Mary on the Hill parish in Augusta, Georgia. Prompted by its pastor, Fr. James Costigan, the parish council decided to use a shared praxis approach to structure a program of education and decision making regarding the renovation of the parish church. Over two hundred people from the parish volunteered to participate and made a significant time commitment. The program engaged participants in expressing their praxis as a faith community and in describing their attitudes and sentiments toward their present worship space. Movement 2 entailed a critical review of the space, what they wished to change and why, what they would like to keep the same and why, and a sharing of significant memories they had of the space and the functions it should more adequately fulfill in the future. Movement 3 made accessible to participants the resources of a liturgist, a liturgical designer, an architect, and myself as a pastoral consultant.

Our service was to speak from our particular expertise and with a focus on this worship space about liturgical and pastoral developments, how they could be reflected in this space, what changes seemed advisable from the perspective of our disciplines, and why, etc. As such expertise was made accessible, a movement 4 dynamic of dialectical appropriation was constantly operative throughout. By way of movement 5, participants, having given parameters to the liturgical designer and architect coming out of the first four movements, finally reached a decision with sufficient consensus to proceed with a plan to refurbish their worship space.

125. For a more detailed reflection on its potential as a style of evangelization, see my "Shared Praxis: An Ordinary Approach to Evangelization."

Chapter 12. Liturgy and Preaching

1. There is significant need for Catholic consciousness to move beyond thinking of liturgy as synonymous with the Mass, and I certainly do not intend my focus here to encourage this limited understanding of "the liturgy." Yet, although the liturgy is far broader than the Mass, it functions as the central liturgical act of worship. There is an old Catholic tradition of referring to the Eucharist as the *sacramentum sacramentorum,* the sacrament of sacraments, and in the traditions of Eastern Catholicism, the word *liturgy* is used only to refer to the celebration of Eucharist. In its *Constitution on the Sacred Liturgy* (hereafter referred to as *C.S.L.*), Vatican II made it clear that liturgy includes all expressions of the public prayer of the church, yet it uses the term *the liturgy* most often to mean the Mass. See, e.g., pars. 7–10 of *C.S.L.,* in Abbott, *Documents,* pp. 140–43.

Jungmann, a great leader in the Catholic catechetical and liturgical renewal movements, wrote, "The worship of the Church is accomplished most perfectly in the celebration of the Eucharist because the Church is 'gathered' most intensively in the one bread of the Eucharist and is most truly itself." (*Encyclopedia of Theology: The Concise Sacramentum Mundi*, "Liturgy," by Joseph A. Jungmann, p. 853.)

2. *C.S.L.*, in Abbott, *Documents*, p. 149.

3. Ibid., p. 141.

4. Ibid., p. 149.

5. Randolph C. Miller writes, "Worship as experienced in community is essential as a base for religious education in all the major traditions" ("Guest Editorial," p. 322).

6. See von Rad, *Old Testament Theology*, vol. 2, p. 418.

7. This, however, did not become a law in the West until the eleventh century. See Dix, *Liturgy*, pp. 485–88, for an overview of the introduction of the Creed into eucharistic liturgy.

8. *C.S.L.*, in Abbott, *Documents*, p. 159.

9. Harris, *Fashion Me a People*, p. 95.

10. *C.S.L.*, in Abbott, *Documents*, pp. 142, 143, 144.

11. For this insight I am indebted to a comment Fr. Richard Ling made in response to an earlier draft of this chapter. In fact, this final version owes much to Dick Ling's comments.

12. There are signs of such analysis afoot; my intention in this chapter is to contribute to it. See Maria Harris, *Fashion Me a People*, esp. chap. 5; Bryce, "The Interrelationship Between Liturgy and Catechesis"; Kavanagh, "Teaching Through Liturgy"; Westerhoff and Neville, *Learning Through Liturgy;* Westerhoff and Willimon, *Liturgy and Learning Throughout the Life Cycle;* Browning and Reed, *The Sacraments in Religious Education and Liturgy;* and Mark Searle, "The Pedagogical Function of Liturgy."

13. Alves, *Religion*, p. 75.

14. Oosdyke, "Acquiring a Sense of Liturgy in Contemporary Times," p. 329. Oosdyke offers an insightful review of four challenges posed by "contemporary lifestyles . . . to traditional worship," namely, "activism, individualism, injustice, and a confused understanding of work" (pp. 324ff.).

15. Writing of the "symbolic crisis" in liturgy, David Power calls for an attitude of "demystification" and "suspicion," "because symbols express and effect the distribution of power (personal, social, creative, organizational, traditional, transformative). The deployment of such power has been too closely identified with ecclesiastical, social and political systems, which block its more general communication and sharing. . . . One has to be suspicious of the ways in which the Christian symbol system has evolved or liturgy is celebrated" (*Unsearchable Riches*, p. 25).

16. Schillebeeckx, *Christ the Sacrament*, p. 4.

17. *C.S.L.*, in Abbott, *Documents*, p. 141.

18. Schillebeeckx describes a sacrament as "a divine bestowal of salvation in an outwardly perceptible form which makes the bestowal manifest; a bestowal of salvation in historical visibility" (*Christ the Sacrament*, p. 5).

19. Ibid.

20. Ibid., p. 42.

21. Ibid., p. 43.

22. Ibid., pp. 43–44.

23. Emphasis added; National Conference of Catholic Bishops, "Environment and Art," p. 5.

24. I take this phrase from Schmemann's wonderful book on liturgy *For the Life of the World*.

25. Power writes, "Liturgy and sacrament when they are celebrated as acts of faith . . . transform human experience . . . by bringing it to expression and . . . relating it to the memory of Jesus Christ, to his presence in the Church through the Spirit" (*Unsearchable Riches*, pp. 3–4).

26. See Sölle, *Christ the Representative*, for a very insightful development of this theme.

27. Hughes, "Liturgy, Justice, and Peace," p. 192.

28. For my distinction between "core" and less essential liturgical symbols, I am indebted to a comment by Paul Covino. The distinction implies, as does the quote below from Vatican II, that there is a "hierarchy" of liturgical symbols—a helpful notion when dealing with the task of inculturation. For Christian communions like the Western rite of

Catholicism who are committed to a consistent liturgical rite as a mark of the church's unity, inculturating the liturgy to adequately reflect the cultures of particular peoples poses a challenge task. Vatican II, however, gave at least some helpful guidelines in this regard in Pars. 37–40 of the *C.S.L.* I quote in part: "Even in the liturgy, the Church has no wish to impose a rigid uniformity in matters which do not involve the faith or the good of the whole community. . . . Provided that the substantial unity of the Roman rite is maintained, the revision of liturgical books should allow for legitimate variations and adaptations to different groups, regions, and peoples, especially in mission lands" (Abbott, *Documents*, p. 151).

29. See M. Farley, "Beyond the Formal Principle."

30. I am indebted to Dick Ling for this analogy.

31. Rahner, *Theological Investigations*, vol. 14, p. 156. (I am indebted to Browning and Reed, *The Sacraments*, p. 11 for this quotation.)

32. McBrien, *Catholicism*, vol. 2, Glossary, p. xlv.

33. Kavanagh, *On Liturgical Theology*, p. 120.

34. Council of Trent, "Canons on the Sacraments in General," canons 6 and 8; see *The Church Teaches*, pp. 263–64.

35. The importance of the sign being truly significant for participants in the sacraments is a constant theme in Aquinas's sacramental theology. See *Summa Theologica*, III, 60, 1–8; vol. 4, pp. 2339–46. See also McBrien, *Catholicism*, vol. 2, pp. 734–36, for commentary on Aquinas's and Trent's position.

36. See Council of Trent, "Decree on Justification," chap. 7 (*The Church Teaches*, pp. 233–34.

37. Rahner explains, "Sacraments are nothing else but God's efficacious word to [humankind], the word in which God offers [Godself] to [us] and thereby liberates [our] freedom to accept God's self-communication by [our] own act" (*Foundations*, p. 415).

38. *C.S.L.*, in Abbott, *Documents*, p. 141.

39. Virgil Michel is a particularly significant example among North American liturgists. See Marx, *Virgil Michel and the Liturgical Movement*. In an excellent review essay, "Eucharist and Justice: Assessing the Legacy of Virgil Michel," Himes points out that for Michel the correlation between liturgy and social reform found its legitimation in the then being revived notion of the "Mystical Body of Christ." Michel's perception was that "the mystical body was the message needed for the Christian renewal of society and the liturgy was the method of communicating the message to believers" (p. 202). Michel was convinced "that the liturgical movement, despite its progress, was doomed unless it made the connection between worship and public life" (p. 208). Because the "mystical body" symbol reflected commitment to community and to individual dignity and participation, to approach the liturgy as the action of the whole Body of Christ would prompt commitment on a "natural level" to what was being enacted "supernaturally" in the liturgy. Himes writes, "In sum, for Michel, involvement in the liturgical life of the mystical body teaches the value of material things, fosters participation in communal activity, promotes a spirit of solidarity among persons, and encourages a disposition toward selflessness in response to the legitimate needs of the community" (p. 210).

40. See Hughes, "Liturgy, Justice, and Peace," p. 192.

41. Himes, "Eucharist and Justice," p. 213.

42. See, e.g., Searle, ed., *Liturgy and Social Justice*; Henderson et al., *Liturgy, Justice and the Reign of God*; Segundo, *The Sacraments Today*; Avila, *Worship and Politics*; Himes, "Eucharist and Justice"; J. Egan, "Liturgy and Justice: An Unfinished Agenda"; Hughes, "Liturgy, Justice, and Peace"; Seasoltz, "Justice and the Eucharist"; White, "Moving Christian Worship Toward Social Justice"; Happel, "Worship as a Grammar of Social Transformation"; Miller, "Moral Significance of Worship." Among feminist theologians, there has been until lately an absence of attention to liturgy as a source of liberation, understandable in light of women's historical experience of liturgy as a male-dominated activity in which they were denied full participation. More recently, however, fine works on liturgy from a feminist perspective have appeared. See, e.g., Ruether, *Women-Church*; Clark, Ronan, Walker, *Image-Breaking/Image-Building*; S. and T. Neufer Emswiler, *Women and Worship*.

43. Imbelli, "Trinitarian 'Politics,'" p. 231.

44. "An ecclesiastical culture of clericalism and the plight of women in the Catholic community are but the two most graphic examples of how our eucharistic rituals . . . reinforce rather than challenge the church's present life, encode a variety of messages which block people's vision of a just and participatory community of disciples" (Himes, "Eucharist and Justice," p. 218).

45. Himes encourages communities and their liturgists to ask such questions as,

What do the symbols say in our society? What do sacraments communicate to the unemployed and underemployed? To women? To those stigmatized by our culture due to illness, lifestyle or race? What is communicated to people when they gather at eucharist if they are removed from the pain of others in the society? Likewise, we can ask of the liturgical event, "who plays what roles?" Who is excluded from a role? Who is excluded from the group entirely? What patterns of human interaction are reinforced by the ritual? Subverted by it? What language is used to articulate the group's understanding of themselves? Of God? What qualities of God and the gospel life are constantly praised and held up before the community? What attributes of the divinity, what dimensions of the gospel, are rarely mentioned? (Ibid., pp. 216, 217–18)

46. See Dix, *Liturgy*, p. 13. Kavanagh claims that the communal action of the liturgy lasted into the Middle Ages with Sunday worship as a day-long celebration for the whole community. See *On Liturgical Theology*, chap. 4.

47. *C.S.L.* #14, in Abbott, *Documents*, p. 144.

48. National Conference of Catholic Bishops (hereafter N.C.C.B.), "Environment and Art," p. 10.

49. Kavanagh, *On Liturgical Theology*, pp. 97–98.

50. N.C.C.B., "Environment and Art," p. 8.

51. Ibid., p. 4.

52. Ibid., p. 19. Regarding the presider's chair, the General Instruction of the Roman Missal (hereafter G.I.) states, "Every appearance of a throne should be avoided" (Instruction 271, *The Sacramentary*, p. 42*).

53. The ecclesiology reestablished by Vatican II of the church as the "people of God" and the Body of Christ, and the emerging understanding of ministry outlined in chap. 11, now need to be reflected in the physical space that Catholic communities use for their worship. The arrangement of pews so that participants have little eye contact, positioning the altar in a removed sanctuary often with an altar railing dividing it from the "body" of the church, and situating the presider's chair behind the altar or in a thronelike position, etc., are all inappropriate. A most helpful short essay on the liturgical space now called for by contemporary understandings of church, ministry, and liturgy is Richstatter, "Your Parish Church."

54. Explaining the sense of *kyros* experienced in the liturgy, as distinct from *chronos* or measured time, Baumer writes, "Clock time is the temporal rhythm of minute following minute that gets someone through the day. Felt time, on the other hand, is that time that is not measured in seconds or minutes or hours. Felt time is measured in feelings, e.g., love, anxiety or anticipation" (*Homiletic as Rhetorical Genre*, p. 133).

55. White, *Christian Worship*, p. 76. See ibid. p. 37 on the need for "constancy" and "diversity" in worship.

56. This principle obviously poses a serious challenge for the church. Our scriptures and traditions first came to expression in a patriarchal culture, and their language and worldview reflect that ideology. But now that we are aware of how language both expresses and forms us, we must engage the challenge of appropriating those symbolic sources of God's revelation without perpetuating and repeating the cultural biases of the contexts in which they first emerged. And there are significant signs of achievement in this regard. The inclusive language lectionary prepared by the National Council of Churches is a case in point. See *An Inclusive Language Lectionary: Readings for Year A* (1983); *Readings for Year B* (1984); *Readings for Year C* (1985). See also *Lectionary for the Christian People*, published by Pueblo. Hymnals are also emerging that are linguistically inclusive and nonmilitarist. See, e.g., Duck and Bausch, eds., *Ever Flowing Streams;* S. and T. Neufer Emswiler, *Sisters and Brothers Sing*. For a study program on the what, why, and

how of "inclusive language," see my own handbook, *Language for a "Catholic" Church.* See also Clanton, *In Whose Image.*

57. See Haring, *Free and Faithful in Christ,* vol. 2.

58. Cooke, *Sacramentality,* p. 163. In a similar vein, Avila insists that liturgy should stimulate "a kind of prophetic crisis that calls into question the status quo in order to provoke change in thinking and action" (*Worship and Politics,* p. 76).

59. See Browning and Reed, *The Sacraments in Religious Education and Liturgy,* p. 8. See pp. 4–11 for a helpful overview of the shift in sacramental theology from a substantialist to what they call a "phenomenological" perspective.

60. See N.C.C.B., "Environment and Art," p. 5.

61. J. Powers, *Spirit and Sacrament,* p. 28.

62. *C.S.L.,* in Abbott, *Documents,* pp. 141, 158.

63. Merton describes the "manifest function" of sacred symbols as explicit, expressed, and conscious in the minds of participants. The "latent function" is not recognized by participants but nonetheless is powerfully formative for them. See *Social Theory and Social Structure,* pp. 115–20.

64. Ricoeur writes, "I define symbol as: any structure of signification in which a direct, primary, literal meaning designates, in addition, another meaning which is indirect, secondary, and figurative and which can be apprehended only through the first" ("Existence and Hermeneutics," p. 20).

65. Power writes, "Symbols in the cultural sense have to do with the world as meaningful whereas the kind of signs from which they are separated have to do with making living in the world functional" (*Unsearchable Riches,* p. 63).

66. Langer writes, "The logical relation between a sign and its object is a very simple one; they are associated . . . to form a pair. . . . They stand in a one-to-one correlation" (*Philosophy in a New Key,* p. 57).

67. Distinguishing them from signs, Langer explains, "Symbols are not proxy for their objects, but are vehicles for the conception of objects. . . . In talking *about* things we have conceptions of them, not the things themselves; and it is the conceptions, not the things, that symbols directly 'mean'" (ibid., pp. 60–61). And Clifford Geertz describes a symbol as "any object, act, event, quality or relation which serves as a vehicle for a conception—the conception is the symbol's 'meaning'" ("Religion as a Cultural System," p. 5).

68. We find a clue to the meaning of *symbol* in the etymology of the word. It comes from the Greek *sum ballein,* literally, "to bring together." In ancient law the word referred to a treaty, the bringing together of two sides in common commitment. This is also reflected in its first ecclesial usage where *symbol* was used to describe an agreed-upon creedal formula, i.e., the common profession of faith to which the community committed itself together. It is interesting to note that in the ancient catechumenal process, the handing over of the baptismal creed to the catechumens was called the *traditio symboli,* literally, "handing over the symbol."

69. Langer, *Problems of Art,* p. 130.

70. Greeley writes that a symbol is "an act of the creative imagination that tries to communicate not merely to our intellects but to our emotions and to our whole persons" (*The New Agenda,* p. 59).

71. Ricoeur, *Interpretation,* p. 55. Ricoeur explains that "the symbol hesitates on the dividing line between *bios* and *logos* in that they are rooted in the experience of life but are sources of discourse and meaning" (p. 59).

72. Fuchs, "Inhabiting the Symbol," pp. 163–64.

73. Langer writes: "Symbolism is the recognized key to that mental life which is characteristically human and above the level of sheer animality" (*Philosophy in a New Key,* p. 28).

74. Berger writes, "Any human experience that is to be communicated to others and preserved over time must be expressed in symbols" (*Imperative,* p. 50).

75. Sullivan, *Psychology,* p. 16.

76. Delattre, "The Rituals of Humanity," p. 5.

77. Fuchs, "Inhabiting the Symbol," p. 172.

78. Clifford Geertz offers a much quoted description of religion along these lines: "Our religion is (1) a system of symbols which acts to (2) establish powerful, pervasive and

long-lasting moods and motivations in [people] by (3) formulating conceptions of a general order of existence and (4) clothing these conceptions with such an aura of factuality that (5) the moods and motivations seem uniquely realistic" ("Religion as a Cultural System," p. 4).

79. Geertz says that religious symbols reflect "the relatively modest dogma that God is not mad" (ibid., p. 13). He footnotes Salvador de Madariaga for this phrase.

80. Tillich highlights this point when he claims that religious symbols "not only point beyond themselves to something else, they also participate in the power of that to which they point." I am indebted to Browning and Reed, *The Sacraments*, pp. 175–76, for this insight and quote from Tillich. They footnote Tillich, "Theology and Symbolism," p. 109.

81. As an anthropologist, Geertz argues that the sacred rituals of a religious community (which he calls "consecrated action") are both the primary expression and the most formative source of a community's identity in faith. This is so because in ritual, "the moods and motivations which sacred symbols induce in people and the general conceptions of order of existence which they formulate for people, meet and reinforce one another" ("Religion as a Cultural System," p. 28).

82. *C.S.L.*, in Abbott, *Documents*, p. 141.

83. Ibid., p. 142.

84. Ibid.

85. Warren, *Faith*, p. 72.

86. This is one reason why as a Catholic religious educator I am deeply committed to the full inclusion of women in all functions of ministry in the Catholic church, and especially in ordained ministry to preside at liturgy. To exclude women from full participation in this central action of the life of the church is profoundly miseducational for both the women and the men who participate in liturgy, and for the wider culture, who can find in such exclusion a "sacred canopy" to legitimate its own sexism.

87. J. Powers, *Spirit and Sacrament*, p. 28 (emphasis added).

88. *Jerome Biblical Commentary*, 2:432.

89. See Power, *Unsearchable Riches*, pp. 213–16, for a threefold schema of criteria "for validating sacramental practice." See also Browning and Reed, *The Sacraments*, p. 129; they offer a list of questions to be asked about liturgical events that suggest criteria for worship "in Spirit and truth."

90. *C.S.L.* 11, in Abbott, *Documents*, p. 143.

91. Instruction 24, *The Sacramentary*, p. 22*.

92. See *The Sacramentary*, p. 360. For the caution that establishing a "generative theme" may not be wise as a general procedure, I am indebted to the advise of Paul Covino.

93. Ibid., p. 362.

94. J. Egan writes insightfully: "To envisage the liturgy as rehearsing and celebrating a story of God independent of the stories of the people who participate is simply to perpetuate the split between faith and life, between the actions of the liturgy and the manifold activities that make up our lives as human beings" ("Liturgy and Justice," p. 252).

95. For a fine resource for creating a worship service for children, see Stewart and Berryman, *Young Children and Worship*.

96. Marty, *The Word*, p. 26.

97. Instruction 41, *The Sacramentary*, p. 24*.

98. Ibid.

99. Ibid., Instruction 42, p. 24*.

100. Ibid., Instruction 25, p. 25*.

101. Ibid., Mass of Dec. 29, p. 51.

102. Schmemann, *For the Life of the World*, p. 34.

103. *The Sacramentary*, p. 371.

104. See Oosdyke, "Acquiring a Sense of Liturgy," pp. 328–29.

105. *The Sacramentary* wisely advises that the money collected is "to be laid in a suitable place but not on the altar" (Instruction 49, p. 25*). I have always felt uncomfortable with the symbol of leaving the money from the collection anywhere near the altar or even in the sanctuary throughout the liturgy of Eucharist. We should never be encouraged to presume that our money is made "holy" by its presence at the altar. Better

to remove the collection to the sacristy immediately after its being offered, thus reminding us that the work of justice is still to be done, and much of our money to be questioned.

106. Ibid., Instruction 54, pp. 25–26*.

107. See Ibid., p. 26*.

108. Dix, *Liturgy*, pp. 105–6.

109. Instruction 56C, *The Sacramentary*, p. 26*.

110. Ibid., Instruction 56H, pp. 26–27*. Dinter points out that the still-too-common
practice in which "the priest at the altar receives 'his' host and drinks from 'his' chalice
and then turns or sends an assisting priest or eucharistic minister to the tabernacle to
communicate the faithful from the reserved sacrament" is clearly discouraged by this
directive of Instruction 56H ("Standing in the Way of Worship," p. 368).

111. Instruction 56K, *The Sacramentary*, p. 27*.

112. Ibid., Instruction 57B, p. 27*.

113. Hughes, "Liturgy, Justice, and Peace," p. 196.

114. *Fulfilled in Your Hearing* (hereafter referred to as *F.I.Y.H.*) states: "Just as the
homily flows out of the Scriptures of the Liturgy of the Word, so it should flow into the
prayers and actions of the Liturgy of the Eucharist which follows" (p. 35). (Note: This
significant document on preaching was issued by the N.C.C.B. and proposed by their
Committee on Priestly Life and Ministry).

115. *F.I.Y.H.* describes "the understanding of the homily that is central to this document" as "a scriptural interpretation of human existence which enables a community to
recognize God's active presence, to respond to that presence in faith through liturgical
word and gesture, and beyond the liturgical assembly, through a life in conformity with
the Gospel" (p. 29).

116. See Buttrick, *Homiletic*, passim.

117. These are the four components that Steimle et al. also outline as constitutive of
a good sermon. Their excellent book is about how to hold all four in balance. See *Preaching the Story*, especially the Introduction.

118. Steimle et al. write that when either one component is overemphasized, then
"the content-centered view tends toward incomprehensible jargon and toward a mecha-
nization of the grace of God; the preacher-centered view toward egotism and subjectivism; the institutional view toward the promotion of something other than the gospel; and
the need-centered view toward superficiality" (ibid., pp. 8–9).

119. See ibid., pp. 12–13.

120. *F.I.Y.H.* makes a bold statement on monological preaching: "To preach in a way
that sounds as if the preacher alone has access to the truth and knows what is best for
everyone else, or that gives the impression that there are no unresolved problems or
possibility for dialogue, is to preach in a way that may have been acceptable to those who
viewed the church primarily in clerical terms. In a church that thinks and speaks of itself
as a pilgrim people, gathered together for worship, witness and work, such preaching will
be heard only with great difficulty, if at all" (p. 5).

121. Black churches still have a rich tradition of active participation in the sermon,
where "preaching with" the congregation is still alive. This is very much in keeping with
the practice of the early church. We have a clear record that Augustine's audience at
Hippo participated actively with applause, acclamation, laughter, sighing, waving of arms
and beating of breast, shouting out in anticipation of his next point, group recitation of
scripture passages he alluded to, etc. See van der Meer, *Augustine the Bishop*, pp. 339–41,
428–29. (For this note I am indebted to the research of William Harmless. See *Augustine
and the Ancient Catechumenate*, chap. 4.)

122. This is a central theme in Martin Marty's short but excellent book, *The Word:
People Participating in Preaching*. Marty gives an insightful rationale for "preaching with"
people based on Trinitarian theology. He writes,"God speaks the creative Word, Jesus is
the Word, the Holy Spirit as hearer is agent of our participation. Here is where the notion
of our preaching-*with* as hearers has its analogy in the very picture of God which Christians enjoy" (ibid., p. 45).

123. *F.I.Y.H.*, p. 25.

124. See Baumer, *Homiletic as Rhetorical Genre*, esp. chap. 6.

125. See ibid., p. 227.

126. *F.I.Y.H.*, p. 15.

127. See Buttrick, *Homiletic*, pp. 23, 305. Buttrick writes insightfully, "In speaking of 'moves,' we are deliberately changing terminology. For years, preachers have talked of making *points* in sermons. The word 'point' is peculiar; it implies a rational, at-a-distance pointing at things, some kind of objectification. Of course, for many decades preachers did seem to suppose that there were fixed truths 'out there' to be talked about or pointed. Instead, we are going to speak of moves, of making moves in a *move*ment of language" (ibid., p. 23).

128. *F.I.Y.H.*, pp. 24–25.

129. Ibid., p. 10.

130. Ibid.

131. *F.I.Y.H.* offers a very helpful schema for facilitating a "homily preparation group." See pp. 36–38.

132. Ibid., pp. 34, 27.

133. Here Niedenthal suggests what the preacher is to effect in movement 1. "The listener must feel, 'Why, that preacher understands what it's like to face what I have to face!' If this recognition is to occur, the preacher must learn how to focus the listener's story so that the listener can recognize it" ("Focusing the Listener's Story," p. 76).

134. See *F.I.Y.H.*, p. 11. The document goes on to insist that every preacher have "the basic tools and methods" to ensure an accurate understanding of the Scriptures.

> Surely every preacher ought to have a basic library to turn to in the preparation of homilies. A good Bible dictionary will help in picturing the background of a passage; a concordance will locate other passages that are related; a 'theological' dictionary of Scripture will trace ideas that recur through Old and New Testaments; Gospel parallels will set similar texts that occur in more than one Gospel side by side. Standard commentaries on the major books of the Bible that appear in the lectionary should also be ready at hand, as well as exegetical commentaries based on the lectionary itself. (p. 12)

Chapter 13. The Church's Ministry of Peace and Justice

1. See Donahue, "Biblical Perspectives on Justice," p. 104, note 3.

2. See Heschel, *The Prophets*, pp. 199–200.

3. Brueggemann, "Voices of the Night," p. 5.

4. H. H. Schrey writes, "It can be said without exaggeration that the Bible, taken as a whole, has one theme: The history of the revelation of God's righteousness" (quoted in Donahue, "Biblical Perspectives," p. 68).

5. Donahue, "Biblical Perspectives," pp. 69, 71. Heschel writes, "In its fundamental meaning *mishpat* refers to all actions which contribute to maintaining the covenant, namely, the true relation between man [*sic*] and man [*sic*], and between God and man [*sic*]" (*The Prophets*, p. 210).

6. Miranda, *Marx and the Bible*, p. 51.

7. Donahue, "Biblical Perspectives," p. 69.

8. Leech writes, "The entire edifice of Jewish social ethics is based on God's action; because God has behaved in this way, so must God's people" (*Experiencing God*, p. 52).

9. Donahue, "Biblical Perspectives," p. 72.

10. Heschel, *The Prophets*, p. 201.

11. Brueggemann, "Voices of the Night," p. 5.

12. Donahue writes, "The prophet is one who is called not only to speak on behalf of Yahweh, but one who speaks on behalf of those who have no voice" ("Biblical Perspectives," p. 74).

13. Ibid., p. 78.

14. Von Rad, "Shalom in the Old Testament," in *Theological Dictionary*, abridged, p. 208.

15. King, "Micah," p. 288. Micah 6:8 is the climax of a passage that begins in 6:1. It is constructed as a covenant lawsuit that Yahweh brings against Israel, and indeed against all humanity (note: as the charge is first presented it is clearly Israel that is on trial, but in 6:8 the one addressed is *Adam*—all humankind).

In vv. 1–2, Yahweh summons Israel to stand trial. Yahweh is both judge and prosecutor. The mountains as foundations of the earth are God's witnesses. Israel stands accused of unfaithfulness. In vv. 3–5, the plaintiff Yahweh lays out the charge by appealing not to statutes written in law books but to the memory of Israel. The people have forgotten the mighty saving deeds of God on their behalf; they have failed to remember how God freed them from the slavery of Egypt and brought them into this fair land, their inheritance. In vv. 6–7 we hear the defendant's feeble plea. But Israel has no case. Its very response shows how accurate the charge is, how much the people have forgotten. Israel implicitly recognizes its guilt and presumes that Yahweh wants a religious sacrifice in recompense. They ask, How great must the sacrifice be? Does Yahweh's wrath demand even the sacrifice of their firstborn? But that attitude is precisely Israel's sin. They have forgotten that sacrifice offered in worship without living the justice, love, and peace demanded by the covenant is a sham. This brings Yahweh to the indictment, for Yahweh has already shown Israel what is "good." The prophetic attorney gives the classic summary of what Yahweh asks of all humankind.

16. In *Kingdom of God in History*, Viviano writes, "I realized that the best New Testament basis for such concern [i.e., social justice] was precisely Jesus' proclamation of the kingdom of God" (p. 9). Later he adds, "Thus we can see how the theme of the kingdom does provide a theological basis for social justice concerns and action on the part of Christians, in that it points to a realm of divine justice here on earth" (p. 22).

17. These are the oft-quoted lines of the Second General Synod of Catholic Bishops (1971) from their statement "Justice in the World," Gremillion, *The Gospel of Peace and Justice*, p. 514.

18. N.C.C.B. *The Challenge of Peace*, p. 8.

19. Richard McCormick, pushing back against Stanley Hauerwas's negative assessment of the natural law tradition, writes,

If Christian convictions on . . . moral questions are indeed in principle available to human insight (sharable by others than Christians), is it not more productive in a pluralistic society to urge one's convictions in the public forum in terms of what is sharable in that forum? . . . Or negatively, are Christians not argued right out of the current controversy by presenting their convictions in terms of particular and often unsharable warrants. If we argue our conviction in terms of a unique community story, others need only assert that their story is not ours. ("Scripture, Liturgy, Character and Morality," pp. 297–98)

20. Pope John XXIII, "Pacem in Terris," pars. 11–27, in Gremillion, *The Gospel of Peace and Justice*, pp. 203–6.

21. Ibid., p. 207.

22. See, *Pastoral Constitution*, in Abbott, *Documents*, pp. 236, 237.

23. Ibid., p. 226.

24. Ibid., p. 284.

25. Ibid., p. 286.

26. N.C.C.B., *Economic Justice*, p. 35.

27. Ibid.

28. Ibid., p. 36.

29. Hollenbach, *Claims in Conflict*, p. 151.

30. N.C.C.B., *Economic Justice*, p. 36. The pastoral is quoting from the *Pastoral Constitution*, par. 69.

31. Ibid., p. 36.

32. Ibid., p. 37.

33. Hollenbach gives a helpful summary when he writes,

In summary, there are three distinct but complementary notions of justice in the tradition—commutative, distributive, and social. Commutative justice guarantees the equal dignity of persons in interpersonal or private transactions. . . . Distributive justice orders the exercise of competing rights claims in such a way that no one (or at least a minimum number of persons) is excluded from participation in those goods which are essentially social. . . . Social justice, . . . is the ordering of rights through legislation and other forms of governmental activity. (*Claims in Conflict*, p. 155)

34. N.C.C.B., *The Challenge of Peace*, p. 9.
35. Ibid.
36. See ibid. p. 35. It refers to the *Pastoral Constitution*, #49.
37. Ibid., p. 24.
38. See ibid., pp. 24, 27–28.
39. The pastoral, following the tradition, distinguishes between *ius ad bellum* criteria (i.e., "*when* conditions exist which allow the resort to force," p. 28) and *ius in bello* criteria (i.e., "*how* even a justified resort to force must be conducted", ibid.). In brief, the *ius ad bellum* criteria are that the war (a) be in a "just cause," (b) be declared by the "competent authority," (c) be of "comparative justice" in that "the rights and values" threatened "justify killing," (d) be waged for the "right intention," (e) be a "last resort," (f) have a "probability of success," and (g) be marked by "proportionality" in "that the damage to be inflicted and the cost incurred by war must be proportionate to the good expected by taking up arms" (ibid., pp. 28–31).

The pastoral lists the *ius in bello* criteria as twofold: "proportionality"—this time meaning that the destruction actually done must never outweigh the good hoped for—and "discrimination"—meaning that "the lives of innocent persons may never be taken directly" (see ibid., pp. 31–34).

40. Ibid., pp. 36–37.
41. Ibid., p. 41.
42. Ibid., p. 44.
43. Ibid., p. 50.
44. See ibid., p. 70.
45. Ibid., p. 74.
46. The phrase *institutionalized violence* was first used, I believe, by the Latin American Episcopal Conference (CELAM) in its Second General Assembly held at Medellin, August–September 1968. See, e.g., the Medellin document "Peace" in Gremillion, *The Gospel of Peace and Justice*, pp. 455–64, esp. par. 16, p. 460.
47. *Pastoral Constitution*, in Abbott, *Documents*, p. 290.
48. N.C.C.B., *The Challenge of Peace*, p. 71.
49. Ibid., p. 37.
50. "Justice in the World," in Gremillion, *The Gospel of Peace and Justice*, p. 520.
51. This is the subtitle of Au's excellent book on this topic, *By Way of the Heart*.
52. Ibid, p. 18.
53. *Constitution on the Church*, in Abbott, *Documents*, p. 67.
54. See ibid., p. 65.
55. Au, *By Way of the Heart*, pp. 6, 7.
56. This phrase came into currency in Catholic church documents with the Latin American Bishops Conference (CELAM) held at Puebla in 1979. see, e.g., part 4, chap. 1, of the "Final Document" in Eagleson and Scharper, eds. *Puebla and Beyond*, pp. 263–67. Donal Dorr argues convincingly, however, that "the *reality* that is designated by the term" (i.e., *option for the poor*), "i.e., the stances taken by the Church in relation to the issue of poverty and oppression in society" and its care for "those who are victims of a society that is structurally unjust," has a substantial basis in the past 100 years of Catholic social teaching. See *Option for the Poor*, pp. 2–3.
57. N.C.C.B. *Economic Justice*, pp. x–xi.
58. Concerning this challenging choice, Dorr writes,

An option for the poor . . . means a series of choices, personal or communal, made by individuals, by communities, or even by corporate entities such as a religious congregation, a diocese, or a Church (as represented by its central administration, and, in varying degrees, by its ordinary members). It is the choice to disentangle themselves from serving the interests of those at the "top" of society and to begin instead to come into solidarity with those at or near the bottom. Such solidarity means commitment to working and living within structures and agencies that promote the interests of the less favoured sectors of society. These . . . include . . . [the] economically poor, the groups that are politically marginalised or oppressed, people discriminated against on sexual grounds, peoples that have been culturally silenced or oppressed, and those who have been religiously disinherited or deprived. (*Option for the Poor*, pp. 3–4)

59. This phrase was first used, I believe, by Joseph Cardinal Bernardin. See "Enlarging the Dialogue on a Consistent Ethic of Life."

60. See Troeltsch, *The Social Teachings of the Christian Churches*, esp. vol. 1, pp. 328–82.

61. In a resonant and classic typology, H. Richard Niebuhr depicted five ways of understanding the relationship between "Christ and Culture." They are as follows: "Christ against culture" (a radical position that places the two in opposition); "Christ of culture" (no tension at all between Christ and the world); "Christ above culture" (a synthesis position in which Jesus as human is *of* culture, but as divine is *above* culture); "Christ and culture in paradox" (sees an unbridgeable dualism between the "two kingdoms"); and "Christ as transformer of culture." (See *Christ and Culture*.)

62. *Pastoral Constitution*, in Abbott, *Documents*, p. 289.

63. Ibid., p. 226.

64. *Decree on the Laity*, in ibid., p. 495.

65. See Pope Paul VI, *Evangelization*, p. 23.

66. Ibid., pp. 24, 21.

67. Ibid., pp. 9, 22.

68. Ibid., pp. 15, 16.

69. Ibid., p. 23. Note that *Evangelii Nuntiandi* frequently grounds this justice and liberation purpose of evangelization in the symbol of God's reign (see #8, 34, etc.).

70. "Justice in the World," in Gremillion, *The Gospel of Peace and Justice*, p. 522.

71. "Declaration on Non-Christian Religions," in Abbott, *Documents*, pp. 662–65.

72. Pope John Paul II, quoted in "The Jews and Judaism in Preaching and Catechesis," in *The Living Light*, p. 114. This is an official Vatican document from the Roman Commission for Religious Relations with the Jews. I recommend it to all Christian ministers and religious educators as a helpful resource on avoiding anti-Semitism in pastoral ministry. See *The Living Light*, 22:2 (Jan. 1986), pp. 113–23. Note also Eugene Fisher, "Implementing the Vatican Document: Notes on Jews and Judaism in Preaching and Catechesis," ibid., pp. 103–11, for an excellent commentary.

73. *The 32nd Congregation of the Society of Jesus*, pp. 421, 412.

74. Marty, *Public Church*, p. 3.

75. See McBrien, *Caesar's Coin*, pp. 63–67, for a discussion of whether the separation is a "wall" or a "line." I recommend this whole work as an excellent discussion of the relationship between religion and politics in America.

76. *Pastoral Constitution*, in Abbott, *Documents*, p. 286.

77. This has been the intent of the N.C.C.B. in their recent pastoral letters. Of their pastoral *The Challenge of Peace* they state, "We want it to make a contribution to the wider public debate in our country on the danger and dilemmas of the nuclear age" (p. 3).

78. Moran, *Interplay*, p. 19.

79. O'Hare, "Peace, Justice, and the Middle Class" (p. 45).

80. See ibid. O'Hare explains, "Radical faith calls for absolute selfless love, repudiating the social interests of one's class. It calls for non-violence and a sheer identity between confession of faith and lifestyle" (ibid., p. 43). Consequently, for "middle-class" congregations he recommends "an honest, yet gradualist means for radical faith to influence religious consciousness" (ibid., p. 44).

81. From my own experience I have learned that a program in a Catholic parish on world hunger is far more likely to attract attendance and to move people to action if it is entitled and structured around a theme like "The Responsibilities of Eucharist Today."

82. Freire explains that if knowledge is merely "transmitted," "even if . . . transmitted with the intention of liberating [people]," it becomes an oppressive ideology and source of control. See *Politics*, p. 85–86.

83. Maria Montessori was convinced that young children have an amazing—she would say God-given—capacity for peace and justice that must be nurtured from the very beginning. Montessori wrote of peace, "The child would appear among us as the teacher of peace. We must gather around him [or her] to learn the mystery of humanity, to

discover in him [or her] the mystery of fundamental goodness that our outer lives and acts belie" (*Education and Peace,* p. 142). Of justice, she wrote, "The child possesses immeasurable abilities and unsuspected powers of intelligence. His [or her] heart is so sensitive to the need for justice that we must call him [or her], as Emerson also did, 'the Messiah who forever returns to dwell among fallen [people], to lead them to the Kingdom of Heaven'" (ibid., p. 142).

84. A most helpful resource for bringing a justice and peace perspective to a whole school curriculum is the "infusion method." See *The Infusion Leadership Manual.* Copies available from Justice/Peace Education Council, 20 Washington Square North, New York City, NY 10011. See also, Loretta Carey, "Adapting the Infusion Method."

85. A complete list is given in "The Covenant" from the Paulist Center Community, 5 Park Street, Boston, MA 02108.

86. Hollenbach writes, "First, some immediate experience of the suffering of the victims of injustice is important if one's heart is to remain sensitive to the continuing need for action" ("Courage and Patience," in O'Hare, *Justice,* p. 8).

87. An example of this are the "storefront meetings" held regularly by the Catholic Worker community in Boston with which I have been associated. At these meetings all guests are invited to comment and reflect on the service offered at "Haley House."

88. In this regard I appreciate the reflective dynamic built into the Catholic Worker movement from the beginning and especially by Peter Maurin's "roundtable discussions." At Haley House in Boston I have experienced this aspect of the Worker movement as meetings entitled "Clarification of Thought." These are evenings of communal resourcing and discernment that increasingly entail a dynamic of critical reflection on present praxis.

89. Butkus, *Dangerous Memory,* p. 327.

90. Moran, *Interplay,* p. 144.

91. Unpublished lecture at Boston College, Summer School, July 1981.

92. This is a constant theme, e.g., in Foucault's *Power/Knowledge.*

93. I first heard this question raised by Metz. See *Faith in History and Society.*

Chapter 14. Pastoral Counseling

1. The reader will note *pastoral care* as a new term in this book. In my own seminary training the term was never used. The typical Catholic seminary was not influenced by the fourfold division of the theological curriculum—Bible, systematics, church history, and pastoral (also called practical or applied) theology—that prevailed in Protestant seminaries from the 18th c. forward. (See Farley, *Theologia,* esp. chaps. 3, 4.) In this division the fourth "specialty" was often designated "pastoral care" (esp. in the United States) but without much consensus on what it entailed (e.g., Should it include religious education, liturgy, preaching, canon law?). Because *pastoral care* is typically used now to designate the general enterprise of which pastoral counseling is a part, I follow this pattern here. However, I see the term as interchangeable with *ministry* as I have used the term throughout.

2. My friend and colleague Claire Lowery writes, "Pastoral counseling, when it over-professionalizes, loses two things: first, a faith basis that people who come to pastors or ministers expect, and second, a community basis, a believing and sustaining community that would nourish both client and counselor" ("The Pastoral Care and Counseling Relationship," p. 207).

3. See Hiltner, *Pastoral Counseling.* Throughout this chapter my references will be to the 1981 printing of Hiltner's book.

4. These are some of the books I have found most helpful on pastoral counseling: Don Browning, *The Moral Context of Pastoral Care* (1976); Don Browning, ed., *Religious Ethics and Pastoral Care* (1983); Donald Capps, *Pastoral Care and Hermeneutics* (1984); Howard Clinebell, *Basic Types of Pastoral Care and Counseling* (1984, rev. and enlarged ed.), and *Growth Counseling* (1979); James Fowler, *Faith Development and Pastoral Care* (1987); Charles V. Gerkin, *The Living Human Document* (1984), and *Widening the Horizons,* (1986); Seward Hiltner, *Pastoral Counseling* (1949); E. Brooks Holifield, *A History of Pastoral Care*

in America (1983); Paul W. Pruyser, *The Minister as Diagnostician* (1976); Robert J. Wicks, Richard D. Parsons, Donald E. Capps, eds., *Clinical Handbook of Pastoral Counseling* (1985).

5. Fowler, *Faith Development and Pastoral Care*, p. 21. Though still quite comprehensive, Browning is more precise than Fowler in his use of the term *pastoral care*. Making distinctions between pastoral care, pastoral counseling, and pastoral psychotherapy, Browning writes, "Pastoral care is clearly the most inclusive activity of the three. It is the more or less unstructured general work with youth, couples, adults and other such groups in various types of informal and formal conversations, dialogues, and other communicative interactions. Pastoral care in this sense occurs on the street corner, at the end of a committee meeting, in the hospital room, in and around the funeral and in many other more or less marginal situations" ("Introduction to Pastoral Counseling," p. 5). See also his *The Moral Context of Pastoral Care*, pp. 104–14.

6. Gerkin, *Widening the Horizons*, p. 23.

7. Clinebell, *Pastoral Care and Counseling*, pp. 25–26. The Association of Pastoral Counselors defines pastoral counseling as "a process in which a pastoral counselor utilizes insights and principles derived from the disciplines of theology and the behavioral sciences in working with individuals, couples, families, groups, and social systems toward the achievement of wholeness and health" (quoted in Strunk, "A Prolegomenon to a History of Pastoral Counseling," p. 15).

8. Ibid., p. 373.

9. In the Catholic traditions this function is often given liturgical form in the sacrament of reconciliation. On this, Clinebell makes an interesting comment: "The need for Protestant equivalents of the sacrament of reconciliation, integrated with skilled counseling is great in our society where guilt proliferates and corporate ways of moving from guilt to reconciliation (in the confessional phase of public worship, for example) lack healing power for many people" (*Pastoral Care and Counseling*, p. 147).

10. My listing of these five functions is suggested by Clinebell; see ibid., pp. 42–43.

11. There is a general assumption that "spiritual direction" is a particularly Catholic activity, and this has some historical warrant. Including spiritual direction in the functions of pastoral counseling may help Protestant counselors to see that spiritual direction is integral to their ministry. It also suggests additional resources to enhance their pastoral counseling—the rich tradition of great spiritual literature and mentors (Julian of Norwich, John of the Cross, Teresa of Avila, Ignatius of Loyola, etc.) that should be the common inheritance of all Christians. Likewise, I refuse to draw a line of division between pastoral counseling and spiritual direction, a tendency in some Catholic literature, because I believe that spiritual directors cannot avoid some partoral counseling with directees; surely psychological health goes hand-in-hand with spiritual well-being. This alerts spiritual directors to attend to the literature of pastoral counseling as an invaluable resource in sponsoring people's spiritual journeys.

12. Clinebell writes, "It is a purpose of this book to describe a new holistic growth and liberation centered paradigm for pastoral care and liberation counseling with spiritual and ethical wholeness at its center" (*Pastoral Care and Counseling*, p. 17). Elsewhere, he defines "growth counseling" as "a human-potentials approach to the helping process that defines the goal as that of facilitating the maximum development of a person's potentialities at each life stage, in ways that contribute to the growth of others as well as to the development of a society in which all persons will have an opportunity to use their full potentials" (*Growth Counseling*, p. 18).

13. Hiltner, *Pastoral Counseling*, pp. 51, 60, 78.

14. Gerkin, *Widening the Horizons*, p. 19.

15. Gerkin, *The Living Human Document*, p. 26.

16. Ibid., p. 28. Donald Capps also proposes what he calls "a hermeneutical model of pastoral care." See *Pastoral Care and Hermeneutics*, passim.

17. See Gerkin, *The Living Human Document*, p. 38 and passim.

18. Ibid., p. 21.

19. Clinebell, *Pastoral Care and Counseling*, p. 33.

20. Ibid., pp. 31–32.

21. Gerkin, *Widening the Horizons*, p. 18.

22. "The setting and context of a pastor's counseling give it uniqueness in profound ways. The setting is the life of a gathered community of faith, a congregation. The

context is pastoral care and the other functions of the general ministry through which pastoral care can occur" (Clinebell, *Pastoral Care and Counseling*, pp. 68–69).

23. Clinebell writes:

The heart of our uniqueness is our theological and pastoral heritage, orientation, resources, and awareness. This is our frame of reference and the area of our special expertise. . . . This consciousness should help pastors recognize the spiritual dimensions present in every counseling situation. This transpersonal awareness is central in all counseling that is truly pastoral. . . . The counseling pastor's working premise that spiritual growth is an essential objective in all caring and counseling is unique among the helping professions. (Ibid., p. 67)

24. Ibid., p. 58.

25. Ibid., p. 59.

26. See Browning, *Religious Ethics and Pastoral Care*, and *The Moral Context of Pastoral Care*.

27. Browning writes, "Pastoral care in a pluralistic age must be guided by a critically and philosophically oriented practical moral theology or theological ethics. This will be necessary for handling issues of care for the diverse publics within specific churches, and it will be necessary for addressing the issues of care for the diversity found in the public world outside the church" (*Religious Ethics*, p. 17).

28. Clinebell, *Pastoral Care and Counseling*, pp. 121–22. For the other six guidelines, see ibid., p. 123.

29. Gerkin, *Widening the Horizons*, p. 101. In *The Living Human Document*, Gerkin writes: "Pastoral counseling may . . . be understood as a dialogical hermeneutical process involving the counselor and the counselee in communication across the boundaries of language worlds" (ibid. p. 128). Gerkin names those worlds as psychology and theology. I add sociology and wish to make more explicit that the primary language context for such hermeneutics is always the language of the counselees as they name and reflect upon their own praxis.

30. There is an emerging literature that reclaims the "practical" as constitutive of all Christian theology and claims that "pastoral" or "practical" theology as a discipline deserves equal status alongside Bible, systematics, and church history instead of its stereotypically "poor relation" status as a "delivery system" for the theory of the more "serious" religious disciplines. See, e.g., Browning, ed., *Practical Theology;* and Mudge and Poling, eds., *Formation and Reflection*. In the Browning collection, Tracy offers a pithy description of practical theology; it is "the mutually critical correlation of the interpreted theory and praxis of the Christian fact and the interpreted theory and praxis of the contemporary situation" ("The Foundations of Practical Theology," p. 76). I also note that the terms "practical" and "pastoral" for this emphasis in theology are more typically Protestant and Catholic respectively.

31. Clinebell, *Pastoral Care and Counseling*, p. 324.

32. Years ago Hiltner referred to counseling as "emotional re-education" in that "it should teach people how to help themselves."
See *Pastoral Counseling*, pp. 19–20. And Clinebell says, "Counseling and therapy are simply methods of re-education to help persons replace faulty learning with creative learning of attitudes, ideas, relationship skills, and values" (*Pastoral Care and Counseling*, p. 324). Clinebell names the educational dimensions of pastoral counseling as threefold: "(1) discovering what facts, concepts, values, beliefs, skills, guidance, or advice are needed by persons in coping with their problems; (2) communicating these directly or helping persons discover them (e.g., through reading); (3) helping persons utilize this information to understand their situation, make wise decisions, or handle problems constructively" (ibid., p. 325).

33. Steckel, "Directions in Pastoral Counseling," p. 27. Steckel adds, however, that in the contemporary scene "eclecticism has gained adherents in pastoral counseling. There are still vigorous advocates for particular therapeutic orientations, but they seem increasingly embattled. From the theoretical side, they are charged with expanding theory into ideology or covert theology. And from the practical side, they are charged with procedural dogmatism and rigidity" (ibid., p. 28).

34. The work of Jurgen Habermas was the original inspiration for my own understanding of critical reflection and is still a primary influence on how I intend it to be done in a shared praxis approach. It is significant that Habermas sees Freud's work as paradigmatic of a "critical science," akin to what he intends for a critical sociology apropos society. Habermas claims that the dynamic of psychoanalysis employed by the therapist with a client is to be employed as critical reflection by the social scientist toward social praxis. Reversing the point here, what religious educators do as critical reflection with a group of participants in a teaching/learning event, the pastoral counselor is to do with a counselee in a counseling event. See Habermas, *Knowledge and Human Interests,* esp. chap. 10.

35. For this claim and indeed for other insights, I note my indebtedness to the work of Dr. Joe F. Stewart and his dissertation "Shared Praxis: A Therapeutic Approach," (Perkins School of Theology, Dallas, Texas, Dec. 1986). In his doctoral research project, Stewart employed the shared praxis approach with a constant group of people over eight weeks to investigate its suitability for group counseling. He writes, "The purpose of the practicum was to determine how Thomas Groome's Shared Praxis Methodology could be appropriated in pastoral counseling from the context of Christian Education" (dissertation abstract, p. 1). In general, Stewart's findings were that shared praxis "is appropriate for use in pastoral educative counseling," that it is especially appropriate for group therapy, but its potential use in one-on-one counseling is yet to be investigated. He opines that it is more likely to be effective with people in crisis than people with chronic emotional disorders. Stewart writes, "Depressed clients would probably not respond well to this counseling approach, nor would those limited by lack of motivation, low intelligence, poor verbal abilities, or those who refuse to work on their own" (from the "Individual Praxis Evaluation," appended to the dissertation). This claim would need further investigation using the process in a one-on-one situation. Stewart also emphasizes that for its use in group therapy "leaders need to have training in group dynamics" (ibid., p. 103).

I focus on one-on-one counseling here only for convenience of description, and because I have already given many examples of using shared praxis with groups of people in Part II of this work. I'm well aware of a significant shift in pastoral counseling toward group work. Steckel writes, "as new theoretical formulations have emerged—family systems theory, for example—it is increasingly argued that one-to-one counseling is simply unproductive in many instances, since the relevant pathology is woven into the fabric of the entire system" ("Directions in Pastoral Counseling," p. 31).

36. I appreciate this notion from my own Gaelic roots; it is the typical translation of the Gaelic *anam cara.* However, *anam* means much more than "soul" (as in body/soul); it refers to the very core and heart of a person. The *anam cara* goes back to an ancient practice in Celtic spirituality of having a friend with whom one could talk in total trust and absolute honesty about the affairs of one's heart—one's very "self."

37. Gerkin, summarizing the insight of Boisen on this matter, writes as follows:

Anton Boisen's image of the human person as a 'document' to be read and interpreted analogous to the interpretation of a historical text has, up to the present, simply been taken as an admonition to begin with the experience of persons in the development of ministry theory. That certainly was central to Boisen's intention. Boisen, however, meant more than that. He meant that the depth experience of persons in the struggles of their mental and spiritual life demanded the same respect as do the historic texts from which the foundations of our Judeo-Christian faith tradition are drawn. (*The Living Human Document,* p. 38)

38. Clinebell lists six responses by the counselor that seem appropriate at different times in a counseling event. He summarizes them as follows:

An *evaluative* response is one that carries the counselor's value judgment; an *interpretive* response is one that intends to teach or explain the dynamics of a person's behavior (the 'why'); a *supportive* response is one that seeks to reassure, inspire, or undergird a person; a *probing* response is one that questions; an *understanding* response is one that reflects understanding and empathy for the counselee's feelings and attitudes; an *advising* response is one that offers what the counselor believes to be a constructive suggestion about coping with a problem. (*Pastoral Care and Coun-*

seling, pp. 94–95; Clinebell footnotes Elias H. Porter Jr. for suggesting the first five of these responses.)

It seems to me that *interpretive* responses are appropriate in movement 2 activity as long as they are offered more as questions to prompt reflection than as explanatory pronouncements, and they should invite the counselee's own active interpretation as well (e.g., "Is it possible that your love for *x* is part of the reason why you are feeling so guilty?"). So too are *supportive, understanding,* and *probing* responses appropriate in movement 2, the last to enable people to uncover the social and personal causes of present praxis. *Evaluative* responses could also be appropriate here (e.g., "This is certainly something that you will want to get cleared up") but obviously must be handled with caution and without moralizing. The style of shared praxis would suggest reserving *advising* kinds of responses (e.g., "Let me recommend that you talk to your father about your feelings— have it out with him") until the later movements. (Note: these last two examples are borrowed from Clinebell. See ibid., p. 96.)

39. Ibid., p. 56.
40. Ibid., p. 110.

Part IV. Prologue.

1. Readers may find my article "The Spirituality of the Religious Educator" helpful ancillary reading to chap. 15.
2. Rahner, *Concern for the Church,* p. 143.
3. Dr. Katherine Zappone argues convincingly that the holiness and wholeness that is Christian spirituality must be grounded in "the relational component of life." We can be holy and whole only in relationship that has "four distinct though interconnected dimensions, namely, relations with self, God, others and the natural world" (*Reconstructing Relationality,* p. 1 and passim).
4. Weaving theological convictions and spiritual commitments into one statement is faithful to a unity that was evident in the first millennium of the Church's history. Up until about the year 1200, theology was a prayerful reflection on the *sacra pagina* (sacred pages, i.e., of Scripture) and an attempt to understand one's life in faith with the purpose of spiritual wisdom—to bring oneself and others into deeper union with God. Conversely, one's spirituality shaped how one did and taught theology. It was only in the post-Scholastic era that theology became severed from spirituality, to the detriment of both. The widespread revision of theological method, especially reflected in liberation theologies and their attention to historical praxis, bodes well for the reuniting of theology and spirituality in our time. Though he is not identified as a liberation theologian, the work of Karl Rahner is an inspiring example of a unifying of theology and spirituality.
5. As I said in the preface and indicated throughout this work, a shared praxis *approach* is my own firm commitment as a Christian religious educator; it is my way of putting together as pedagogical and ministerial style some of my foundational convictions. Undoubtedly the commitments reflected in it can be existentially realized other than by the "movements" as I have outlined them, and within its movements many different "methods" can be used that are appropriate to the approach. But I'm convinced that whatever methods one uses, one's work of Christian religious education is to realize the commitments that I draw together as constitutive of a shared Christian praxis approach. For example, I believe all methods of Christian religious educators should engage people as agent-subjects-in-relationship, promote participation and dialogue, honor God's self-disclosure in people's own lives, bring people to name and reflect on their own reality, make accessible Christian Story/Vision with hermeneutics appropriate to the tradition and adequate to people's lives, enable people to make the tradition their own in their historical context, invite people to decision for faith that is lived and truth that is whole. Thus, to state the theological and spiritual foundations I intend to be operative in a shared Christian praxis approach is to articulate my creed as a Christian religious educator.
6. This is an awkward construct and perhaps a temporary one until Christians can solve the problem of how to name the First Person of the Blessed Trinity, while honoring

our Trinitarian doctrines, now that we are well advised to avoid exclusively male imagery for God. (See my *Language for a "Catholic" Church*, chapter 3.) I believe "God the Creator" is also a candidate, but it refers more to a function than a person, and though it reflects God's "first gift" of creation, it does not as readily reflect God's "second gift" of redemption/divinization. (For this note, I am indebted to comments made by Robert Imbelli to an earlier draft of the manuscript.)

Chapter 15. My Pedagogical Creed as a Christian Religious Educator

1. I deliberately limit my footnoting throughout the Creed because many of its themes have already had substantial attention. In the articles on theological anthropology, there are strong echoes of Rahner, as here, for example. Rahner writes, "Now we are coming to the innermost center of the Christian understanding of existence when we say: Man [*sic*] is the event of a free, unmerited and forgiving, and absolute self-communication of God" (*Foundations*, p. 116).

2. Here I am endeavoring to balance a dual affirmation of what the Scholastic theological tradition calls "uncreated" and "created" grace. *Uncreated grace* refers to God's "original" graciousness toward human beings: God, in the act of creative self-giving, disposes our human existence to receive God's outreach in love. *Created grace* refers to the ongoing assistance that God gives to heal and strengthen us beyond our "natural" powers and that enables us to cooperate freely with what God is doing through us.

3. Nelson refers to Scripture and tradition as "the residue of how previous generations responded to God" (*How Faith Matures*, p. 92). Nelson adds, "The residue is not God, but it may guide us to our own experience with God" (ibid.).

4. This is why the doctrine of Chalcedon—that Jesus is consubstantial with God in divinity and with us in humanity—must stand at the center of Christian faith, not as an abstract idea or a baffling mystery but as a hopeful symbol of the at-one-ment that Jesus makes possible between God and humankind. See also chapter 9, note 12.

5. As noted in chap. 13, I take this phrase from the Apostolic Exhortation of Pope Paul VI *On Evangelization in the Modern World* (*Evangelii Nuntiandi*).

6. By affirming this turn to the historical Jesus, I am not recommending a naive reading of the Gospels as was often the practice during the "first quest" for the historical Jesus. That "first quest" began with Reimarus (1694–1768), found its high point in Strauss's book *The Life of Jesus* (1835), was expanded upon by Renan, von Harnack, et al., and ended, probably, with Wilhelm Wrede's work *The Messianic Secret in the Gospels* (1901). I write here, instead, in the spirit of what is usually called the "new quest" for the historical Jesus, which does not look for a biography of Jesus or for access to an "uninterpreted" Jesus but contends that there is continuity between the teachings of the historical Jesus and the beliefs that the early church held about him. This movement began with Ernst Kasemann's ground-breaking essay of 1953 "The Problem of the Historical Jesus," and Bornkamm's *Jesus of Nazareth* (1960) was probably its first major work (followed by Cullmann, Dodd, Jeremias, Brown, etc.). The new quest employs redaction criticism to analyze the editing and selecting that went on in the actual writing process (stage three), form criticism that analyzes the smaller pericopes and their *Sitz im Leben* (situation in life) from the precanonical tradition between the time of Jesus and the writing of the first Gospel (stage two). Exponents of the "new quest" are confident that those critical tools (along with source criticism, literary criticism, etc.) give evidence of how Jesus was first preached and, indirectly at least, how he was perceived in the course of his own historical ministry (stage one).

7. See McBrien, *Catholicism*, vol. 1, pp. 375–82, for a review of five of the "partial Jesuses" that are often the selected preference of Christians.

8. Aristotle, *Nichomachean Ethics*, book 3, chap. 6:12, p. 147.

9. My articulation here obviously reflects my Trinitarian faith, which is indeed my own Christian confession. But many of the great religious traditions of the world express an awareness of God's Spirit in one way or another. In the Hebrew Scriptures, e.g., God's Spirit is the power of Yahweh as life-giving breath (*ruah*) in the world to sustain and lead all people and all creation to a share in divine life, wisdom, and holiness. And I'm con-

vinced that Christian pneumatology has its substructure in the natural experiences of people of the ubiquitous presence of a life-giving Spirit that is gift to human lives.

10. The history of Trinitarian doctrine has been marked by a controversy between Eastern and Western Christianity, often referred to as "the filioque debate." The "filioque" and Western position contends that the Holy Spirit proceeds from the Father *and* the Son—the doctrine of "Double Procession." It was challenged by the Eastern churches who, anxious to maintain that there is a single "font of divinity" in the Godhead, favored the original formula of the Nicene-Constantinopolitan Creed that the Holy Spirit proceeds "from the Father alone" and rejected the "filioque" clause in the Creed. The Council of Florence (1439), however, did not require the filioque clause in the recitation of the Creed, and in Western Christianity it is now theologically acceptable to say either that the Spirit proceeds from the Father *and* the Son or from the Father *through* the Son.

11. This list of the "gifts of the Holy Spirit" has emerged over history in Christian theological and catechetical tradition and has pointed, ironically, to Isa. 11:1–3 as its classic source.

12. Robert Imbelli writes, "Christian trinitarianism fosters the transformation of the political, just as it summons us to the transformation of every dimension of human existence. . . . trinitarian faith neither fuses nor divorces religion and politics; rather it calls both to transformative dialogue" ("Trinitarian 'Politics,'" p. 231).

13. See the *Constitution on the Church,* in Abbott, *Documents,* chap. 1, entitled "The Mystery of the Church." My quote here is from Pope Paul VI and is footnoted to the above title of the *Constitution*'s first chapter. See ibid., p. 14.

14. I have footnoted Elisabeth Schüssler Fiorenza throughout this work for the phrase "inclusive discipleship of equals," but the model of the church as a "community of disciples" was first popularized by Avery Dulles. See *A Church to Believe In,* chap. 1. Dulles cites Pope John Paul II's encyclical *Redemptor Hominis* (1979) as a source of this model in his own thinking. See ibid., p. 7.

15. Vatican II's *Dogmatic Constitution on Divine Revelation* gives what initially sounded like an amazing admission by a church that had so strenuously claimed to have "the fullness of truth." The *Constitution* states, "As the centuries succeed one another, the Church constantly moves forward toward the fullness of divine truth until the words of God reach their complete fulfillment in her [*sic*]" (Abbott, *Documents,* p. 116).

16. Pope Paul VI, *Evangelization,* p. 15.

17. I take this list of the forms of the church's diakonia from Letty Russell (see *Future,* p. 118).

18. The tendency of the "right" can be to divinize the church to the point that its humanity is forgotten, to make it into a "perfect society" (Bellarmine's phrase) beyond question or critique. The tendency of the "left" can be to overlook its divine dimension and see it entirely as a human construction and for purely social purposes. Both extremes, I believe, should be avoided. As with the Christological doctrine of two natures but one person in Jesus, so too the church's divine and human elements are to be affirmed, with the two dimensions neither subsuming each other nor being dichotomized as if there were two churches.

19. This has been *the* central theme throughout Part III of this work. For a summary, see my essay "Parish as Catechist."

Bibliography of Sources Quoted or Cited

Abbercrombie, Nicholas. *Class, Structure and Knowledge*. Oxford: Basil Blackwell, 1980.

Abbott, Walter M., ed. *The Documents of Vatican II*. Translated by Joseph Gallagher. New York: America Press, 1966.

Ackermann, Robert. *Theories of Knowledge*. New York: McGraw-Hill, 1965.

Alves, Rubem A. *Tomorrow's Child: Imagination, Creativity and The Rebirth of Culture*. San Francisco: Harper & Row, 1972.

———. *What is Religion?* Translated by Don Vinzant. Maryknoll, NY: Orbis Books, 1984.

Anderson, Bernhard W. *The Living Word of the Bible*. Philadephia: Westminister Press, 1979.

The Apostolic Fathers. Edited by Jack N. Sparks. Nashville: T. Nelson, 1978.

The Apostolic Tradition of Hippolytus. Translated by Burton S. Easton. Cambridge: Cambridge Univ. Press, 1934.

Aquinas, Thomas. *The Catechetical Instructions of St. Thomas Aquinas*. Translated by Joseph B. Collins. New York: Joseph F. Wagner, 1947.

———. *Commentary on Aristotle's Physics*. Translated by Richard J. Blackwell, Richard J. Spath, and W. Edmund Thirlkel. New Haven, CT: Yale Univ. Press, 1963.

———. *On the Power of God*. Translated by Father Lawrence Shapcote of the English Dominican Fathers. London: Burns, Oates & Washbourne, 1932–34.

———. *The Soul*. Translated by John Patrick Rowan. St. Louis: B. Herder, 1949.

———. *Summa Contra Gentiles*. Translated by A. C. Pegis (book 1), J. F. Anderson (book 2), V. J. Bourke (book 3), and C. J. O'Neil (book 4). Notre Dame, IN: Univ. of Notre Dame Press, 1955–57.

———. *Summa Theologica*. 5 vols. Translated by the Fathers of the English Dominican Province. Westminster, MD: Christian Classics, 1981.

———. *The Teacher*. In *Basic Writings in Christian Education*. Edited by Kendig B. Cully. Philadelphia: Westminster Press, 1960.

———. *The Teacher (De Magistro)*. In *The Philosophy of Teaching of St. Thomas Aquinas*. Translated by Helen Mayer. Milwaukee: Bruce, 1929.

———. *Truth (De Veritate)*. Translated by Robert W. Mulligan (vol. 1), James V. McGlynn (vol. 2), and Robert W. Schmidt (vol. 3). Chicago: Henry Regnery, 1952.

Arieti, Silvaro. *Creativity: The Magic Synthesis*. New York: Basic Books, 1976.

Aristotle. *The 'Art' of Rhetoric*. Loeb Classical Library. 1926.

———. *De Anima*. Translated by R. W. Hicks. New York: Arno Press, 1976.

———. *The Basic Works of Aristotle*. Edited and with an Introduction by Richard McKeon. New York: Random House, 1941.

———. *Metaphysics*. Loeb Classical Library. 1935.

————. *Nicomachean Ethics*. Loeb Classical Library. 1982.

————. *On the Soul*. Loeb Classical Library. 1957.

————. *Parts of Animals*. Loeb Classical Library. 1937.

————. *Parva Naturalia: On Memory and Recollection*. Loeb Classical Library. 1957.

————. *The Physics*. 2 vols. Loeb Classical Library. 1929–34.

————. *The Poetics*. Loeb Classical Library. 1927.

Aronowitz, Stanley. "Mass Culture and the Eclipse of Reason: The Implications for Pedagogy." *College English* (Apr. 1977): 768–74.

Assmann, Hugo. *Theology for a Nomad Church*. Translated by Paul Burns. New York: Orbis Books, 1976.

Au, Wilkie. *By Way of the Heart: Toward a Holistic Christian Spirituality*. New York: Paulist Press, 1989.

Augustine. *Answer to Skeptics*. Translated by Denis J. Kavanaugh. In *Writings of Saint Augustine*, vol. 1. The Fathers of the Church. New York: CIMA, 1948.

————. *Augustine: Earlier Works*. Selected and translated by John H. S. Burleigh. Library of Christian Classics, vol. 6. Philadelphia: Westminster Press, 1953.

————. *Augustine: Later Works*. Selected and translated by John Burnaby. Library of Christian Classics. Ichthus ed. Philadelphia: Westminster Press, 1955.

————. "The Catholic and Manichaean Ways of Life." In *The Fathers of the Church*, vol. 56. Translated by Donald Gallagher and Idella Gallagher. Washington, DC: Catholic Univ. of America Press, 1965.

————. *City of God*. Edited by Vernon J. Bourke. Translated by Gerald G. Walsh et al. Garden City, NY: Doubleday, Image Books, 1958.

————. *The Confessions of Saint Augustine*. Translated by John K. Ryan. Garden City, NY: Doubleday, Image Books, 1960.

————. *Divine Providence and the Problem of Evil (De Ordine)*. Translated by Robert P. Russell. In *Writings of St. Augustine*, vol. 1. The Fathers of the Church. New York: CIMA, 1948.

————. *The Enchiridion on Faith, Hope and Love*. Gateway ed. Translated by Henry Paolucci. Chicago: Regnery, 1961.

————. *The Essential Augustine*. Edited by Vernon J. Bourke. Indianapolis: Hackett, 1981.

————. "The First Catechetical Instruction (De Catechizandis Rudibus)." Translated by Joseph P. Christopher. In *Ancient Christian Writers*, vol. 2. Westminster, MD: Newman Press, 1962.

————. *Homilies on the Gospel of John*. Translated by John Gibb. In *Nicene and Post-Nicene Fathers*, vol. 7. New York: Charles Scribner's Sons, 1888.

————. *The Literal Meaning of Genesis*. 2 vols. Translated by John H. Taylor. In *Ancient Christian Writers*, nos. 41–42. New York: Newman Press, 1982.

————. "The Magnitude of the Soul *(De Quantitate Animae).*" Translated by John J. McMahon. In *Writings of Saint Augustine*, vol. 2. The Fathers of the Church. New York: CIMA, 1947.

————. *On The Measure of the Soul*. Translated by Francis Tourscher. Philadelphia: Peter Reilly, 1933.

————. *The Teacher*. In *Ancient Christian Writers*, no. 9. Translated by Joseph M. Colleran. New York: Newman Press, 1949.

————. *The Trinity*. In *The Fathers of the Church*, vol. 45. Translated by Stephen McKenna. Washington, DC: Catholic Univ. of America Press, 1963.

———. *The Works of Aurelius Augustinus.* Edited by Marcus Dods. Edinburgh: T. & T. Clark, 1871–76.

Aulen, Gustaf. *Christus Victor.* Translated by A. G. Herbert. New York: Macmillan, 1967.

Avila, Rafael. *Worship and Politics.* Translated by Alan Neely. Maryknoll, NY: Orbis Books, 1981.

Bacon, Francis. *Novum Organum.* Edited by Thomas Fowler. Oxford: Oxford Univ. Press, 1889.

Bainton, Roland H. *Christianity.* Boston: Houghton Mifflin, 1987.

Baldwin, James Mark, ed. 3 vols. in 4. *Dictionary of Philosophy and Psychology.* Gloucester, MA: Peter Smith, 1960.

Bandas, Rudolph G. *Catechetical Methods.* New York: J. F. Wagner, 1929.

Baronowski, Arthur. *Creating Small Faith Communities.* Cincinnati: St. Anthony Messenger Press, 1988.

Barr, James. *The Bible and the Modern World.* New York: Harper & Row, 1973.

Barrett, William. *Death of the Soul: From Descartes to the Computer.* Garden City, NY: Doubleday, Anchor Books, 1986.

Baum, Gregory. *The Priority of Labor.* New York: Paulist Press, 1982.

Baumer, Fred A. *Toward the Development of Homiletic as Rhetorical Genre.* Ph.D. diss., Northwestern Univ., June 1985.

Bausch, William J. *Traditions, Tensions, Transitions in Ministry.* Mystic, CT.: Twenty-third Publications, 1982.

Belenky, Mary Field, Blythe Clinchy McVicker, Nancy Rule Goldberger, and Jill Mattuck Tarule. *Women's Ways of Knowing: The Development of Self, Voice, and Mind.* New York: Basic Books, 1986.

Bellack, Arno. "History of Curriculum Thought and Practice." *Review of Educational Research* 39:3 (June 1969): 283–90.

Bellah, Robert, et al. *Habits of the Heart.* San Francisco: Harper & Row, Perennial Library, 1985.

Benjamin, Walter. *Illuminations.* Edited and with an Introduction by Hannah Arendt. Translated by Harry Zohn. New York: Harcourt, Brace & World, 1968.

Berger, Peter L. *The Heretical Imperative.* New York: Doubleday, Anchor Books, 1979.

———. *Invitation to Sociology: A Humanistic Perspective.* Garden City, NY: Doubleday, 1963.

———. *The Sacred Canopy.* Garden City, NY: Doubleday, Anchor Books, 1969.

Berger, Peter L., and Thomas Luckmann. *The Social Construction of Reality.* Garden City, NY: Doubleday, 1966.

Berkeley, George. *A Treatise Concerning the Principles of Human Knowledge.* LaSalle, IL: Open Court, 1950.

Bernardin, Joseph Cardinal. "Enlarging the Dialogue on a Consistent Ethic of Life." *Origins* 13:43 (Apr. 5, 1984): 705, 707–9.

Bernstein, Richard J. *Beyond Objectivism and Relativism.* Philadelphia: Univ. of Pennsylvania Press, 1983.

———. *Praxis and Action.* Philadelphia: Univ. of Pennsylvania Press, 1971.

Bernstein, Richard J., ed. *Habermas and Modernity: Studies in Contemporary German Social Thought.* Cambridge, MA: MIT Press, 1985.

Bettenson, Henry, ed. *Documents of the Christian Church.* 2d ed. New York: Oxford Univ. Press, 1963.

Blanshard, Brand. "Wisdom." In *The Encyclopedia of Philosophy,* vol. 8, edited by Paul Edwards. New York: Macmillan, 1967.

Bloom, Benjamin S., et al. *Taxonomy of Educational Objectives: Cognitive Domain.* New York: Longmans, Green, 1956.

Boesak, Allan. *Farewell to Innocence: A Socio-ethical Study on Black Theology and Power.* Maryknoll, New York: Orbis Books, 1977.

Boff, Leonardo. *Church, Charism and Power.* New York: Crossroad, 1985.

———. *Ecclesiogenesis: The Base Communities Reinvent the Church.* Maryknoll, NY: Orbis Books, 1986.

Bonhoeffer, Dietrich. *The Cost of Discipleship.* New York: Macmillan, 1969.

Bonino, Jose Miguez. *Christians and Marxists.* Grand Rapids: Eerdmans, 1976.

Bornkamm, Gunther. *Jesus of Nazareth.* Translated by Irene McLuskey and Fraser McLuskey with James M. Robinson. New York: Harper, 1960.

Botkin, James W., Mahdi Elmandjra, and Mircea Malitza. *No Limits to Learning.* New York: Pergamon Press, 1979.

Bower, William Clayton. "A Curriculum for Character and Religious Education in a Changing Culture." *Religious Education* 25 (Feb. 1930): 130–33.

Bowman, Locke E., Jr. *Teaching for Christian Hearts, Souls, and Minds: A Constructive Holistic Approach to Christian Education.* Harper & Row: San Francisco, 1990.

Boyack, Kenneth, ed. *Catholic Evangelization Today: A New Pentecost for the United States.* New York: Paulist Press, 1987.

Boydston, Jo Ann, ed. *Guide to the Works of John Dewey.* Carbondale, IL: Southern Illinois Univ. Press, 1970.

Boys, Mary C. "Access to Traditions and Transformation." In *Tradition and Transformation in Religious Education,* edited by Padraic O'Hare. Birmingham, AL: Religious Education Press, 1979.

———. *Biblical Interpretation in Religious Education.* Birmingham, AL: Religious Education Press, 1980.

———. *Educating in Faith: Maps and Visions.* San Francisco: Harper & Row, 1989.

Boys, Mary, ed. *Educating for Citizenship and Discipleship.* New York: Pilgrim Press, 1989.

Bracken, Harry M. *Berkeley.* London: Macmillan, 1974.

Braxton, Edward K. *The Wisdom Community.* New York: Paulist Press, 1980.

Brennan, Margaret. "Sing a New Song unto the Lord: The Relationship Between Spirituality and Social Responsibility." In *Education for Peace and Justice,* edited by Padraic O'Hare. San Francisco: Harper & Row, 1973.

Brown, Raymond E. "Bishops and Theologians: 'Dispute' Surrounded by Friction." *Origins* 7:43 (Apr. 13, 1978): 673–82.

———. *The Churches the Apostles Left Behind.* New York: Paulist Press, 1984.

———. *The Gospel According to John.* 2 vols. Anchor Bible Series, vol. 29. Garden City, NY: Doubleday, 1966.

———. *Priest and Bishop.* Paramus, NJ: Paulist Press, 1970.

Brown, Robert McAfee. *Theology in a New Key.* Philadelphia: Westminister Press, 1978.

Browning, Don S. "Introduction to Pastoral Counseling." In *Clinical Handbook of Pastoral Counseling,* edited by Robert J. Wicks, et al. New York: Paulist Press, 1985.

———. *The Moral Context of Pastoral Care.* Philadelphia: Westminister Press, 1976.

———. "Pastoral Theology in a Pluralistic Age." In *Practical Theology,* edited by Don S. Browning. San Francisco: Harper & Row, 1983.

————. "Practical Theology and Religious Education." In *Formation and Reflection: The Promise of Practical Theology*, edited by Louis S. Mudge and James N. Poling. Philadelphia: Fortress Press, 1987.

————. *Religious Ethics and Pastoral Care*. Philadelphia: Fortress Press, 1983.

Browning, Don S., ed. *Practical Theology*. San Francisco: Harper & Row, 1983.

Browning, Robert L., and Roy A. Reed. *The Sacraments in Religious Education and Liturgy*. Birmingham, AL: Religious Education Press, 1985.

Brueggemann, Walter. *The Creative Word*. Philadelphia: Fortress Press, 1982.

————. *The Prophetic Imagination*. Philadelphia: Fortress Press, 1978.

————. "Voices of the Night—Against Justice." In *To Act Justly, Love Tenderly, Walk Humbly*, by Walter Brueggemann, Sharon Parks, and Thomas H. Groome. New York: Paulist Press, 1986.

Bryce, Mary Charles. "The Interrelationship Between Liturgy and Catechesis." *American Benedictine Review* 28 (Mar. 1977): 1–29.

Buber, Martin. *Between Man and Man*. Translated by R. G. Smith. London: Kegan Paul, 1947.

————. *I and Thou*. Translated by Walter Kaufmann. New York: Charles Scribner's Sons, 1970.

————. *Tales of the Hasidim, The Early Masters*. Translated by Olga Marx. New York: Schocken Books, 1947–48.

Burghardt, Walter. "Free Like God: Recapturing an Ancient Anthropology." *Theology Digest* 26:4 (Winter 1978): 343–64.

Burnet, John. *Aristotle on Education*. Cambridge: Cambridge Univ. Press, 1936.

Bushnell, Horace. *Christian Nurture*. New Haven, CN: Yale Univ. Press, 1967.

Butkus, Russell. *Dangerous Memory: Toward a Pedagogical Strategy for Social Justice Education*. Ph.D. diss., Boston College, June 1985.

Buttrick, David. *Homiletic: Moves and Structures*. Philadelphia: Fortress Press, 1987.

Calvin, John. "The Catechism of the Church of Geneva." In *Basic Writings in Christian Education*, edited by Kendig B. Cully. Philadelphia: Westminster Press, 1960.

————. *Institutes of the Christian Religion*. 2 vols. Edited by John T. NcNeill. Translated by Ford Lewis Battles. Library of Christian Classics, vols. 20–21. Philadelphia: Westminster Press, 1960.

————. *Instruction in Faith (1537)*. Translated by Paul T. Fuhrmann. Philadelphia: Westminster Press, 1949.

Campbell, Peter A., and Edwin M. McMahon. *Bio-Spirituality*. Chicago: Loyola Univ. Press, 1985.

Canon Law Society of America, "Consensus Statement from the Symposium on Women and Church Law." In *Sexism and Church Law*, edited by James Coriden. New York: Paulist Press, 1977.

Capps, Donald. *Pastoral Care and Hermeneutics*. Philadelphia: Fortress Press, 1984.

Carey, Loretta. "Adapting the Infusion Method." *Momentum* 13:3 (Oct. 1982): 40–42

Carmody, John. "The Realism of Christian Life." In *A World of Grace*, edited by Leo J. O'Donovan. New York: Crossroad, 1984.

Carr, Anne E. "Starting with the Human." In *A World of Grace*, edited by Leo J. O'Donovan. New York: Crossroad, 1984.

A Catechism of Christian Doctrine: Prefaced and Enjoined by Order of the Third Plenary Council of Baltimore (The Baltimore Catechism). New York: D. and J. Sadlier, 1885.

The Catechism of the Council of Trent. Translated by J. Donovan. New York: Christian Press Association, 1829.

Catholic Biblical Association Task Force on the Role of Women in Early Christianity. "Women and Priestly Ministry." *Catholic Biblical Quarterly* 41:4 (Oct. 1979): 608–13.

Cavalier, Wayne, and William Lowe. "Socialization and Shared Praxis." *The Living Light* 22:3 (Mar. 1986): 222–30.

Cavalletti, Sofia. *The Religious Potential of the Child.* New York: Paulist Press, 1983.

Champlin, Joseph. *The Marginal Catholic: Challenge, Don't Crush.* Notre Dame, IN: Ave Maria Press, 1989.

The Church Teaches: Documents of the Church in English Translation. Translated and compiled by John F. Clarkson, et al. Rockford IL: Tan Books, 1973.

Cicero, Marcus Tullius. *De Finibus Bonorum et Malorum.* Loeb Classical Library. 1914.

————. *De Natura Deorum Academica.* Loeb Classical Library. 1933.

Clanton, Jann Aldredge. *In Whose Image: God and Gender.* New York: Crossroad, 1990.

Clark, Linda, Marian Ronan, and Eleanor Walker. *Image Breaking/Image Building: A Handbook for Creative Worship with Women of Christian Tradition.* New York: Pilgrim Press, 1981.

Clausen, J. A., ed. *Socialization and Society.* Boston: Little, Brown, 1968.

Cleary, Edward L. *Crisis and Change: The Church in Latin America Today.* Maryknoll, NY: Orbis Books, 1985.

Clement of Alexandria. "Christ the Educator." In *Basic Writings in Christian Education,* edited by Kendig B. Cully. Philadelphia: Westminster Press, 1960.

Clinebell, Howard. *Basic Types of Pastoral Care and Counseling.* Rev. and enlarged ed. Nashville: Abingdon Press, 1984.

————. *Contemporary Growth Therapies.* Nashville: Abingdon Press, 1981.

————. *Growth Counseling.* Nashville: Abingdon Press, 1979.

Coe, George Albert. *A Social Theory of Religious Education.* New York: Arno Press and the New York Times, 1969.

Coleman, John A. *An American Strategic Theology.* New York: Paulist Press, 1982.

Coleman, Lyman. Serendipity Personal Growth Programs. Waco, TX: Creative Resources, 1975.

Cone, James H. *Black Theology and Black Power.* New York: Seabury Press, 1969.

————. *Speaking the Truth.* Grand Rapids: Eerdmans, 1986.

Congar, Yves M. *A History of Theology.* Edited and translated by Hunter Guthrie. Garden City, NY: Doubleday, 1968.

————. "The Magisterium and Theologians—A Short History." *Theology Digest* 25:1 (Spring 1971): 15–20.

Conn, Walter E., ed. *Conversion: Perspectives on Personal and Social Transformation.* New York: Alba House, 1978.

Connerton, Paul, ed. *Critical Sociology.* New York: Penguin Books, 1976.

Cooke, Bernard. *Ministry to Word and Sacraments.* Philadelphia: Fortress Press, 1976.

————. *Sacraments and Sacramentality.* Mystic, CT: Twenty-third Publications, 1983.

Copleston, Frederick. *A History of Philosophy.* 9 vols. in 3. Garden City, NY: Image Books, 1985.

Cornford, Francis MacDonald. *Before and After Socrates.* Cambridge: Cambridge Univ. Press, 1932.

Cox, Harvey. *Religion in the Secular City*. New York: Simon & Schuster, 1984.

Crawford, Marisa L., and Graham Rossiter. *Teaching Religion in the Secondary School*. Sydney, Australia: Province Resource Group, Christian Brothers, 1985.

Crossan, John Dominic. *The Dark Interval: Towards a Theology of Story*. Niles, IL: Argus Communications, 1975.

———. *In Parables*. New York: Harper & Row, 1973.

Crowe, Frederick E. *The Lonergan Enterprise*. Cambridge, MA: Cowley Publications, 1980.

———. *Old Things and New: A Strategy for Education*. The Lonergan Workshop *Journal*, supplementary issue, vol. 5. Edited by Fred Lawrence. Atlanta: Scholars Press, 1985.

Cully, Kendig Brubaker, ed. *Basic Writings in Christian Education*. Philadelphia: Westminster Press, 1960.

Curley, E. M. *Descartes Against the Skeptics*. Cambridge, MA: Harvard Univ. Press, 1978.

Curtis, Bernard, and Wolfe Mays, eds. *Phenomenology and Education*. London: Methuen, 1978.

Daley, Leo C. *The Writings of Saint Augustine*. New York: Monarch Press, 1965.

Daly, Mary. *Gyn/Ecology: The Metaethics of Radical Feminism*. Boston: Beacon Press, 1978.

Danziger, Kurt. *Readings in Child Socialization*. London: Pergamon Press, 1970.

Davaney, Sheila Greene. "Problems with Feminist Theory: Historicity and the Search for Sure Foundations." In *Embodied Love: Sensuality and Relationship as Feminist Values*, edited by Paula M. Looey, Sharon A. Farmer, and Mary Ellen Ross. San Francisco: Harper & Row, 1987.

David, Thomas G., and Benjamin D. Wright, eds. *Learning Environments*. Chicago: Univ. of Chicago Press, 1975.

Delattre, Roland. "The Rituals of Humanity." *Prospects: An Annual of American Studies* 5 (1979).

Deleuze, Gilles, *Kant's Critical Philosophy*. Translated by Hugh Tomlinson and Barbara Habberjam. Minneapolis: Univ. of Minnesota Press, 1984.

Denzinger, Henry. *The Sources of Catholic Dogma*. Translated by Ray J. DeFerrari. New York: B. Herder Books, 1957.

Derrida, Jacques. *Dissemination*. Translated by Barbara Johnson. Chicago: Univ. of Chicago Press, 1981.

Descartes, René. *Discourse on Method*. In *The Philosophical Writings of Descartes*, vol. 1. Translated by John Cottingham, Robert Stoothoff, and Dugald Murdoch. New York: Cambridge Univ. Press, 1985.

———. *Meditations on First Philosophy*. In *The Philosophical Writings of Descartes*, vol. 2. Translated by John Cottingham, Robert Stoothoff, and Dugald Murdoch. New York: Cambridge Univ. Press, 1984.

———. *The Passions of the Soul*. In *The Philosophical Writings of Descartes*, vol. 1, Translated by John Cottingham, Robert Stoothoff, and Dugald Murdoch. New York: Cambridge Univ. Press, 1985.

———. *Principles of First Philosophy*. In *The Philosophical Writings of Descartes*, vol. 1. Translated by John Cottingham, Robert Stoothoff, and Dugald Murdoch. New York: Cambridge Univ. Press, 1985.

———. *Rules for the Directions of the Mind*. In *The Philosophical Writings of Descartes*, vol. 1. Translated by John Cottingham, Robert Stoothoff, and Dugald Murdoch. New York: Cambridge Univ. Press, 1985.

Dewey, John. *Art as Experience*. New York: Paragon Books, 1934.

———. *Democracy and Education*. New York: Macmillan, 1916.

————. *Experience and Education.* New York: Collier Books, 1938.

————. *How We Think.* Boston: D. C. Heath, 1910.

————. *Liberalism and Social Action.* New York: G. P. Putnam & Sons, 1935.

————. "My Pedagogic Creed." In *Dewey on Education,* compiled by Martin S. Dworkin. Classics in Education, no. 3. New York: Teachers College Press, 1971.

————. *Reconstruction in Philosophy.* Enlarged ed. Boston: Beacon Press, 1948.

Dictionary of Philosophy. Edited by Dogobert Runes. New York: Philosophical Library, 1983.

"The Didache: The Teaching of The Twelve Apostles." Translated by James A. Kleist. In *Ancient Christian Writers,* vol. 6. Westminster, MD: Newman Press, 1948.

Dinter, Paul E. "Standing in the Way of Worship." *Commonweal,* June 16, 1989.

Dix, Dom Gregory. *The Shape of the Liturgy.* Notes by Paul V. Marshall. San Francisco: Harper & Row, 1945.

Donahue, John R. "Biblical Perspectives on Justice." In *The Faith That Does Justice,* edited by John C. Haughey. New York: Paulist Press, 1977.

Donovan, Josephine. *Feminist Theory: The Intellectual Traditions of American Feminism.* New York: Continuum, 1988.

Donovan, Vincent J. *Christianity Rediscovered: An Epistle from the Masai.* Notre Dame, IN: Fides/Claretian, 1978.

Dorr, Donal. *Option for the Poor: A Hundred Years of Vatican Social Teaching.* Maryknoll, NY: Orbis Books, 1983.

Dosh, Terence. "Clericalism." *Ministries* (Oct. 1981): 21–23.

Doyle, Walter. "Learning and the Classroom Environment: An Ecological Analysis." *Journal of Teacher Education* 28 (1977): 51–55.

Dreitzel, Hans Peter, ed. *Childhood and Socialization.* New York: Macmillan, 1973.

Duck, Ruth C., and Michael G. Bausch, eds. *Ever Flowing Streams.* New York: Pilgrim Press, 1981.

Dulles, Avery. *A Church to Believe In.* New York: Crossroad, 1982.

————. "The Meaning of Faith Considered in Relationship to Justice." In *The Faith That Does Justice,* edited by John C. Haughey. New York: Paulist Press, 1977.

————. *Models of the Church.* Garden City, NY: Doubleday, 1974.

————. *Models of Revelation.* Garden City, NY: Doubleday, 1983.

————. *The Resilient Church.* Garden City, NY: Doubleday, 1977.

————. "What is Magisterium?" *Origins* 6:6 (July 1, 1976): 81–87.

Dunning, James. "Method Is the Medium Is the Message: Catechetical Method in the RCIA." In *Precatechemunate,* vol. 1 of *Christian Initiation Resources Reader.* New York: William H. Sadlier, 1984.

Durant, Will. *The Story of Philosophy.* New York: Pocket Books, 1961.

Durka, Gloria, and Joan Marie Smith, eds. *Aesthetic Dimensions of Religious Education.* New York: Paulist Press, 1979.

Durkheim, Emile. *The Rules of Sociological Method.* New York: Free Press, 1964.

Dych, William V. "Theology in a New Key." In *A World of Grace,* edited by Leo J. O'Donovan. New York: Crossroad, 1984.

Dykstra, Craig. *Vision and Character.* New York: Paulist Press, 1981.

Eagleson, John, and Philip Scharper, eds. *Puebla and Beyond.* Maryknoll, NY: Orbis Books, 1979.

Eby, Frederick. *Early Protestant Educators.* New York: McGraw-Hill, 1931.

Egan, Gerard. *Change Agent Skills in Helping and Human Service Settings.* Monterey, CA: Brooks/Cole, 1985.

Egan, John. "Liturgy and Justice: An Unfinished Agenda." *Origins* 13:15 (Sept. 22, 1983): 245–53.

Eisner, Elliot. *The Educational Imagination*. New York: Macmillan, 1979.

Elliott, Harrison S. *Can Religious Education Be Christian?* New York: Macmillan, 1953.

Emswiler, Sharon Neufer, and Tom Neufer Emswiler. *Sisters and Brothers, Sing!* Normal, IL: Wesley Foundation, 1977.

———. *Women and Worship*. New York: Harper & Row, 1984.

The Encyclopedia of Philosophy. 8 vols. Edited by Paul Edwards. New York: Macmillan and The Free Press, 1967.

Encyclopedia of Theology: The Concise Sacramentum Mundi. Edited by Karl Rahner. New York: Seabury Press, 1975.

Endo, Shusaku. *A Life of Jesus*. Translated by Richard A. Schubert. New York: Paulist Press, 1978.

Erikson, Erik H. *Childhood and Society*. 2d ed. New York: W. W. Norton, 1963.

"Eucharist and Ministry." *Lutherans and Catholics in Dialogue,* vol. 4. Washington, DC: USCC, 1970.

Facker, Gabriel. *The Christian Story*. Grand Rapids: Eerdmans, 1978.

Fahey, Michael A. "On Being Christian Together." In *A World of Grace,* edited by Leo. J. O'Donovan. New York: Crossroad, 1984.

Farley, Edward. *Theologia*. Philadelphia: Fortress Press, 1983.

Farley, Margaret. "Beyond the Formal Principle: A Reply to Ramsey and Saliers." *Journal of Religious Ethics* 7:2 (Fall 1979): 191–202.

Ferrier, J. F. *Institutes of Metaphysics*. Edinburgh: Univ. of St. Andrews Press, 1854.

Fiorenza, Elisabeth Schüssler. *Bread Not Stone: The Challenge of Feminist Biblical Interpretation*. Boston: Beacon Press, 1984.

———. *In Memory of Her*. New York: Crossroad, 1983.

Fiorenza, Francis Schüssler. *Foundational Theology: Jesus and the Church*. New York: Crossroad, 1984.

Fischer, Kathleen R. *The Inner Rainbow: The Imagination in Christian Life*. New York: Paulist Press, 1983.

Fisher, Eugene. "Implementing the Vatican Document: Notes on Jews and Judaism in Preaching and Catechesis." *The Living Light* 22:2 (Jan. 1986): 103–11.

Fitzmyer, Joseph A. *A Christological Catechism: New Testament Answers*. New York: Paulist Press, 1982.

———. *The Gospel According to Luke, 1–9*. The Anchor Bible Series, vol. 28. Garden City, NY: Doubleday, 1981.

———. *The Gospel According to Luke 10–24*. The Anchor Bible Series, vol. 28a. New York: Doubleday, 1985.

Flax, Jane. "Political Philosophy and the Patriarchal Consciousness: A Psychoanalytic Perspective on Epistemology and Metaphysics." In *Discovering Reality,* edited by Sandra Harding and Merrill B. Hintikka. Boston: D. Reidel, 1983.

Flynn, Marcellin. *Catholic Schools and the Communication of Faith*. Homebush, N.S.W., Australia: St. Paul Publications, 1979.

———. *The Effectiveness of Catholic Schools*. Homebush, N.S.W., Australia: St. Paul Publications, 1985.

———. *Some Catholic Schools in Action*. Sydney, Australia: Catholic Education Office, 1975.

Foucault, Michel. *The History of Sexuality: Volume I*. Translated by Robert Hurley. New York: Vintage Books, 1978.

————. *Power/Knowledge: Selected Interviews and Other Writings 1972–77.* Translated and edited by Colin Gordon. New York: Pantheon Books, 1980.

Fowler, James W. *Becoming Adult, Becoming Christian.* San Francisco: Harper & Row, 1984.

————. *Faith Development and Pastoral Care.* Philadelphia: Fortress Press, 1987.

————. *Stages of Faith.* San Francisco: Harper & Row, 1981.

Frankl, Victor E. *Man's Search for Meaning.* Translated by Isle Lasch. New York: Pocket Books, 1963.

Freire, Paulo. *Cultural Action for Freedom.* Cambridge, MA: Harvard Educational Review, 1970.

————. *Education for Critical Consciousness.* New York: Seabury Press, 1973.

————. *Pedagogy of the Oppressed.* Translated by Myra Bergman Ramos. New York: Seabury Press, 1970.

————. *Pedagogy in Process: The Letters to Guinea-Bissau.* Translated by Carman St. John Hunter. New York: Seabury Press, 1978.

————. *The Politics of Education: Culture Power and Liberation.* Translated by Donaldo Macedo. South Hadley, MA: Bergin & Garvey, 1985.

Fuchs, Michael. "The Church and the Task of Inhabiting the Symbol." *Religious Education* 76:2 (Mar.–Apr. 1981): 162–77.

Gadamer, Hans-Georg. *Philosophical Hermeneutics.* Translated and edited by David E. Longe. Berkeley: Univ. of California Press, 1976.

————. "On the Scope and Function of Hermeneutical Reflection." *Continuum* 8:1–2 (Spring–Summer 1970): 77–95.

————. *Truth and Method.* New York: Seabury Press, 1975.

Gatt-Fly. *Ah-hah!: A New Approach to Popular Education.* Toronto: Between the Lines, 1983.

Gaylor, Christine G., and Annelle Fitzpatrick. "The Stages of Consciousness Raising." *Human Development* 8:3 (Fall 1987): 6–11.

Geertz, Clifford. *The Interpretation of Cultures.* New York: Basic Books, 1973.

————. "Religion as a Cultural System." In *Anthropological Approaches to the Study of Religion,* edited by Michael Banton. London: Tavistock Publications, 1966.

Gendlin, Eugene T. *Focusing.* New York: Bantam Books, 1981.

Gerkin, Charles V. *The Living Human Document.* Nashville: Abingdon Press, 1984.

————. *Widening the Horizons.* Philadelphia: Westminster Press, 1986.

Geuss, Raymond. *The Idea of a Critical Theory: Habermas and the Frankfurt School.* Cambridge: Cambridge Univ. Press, 1981.

Gilligan, Ann Louise. *The Feminist Imagination: Toward a Feminist Theological Pedagogy.* Ph.D. diss., Boston College, 1986.

Gilligan, Carol. *In a Different Voice: Psychological Theory and Women's Development.* Cambridge: Harvard Univ. Press, 1977.

Giroux, Henry A. *Theory and Resistance in Education.* South Hadley, MA: Bergin & Garvey, 1983.

Goethals, Gregort T. *The TV Ritual: Worship at the Video Altar.* Boston: Beacon Press, 1981.

Goldberg, Michael. *Theology and Narrative: A Critical Introduction.* Nashville: Abingdon, 1982.

Goldbrunner, Josef. *Holiness Is Wholeness and Other Essays.* Notre Dame, IN: Notre Dame Univ. Press, 1964.

Gordon, William J. J. *Synectics: The Development of Creative Capacity.* New York: Harper & Row, 1961.

Gordon, William J. J., and T. Poze. *The Metaphorical Way.* New ed. Cambridge: Porpoise Books, 1979.

Goslin, David A., ed. *Handbook of Socialization Theory and Research.* Chicago: Rand McNally, 1969.

Grant, Robert, with David Tracy. 2d ed. *A Short History of the Interpretation of the Bible.* Philadelphia: Fortress Press, 1984.

Grassi, Joseph A. *The Teacher in the Primitive Church and the Teacher Today.* Santa Clara, CA: Univ. of Santa Clara Press, 1973.

Greeley, Andrew. M. *The New Agenda.* New York: Doubleday, Image Books, 1973.

———. *The Religious Imagination.* New York, William H. Sadlier, 1981.

Gremillion, Joseph, ed. *The Gospel of Peace and Justice.* Maryknoll, NY: Orbis Books, 1976.

Griffith, Colleen M. "Does Matter Matter." Unpublished paper. Harvard Divinity School, spring semester, 1986.

———. "Toward a Contemporary Theology of Bodiliness." Diss. proposal, Harvard Divinity School, Feb. 1987.

Grimmitt, Michael. *Religious Education and Human Development.* Great Wakering, U.K.: McCrimmon, 1987.

Grisar, Joseph. *Mary Ward.* London: The Month, n.d.

Groome, Thomas H. *Christian Religious Education: Sharing Our Story and Vision.* San Francisco: Harper & Row, 1980.

———. "Conversion, Nurture and Educators." *Religious Education* 76:5 (Sept.–Oct. 1981): 482–97.

———. "From Chauvinism and Clericalism to Priesthood: The Long March." In *Women and Religion: A Reader for the Clergy,* edited by Regina Coll. New York: Paulist Press, 1982.

———. *Language for a "Catholic" Church.* Kansas City, MO: Sheed & Ward, 1991.

———. "Parish as Catechist." *Church* 6:3. (Fall 1990): 23–27.

———. "A Religious Educator's Response. In *The Education of the Practical Theologian,* edited by Don S. Browning, et al. Atlanta: Scholars Press, 1989.

———. "Shared Praxis: An Ordinary Approach to Evangelization." In *Catholic Evangelization Today: A New Pentecost for the United States,* edited by Kenneth Boyack. New York: Paulist Press, 1987.

———. "The Spirituality of the Religious Educator." *Religious Education* 83:1 (Winter 1988): 9–20.

———. "Theology on Our Feet: A Revisionist Pedagogy for Healing the Gap Between Academia and Ecclesia." In *Formation and Reflection,* edited by Lewis Mudge and James Poling. Philadelphia: Fortress Press, 1987.

———. "Walking Humbly With Our God." In *To Act Justly, Love Tenderly, Walk Humbly,* Walter Brueggemann, et al. New York: Paulist Press, 1986.

Groome, Thomas H., et al. The Coming to Faith Religion Curriculum. Grades 1–8. Standard and Parish eds. New York: Sadlier, 1989–90.

———. The God with Us Religion Curriculum. Grades K–8. Standard and Parish eds. New York: Sadlier, 1983–84.

Gula, Richard M. *To Walk Together Again: The Sacrament of Reconciliation.* New York: Paulist Press, 1984.

Gutierrez, Gustavo. *On Job: God-talk and the Suffering of the Innocent.* Translated by Matthew J. O'Connell. Maryknoll, NY: Orbis Books, 1986.

———. *A Theology of Liberation.* Translated by Caridad Inda and John Eagleson. Maryknoll, NY: Orbis Books, 1973.

Habermas, Jurgen. *Communication and the Evolution of Society.* Translated by Thomas McCarthy. Boston: Beacon Press, 1979.

————. *Knowledge and Human Interests.* Translated by Jeremy J. Shapiro. Boston: Beacon Press, 1971.

————. "A Reply to My Critics." In *Habermas: Critical Debates,* edited by John B. Thompson and David Held. Cambridge, MA: MIT Press, 1982.

————. *Theory of Communicative Action,* vol 1. Translated by Thomas McCarthy. Boston: Beacon Press, 1984.

————. "Toward a Theory of Communicative Competence." *Inquiry* 13 (1970): 360–75.

Hanigan, James P. *What Are They Saying About Sexual Morality?* New York: Paulist Press, 1982.

Happel, Stephen. "Worship as a Grammar of Social Transformation." *Proceedings of the Catholic Theological Society of America* 42 (1987): 60–87.

Happel, Stephen, and David Tracy. *A Catholic Vision.* Philadelphia: Fortress Press, 1984.

Harding, Sandra. *The Science Question in Feminism.* Ithaca, NY: Cornell Univ. Press, 1986.

Harding, Sandra, ed. *Feminism and Methodology.* Bloomington: Indiana Univ. Press, 1987.

Harding, Sandra, and Merrill B. Hintikka, eds. *Discovering Reality.* Boston: D. Reidel, 1983.

Haring, Bernard. *Free and Faithful in Christ: Moral Theology for Clergy and Laity.* New York: Seabury Press, 1978.

Harmless, William, S.J. *Augustine and the Ancient Catechumenate: A Catechetical Perspective.* Ph.D. diss., Boston College, 1990.

————. "Augustine's Lenten Catechesis." Unpublished paper. Boston College, Spring semester, 1988.

Harris, Maria. "Art and Religious Education: A Conversation." *Religious Education* 88:3 (Summer 1988): 453–73.

————. *Fashion Me a People.* Louisville, KY: Westminster/John Knox Press, 1989.

————. *Teaching and Religious Imagination.* San Francisco: Harper & Row, 1987.

Hartshorne, Charles. *Creative Synthesis and Philosophic Method.* LaSalle, IL: Open Court, 1970.

Hartsock, Nancy C. M. "The Feminist Standpoint: Developing the Ground for a Specifically Feminist Historical Materialism." In *Discovering Reality,* edited by Sandra Harding and Merrill B. Hintikka. Boston: Reidel, 1983.

Hater, Robert J. *The Ministry Explosion: A New Awareness of Every Christian's Call to Ministry.* Dubuque, Iowa: William C. Brown, 1979.

Hauerwas, Stanley. *Vision and Virtue.* Notre Dame, IN: Fides, 1974.

Haughey, John C., ed. *The Faith That Does Justice.* New York: Paulist Press, 1977.

Hayward, Carter. *The Redemption of God.* Washington, DC: Univ. Press of America, 1982.

Hegel, G. W. F. *The Phenomenology of Mind.* 2d ed. Translated by J. B. Baillie. London: George Allen & Unwin, 1949.

————. *Reason in History: A General Introduction to the Philosophy of History.* Translated by Robert S. Hartman. New York: Liberal Arts Press, 1953.

Heidegger, Martin. *Basic Writings.* Translated by David Farrell Krell. New York: Harper & Row, 1977.

————. *Being and Time.* Translated by John Macquarrie and Edward Robinson. New York: Harper & Row, 1962.

————. *Discourse on Thinking.* Translated by John M. Anderson and E. Hans Freund. New York: Harper & Row, Harper Torchbooks, 1966.

————. *On Time and Being.* Translated by Joan Stambaugh. San Francisco: Harper & Row, 1972.

————. *On the Way to Language.* New York: Harper & Row, 1971.

Held, David. *Introduction to Critical Theory: Horkheimer to Habermas.* Berkeley: Univ. of California Press, 1980.

Hellwig, Monica K. *Understanding Catholicism.* New York: Paulist Press, 1981.

Henderson, Frank, et al. *Liturgy, Justice and the Reign of God: Integrating Vision and Practice.* New York: Paulist Press, 1988.

Heschel, Abraham J. *The Prophets.* 2 vols. New York: Harper & Row, 1962.

Hilgard, Ernest R. "The Trilogy of Mind: Cognition, Affection, and Conation." *Journal of History of Behavioral Sciences* 16 (1980).

Hill, William Fawcett. *Learning Through Discussion.* Rev. ed. Beverly Hills, CA: Sage, 1969.

Hiltner, Seward. *Pastoral Counseling: How Every Pastor Can Help People to Help Themselves.* Nashville: Abingdon Press, 1949.

Himes, Kenneth R. "Eucharist and Justice: Assessing the Legacy of Virgil Michel." *Worship* 62:3 (May 1988): 201–24.

Holifield, E. Brooks. *A History of Pastoral Care in America.* Nashville: Abingdon Press, 1983.

Holland, Joe, and Peter Henriot. *Social Analysis: Linking Faith and Justice.* Rev. ed. Maryknoll, NY: Orbis Books, 1983.

Hollenbach, David. *Claims in Conflict: Retrieving and Renewing the Catholic Human Rights Tradition.* New York: Paulist Press, 1979.

————. "Courage and Patience: Education for Staying Power in the Pursuit of Peace and Justice." In *Education for Peace and Justice,* edited by Padraic O'Hare. San Francisco: Harper & Row, 1983.

Horkheimer, Max. *Critique of Instrumental Reason.* New York: Seabury Press, 1974.

————. *Eclipse of Reason.* New York: Oxford Univ. Press, 1947.

Horkheimer, Max, and Theodor W. Adorno. *Dialectic of Enlightenment.* New York: Herder & Herder, 1972.

Hough, Joseph C., Jr., and John B. Cobb, Jr. *Christian Identity and Theological Education.* Chico, CA: Scholars Press, 1985.

Howe, Reuel L. *The Miracle of Dialogue.* New York: Seabury Press, 1963.

Huebner, Dwayne. "Curriculum as Concern for Man's Temporality." In *Curriculum Theorizing,* edited by Willam Pinar. Berkeley, CA: McCutchen, 1975.

————. "Religious Education: Practicing the Presence of God." *Religious Education* 82:4 (Fall 1987): 569–77.

————. "Toward a Remaking of Curricular Language." In *Heightened Consciousness, Cultural Revolution, and Curriculum Theory,* edited by William Pinar. Berkeley, CA: McCutchen, 1974.

Hughes, Kathleen. "Liturgy, Justice, and Peace." In *Education for Peace and Justice,* edited by Padraic O'Hare. San Francisco: Harper & Row, 1983.

Hume, David. *A Treatise of Human Nature.* 2d ed. Edited by L. A. Selby-Bigge. With text revised and variant readings by P. H. Nidditch. Oxford: Clarendon Press, 1978.

Husserl, Edmund. *Ideas.* Translated by W. R. Boyce Gibson. London: Collier-Macmillan, 1962.

Hussey, M. Edmund. "Needed: A Theology of Priesthood." *Origins* 17:34 (Feb. 4, 1988): 577–83.

Ihde, Don. *Hermeneutic Phenomenology: The Philosophy of Paul Ricoeur.* Evanston, IL: Northwestern Univ. Press, 1971.

Imbelli, Robert. "Trinitarian 'Politics.'" *Review for Religious* (Mar.–Apr. 1989).

An Inclusive Language Lectionary: Readings for Year A, B and C. Atlanta: John Knox Press, 1983.

Jacoby, Russel. *Social Amnesia.* Boston: Beacon Press, 1975.

James, William. *Pragmatism.* New York: Longmans, Green, 1908.

Jay, Martin. *The Dialectical Imagination.* Boston: Little Brown, 1973.

The Jerome Biblical Commentary. 2 vols. Edited by Raymond E. Brown, et al. Englewood Cliffs, NJ: Prentice-Hall, 1968.

John Paul II, Pope. "Catechesi Tradendae: Apostolic Exhortation on Catechesis." *The Living Light* 17:1 (Spring 1980): 44–89.

———. *Redemptor Hominis.* Washington, DC: USCC, 1983.

———. "Relating Truth and Freedom." *Origins* 18:21 (Nov. 3, 1988): 347–48.

Justin Martyr. "Apology I.65." In *The Fathers of the Church,* translated by Thomas B. Falls. New York: Christian Heritage, 1948.

Kant, Immanuel. *Critique of Practical Reason.* Translated by Lewis White Beck. Indianapolis: Bobbs-Merrill, 1956.

———. *Critique of Pure Reason.* Unabridged ed. Translated by Norman Kemp Smith. New York: St. Martins Press, 1965.

———. *Kant's Critique of Practical Reason and Other Works on the Theory of Ethics.* Translated by Thomas K. Abbott. New York: Longmans, Green, 1909.

Kasemann, Ernst. "The Problem of the Historical Jesus." In *Essays on New Testament Themes.* Studies in Biblical Theology, 41. London: SCM Press, 1964.

———. *The Testament of Jesus.* Philadelphia: Fortress Press, 1968.

Kaufman, Gordon D. *An Essay on Theological Method.* Rev. ed. Missoula, MT: Scholar's Press, 1979.

———. *Theology for a Nuclear Age.* Philadelphia: Westminister Press, 1985.

Kavanagh, Aidan. *Elements of Rite: A Handbook of Liturgical Style.* New York: Pueblo, 1982.

———. *On Liturgical Theology.* New York: Pueblo, 1984.

———. "Teaching Through the Liturgy." *Notre Dame Journal of Education* 5 (1974): 35–49.

Kavanaugh, John Francis. *Following Christ in a Consumer Society.* Maryknoll, NY: Orbis Books, 1981.

Kearney, Richard. *Modern Movements in European Philosophy.* Manchester, U.K.: Manchester Univ. Press, 1986.

———. *The Wake of Imagination.* London: Hutchinson, 1988.

Keller, Evelyn Fox. *Reflections on Gender and Science.* New Haven, CT: Yale Univ. Press, 1985.

Kelsey, Morton T. *Caring: How Can We Love One Another?* New York: Paulist Press, 1981.

Kinast, Robert. *Caring for Society: A Theological Interpretation of Lay Ministry.* Chicago: Thomas More Press, 1985.

King, Philip J. "Micah." In *The Jerome Biblical Commentary,* vol. 1, edited by Raymond E. Brown, et al. Englewood Cliffs, NJ: Prentice-Hall, 1968.

Kleissler, Thomas H., Margo A. LeBert, and Mary C. McGuinness. *Small Christian Communities: A Vision of Hope.* New York: Paulist Press, 1991.

Kolbe, Kathe. *The Conative Connection: Uncovering the Link Between Who You Are and How You Perform.* Reading, MA: Addison-Wesley, 1990.

Kraft, Charles. *Christianity in Culture.* Maryknoll, NY: Orbis, 1979.

Laeuchli, Samuel. *Power and Sexuality: The Emergence of Sexuality at the Synod of Elvira.* Philadelphia: Temple Univ. Press, 1972.

Lamb, Matthew L. "Liberation Theology and Social Justice." *Process Studies* 14:3 (1985): 102–23.

———. *Solidarity with Victims.* New York: Crossroad, 1982.

Langer, Susanne K. *Philosophy in a New Key.* 3d ed. Cambridge, MA: Harvard Univ. Press, 1960.

———. *Problems of Art: Ten Philosophical Essays.* New York: Scribners, 1957.

Lasch, Christopher. *The Culture of Narcissism.* New York: Warner Books, 1979.

Lavine, T. Z. *From Socrates to Sartre.* New York: Bantam Books, 1984.

Lea, Henry Charles. *History of Sacerdotal Celibacy in the Christian Church.* 4th ed. New York: Univ. Books, 1966.

Leckey, Dolores. "What the Laity Need." *Origins* 12:1 (May 20, 1982): 9–15.

Lee, Bernard J., and Michael A. Cowan. *Dangerous Memories: House Churches and Our American Story.* Kansas City, MO: Sheed and Ward, 1986.

Lee, James Michael. *The Content of Religious Instruction: A Social Science Approach.* Birmingham, AL: Religious Education Press, 1985.

———. "Lifework Spirituality and the Religious Educator." In *The Spirituality of the Religious Educator,* edited by James Michael Lee. Birmingham, AL: Religious Education Press, 1985.

Leech, Kenneth. *Experiencing God: Theology as Spirituality.* San Francisco: Harper & Row, 1985.

Legrand, Herve-Marie. "The Presidency of the Eucharist." *Worship* 53 (Summer 1979): 413–38.

Leo I, Pope (Leo the Great). *Letters. The Fathers of the Church,* vols. 34, 37. Translated by Edmund Hurt. New York: Fathers of the Church, 1957.

Lescoe, Francis, J. *Existentialism: With or Without God.* New York: Alba House, 1974.

Leyden, W. von. *Remembering: A Philosophical Problem.* London: Gerald Duckworth, 1961.

Leypoldt, Martha M. *40 Ways to Teach in Groups.* Valley Forge, PA: Judson Press, 1967.

Lindbeck, George A. *The Nature of Doctrine.* Philadelphia: Westminister Press, 1984.

Little, Sara. *To Set One's Heart: Belief and Teaching in the Church.* Atlanta: John Knox Press, 1983.

Lobkowicz, Nicholas. *Theory and Practice: History of a Concept from Aristotle to Marx.* Notre Dame, IN: Univ. of Notre Dame Press, 1967.

Locke, John. *An Essay Concerning Human Understanding.* Abridged and edited by A. S. Pringle-Pattison. Oxford: Clarendon Press, 1924.

———. *Second Treatise of Government.* Edited by C. B. Macphearson. Indianapolis: Hackett, 1980.

Loder, James. *The Transforming Moment: Understanding Convictional Experiences.* San Francisco: Harper & Row, 1981.

Lonergan, Bernard J. F. "Aquinas Today: Tradition and Innovation." *Journal of Religion* 55:2 (Apr. 1975): 165–80.

———. *Collection Papers.* [Commonly referred to as *First Collection.*] Edited by F. E. Crowe. New York: Herder & Herder, 1967.

———. *Insight: A Study of Human Understanding.* San Francisco: Harper & Row, 1978.

———. *Method in Theology.* New York: Seabury Press, 1972.

———. *A Second Collection: Papers.* Edited by William F. J. Ryan and Bernard J. Tyrrell. London: Darton, Longman & Todd, 1974.

————. "Theology in Its New Context." In *Conversion: Perspectives on Personal and Social Transformation,* edited by Walter E. Conn. New York: Alba House, 1978.

————. *A Third Collection.* Edited by Frederick E. Crowe. New York: Paulist Press, 1985.

————. *Verbum: Word and Idea in Aquinas.* Edited by David B. Burrell. Notre Dame, IN: Univ. of Notre Dame Press, 1967.

Loughlin, Catherine E., and Joseph H. Suirna. *The Learning Environment.* New York: Teachers College, 1982.

Lowery, Claire E. "The Pastoral Care and Counseling Relationship." In *Education for Peace and Justice,* edited by Padraic O'Hare. San Francisco: Harper & Row, 1983.

Luther, Martin. *Christian Liberty.* Rev. ed. Translated by W. A. Lambert. Edited by Harold J. Grimm. Philadelphia: Fortress Press, 1957.

————. *Dr. Martin Luther's Large Catechism.* Translated by John N. Lenker. Minneapolis: Augsburg, 1935.

————. *The Short Catechism.* Translated by Henry Wace and C. A. Buchheim. In *Early Protestant Educators,* edited by Frederick Eby. New York: McGraw-Hill, 1931.

Luzbetak, Louis J. *The Church and Cultures.* Maryknoll, NY: Orbis, 1979.

Lynch, James J. *The Broken Heart: The Medical Consequences of Loneliness.* New York: Basic Books, 1977.

McBrien, Richard P. *Caesar's Coin: Religion and Politics in America.* New York: Macmillan, 1987.

————. *Catholicism.* 2 vols. Minneapolis: Winston Press, 1980.

————. *Ministry: A Theological, Pastoral Handbook.* San Francisco: Harper & Row, 1987.

McCarthy, Thomas. *The Critical Theory of Jurgen Habermas.* 2d ed. Cambridge, MA: MIT Press, 1982.

McCormick, Richard A. "Scripture, Liturgy, Character and Morality." *Readings in Moral Theology 4,* edited by Charles E. Curran and Richard A. McCormick. New York: Paulist Press, 1984.

McDougall, William. *An Introduction to Social Psychology.* London: Methuen, 1908.

————. *Physiological Psychology.* London: J. M. Dent, 1905.

McFague, Sallie. *Models of God.* Philadelphia: Fortress Press, 1987.

MacIntyre, Alasdair. *After Virtue.* Notre Dame, IN: Univ. of Notre Dame Press, 1981.

McKeon, John F. X. "Synectics in Shared Christian Praxis." *The Living Light* 24:4 (June 1988): 340–53.

Mackey, James P., ed. *Religious Imagination.* Edinburgh: Edinburgh Univ. Press, 1986.

Macquarrie, John. *Principles of Christian Theology.* New York: Charles Scribner's Sons, 1977.

Maney, Thomas. *Basic Communities.* Minneapolis: Winston Press, 1984.

Mann, Peter. *Through Words and Images.* New York: CTNA, 1983.

Mannheim, Karl. *Ideology and Utopia.* New York: Harcourt, Brace & World, 1936.

Marthaler, Berard L. *The Creed.* Mystic, CT: Twenty-third Publications, 1987.

————. "Socialization as a Model for Catechetics." In *Foundations of Religious Education,* edited by Padraic O'Hare. New York: Paulist Press, 1978.

Martos, Joseph. *Doors to the Sacred.* Garden City, NY: Doubleday, 1981.

Marty, Martin E. *Public Church.* New York: Crossroad, 1981.

————. *The Word: People Participating in Preaching.* Philadelphia: Fortress Press, 1984.

Marty, Martin E., and Dean G. Peerman, eds. *A Handbook of Christian Theologians.* Cleveland: Fontana Books, 1965.

Marx, Karl. *Capital: A Critique of Political Economy.* Translated from the 3d German ed. by Samuel Moore and Edward Aveling. New York: International Publishers, 1967.

————. *A Contribution to the Critique of Political Economy.* Edited by M. Dobb. Translated by S. W. Ryazanskaya. New York: International Publishers, 1970.

————. *Economic and Philosophic Manuscripts of 1844.* Translated by Martin Milligan. Moscow: Foreign Language Publishing House, 1961.

Marx, Karl, and Friedrich Engels. *The German Ideology.* 3d rev. ed. Moscow: Progress Publishers, 1976.

————. *Manifesto of the Communist Party.* Authorized English translation edited and annotated by F. Engels. New York: International Publishers, 1948.

Marx, Paul B. *Virgil Michel and the Liturgical Movement.* Collegeville, MN: Liturgical Press, 1957.

Mayer, Mary Helen. *The Philosophy of Teaching of St. Thomas Aquinas.* Milwaukee: Bruce, 1929.

Mead, G. H. *Mind, Self and Society.* Chicago: Univ. of Chicago Press, 1934.

Meer, Frederik van der. *Augustine the Bishop.* Translated by Brian Buttershaw and G. R. Lamb. London: Sheed & Ward, 1961.

Melchert, Charles F. "Does the Church Really Want Religious Education?" *Religious Education* 69:1 (Jan.–Feb. 1974): 12–22.

————. Review of *Does the Church Really Want Religious Education?* edited by Marlene Mayr. In *Religious Education* 83:3 (Summer 1988): 477–78.

Merleau-Ponty, Maurice. *Phenomenology of Perception.* Translated by Colin Smith. London: Routledge & Kegan Paul, 1962.

Merton, Robert K. *Social Theory and Social Structure.* Glencoe, IL: Free Press, 1957.

Metz, Johann Baptist. *Faith in History and Society.* Translated by David Smith. New York: Seabury Press, 1980.

Miles, Margaret R. *Image as Insight.* Boston: Beacon Press, 1985.

————. *Practicing Christianity.* New York: Crossroad, 1989.

Miller, Donald. "Moral Significance of Worship." *Religious Education* 75:2 (1980): 193–203.

Miller, Donald E. *Story and Context: An Introduction to Christian Education.* Nashville: Abingdon Press, 1987.

Miller, Randolph Crump. "Guest Editorial." *Religious Education* 84:3 (Summer 1989).

————. *The Theory of Christian Education Practice.* Birmingham, AL: Religious Education Press, 1980

Miranda, Jose. *Communism in the Bible.* Translated by Robert R. Barr. Maryknoll, NY: Orbis Books, 1982.

Miranda, Jose P. *Marx and the Bible.* London: SCM Press, 1977.

Mohler, James. *The Origin and Evolution of the Priesthood.* New York: Alba House, 1970.

Mondin, Battista. *St. Thomas Aquinas' Philosophy.* The Hague: Martinus Nijhoff, 1975.

Monette, Maurice L. *The Supper Table: Programs for Community Spirituality.* Kansas City, MO: Sheed & Ward, 1985.

Montessori, Maria. *Education and Peace.* Translated by Helen R. Lane. Chicago: Regnery, 1972.

———. *The Montessori Method.* New York: Schocken Books, 1969.

———. *Spontaneous Activity in Education.* Introduction by John J. McDermott. New York: Schocken Books, 1965.

Moore, Mary Elizabeth. *Education for Continuity and Change.* Nashville: Abingdon Press, 1983.

Moore, Sebastian. *The Fire and the Rose Are One.* New York: Seabury Press, 1980.

Moos, Rudolf. *Evaluating Educational Environments: Methods, Procedures, Findings and Implications.* San Francisco: Jossey-Bass, 1979.

Moran, Gabriel. *Interplay: A Theory of Religion and Education.* Winona, MN: Saint Mary's Press, 1981.

———. "The Intersection of Religion and Education." In *Who Are We? A Quest for a Religious Education,* edited by John Westerhoff III. Birmingham, AL: Religious Education Press, 1978.

———. "Of a Kind and to a Degree." In *Does the Church Really Want Religious Education?* edited by Marlene Mayr. Birmingham, AL.: Religious Education Press, 1988.

———. *No Ladder to the Sky: Education and Morality.* San Francisco: Harper & Row, 1987.

———. *Religious Body.* New York: Seabury Press, 1974.

———. *Religious Education Development: Images for the Future.* Minneapolis: Winston Press, 1983.

———. *Religious Education as a Second Language.* Birmingham, AL: Religious Education Press, 1989.

———. "Two Languages of Religious Education." *The Living Light* 14:1 (1977): 7–15.

Mudge, Louis S., and James N. Poling, eds. *Formation and Reflection: The Promise of Practical Theology.* Philadelphia: Fortress Press, 1987.

Mumford, Lewis. *Art and Technics.* New York: Columbia Univ. Press, 1952.

Murphy, Roland. "Concept of Old Testament Wisdom." In *The Jerome Biblical Commentary,* vol. 1, edited by Raymond E. Brown, et al. Englewood Cliffs, NJ: Prentice-Hall, 1968.

Murray, John Courtney. *We Hold These Truths: Catholic Reflections on the American Proposition.* New York: Sheed & Ward, 1960.

National Conference of Catholic Bishops. *The Challenge of Peace: God's Promise and Our Response.* Boston: Daughters of St. Paul, 1983.

———. *Economic Justice for All.* Washington, DC: USCC, 1986.

———. *Fulfilled in Your Hearing: The Homily in the Sunday Assembly.* Washington, DC: USCC, 1982.

———. *The Rite of Christian Initiation of Adults.* Washington, DC: USCC, 1988.

National Conference of Catholic Bishops. Bishops' Committee on the Liturgy. "Environment and Art in Catholic Worship." Washington, DC: USCC, 1977.

Neaves, Norman. "Preaching in Pastoral Perspective." In *Preaching the Story,* edited by E. Steimle, M. Niedenthal, and C. Rice. Philadelphia: Fortress Press, 1980.

Nelson, C. Ellis. *How Faith Matures.* Louisville, KY: Westminster/John Knox Press, 1989.

———. *Where Faith Begins.* Richmond, VA: John Knox Press, 1971.

The New Catholic Encyclopedia. 16 vols. New York: McGraw-Hill, 1967.

Newman, John Henry Cardinal. *On Consulting the Faithful in Matters of Doctrine.* Kansas City, MO: Sheed & Ward, 1961.

———. *An Essay on the Development of Christian Doctrine.* Westminster, MD: Christian Classics, 1968.

Niebuhr, H. Richard. *Christ and Culture.* New York: Harper & Row, Harper Torchbooks, 1956.

———. *The Meaning of Revelation.* New York: Macmillan, 1941.

Niebuhr, Reinhold. *The Nature and Destiny of Man.* 2 vols. New York: Charles Scribner's Sons, 1943.

Niedenthal, Morris J. "Focussing the Listener's Story." In *Preaching the Story,* edited by E. Steimle, M. Niedenthal, and C. Rice. Philadelphia: Fortress Press, 1980.

Nouwen, Henri J. M. *The Living Reminder.* New York: Seabury Press, 1977.

O'Brien, Maureen R. *Religious Education and the Public Church: The Contribution of The Challenge of Peace.* Ph.D. diss., Boston College, 1990.

O'Connor, D. J., and Brian Karr. *Introduction to the Theory of Knowledge.* Minneapolis: Univ. of Minnesota Press, 1982.

O'Donovan, Leo J., ed. *A World of Grace.* New York: Crossroad, 1981.

Ogden, Schubert M. *Faith and Freedom.* Nashville: Abingdon Press, 1979.

O'Halloran, James. *Signs of Hope: Developing Small Christian Communities.* Maryknoll, New York: Orbis, 1991.

O'Hare, Padraic. *Foundations of Religious Education.* Ramsey, NJ: Paulist Press, 1978.

———. "Hospitality as a Paradigm for Youth Ministry." In *Occasional Paper,* no. 10. Naugatuck, CT: Center for Youth Ministry Development, 1986.

———. "Peace, Justice, and the Middle Class." *PACE* 16 (Nov. 1986): 43–51.

O'Hare, Padraic, ed. *Education for Peace and Justice.* New York: Harper & Row, 1983.

———. *Traditions and Transformation in Religous Education.* Birmingham, AL: Religious Education Press, 1979.

O'Leary D. J., and T. Salinow. *Love and Meaning in Religious Education.* Oxford: Oxford Univ. Press, 1982.

Oliver, Donald W. and Kathleen Waldron Gersham. *Education, Modernity and Fractured Meaning: Toward a Process Theory of Teaching and Learning.* Albany: State Univ. of New York, 1989.

Olson, David, ed. *Common Sense.* Toronto: Routledge & Kegan Paul, 1980.

O'Meara, Thomas Franklin. "A History of Grace." In *A World of Grace,* edited by Leo J. O'Donovan. New York: Crossroad, 1984.

———. *Theology of Ministry.* New York: Paulist Press, 1983.

Oosdyke, Mary Kay. "Acquiring a Sense of Liturgy in Contemporary Times." *Religious Education* 84:3 (Summer 1989): 323–37.

Orsy, Ladislas. *The Church: Learning and Teaching.* Wilmington, DE: Michael Glazier, 1987.

Osborne, Kenan B. *Priesthood.* New York: Paulist Press, 1988.

Ostdiek, Gilbert. *Catechesis for Liturgy: A Program for Parish Involvement.* Washington, DC: Pastoral Press, 1986.

Pagels, Elaine. *The Gnostic Gospels.* New York: Vintage Books, 1979.

Palmer, Deidre. *Religious Education for a Discipleship of Equals.* Ph.D. diss., Boston College, 1989.

Palmer, Parker J. *The Company of Strangers.* New York: Crossroad, 1981.

———. *To Know as We Are Known.* San Francisco: Harper & Row, 1983.

———. *The Promise of Paradox.* Notre Dame, IN: Ave Maria Press, 1980.

———. "The Violence of Our Knowledge: A Christian Response." *The Auburn News* (Fall 1983): 1–6.

Palmer, Richard E. *Hermeneutics.* Evanston, IL: Northwestern Univ. Press, 1969.

Pannenberg, Wolfhart. *Theology and the Kingdom of God.* Philadelphia: Westminster Press, 1969.

Parent, Neil A., ed. *Adult Learning and the Parish.* Dubuque, IA: Religious Education Division, W. C. Brown, 1985.

Parks, Sharon. *The Critical Years: The Young Adult Search for a Faith to Live By.* San Francisco: Harper & Row, 1986.

Paul VI, Pope. *Apostolic Letter, Ministeria Quaedam (1972).* In *The Rites of the Catholic Church as Revised by the Second Vatican Council.* New York: Pueblo, 1976

———. *On Evangelization in the Modern World.* Washington, DC: USCC, 1975.

Pegis, Anton, ed. *Basic Writings of Saint Thomas Aquinas.* 2 vols. New York: Random House, 1945.

Pelikan, Jarislav. *The Vindication of Tradition.* New Haven, CT: Yale Univ. Press, 1984.

Percival, Henry R., ed. *The Seven Ecumenical Councils of the Undivided Church: Their Canons and Dogmatic Decrees.* New York: E. S. Gorham, 1901.

Perkins, Pheme. *Hearing the Parables of Jesus.* New York: Paulist Press, 1981.

———. *Jesus as Teacher.* New York: Cambridge Univ. Press, 1990.

Perrin, Norman. *Jesus and the Language of the Kingdom.* Philadelphia: Fortress Press, 1976.

Philibert, Paul. "The Promise and Perils of Memorization." *The Living Light* 17 (Winter 1980): 299–310.

Piaget, Jean. *Science of Education and the Psychology of the Child.* Translated by Derek Coltman. New York: Viking Press, 1972.

———. *To Understand Is to Invent: The Future of Education.* New York: Penguin Books, 1973.

Plato. *Menno.* In *Great Dialogues of Plato.* Translated by W. H. D. Rouse. New York: New American Library, 1956.

———. *Phaedo.* In *The Dialogues of Plato,* vol. 1, translated by B. Jowett. New York: Random House, 1892.

———. *The Phaedo.* Translated by David Gallop. Oxford: Clarendon Press, 1975.

———. *The Republic.* In *Great Dialogues of Plato,* translated by W. H. D. Rouse. New York: New American Library, 1956.

———. *Theaetetus.* Loeb Classical Library. 1977.

———. *Timaeus.* In *Plato,* vol. 9. Loeb Classical Library. 1929.

Plotinus. *The Essential Plotinus.* 2d ed. Translated by Elmer O'Brien. Indianapolis: Hackett, 1964.

Polanyi, Michael. *Knowing and Being.* Chicago: Univ. of Chicago Press, 1969.

Pontifical Biblical Commission. "Can Women Be Priests?" *Origins* 6:6 (July 1, 1976): 92–96.

Power, David N. "The Basis for Official Ministry." *The Jurist* 41:2 (1981): 314–42.

———. *Gifts That Differ: Lay Ministries Established and Unestablished.* New York: Pueblo, 1980.

———. *Unsearchable Riches.* New York: Pueblo, 1984.

Powers, Bruce P. *Christian Leadership: A Fresh Look at Leadership that Gives Life.* Nashville: Broadman Press, 1979.

Powers, Joseph M. *Spirit and Sacrament: The Humanizing Experience.* New York: Seabury Press, 1973.

Pruyser, Paul W. *The Minister as Diagnostician.* Philadelphia: Westminster Press, 1976.

Pseudo-Dionysius. *Pseudo-Dionysius: The Complete Works*. Translated by Colon Luibheid. New York: Paulist Press, 1987.

Quitslund, Sonya A. "A Feminist Perspective on Kings and Kingdom." *The Living Light* 19:2 (Summer 1982): 134–39.

Rad, Gerhard von. *Old Testament Theology*. 2 vols. Translated by D. M. G. Stalker. New York: Harper & Row, 1965.

Rahner, Karl. *Belief Today*. New York: Sheed & Ward, 1967.

———. "Christianity and the New Earth." Translated by Francis J. Goetz and C. Lee Miller. *Theology Digest* 15:4 (Winter 1967): 275–82.

———. *Concern for the Church*. Translated by Edward Quinn. New York: Crossroad, 1981.

———. *Foundations of Christian Faith*. Translated by William V. Dych. New York: Seabury Press, 1978.

———. *The Shape of the Church to Come*. Translated by Edward Quinn. New York: Seabury Press, 1974.

———. *Theological Investigations*. 20 vols. Translated and with an Introduction by Cornelius Ernst. Baltimore: Helicon Press, 1961–83.

———. "Toward a Fundamental Interpretation of Vatican II." *Theological Studies* 40:4 (Dec. 1979): 716–27.

Rahner, Karl, and Herbert Vorgrimler. *Dictionary of Theology*. New rev. ed. Translated by Richard Strachan, et al. New York: Crossroad, 1981.

Ramsey, Ian. *Models and Mystery*. London: Oxford Univ. Press, 1964.

Ramsey, Paul. "Liturgy and Ethics." *Journal of Religious Ethics* 7:2 (Fall 1979): 139–71.

Reagan, Charles E., and David Stewart, eds. *The Philosophy of Paul Ricoeur: An Anthology of His Work*. Boston: Beacon Press, 1978.

Reber, Robert E. "Vocation and Vision: A New Look at the Ministry of the Laity." *The Auburn News* (Fall 1986).

Rice, Charles L. "The Preacher's Story." In *Preaching the Story*, edited by E. Steimle, M. Niedenthal, C. Rice. Philadelphia: Fortress Press, 1980.

Ricoeur, Paul. "Creativity in Language." Translated by David Pellauer. *Philosophy Today* 17:2 (Summer 1973): 97–111.

———. "Existence and Hermeneutics." In *The Conflict of Interpretations*, edited by Don Ihde. Evanston, IL: Northwestern Univ. Press, 1974.

———. *Freud and Philosophy: An Essay on Interpretation*. Translated by Denis Savage. New Haven, CT: Yale Univ. Press, 1970.

———. *Interpretation Theory: Discourse and the Surplus of Meaning*. Fort Worth, TX: Texas Christian Univ. Press, 1976.

———. "The Model of the Text: Meaningful Action Considered as a Text." *Social Research* 38 (Autumn 1971).

The Rite of Christian Initiation of Adults: Study Edition. Washington, DC: USCC, 1988.

The Rites of the Catholic Church as Revised by the Second Vatican Council. New York: Pueblo, 1976.

Roberts, Alexander, and James Donaldson, eds. *The Ante-Nicene Fathers: Translations of the Writings of the Fathers Down to A.D. 325*. 10 vols. Grand Rapids: Eerdmans, 1979.

Robinson, Edward. *The Original Vision: A Study of the Religious Experience of Childhood*. New York: Seabury Press, 1983.

The Roman Catechism. Translated and annotated by Robert J. Bradley and Eugene Kevane. Boston: St. Paul Edition, 1985.

Rossiter, Graham. "The Need for a 'Creative Divorce' Between Catechesis and Religious Education in Catholic Schools." *Religious Education* 77:1 (Jan.–Feb. 1982): 21–40.

————. "Perspectives on Change in Catholic Religious Education Since the Second Vatican Council." *Religious Education* 83:2 (Spring 1988): 264–76.

Rossiter, Graham, and Marisa Crawford. *Teaching Religion in the Secondary School.* Sydney, Australia: Christian Brothers Resource Group, 1985.

Ruben, David Hillel. *Marxism and Materialism: A Study in Marxist Theory of Knowledge.* Garden City, NJ: Humanities Press, 1977.

Ruether, Rosemary Radford. *Sexism and God Talk: Toward a Feminist Theology.* Boston: Beacon Press, 1983.

————. *Women-Church: Theology and Practice of Feminist Liturgical Communities.* San Francisco: Harper & Row, 1985.

Ruether, Rosemary Radford, ed. *Religion and Sexism: Images of Woman in the Jewish and Christian Traditions.* New York: Simon & Schuster, 1974.

Russell, Letty M. *Christian Education in Mission.* Philadelphia: Westminster Press, 1967.

————. *The Future of Partnership.* Philadelphia: Westminister Press, 1979.

————. *Growth in Partnership.* Philadelphia: Westminister Press, 1981.

The Sacramentary. English translation by the International Commission on English in the Liturgy. New York: Catholic Books, 1974.

Sacramentum Mundi. 6 vols. Edited by Karl Rahner. New York: Herder & Herder, 1968.

Sacred Congregation for the Doctrine of the Faith. "Declaration on the Question of the Admission of Women to the Ministerial Priesthood." *Origins* 6:3 (Feb. 1977): 517–24.

Sand, Ole. "Curriculum Change." *The Curriculum: Retrospect and Prospect.* In *The Seventieth Yearbook of the National Society of Education,* part 1, edited by Robert M. McClure. Chicago: Univ. of Chicago Press, 1971.

Sanders, James A. "Adaptable for Life." In *Magnalia Dei: The Mighty Acts of God,* edited by Frank M. Cross, Werner E. Lemke, and Patrick D. Miller, Jr. New York: Doubleday, 1976.

————. *God Has a Story Too.* Philadelphia: Fortress Press, 1979.

Sanders, Norris M. *Classroom Questions: What Kinds?* New York: Harper & Row, 1966.

Sartre, Jean-Paul. *Being and Nothingness.* Translated by Hazel E. Barnes. New York: Philosophical Library, 1956.

————. *Existentialism and Human Emotions.* Translated by Bernard Frechtman and Hazel E. Barnes. New York: Philosophical Library, 1957.

Sawicki, Marianne. *The Gospel in History.* New York: Paulist Press, 1988.

Schillebeeckx, Edward. *Christ.* New York: Crossroad, 1981.

————. *Christ, the Sacrament of the Encounter with God.* Kansas City: Sheed, Andrews & McMeel, 1963.

————. *The Church with a Human Face: A New and Expanded Theology of Ministry.* New York: Crossroad, 1985.

————. *Jesus.* New York: Seabury Press, 1979.

————. *Ministry.* New York: Crossroad, 1981.

Schillebeeckx, Edward, and Bas van Iersel. *Jesus Christ and Human Freedom.* New York: Herder & Herder, 1974.

Schineller, Peter. *A Handbook on Inculturation.* New York: Paulist Press, 1990.

Schiro, Michael. *Curriculum for Better Schools: the Great Ideological Debate.* Englewood Cliffs, NJ: Educational Technology Publications, 1978.

Schmemann, Alexander. *For the Life of the World*. Crestwood, NY: St. Vladimer's Seminary Press, 1982.

———. *Introduction to Liturgical Theology*. Translated by Asheleigh E. Moorhouse. Crestwood, NY: St. Vladimer's Seminary Press, 1986.

Schmidt, Stephen A. "Toward a Strategy for Public Christian Education." *Religious Education* 82:3 (Summer 1987): 469–85.

Schreiter, Robert J. *Constructing Local Theologies*. Maryknoll, NY: Orbis Books, 1986.

———. "Faith and Cultures: Challenges to a World Church." *Theological Studies*, 50:4 (Dec. 1989): 744–60.

Schroyer, Trent. *The Critique of Domination*. New York: George Braziller, 1973.

Scott, Kieran. "Collapsing the Tensions." *The Living Light* 18:2 (1982):167–69.

———. "Communicative Competence and Religous Education." *Lumen Vitae* 35 (1980): 76–96.

Searle, Mark. "The Pedagogical Function of Liturgy." *Worship* 55:4 (July 1981): 332–59.

Searle, Mark, ed. *Liturgy and Social Justice*. Collegeville, MN: Liturgical Press, 1980.

Seasoltz, Kevin R. "Justice and the Eucharist." *Worship* 58 (1984): 507–25.

Seguel. Mary Louise. *The Curriculum Field: Its Formative Years*. New York: Teachers College, 1966

Segundo, Juan Luis. *The Sacraments Today*. Maryknoll, NY: Orbis Books, 1974.

Seymour, Jack L., Robert T. O'Gorman, and Charles R. Foster. *The Church in the Education of the Public*. Nashville: Abingdon Press, 1984.

Seymour, Jack L., and Donald E. Miller. *Contemporary Approaches to Christian Education*. Nashville: Abingdon Press, 1982.

Shaw, Bernard. *Saint Joan, A Chronicle, and The Apple Cart, A Political Extravaganza*. London: Constable, 1924.

Shor, Ira. *Critical Teaching and Everyday Life*. Boston: South End Press, 1980.

Shorter, Alyward. *Toward a Theology of Inculturation*. Maryknoll, NY: Orbis, 1988.

Smith, Wilfred Cantwell. *Belief and History*. Charlottesville: Univ. Press of Virginia, 1977.

———. *The Meaning and End of Religion*. New York: Harper & Row, 1978.

Society of Jesus. *Documents of the 31st and 32d General Congregations of the Society of Jesus*. St. Louis, MO: Institute of Jesuit Sources, 1977.

Sölle, Dorothee. *Christ the Representative*. Philadelphia: Fortress Press, 1967.

Solomon, Robert C. *Introducing Philosophy: Problems and Perspectives*. New York: Harcourt Brace Jovanovich, 1977.

Sparks, Jack N. *The Apostolic Fathers*. Nashville: Thomas Nelson, 1978.

Spinoza, Baruch. *The Ethics and Selected Letters*. Edited by Seymour Feldman. Translated by Samuel Shirley. Indianapolis: Hackett, 1982.

Steckel, Clyde J. "Directions in Pastoral Counseling." In *Clinical Handbook of Pastoral Counseling*, edited by Robert J. Wicks, et al. New York: Paulist Press, 1985.

Steeman, Theodore M. "Durkheim's Professional Ethics." *Journal for The Scientific Study of Religion* 2:2 (Spring 1963): 163–81.

Steimle, Edmund A., Morris J. Niedenthal, and Charles L. Rice. *Preaching the Story*. Philadelphia: Fortress Press, 1980.

Stewart, Joe F. "Shared Praxis: A Therapeutic Approach." Ph.D. diss., Perkins School of Theology, Dallas, TX, 1986.

Stewart, Sonja M., and Jerome W. Berryman. *Young Children and Worship*. Louisville, KY: Westminster/John Knox Press, 1989.

Stout, George Frederick. *A Manual of Psychology*. In *Significant Contributions to the History of Psychology 1750–1920*. Series A: Orientations, vol. 9. Edited by Daniel N. Robinson. Washington, DC: Univ. Publications of America, 1977.

Strauss, David Friedrich. *The Life of Jesus Critically Examined*. Translated from the 4th German ed. by Marian Evans. St. Clair Shores, MI: Scholarly Press, 1960.

Strunk, Orlo. "A Prolegomenon to a History of Pastoral Counseling." In *The Clinical Handbook of Pastoral Counseling*. Robert J. Wicks, et al. New York: Paulist Press, 1985.

Sullivan, Edmund V. "Common Sense from a Critical Historical Perspective." In *Common Sense*. Edited by David Olson. Toronto: Routledge & Kegan Paul, 1980.

————. *A Critical Psychology*. New York: Plenum Press, 1984.

Surlis, Paul J. "Youth Ministry and the Politicization of Youth." *The Living Light* 18:3 (Fall 1981): 253–60.

Sutherland, William F. *A Critical Examination of Shared Praxis in Religious Education*. Ph.D. diss., Univ. of Pittsburgh, 1984.

Swidler, Leonard, and Arlene Swidler, eds. *Women Priests: A Catholic Commentary on the Vatican Declaration*. New York: Paulist Press, 1977.

Taylor, A. E. *Aristotle*. New York: Dover Publications, 1955.

Taylor, Charles. "Overcoming Epistemology" In *After Philosophy*. Edited by Kenneth Baynes, et al. Cambridge, MA: MIT Press, 1987.

Tertullian. "De Exhortatione Castitatis." In *Documents of the Christian Church*. 2d ed. Edited by Henry Bettenson. New York: Oxford Univ. Press, 1963.

Theological Dictionary of the New Testament. 10 vols. Edited by Gerhard Kittel. Edited and translated by Geoffrey W. Bromiley. Grand Rapids: Eerdmans, 1967.

Theological Dictionary of the New Testament. Abridged in one volume by Geoffrey W. Bromiley. Edited by Gerhard Kittel and Gerhard Freidrich. Translated by Geoffrey W. Bromiley. Grand Rapids: Eerdmans, 1985.

Thomas, Stephen N. *The Formal Mechanics of Mind*. New York: Cornell Univ. Press, 1978.

Thompson, Norma H., ed. *Religious Education and Theology*. Birmingham, AL: Religious Education Press, 1982.

Thompson, W. M. *Christ and Consciousness*. New York: Paulist Press, 1976.

Thompson, William. "The Hope for Humanity: Rahner's Eschatology." In *A World of Grace*, edited by Leo J. O'Donovan. New York: Crossroads, 1984.

Tillich, Paul. *Dynamics of Faith*. New York: Harper and Row, 1957

————. *A History of Christian Thought*. New York: Harper & Row, 1968.

————. *Theology and Culture*. New York: Oxford Press, 1959.

Tonnies, Ferdinand. *Community and Society*. Translated by Charles P. Loomis. New York: Harper & Row, 1963.

Torrance, Thomas F., ed. and trans. *The School of Faith: The Catechisms of the Reformed Tradition*. London: James Clarke, 1959.

Torres, Sergio, and John Eagleson, eds. *The Challenge of Basic Christian Communities*. Translated by John Drury. Maryknoll, NY: Orbis Books, 1981.

Toton, Suzanne D. "The Public and Political Responsibility of Christian Education." *Religious Education* 82:4 (Fall 1987): 606–23.

Tracy, David. *The Analogical Imagination*. New York: Crossroad, 1981.

————. *Blessed Rage for Order*. New York: Seabury Press, 1975.

————. "The Foundations of Practical Theology." In *Practical Theology*, edited by Don S. Browning. San Francisco: Harper & Row, 1983.

————. *Plurality and Ambiguity: Hermeneutics, Religion, Hope.* San Francisco: Harper and Row, 1987.

Trible, Phyllis. *God and the Rhetoric of Sexuality.* Philadelphia: Fortress Press, 1978.

Troeltsch, Ernst. *The Social Teachings of the Christian Churches.* 2 vols. Translated by Olive Wyon. London: George Allen, 1931.

Troifontaines, Roger. *What Is Existentialism?* Albany, NY: Magi Books, 1968.

Tyler, Ralph W. *Basic Principles of Curriculum and Instruction.* Chicago: Univ. of Chicago Press, 1949.

Vatican Commission on Relations with the Jews. "The Jews and Judaism in Preaching and Catechesis." *The Living Light* 22:2 (January 1986): 113–23.

Viviano, Benedict T. *The Kingdom of God in History.* Wilmington, DE: Michael Glazier, 1988.

von Leyden, W. See Leyden, W. von.

von Rad, Gerhard. See Rad, Gerhard von.

Vorgrimler, Herbert. *Understanding Karl Rahner.* New York: Crossroad, 1986.

Waddy, Lawrence. "God's Tumbler." In *Drama in Worship.* New York: Paulist Press, 1978.

Warner, Sylvia Ashton. *Teacher.* New York: Simon & Schuster, Touchstone Edition, 1986.

Warnock, Mary. *Imagination.* Berkeley: Univ. of California Press, 1976.

————. "Religious Imagination." In *Religious Imagination,* edited by James P. Mackey. Edinburgh: Edinburgh Univ. Press, 1986.

Warren, Michael. *Faith, Culture and the Worshiping Community.* New York: Paulist Press, 1989.

————. *Sourcebook for Modern Catechetics.* Winona, MN: St. Mary Press, 1983.

Weber, Max. *From Max Weber: Essays in Sociology.* Edited by H. H. Gerth and C. W. Mills. New York: Oxford Univ. Press, 1976.

————. *The Protestant Ethic and the Spirit of Capitalism.* London: Charles Scribner's Sons, 1958.

————. *The Sociology of Religion.* Boston: Beacon Press, 1963.

Weil, Marsha, and Bruce Joyce. *Information Processing Models of Teaching.* Englewood Cliffs, NJ: Prentice-Hall, 1978.

Welch, Sharon D. *Communities of Resistance and Solidarity: A Feminist Theology of Liberation.* Maryknoll, NY: Orbis Books, 1985.

Wellmer, Albrecht. *The Critical Theory of Society.* New York: Herder & Herder, 1971.

Westerhoff, John H. *Will Our Children Have Faith?* New York: Seabury Press, 1976.

Westerhoff, John H., ed. *Who Are We? The Quest for a Religious Education.* Birmingham, AL: Religious Education Press, 1978.

Westerhoff, John H., and Gwen Kennedy Neville. *Learning Through Liturgy.* New York: Seabury Press, 1978.

Westerhoff, John H., and William M. Willimon. *Liturgy and Learning Throughout the Life Cycle.* New York: Seabury Press, 1980.

White, James F. *Introduction to Christian Worship.* Rev. ed. Nashville: Abingdon Press, 1990.

————. "Moving Christian Worship Toward Social Justice." *The Christian Century* 104 (1987): 558–60.

Whitehead, Alfred North. *The Aims of Education and Other Essays.* New York: Free Press, 1929.

Whitehead, Alfred North, and Bertrand Russell. *Principia Mathematica.* 3 vols. 2d ed. Cambridge: Cambridge Univ. Press, 1950.

Whitehead, Evelyn Eaton, and James D. Whitehead. *Seasons of Strength.* Garden City, NY: Image Books, 1986.

Whitehead, James D., and Evelyn Eaton Whitehead. *The Emerging Laity.* Garden City, NY: Doubleday, 1986.

———. *Method in Ministry.* New York: Seabury Press, 1980.

Wicks, Robert J., Richard D. Parsons, and Donald E. Capps, eds. *Clinical Handbook of Pastoral Counseling.* New York: Paulist Press, Integration Books, 1985.

Wilber, Ken. *A Sociable God: Toward a New Understanding of Religion.* Boulder, CO: New Science Library, 1984.

Wilder, Amos Niven. *Theopoetic: Theology and the Religious Imagination.* Philadelphia: Fortress Press, 1976.

Wilder, Anne. *Early Christian Rhetoric.* Cambridge MA: Harvard Univ. Press, 1971.

Williamson, William B. *Language and Concept in Christian Education.* Philadelphia: Westminster Press, 1970.

Wingeier, Douglas E. *Working Out Your Own Beliefs: A Guide for Doing Your Own Theology.* Nashville: Abingdon Press, 1980.

Woozley, A. D. *Theory of Knowledge.* London: Hutchinsons Univ. Press, 1949.

Wrede, William (Wilhelm). *The Messianic Secret in the Gospels.* Translated by J. C. G. Greig. Cambridge: J. Clarke, 1971.

Wyckoff, D. Campbell. "Understanding Your Church Curriculum." *The Princeton Seminary Bulletin* 63:1 (1970): 77–84.

Zappone, Katherine E. *The Hope for Wholeness: A Spirituality for Feminists.* Mystic, CT: Twenty-Third Publications, 1991.

———. Katherine E. *Reconstructing Relationality: Spirituality and Religious Education.* Ph.D. diss., Boston College, 1986.

Index